H. H. Asquith

Letters to Venetia Stanley

H. H. Asquith
Letters to Venetia Stanley

———————✳———————

SELECTED AND EDITED BY

MICHAEL AND ELEANOR BROCK

But who can take a dream for a truth?
ROBERT BROWNING, *The Statue and the Bust*

Oxford   New York

OXFORD UNIVERSITY PRESS

1982

Oxford University Press, Walton Street, Oxford OX2 6DP

London Glasgow New York Toronto
Delhi Bombay Calcutta Madras Karachi
Kuala Lumpur Singapore Hong Kong Tokyo
Nairobi Dar es Salaam Cape Town
Melbourne Auckland

and associates in
Beirut Berlin Ibadan Mexico City Nicosia

British Library Cataloguing in Publication Data
Asquith, Herbert Henry, Earl of Oxford & Asquith
H. H. Asquith: letters to Venetia Stanley.
1. Asquith, Herbert Henry, Earl of Oxford &
Asquith–Correspondence, reminiscences, etc.
I. Title   II. Brock, Michael
III. Brock, Eleanor
941.083'092'4   DA566.9.07
ISBN 0–19–212200–2

Library of Congress Cataloging in Publication Data
Asquith, H. H. (Herbert Henry), 1852–1928.
H. H. Asquith, letters to Venetia Stanley.
Includes letters between Venetia Stanley and Edwin Montagu.
Bibliography: p. 615.
Includes index.
1. Asquith, H. H. (Herbert Henry), 1852–1928.
2. Montagu, Venetia Stanley, 1887–1948.
3. Montagu, Edwin Samuel, 1879–1924.
4. Prime ministers – Great Britain – Correspondence.
5. Asquith family.   6. Stanley family.
I. Montagu, Venetia Stanley, 1887–1948.
II. Brock, Michael.   III. Brock, Eleanor.
IV. Montagu, Edwin Samuel, 1879–1924.
V. Title.
DA566.9.A685A4 1982 941.083'092'4 [B] 82–6348   AACR2
ISBN 0–19–212200–2

Set by Western Printing Services Ltd
Printed in Great Britain by
The Thetford Press Ltd,
Thetford, Norfolk

To
Katharine Brock

Contents

✳

Introduction, p. 1; Women's Suffrage, p. 26; The 1914 Naval Estimates, p. 35; Ulster I: 'Worse things than bloodshed'? p. 38; Ulster II: The Curragh 'Mutiny', p. 56; The 1914 Budget, p. 63; Ulster III: 'The last of the Home Rule Bill', p. 69; Ulster IV: The Amending Bill, the Conference, and Bachelor's Walk, p. 83; Sarajevo: 'An "obituary" on the Austrian royalties', p. 91.

Introduction, p. 111; Ulster V: The Amending Bill Postponed, p. 134; The Decision for War, p. 141; The First Days of War: A. Kitchener, p. 152; B. The Expeditionary Force, p. 154; Sir John French: 'I am sure he is our best man', p. 164; Kitchener's 'indifference to the Territorials', p. 166; 'The "strangulation" of Germany', p. 169; Ulster VI: 'A really great achievement?', p. 173; 'The Germans are coming round in a big enveloping movement', p. 177; Directing the War Effort: 'A united and *most* efficient cabinet', p. 183; 'A lasting business which will try all our mettle', p. 190; 'The French plan of campaign has been badly bungled', p. 193; 'Bad news . . . from French', p. 207; The B.E.F. in Retreat: 'The only thing . . . was for Kitchener to go there', p. 211; 'The Irish breast high for loyalty and recruiting', p. 236; The Three Cruisers, p. 252; 'The Americans are making themselves disagreeable about the . . . cargoes', p. 254; Weaponry: 'Almost every "lesson" learned in the Boer War has to be . . . reversed in this', p. 264; The First Lord of the Admiralty, p. 283; 'A royal row . . . about . . . the Welsh Army Corps', p. 288; Sir Edgar Speyer, p. 292; Fisher: 'Winston won't have anybody else', p. 294; Coronel: 'If the Admiral had followed his instructions', p. 307; 'Haldane . . . is violently attacked . . . as a thinly veiled friend of Germany', p. 322; 'A diversion on a great and effective scale', p. 344.

✳

Illustrations

✳

Drawings in Text

We wish to thank all those named above who have allowed reproduction of these likenesses. The etching of Lord Fisher was commissioned by the late Sir Laurence Brock on behalf of a group of colleagues, and is in our possession. — M. G. B., E. H. B.

Maps

Preface

THE editing of H. H. Asquith's letters to Venetia Stanley was begun with great energy and devotion by her daughter, the late Mrs Judith Gendel.[1] We were asked, after Mrs Gendel's untimely death, to take on the work; and we have tried to produce an edition which would be useful both for general readers and for scholars.

More than 560 of Asquith's letters to Venetia, running to some 300,000 words, have survived in the Montagu Papers. Almost all were written between January 1912 and May 1915.[2] Something over half of this material is published here. Our aim was to exclude much of the repetition and some of the gossip in the Letters without giving a distorted view of the series as a whole. In a very few instances, none of them important, a phrase has been omitted because reproducing it might have wounded those now living. We have been sparing in selecting from what Asquith wrote early in the friendship before he started to discuss politics with Venetia, whereas almost every word has been included from the Letters of July and August 1914. As Venetia's replies to Asquith have disappeared, some of the letters which passed between her and Edwin Montagu in 1915 have been given to complete the story.

The modern world is a long way from Asquith's, whether in politics or social arrangements. We have outlined the story on the personal side in three introductory passages and an epilogue, and have provided comments on the principal public issues discussed in the Letters. These comments are clustered most thickly around themes such as the political confrontation over Home Rule for Ireland, the decision for war in August 1914, and the early part of the Dardanelles campaign, where Asquith's remarks add materially to the historical record. No issue has been selected for comment, however important, unless he was closely concerned with it. In compiling the Biographical Notes and the Index we have concentrated on summarizing the record as it stood in 1915. Source references have been kept to a minimum; but we have tried to provide them where a scholar might not be able to discover the source from the context. The conventions and abbreviations used are described in the Editorial Note.

As the Acknowledgements show, we have received a great deal of help while preparing these letters for publication. Two people have done more than help us. This book owes its existence to Mark Bonham Carter and

Milton Gendel, the first holding the copyright of Asquith's Letters to Venetia and the second the Letters themselves.[3] Both have been unstinting in their help and encouragement to us. For that, and for their patience in the face of many delays, we are deeply grateful. If the editing has any merits, their aid, and that of many others, does much to account for these. The faults lie at our door.

Oxford   M. G. B.
May, 1982   E. H. B.

---

[1] A short memoir by Mr Patrick Leigh Fermor, written soon after her death in 1972, is reprinted on pp. 611–12.

[2] A schedule of the Letters, showing which have been selected in whole or part, is given in Appendix 2.

[3] We must also thank Mr Bonham Carter for permission to quote from the other letters in the Bonham Carter MSS, and from the Asquith MSS in the Bodleian Library, Oxford, and Mr Gendel for allowing reproduction of some of the letters which passed between Venetia and Edwin Montagu, and which are in his copyright.

Acknowledgements

WE wish to express our humble thanks for the gracious permission of Her Majesty The Queen to use material in the Royal Archives.

We are greatly indebted to the following for allowing us either to consult papers in their possession, or to use copyright material, or, in many cases, for giving both these permissions: Sir Richard and Lady Acland; the Trustees of the Beaverbrook Foundation and the House of Lords Record Office (Beaverbrook, Bonar Law, and Lloyd George Papers); the University of Birmingham (Austen Chamberlain Papers); the Curators of the Bodleian Library, Oxford; the Syndics of the Cambridge University Library; the Hon. Edward Carson; the Master and Fellows of Churchill College, Cambridge (Chandos and Hankey Papers); the Rt. Hon. the Earl of Crawford and Balcarres, P.C.; His Grace the Archbishop of Canterbury and the Trustees of Lambeth Palace Library (Randall Davidson Papers); Lord Elibank; Lord Gainford; the Rt. Hon. the Earl Haig, O.B.E.; the Executors of the late Mrs Sylvia Henley; the Dean and Chapter of Durham (Hensley Henson Papers); the Imperial War Museum; Lord Kennet (Lady Scott's diaries, and H. H. Asquith's letters to Lady Scott); Mrs David Hankinson and the Viscountess Chandos (diary of the late Sir Alan Lascelles, P.C.); Mr Patrick Leigh Fermor, D.S.O., O.B.E.; the Rt. Hon. the Earl Lloyd George of Dwyfor; the Executors of the late Mrs Adelaide Lubbock; Mr David McKenna, C.B.E.; the Master and Fellows of Magdalene College, Cambridge (A. C. Benson diary); Mrs D. M. Maxse; the Warden and Fellows of New College, Oxford (the Milner Papers); Mr A. B. L. Munro-Ferguson; the University of Newcastle (Runciman of Doxford Papers); the Warden and Fellows of Nuffield College, Oxford (Emmott and Pease Papers); the Rt. Hon. the Earl of Oxford and Asquith, K.C.M.G.; Lord Ravensdale, M.C.; Viscount Rothermere; the Most Hon. the Marquess of Salisbury, D.L.; the Trustees of the National Library of Scotland; Mrs J. Simon (Emmott Papers); Mrs Anne Symonds (typescript of letters to Hilda Harrisson); the Hon. Colin Tennant (Glenconner Papers); the Master and Fellows of Trinity College, Cambridge; the State Library of Victoria (Papers of Margaret Stanley); the Trustees of the National Library of Wales.

Quotations from Crown Copyright records are reproduced by kind permission of the Controller, Her Majesty's Stationery Office. We thank Lord Oxford and Asquith, the Hon. John Jolliffe, and Messrs. Collins for allowing us to reproduce part of the letter to Conrad Russell on p. 202 of *Raymond Asquith: Life and Letters* (1980).

We are grateful to the following for the generous help they gave us with family or personal reminiscences: Sir Isaiah Berlin, O.M., C.B.E., F.B.A.; Lord David Cecil, C.H.; Lady Diana Cooper; Mrs James de Rothschild; the Hon. Mrs Laura Grimond; the Hon. John Jolliffe; the Rt. Hon. Harold Macmillan, P.C., O.M., F.R.S.; the Rt.

Hon. the Earl of Oxford and Asquith; Lord Rothschild, G.B.E., G.M., F.R.S.; Mr John Sparrow, O.B.E. We should also mention the help which we received from the late Mrs Sylvia Henley.

We extend our thanks to Lord and Lady Stanley of Alderley for their help and hospitality; to Mr Simon Bainbridge and Mrs Katharine Brock for reading the typescript and for the useful comments which they made on it; to Mr David Brock for help with the family trees and with the maps; and to Mr Richard Brain for going so far beyond the call of duty in making our typescript fit for the press. We are indebted to the British Academy for a research grant. We were given excellent facilities, during a period of leave, by the Rockefeller Foundation and the staff of the Villa Serbelloni, and by the Hebrew University, Jerusalem. In Wolfson College, Oxford, in the School of Education of the University of Exeter, and in Nuffield College, we have met with great forbearance and with expert secretarial help; and we are grateful.

We wish to thank the following for the trouble which they have taken on our behalf, especially in answering our enquiries: Dr David Aldridge; the Revd. P. A. Apps; Lady Archibald; Dr Anne Barton; Dr Alan Bell; Lady Berlin; Mr George Brock; Mrs Nathalie Brooke; the Revd. Robert Brown; Mr William Calder; M. François-Xavier Camenen; Professor Barbara Campbell; the Revd. Professor Sir Owen Chadwick, K.B.E.; Lord Clark, O.M., C.H., K.C.B., F.B.A.; Professor John Clive; Lord Coleraine; the Revd. Prebendary N. J. Davey; the Rt. Hon. the Earl and Countess de la Warr; Mrs Honor Ellis; General Sir Anthony Farrar-Hockley, K.C.B., D.S.O., M.C.; Mr Matthew Fforde; Mr Geoffrey Finlayson; Professor Isaiah Friedman; Professor Shmuel Galai; Dr Dennis Gath; Professor François Goguel; Professor Richard Gombrich; Dr Brian Harrison; Mr W. D'Arcy Hart; Mr Michael Hart; Dr Cameron Hazlehurst; Mr George Howard, D.L.; Mr Clive Hughes; M. Serge Hurtig; Mr Benjamin Jaffe; Professor E. T. James; the Rt. Hon. Roy Jenkins, P.C.; Professor John Jones; Mrs Anita Leslie-King; Mr E. Lewis; the Rt. Hon. the Countess of Longford, C.B.E.; Dr John McCaffrey; Mr David McKenna; Mr Michael Maclagan; Mr H. Margary; Dr Colin Matthew; Mr Ivor Montagu; Mrs Morawiak; the Revd. Professor Dennis Nineham; Mr David Parsons; Dr John Penney; Dr H. J. O. Pogge von Strandmann; the Revd. John Porteous; Mr T. I. Rae; Mr Adam Ridley; Professor Keith Robbins; Mr Kenneth Rose; the Dowager Duchess of Rutland, J.P.; Professor Michael Rutter; Mrs Dorothy Silberston; the Revd. R. W. H. Simmons; Captain R. W. J. Smith; Mrs Zara Steiner; Professor Barry Supple; Dr Geza Vermes; Professor John Vincent; Mr D. P. Waley; Mr David Walker; Dr John Walsh; Mrs Elizabeth Wansbrough; Mrs Frances Wicks; Dr Philip Williams; the Rt. Hon. the Lord Windlesham, P.C.; Mrs Rosemary Wolff; Mrs Christine Woodland; Dr C. J. Wrigley; Brigadier Peter Young, D.S.O., M.C.; Mr Philip Ziegler.

We have received advice and help from the library, archive, and administrative staffs of many institutions. We are especially grateful to those who answered our enquiries from Cheshire County Record Office; the Regimental Museum, the Cheshire Regiment; Chester City Record Office; Site Services, I.C.I. Ltd., Pharmaceuticals Division, Alderley Park; Kent County Record Office; Lymington

District Library; the Regimental Association, the Middlesex Regiment (D.C.O.); the Navy Records Society; the University College of North Wales; Queen's College, Harley Street; the University of Reading; Surrey County Library; the Humanities Research Center, University of Texas; West Sussex Record Office.

Editorial Note

ASQUITH'S LETTER.

Asquith's early Letters to Venetia usually began 'Dearest Venetia' and were signed 'H.H.A.'. From the middle of 1912 onwards he nearly always omitted the initials at the end: when he used any preface it was generally 'My Darling'. As most of the Letters were on paper headed 10 Downing Street (even if Asquith wrote some of them elsewhere) the address has been printed only where this was not the case. Nicknames and Christian names occur frequently; the people concerned are identified in the Index.

Asquith sometimes composed a Letter on more than one day. In these cases each day's contribution has been given a separate number. When he enclosed a document by someone else this carries the number of the Letter with which it was enclosed, with a, b, or c added. He dated almost all of his letters. For a few, such as Letter 75 where he wrote simply 'Whitsuntide', the placing has been a matter of judgement. When he wrote to Venetia more than once a day each Letter carries a roman numeral in square brackets. In a few of these instances only one of the Letters has been selected. Thus Letter 211, the only one selected for 16 November 1914 but the second he wrote her that day, is dated 16 Nov. 1914 [ii].

Asquith's punctuation and spelling have been left as in the original, except where the punctuation might mislead the reader. Names of ships, and titles of books and newspapers, have been conventionally italicized.

Within a Letter, where one or more paragraphs, or a substantial part of one, have been omitted, this has been indicated by a line space.

THE MONTAGU–STANLEY CORRESPONDENCE

Edwin Montagu and Venetia Stanley began to correspond at the end of 1909. Many of the surviving letters are impossible to date, and it may be conjectured that a number have not survived, especially from those written in 1914.

The 1915 letters between Edwin and Venetia included in this volume (and two enclosures in their letters, one from Margot Asquith to Edwin and one from Asquith to Margot) are numbered as a separate series with roman numerals. When written on the same day as a letter (or letters) from

Asquith to Venetia, the roman-numbered letter is always placed after Asquith's. The index entries for Edwin and Venetia show where these letters come in the volume.

Edwin wrote on the headed paper of his house, 24 Queen Anne's Gate, S.W., unless otherwise stated; where no address is given on Venetia's letters as printed here, it is not known where she wrote from.

No attempt has been made to regularize the punctuation of the letters of Edwin and Venetia (let alone Margot's). Edwin's writing is extremely hard to decipher.

MANUSCRIPT SOURCES

Where the source has not been given it is:

(i) the Montagu MSS for Asquith's letters to Venetia, and for those which passed between Venetia and Edwin;

(ii) the Bonham Carter MSS for any other letter from or to Asquith, for the letters and diaries of Margot Asquith, for the letters, diaries, and lecture notes of Violet Asquith, and for letters from Venetia to Violet.

ABBREVIATIONS USED

The following abbreviations have been used for convenience:

	Cited as
H. H. Asquith (Earl of Oxford and Asquith), *Memories and Reflections*, 1852–1927, 2 vols. (1928).	*Memories and Reflections*
Margot Asquith, *Autobiography*, 2 vols. (1920, 1922). This book has also appeared in several other editions, British and American. The one-volume abridged edition (1962) contains a valuable Introduction by Mark Bonham Carter.	Margot Asquith, *Autobiography*
The Asquith Papers, Bodleian Library, Oxford.	Asquith MSS
British Documents on the Origins of the War, 1898–1914, ed. G. P. Gooch and H. Temperley, 11 vols. (1926–38).	*Brit. Docs. War*
British Library, Additional Manuscripts.	B L Add. MSS
Winston Churchill: Companion Documents. Each volume of the biography started by Randolph Churchill, and now being completed (from 1914) by Martin Gilbert, has been accompanied by Companion Documents. Details for the volumes cited are:	*Churchill: Companion Docs.*

    1901–1914, 3 vols., continuous pagination (1969)
    1914–1916, 2 vols., continuous pagination (1972)
    1922–1929, 1 vol. continuous pagination (1979)
    1929–1935, 1 vol. continuous pagination (1981)

Gainford Papers, Nuffield College, Oxford: J. A. Pease's diary.

Pease, diary

Hankey Papers, Churchill College, Cambridge: M. P. A. Hankey's diary.

Hankey, diary

M. P. A. Hankey, *The Supreme Command, 1914–1918*, 2 vols. (1961).

Hankey, *Supreme Command*

Inside Asquith's Cabinet: from the Diaries of Charles Hobhouse, ed. E. David (1977).

Hobhouse, *Diaries.*

Roy Jenkins, *Asquith* (revised edition, 1978). First published 1964. The revised edition contains the passages excised earlier 'in deference to Lady Violet Bonham Carter'.

Jenkins, *Asquith.*

Lady Kennet, *Self-Portrait of an Artist* (1949). Posthumously published; consists, for years from 1913 onwards, of extracts from the diaries (now in Cambridge University Library) of Lady Scott, later Lady Kennet, for whom see p. 634.

Self-Portrait of an Artist.

David Lloyd George, *War Memoirs* 2 vols. (1938). Originally published in 6 volumes (1933–36). In the two-volume edition pagination is continuous.

Lloyd George, *War Memoirs.*

A. J. Marder, *From the Dreadnought to Scapa Flow*: vol. 2, *The War Years to the Eve of Jutland* (1965).

Marder ii

West Sussex Record Office, Leo Maxse Papers.

Leo Maxse MSS

Parliamentary Debates, 5th Series (House of Commons, unless otherwise stated.)

Parl. Deb.

Public Record Office, Cabinet Papers.

P.R.O. CAB.

Royal Archives; George V.

R A GV

The papers of John Satterfield Sandars, Bodleian Library, Oxford. All the papers cited are from MSS Eng. hist. *c.*767.

Sandars MSS

J. A. Spender and Cyril Asquith, *Life of H. H. Asquith, Lord Oxford and Asquith* 2 vols. (1932).

Spender and Asquith

Titles

References to the peerage in this volume accord with those in G.E.C.'s *Peerage,* 2nd edition.

PART 1

The Master of the Commons

THE letters in this volume were written by a great statesman to a girl of less than half his age. Beatrice Venetia[1] Stanley, who belonged to a prominent Liberal family, first appeared in H. H. Asquith's circle as the childhood friend of his elder daughter, Violet. He was then the coming man of British politics. He had a complete armoury of the skills which a political leader needed in the era when Britain had gone half-way towards democracy and universal suffrage, being a master both of parliamentary debate and of platform speaking. Trained in the law, he cut through governmental problems with extraordinary speed. A spell as Home Secretary had proved his executive capacity. When the Liberals' long stay in the wilderness ended in December 1905 he became Chancellor of the Exchequer and heir apparent to the premiership.

Asquith was credited, as he later wrote, with 'a slight weakness for the companionship of clever and attractive women' (Letter 342). By 1907, when Venetia was 20, she was enrolled in what his wife, Margot, banteringly called his 'little harem'.[2] In January 1908 Pamela Jekyll drew a diagram for him showing his heart as divided between 'Viola [Tree], Dorothy [Beresford], Lilian [Tennant], Venetia, and me'.[3] By midsummer 1912 the others had dropped out and Venetia reigned unchallenged. By the spring of 1914 his love for her dominated his thoughts. It became ever more intense until 12 May 1915, when she shattered the dream by telling him of her engagement to one of his cabinet colleagues. He had become Prime Minister at the age of 55, three months after Pamela Jekyll drew her diagram; and his premiership outlasted even the long romance with Venetia, for he did not leave 10 Downing Street until December 1916. Part 1 of this volume is concerned with the pre-war phase of the friendship, that is, with the world which fell apart when London learned, on 24 July 1914, of the ultimatum sent from Vienna to Belgrade.

Venetia's special relationship with the Prime Minister and his family may be dated from December 1909, when Violet Asquith's admirer, Archie Gordon, died as a result of a motoring accident, and Venetia, by now Violet's closest woman friend, proved how effective she could be in the role of comforter. The earliest of Asquith's extant letters to her were written in September 1910 and in the second general election of that year she came with Violet to some of his election meetings. In January 1912 he took a holiday in Sicily with Edwin Montagu, a junior member of his Government who had been one of his Private Secretaries. The two were joined there by Violet and Venetia. A few weeks after their return Venetia was the Prime Minister's weekend guest at a house, Hurstly, which he had been lent on the edge of the New Forest, near Lymington. He recorded three years later,

I was sitting with her in the dining room on Sunday morning – the others being out in the garden or walking – and we were talking and laughing just on our old accustomed terms. Suddenly, in a single instant, without premonition on my part or any challenge on hers, the scales dropped from my eyes; the familiar features and smile and gestures and words assumed an absolutely new perspective; what had been completely hidden from me was in a flash half-revealed, and I dimly felt, hardly knowing, not at all understanding it, that I had come to a turning point in my life (Letter 385).

The half-revelation near the New Forest was completed a few weeks later at Ewelme Down in Oxfordshire;[4] but the romance did not develop with dramatic speed. Though Venetia was by now Asquith's most regular correspondent, his average rate of writing to her did not reach a letter a week. Venetia wrote to Edwin Montagu in November 1912:

I spent most of last week . . . at Downing Street. I saw not very much of the P.M. Do you remember saying how much he varied in his liking for me, and that sometimes he quite liked me and at others not at all? Well, this was one of the not at all times. He was horribly bored by my constant presence at breakfast, lunch and dinner.

Venetia's account probably exaggerates Asquith's lack of interest; but in August 1913 he had forgotten the date of her birthday.* At this stage there was nothing obsessional about his love for her: when they were apart what Violet called his 'boundless capacity for happiness' had full play.[5] From the Admiralty Yacht, during a Mediterranean cruise in May 1913, Violet reported to Venetia: 'Father bird happy, making lists of women's names beginning with P, and as sunburnt as a strawberry.' Asquith still did not consult Venetia, nor write much to her about politics; and during 1913 his letters to his wife Margot, whenever he was away from her, were more informative than those to Venetia.

Early in 1914, as the problem of Ulster in a Home Rule Ireland loomed ever closer, the conversations and letters began to change in character. Asquith later reminded Venetia of

the stage . . . when we began to talk not only of persons and books but of . . . my

---

* He asked for the date in good time: see Letter 18.

interests, politics, etc., and I began to acquire the habit, first of taking you into confidence, and then of consulting and relying on your judgment (Letter 386).

Asquith composed the King's Speech for the 1914 session while staying with the Stanleys at Alderley[6] for New Year; and Venetia made clear to him that she would have liked to be shown the draft (Letter 208). He now began to write about three times a week; and by the end of March 1914 he was discussing the problems of the premiership with her. He looked back to the Curragh affair in that month as one during which she had been his regular 'counsellor' (Letter 354 and pp. 56–8).

It is almost certain that Asquith never became Venetia's lover in the physical sense;* and it is unlikely that he even wished for this. The romantic ardour which he sustained is not easy to envisage in our age of 'permissiveness' and post-Freudian introspection. By the middle of 1914 he was deeply in love. He was becoming dependent on Venetia and the signs are that this had begun to alarm her. When he stayed for Whitsun at the other Stanley estate, Penrhos, near Holyhead,[7] his chances of resolving the Home Rule crisis were fading and she saved him, in his own later words, 'from something very like despair' (Letter 126); but before he left she seems to have warned him that he could not long remain the only man in her life. He wrote that he took south 'some bright memories, and a *sad* heart' (Letter 73). A year later, when she was engaged to be married and the spell had been broken, he wondered, in anguish of spirit, why he had not 'had the courage to act upon' this *'Nunc Dimittis* letter'.[8] One reason was that Venetia had become too fond of 'the Prime', and too flattered by his attentions, to persevere in any of her warnings to him. Such episodes ended in her making him 'happy again', as she later wrote, by saying 'anything he wanted' (Letter xxv). He spent an hour in her company on 23 June 'and every cloud was lifted' (Letter 84). By 3 July he was writing, 'there can never any more be any misunderstanding between us' (Letter 89). The threat of an Irish civil war which was now developing made his need for her support still sharper. From the end of June 1914 he wrote almost every day if they were apart. Some days brought her several letters: on some he both met her and wrote. On 14 July, oppressed by the Irish crisis, he implored, 'Do keep close to me beloved in this most critical time of my life' (Letter 96).

* * *

Nearly all British Prime Ministers have suffered from loneliness: many have unburdened themselves to confidantes and found solace in romantic attachments. Asquith, as has been mentioned, already had a well-developed

---

* Although at the time Lady Diana Manners thought differently. She was apparently invited to replace Venetia, but did not respond: P. Ziegler, *Diana Cooper* (1981), pp. 60, 195.

taste for such solace when he became premier. He was experienced in giving his relationships with women a romantic tinge without allowing anything too intense. Why did this one friendship go so completely beyond his control? The first part of any answer must be that Venetia was uniquely suited, by family background and by temperament, to be this Prime Minister's 'life-giver'.[9] The Stanleys of Alderley were intellectually tough and adventurous, yet impeccably Liberal. Venetia's mother, Lady Sheffield, was Asquithian to the point of taking a prominent part against women's suffrage. Though Venetia was first cousin to Clementine Churchill the Government did not include any of her immediate family. Thus she belonged close to the centre of Liberal politics without having an embarrassing tie with any of the premier's colleagues. Her family training had equipped her for discussion with a man of Asquith's calibre. Bertrand Russell has left a picture of the Stanleys of her parents' generation in their prime:

Lyulph [Venetia's father] was a free-thinker, and spent his time fighting the Church on the London School Board. . . . Algernon [Lyulph's brother] was a Roman Catholic priest, a Papal Chamberlain and Bishop of Emmaus. Lyulph was witty, encyclopaedic, and caustic. Algernon was witty, fat, and greedy. . . . At the Sunday luncheons there would be vehement arguments, for among the daughters and sons-in-law there were representatives of the Church of England, Unitarianism, and Positivism. . . . I used to go to these luncheons in fear and trembling, since I never knew but what the whole pack would turn upon me. I had only one friend whom I could count on among them . . . my uncle Lyulph's wife, sister of Sir Hugh Bell.[10]

Venetia possessed all the accomplishments of the girls of her circle. She had been well educated by governesses and tutors and had the wide knowledge of English literature which Asquith required in his girl friends. Her memory was retentive. Her upbringing had given her enough independence to defy the stuffier conventions, but not enough to strike out decisively on her own. Unlike another of her cousins, Gertrude Bell, she had not the self-confidence of a 'college girl'. She did not feel the wild urges of a rebel. She would never have emulated the actress Lillah McCarthy in scribbling 'Votes for Women' across the Prime Minister's blotter.[11] With all her strong intelligence she had a curious lack of determination and initiative; she would drift pleasantly with the stream until action was imperative. She was attractive, but not outstandingly beautiful. In the simple psychological categories used in her circle she was classed as rather 'masculine' in outlook. When she helped at a summer camp for a Hoxton boys' club in 1913 she 'played football for the first time', and reported to Edwin Montagu, 'It's, I think, far the most thrilling game I've ever played: it intoxicated me.' There was no queue of eligible suitors seeking her hand in marriage. Despite its old-fashioned phrasing a passage in Sir Lawrence Jones's *An Edwardian Youth* conveys vividly how a young man saw her at this time:

Venetia had dark-eyed, aquiline good looks and a masculine intellect. I delighted in her and we were close friends; but she permitted herself, in the morning of her youth, no recourse to her own femininity. She carried the Anthologies in her head, but rode like an Amazon, and walked the high garden walls of Alderley with the casual stride of a boy. She was a splendid, virginal, comradely creature, reserving herself for we knew not what use of her fine brain and hidden heart.

Thus Venetia was not one to inspire men of her own age with romantic ideas, if young Jones was at all typical. When he was advised by an unnamed 'cabinet minister' to marry Venetia, he merely wondered, 'How can a man so obtuse be fit to govern?'[12]

Venetia was kept single, however, not by the absence of any suitors, but by the highly ineligible character of the one she had. Edwin Montagu fell in love with her almost when Asquith did and proposed to her in the summer of 1912. She refused him but remained his friend and comforter. It was her acceptance of this proposal when it was renewed early in 1915 which brought her close friendship with Asquith to an end. Edwin thus played a leading role in the drama which underlay these letters.

In some ways Edwin's attachment to Venetia ran parallel to Asquith's. Both men admired the help she gave Violet after Archie Gordon's accident and death; both were with her on the Sicilian holiday; both were in love with her soon after it. Both found a life-giving quality in her.* With her they could relax and recharge their batteries. Though moody, neurotic, and ugly, Edwin had remarkable sensitivity and charm.[13] Only eight years older than Venetia he was already a rising politician: he was to be Secretary of State for India while still in his thirties. The death of his millionaire father, Lord Swaythling, in 1911 had left him in easy circumstances. Like Venetia he had outdoor interests (both were keen bird-watchers); and he was quicker than Asquith to discern Venetia's interest in politics. She told him in 1912:

. . . I always like you to talk to me about these more important and vital issues in your life rather than permanently to stick to . . . whether Cynthia is nicer than Katharine, or Cys cleverer than Raymond! . . . If, as you say, it made a difference to you to talk about it . . . I am glad that I should have been of some use.[14]

The letters which passed between Edwin and Venetia in the spring of 1912 concerned the state of the Government as well as the chances of seeing a roseate tern on the Anglesey Skerries.

---

* They were not alone in this. In 1958 Brendan Bracken named her as among the very few who had been able to bring Winston Churchill out of one of his depressions: C. E. Lysaght, *Brendan Bracken* (1979), p. 332.

Venetia almost accepted Edwin in 1912. Indeed, with characteristic indecision, she did so at first and went back on it.[15] Even then she gave him the
impression that the verdict might not prove final. One appalling obstacle to
their marrying was a condition attaching to his income from his father's
will. Lord Swaythling had died in 1911 and left the bulk of his fortune in
trust for his children with the much publicized[16] proviso that if any of them
abandoned the Jewish faith, or married out of it, they would lose their share.
Apart from that share Edwin's income was very small for someone who had
embarked on political life. Thus his proposal to Venetia invited her either to
live in comparative poverty or to change her religion for money. Venetia's
circle was not free of anti-Semitism; and in 1912 this flight from Christianity to Judaism, largely for financial motives, would have represented a
painful defiance of convention even for a free-thinking Stanley.

Venetia's refusal did not lessen her concern for Edwin. When he was in
India at the end of 1912 she wrote:

Why don't you hurry up your journeys a bit and get home by about March 10th? If
they knew you were going to be back by then perhaps they would postpone the
Indian Finance Debate (it will be a great crush, won't it, to get it in before the
February adjournment and your return would be an excellent reason for delaying it
a little).

Edwin sank into gloom but remained constant. When Venetia invited him
to Penrhos in November 1913 he declined in terms which foreshadowed
what Asquith was to experience.

There come times when . . . the yearning for what I cannot have becomes so
poignant that I cannot trust myself to behave naturally. I have found recently that
coming to see you, although the perfect unscarredness of your emotions ought to
help me, leaves behind it feelings of despair and jealousy.

A fortnight later he was writing:

I shall remember all my life, however much you may have regretted it since, that
you once consented to marry me . . . . Now please remember, whatever happens,
that I shall never change, and that if you do, there it is.

*   *   *

Thus Venetia both outshone and outlasted the rest of Asquith's 'little
harem'. She had started with the advantage of being Violet's closest friend;
and Edwin's ineligibility as a suitor kept her single. With his taste for
intelligent and attractive girls who might be willing to hold hands, Asquith
found in her an admirable comforter and confidante; and he might well end
by regarding her as more than what Violet called a 'companion in
brightness'.[17] Experienced though he had become in the conduct of an
amitié amoureuse, his record showed his tendency to plunge head over

heels into romance, in the belief that he had found his ideal woman. He fell in love with Helen Melland when he was 18, became secretly engaged to her at 22, and married her, before he had an assured income, at 24. When he was 38 he fell in love with Margot Tennant. 'You have made me a different man,' he told her in July 1891, 'and brought back into my life the feeling of spring.'[18] Less than two months after this was written his wife died of typhoid. He embarked without delay on a siege of Margot, which ended with their marriage in May 1894, when she was 30.*

This romanticism was complemented in Asquith by considerable caution and self-knowledge. The balance was tipped towards romance in the spring of 1912, and still more during 1914, by the fact that the politics of those periods subjected him to unusual strain. The Prime Minister needed a secret place in which he could, at will, either escape from his problems or discuss them. When a man falls in love and moves through the looking-glass, where 'the familiar features assume an absolutely new perspective', that need is met.

Asquith told Venetia three years later that his love for her had rescued him from 'sterility, impotence, and despair' (Letter 339).† By all accounts he was in a bad way in the spring of 1912. In February there were rumours that he meant to resign. When he told the Commons late in March that the talks on the coal strike had broken down he could scarcely master his emotion. In mid-April, he 'said that he . . . was absolutely done up and must go away for a change'.‡[19] In the same month a correspondent wrote to Balfour that Asquith's 'nerve and virility [were] atrophied and gone'. In May Tyrrell of the Foreign Office was recorded as saying that the cabinet 'were really anxious to find an occasion for resignation'.[20] Some of these reports should be discounted as the concoctions of the Opposition; but in January 1912, after six years of office, Asquith himself implied privately that it was time for a change. 'No set of men', he wrote to Lady Horner,

---

* A psychological theory has been propounded (the Phaeton Theory) to the effect that clever orphaned children, especially boys who lose their fathers, may develop both intense ambition and an incapacity to form stable personal relationships. In *The Fiery Chariot* (1970) Lucille Iremonger has applied this theory to many British Prime Ministers, Asquith among them. The boy is said to acquire a substitute father (in Asquith's case his headmaster, in Lloyd George's Uncle Lloyd), who drives him harder than his natural father would have done, and who cannot fill the more personal side of a father's role. For a critique see the article by Hugh Berrington, *British Journal of Political Science* July 1974, iv. 345–69. The Phaeton Theory was originally formulated about bastards and there are difficulties about applying it to orphans such as Asquith.

† During the last sixty years the explicitly sexual connotations of certain terms have driven them from general use. There has been a change of usage since Asquith's time in the case of words such as 'sterility', 'impotence', 'intimacy', 'lover', and 'affair'.

‡ Asquith enjoyed exceptionally good health. This occasion, on which he was diagnosed as suffering briefly from high blood-pressure, was the only one during his peacetime premiership when he was troubled by more than a passing infection.

'ought, under modern conditions, to be in office for more than six years together.'[21]

Asquith was bound to be upset by the coal strike. He was the master of Parliament, but not of the forces outside it. He dealt more confidently with the Tory peers than with the miners. Yet at first sight it seems odd that events in the spring of 1912 should have brought him lower than the Ulster crisis was to do two years later. In the preceding eighteen months he had led his party to their third successive election victory, curbed the Conservative majority in the Lords, and seen the Conservative leader, A. J. Balfour, displaced. He had dominated that general election campaign; his ascendancy in the Commons was judged to surpass even that of Gladstone. It took more than the coal strike to outweigh all this. After a political ascent almost free from set-backs Asquith was suffering from a degree of disillusionment. He had completed nearly four years as Prime Minister and had not turned 60. The excitement and sense of achievement which the highest promotion brings had worn off. In one of his sonnets to Venetia he wrote (Letter 291) of:

> Fame's mocking foil, and Power's grim deceit.

It is those who reach the heights late after a hard struggle who are apt to enjoy them most. Disraeli was a prey to many ills, but not to disillusionment. He relished the premiership to the end, writing to Lady Bradford after more than four years of it,

> I . . . cannot at all agree with the great king that all is vanity.[22]

Dizzy had struggled up the greasy pole for a lifetime with many slips, and had not reached a firm place at the top until his seventieth year.

The main clue to Asquith's mood of despair lay not in politics, however, but in his harassing family life. The strain which made him need the romance with Venetia was not solely political in origin. The problems of the coal strike passed: those of his home did not. Thus, while his love for Venetia developed slowly during the eighteen months between the strike and the final Home Rule crisis, it did not recede; there was no moving back through the looking-glass. Even when politics put the master of 10 Downing Street under no particular stress, its other occupants could be guaranteed to keep him from his rest. He had married Margot as an open-eyed romantic. He knew that her health and nerves were not good. 'I know too,' he told Mrs Horner in September 1892, 'that she does not love me, at least not in the way that I love her. Her passion long since went elsewhere; and, whomever she marries, her husband will have to win his way. I am under no illusions.'[23] He cannot have realized, however, quite what a strain it would be to live with Margot in her middle age. She had fine qualities, but not those most needed in a Prime Minister's wife. In youth she and her sisters had held the middle of London's social stage. She had no notion of adapting to a quieter supporting role, or of becoming her hard-pressed husband's restful confidante. Late one evening in May 1915, when Venetia had gone out of Asquith's life, he told Violet what Margot's partner had to endure. She noted in her diary:

Poor darling; he said: 'I have sometimes walked up and down that room till I felt as tho' I were going mad. . . . When one needed rest to have a thing like the *Morning Post* leader flung at one – all the obvious reasons for and against things more controversially put even than by one's colleagues.' Venetia rested him from all this.

The restraints and reticences expected of someone in her position were alien to Margot. She did not realize that the candour with which she had taken the great houses by storm was not thought suitable in the mistress of 10 Downing Street. She proffered medical and dental advice unasked. 'For God's sake,' she adjured Lord Rosebery in August 1913, 'take pure liquid paraffin every day.'[24] She became unpopular and a prey to constant nervous illnesses. 'Margot I find rather trying as a visitor', Pamela McKenna told a friend in September 1912;

she criticizes everything incessantly . . . and always in the unkindest way; . . . but I know she never means to be wounding and I do feel so sorry for her, as she makes herself terribly unhappy.[25]

In October 1913 a young man noted in his diary after his first visit to The Wharf, 'It is rather sad that she, who must once have had more friends than she could count, should now have so many enemies.'[26] Margot came away from a visit, Cynthia Asquith noted two years later, 'leaving a wake of weeping, injured people'.[27] The criticisms were not always received merely with tears. During the second 1910 election campaign Margot wrote to Lloyd George criticizing his speeches. She had not consulted her husband. Lloyd George was furious and had to be pacified by the Chief Whip.

Henry James once commented on the 'rigid intellectual economy'[28] which he had observed Asquith practising in hours of relaxation. The Prime Minister told old jokes and familiar stories. This maddened Margot. 'I am horribly impatient,' she noted in 1905; 'and it is only by strong self-control that I ever listen at all, when I see a familiar route traversed step by step.' Asquith probably regarded guests as a welcome distraction; and Margot enjoyed entertaining. But there was little relief to be found that way. Lavish hospitality increased the Prime Minister's recurrent money worries, for Margot was very extravagant; and she was left lamenting to Edith Lyttelton, 'I ought to have my *own* husband and my *own* children in a home of my *own*. I have only been alone with Henry and my children three weeks in nineteen years.'[29]

This was the heart of the trouble. Her daughter Elizabeth was only just 'coming out'; her son Anthony ('Puffin') was still at his preparatory school. She felt that the three of them were being crowded out of her husband's life by her brilliant stepdaughter. Violet had been a child of 4 when her mother died. She adored her father and was too young, and too closely beset by her own emotional troubles, to make much allowance for her stepmother's difficulties. There had been trouble between Margot and Violet for years. 'It is a grief to me', Asquith wrote to Margot in December 1909, 'that the two women I care for most should be on terms of chronic misunderstanding.' The Prime Minister had to cope with two clever, temperamental competitors for his affection. Neither had undergone the social discipline of being educated at school. Both suffered in these years from recurrent ill health. Each chafed at being locked to the other in what has been traditionally regarded as the most difficult family relationship. 'I always tell everyone of temperament', Margot noted in August 1912, '*never* to be a step-mother.'

Most of the political troubles which put Asquith under strain had the side-effect of intensifying Margot's misery. During the House of Lords crisis in 1911 some Conservative hostesses maintained a social boycott against the Liberals. It was far from complete, and in some cases it soon lapsed, though it was to be revived and extended in 1914 during the final struggle over Home Rule; but it grieved Margot acutely. In January 1913 she wrote to Ettie Desborough, her friend since girlhood: 'I cried when you never sent me one line for Xmas: since life divided into deep devotion for twenty years and impatient hate for these last years, I have quite lost my nerve.'[30]

*   *   *

During the pre-war period Asquith's friendship with Venetia seems to have benefited him. It improved his morale and helped him with a personal problem. For some years his associates had been aware that he was apt to drink too much; and their disquiet had become serious during 1911. In November 1904 he was said to have received a severe warning about his champagne consumption from Haldane, who was no teetotaller. In December 1907 he was described by Munro-Ferguson as having 'a character deteriorated . . . by a free use of wine which he cannot carry'.[31] On 1 July 1909 C. E. H. Hobhouse noted, 'Asquith has . . . been drinking during the last week or two pretty hard.' In April 1911 Asquith was at his best in the House until dinner time, according to Churchill, ' – but thereafter!' Those comments came from well-informed Liberals and they cannot all be attributed to the malice of critics or rivals.[32] Churchill's remark followed a culminating incident during the committee stage of the Parliament Bill when Asquith appeared on the front bench too drunk to speak and a scandal was narrowly averted.[33]

Political opponents continued to refer to Asquith as a 'drunken time-server' throughout his later premiership;[34] but with close observers his reputation for sobriety seems to have improved markedly during his romantic attachment to Venetia. It is impossible to be sure about this; until Haig wrote his wartime diary it was not the practice to record the premier's dining habits glass by glass. In December 1912, however, J. A. Pease noted after a visit to the Asquiths at The Wharf:

All Asquith took for dinner in the way of liquor was a whiskey and soda and a glass of mild port from the wood; at 12 a tumbler of perrier water; and I am told except when dining out he rarely takes more.[35]

After meeting Asquith at a theatrical supper party in June 1914 Arnold Bennett, who was no uncritical admirer, commented: 'He drank a little, but more mineral water than champagne.'[36] Active as Asquith's social life was, comparatively few people were well placed to observe him throughout the evening. What was soon apparent to a wide circle was that all doubts about his will to govern should be put aside. The new note was struck by Max Beerbohm's cartoon of 1913 (opposite p. 172). The Prime Minister sits at ease, disregarding the threats of those who surround him – Sir Edward Carson, a peer with a horsewhip, a German officer, a syndicalist, and a suffragette with an axe. The caption is:

> Come one, come all, this rock shall fly
> From its firm base as soon as I.

Asquith did not suffer in reputation from his attachment to Venetia: it remained a secret to an extent which may seem remarkable today. The gossip columns of the press were then less prominent than they have since become; and local papers showed little interest in the Prime Minister's companions. When Venetia went to Asquith's election meetings at Burnley and Accrington in December 1910 the *Burnley Gazette* merely reported that 'Miss Valentia Stanley' had joined Miss Asquith. When Asquith, Violet, and Venetia travelled to Penrhos together for Whitsun in 1914 the *Holyhead Chronicle's* report did not mention the third member of the party.

Asquith was safeguarded against his friends' realization that he was deeply in love by the very notoriety of his liking for feminine company. Nearly everyone assumed that Venetia was just another in the 'little harem'. Suggestions that the Prime Minister's recreations were apt to be frivolous, and occasionally undignified, had been current for years, and were not entirely confined to Conservative circles. Maud Allan, whose daring dance in *The Vision of Salome* became the talk of London in 1908, was invited to a Downing Street garden party. As Edwin Montagu pointed out to Asquith, this was an imprudent invitation: the Nonconformist

Liberals had objected to encountering Miss Allan while with their wives and were not abashed in their protests by the fact that they had recognized her without difficulty.[37] The Prime Minister's verse in a music-hall song ridiculing the follies of the great was given the refrain:

> For strolling abroad
> In the garden with Maud
> Is a thing that I know I could do.[38]

The premier appeared to Lord Lovat in December 1913 to be 'incapable of doing anything except drift', because of 'drink, bridge, and holding girls' hands'.[39] In February 1914 Ethel Smyth, incensed at Asquith's opposition to women's suffrage, wrote:

I think it disgraceful that millions of women shall be trampled underfoot because of the 'convictions' of an old man who notoriously can't be left alone in a room with a young girl after dinner.[40]

In the following July the Archbishop of Canterbury was privately critical of a premier 'who continued to play bridge with young women until the small hours of the morning'[41] when civil war was round the corner. Very few people knew that references to girls in the plural were by now wide of the mark, since the 'little harem' had been dispersed, to be succeeded by a single great romance.

Margot knew. She wept when she saw Asquith off to Sicily in January 1912, and confided to her diary that she was jealous of those who had gone with him. He wrote from Taormina to reassure her:

Why should you think anything you have written has 'alienated' me? It could not, even for a moment, and even tho' I thought some things you said (or suggested) a little less than just. I love you always wherever I am; and you know well that no one ever does or ever could take your place.

Margot prided herself on refusing to monopolize her husband. She wrote many years afterwards:

Some of my friends . . . wondered why I was not jealous of the women he was fond of. On the contrary, I welcomed them, as they fitted the theory which I have always held about wives. . . . No woman should expect to be the only woman in her husband's life. The idea of such a thing appears to me ridiculous. . . . I not only encouraged his female friends, but posted his letters to them if I found them in our front hall.[42]

Margot's reminiscences do not always provide a reliable guide to her past attitudes. But to an extent the facts bear out what she wrote. Venetia proved the exception to the rule, however. At an early stage she was classed by Margot as 'Violet's squaw',[43] and suspected accordingly. Margot saw the

The Asquith family and friends at Glen, Easter 1904. Left to right: Elizabeth Asquith, H. H.
Asquith, Olive Macleod (standing at back), Margot Asquith (seated, foreground), Katharine
Horner (later Mrs Raymond Asquith), Violet Asquith, H. T. Baker (standing at back), Arthur
Asquith, Cyril Asquith (in front), Edward Horner, Raymond Asquith.

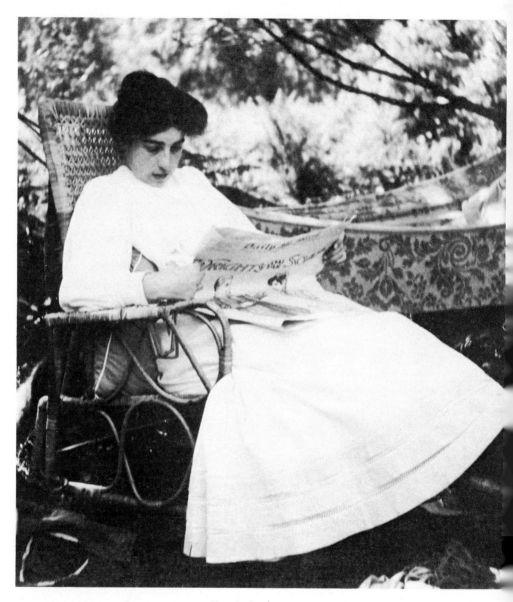

Venetia Stanley, 1908

two girls as conspiring to keep her out of things. The growth of Asquith's attachment did not escape the eye of a wife who loved him deeply, and who never lost a chance to criticize Venetia. By March 1914 Margot knew that this friendship had become far more intense and serious than the others had ever been. Assuming that Edwin Montagu was out of the running as Venetia's suitor, she wrote to him on 21 March:

If Venetia had an ounce of truth and candour . . . I should smile; but she is even teaching Henry* to avoid telling me things. . . . I'm far too fond of H. to show him how ill and miserable it makes me. . . . Good God, to think you proposed to her! A woman without refinement or any imagination whatever. . . . Oh, if only Venetia would marry. How I loathe girls who can't love but claim and collect like a cuckoo for their own vanity. Venetia's head is completely turned.[44]

Margot was right to see Venetia's marriage as the most likely ending to the friendship. Not being a love-affair in the physical sense, it did not follow any recognizable sequence of passion and satiety. As almost all Venetia's letters to Asquith have disappeared her attitude at each stage is hard to gauge. She felt affection for her devoted admirer. 'The P.M.', she told Montagu in December 1912, 'was at his very best, most lovable and most foolish.' She liked being the great man's confidante and always in the know. Whatever her disquiet by June 1914 she was not minded simply to loosen her ties with Asquith and drift away. But the Austrian ultimatum to Belgrade ended many things and led, by the strangest ways, to the change for which Edwin Montagu was waiting.

*   *   *

Asquith was an extremely assiduous correspondent. Except for business notes his letters went almost entirely to his women friends.[45] Most of these personal letters are of no great political interest. They represented one of his recreations. He sought from his correspondence 'not counsel,' in Desmond MacCarthy's words, 'but comfort, communication, and relief'.[46] He told a cabinet colleague in 1912 that 'he knew how to write to people in accordance with the prospect of letters being retained or destroyed; and he wrote accordingly'.[47] The Letters written to Venetia from March 1914 to May 1915 are the exception to all this. Although Asquith knew that they were being kept he filled them with personal, political, and military secrets of every kind; and they include constant appeals for Venetia's counsel. They constitute the most remarkable self-revelation ever given by a British Prime Minister; and it is not likely that they will come to be matched, if only

---

* Asquith's Christian names were Herbert Henry. Few people except Margot called him Henry. It was not then usual among the professional class for a man to be known outside his family by his Christian name.

because Asquith's refusal to use the telephone would not be encountered nowadays among premiers.

There are limits to what even a series such as this can reveal about a statesman. Love-letters, from their very nature and purpose, provide a slightly distorted picture of the writer. What was written to amuse Venetia, usually in moments of comparative relaxation, could hardly give an adequate account either of the premier's administrative grasp or of his parliamentary mastery. He could not risk boring Venetia with the first; and he wanted her to derive her knowledge of the second, not from what he told her, but from attendance in the gallery of the Commons. The Letters show Asquith's attitudes and interests. They indicate his limitations, since they help to confirm the accepted view that his statesmanship was not of the most imaginative kind. What is absent is any indication of the scope of his achievement. It is necessary when reading them to keep in mind that he has seldom been equalled as a peacetime Prime Minister. Britain obtained a recognizably democratic electoral system with the Third Reform Act of 1884. During the sixty years between then and the end of the Second World War the Conservatives lost office quite often; but they faced opponents who held substantial power only once, from the general election of 1906 to the wartime party truce of 1914. Asquith dominated British politics during those eight crucial years;[48] for six of them he was Prime Minister. The administration over which he presided founded Britain's welfare state, reorganized its defences, and modernized its parliamentary arrangements by curbing the House of Lords.

These battles had been fought and won before most of the pre-war Letters were written. In March 1914, when political questions first feature in them on a large scale, Asquith's peacetime premiership had, as it turned out, only a few months to run. The Letters which he wrote between the Curragh 'Mutiny' of that March and the Austrian ultimatum of July depict, not achievement, but mounting embarrassments. He had made a serious misjudgement on Irish Home Rule and in these weeks he was suffering from its results. He shared these embarrassments with Venetia and they must now be described.

The Liberals had been committed since 1886 to Home Rule for Ireland, that is, to giving the Irish their own parliament. A large majority of the Lords opposed this policy, so that until 1911 there had been little possibility of carrying it out and little need for the Liberal leaders to face the difficulty of including the Ulster Protestants in a Home Rule Ireland. The two elections of 1910 brought the prospect of action. Thereafter Asquith had not only the power to enact Home Rule, but an increased inducement to do so. On the one hand, his double victory at the polls ensured the passage of the Parliament Act by which he could overrule the Conservative peers. On the other it left him dependent for his majority on Irish Nationalist M.P.s. The Home Rule Bill was introduced in 1912 and was due to become law under the provisions of the Parliament Act in 1914.

There was little prospect that Belfast could be put under Dublin at a stroke. But the Liberals were as strongly opposed as their Irish Nationalist allies to the permanent partition of Ireland. They had therefore to engraft on to the Home Rule Bill some form of special treatment which would keep the Protestant parts of Ulster as a special entity for a limited period. According to Liberal theory, once the Dublin government had established itself, the Protestants of the north would lose their hostility to it. The problem was whether to introduce this concession to the Ulster counties early or late.

By grasping the nettle early Asquith could have brought his Ulster proposals under the provisions of the Parliament Act, and so made them immune against the Tory majority in the Lords. This drastic course would have been far from safe. It would not have appeased the Conservatives, whose object at the early stage was not merely to save Ulster but to defeat Home Rule. It would have embittered John Redmond, and weakened his position against the anti-British extremists on his flank at the outset of the battle. He and his Irish Nationalists were committed to treating Ireland as a unit from the start; and they shared in the general belief that a Home Rule Ireland deprived initially of Ulster's industries might well prove a failure. The tactics of decisive action in 1912 would have had the great advantage, however, that they did not depend on the consent of the Opposition. If in 1912 the Liberals could have devised a government for Ulster which middle-of-the-road British voters thought fair, and which did not drive the Irish Nationalists to revolt, they could have been sure of putting it on the statute-book, and they would have made the Conservative leaders think twice before backing Ulster's Protestant diehards.

Asquith, who was always inclined to postpone the evil day, chose the other course of delaying the concession to Ulster until 1914,[49] in the belief that by then the imminent enactment of Home Rule would make the Protestants of the north more reasonable. This may not have been the wrong choice; but the grounds on which it was made were quite unrealistic. Asquith adopted it under the mistaken belief that when the Bill was close to the statute-book the Ulstermen would see the inescapable prospect of being ruled from Dublin and would come to heel. They saw no such prospect. They had the wholehearted backing of the Conservative party and they meant to keep Protestant Ulster out of the clutches of the south for good. They were prepared to establish their own provisional government in Belfast and to protect it by armed force; and they knew that no British cabinet, least of all Asquith and his pacific Liberals, could order that they should be shot down for insisting on staying in the United Kingdom and under the Union Jack. The near certainty that Home Rule would reach the statute-book persuaded them, not to compromise, but to form their own army and administration, and to adopt a fighting stance.

Asquith acknowledged throughout that bringing Ulster into a Home Rule Ireland would provoke 'tumult and riot'.[50] This admission was far short of the facts. Bringing Ulster into a Home Rule Ireland would provoke, not disorder, but well-organized defiance. There was nothing disorderly about Carson's army in 1914. The Prime Minister was committed to negotiating with people who had little wish to co-operate in a settlement.[51] By holding out they could both humiliate the Government and ensure, as they believed, that the six 'Protestant' counties should be permanently excluded from the Home Rule area; if Asquith could not order the army to fire on Ulstermen he could not impose Home Rule on Ulster.

It is no coincidence that most of the peacetime Letters show Asquith in the toils. As the strain and his apprehensions increased so did his need for Venetia. Even his calm and experience were not proof against the shock of realizing how mistaken his analysis had been. By the end of June 1914 he faced a surrender such as few political leaders have survived. A final attempt at an Ulster settlement was made at the Buckingham Palace Conference in July. When that failed Asquith saw himself as heading for political disaster. But in politics, as he was fond of saying, 'the Expected does not Happen' (Letter 52). On the day on which the conference broke down the Foreign Secretary learned the terms of the Austrian ultimatum to Serbia.

Notes to the Introduction to Part 1

1. For an earlier Venetia Stanley see Aubrey's *Brief Lives*, ed. O. L. Dick (1958), pp. 100–101. This famous 17th-century beauty was a granddaughter of the 12th Earl of Derby (d. 1572).
2. Diary, 1915–16 vol., p. 213.
3. Pamela Jekyll married Reginald McKenna, 3 June 1908. For Viola Tree's wedding see Letter 3. Dorothy Beresford's father was the parson at Easton Grey: see Appendix 3. Lilian Tennant was the daughter of one of Margot's cousins.
4. See Appendix 3.
5. Asquith to Venetia, 19 Aug.; not selected. Lady Violet Bonham Carter's lecture notes (undated), 'Great Figures I Have Known'.
6. See Appendix 3.
7. See Appendix 3.
8. To Venetia, 3 June 1915; not selected.
9. See Letter 99.
10. *Autobiography*, i (1967). 34. Venetia's father had succeeded as Lord Stanley of Alderley in 1903, and as Lord Sheffield in 1909.
11. Lillah McCarthy, *Myself and My Friends* (1933), p. 149.
12. *An Edwardian Youth* (1956), p. 214.

13. Duff Cooper, *Old Men Forget* (1953), p. 52; Diana Cooper, *The Rainbow Comes and Goes* (1958), p. 138; J. M. Keynes, *Essays in Biography* (1933), pp. 55–8.
14. Dated 'Tuesday' only; reply to his letter of 11 Mar. 1912.
15. See Edwin to Venetia, 8 and 26 Aug., and 22 Sept. 1912.
16. See, for instance, the *Nation*, 11 and 18 Mar. 1911, editorial note and reply by G. K. Chesterton.
17. To Venetia, 17 Nov. 1912.
18. 22 July.
19. Austen Chamberlain, *Politics from Inside* (1936), p. 475.
20. K. Young, *Balfour* (1963), p. 332.
21. 5 Jan.: Earl of Oxford's MSS.
22. *Letters to Lady Bradford and Lady Chesterfield*, ed. Marquess of Zetland (1929), ii. 200.
23. 11 Sept.: Earl of Oxford's MSS.
24. 14 Aug.: Rosebery MSS, Nat. Library of Scotland, 10124, ff. 55–6.
25. To Pease, 11 Sept.: Gainford MSS, Nuffield College, Oxford. For Pamela McKenna, see n. 3 above.
26. Diary of Alan Frederick Lascelles.
27. *Diaries, 1915–18* (1968), p. 68.
28. Spender and Asquith, i. 217.
29. Undated, 1913: Chandos MSS, Churchill College, Cambridge. Asquith's financial worries did not start only when he had left office. See, for instance, his letters to Lord Glenconner 20 Oct., 18 Dec., and 20 Dec. 1913, and Margot to Glenconner, 20 Dec. 1913 (all Glenconner MSS); Asquith to Margot, 28 Dec. 1913; C. Addison, *Four and a Half Years* (1934) i. 237.
30. N. Mosley, *Julian Grenfell* (1976), p. 217. See also Margot Asquith, *More Memories* (1933), pp. 182–3; Margot to the Marquess of Salisbury, 15 and 26 May 1914: Hatfield House MSS, 4M/74/226, 232–3.
31. Stephen Koss, *Haldane* (1969), p. 54. Ronald Munro-Ferguson was writing to Rosebery, whom he admired, speculating on the possibility of keeping Asquith out of the premiership (Rosebery MSS, 10020 f. 28).
32. Hobhouse, *Diaries*, p. 79; Randolph Churchill, *Churchill: Young Statesman, 1901–1914* (1967), p. 344.
33. See Lloyd George, *Family Letters, 1885–1936* (1973), ed. K. O. Morgan, p. 155; *A Good Innings: Private Papers of Visc. Lee of Fareham* (1974), p. 98. An Opposition speaker referred at 2 a.m. to 'the very happy manner in which the Prime Minister in the earlier hours of the evening chose to withdraw from the barricades'. He was called to order by the Chairman: *Parl. Deb.* XXIV. 1221.
34. N. Mosley, *Julian Grenfell* (1976), p. 217.
35. Diary, 2 Dec., Gainford MSS.
36. *Journals*, ed. Newman Flower, ii (1932), 91.
37. S. D. Waley, *Edwin Montagu* (1964), p. 30. For a Conservative comment on this incident, and for a story about Asquith in Venice, see the diary of Lord Balcarres (succ., 1913, as Earl of Crawford), 15 Feb. 1909 and 18 Nov. 1912.
38. Buckmaster, *Roundabout* (1969), p. 165.
39. S. R. Williamson, jr., *Politics of Grand Strategy* (1969), p. 311; from Henry Wilson's diary.
40. 11 Feb., to the Archbishop of Canterbury: Randall Davidson MSS, Lambeth Palace.
41. Hensley Henson's diary, 18 July 1914: vol. 19, p. 232, the Dean and Chapter Library, Durham.
42. *Off the Record* (1943), pp. 121–22.
43. Margot's narrative about Christmas, 1909.
44. Montagu MSS.

45. Raymond Asquith told his wife, 22 Aug. 1916, that during ten months on the Western Front he had not received 'a line of any description' from his father: *Raymond Asquith*, ed. John Jolliffe (1980), p. 287.
46. *Portraits* (1931), p. 4.
47. Pease, diary, 3 Dec.: Gainford MSS.
48. See Visc. Samuel, *Memoirs* (1945), p. 87; G. K. A. Bell, *Randall Davidson* (3rd edn., 1952) p. 868 (Rosebery's view).
49. When the Bill was being prepared in Feb. 1912 Asquith seems to have toyed with an early concession to Ulster: Hobhouse, *Diaries*, p. 111. By Sept. 1913 he was saying that he had always believed in delaying the concession until the final stage: *Churchill: Companion Docs., 1901–1914*, p. 1400.
50. Asquith's memo for the King, mid-Sept. 1913, quoted in P. Jalland, *The Liberals and Ireland* (1980), p. 140.
51. By 1914 Bonar Law and Carson had, in effect, abandoned those Irish Conservatives who did not live in the six 'Protestant' counties of Ulster. This made it very difficult for them to compromise on the six counties.

Archerfield House,[1]
Dirleton, R.S.O.
Scotland.

10 Sept 1910

> Slowly Venetia plods the heavenward road:
> Drawn by the carrot, driven by the goad:
> The flattery, *this*, of blind and fatuous friends –
> The candour, *that*, which pierces and amends.[2]

[1] See Appendix 3. (R.S.O. was a postal term standing for Railway Sub-Office.)

[2] On such verses see Venetia to E. S. Montagu, 11 Dec. 1912: '[The Prime's] "Muse", as he chooses to call it, has burst into song again, which is always I think a sign that he has superabundant spirits and vitality.'

2

1 Ap 1912

Dearest Venetia,

I stupidly forgot on Friday that I was bound to go to-night to Grillions[1] to dine, and see one or two men there. I hope this hasn't put you off anything nice.

I want to see you (& *must*) before you go, and I hear from Violet that you might be able to come here (H. of C) to-morrow (Tuesday) to hear the Budget: in any case after it, at tea time, in my room.

Cassandra-Tante[2] gives his (or her) annual Budget dinner[3] in the evening: so that is taken up.

You will come, won't you?

What did Lord Byron say when he heard the news of the Battle of Waterloo?[4] I had a dullish Sunday (compared with some),[5] and drove back this morning nearly 100 miles in unbroken solitude!
But 'More true joy Marcellus, exiled, feels
  Than Caesar, with a Senate at his heels'.[6]

I have got such a good metaphor about you, which I will tell you in confidence.

Ever yr loving
HHA

[1] Founded in 1812 and named after proprietor of the hotel where it first met. Asquith had been a member since 1893. Weekly dinners were held during the session of Parliament.

[2] E. S. Montagu, after being Asquith's Parliamentary Private Secretary (to use modern parlance), had become Parliamentary Under-Secretary, India; he was to become Financial Secretary to the Treasury, Feb. 1914. The double nickname referred to his gloomy prophecies. *Tante*, a novel by Anne Douglas Sedgwick, had been published in 1911. It concerns 'the most

famous of living pianists' who 'sees life as a dark riddle [and] counts herself as of the entombed'. Montagu had announced 'that he had all sorts of hidden affinities and resemblances to that moody and tempestuous genius' (H.H.A. to Viola Tree, 10 Mar. 1912: Parsons MSS, B L, provisionally Add. MSS 59895).

³ Lloyd George was to introduce the budget on 2 Apr. Asquith cried off Montagu's dinner at the last moment – a sure sign in him of unusual fatigue (Venetia to Montagu, 3 Apr.) See p. 7.

⁴ 'I'm damned sorry for it. I didn't know but I might live to see Lord Castlereagh's head on a pole but I suppose I shall not now.'

⁵ See p. 2.

⁶ Pope, *An Essay on Man*, Ep.iv. 257.

3

13 July 1912

You have not really been to 'dumb forgottenness' (is this a new reading?) a prey – so far at least as I am concerned. I suppose you have in your mind the Violets, Bongies, Tantes, and all that faithless crew? Yesterday was Friday, but alas! I had no drive.[1]

You must be very conscious just at present of your privileges as a many-uncled niece, as I was last night of mine as a many-nieced uncle.[2] We had a huge family dinner party in honour of Frances Tennant[3] – from 25 to 30 'sat down', as the papers say. There was every species of Tennant, Asquith, Lister,[4] Lubbock[5] &c and a sprinkling of carefully selected outsiders such as the millionaire Moore, Hugh,[6] Tante &c. It was quite a success – as also was our garden party the day before at which not a single suffragette was allowed to penetrate, tho' 4 or 5 made the attempt & were winnowed off at the front door.

Viola's wedding was a very pretty one & terribly crowded.[7] A rather improper looking lady created a sensation by her appearance at the garden party – she turned out to be the Marchesa di Rudini, daughter of the late Labby. I played Bridge with her years ago at Rome.[8] She insisted on coming also to lunch yesterday,[9] where I sat between her & Mrs Hamlyn[10] – a good study in piquant contrasts. We are going to a dismal official luncheon to-day at the Palace to meet the Colonials,[11] of whom I feel that I have already seen about as much as I want, and then to Esher for Sunday with Edgar.[12] I think of motoring all the way on Wed to Penrhos: anyhow we shall be there in time for dinner. I quite agree about *Mr Perrin*: it is redeemed by the end; the girl is a thundering bore. But I think there is a lot of promise in it. I know *Spanish Gold* & its successor.[13] You have got hold of the *Medea* lines[14] – or some of them. They are not intended for Tante, who by the way made quite a good speech on Thursday.[15] I am glad you have spoken to him. I must now try & think of something to say at Dublin[16] – or about the Royal Society whose 250th birthday I have to toast at the Guildhall on Tuesday.

Dear love. *Your*

[1] Asquith made regular excursions on Friday afternoons in his chauffeur-driven car. Venetia seems already to have become his usual companion on these.

[2] Venetia's sister Blanche had just been married to Eric Pearce-Serocold at Alderley amid a large gathering of the Stanley family. Margot Asquith had been the youngest but one among twelve brothers and sisters and she had three half-sisters through her father's second marriage. See the family trees in N. Crathorne, *Tennant's Stalk* (1973).

.[3] Frances Tennant was to be married to Guy Charteris on 23 July.

[4] Margot's sister Charlotte, 'Charty' (d. 1911), had married, 1877, the 4th Lord Ribblesdale. For the three Lister daughters see Letters 5, n. 4; and 12, n. 3.

[5] Margot's father had died in 1906 and in 1907 her stepmother, Marguerite, had married Geoffrey Lubbock.

[6] George Gordon Moore, an American, and Hugh Godley. The latter was a close friend of both Violet Asquith and Venetia (see Letter 74, n. 2).

[7] Viola Tree had married Alan Parsons on 11 July. For her friendship with Asquith see p. 1. Hugh Godley reported the wedding to Violet as 'a very vulgar affair'.

[8] Henry Labouchere, the Victorian radical, had died in the previous January, leaving a large sum to his only daughter, the Marchesa.

[9] In the midst of the festivities mentioned, and immediately before this lunch party, Asquith 'made one of the best speeches he's ever made . . . and it came after a really good one of Balfour's' (Montagu to Venetia, 14 July). It was on the second reading of the Government's Franchise and Registration Bill (see p. 26).

[10] Margot had been her friend since their Leicestershire hunting days. Part of the Asquiths' honeymoon in 1894 had been spent at her house, Clovelly Court (see Appendix 3).

[11] A Canadian mission, headed by Borden, the Prime Minister, was in London to discuss naval policy.

[12] Sir Edgar Vincent's home at Esher, for which see Appendix 3.

[13] *Mr. Perrin and Mr. Traill* by Hugh Walpole had been published in 1911, *Spanish Gold* by 'George Birmingham' (Canon J. O. Hannay) in 1908.

[14] Asquith often set literary puzzles in these early letters. Venetia had identified a passage from this play by Euripides.

[15] Like Asquith's (n. 9 above), on the second reading of the Franchise and Registration Bill.

[16] Asquith went to Ireland via the Stanleys' house at Penrhos: see Appendix 3. In his Dublin speech, 19 July, he said that he did not 'believe in the prospect of a civil war' in Ireland. On 27 July at Blenheim Palace Bonar Law could 'imagine no length of resistance to which Ulster will go in which I shall not be ready to support them'. See illustration facing p. 332.

4

The Wharf,
Abingdon.[1]

14 Aug 1912.

It is an age since I heard from you or of you – or even about you. It is time you made some sign. Have you been cultivating new acquaintances, or (what would be much worse) playing fast & loose with old ones? Step into the confessional & let me know the worst.

I know (for he spent Monday night here) that the Assyrian has been coming down among you like a wolf on the fold. Did the 'sheen of his spear' dazzle your vision? and what happened? Tell me all about it.[2]

This place is getting into working order, & is now quite habitable, tho' the persistent rains do not allow it to appear to the best advantage. I spent Friday to Monday with the George Mussings at a place called Springs about 10 miles further down the river. The Herbert Gladstones, Basil Blackwood & Harry Paulton were there: also a rather attractive young woman, a daughter of Lord Methuen, Kitty by name, who is alleged to have ravaged & consumed the hearts of the military in S. Africa during the last three years.[3]

We have had staying here the Eric Drummonds who left to-day – both of them very nice tho' not particularly exciting. The proximity of the river has tempted me to paraphrase Sir J. Denham's famous lines wh. I have often quoted to you –

> 'How deep, how clear, ungentle & yet dull:
> Rage without strength, o'erflowing but not full.'[4]

That wd. describe certain kinds of writing & speaking: Bonar Law's for example.[5]   Dear love. *Your*.

[1] See Appendix 3.

[2] Montagu had just proposed to Venetia: see p. 5. Byron's poem 'The Destruction of Sennacherib' may have prompted Asquith to call Montagu, who was swarthy, 'the Assyrian'. For the latter's 'ugliness . . . and dark eyes' see Duff Cooper, *Old Men Forget* (1953), p. 52.

[3] Viscount Gladstone had been Governor-General, South Africa, since Dec. 1909, Lord Methuen C.-in-C. there, 1908–12. Paulton had been a Liberal M.P., 1885–1910, and Assistant Private Secretary to Asquith, 1893–5. Basil Blackwood was the third son of the 1st Marquess of Dufferin and Ava (d. 1902). Kitty Methuen was to marry into Asquith's circle in 1915: see Letter 376.

[4] Though deep, yet clear; though gentle, yet not dull;
         Strong, without rage, without o'erflowing full.
                    Sir John Denham, 'Cooper's Hill'.

[5] Bonar Law had been elected leader of the Conservatives in the Commons in Nov. 1911.

5

In train
Inverness to Edinburgh.

14 Sept '12.

I am in your debt for two delightful letters, & should have answered the first long ago, but that I was looking forward to seeing you & having talks at Dornoch, not expecting you to turn out a treacherous tenant. I treasure the little box *very* much. It is just a fortnight since I came to Scotland, & I am now on my way South with the prospect of Sunday at Glen[1] & Monday night at Crewe. . . .

. . . I passed on to Balmoral, the rigours of which were alleviated by the company of H. Gladstone & R. Lister, and after three days of 'duty' went for the night to the Beattys at Invercauld. It is (unlike Balmoral) a really beautiful place, & my fellow guests were the Lyttons, the Winstons, & Mdlle Beauxyeux, otherwise known as The Bud.[2] Thence I made my way in the Rolls Royce to Dallas and enjoyed the society of my two surviving nieces: Die Wunderschöne & La Difficile.[3] We drove over on Sunday to see Laura & Diana at Beaufort – a most unlovely specimen of the modern Scotch Baronial style.[4] The last stage of my wandertäge was spent at Oversteps, whither I went on Monday with Eliza & joined Margot & Puffin. The McKennae[5] were in full battle array – Pamela, Reggie, & Ernest: you would have revelled in the environment & were most wrong to miss it. The Assyrian, after many vacillations, also played us false. Did he find his way (or will he) to Penrhos – I wonder? The golf at Dornoch was very good, & the weather the best we have had this summer. We paid a visit to Skibo – only 3 miles off – a marvellous millionaire's pot pourri,[6] with amongst other attractions a small arm of the sea, heated to 75 degrees, and covered in with a sliding glass roof, which according to our host stupefied the late Edward the Peacemaker. He (i.e. Carnegie) keeps a stud of 13 motors, & Margot took the opportunity to charter 2 of them for our use, in one of wh. (a well appointed Rolls Royce) I made the journey of about 70 miles to Inverness this morning.[7] . . .

[1] See Appendix 3.

[2] Sir Reginald Lister, Lord Ribblesdale's younger brother, was less staid than some Balmoral guests. In 1908, when he had been Counsellor at the Paris Embassy, and George V, then still Prince of Wales, had visited Paris, he had persuaded the Prince to sample Parisian night life. They had started at a play which the Prince recorded as 'the hottest thing I have ever seen on the stage', and moved on 'to the Bal Tabarin and the Abbaye at Montmartre and other places'. Invercauld House, which the Beattys rented, is quite near Balmoral. Beatty was then Churchill's Naval Secretary. He had ample means through his wife, daughter of Marshall Field, the Chicago millionaire. 'The Bud' was Mrs Churchill's sister, Nellie Hozier.

[3] Two of Frank Tennant's three daughters, Geraldine and Kathleen, were still unmarried.Geraldine (Dinah, Die Wunderschöne) m., Feb. 1915, Sir Iain Colquhoun, 7th Bt.; Kathleen (Kakoo) m., Jan. 1916, John, Marquess of Granby, who succ., 1925, as 9th Duke of Rutland. At Dallas Lodge, Moray, a small shooting lodge had been added to a late 17th-century Round-square.

[4] Two of Charlotte Ribblesdale's three daughters. Laura had married Lord Lovat in 1910. Beaufort Castle, Inverness-shire, was built 1880 (and partly rebuilt after a fire, 1936).

[5] Asquith liked comic plurals for surnames. Reginald McKenna was Home Secretary, Pamela his wife, and Ernest his brother.

[6] See Appendix 3. The swimming pool at Skibo, though large, does not quite measure up to Asquith's description.

[7] 'I had the boldness to ask for 2 of his 11 motors; . . . he was delighted and lent us both' (Margot's Diary, 14 Sept.).

6

6 Jan. 1913

You don't need to be told how much I enjoyed my time with you. It was in every way & at every moment delightful, tho' (as you may guess) if one could have chosen, I should have liked – without any reflection on the charming & attractive qualities of those who were there – more opportunities of being with *you*. But it would be ungrateful to complain: & I shall always remember our mist- & rain-blurred survey of the three counties, thro' wh. we drove on Saturday.[1]

I purposely keep back, when we are together, so much: more, I dare say, than you suspect.

But I am looking forward to the 18th (or 17th): send me a few names of people to ask. Will they include Mr Solicitor?[2] I will write you a *real* letter very soon. This is only a signal, but it conveys *much*. Dear love

Your

[1] From 3 to 5 Jan. 1913 Asquith stayed with the Stanleys at Alderley: see Appendix 3. Venetia wrote to E. S. Montagu, 7 Jan.:

It was his maiden visit here and though it rained as it only can rain here we had great fun. He and I went for a very dank, chilly, misty drive over the hills to Buxton and he put me through a sharp examination in scripture. As you know, it is not my subject and a few questions revealed the horrid fact that I couldn't name more than 2 of the 12 Apostles! This was a good deal used. I played a lot of chess with him and a certain amount of bridge, at both of which I was fairly successful. He seemed very well, I thought, though rather bored by the prospect of the coming Session.

[2] Sir John Simon.

7

Tu. 7 Jan 1913

I wish I had stayed (if you would have had me) at Alderley over Monday evening. It was dismally dull here, tho' I dined at Grillion's in company with Mr Solicitor! Harcourt & G. Murray & Welby were there, & we had some quite good talk: amongst other things & people, of Blowitz, the great *Times* correspondent in Paris from 1875 to 1900. I quoted Gambetta's remark about him – that he was the *four* worst things: 'Juif, Polonais, Catholique, décoré'.[1] Which do you think the most objectionable of the four? I am afraid, the first?[2] . . .

. . . I am bothered with various things – the latest being certain follies wh. Rufus Isaacs & Ll. George have committed in regard to Marconi shares.[3] Mr Sol[r] has the happy gift of being impeccable. But it is a great rest & refreshment to think & dream of – what you will *never* guess. Dear love –

Your

[1] H. G. S. de Blowitz was a Roman Catholic of Jewish extraction, born in Bohemia. He became a French citizen during the Franco-Prussian War and was decorated for helping the French Government to deal with the Commune in Marseilles in Apr. 1871: de Blowitz, *My Memoirs* (1903).

[2] Venetia's friendship with Edwin Montagu may have given Asquith a particular interest in her attitude to Jewish people. See pp. 5–6.

[3] In Oct. 1912 Isaacs and Lloyd George denied in the Commons that they had ever had any interest in the English Marconi Company. They did not reveal that they had been dealing in American Marconi shares. It is not clear whether Asquith knew of these dealings when the denials were made, or learned of them only a few days before this letter was written. See Jenkins, *Asquith*, pp. 250–5.

8

Thurs. 16 Jan 1913

. . . I am depressed at the thought of absence & separation – & all sorts of possibilities. In any case, as Dryden says, not 'Heaven itself upon the past has power'.[1] And for the *future* – I have faith & try to have hope.

Dear love. *Your*

[1] Not Heav'n itself upon the past has pow'r;
But what has been, has been, and I have had my hour.
Dryden, *Translations from Horace, Ode 29 of Book iii.*
A favourite quotation: see Letters 76, 152, and 318.

9

Monday 20 Jan. 13

It was a real delight to get your dear little pencil letter when I returned from the Coast to-day. I thought you might like to have the notes,[1] which were purposely put together (in my ramshackle fashion) on the back of a letter of yours – which undoubtedly brought them good luck. . . .

9a[2]

Alderley

. . .I am afraid I may just miss Violet, and so escape her hours of conversation about America, which I very much regret as I am afraid she may have become bored by talking of it by the time I get home. Have you heard from her? I havent. I loved the cutting. It would be fun to see the American papers & what they have to say. Here we have 3 inches of snow on the ground, with signs of more, and most of us in bed with colds. I have escaped so far. We have no one here except an Australian Rhodes scholar, an officer in the Office of Works who is inspecting Delamere Forest and has been here since Friday. His name is Robinson. I think regretfully of last Sunday and wish that it had been here that you were bringing Bluey and Oc.[3]

Fanny Parnell's poem is very remarkable, but I suppose it is open to your criticism. It is one of the few good poems in the book.[4]

Do you see that the Assyrian has 'acquired' (in the words of *The Times*) a house in Queen Annes Gate?[5] Do you think he will entertain us there lavishly. I fear not.

Yrs.

Venetia

[1] For his speech in the third reading debate on the Home Rule Bill (15 Jan.).

[2] From Venetia to Asquith, returned to her as indicated in Letter 9. The original sheet with Asquith's notes on the back has since disappeared, the text of 9a being taken from a copy made by Judy Gendel. This is the only passage to have survived from the whole series of Venetia's letters to Asquith during this period.

[3] Harold Baker and Arthur Asquith. Baker had been 'nicknamed "Bluetooth" or "Bluey" after the early King of Denmark, but for what precise reason both he and everyone else had forgotten': Cynthia Asquith, *Diaries, 1915–1918* (1968), p. 486.

[4] No. 568 in *The Oxford Book of Victorian Verse*. It starts:
              'Shall mine eyes behold thy glory, O my country?'
Asquith had called it 'rather too throbbing and strident'.

[5] No. 24: see *The Times*, 9 Jan.

Women's Suffrage (Letter 10)

ASQUITH opposed women's suffrage though most of his cabinet and of the Liberals in the Commons supported it in some form or other. In 1912 the cabinet introduced a bill to abolish plural voting and to extend the suffrage to the two and a half million men who did not yet have the vote. They promised that there would be a free vote in the committee stage on an amendment to give women the same voting rights as men. On 22 January 1913 they 'agreed to differ' on this amendment, and decided that there would be no ministerial resignations whatever the result.

If a bill is amended so substantially during its passage through the House that its whole character is changed, the Speaker may rule that it must be withdrawn and reintroduced. On 27 January Speaker Lowther announced that this would be his ruling if the women's suffrage amendment were passed. The precedents were not clear; and, although *The Times* had pointed out that the ruling might go this way (29 Jan. 1912), the Government were taken by surprise. They lost prestige; but Asquith was greatly relieved

(Letter 11). If the Speaker had decided the other way, and the women's suffrage amendment had then been carried, he would have been obliged to use much energy and parliamentary time in trying to put it on to the statute-book. He naturally recoiled from the prospect of having to do this against his own convictions; and, like the Irish Nationalists, he deprecated any measure which might complicate the passage of Home Rule (see p. 37).

There is some irony about the accusation by the militant suffragettes of the Women's Social and Political Union (*Suffragette*, 31 Jan.) that Asquith had been in collusion with the Speaker. Bonar Law made the enquiry in the House (23 January) which elicited the announcement.[1] The Speaker merely gave the cabinet advance information, as a courtesy, of what he was going to say.

[1] D. Morgan, *Suffragists and Liberals* (1975), ch. 8.

10

Wed 22 Jan 1913

. . . Everybody here is in a tumult of intrigue & counter-intrigue about the women, who come to the front on Friday. The Lobbies are full of missionaries & Maenads trying to seduce our poor spineless wind-tossed waverers & wobblers. I don't see anything of it first-hand, but from what I hear it is a rather pitiful exhibition of so-called masculinity. I am going to speak on Monday, & shall not mince my words. I don't know what will happen but with all these fluid flaccid indeterminate elements, I am not without hope of turning the scale. . . .

11

27 Jan 13

. . . The Speaker's coup d'état has bowled over the Women for this Session: a great relief – but I dare say the militants will now take again to the war-path. . . .

12

The Wharf,
Sutton Courtney,
Berks.

Tu. 18 Feb 13

Your letter of Friday arrived here this morning and was as welcome as – I was going to say 'the flowers that bloom in the spring'. But looking out of the window upon our spacious lawns & parterres, I can only see a single yellow crocus – 'fair as a bulb, when only one Is shooting thro' the ground'. Sir F. Crisp, who promised to be our horticultural providence, has certainly not earned the baronetcy which was prematurely bestowed upon him on New Year's Day.[1] . . .'

. . . I motored yesterday to Easton Grey[2] to see Lucy & Laura Lovat, & heard the surprising news of Diana Lister's engagement to young Percy Wyndham. She is only 19, but perhaps it is better that she shd. get married, as she is a homeless wanderer on the face of the Shires, & not very well able to look after herself.[3] Do you know him? Tho' only 25, I understand he has had a good many experiences.

Bongie[4] & Bluetooth wd. tell you all our London news – particularly how the latter & I championed the far-away Assyrian, who was left without a stain on his character.[5] On Friday we gave a huge dinner party to welcome Anne Islington,[6] it was (considering its size & complexity) quite a success – notwithstanding that Maud Cunard imported a tail of her own of rather shady foreigners. By the way, Crewe tells me to-day that Tante is already firing off neurotic telegrams on the subject of the proposed inquiry.[7] He sent me a series of silhouettes – etched in vitriol – of the members of the Viceroy's Council, a few days ago. Now I must stop. Write again *without* delay. No Nest is forthcoming – except Glen, wh. is too far off – so we still stay on here for a while – Dear love – Your.

Will you please give enclosed to Bongie?

[1] Vice-President of the Linnean Society of London, 1881–1906.

[2] See Appendix 3.

[3] Diana's mother had died in 1911 and her father, Lord Ribblesdale, was financially embarrassed. Wyndham had first met her on 24 Jan. when hunting and had proposed on 12 Feb. 'Diana', Lady D'Abernon noted some years later, 'is very pretty and has the charm of all the Listers.' The three Lister sisters increased Asquith's Tory connections. Laura Lovat's husband was a Conservative peer, and Diana's fiancé the son of an Opposition front-bencher. A year later Barbara's husband won a by-election against a new member of Asquith's cabinet (see Letters 38 and 115 n. 4).

[4] Maurice Bonham Carter. The nickname had been given him at school. It may have owed its popularity to the Yonghy-Bonghy-Bò of Edward Lear's *Laughable Lyrics* (1876).

⁵ Edwin Montagu was in India on government business from Oct. 1912 to Mar. 1913. In his absence the Opposition called for a Select Committee to investigate the position of Samuel Montagu & Co. in buying silver for the Indian coinage. The firm had been appointed as buyers by the India Office in an effort to break 'the Indian silver ring'. Edwin was not involved in this decision; and rumours of scandal, which had arisen in the aftermath of the Marconi disclosures (Letter 7, n. 3), were dispelled without great difficulty. Asquith promised a general inquiry into the financial controls exercised by the India Office and the motion for a Select Committee was not pressed to a division.

⁶ Lord Islington had resigned from the Governorship of New Zealand, which he had held since 1910, to chair a Royal Commission on the Indian public services (the proposed inquiry which prompted Montagu's telegrams). Lady Islington had once been one of Margot's protégées and remained a close friend.

⁷ For the proposed inquiry see n. 5 above. Montagu's embarrassment is understandable in view of the position of one of his cousins, Sir Stuart Samuel. In 1913 an M.P. who entered into official relations with the Government had to resign his seat and stand for re-election (see Letter 38, n. 2). Sir Stuart, who was a Liberal Member, had sought silver buying business for the family firm from the India Office in a way which could be held to entail his resignation. He had declined to resign when urged to do so by the *Jewish Chronicle* in Nov. 1912; and in Feb. 1913 the question of law was referred to the Judicial Committee of the Privy Council. The Committee ruled that the seat must be vacated, whereupon Sir Stuart resigned and was re-elected with a reduced majority.

13

Ap. 1913.

Venetia, though a Christian child,
Sprung from an Aryan stem –
Frequents – too easily beguiled! –
The silken tents of Shem.¹

¹ Edwin Montagu's house was known to Asquith and Venetia as 'the silken tent': see the reference in Letter 41 to its silken curtains. The Hebrews were supposed to be descended from Shem, the eldest of Noah's three sons (hence Semite).

14

The Wharf,
Abingdon.

April 1913

To stir V—a's pulse (an arduous feat)
Out of its normal metronomic beat,
Two Statesmen, & two only, have the Knack –
Sir J—n the Wily, & the Wilier M—c.¹

¹ Sir John Simon and Reginald McKenna. Churchill wrote to his wife from Penrhos, 14 July 1911: 'Much chaff by Violet and the P.M. of Venetia, who is alleged to have flirted with McKenna to the effect that on his saying to her at golf "Come along, my little mascot", she

replied (she denies this) "I wish I were and then I could hang on your watch chain".' McKenna is called 'the mascot tamer' in the Letters.

15

7 Ap. 1913

. . . The congested Wharf[1] found room for Clemmie Churchill, Robert Ross, and the Assyrian. The last named was in an introspective and sombre mood: declared that he had never known what it was to be free from physical & mental pain: and complained that he amused nobody & that nobody amused him. Apart from this, he seemed to be in quite good spirits, and played Bridge with zest & determination. Ross proved to be a very agreeable companion & what John Burns calls a 'good Raconter'.[2] It was a lovely tho' windy day, & I missed you very much. We drove back this morning in Tante's Rolls Royce which devours the ground. Did you read Mr Solicitor's speech, about the man with trousers & without a shirt &c &c? Quite a series of rich, ripe, Falstaffian touches.[3] I thought of our conversation on Friday. Come soon. Dear love –

Your

[1] 'The Wharf I . . . thought very nice,' Venetia reported to Edwin Montagu in Nov. 1912, 'though as a solitary country place for a large gregarious family full of the most obvious drawbacks.'

[2] Ross had been Oscar Wilde's close friend and was his literary executor. In 1915–16 Lord Alfred Douglas made bitter, and well publicized, attacks on the Asquiths for their friendship with Ross (see Jenkins, *Asquith*, pp. 379–80). Burns was President of the Local Government Board, Dec. 1905–Aug. 1914, being the first artisan to reach the cabinet. He was largely self-educated, having left school at the age of 10.

[3] Speaking at Oswestry on 4 Apr., Simon had ridiculed the Conservatives' new policy of tariffs without food taxes (the equivalent of trousers without a shirt). During the second 1910 election campaign Balfour offered to submit the food taxes issue to a referendum. At the end of 1912 the Conservative leaders abandoned this referendum offer and announced that their party would impose food taxes if the Dominions called for them. The move was denounced in the Northcliffe press and caused uproar in the Conservative party. Bonar Law and Lansdowne were persuaded to remain as leaders while eating their words. The Conservatives now promised that there would be no food taxes until, after a spell of office, they had won a second election on that specific issue. These shifts and compromises presented the Liberals with a large target.

16

A Summer Day
July 1913

———

V x x a loquitur:

I fence with Mistress Katharine,[1]
Betimes, in Downing Street:
Eurhythmics[2] call me next – a whirl
Of body arms and feet.

Alert, but hungry, off I speed
To luncheon – *tête à tête* –
Where the Assyrian's groaning board
Is spread, in Queen Anne's Gate.[3]

Then to the City – to select
Rare fine-spun lingerie,
And thence, magnetically drawn,
I reach the Gallery.

A jaded House quaffs wearily
An outworn Session's dregs,
But my fresh heart leaps up to see
Grim T—e[4] on his legs.

The day rolls on: another treat
Is yet in store for me:
Lurking (I know) in Mansfield Street
Lord S—d[5] waits for tea.

'Tis 7 o'clock: my peignoir donn'd,
My priceless H—k[6] I dandle,
While Mrs B—r combs my hair,
And tells the latest scandal.

The gong's last note reverberates,
I join the Sh—d table,
Bong—e to left, Ge—f—y to right,[7]
I've scaled the tower of Babel.

A hasty rubber: off I hie
Where Beecham rules the scene:
And sample for the 20th time
Nijinsky, Chaliapine.[8]

The night is young: a rout, a dance
A supper, still remain:
I go to bed at ½ past 3 –
To do it all again.

[1] Mrs Raymond Asquith. 'I've taken to fencing,' Venetia told Edwin Montagu (21 Nov. 1912); 'Katharine and I do it three times a week: it's such fun. I am trying to make Violet start too, partly because I think she would like it, and also because I think the Downing Street garden would be such a good place to do it in in the summer.'

[2] A system of training body-movements so that they would be, not merely an accompaniment to music, but an expression of it; devised by Émile Jacques-Dalcroze (1865–1950), who used it originally for professional students of music, but from 1905 more generally.

[3] For Montagu's house see Letter 9a.

[4] Tante, i.e. Montagu.

[5] Lord Sheffield, Venetia's father. For No. 18 Mansfield Street, the Stanleys' London house, see Appendix 3.

[6] Huck, Venetia's dog.

[7] Maurice Bonham Carter and Venetia's cousin, Geoffrey Howard. The latter was well known for his loud voice.

[8] Beecham had been conducting, and Nijinsky dancing, for the London seasons of the Ballets Russes since 1911. The Grand Season at Drury Lane in 1913 included opera and ballet, Chaliapine being one of the opera stars.

17

Hopeman Lodge,[1]
Hopeman,
Morayshire.

21 Aug 1913

Our letters seem to have got into a bad habit of crossing. I wrote to you on Tuesday, not thinking that you were going to Ireland before Thursday, and gave a fairly full account of our manner & custom of living here. Thank you very much for your Killarney letter, which arrived this morning. I know the place: it is quite one of the gems of Europe. Yes, it is depressing to read how, & with who, you have been spending your time. You are really not to be trusted so far out of reach of warning voices & gently guiding hands, and a weekly Friday afternoon sermon. Do you miss it? However, I applaud your candour in making a full (is it full?) confession, but penance comes before absolution – as the minions of the Pope's household, with whom you have been consorting, have doubtless told you.[2] I have been thinking of a mild and minor privation suitable to a first offender (tho' alas! you have long since lost all claim to that title). On the whole, I think it must take the form of abstaining from tête-à-tête's with Bongie during his stay at Penrhos, and spending a daily 2 hours in walking & talking with Mr Stopford Brooke.[3] You see how easily I let you down.

Cys has arrived here, minus all his luggage, & having very narrowly escaped drowning at Clovelly.[4] Violet & I engaged in a foursome at Lossie yesterday with Ramsay Macdonald (who lives there) & Somervell.[5] Violet rather lost her heart to the brindle-haired Labour leader.[6]

The Assyrian writes (with characteristic cold-bloodedness) that the sudden death of his host 'rather complicates' his plans:[7] he still hopes to be with us to-morrow. Don't you wish you had the wings of a dove? This is in most ways an ideal resting place.

Dear love. Always.

[1] See Appendix 3.

[2] Killarney House is in County Kerry.

[3] Stopford Augustus Brooke (1832–1916) was a preacher and man of letters of Unitarian views. His son Stopford William Wentworth Brooke (1859–1938) had been a Liberal M.P., 1906–10.

[4] See Letter 3, n. 10.

[5] Cyril Asquith had just obtained a first class in Greats at Oxford where he had been friendly with Donald Somervell (Attorney-General, 1936–45; Lord Justice of Appeal, 1946–54; Lord of Appeal in Ordinary, 1954–60).

[6] 'He is very good looking and fluent – rather vain', she wrote to Venetia, 21 Aug. MacDonald was expelled from the Moray Golf Club in 1916 because of his supposedly unpatriotic attitude to the war. After that he never played on the Lossiemouth links.

[7] Montagu's letter to Venetia about this is hardly cold-blooded: 'I have had an awful time; my poor friend, a splendid old boy, died literally in my arms. . . . This is a wonderful family believing without affectation that death is but an incident. I like death less and less the more I come to it and my friends' faith does not inspire me: it frightens me.'

18

Hopeman Lodge,
Hopeman,
Morayshire.

22 August 1913

V.S. aet. XXVI

———

> While friends, unthinking, join to celebrate
> With posies, presents, prayers, this famous date;
> I, only I, explore in pensive mood
> The secret of V—a's spinsterhood:

Contemn the craven crew, who dare not rise
To risk the gain or loss of such a prize;
And envy him (not born, like me, too soon)
For whom the partial gods reserve the boon.

19

Hopeman Lodge,
Hopeman,
Morayshire.

3 Sept 1913

. . . Dorothy's engagement is the 'big gooseberry' of the dull season. Less considerate than you, I made Violet & Elizabeth guess; result, a pitiable display of wild & futile conjecture. Isn't the fiancé what Violet calls your Sylvia's 'discard'? It gives one a certain sombre satisfaction to think that he is a brewer. Are they going to live on the past profits of this sinful trade? Or is he going to confine his energies in the future to the production of ginger pop? It is quite a good situation.[1]

Tante came to us on Sat & left again on Sunday. He was in his best form, & complained bitterly of Violet's 'warped sense of humour'. Beb & Cynthia arrive to-day: also Blue-tooth, who no longer objects to be in the same house with the 'moonfaced wanton'. The weather has been cold & grey for 3 days, but seems to be upon the mend. Mrs Birrell hit a male suffragette (who was pouncing upon her Augustine) with an umbrella on the head – much to Violet's envy, who now wishes she had used her cleek upon my assailant.[2] How sad about the Kenmares' house![3]

Dearest love. Always.

[1] Lady Dorothy Howard's mother, the widow of the 12th Earl of Carlisle and Venetia's aunt, was a prominent crusader for teetotalism. Venetia's sister Sylvia was married to Anthony Henley, elder brother to Lady Dorothy's fiancé. Venetia wrote of the fiancé to Montagu, 10 Sept.: 'I think it's larks his being a brewer and a Conservative and an anti-suffragist.'

[2] Asquith had been assaulted on the Lossiemouth golf links by suffragettes who tried to tear off his clothes. Violet protected him until the detectives came up. She said, many years later, that she had thrown away her club to escape the temptation of using it (*Observer*, 22 Nov. 1969). A cleek corresponded roughly to the number 2 iron of a modern golf-bag.

[3] Killarney House had been gutted by fire on 31 Aug.

20

8 Dec 13 midnight

This was one of the most delightful Sundays I can ever remember. After all the speechifying, & the limelight, and the butter-boats of appreciation &

adulation, and the conversations with Uncle Hugh & Aunt Florence[1] – and all the rest – the change, & the joy of being with you, and of realising things as they are, or as one hopes they are, was *everything*. I only hope you felt anything like the same. . . .

[1] Asquith spoke to the conference of the National Liberal Federation at Leeds on 27 Nov. Lady Sheffield's brother, Sir Hugh Bell, had a country house at Rounton, Northallerton. For 'Aunt Florence', his second wife, see p. 117.

21

15 Dec 1913

I got back from the Wharf soon after noon, and was delighted to find your yesterday's letter. We were much more lucky than you seem to have been (apart from your excursions into Swiss geography & history) as we had brilliant sunshine all day, & after the sun set an unclouded full moon.

The Assyrian was in good form, but had to leave on Sunday afternoon for one of his shooting expeditions. He seems to have told Margot that he now realised that Viola was the sort of woman whom he ought to have married, & to have compared her favourably with the unsatisfying and elusive young females who have so far played, in turn, the part of pole-star to his rather vagrant heart. I hope this won't rankle too sorely in your susceptible bosom. As I told Viola (by way of warning), his i.e. the A's 'Sentimental Journey' has hitherto been a series of jolts and bumps from one milestone to another. Perhaps you think this was an exaggerated way of putting it? and that there was at any rate one fairly prolonged spell of more or less tumultuous constancy?[1]

I am very much afraid that the chances of seeing you next Sunday dwindle to an even finer point. There are all sorts of complications about Eliz[th], Puffin, &c &c. You know how I long to be with you – don't you?

Dearest love

[1] Viola Parsons (née Tree). For Montagu's proposal to Venetia see p. 5.

The 1914 Naval Estimates
(Letters 22, 24–28, 33, 34 and 47)

THE Naval Estimates for 1914 created a political crisis of which the anti-armament delegation mentioned in Letter 22 gave a foretaste. When the cabinet discussions began early in December 1913, Churchill, the First Lord of the Admiralty, deployed a strong case. The Government was committed to an extremely expensive programme of converting fleet units to oil fuel. If

Churchill had resigned he would probably have taken the two junior ministers at the Admiralty and the Sea Lords with him. On the other hand, the
demand in the Liberal party for a reduction in these estimates had grown
very strong. The National Liberal Federation conference had carried, without dissent and amid cheers, a motion viewing 'with grave anxiety the
continued growth in armaments' (27 November). 'The principle of Liberalism', one speaker said, 'must be got into the Admiralty and must remain
there.' Many Liberals had long been sceptical about the possibility of
German aggression. Germany had led Europe in schemes of social welfare.
'Social democracy', pronounced the Liberal *Nation*, 'with its twenty per
cent of soldiers in the German army, will stop war and the growth of
German armaments.' After the Reichstag elections of 1912, and the co-
operation between Britain and Germany over the Balkan Wars, this was
easy to believe. It was abhorrent to Liberals to treat Germany as a potential
enemy, and Russia, a repressive and backward power given to anti-Jewish
pogroms, as a close friend. Liberal editors were apt to treat accounts of
Germany's warlike spirit and preparations as the work of dupes or knaves.[1]
They put some of their own foreign correspondents in the first category. To
the second they consigned those jingo newspapers which used war scares to
build circulation. They regarded the demand for conscription primarily as
an effort to destroy Liberalism and civil liberty.

The belief that war had become less likely was not confined to Liberals.
The Great Illusion by Norman Angell which had appeared in 1910 enjoyed a
great vogue. It influenced Lord Esher, who was regarded in Conservative
circles as an authority on defence matters. In March 1912 he told an
audience of service officers, chaired by the C.I.G.S., that war 'becomes
every day more difficult and improbable'.[2] According to Angell each European nation had become so dependent economically on the others that the
folly of war was obvious: the winners would lose like the rest. This euphoria
was to remain unabated for some months. At the end of May 1914 Britain
and Germany reached agreement on the Baghdad railway question, the
Committee of Imperial Defence being advised to 'act on the assumption that
the present international situation is likely to continue for the next three to
four years'. Conservative papers sent greetings to the Kaiser in June,[3]
Conservative spokesmen having long made clear that the Ulster Protestants
would rather be ruled by the Kaiser than by Roman Catholics from Dublin.[4]
By then Sir Edward Grey, the Liberal Foreign Secretary, was almost equally
optimistic. He thought in late June 'that the German government are in a
peaceful mood and that they are very anxious to be on good terms with
England'.[5]

Some of the warnings which were sounded failed even to reach Liberal
editors and ministers: others came from sources in which they had little

confidence. In January 1913 the British Ambassador at Vienna had written to Nicolson, Grey's Permanent Under-Secretary, about the instability resulting from the Balkan Wars. 'Serbia', he warned, 'will some day . . . bring about a universal war on the continent. . . . The next time a Serbian crisis arises . . . Austria-Hungary will refuse to admit any Russian interference . . . and . . . will proceed to settle . . . with her little neighbour *coûte que coûte.*'[6]

Lord Fisher, lately the First Sea Lord, had written as early as 1911 that 'Armageddon' would start in 1914 as soon as the widening of the Kiel Canal had been completed.[7] Others pointed out that Russia's recovery from the débâcles of 1905–06, and the adoption of three-year army service in France, would soon reduce Germany's military lead, and give the war party in Berlin an inducement to strike while still strong.[8] These views were easily disregarded as irresponsible jingo scaremongering.[9] It was hard to regard Fisher's prophecies as entirely judicious, for instance, when he interlarded them with assertions that the British were the ten lost tribes of Israel.

The Liberals had strong reasons for disliking defence estimates which they regarded as unnecessarily high. If they were to win the 1915 election they needed a good budget in 1914. High spending on defence was hamstringing plans for social reform. A successful budget would help Lloyd George, the Chancellor of the Exchequer, to recover from the Marconi affair. This was the background to the interview with the *Daily Chronicle* on 1 January 1914 in which he decried 'the overwhelming extravagance in our expenditure on armaments'. Characteristically, Asquith referred to this interview as 'heedless folly' (Letter 24). Others thought it a bid for radical and Labour support.

As a thrusting ex-Tory, whom many Liberals thought too warlike, Churchill was vulnerable to Lloyd George's attack. Yet Asquith succeeded, after long cabinet discussions, in securing agreement to the estimates with no more than minor concessions by the Admiralty. He was well placed to use his skill as a chairman. Lloyd George wanted concessions made to Ulster on Home Rule. On that issue his main cabinet ally was Churchill: he could not afford a breach with the First Lord. Moreover few Liberals would have forgiven any move which gave Churchill good cause to resign, however much they disliked his estimates. A weakened ministry would have little chance of establishing Home Rule. Indeed Asquith allowed his colleagues to know that he would dissolve Parliament rather than carry on with such a cabinet. The Home Rule and Welsh Disestablishment Bills were due to become law in 1914 under the Parliament Act. If there were resignations and a dissolution now, all the work done to enact these measures would be lost and the Parliament Act would begin to look something of a nullity. No minister was prepared to fight the estimates to the point of becoming known as the rebel who had forced on a dissolution.

[1] See R. C. K. Ensor, *England, 1870–1914* (1936), p. 484, n. 1; P. Gibbs, *Adventures In Journalism* (1923), pp. 204–10. For the proceedings of the peace societies in 1914 see *Manchester Guardian*, 19 May, 10d; 20 May, 10b; 10 June, 10e.

[2] *The Influence of King Edward and Other Essays* (1915), p. 147.

[3] In October 1913 the Kaiser had been eulogized by a Northcliffe paper, the *Evening News* (17 Oct.), and by L. J. Maxse in the *National Review*, lxii. 298.

[4] Bonar Law, 1 Jan. 1913 (*Parl. Deb.* xlvi. 464, 471). See also *Morning Post*, 19 Dec. 1910; 9 Jan. 1911 (Andrews, Craig) and A. T. Q. Stewart, *The Ulster Crisis* (1967), p. 226. There was little response from Germany where the Ulster movement was not popular: F. Prill, *Ireland, Britain, and Germany, 1871–1914* (1975), p. 134.

[5] Keith Robbins, *Grey* (1971), p. 287.

[6] H. Nicolson, *Lord Carnock* (1930), p. 390.

[7] R. H. Bacon, *Fisher* (1929), ii. 139. Fisher put 'the date of . . . Armageddon' at Oct. 1914, as he expected the Germans to complete their harvest before declaring war.

[8] See J. S. Sandars to A. J. Balfour [Sept. 1911], B L Add. MSS 49767, ff. 182–3; *National Review*, lxii. 49 (Sept. 1913). This point was better appreciated on the Continent than in England: see I. V. Bestuzhev, *Journal of Contemporary History*, i, no. 3, 96 (report in 1912 by the Russian military agent in Berlin that 'the critical moment' would come just after the spring of 1914).

[9] See A. G. Gardiner's 'Open Letter to Lord Northcliffe', *Daily News*, 5 Dec. 1914. In Dec. 1912 the *Nation* (xii. 421) had thought Lord Roberts's conscription scheme 'more than anything else a plot for the destruction of Liberalism and . . . civil freedom'.

22

17 Dec 1913

. . .I have spent most of the day in receiving deputations from anti-armament MP's,[1] and Nonconformist divines anxious about 'single-school areas'.[2] They were both rather trials of patience – people telling you at great length things which you know as well as they do, with a plentiful fringe of banal rhetoric. . . .

[1] 40 MPs attended. They were said to represent a further 60.

[2] Areas in which the only school was under Church of England management. The discussions about this problem are described in G. Sherington, *English Education, Social Change and War, 1911–1920* (1981), ch. 2.

Ulster I: 'Worse things than bloodshed'?
(Letters 23–48)

ASQUITH's difficulties over Ulster's place in a Home Rule Ireland have been described on pp. 14–16. He had been in touch with Bonar Law on the problem since October 1913. The talks initiated then broke down after his interview

with Carson on 2 January 1914 (Letter 23). The Opposition insisted on the
total and permanent exclusion of Ulster from the Home Rule scheme. At
first the Liberals would not go beyond an arrangement whereby the excluded area would have special powers of veto in the Irish parliament. This
was the formula put to Redmond on 2 February (Letters 29–31). The cabinet
were soon driven further by their overriding need to publish proposals
which moderates outside Ireland would regard as fair. They secured a
measure of assent from the Nationalist leaders to a scheme whereby each of
the more Protestant counties of Ulster could hold a referendum and exclude
itself from Home Rule Ireland for six years. The period of exclusion would
include two general elections, so that it gave the Conservatives two chances
to save Ulster. Asquith announced this 'final' concession on 9 March
(Letter 43).

The cabinet needed to show that they were firm as well as moderate.
Churchill, who wanted to rehabilitate himself with his party after the naval
estimates crisis,[1] undertook this task. In a speech at Bradford on 14 March
he made plain that Home Rule, in its amended form, was to go into effect
whether Carson's Ulster Volunteers liked it or not (Letters 46 and 47).
Coercion was not ruled out: there were, Churchill declared in a characteristic phrase, 'worse things than bloodshed even on an extended scale'. On 17
March a cabinet committee reported that troops should be moved to reinforce the guards on the Ulster arms depots and orders to this effect were
issued on the following day.[2] General Sir Arthur Paget, the Commander-in-
Chief in Ireland, feared that what counted as firmness in London became
provocation across the Irish Channel; and after a day or two of his blundering it was not only the Ulstermen who had been provoked (Letters 49–51).

[1] 'In order to strengthen myself with my party, I mingled actively in the Irish controversy':
Churchill, *The World Crisis, 1914* (1923), p. 178.
[2] For the background to this report see P. Jalland, *The Liberals and Ireland* (1980), pp.
219–23.

23

Lympne[1]

Sat 3 Jan 14

It was a delightful surprise to get your little pencil note this morning, and
dear of you to write it. Of course I enjoyed Alderley – in spite of anxieties
about Cys[2] & other things; but from my point of view it is rather tantalising
to be there when you are doubling the parts of Martha & Granville Barker.[3]
But I carry about some memories of your little room which 'flash upon
the inward eye, that is the bliss of solitude'. You say it would be nice for

us to be abroad together again.[4] So say I – but in what sort of 'juxta-position'?

Very good news of Cys: the Doctor says he will now only telegraph on alternate days.

I wrote a Collins to your Mother & told her (apart from pleasure) that I had learnt 3 solid things at Alderley this time (1) how to play 'Commerce'[5] (2) that there were fools who thought Gibbon wrote Junius (this was from a book I took up to console me in my bedroom the night you disappeared) (3) that there are quite intelligent people who are under the sway of Dogs!

The Assyrian & I had a peaceful but gloomy journey to London, and after lunch I 'perched' for an hour at 24 Q. A. Gate – not in his company, but in that of – you can perhaps guess Who.[6] I motored here in twilight & silence, and wished I were elsewhere. My nieces are kind & welcoming,[7] but –. I go back to London Monday: *do* write – now & always   *dearest Love*

[1] See Appendix 3.

[2] Cyril Asquith had developed dysentery, with a very high fever, a week after arriving in Egypt. Typhoid was feared at first 'which, if it had developed, he couldn't possibly have lived through' (Violet Asquith to Venetia, 14 Jan. 1914).

[3] Harley Granville-Barker (1877–1946), the leading London actor, playwright, and producer. During the New Year house party at Alderley Venetia came in for the household work falling on the only daughter still unmarried; and she was much concerned with the plays which the children acted. Asquith reported to Margot (3 Jan.): 'The Arthur Stanley children . . . are born actors with the Kemble blood in their veins, and were well coached by their mother.'

[4] See Letter 25, n. 1.

[5] His instruction in this old-fashioned game may have been prolonged. The Christmas Day session, as Venetia reported to Edwin Montagu, began 'immediately after dinner' and ended after midnight. The players were apparently refreshed with punch: see Letter 242. A 'Collins' was a letter of thanks to a hostess, named after Mr Collins's letter in *Pride and Prejudice*.

[6] For this meeting with Carson see pp. 38–9.

[7] Dinah and Kakoo, Frank Tennant's younger daughters. See Letter 5, n. 3.

24

Tu. 6 Jan 1914

I have not heard from you yet since you crossed the Channel,[1] but I am hoping for a letter to-morrow. I dined quite alone last night, which I rather liked. . . .

I have had quite a stream of visitors this morning, mostly of the official type: Illingworth, Edward Grey, the Arch Colonel, and the Infant Samuel.[2] They all mutter severe things about Ll. George, & the heedless folly of his 'interview', which has set all Europe (not to mention the poor Liberal party here at home) by the ears. I find that Winston does not return from his Paris fleshpots till Friday: meanwhile he preserves a dignified and moody silence. The Assyrian (after his fashion) has beaten a retreat into the fens and thickets of Cambridgeshire[3] . . .

[1] Venetia was in Chamonix with her brother Oliver.
[2] The Chief Whip, Foreign Secretary, War Secretary (J. E. B. Seely), and Postmaster-General. See p. 37.
[3] Montagu sat for the Chesterton Division of Cambridgeshire.

25

9 Jan 14

It was delicious to get your charming long letter of 6th this morning. (By the way, I gave you a much needed holiday in the way of letter-reading yesterday. I thought it was only fair.) As regards conditions of foreign travel I agree that we had a very good time in Sicily.[1] I wouldn't go so far as to say 'it answered *every* requirement'. I can imagine even more ideal conditions – but I fear they are not likely to be realised in the way I should picture them. Meanwhile we will still hope that sometime this year the *Enchantress* may come to our aid & provide at any rate a good second-best.[2]

That assumes that the good ship is likely to be at our disposal, which after the hour's talk I have just had with Winston seems to me to be by no means certain. He has been hunting the boar in Les Landes,[3] and has come back with his own tusks well whetted, and all his bristles in good order. There will be wigs on the green, before his tussle with Ll. G is over. A fallen wig *can* be readjusted, but the process of putting it on again & looking as tho' nothing had happened, is as a rule neither easy nor dignified. You see I speak to you in allegories, but I know no one who is more skilled in reading between (and behind) the lines.

I will now tell you something about my own doings – actual & future. I dined with Lady C Hatch – a rather dismal function of dim people, with baddish Bridge: as the result of 3 strenuous rubbers I lost 1/-! I had another solitary drive yesterday (if only you were here instead of being mewed up in a beastly far-away inn!) and dined with the M°Kennae. Your friend was in his best form – cheerful fluent & assured – just as you remember him on a famous & fateful afternoon. Bluey was there – as always – & Frances Horner & Lady Scott.[4] It was quite nice, if not wildly exciting. To-night I attend the Assyrian's banquet in honour of Lady Sheffield, & I suppose of La Reine Pédauque & her vice-regal spouse.[5] They are dining with me here on Monday. I go to Easton Grey for Sunday. *Tuesday morning* I mean to start for Antibes, & find that I shall have Lady Scott & Lady Muriel Paget as travelling companions; don't you envy me? I shall be there (Hôtel du Cap d'Antibes) from Wed to Sunday 18th when I return here with Puffin. So I hope I shan't miss much of you: I dine with your family 20th. *Do write* & be clever in hitting off posts & addresses: it makes *so* much difference to me.

I can't say that the account you give of your present way of life makes me long to share its externals, much as I should love to be in your company. I heard from Violet this morning – the first letter giving an account of Cys's illness, which seems at first to have been rather alarming. The papers to-day announce that I am going to Paris on a mission! There are enough rocks ahead without that. Meanwhile now as always you are 'a very present help'.[6]

All my love

[1] A reference to the Sicilian holiday, for which see p. 2.

[2] The Admiralty Yacht. Cruising in it is depicted in Violet Bonham Carter, *Winston Churchill as I Knew Him* (1965), ch. 19. From the *Enchantress* off the west of Scotland Venetia wrote to Edwin Montagu: '(Off Colonsay, 10 Sept. 1913) A most wonderful lonely enchanted place with delicious sandy and rocky little bays, looking quite glorious yesterday in brilliant clear weather, and even today full of charm and mystery in spite of thick obliterating Scotch mist . . . I am always very happy here. I love the life with long intervals of drifting about and then one goes to divine inaccessible places.'

[3] He had been with his friend the Duke of Westminster.

[4] Widow of the explorer. In 1915 she became one of Asquith's closest friends.

[5] Arthur Stanley, Venetia's eldest brother, had just been appointed Governor of Victoria. The nickname for his wife referred to the alleged claim of the Stanleys to trace their descent from Charlemagne: Bertha, Charlemagne's mother, was supposed to have been goose-footed. Anatole France's novel, *La Rôtisserie de la Reine Pédauque*, had been published in 1893.

[6] Psalm 46.1.

26

21 Jan 14

. . . I had a long interview after we parted yesterday with my two colleagues[1] – *à trois*. It was interesting & at moments rather dramatic. What Mr G.[2] called 'bridge-building' is going on to-day but I am not very sanguine about the success of that particular operation! Write to me if you can't see me.   Dearest love.

[1] Lloyd George and Churchill.

[2] Gladstone.

27

27 Jan 1914

. . . Grim realities were not slow in presenting themselves – 'Gorgons & Hydras and Chimaeras dire' – as Milton says.[1] A letter (of rather a neurotic kind) from the highest quarters:[2] a visit (near mid-night) from the Lord Chancellor, with a somewhat nebulous report of his Windsor Sunday; and in the course of this morning successive calls from Winston & Ll. G. . . .

And now as I am writing we are in the full stress of Cabinet discussion. Happily Huck is not present, but the bigger breed have their ears well laid back, & from time to time give tongue. (Some considerable time, say $\frac{1}{2}$ or $\frac{3}{4}$ of an hour, has elapsed since I wrote the last sentence, full of animated sound, including a few mellow and melodious *glapissements* from 'Sweetheart'.[3]) We shan't decide anything to-day & shall meet again to-morrow. But the air is more than a trifle thunderous. Are you angry that I said you were apt to be 'unsurprised'?   Dearest love.

[1] *Paradise Lost*, ii. 628.

[2] The King wrote (26 Jan.): 'Ulster will never agree to send representatives to an Irish parliament in Dublin.' Asquith would have been well advised to heed this warning; but in private he took a patronizing view of the King, writing (Sept. 1912) to Margot: 'He is a nice little man with a good heart and tries hard to be just and open minded. It is a pity he was not better educated.' For Queen Mary's view of the defects in George V's education see H. Nicolson, *Diaries and Letters, 1945–62* (1968), p. 167.

[3] Earl Beauchamp, First Commissioner of Works. Asquith often referred to the less important members of his cabinet as 'beagles', 'bobtails', and 'trays'. See *King Lear*, III. vi:

> The little dogs and all,
> Tray, Blanch, and Sweetheart, see they bark at me.

28

28 Jan 14

. . . To-day we have had another & more satisfactory Cabinet (for yesterday was mainly given to sniping from opposite sides of the hedge), and I have good hopes that to-morrow we shall arrive at a settlement. I hear from Illingworth, who goes scouting about, that the Impeccable is the real & only stubborn Irreconcilable.[1] I should be sorry if we had to give him permanently the 2 extra syllables. I am hoping to see you again Friday. . . .

[1] 'The loss of W.C.,' Simon ('the Impeccable') wrote to Asquith, 'though regrettable, is *not* by any means a splitting of the party – indeed large Admiralty estimates may be capable of being carried *only* because W.C. has gone.' The protest against Churchill's estimates sent to Asquith on 29 Jan. was signed by Beauchamp, Hobhouse, McKenna, Runciman, and Simon.

29

. . . I had Birrell with me at the Leviathan[1] interview. I developed the situation with such art as I could master, until the psychological moment arrived for discharging my bomb. My visitor shivered visibly & was a good deal perturbed, but I think the general effect was salutary. He wisely refused to commit himself on the spot, & promises further communication in a day or two. . . .

¹ A nickname for John Redmond. It seems to have been Asquith's invention and something close to a code-word. For the 'bomb' see p. 39.

30

After I wrote to you yesterday I spent rather an unprofitable afternoon, listening to and interrupting a Miners' deputation for the best part of 2 hours on Minimum Wage & other equally exhilarating topics, and then going for a solitary drive in the gloaming. I didn't get as far as the Hale, but I passed Venetius's tasty little villa, and fancied I caught a hasty glimpse of him at work in his garden – as an ex-horny-hand ought from time to time to be.[1] I dined with Cassel & played Bridge with Lady Lewis Lady Paget & Winston. The 'First Lord' made every conceivable blunder: happily I was not his partner, & came home with a slightly replenished pocket. (I have been interrupted by a call from Crewe, in the course of which I broke to him that he might have to part with the services of his Assyrian Curate – called by Providence to a higher sphere – *strictly entre nous*. I am not sure that after all it may not be the Treasury. On the whole he (i.e. C.) prefers Bluetooth to the rest as a successor.[2] Then in came Birrell, who had just had a rather gloomy second interview with our Leviathan. The 'breadcrumb' stage has not yet been reached – if it ever will be.[3] I must brace myself to fresh culinary efforts (I fear) to-morrow aft. before I make tracks for Windsor. Birrell, none the less, is in excellent form & I am glad to say is staying to lunch. I break off for the moment here.)

I have now been at the Mansion House at a meeting to organise the celebration of 100 years' peace between us & the Yankees.[4] A pretty dismal affair, as no one could by possibility rise above the level of platitude. Old Bryce made rather a good speech: he is 76 & looks like Father Time, but could still shew you the way up the Mauvais Pas – or higher, & discourse at a moment's notice & at any required length on any topic human or divine.[5]

H. H. Asquith at Penrhos, 1911

H. H. Asquith and Venetia Stanley,
February 1910

Venetia Stanley,
about 1904

Winston Churchill
and Venetia Stanley
at Penrhos, Whitsun
1910

Since I came back I have been visited by Spender & the Infant Samuel, as we call him. I am dining to-night with the Winstons. I have been trying for some strange reason to read at nights a History of the Wars of the Roses, but find it a desperate tangle of small men & events. I wonder how you have spent your day? hunting & holla'ing – I suppose. I will tell you to-morrow whether Sunday is possible. I long to see you again: like the erring but forgiven Thomas I think seeing is believing – at least sometimes.

All my love

[1] See Letter 81, n. 2.

[2] Montagu was promoted in Feb. from being Parliamentary Under-Secretary, India, to be Financial Secretary to the Treasury. For 'Bluetooth' see Letter 37, n. 2.

[3] In the final stage of his cooking Asquith would have to agree with the Nationalist leaders exactly what powers of veto Ulster would command in the Irish parliament, and – a still more contentious question – exactly what area should be designated as 'Ulster' for this purpose.

[4] The Treaty of Ghent to end the war of 1812 was signed in Dec. 1814.

[5] Viscount Bryce was Ambassador in Washington, 1907–13. He had been a notable mountaineer. Mount Bryce in the Canadian Rockies is named after him.

31

5 Feb 14

Thank you for very dear letter this morning. When you say you would like to be me, with 'crowded hours' &c, I wonder if you realise what it means in the course of the working hours of one day to have to tackle (1) your Cabinet (2) your deep-sea fishes[1] (3) your Sovereign. All of which adventures come within to-day's programme. But I *love* your confidence. Of course I would have shewn you the 'paragraph',[2] if you had given me a hint that you.wanted to see it. There is nothing (as you know) that I would not shew you: so great & deep is my trust.

I dined at the Churchills' last night. Winston slept placidly in his arm chair while I played Bridge with Clemmie, Goonie & the Lord Chief Justice[3] being our antagonists. With some feelings of compunction I went home with £3 of poor Goonie's money in my pocket. This morning we had another Cabinet which did not come to very much, as Winston's field of discussion is quite inexhaustible. A rather unsatisfactory communication (tho' very well put) from the Leviathan.[4] . . .

[1] The leading Irish Nationalists (cf. 'Leviathan').

[2] See Letter 35, n. 1.

[3] Lady Gwendeline Churchill, Goonie, was Winston's sister-in-law. Rufus Isaacs had been appointed Lord Chief Justice and created Lord Reading in Oct. 1913.

[4] See D. Gwynn, *Redmond* (1932), p. 253. Redmond kept a record of nearly all his interviews and correspondence with Asquith.

32

6 Feb 14

I did not get any letter from you to-day, but yesterday was no doubt a 'hunting day', and you have already admitted the accuracy of my unvarnished account of the calls & cares of that phase of your life.

The enclosed 2 cuttings – one of wh. was sent me by your Mother – shew a good deal of imagination, especially the one which accounts for my pilgrimages to Alderley by a consuming desire to deal with 'the Nonconformist grievance in single-school areas'. I think (if you were so minded) you could supply a better reason.

I spent about an hour & a half with the Sovereign before dinner and we covered a good deal of ground. I spoke to him very faithfully, but I am not sure that I produced an abiding impression.[1] Esher (who was at dinner) told me that the King liked me but (how unlike you!) was rather afraid of me! I am sure you will find that impossible to believe & difficult to imagine. We finished up our talk on very friendly terms, and at dinner I had the privilege of sitting between the Queen (who told me she hated music) & Lady Ampthill – Beauchamp's sister, of whom there is not much to be said. The nicest person there was Ld. Granville, who is now Secretary of the Embassy at Paris. We didn't play Bridge, and I left fairly early this morning.

Birrell tells me that the latest story is that Carson has fallen desperately in love. The Siren is a young & beautiful Ulster lady, who was much moved & attracted by his speeches, and his noble & commanding demeanour. Carson hoped, & still hopes, that he had struck a tenderer chord, but apparently she is prepared to yield her homage, but not her heart – not to speak of her hand.[2] It will be curious to see what effect, if any, this little tragi-comedy has upon the political situation.

I understand you are coming up in any case on Sat. night: so I shall see you Sunday even though (as I fear) a golfing expedition is impossible. It will be a great joy to have you once more within range – my deep & dearest love.

[1] The King warned Asquith that if the negotiations on Ulster failed many army officers would resign. He added that 'although at the present stage . . . he could not rightly intervene, the time *would* come when the Bill was presented for Assent, and then he should feel it his duty to do what in his own judgement was best for his people generally': R A GV K 2553 (3) 83 (the remark is not correctly recorded in Harold Nicolson, *George V* (1952), p. 233). Asquith argued that the ministry should either be dismissed at once or assured against trouble over the Royal Assent. The King did not accept this argument.

[2] Ruby Frewen, thirty years Carson's junior, whom he had first met at Homburg in the summer of 1912. He married her in Sept. 1914. His first wife had died in Apr. 1913.

33

11 Feb 14 [i]

. . . We are just going to have a Cabinet – indeed I am already late for it: and from what the Impecc^{ble} said to me last night I think it will bring the heavy laden & storm tossed ship safely into port. There are lots of things I shd. love to talk about – but how can I? And I console myself as best I can with the thoughts of Friday.

Dearest love

34

11 Feb 14 [ii]

Since I wrote to you this morning, the ship very nearly foundered as she was entering port. . . . By extra-careful steering, however, the calamity was averted, and after countless adventures the much-battered hulk, with her very slightly-diminished freight, lies safe in her desired haven. . . .

The event of this afternoon's debate with us was Carson's speech. He followed a somewhat arid display by the Impeccable, and was really very impressive. I wrote him a line of congratulation,[1] and you may like to see his answer: also a rather nice letter from old Bryce.[2] Aren't you ever coming again to our debates?

Dearest love.

34a

Private.

Febry 11.14.

My dear Prime Minister –
Your letter is more than generous & I am grateful.

Yrs vy sincerely,
Edward Carson

[1] Published in I. Colvin, *Carson*, ii (1934). 283. The speech suggested that Carson was working more for the exclusion of Ulster than for the complete defeat of Home Rule. It 'ought to be helpful', Asquith told the King, 'towards an ultimate settlement': R A GV K 2553 (3) 85. On 11 Feb. 1935 Margot Asquith wrote to Winston Churchill: 'I cd not help thinking how much Henry wd have enjoyed yr speech this afternoon, and how *certainly* he would have told you so. Your Policy? – No, but yr speech – Yes.'

[2] See Letter 30. Bryce's letter is missing.

35

12 Feb 1914

. . . Yes – that was the Alderley paragraph, that you were *so* incurious about. I had a letter yesterday from High Quarters expressing delight at it, & its effect: soon it will come to be thought to have been composed & to have originated there (instead of in a rather gloomy half-hour at Alderley)[1]: just as George IV gradually persuaded himself that he had been in command at the Battle of Waterloo. . . .

Bonar Lisa was rather spitfire last night, & looking back I am inclined to be satisfied with the debate. The fate (immediate, not ultimate) of Shem will be decided this afternoon.[2]. . .

[1] The Home Rule paragraph in the Speech from the Throne contained an appeal for 'the spirit of mutual concession'. It was soon being said that the King had insisted on this passage despite ministerial objections.
[2] See Letter 30, n. 2.

36

The Wharf,
Sutton Courtney,
Berks.

Sunday 15 Feb 1914

. . . You would see that I got into the House in time to devote 5 or 6 faithful minutes to that prime ass Leif Jones.[1] I couldn't forgive him for curtailing our drive. The Court was not very amusing – a scanty display of beauty: young Mrs Jimmy Rothschild looked about the best: and no diverting incidents. I noticed that not a single woman, could make a decent curtsey with her legs tied & manacled as they are now.[2]. . .

[1] Leif Jones was prominent in the temperance movement. He asked why a Licensing Bill, to which the Liberals had been long committed, was not mentioned in the Speech from the Throne. Asquith replied that no room could be found for one in the 1914 legislative programme.
[2] Hobble skirts were in fashion. According to evidence given in Westminster County Court in Jan. 1911 wearing them was liable to impede such actions as boarding a bus (*The Times*, 1 Feb. 1911, 12c).

37

16 Feb 1914

. . . You would have been amused at the breakfast discussion this morning at the Wharf between Goonie Churchill & Leonie Leslie.[1] The former strongly maintained that the Assyrian had 'charm', to which the others replied that he had never taken his eyes off her (Goonie) during the whole of dinner last night, meanwhile preserving almost unbroken silence with his neighbour. I drove up alone, as Margot is staying on for another night.

I am sorry your golf was so disappointing, tho' I expect it was better than Goonie's at Huntercombe. We *must* play together again soon. You don't say what sort of a course it is.

I have just had an interview with Charles Roberts, who must be almost a cousin of yours, & to whom I have given the Assyrian's place at the India Office. Bluetooth (or 'Pluto' as Mrs Leslie calls him) wd. have looked too much like a job,[2] and Roberts is better for this than either of the other two possible outsiders – Dr Addison & Neil Primrose. I hardly know him, but I was favourably impressed, and I shall be curious to see whether he sprouts or shrivels in the refrigerating atmosphere maintained by Crewe. I managed with some difficulty at question time to extricate the 'corrupt' Gulland from the scrape into which he got at Wick,[3] and the evening promises to be placid I shall dine at Grillions.

The Ex-Master came to see me & rehearsed the Apologia he is going to deliver in the Lords to-morrow.[4] I am glad to say that I cut a lot of it out, and hacked & re-hashed much of the rest. You ought to go & hear it, as there is sure to be a lively time. I must see you soon beloved. As you say an hour a week is ridiculous – but I really give you many other hours, don't I?

All love.

[1] Mrs Leslie was Winston's aunt.
[2] Roberts's wife, Lady Cecilia (née Howard) was Venetia's first cousin. Harold Baker ('Bluetooth'), then Financial Secretary to the War Office, was a personal friend of the Prime Minister, whose taste for the classics and rejection of women's suffrage he shared.
[3] The Liberal sitting for Wick Burghs had been appointed Lord Advocate and re-elected. Wick had applied for a harbour grant. During the by-election campaign Gulland, the Government's Scottish Whip, had used words which could be construed as a promise that the Lord Advocate, if re-elected, would make sure of the grant to Wick.
[4] Lord Murray of Elibank (cr. 1912), the Master of Elibank, Liberal Chief Whip 1910–12, had been involved in the Marconi purchases. See Letter 7, n. 3.

38

I have not heard from or of you to-day: which is unsatisfying. I suppose you went to the H. of Lords, in which case you might have looked in here on your way out.

I have had a pretty dreary day, what with dull things and dull people. The Bucks election went fairly well, tho' we ought to have knocked a little more paint off the majority.[1] I am much more interested in Bethnal Green, where both our motors have been engaged all day in bringing Masterman's sheep to the shambles.[2]

Sir F. Bertie of Paris came to lunch: also Frances & Dinah, & Ribblesdale. Frances goes off to Costebelle for 3 weeks or a month, & looks as if she needed it. I sat next Lady Wemyss whom I had not seen for an age. She looks older, but reports that the Doctor says her husband's pulse is like that of a boy.[3] She was devoted to Alfred Lyttelton[4] & misses him sorely. I am thinking of dining here (H. of C.) to-night, as I have nowhere to go to.

I shall come for you immediately after lunch to-morrow – say about ¼ to 3. I *so* much want & need to see you again beloved.

[1] The Conservatives had held South Bucks since the election of Jan. 1910. In Dec. 1910 the Liberals had not contested it.

[2] Masterman was standing for re-election in South West Bethnal Green where he had won a by-election in July 1911 by 184. Under a provision which had originated in 1707 (modified in 1919 and finally repealed in 1926) his promotion to the cabinet entailed his vacating his seat. As one of the master minds for the national insurance scheme he was the scapegoat for its unpopularity. He lost Bethnal Green by 20 votes through the intervention of a Socialist candidate. 'Not exactly a blow,' Asquith told his daughter Violet (20 Feb.), 'for there was a substantial Home Rule majority; but it is a bore, especially for Masterman.' See also Letter 70, nn. 4–5.

[3] Grace, second wife of the 8th Earl. He was 95 and had been in Parliament, except for one year, since 1841. He died on 30 June 1914. His granddaughter Cynthia was married to Asquith's second son, Herbert.

[4] The Conservative statesman, who had died, aged 56, in July 1913. Màrgot's much loved sister Laura (d. 1886) had been his first wife.

39

I should be deeply depressed about Friday, and cursing that infernal soldier with imprecations not loud but intense, were it not that I can look back upon our delicious time together yesterday, & forward to Saturday & Sunday. All the same I hate to break the continuity of our Fridays, which have now gone on so long, and been so uniformly full of happy hours.

It was sad to have to leave you so soon, and when I got back to the House I found the Assyrian lying in wait, with a number of dullish business problems. Not that he finds them dull: for the present at any rate every sum in Treasury arithmetic is irradiated in his eyes with a special glamour – 'the light that never was on sea or shore'.[1]

We dined at Cassel's and I played Bridge with Mrs Keppel, Julia Maguire,[2] & Ruggles,[3] and won a little money. Rather an odd company – Lichnowsky, Mr & Mrs Joshua (!),[4] Lady Hindlip, H. Stonor &c. One sees more & more that millionaires take their pleasures sadly: poor Cassel lost the only thing he cared for when his daughter died, and now he has had to give up smoking wh. was his greatest resource, for fear of headaches! I wonder how you got on at Hugh's. Did you talk with Ettie and get anywhere near private things?[5] We have to dine at a banquet at the Crewes' to-night, which is a great bore, and like the soldiers in Wolfe's poem I 'ruefully think of the morrow'.[6]   Bless you *beloved*

[1] For Montagu's promotion to be Financial Secretary to the Treasury see Letters 30, n. 2, and 35. Wordsworth's phrase ends 'sea or land': 'Elegiac Stanzas Suggested by a Picture of Peele Castle in a Storm'.

[2] Mrs Alice Keppel had been an intimate friend of Edward VII in his later years. Asquith often encountered Mrs Julia Maguire, a granddaughter of the great Sir Robert Peel and wife of the Vice-President of the British South Africa Company, as she was friendly with both Sir Ernest Cassel and Sir Edgar Vincent (Lord D'Abernon).

[3] Sir Evelyn Ruggles-Brise, the prison reformer. See Letter 216, n. 3.

[4] For Lichnowsky, German Ambassador, see Letter 79, n. 1. Mrs Joshua (née Hirsch) was sister to Lady Lewis, wife of the 2nd baronet. Asquith's friendship had been chiefly with the 1st baronet (d. 1911) and his wife. Mr Joshua was a business man.

[5] Ettie Desborough had been admired by Lord Archie Gordon. The latter's death after a car accident in Dec. 1909 (see p. 1) had led Violet to make Ettie something of a confidante.

[6] 'The Burial of Sir John Moore': the soldiers thought 'bitterly'. Asquith corrected his mistake in the next letter.

40

26 Feb 14 [ii]

. . . Lord Knollys came to lunch – I forget whether you know him. He is a real typical survival of the mid-Victorians, and having spent his whole life in Courts, & in the service of royalties, remains a sound & strong Liberal. Naturally he is not very fond of the Powers that now are.[1] . . .

[1] Knollys was born a few weeks after Victoria came to the throne. He had been Edward VII's Private Secretary, and then joint Private Secretary, with Lord Stamfordham, to George V until Mar. 1913. In Nov. 1910 the Liberals wanted the King's promise to create peers should a creation be needed to pass the Parliament Bill. By arguing that there was no alternative Knollys persuaded George V to give this secret promise. According to Knollys, if the King refused and Asquith resigned, Balfour would decline to form a government. This assurance

ran counter to some crucial evidence about Balfour's attitude which Knollys suppressed. The evidence did not come even to the King's eyes until Nov. 1913; but Knollys's pro-Government stance was well known before the Parliament Bill crisis ended. Asked by Lady Desborough about congenial fellow guests, Balfour replied: 'My Dear Ettie, I should enjoy meeting any man in England, except Lord Knollys: him I will not meet.' In Feb. 1914 Knollys was bitter about the circumstances of his 'retirement' in the previous year. He was too good a courtier to be a Liberal partisan. His Liberalism consisted largely in the belief that the King's government should have the King's support even when it consisted of Liberals and radicals. So far from repenting of his devious course in Nov. 1910 he thought, with some reason, that he had saved the King from becoming involved in politics on the losing side. He probably feared that too active a royal concern for the Ulster Protestants entailed risks of a similar involvement.

41

24 Queen Anne's Gate,
S.W.
                                                                    3 March 1914

This is an odd address to write to you from, isn't it? I have been perching here for the best part of 2 hours (it is now about 6), and taking part in one of the most interesting conversations (*à deux*) that I have had for a long time. You know from what I told you on Sunday[1] who did the other part of the talk. You would have been amused – perhaps more than amused – if you had been ensconced behind one of the silken curtains. I am sure at any rate that you would have been amazed at the frankness on both sides.[2] I will tell you more about it, if you care to know, when we meet. Perhaps to-morrow before dinner? . . .

Weren't you surprised to find me lunching at Winston's? I hardly took you in before you were gone, and I suppose you have been fribbling all the afternoon at hat and dress shops with The Bud. I had a fairly amusing talk with her at lunch, when she told me how you all (for I feel sure you were one of the guilty) put opium into Raymond's pipes. What nights! The debate to-night is off, and I have engaged to make my 'statement' on Monday next: so mind you get a place. I shall be bitterly disappointed if you are not there.[3] I wonder what you are doing to-night. I suppose I ought not to think so much about you – but I am quite unrepentant, beloved.

[1] Venetia had been at The Wharf on Sunday, 1 Mar.
[2] Asquith had met Carson after a report from Stamfordham that Carson's sole object was a settlement which would satisfy Ulster. Montagu's house was chosen as before (Letter 23, n. 6) in order to foil reporters.
[3] Asquith was due to move the second reading of the Home Rule Bill and to announce the Government's plans for Ulster, on 9 Mar.

42

7 March 1914

. . . This morning I have had here Birrell & Lloyd George & Illingworth – all in quite good spirits.[1] . . . The mystery of the leakage is still unpenetrated: I can see that Ll. G. suspects Winston, who preserves an unbroken silence in regard to the incident.[2] . . .

[1] Because they believed their settlement terms, while probably unacceptable to Bonar Law and Carson, to be highly attractive to moderate and cross-bench opinion. Redmond had just accepted that the exclusion of Ulster, originally put at 3 years, should be extended to 6.
[2] The Ulster plan was published in the *Daily News* on 5 Mar., the day after the cabinet had agreed to it. See Jenkins, *Asquith*, pp. 303–5.

43

9 March 1914

Thank you for your nice Sunday letter, which gave me just the details I like to know of your downsittings and uprisings (including the marking of chemises! which I did not know to be one of your accomplishments).

I am very glad you were at the Wharf last Sunday, and not this. It poured continuously for nearly 48 hours, & we were reduced to motoring to Sir Sympne's at Fritwell. We found him returning from a father's Sunday walk with his two girls and the family deerhound. He has an Irish governess whose name I forget, but who rules the whole establishment. She had been hunting ! with the Bicester on Saturday in the company of F. E. Smith[1] who had told her which of my colleagues in the Cabinet were loyal, & which (a large majority) were otherwise.

Violet did a really good performance, sprinting from Brindisi the whole way to Charing Cross where she arrived at 3.30 this aft., just in time to find standing room in Mrs Lowther's[2] Gallery. I was bitterly disappointed that you were not there: why didn't you disguise yourself as a pressman? There was a huge crowd, but I did not count to excite them: so I adopted a rather funereal tone.[3] Bonar Law was really at his worst.[4] I am going to dine at Grillion's, but I have hopes that we shall meet at dinner to-morrow night. Can I come Wed. before dinner? I have lots to say to you darling – & so I hope have you to me. Bless you – all my love.

Of course you must come to dinner Thurs. and bring the Bud.

[1] F. E. Smith and Simon both had country houses in Oxfordshire. Smith's was at Charlton. 'Sympne' on the analogy of Lympne (pronounced 'Lim').
[2] Wife of the Speaker.
[3] The Liberals and Nationalists found nothing to cheer in Asquith's speech. They thought

that the Government had gone, in Redmond's words, 'to the very extremest limit of concession'.
   [4] Lord Hugh Cecil thought that Bonar Law had dismissed the Government's offer too
brusquely. 'Our success depends', Cecil told Carson (13 Mar.), 'on winning a general election;
and to do that we must assume an attitude which the ordinary citizen will regard as . . .
reasonable.'

44

10 March 1914.

   . . . I think the *general* effect of yesterday's proceedings was not bad, tho'
it is too soon yet to say whether there is a real chance of *rapprochement*. I
still feel bitterly resentful with Fate for upsetting next Sunday – wh. wd.
have been heavenly. Darling be dear and kind – all love.

45

Sat 14 March 14.

   . . . I have been busy with Thring[1] & Birrell this morning over the Irish
amendments. When Thring had gone I talked to B. about the Lord Lieutenancy. He is very anti- Aberdeens, and would like to see them booted at the
first opportunity.[2] I told him that Lucas[3] had been suggested, & that I feared
he was rather farouche for the job. 'Farouche' said B 'I should think so. You
know what he said when some lady asked him why he didn't marry?' I:
'No.' B: 'He said he had 3 reasons. First, I have a wooden leg.' The Lady:
'Oh that doesn't matter.' Lucas: 'Second, I always sleep between blankets.'
Lady: 'That *does* sound rather uncomfortable.' Lucas: 'Third, I always
scream when I wake up in the morning.' This settled the lady. Not perhaps
fit for publication, but I thought it would amuse you. Otherwise Birrell was
rather favourable to the idea. Darling we have had some delicious times
together this last week. Bless you. All my love.

   [1] Sir Arthur Thring was First Parliamentary Counsel, 1903–17, and thus the principal
draftsman for important bills.
   [2] Aberdeen had been Lord-Lieutenant since 1906. His wife was a very active consort.
   [3] Auberon Herbert, 8th Baron Lucas, then Parliamentary Secretary, Board of Agriculture.
While acting as *The Times* correspondent in the South African war he had received a wound in
the foot which led to his leg being amputated below the knee. He had been brought up in the
New Forest and was fond of open-air life. He seemed to John Buchan 'a gipsy to the core'. 'His
courage', G. K. Chesterton wrote, 'was . . . casual and . . ., in a quiet way, crazy.' Joined
Royal Flying Corps when coalition formed, May 1915. Did not return from a flight over the
German lines, Nov. 1916.

46

. . . We had a regular rough & tumble in the House just now at question time, which you would rather have enjoyed. Carson denounced our olive-branch as a 'hypocritical sham', & it looks as if the thing had broken down.[1] All our people (including myself) are very pleased with Winston's speech, which was quite opportune.[2] I am going to dine at Grillion's & have called a Cabinet for to-morrow morning to discuss the new situation. What are you doing to-morrow? and when shall I see you. *Dearest* love.

[1] Bonar Law and Carson having rejected the Government's concession, Asquith had to steady his followers by showing a firm front. He put his authority behind Churchill's Bradford speech (see n. 2 below and p. 39) and answered 26 Opposition questions on the Ulster proposals within fifteen minutes, refusing any detailed information. To Bonar Law's protest he replied: 'If our general proposal is rejected it will obviously be a waste of time to formulate for discussion all ancillary and consequential points of machinery and detail.' Bonar Law then demanded time for a censure debate and this was fixed for 19 Mar.

[2] See p. 39. Asquith may have contemplated using force against the Carsonites. More probably he relied on the suggestion that he might do so to bring them to heel.

47

I got cold on Sat & Sunday which made my cough worse: so to-day I have stayed in the house & even swallowed a dose of Parky's stuff.[1] I hoped to have seen you at any rate for a moment, as Violet said you were coming in after lunch. It is disappointing, as I fear I may not be able to see you to-morrow. Mind you get a place in the gallery for Thursday.

I dined at Grillion's & talked with Mr Justice Darling (for a change) & Sir G. Murray who has just returned from India. John Fortescue was there – the dried up spinsterised librarian of Windsor – who we learn to-day has become engaged to a girl of 24. She has been or is an actress, & is a sister of Stella Campbell's husband.

We had a Cabinet to-day instead of to-morrow, in view of what happened in the House yesterday. There was great harmony, and Winston preened himself & was stroked by the others – all on account of his Bradford speech. And those Navy Estimates, with all the memories which cluster around their cradle, promise to go through on oiled castors, with hardly a murmur of protest. Am I not right in my fixed belief that the Expected rarely happens? The Granville Barkers came to lunch & Maggie Ponsonby[2] who is really good company. I forget whether you know her. I have spent a quiet solitary afternoon reading a book by a Jew called Hirsch about the fortunes of his race in the Middle ages.[3] Do write to me darling – all love. . . .

[1] Dr T. W. Parkinson was the Asquiths' doctor.

[2] Unmarried daughter of Sir Henry Ponsonby (d. 1895), Queen Victoria's Private Secretary. Margot wrote (*Autobiography*, i. 188) that Magdalen Ponsonby, though 'socially . . . uncouth, had a touch of her father's genius'.

[3] Probably part of the 6-vol. *History of the Jews* by Heinrich Hirsch Graetz (English translation, 1891–8). Possibly Asquith misstated the author's name entirely: *The Jews and the English Law* by H. S. Q. Henriques was published in 1908.

48

19 March 14

We have had the exciting part of the debate, which ended in the exit of Carson[1] en route for Belfast amidst the tumultuous cheering of the Tories. He was very rude to Winston. My voice was in bad condition and I had some difficulty in keeping it up. Violet is here & reported your proceedings at Selfridge's, which I am very sorry to have missed.[2] You must tell me all about it to-morrow: I will call for you after lunch. I had the best part of an hour with the Sovereign at Buck^m Palace this morning. He is as you may imagine in rather a gloomy mood, and has exaggerated notions of the fighting quality of the 'Volunteers'.[3] His own scheme is to have a recurring plebiscite every 3 years, which I was obliged to tell him would please nobody, and keep the whole place in a condition of chronic ferment. He was very nice & considerate on the whole. . . .

. . . It was delicious having you last night – tho' the conditions might have been better.

All love – darling.

[1] Carson was well informed, by Sir Henry Wilson and others, about the Government's plans for military measures in Ulster. He told the Commons that these were highly provocative and went to Belfast to make sure that his Ulster Volunteers were not provoked into premature action.

[2] Venetia took part in a charity sale and bought Asquith a blue muffler for wear 'in the motor': Letter 423.

[3] The King may have exaggerated the ability of the Ulster Volunteers to fight regular troops; but his warning to Asquith (Letter 32, n. 1), that some regular officers might be unwilling to fight the Volunteers was well justified.

Ulster II: The Curragh 'Mutiny' (Letters 49–55 and 61)

THE cabinet's plans for reinforcing the Ulster arms depots (see p. 39) were extensive and elaborate. The Ulster Volunteers bearing arms were already thought to outnumber the regular troops in Ireland and even the simplest military moves in Ulster might lead to counter-action. Extended contingency plans were therefore needed. But a group of ministers, who would have included Churchill but not Asquith, may have gone beyond precautions and seen the troop movements as a chance to show that the Ulster Volunteers did not rule Ulster. The orders given by the Admiralty comprehended not merely the four small ships which might be needed to transport the reinforcements to the arms depots and installations, but the Third Battle Squadron, then off the north-west coast of Spain, which was to steam to Lamlash and so be conveniently near Belfast. Asquith did not know that Churchill had moved the Battle Squadron until it was well on the way.

When Sir Arthur Paget was in London (18 and 19 March) collecting his instructions he secured the agreement of the Secretary of State for War, Colonel John Seely, that 'where officers have direct family connexion with the disturbed area in Ulster, . . . they should be permitted to remain behind' if their units were ordered north. Any other officer refusing to take part in these operations would be dismissed the service. On the morning of 20 March Paget told seven of his senior officers of this decision. He intended, he wrote later, that the seven should 'inform those officers subordinate to themselves' of the position. One of his hearers was Brigadier General Hubert Gough, who had strong Ulster sympathies, though not an Ulster domicile. Gough commanded the cavalry brigade at the Curragh. His officers were in fashionable regiments and a number of them could forfeit their commissions without making great financial sacrifices.

Gough canvassed his officers in the afternoon and reported to headquarters in Dublin that they needed more information. 'If the duty involves the *initiation* of active military operations against Ulster,' the report continued, sixty officers 'would respectfully, and under protest, prefer to be dismissed'. He had five officers who 'claimed protection' because of Ulster domicile. Between 11 and 12 o'clock that evening (20 March) Asquith was summoned from the bridge table at Lord Sheffield's to be shown a telegram from Paget that Gough and 57 of his officers would 'prefer to accept dismissal if ordered north'. Gough and his commanding officers were at once summoned to London (Letter 49). Paget's telegram ended all notions of using the armed forces that weekend to overawe the Ulstermen; and at 5.30 p.m. on 21 March the Third Battle Squadron, then abreast of the Scillies, received fresh, and innocuous, orders. The troop movements were all completed without incident.

On 23 March the cabinet approved a statement authorizing Gough to tell his officers that the whole affair was a 'misunderstanding': the Army Council and Commander-in-Chief had meant to assure themselves solely that 'lawful commands . . . for the protection of public property and the support of the civil power . . . or for the protection of . . . lives and private property' would be obeyed. Seely, who had been with the King during the cabinet meeting, returned as it broke up. He and Morley there and then added two further paragraphs to the statement. The right of the Government 'to use all the forces of the crown in Ireland . . . to maintain law and order' was stated in the first. The second recorded that the Government 'have no intention whatever of taking advantage of the right to crush political opposition to the policy or principles of the Home Rule Bill'.

When Gough was shown the statement, with these additions, he wrote: 'In the event of the present Home Rule Bill becoming law, can we be called upon to enforce it on Ulster under the expression of maintaining law and order?' Gough told French, the C.I.G.S., and Ewart, the Adjutant-General, that unless they read the statement as answering his question in the negative, he and his colonels 'would prefer to leave the army immediately'. French wrote beneath the demand for this interpretation: 'That is how I read it. J.F.' Armed with these assurances Gough caught the night mail to Ireland.

Asquith's parliamentary position was by now most uncomfortable. He could not accept Seely's two 'peccant paragraphs' as Balfour called them, still less French's minute. It no longer looked as if the army could be used to coerce Ulster; but the Government's right so to use it had to be maintained. The Opposition would charge the cabinet with trying to smash the Volunteers by provoking these loyal Ulstermen to premature action. Even Asquith would find difficulty in explaining why a plan to reinforce arms depots had involved a cavalry brigade, to say nothing of eight battleships. Presenting a firm front to Carson and Co. not merely showed the extreme difficulty of using the army to control Ulster, but led to the resignations of the Secretary of State for War, the C.I.G.S., and the Adjutant-General. The Opposition's success might be expensive, however. Carson's Ulstermen depended for salvation on the British electorate. Bonar Law and Carson could pay a high price for any development which was 'going to do them harm in the country' (Letter 52).

49

21 March 1914[1]

. . . I found here Winston, the Arch Colonel, Sir John French & Gen[l] Ewart – with some pretty alarming news. The Brigadier and about 57 officers of the Cavalry Brigade at the Curragh had sent in their resignations sooner than be employed in 'coercing' Ulster. The Brigadier – Gough – is a distinguished Cavalry officer, an Irishman, & the hottest of Ulsterians, and there can be little doubt that he has been using his influence with his subordinates to make them combine for a strike. We sent orders for him & the 3 Colonels to come here at once & they will arrive this evening. Meanwhile, from what one hears to-day it seems likely that there was a misunderstanding. They seem to have thought, from what Paget said, that they were about to be ordered off at once to shed the blood of the Covenanters, and they say they never meant to object to do duty like the other troops in protecting depots &c & keeping order. This will be cleared up in a few hours: but there have been all sorts of agitations & alarums in high quarters, and I had a visit this morning from Stamfordham who wore a very long face.[1] I took the opportunity of saying that the main responsibility for all this mutinous [*sic*] rested with Lord Roberts, who is in a dangerous condition of senile frenzy.[2] . . .

[1] The King knew nothing about the doings at the Curragh until he opened his morning paper on 21 Mar. In the various appeals to the officers there his name was reported to have been freely used.

[2] Earl Roberts, who was an Irishman, had advised the Ulster Volunteers and found them their commander (Lt.-Gen. Sir George Richardson).

50

22 March 1914

Thank you so much darling for your sweet little pencil letter. Yes – this has been a *very* unsatisfactory week: I have never wanted you more, and yet when together we have always been at a distance; and a thousand things come & go which can never be put properly on paper, but which all the more I wish to share with you. We will arrange to have a good talk before Dinner some day very soon – perhaps Tuesday? . . .

The military situation has developed, as might have been expected, and there is no doubt if we were to order a march upon Ulster that about half the officers in the Army – the Navy is more uncertain – would strike. The immediate difficulty in the Curragh can, I think, be arranged but that is the permanent situation, & it is not a pleasant one. Winston is all for creating a temporary Army *ad hoc* – but that of course is nonsense.[1] I had an hour with the King this afternoon who is a good deal perturbed, & afterwards (contrary to my settled practice) I saw Geoffrey Robinson of the *The Times*, & gave him a few hints of a quieting kind.[2] I have now a letter from Bonar Law who is going to raise the whole thing in the House to-morrow. If I add that I had also a visit from the Abp. of Canterbury,[3] you will see that a Sunday in

London is not a day of rest. This will be the third successive Monday that we have a 'crisis' in the House. . . .

¹ The Irish Nationalists created a 'temporary army'; and the National Volunteers soon outnumbered their opponents in Ulster (see p. 69).

² The statement appeared exclusively in *The Times* on 23 Mar., much to the annoyance of the Liberal newspaper editors. It was economical in facts and Asquith had some trouble later in explaining this reticence. Robinson (who changed his name to Dawson in 1917) was Editor of *The Times*, 1912–19 and 1923–41.

³ Asquith told the Archbishop, in effect, that if Bonar Law proposed amending the scheme of 9 Mar. (p. 39), so that the counties voting to be excluded for a term of years were allowed to vote again on exclusion at the end of that term, he would do all he could to secure the agreement of his colleagues. The Archbishop (who was an experienced political mediator) reported that Law thought this 'practically the best line of solution': the Government should put it forward; if they did Law would 'take the risks for himself in accepting it'.

51

23 March 1914

What with Paget's tactless blundering, and Seely's clumsy phrases, and the general Army position, I had rather a tough job to handle. A.J.B. who is the only quick mind in that ill-bred crowd, hit the right nail, or rather touched the sore spot.¹ The whole thing – wh. need never have happened, and could have been stopped on the threshold, is a stupid misadventure. . . .

We had a Cabinet this morning with a lot of talk about this wretched Paget-Gough affair. E. Grey strong in favour of a general election as soon as H. R. Bill is passed and before it comes into operation.². . .

¹ 'Whoever supposed', Balfour asked, 'that General Gough resigned because he had to see that some guns at Dundalk were not taken away or that some small arms . . . somewhere else were not imperilled? . . . Either the government . . ., or one section of the government, thought that the time had come for doing something . . . They came up . . . against facts which they had not foreseen; and they shrank from the consequences, and have been occupied ever since in industriously trying to cover up [their] tracks.'

² 'We cannot and ought not to use force to bring the . . . Bill into operation', Grey wrote to Asquith, 'till the opinion of the country has been taken.'

52

25 March 1914

It is now 7 o'clock & I am writing this from the Treasury Bench while our brindled Lossiemouth friend is making quite a good speech from the Labour benches.¹ I am afraid you have not been here: I wish you had: for never in the whole of my experience at the bar and in Parliament have I seen a strong

& really formidable case (as I told you yesterday) so miserably presented and so coldly backed up. It is quite clear that the Tories are thoroughly cowed over this army business: they think it is going to do them harm in the country. Our people on the other hand are really hot & excited – more than they have been for a long time, and I am beginning to believe that we are going to score out of what seemed an almost impossible situation.[2] So true is it – according to my favourite axiom, of which by this time you must be getting tired – that the Expected does not Happen. . . .

[1] MacDonald spoke on 23 and 25 Mar., emphasizing that the Conservatives must not be allowed to substitute a veto by aristocratic army officers for the defunct veto of the Lords. He and John Ward (Letter 53, n. 2) naturally ignored the evidence that many men in the ranks were as sympathetic to Ulster as were their officers. British uniforms had long been more popular in Belfast than in Dublin and this had affected the attitude of the troops. Seely told the cabinet on 23 Mar. that 'quite as much disaffection was to be found amongst the rank and file as among the officers': Hobhouse, *Diaries*, p. 165.

[2] Asquith told Stamfordham 'that last night's task in the House was the most difficult he ever had to handle': R A GV K 2553 (4) 51.

53

26 March 14

. . . I found the main preoccupation of the Other Party to my interview at the Palace was with his own position, and the 'terrible cross-fire' to wh. he conceives himself to be exposed.[1] He was very indignant about John Ward, & thinks the Speaker should have called him to order. In regard to the Army mess he was easier than I expected.[2]

French offered his resignation but has withdrawn it for the moment at any rate. His position is a very difficult one, but he has been so loyal & has behaved so well that I would stretch a great many points to keep him.[3] We are going to have a Cabinet on the subject to-morrow morning, & I shall have to say something in the House at noon. I hope to come for you soon after lunch, if the Gods are kinder to us than they have been of late. I see so terribly little of you, except afar off . . .

[1] The Opposition leaders had worked hard at alarming the King. In May 1912 he had been told by Bonar Law that the Royal Assent to the Home Rule Bill was by no means 'a purely formal act': giving it would make 'half your subjects think you have acted against them'. George V regarded a general election before Home Rule became law as the only means of relieving him from this burden of responsibility.

[2] On 24 Mar. John Ward, a Labour Member who had been a navvy, read a syndicalist leaflet to the Commons. The argument of this document was that the troops should follow the example of their Tory officers and obey no orders which might infringe the interests of their class. Like MacDonald, Ward was concerned that syndicalist doctrines, which had failed to subvert the Labour party, had received such a boost from the Tories. 'We have to decide', he concluded, 'whether the people . . . are to make the laws . . . absolutely without interference

either from King or army.' When taken as a guest to the National Liberal Club he was cheered for 'saying', as one member put it, 'what we all think'.

³ On 25 Mar. Asquith told the Commons that Seely's resignation had been proffered and rejected, and commented severely on French's answer to Gough's question. An officer's claim to ask hypothetical questions of this kind would, if allowed, 'place the government and the country at the mercy of the army'.

54

30 March 1914

Dearly beloved, your letter which I found here this morning was the greatest solace & joy, as the thought of you & of our delicious drive has been all thro' the wet dreary Sunday at the Wharf. I drove away from you in solitude & missing you so much, but the memory of things you had said 'flashed upon the inward eye'.¹

I started the idea of the two offices at once, & I need not tell you that Winston's eyes blazed, and his polysyllables rolled, and his gestures were those of a man possessed. Even Bluey's wary deep set gaze lighted up². . .

The weather was vile & we could not golf – only trundle about at a snail's pace (in deference to Clemmie's fears)³ in a shut-up motor. When I got back this morning I heard (as I expected) that the Generals (i.e. French & Ewart) had come back to the position that as a matter of personal honour they must go. Poor Seely, who was there, of course was bound to follow suit. French behaved admirably, & when I told him privately that I thought of going to the W.O, he was delighted and promised all his help. So then I proceeded to the King & put my scheme before him. He remarked – naively, as Bonar Law wd say⁴ – that the idea had never occurred to him! but he was quite taken with it and gave it emphatic approval. So after questions – as you will see by the papers – I threw the bombshell on the floor of the House, and I think the effect was all that one cd. have hoped. On the advice of the Impeccable I cleared out at once, not wishing to incur a penalty of £500 for sitting after my seat was legally vacant. So I am no longer an M.P.⁵. . .

¹ Wordsworth, 'I Wandered Lonely as a Cloud'.

² Asquith proposed to become Secretary of State for War, combining that office with the premiership.

³ She had suffered a miscarriage in Feb. 1912, followed by some months of ill health, and shortly afterwards had been in a motoring accident. She was now pregnant again.

⁴ This is probably a reference to Bonar Law's pronunciation, which often amused Asquith. Bonar presumably pronounced the word as 'navely'. See also Letter 404.

⁵ The announcement brought the Liberals to their feet, cheering wildly. The Opposition shouted 'Cromwell'. Having accepted a new office Asquith had to vacate his seat: see Letter 38, n. 2. For Simon's advice see Asquith MSS vol. 25, f. 178. Asquith was re-elected, unopposed, and took his seat again on 14 Apr.

55

7 Ap 14

. . . I have just received a rather hysterical letter from G. R.[1] I *must* see you to-morrow, before we all separate . . .

[1] Georgius Rex: in effect the King's letter was a plea to allow the exclusion of Ulster without time-limit. Asquith replied that the majority in the Commons could 'not be brought to assent' to that; he would continue to seek a 'via media' between the positions of Ministry and Opposition.

56

9 Ap 14

. . . You see I am in rather a growling mood: perhaps I shall improve on the road to Skindles, whither I start in an hour in Violet's company. As we shall be alone during the drive, we may get on to the . . . topic. I saw him[1] for 5 minutes at our dinner table on Tues. night, but as the light was dim & he didn't open his lips – except to take in food – I can hardly be said to have formed even a first impression. He came yesterday afternoon to see Margot & sat with her for an hour. She complains of the way in which his ears protrude, but otherwise thinks him fairly good-looking. He said he 'supposed' V & he were not engaged, but seemed pretty confident that it wd. end as he wishes. Margot says he is 'nice', inarticulate, unimpressive – like a certain type of hunting man, who in old days used to fall in love & propose to her. She is *convinced* that it will not come off. . . .

[1] A young man with whom Violet had contracted a semi-engagement while in Egypt. See also Letter 59.

The 1914 Budget (Letters 57, 60–64, 67, 81, 83 and 94)

LLOYD GEORGE planned another 'people's budget' for 1914. It was to 'throw out of gear the whole Tory line of battle' and so to be the groundwork for a Liberal victory in the 1915 election. The starting-points were a deficit of more than £5,000,000 mainly because of the Naval Estimates, and a report predicting large increases in rates unless local authorities could be given some relief. Such rate increases would fall disproportionately hard on working-class people. The budget provided more than £4,000,000 in grants to local authorities, as the first instalment in a system of central grants. The prosperous were to pay, through a rise of twopence in income tax to 1s.4d. and increased supertax and death duties.

The Liberal Members included some very rich men and the budget provoked a formidable revolt. The malcontents had a strong case because a new valuation system was needed if the grants for local authorities were to be distributed fairly. There was little prospect that the Lords would pass the Valuation Bill. However quickly it reached the statute-book the system which it authorized would take time to erect, and would be doomed if the Conservatives won the election. The Chancellor was therefore raising taxes without any assurance that the proceeds would be used to relieve the worst-hit ratepayers, or indeed any ratepayers at all (Letter 83). The cabinet ended by making a drastic cut in the Finance Bill and abandoning the grant plan except for the education grant. The income tax increase was accordingly cut from twopence to one penny. 'I am so miserable,' Edwin Montagu wrote to Venetia on 25 June; 'I was sent to the Treasury to prevent this sort of thing and I have failed.'

57

The Wharf,
Sutton Courtney,
Berks.

10 Ap 14

. . . The Assyrian came down in the afternoon & spent the night here. . . .

. . . Amidst the open derision of the family (i.e. Violet & Cys) he & I solemnly retired after breakfast to the Barn,[1] and there discussed for the best part of an hour Budget figures & fantasies (for Ll. G., who has forgotten all about land & housing,[2] is in one of his most imaginative & audacious fiscal moods: going to 'sweep the country' &c.). We are going to Huntercombe to golf after lunch. How I wish I were with you or you with me my darling. *Write. All* my love. . . .

[1] The Barn stood in the garden of The Wharf, near the river bank. It is described in Mark Bonham Carter's Introduction to Margot Asquith's *Autobiography*, one-volume edition, 1962, p. xxxii.

[2] Lloyd George had launched the urban part of the land and housing campaign at Glasgow on 4 Feb. 1914. It was easy to attack ducal landlords; but the constructive part of the campaign involved complex proposals on rating and taxation, property law, and compulsory purchase.

58

The Wharf,
Sutton Courtney,
Berks.

11 Ap 14.

I am disappointed to have no letter this morning: perhaps it will come later in the day. Elizabeth arrived last night in very good form, and the Assyrian left to take his gloomy share in the Paschal rites of the family. The details of the menu – bitter herbs, shank bone of lamb, chopped apples, and other such dainties – are set out with gusto in the enclosed which I cut out of the newspaper this morning. Violet accompanied our parting guest (who does not return till Monday) as far as Henley while Cys & I played at Huntercombe. Among other things he seems to have told her that he doubted whether he would ever marry, as he never met a woman who was 'nearly as nice' as himself! It is always difficult to say how far he is serious in these paradoxes as e.g. that he has no further political ambitions, except to be Governor General of India.

Notwithstanding the calendar, when I have spent some time in the company of Tante or Bluey or some others, I feel that I am really younger than these middle aged youths, who are always making their wills (and codicils), and feeling their pulses, and arranging how & where to spend their declining years. There is some truth in the French saying, 'L'homme a l'age des sentiments qu'il ressent: la femme a l'age des sentiments qu'elle inspire'. Judged by that test Mme Recamier, for instance, was in her first youth at 70.

I have been reading a lot of things about The W.O. and the Army – it is like the 'dates of Jewish Kings' & 'whether shawms have strings'[1]: e.g. what infantry regiments have their uniform facings *blue*? My darling you are always in my thoughts. I wonder if you think of me? Bless you beloved.

[1] Arthur Clement Hilton, 'The Vulture and the Husbandman', a parody of 'The Walrus and the Carpenter' by Lewis Carroll.

59

17 Ap. 14

Thank you so much darling for your two letters: the last but one in particular is a great joy to me. I don't know why I assumed you were coming up yesterday. As I go off with Eliz^th this morning to the Wharf, I shall not see you – which is a bitter blow. It seems ages since I felt the touch of your hand. Violet I think stays at Littlestone till Wednesday, but I hope you will

be back before then. I am very curious to know your impressions – first &
second.

The dinner for Violet's birthday was quite a success – tho' the young man
was not one of the guests – I don't know why. The only novelties were the
Morrells & the Ponsonbys.[1] Ottoline's coiffure surpassed in daring &
luxuriance even *your* most adventurous efforts. By the way, isn't it strange
how one has come to love the fringe?

I had a busy day yesterday, and am rapidly becoming accustomed to my
'double life'. I am going to write to-day to Anthony Henley offering him
my job.[2] I think I told you I have an excellent man in Creedy. Elizabeth who
came on a tour of inspection to the W.O. yesterday, & was nearly repulsed
as a suspected suffragette, was much taken with him. Like the excellent
Masterton Smith (& some other people) he seems to have a spouse in the
dim background of his life.[3] I am just going to have half an hour with Lloyd
George over his budget – always a baffling kind of amusement. I miss you so
much beloved. All my love.

[1] Philip Morrell and Arthur Ponsonby were anti-armament Liberal M.P.s. Lady Ottoline
Morrell and Asquith had been close friends from their first meeting in Dec. 1897 until her
engagement to Philip Morrell four years later. She was half-sister to the Duke of Portland.
Ponsonby's father, Sir Henry Ponsonby (see Letter 47, n. 2), had been Queen Victoria's
Private Secretary and one of his brothers was Assistant Private Secretary to George V.

[2] That of Private Secretary to the Secretary of State for War, ranking under Creedy (see
n. 3 below). Henley, who was the husband of Venetia's sister Sylvia, accepted. He had become
a captain in the 5th Lancers, and a Staff College graduate, via Balliol (where he was known as
'Old Honks') and the Bar. He had once walked with Hilaire Belloc from Oxford to London in
$11\frac{1}{2}$ hours.

[3] Creedy was Principal Private Secretary to the Secretary of State for War, 1913–20,
Masterton-Smith to the First Lord of the Amiralty, 1910–17. Creedy went on to be Permanent Under-Secretary of State, War Office, 1924–39; Masterton-Smith held the same position in the Colonial Office, 1921–4.

60

The Wharf,
Sutton Courtney,
Berks.

Sat 18 Ap 1914

I had a whole hour (!) with Ll. G. attended by the faithful Assyrian, and
we played about with millions and tens of millions with good humour &
even gaiety. No one can hop with greater agility from one twig (or even
one tree or forest) to another. Meanwhile the land campaign, housing, re-
peopling the deserted glens, getting fair play from the ground landlord for
the Gorringes[1] &c – all these have receded into a dim background, & are for
the moment as though they had never been.

I drove down with Elizabeth in beautiful weather to Skindles, where we ate plovers' eggs and some other things, and then proceeded to Hunter-combe. We had quite a good level game of 12 holes. Elizabeth has taken out on her own a motor driver's licence, and this morning she is practising the art with Harwood in the smaller car. It will be some time before I shall trust myself to her guidance. . . .

I wonder my darling how you are faring, and I am eager to know what you think & feel about the situation which is before your eyes. I have a nasty week in prospect – Welsh Church, Army Bill, & the Stationery vote (!) which means, I believe, a discussion of Haldane's tampering with the report of his speech.[2] What colleagues I have! when even the Sinless one can be hauled over the coals. Bless you beloved.

[1] Frederick Gorringe Ltd., the department store, then occupied a large site in Buckingham Palace Road.

[2] Haldane had told the Lords that no orders had been or would be issued 'for the coercing of Ulster'. Unwisely he had inserted 'immediate' before 'coercing' in the Hansard report of his speech.

61

22 Ap 14

Thank you so much darling for your letter. I don't think your day sounds wildly exciting – dining with Geoffrey & lunching with Edward:[1] even at the Savoy!

The Assyrian's dinner was rather disappointing, as only one of the Round Tablers[2] turned up, & I had no talk with him. Ramsay MacDonald & Arthur Ponsonby were the novelties of the occasion. After we had gone to the House & duly voted for the destruction of the Welsh Church, & passed the 2nd reading of the Army Bill in 6 minutes, we went back to Queen Anne's Gate & played (i.e. Ass^n, Bluey, Bongie & I) Bridge for an hour or so.

I have had a pretty exhausting day – Cabinet all morning, 35 questions (a record)[3] to answer in the House, & the Committee on the Army Bill where I have been sitting for hours between Jack Tennant & Bluey, & occasionally airing views on the impressment of motors & aircraft, and the liability of soldiers to have their pay stopped for the maintenance of their bastard children &c &c. At any rate it is a change.

I am going as you know to dine with Ll. George & talk Budget: I will try to keep your interests in mind. We had a huge party at lunch to-day including Anne Islington, Ottoline, Crewe, John Burns &c – as incongruous a lot as even we have ever got together, since Pierpont Morgan[4] sat between

Fraü[5] & Eliz[th]. Violet was back but as yet I have had no talk with her. I am hoping to meet you at dinner to-morrow.

Bless you my beloved: think of me.

[1] Geoffrey Howard, Venetia's cousin, and Edward Horner, Katharine Asquith's brother.

[2] A group which had gathered round Milner, and had founded the review *The Round Table*.

[3] Asquith revealed in one of his answers that he had learned about the movement of the battleships towards Ulster on 21 Mar. and had at once countermanded it (see p. 57). The Government's second white paper was issued soon after this question time.

[4] The American financier, who had died in Mar. 1913; or Asquith may possibly have referred to his son. Both were well known in London.

[5] For 'Fraülein', the governess, probably Anna Heinsius, see R. J. Minney, *Anthony Asquith* (1973), p. 20.

62

1 May 14

It is very tantalising to know that you have postponed your journey, & are going to be here, while I shall be rubbing shoulders with the abhorred tribe of pressmen in the Whitehall Rooms.[1] The function begins at 7, and as I had (after meeting the Army Council this morning, and Birrell, and the Impeccable, and Winston, who was very copious & perorative [*sic*] about the Budget, and Redmond Dillon & Co, and exchanging pleasantries at lunch with Maud Cunard & Peggy Crewe, and sustaining my part in a solemn French dialogue with Cambon)[2] to try & compile some not too offensive observations about the newspaper world, you will agree – if you have survived this sentence – that I could not possibly come to see you this afternoon. . . . The only really nice hour I have had this week was yesterday. Send me a line. Dearest love. Don't leave this on your table or in some one else's envelope!

[1] Asquith presided, and made the principal speech, at the 51st anniversary dinner of the Newspaper Press Fund at the Hotel Metropole.

[2] Paul Cambon had been French Ambassador in London since 1898. 'One of his little "poses"', Lord Esher wrote in 1915, 'is inability to speak or understand the English language. He can do both.'

63

The Wharf,
Sutton Courtney,
Berks.

Sunday 3 May 14

. . . We found the Assyrian & Mikky[1] here: the former left early this morning to spend a happy day budgeting with the Chancellor of the

Exchequer at Walton Heath. I have seen more of the young man than ever before, and to me it is quite unthinkable.[2] He is 'nice' & not bad to look at, but has no distinction or edge of any kind, and one never knows without looking carefully round whether he is in the room or not. It is one of the most mysterious cases of *foudroyance* that I can remember. Pauline[3] is here, & we are going to drive into Oxford to fetch Cys. My plans this week are of the vaguest, & I know nothing of yours. I wonder when I shall see you? Take care of yourself darling – All love. . . .

[1] R. S. Meiklejohn, a Principal Clerk in the Treasury, who worked largely for the Prime Minister.

[2] Violet's quasi-fiancé. See Letter 56.

[3] Pauline Stapleton-Cotton (b. 1877).

Ulster III: 'The last of the Home Rule Bill' (Letters 64–71)

ON the night of 24/25 April, 24,600 rifles and several million rounds of ammunition were landed from Germany at Larne and elsewhere in Ulster, and distributed by Carson's followers (Letter 66). There was a conciliatory 'exchange' in the Commons between Churchill and Carson on 28 and 29 April; and on 5 May Asquith met Carson and Bonar Law (Letter 64). Some progress was made on procedure. It was agreed that no purpose would be served by a committee stage for the Home Rule Bill: the Ulster settlement proposals would be embodied in a separate Amending Bill. Asquith did not concede the demand that the Home Rule Bill should remain in the Commons until settlement terms for Ulster had been agreed. On the wider question there was little sign of an accommodation. The Curragh 'mutiny' and the gun-running had left the Conservative leaders in an apparently strong position. They maintained that no settlement could be achieved if the exclusion of Ulster was to be limited in time, while Asquith said that 'he would be no party to the coercion of Ulster'.

Carson's position, while strong, was not quite as strong as it looked. Now that the Conservatives were involved in large-scale gun-running their attempt to convict the Government of trying to coerce Ulster lost much of its moral force: it had come to look, in Churchill's words, 'uncommonly like a vote of censure by the criminal classes on the police'. Some Conservatives still disliked the policy of saving Ulster by ditching their friends in the rest of Ireland. Others wanted a settlement on 'federal' lines (Letter 64). The National Volunteers were growing rapidly. By the end of June they outnumbered Carson's force (Letter 110). They were not under Redmond's secure control, so that their importance inhibited him from agreeing to further concessions. It also made the continued government of southern Ireland from Westminster almost impossible.

By Whitsun, despite stormy scenes, the Home Rule Bill had been pushed through the Commons (Letters 67 and 71).

64

5 May 14

I hoped I should have heard from you to-day: for I have not the least idea how you are, & what you are doing, or when & where we shall meet. *Do* write.

The Budget debate collapsed as Ll. G. landed the House in a well (or luckily) contrived morass of obscurity in which for the moment every one was bogged. Even to-day people seem to be in two minds what it is all about: but so far as I am told, there is no very active hostility. I dined at the House at the annual budget dinner, given this year at the joint expense of the Impeccable & the Assyrian, and sat next the former within easy range of Sir M. Nathan – who is an enthusiastic supporter of the Budget (being, as he is, the real author of the wicked 'scales').[1]

I have had what is called a 'busy' day: a good part of the morning being furtively spent in the silken tents in converse with 2 eminent persons, whom I will not name.[2]

I then had a turn at the War Office, and got some useful stuff from Anthony Henley. Thence to the House where I had to get through a small motion,[3] and afterwards 2 deputations – Panama Exhibition,[4] & Federalism![5] Interviews with Loulou,[6] Ll. George, & others filled up the interstices, and now I am going to dine in Violet's company at the Arch-Colonels's. It is almost like one of your July days. It is possible that with great good luck I might come in the motor for you a little before 6 to-morrow (Wed). But I can't be quite sure. Anyhow I shall try to see you –

Bless you darling.

[1] After a remarkable career in the army and the colonies Sir Matthew Nathan had become Chairman of the Board of Inland Revenue in 1911. The budget proposals included introducing a graduated scale for supertax and making the scale for death duties more severe.

[2] The conversation with Bonar Law and Carson was reported in *The Times* and *Daily Mail* on 6 May. F. E. Smith is said to have leaked the news to the Northcliffe press: H. Montgomery Hyde, *Carson* (2nd edn., 1974), p. 367.

[3] It concerned a standing order to regulate 'blocking motions'.

[4] The all-party deputation asking for Britain to be officially represented at the Exhibition claimed the support of 366 M.P.s (out of 670). The cabinet, told that this would cost £250,000, 'were unanimously against' being represented: Hobhouse, *Diaries*, p. 146.

[5] Under the federal scheme, as it was propounded by members of Milner's Round Table group, there were to be separate legislatures for each part of Britain: Ulster would be free to join the rest of Ireland, but was not to be coerced into doing so. *The Times* (6 May) reported 'upwards of 100 Liberals, and a smaller number of Unionists' as favouring a federal solution. Austen Chamberlain had made a rather similar estimate on 2 Apr.

[6] Lewis Harcourt, the Colonial Secretary.

65

War Office

7 May 1914

. . . We had some quite amusing Bridge last night & Sylvia & I took a little from the super-taxed Derenbergs.[1] I thought you would have come in from the Club,[2] but you were play-going in fashionable company. Altogether you have treated me badly this week, and I don't suppose I shall have more than a glimpse of you at Ottoline's to-night. Anyhow to-morrow afternoon we will have our drive. I had a fairly satisfactory interview with Redmond & Dillon this afternoon. The House is duller than ditch-water. It is a great bore that I have to remain here Sat night but as you say we will motor back together Monday. Waxworks came to lunch & confided to me that one of his great desires was that his Oil King Sir Marcus Samuel shd. be made a Peer! He is a hot Tory Semite.[3]   My dearest love.

[1] Charles Derenberg was on the Stock Exchange and was to be 'hammered' on 30 July 1914 in the panic preceding the outbreak of war. His wife was a professional pianist (Ilona or Eilona Eibenschutz).

[2] Founded in 1910 for poor boys in memory of Lord Archie Gordon. In Westmoreland Place, Hoxton. See also Letter 75.

[3] Sir Reginald Macleod was nicknamed 'Waxworks' 'because of his pink-and-white complexion and white cotton wool side whiskers': L. E. Jones, *An Edwardian Youth* (1956), p. 217. His house, Vinters, Maidstone, was near Sir Marcus Samuel's, The Mote. The latter had been a founder of the Shell Transport and Trading Company in 1897, with which the Dutch oil interests had been amalgamated ten years later; created Lord Bearsted, 1921; Viscount, 1925.

66

11 May 14

Short as it was – far too short – I thought we had a delicious time, and the drive back to-day was a thing to remember. . . .

I found lots of bothers awaiting me, and spent some time with Illingworth & Gulland & Ll. George. The last named came to lunch, where also were Eddie Marsh & Peggy Crewe. She renewed with great vigour her campaign on behalf of 'Sr Edgar' and what she elegantly if rather unkindly calls his 'whitewashing'.[1] We had an uneventful time at the House, where I was rather feebly catechised about the gun-running & its consequences. Bongie has told you about coming to the Naval & Mil^y tournament on Friday aft. I suppose about 3. We have the royal box which will hold 10! I have got to go to the Guildhall function to-morrow wh. is a nuisance: the others are going to the Gala Opera to-night.[2] Bless you darling –   all love.

¹ Sir Edgar Vincent was being considered for a peerage in the forthcoming honours list: see Letter 83. He had been in the 1911 list of those to be ennobled should a mass Liberal creation be required. His financial career had not been one of unbroken success, the Imperial Ottoman Bank in Constantinople having become involved in serious losses during his Governorship (1889–97).
² Where they heard *Tosca*, Act 1; *La Bohème*, Act 1, with Melba and Martinelli; and *Aida*, Act 2, sc. 2.

67

THE INFANT SAMUEL.
(Punch)

12 May 14

. . . I went to the function at the Guildhall this morning for the Denmark royalties. It is I suppose about the 15th thing of the kind I have attended. I sat next old Princess Christian,¹ who showed a nearer approach to general intelligence than I have ever discovered in her before. The luncheon & toasts & getting away were very prolonged, and as I had to change my clothes I was very nearly late here at the House. Happily the Infant Samuel was on his legs dilating on Milk, and a little diluting his subject to give me time.²

We had quite a lively debate, A.J.B. doing his best to wreck the chances of peace.³ Ll. George & Redmond were quite good: also one Whyte who sits for Perth⁴. . . .

¹ Queen Victoria's third daughter.
² He was moving for leave to introduce the Milk Bill.
³ The procedural resolution for the Home Rule Bill was being debated. Balfour made much

of the defects of a Bill which could be brought into effect only through an Amending Bill. He had tried in April to scotch the federal solution. See also Letter 98.

[4] Whyte lost his seat in 1918 and became an authority on Far Eastern affairs; Chairman, Indian Legislative Assembly, 1920–25.

68

13 May 14

. . . The Irish are in rather a panicky mood, but I think they will soon recover their nerves. I have a rather effusive letter to-day from high quarters[1]. . . .

[1] The announcement about the Amending Bill had delighted the King and angered Redmond.

69

19 May 1914

I rather hoped to have heard from you to-day as I am quite in the dark as to your doings this week – beyond that you were dining with the Lyells – I suppose with ulterior views to a ball. Anyhow I hope we may have Friday afternoon together, after I lunch with Maud Cunard, who promises a dazzling array of beauty, charm &c.

I enjoyed my time at Aldershot much more than I expected. The weather was divine, & I have never seen anything so beautiful as the hawthorn rhododendrons azaleas &c all blooming side by side. I drove after lunch on Sunday to Swinley Forest, and played a round of golf with the Lord Chief Justice. Yesterday I participated in all sorts of military functions, bloody & otherwise, & motored back in time to dine with Ll. George. The royalties were quite agreeable, and the Pss Mary, tho' far from forthcoming, is easier to deal with than she used to be. I came across one or two quite intelligent soldiers, and acquired a certain amount of lore in regard to uniforms colours, & other branches of more or less useless knowledge. I had a long talk this morning with Gen[l] Macready who is over from Belfast, and is certainly one of the cleverest of the soldiers. He takes a sane level-headed view of things.[1]

We are in the depths of dullness here over the Welsh Church – positively its last appearance – after a far from lively luncheon downstairs in honour of the S. Buxtons, whose health I proposed.[2] I am now off to War Office. I wonder what you are doing my darling – *do* write to me.   All love.

[1] In *Annals of an Active Life* (1924), i. 190–91, Macready recorded the instructions given to him on this visit: 'If Carson proclaimed his provisional government the only course was to remain on the defensive and do nothing, Mr Asquith being of opinion that a proclamation would be issued by Carson which would clear the air and give an indication as to future action.' Macready's inclination was to 'govern or get out' (p. 198).

[2] Buxton had just been appointed Governor-General of South Africa.

70

Buckhurst,
Withyham,
Sussex.

Sunday 24 May 14.

I thought that we had a delicious drive on Friday, & it braced me up for the huge dinner (nearly 50) of MP's & their wives in the evening. I sat between Lady Susan Townley & Lady Pirrie (of Belfast)[1]: most of them I had never seen before. All the same it was a great success – thanks largely to Lady Tree who 'obliged' with some excellent recitations after dinner. I motored down here after lunch yesterday with Margot & Elizabeth. It is a really beautiful park, with fine gardens & water.[2] . . . I think the two Benson boys – Rex is in India on Hardinge's staff – the two nicest & most desirable young men (with Oc)[3] of my whole acquaintance – manly, good-looking, with charming manners & plenty of intelligence: in fact, ideal sons-in-law. But these things apparently don't happen!

The Ipswich election is quite the worst we have had,[4] & is a smasher for poor Masterman. The odd thing about it seems to be that it was fought about everything & anything except Home Rule. I saw Ll. George on Sat morning, and he was pretty certain that Masterman wd. be beaten. He was told by some of the local people that the Cross which M. wears & flaunts on his waistcoat wd. cost him at least 50 votes![5] It is quite likely that we may finish up at the House to-morrow (Monday) night. In any case I hope we shall go in your company on Wed morning to Shrewsbury & thence by motor. It will be a great joy my darling.   Dearest love.

[1] The wives of the British Minister to Persia and of the Chairman of Harland and Wolff. Lord Pirrie had become a Liberal peer in 1906 and been Comptroller of the Household to the Lord-Lieutenant of Ireland, 1907–13. He was prominent in the Ulster Liberal Association.

[2] See Appendix 3.

[3] Asquith did not conceal in these letters that Arthur was his favourite son.

[4] The Liberals had already lost two seats in by-elections since the start of the 1914 session – South West Bethnal Green by 20 votes (Letter 38, n. 2), and Leith District by 16. Labour interventions accounted for both these defeats. As the next note shows, Ipswich was more serious, though the swing against the Government there (5.1%) was the smallest of the three.

[5] In Dec. 1910 the Liberal now retiring had been 344 votes ahead of the leading Conservative in this double-Member constituency. The by-election winner beat Masterman by 532,

and both his opponents combined by 137. He said that he had won 'on the Home Rule question, and to a lesser extent, perhaps, on that of the Insurance Act'. It was the kind of constituency in which employers aggrieved at paying insurance contributions were prominent: Masterman's connection with national insurance no doubt harmed him (see Letter 38, n. 2), as did the enmity of the *Daily Mail* and *John Bull*. Home Rule seems to have been more important than Asquith made out, however: Carson was the Conservatives' principal eve-of-poll speaker. Lloyd George had made the eve-of-poll speech for Masterman on 22 May. High Churchmanship, if emphasized, was a disadvantage to a Liberal candidate. The Labour intervention at Ipswich was a reprisal for the North East Derbyshire by-election a few days earlier where a Liberal candidature had allowed the Conservatives to capture a Labour seat, and had driven the Labour candidate into third place.

71

25 May 1914

. . . The House was very crowded & rather uproarious but on the whole in a good temper. The Speaker abased himself (I thought) somewhat excessively before Bonar Law,[1] and B. L. made a rasping & ridiculous speech on the topic of the outrages & oppressions we have been inflicting on the minority. I made a hottish reply, and after a melancholy screed from W^m O'Brien we divided on the 3rd reading, and after 2 years saw the last of the Home Rule Bill.[2] . . .

[1] On 21 May during the third reading debate on Home Rule Asquith refused to disclose the contents of the Amending Bill. The Speaker asked Bonar Law whether the resulting uproar from the Conservatives had his 'assent and approval'. 'I would not presume to criticize what you consider your duty, Sir,' Bonar Law replied; 'but I know mine, and that is not to answer any such question.' The Speaker then suspended the sitting on the ground of grave disorder. The retort by Bonar Law, and the apology made to him by the Speaker after the weekend, greatly increased his parliamentary standing. Asquith 'wondered whether he would have said anything so good'. His own calm conduct on 21 May was admired, Gladstone's daughter (Mrs Drew) commenting, for instance, 'The P.M. is really wonderful': L. Masterman, *Mary Gladstone* (1930), p. 477.

[2] Bonar Law was complaining that the Opposition were compelled to debate Home Rule before the Government's Ulster proposals had been published. In reply Asquith pointed out that the complaint came strangely from a Conservative leader: when the Liberals were in opposition they were not protected by a majority in the Lords, and were thus not given three sessions in which to discuss their opponents' measures. (Under the Parliament Act the Commons had to pass a measure in three successive sessions to overrule a Lords majority.) O'Brien led a small group of Irish Members sitting for constituencies in the area of Cork, who had all along favoured concessions to Ulster.

72

May 1914

Locutiones
B.V.S.
valde deflendae
necnon
vehementer cavendae[1]

—

It's up to you

We're out for it

Doggo
Dusty
Soppy

Drat the man

Quite a nut

A Peach

A Dew-drop

Biffo

Darling Huck!

Pretty Mick!

[1] 'Expressions used by B.V.S. which are much to be deplored and emphatically to be guarded against.'

73

Penrhos,
Holyhead.[1]

Sat. June 6. 1914.

Don't forget that 'They have most power to harm us whom we love'.[2] I take with me some bright memories, and a *sad* heart.

[1] See Appendix 3. Asquith had been staying there since 27 May.
[2] Beaumont and Fletcher: *The Maid's Tragedy*, v.iv

74

Nuneham Park,
Oxford.[1]

Sunday 7 June 14.

I left with rather a heavy heart which was not much lightened during the journey, tho' it was a lovely day & for the most part a beautiful drive. I rather hoped I should have got a line from you this morning. I had a good talk with Violet – mainly about Hugh[2] & Bongie, and when we parted at Shrewsbury she was in a slightly tearful mood. I avoided the Black country and came through Bridgnorth & Kidderminster to Stratford on Avon, where I got out of the motor & revisited the Church with the Shakespeare bust and other relics. A typical Dickens verger came up & said 'Have I the honour of addressing our distinguished Prime Minister?' I tried to shake him off with a gruff & uninviting affirmative, but he at once produced an autograph book, where I signed my name below that of our nice old friend Sir James Donaldson, who I regret to say had visited the Church as the guest of Corelli![3]

I found Margot & Elizabeth here: they were close at hand during the suffragette scene at the Court, and say that the young woman did her part very well.[4] We have a characteristic party here: the Eshers, Gerald Lowther (late of Constantinople),[5] Jack Peases, Lionel Earle, a French Countess, and my old private secretary Mark Sturgis[6] with his beautiful fiancée Lady Rachel Wortley. I say beautiful because all the world calls her so: but tho' she has a fine figure and colouring I can see nothing interesting in her face. I sat on one side of her at dinner and when our turn arrived for conversation, the topic upon which we fell was the breeding & feeding of Pigs, by which she means to eke out a slender income in the early days of her married life. She seems to be quite a practical young woman and makes no pretence to charm.

I found here the enclosed from Ll.G. which, as it is probably the longest letter he has ever written with his own hand,[7] I send you as a curiosity: to be destroyed after you have read it, or if not, to be deposited with other documents in your possession in some safe & secret receptacle. We played bridge – not very amusing, and to-day as it promises to be fine we may golf after lunch at Huntercombe. Write on Monday to Downing St.

I muse a great deal over what we said & thought in some of the delicious hours we spent together, and I try at odd moments to piece together what you said into a coherent whole. Not very easy! Do you remember replying to what I thought was a rather penetrating analysis of some aspects of your character: 'I think it is *not unlikely* that it may be *rather* true'?[8] My darling the thought of you is a joy & inspiration to me. All my love.

74a

11 Downing Street,
Whitehall, S.W.

June 5th 1914.

My dear Prime Minister,

I have had a long talk with Elibank. He strongly approves of the suggested arrangement.[9] Had he remained at the Whip's Office he contemplated doing something of the kind himself. He is convinced that under modern conditions of Parliamentary warfare no Chief Whip can attend effectively to the party business in the House & in the country as well. I discussed names with him. He was divided in his mind between Ponsonby & Addison.[10] He thought that Percy would be more likely to accept tranquilly the appointment of an outsider than of one of his own subordinates like Wedgwood Benn.[11] He was of opinion that the proposed rearrangement of functions could be put in such a way to Percy as not to offend his susceptibilities.

He was anxious that Percy should not find out that he (Elibank) had been consulted.

He was insistent on the Chief Whip's authority in the House not being diminished & on his still retaining the position of Prime Minister's confidential adviser.[12]

Ever sincerely,

D. Lloyd George.

[1] See Appendix 3.

[2] Hugh Godley had been Violet's close friend for some years and had at one stage been in love with her. He was nearly ten years her senior. Asquith wrote to Margot, 3 June, that Violet had 'of course' told Hugh 'everything' about her latest attachment (Letter 56), and had 'asked his advice'. Violet wrote to Hugh, 5 June: 'You were what *no* one else could have been – a balm and a stimulus and a delight all rolled into one.'

[3] Asquith had sat for East Fife since 1886. Donaldson had been Principal of St Andrews University during the same period: he was a close friend of the novelist Marie Corelli, who lived in Stratford-on-Avon. Donaldson called her 'my sweet Marie' or 'beloved little lassie'. Asquith must have disapproved either of the friendship, or, more probably, of the novels.

[4] In protest against the forcible feeding of suffragettes on hunger strike, Mary Blomfield shouted, as the King and Queen were passing: 'Your Majesty, won't you stop torturing the women?' She had gained entry to Buckingham Palace without difficulty, her father having been a prominent architect and her Blomfield grandfather Bishop of London. The Queen found the incident 'very unpleasant'.

[5] Lowther had been Ambassador at Constantinople, 1908–13, where he was thought 'an utter dud' according to the youthful T. E. Lawrence.

[6] Asquith's Private Secretary, 1908–10. Later Sir Mark Grant-Sturgis.

[7] Asquith was not the only colleague to joke about Lloyd George's inadequacy as a correspondent. When Churchill mentioned to Campbell-Bannerman that he had received a letter from Ll. G., the response was: 'Keep it: it is the only one extant': T. Jones, *A Diary with Letters, 1931–50* (1954), p. 262.

[8] 'The P.M. used to mock me', Venetia told Edwin, 15 June 1915, 'for my habit of gross under-expression. "Fun" and "rather nice", he said, were my highest terms of praise.'

[9] This referred to Lloyd George's scheme whereby Liberal party organization outside

Parliament would cease to be the responsibility of the Chief Whip. Asquith approved of the scheme and had advised Lloyd George to see the former Chief Whip about it. The difficulties which the Government party was apt to experience in keeping its organization effective were well known. Montagu had suggested a plan of this kind as early as Nov. 1908; and the need for one was increased in 1912 when the Conservatives made such an arrangement, Arthur Steel-Maitland being put in charge of their reorganized party machine. The Ipswich by-election defeat brought this to a head: see C. Beck to Masterman, 26 May; Montagu to Asquith, 27 May, 1914, quoted in C. Hazlehurst, *Politicians at War* (1971), p. 129.

[10] For Ponsonby see Letter 59, n. 1; he had refused appointment as a junior Whip in 1913. For Dr Christopher Addison see Letter 37; he held medical qualifications and had been closely associated with Lloyd George over health insurance.

[11] Percy Illingworth was the Chief Whip, Wedgwood Benn a Junior Whip. Lloyd George had suggested Benn for the party post to be created (Asquith to Margot, 4 June 1914).

[12] It seems that Illingworth objected to the proposal. When war came it had not been put into effect. See G. A. Riddell, *War Diary* (1933), p. 50.

75

For B. V. S.
and *no one* else
————

War Office,
Whitehall,
S.W.[1]

Whitsuntide 1914

With rough justice, the *superficial* aspects of the life of the person in question – more particularly in London – may be described as phases in a pleasure-hunt.

Even the gruffest observer cannot withhold a reluctant tribute to the vitality and versatility which, in the course of an average summer day, can betake itself – successively or at choice – to

	Fencing	Shopping	Ladies gallery-ing
	Swimming	Palming	Gossiping
(Life A)	Tennissing	Polo-watching	Hair-brushing
	Manicuring	Motoring	Dining
	Lunching	Golfing	Dancing
	Play & opera-going		Gambling

On the other side of the account must be set one evening a week given conscientiously to a boys' club.

After a fair but not excessive allowance for sleep, how much time is left for

Reading
Writing

(Life B)   Thinking
                Practising an art
                'Making one's soul' (J. Morley)

The sum does itself, and need not be worked out in detail.

I purposely used the word 'superficial', because it is mere pedantry to suppose that the *two great things* which are needed in human intercourse, and which are not the same the one with the other, are necessarily excluded from Life A, or necessarily included in Life B.

They are (1) Unselfishness (2) Considerateness. Lots of both may be shown in the 'pleasure-hunt'. Both may be conspicuously absent from the austere and untempered pursuit of 'higher things'.

Another admission – perhaps an equally damaging one to the would-be censor – has also to be made. It is due to the different point of view from which the sexes in the modern world regard and judge one another. There are men who lead Life A (at any rate in most of its phases) but as a rule they get no admiration, and little more than tolerance, from any woman who is worth the name. On the other hand, the same life is led by women and girls whom the most fastidious of mankind acknowledge to be the flower of their sex. One reason, of course, is that most, if not all, men have an alternative or at any rate a mixed existence which, without any effort, they can choose if they please: while to a woman (in the social conditions supposed) it involves a continuous exertion of will, and constant mutiny against established routine, to shake herself free, and pursue, in any real or full sense, a self-determined life.

All the same, it is sad to see so much of beauty and charm, and powers that might move & raise the world, running to waste.

One is apt to think with Coventry Patmore

> 'How giv'n for nought her priceless gift,
> How spoil'd the bread & spill'd the wine,
> Which, spent with due respective thrift,
> Had made brutes men and men divine'.[2]

But what is a woman to do who is conscious that she is not making the best or the most of her world?

> To 'get her to a Nunnery'?[3] To give up Society, and take to 'Slumming'? To become a competitor with the less well-off of her sex in professions which are already over-crowded? Or to fold her hands, and bow dumbly to the decrees of Destiny?*

These are all counsels of Despair. Pleasure is a good and not a bad thing:[4] introspection is a dangerous and debilitating habit; there is, as a rule, more harm than good to be got by wrenching one's self out of the groove in which one's life finds its natural & normal course. 'Heroic remedies' will generally be found to partake of the quality of quack medicines.

Simpler & more commonplace expedients are more likely to be of use. For instance:

(1) To be sure that each day (not necessarily at the same hour) one has a fixed time – it might be an hour or less – to one's self for reading & such like occupations.

(2) Always to have on the stocks some definite subject, about which at odd moments to think & read.

(3) To try & really help, & if possible inspire, some chosen friends in their ambitions and work.

(4) To keep secrets, to waste as little time as may be over trivialities and with merely frivolous people, and to put a stopper on ill-natured gossip.

And I should add

(5) To have some one from whom you have no secrets, and upon whose understanding, judgment, and love, you can implicitly rely.

* Wifehood & motherhood (as we constantly see) are not in themselves solutions.

---

[1] Asquith seems to have carried War Office notepaper about with him (see Letter 180). He probably presented this essay to Venetia after the Whitsun break at Penrhos.

[2] Coventry Patmore, *The Angel in the House*. Asquith was addicted to this quotation. See Letter 401; his letter to Viola Tree, *Castles in the Air* (1926), p. 185; and Frances Horner, *Time Remembered* (1933), p. 107.

[3] *Hamlet*, III. i.

[4] Compare Hugh Gaitskell to his daughter Julie, 23 June 1958: 'Pleasure is not only all right but good so long as it is not too selfish or undermining of one's capacity to do whatever it is one *can do*': Philip M. Williams, *Gaitskell* (1979), p. 376.

76

Nuneham Park,
Oxford.

8 June '14

It was a great joy and consolation to get your little letter this morning. Yes, we had a *divine* time, all too short, tho' longer than one could have hoped in this drab & distracting world. When shall we have such another? 'Not Heaven itself upon the past has power'[1] is a quotation with which I try to keep up heart and spirits when I think of the future with all its dim possibilities, in forecasting which (in the things which touch one most keenly & deeply) doubt seems often so much more rational than hope. At any rate you will be glad to know that, in obedience to your wish (only a week ago to-day), I have suspended those prayers to the gods which you forbade.

When shall I see you – really see you – I wonder? On Friday we will have our drive – but before? . . .

---

¹ Dryden, *Translations from Horace, Ode 29 of Book iii.*

77

9 June 1914

I hear from Bongie that you arrived this morning: so that we are once more within range, not I hope like ships that pass in the night. Margot & Eliz & I fancy Violet are going to the State Ball, which I eschew. I am dining with the Club (not yours but Dʳ Johnson's¹) which is celebrating one of its anniversaries. The House was quite dull & eventless, and after interviews with Ll. George Crewe & Haldane, I spent an hour dry-as-dusting at the War Office. I am going to have a talk with Illingworth to-morrow morning.

I drove over this morning from luncheon with Loulou & Jack Pease to Oxford to attend Sir W. Anson's² funeral, or at least the first part of it. There was a rather remarkable congregation in St. Mary's Church where in old times Newman used to preach. Anson, a very cultivated and agreeable man, was a teaching example of the futility of the don in politics. Lord Palmerston once defined dirt as 'matter in the wrong place', and equally misplaced is an Oxford or Cambridge jurist or mathematician in the House of Commons. Tho' a strong & rather warped partisan he never became bitter, and less than a month ago I sat next him & had a nice talk at Grillions. I suppose you are at the Club to-night? And to-morrow? I long to see you again my darling more than I can tell you, and to know your thoughts. Bless you always – all my love.

---

¹ For 'your club' see Letter 65, n. 2. 'The Club' was founded by Sir Joshua Reynolds in 1764, Samuel Johnson being a founder-member.

² Succeeded as 3rd baronet, 1873; Warden of All Souls College, Oxford, 1881 to his death; Conservative M.P. for Oxford University, from 1899; Parliamentary Secretary, Board of Education, 1902–5; P.C., 1911; an authority on constitutional law, he regarded the Parliament Act and what flowed from it as a mutilation of the constitution.

Ulster IV: The Amending Bill, the Conference, and Bachelor's Walk (Letters 78–110)

ASQUITH now tried to obtain some agreement with Carson and Bonar Law on the distribution of Protestants and Catholics in each Ulster county. In private discussions the salient facts were agreed to be that three of the counties of historic Ulster were largely Catholic, four largely Protestant, and two (Fermanagh and Tyrone) almost evenly balanced with the Catholics just in a majority. Within these last two it was not possible to delineate Protestant and Catholic districts. Virtually all the districts were mixed, the Protestants normally occupying the lower-lying, and richer, land. Carson quickly saw the advantage of demanding the exclusion, with no time-limit to it, of the bloc of six counties with substantial Protestant populations. He naturally resisted all suggestions that the right of any one of the six to be excluded should be tested by a county plebiscite (Letter 92). The plan which he opposed was popularly called 'county option'; his demand was for 'a clean cut' (Letter 107). He did not pretend, even in public, to be sure of a majority in each of the counties: were Protestant Ulstermen, he asked, going 'to abandon men in another county just because there may be a majority here or a majority there'?[1]

Carson and Bonar Law were confident of securing the exclusion of Ulster provided that they could keep their followers in hand. None of the Government's manoeuvring had obscured the basic fact mentioned in the Introduction (p. 16): now that the Ulster Protestants had organized their resistance they could not be coerced. On 17 July Asquith told Bonar Law that it 'would be a crime' to allow civil war to start on the issue of whether to divide Tyrone. The people of Ulster, Bonar replied, knew 'that they had a force which would enable them to hold the province; and, with opinion divided in this country, it was quite impossible that any force could be sent against them which could dislodge them; and therefore they knew that they could get their own terms; and it was certain they would rather fight than give way on such a point as this'.[2] Redmond could no more concede the 'clean cut' than Carson could abandon it. All the conciliatory efforts of Asquith, and of a host of coadjutors headed by the King, broke down on the fact that both sides preferred putting Ulster's resistance to the test to backing down on this central issue.

The question of the time-limit was less intractable. If the Liberals won both the general elections due during the next six years the Ulstermen would have to start making their peace with Dublin however long a period of exclusion they had originally been promised.[3] Redmond made clear in conference on 21 July that he would negotiate on the time-limit provided the 'clean cut' disappeared.

The exchange of information on the Ulster counties after Whitsun (Letters 78 and 79) left the parties completely at odds on what the Amending Bill (p. 39) should contain. As introduced in the Lords on 23 June, it reproduced the Government's terms of March: each Ulster county could opt out of Home Rule by plebiscite for six years (Letter 84). As amended by the Tory peers, it provided for the permanent exclusion of all the nine counties of historic Ulster (Letters 87 and 93).

For some weeks the King had pressed for a conference under a neutral chairman (see the oblique references in Letters 84 and 86). The Prime Minister prepared for this by a network of private negotiations on the area to be excluded. By mid-July the geographical part of the dispute had almost been narrowed to Tyrone and Fermanagh (Letters 87 and 91–7). On 16 July Asquith asked the King to convene a conference (Letters 98–101). This met at Buckingham Palace with the Speaker as chairman from 21 to 24 July. There was no agreement on the area to be excluded, so that the problem of the time-limit was not reached (Letters 102, 103, and 107). Asquith then decided to proceed with the Amending Bill in the Commons on 28 July, restoring county option but not the time-limit (Letters 103 and 105). On the Sunday before that date, 26 July, the National Volunteers did some gun-running in daylight at Howth, near Dublin. This led to a brush with regular troops who opened fire in Bachelor's Walk, killing three and injuring thirty-eight (Letters 106 and 107). Asquith had to allow tempers to cool among Redmond's followers and he postponed the second reading debate on the Amending Bill for two days (Letter 108). On 30 July, a few hours before his speech was due, he was asked by Bonar Law and Carson to postpone it during the war crisis in the interests of national unity (Letter 110). He agreed. Ulster had been driven from the main headlines at last.

---

[1] From Herne Hill speech, 4 July: *Daily Telegraph*, 6 July, 11e. Other papers did not report this remark. The Liberal press dealt briefly with Carson: *The Times* may have found the admission embarrassing. From January 1913 onwards (when the Liberals won Londonderry City by 57 votes) the Conservatives were in a parliamentary minority (16 to 17) in the nine counties of historic Ulster.

[2] Robert Blake, *The Unknown Prime Minister* (1955), p. 214.

[3] Similarly Redmond had little to gain from a short period. If the Conservatives won the election due in 1915, they would enact permanent exclusion; if the Liberals won, they would need a second victory before they could bring the Ulster Protestants to accept Home Rule.

78

War Office,
Whitehall,
S.W.

11 June 14

Thank you my darling for your sweet letter. Here is the map which will interest you, and I have written in the percentage of the Protestants & Roman Catholics in each of the counties. I have not yet got any answer to *our* letter.[1] I saw the King for nearly an hour this afternoon: his talk was largely about Ireland & the desirability of bringing the two Irish lots into one room for conference agreement &c. He will be away all next week attending the Ascot functions.

I sat next the Troubetskoy at our huge dinner last night. Her eyes are neither so large nor so liquid as they were 20 years ago, but otherwise she has worn well and tho' a little too cloying she talks quite interestingly.[2] We had not a very interesting lot of guests – Stamfordhams St. Davids &c &c. and the Assyrian & I went to the House to the division at 11. Afterwards, at Violet's solicitation and in response to a rather agitated letter from Lillah, *re* Dunn, I went to the Connaught rooms to the Barker supper in celebration of the 500th night of *The Great Adventure*.[3] There were a lot of actors & actresses with Eddie Marsh, Philip Sassoon and such (including the much debated Dunn)[4] thrown in. After supper they danced. I sat next Ainley (who comes like me from Morley!) and opposite Arnold Bennett, whom I thought a bounder of the first degree. . . .

[1] Probably to Carson with whom Asquith was corresponding. These letters are not in the Carson MSS. For the exchange of maps see Carson to Asquith, 15 May, and 10, 13, and 25 June: Asquith MSS, vol. 39, ff. 178–9, 182–4, and 193.

[2] Princess Amélie Troubetskoy, the American authoress, then aged 50, had married (1896) as her second husband Prince Pierre Troubetskoy, a portrait painter who had emigrated to the United States as a young man.

[3] *The Great Adventure* by Arnold Bennett had opened at the Kingsway Theatre on 25 Mar. 1913, with Henry Ainley and Wish Wynne in the leading parts. It was produced by Harley Granville-Barker, who had married Lillah McCarthy in 1906. 'Lillah was my partner,' Bennett recorded of this supper; 'but Asquith came uninvited and she had to look after him.' Bennett did not know about the 'agitated letter'.

[4] See Letter 83, n. 6.

79

The Wharf,
Sutton Courtney,
Berks.

Sun. 14 June 14

. . . I am not in the best of moods this morning. A contributory cause is the Lichnowsky couple, whom I find rather trying guests. They have neither of them any manners, and he is loquacious and inquisitive about trifles.[1] After dinner last night we went to the barn & she took possession of the piano-stool, and strummed & drummed infernal patches of tuneless music for the rest of the evening.[2] . . .

I had another letter from C.[3] this morning enclosing the long promised map, which is a rather unwieldy affair to look at & hold: I haven't had time yet to examine the details. Did you ever look at yours? . . .

[1] Prince Lichnowsky had been German Ambassador since Oct. 1912. In *The Genesis of the War* (1923) Asquith wrote of the Ambassador's desire for peace and for Anglo-German friendship (and, less sincerely, of his 'most agreeable manners'). Despite a voice described as 'raucous' or 'querulous' Lichnowsky was popular in English society; but his marriage was not happy, so that he and his wife may not have shown at their best when house guests together for the weekend. In Lichnowsky's *My Mission to London* (English edn., 1918) Asquith was depicted as

a jovial *bon-vivant*, fond of the ladies, especially the young and pretty ones. He is partial to cheerful society and good cooking. . . . A pacifist like his friend Grey, and favouring an understanding with Germany, he treated all questions with the cheery calm and assurance of an experienced man of business, whose good health and excellent nerves were steeled by devotion to . . . golf.

(Passage reproduced in Lichnowsky, *Heading for the Abyss* (1928), p. 69.) Lichnowsky, who was an admirer of Britain (and first cousin to the Russian Ambassador in London), carried no weight with the German Government.

[2] As a persistent pianist the Princess was at some disadvantage with a host as unmusical as Asquith. 'In Princess Lichnowsky', Margot wrote in her *Autobiography*, 'I found so much nature, affection, and enterprise that, in spite of black socks, white boots, and crazy tiaras, I could not but admire her.'

[3] Carson wrote (13 June) that the map was 'merely for information' and that he was 'not in a position' to make suggestions (Asquith MSS, vol. 39, f. 184). On 16 June Crewe, pressed in the Lords about the delays to the Amending Bill, revealed that 'some communications' had passed between Carson and the Government; and press reports referred to an interchange of maps. Carson objected; and on 23 June, moving the first reading of the Amending Bill, Crewe read out Carson's objections and his replies.

80

15 June 14

. . . Kakoo arrived at lunch time and she & Oc & I golfed at Hunter-combe. We then punted over to Norah Lindsay's[1] and saw a lot of diving &

swimming by Diana Manners & Angie[2] & other more or less expert perfor-
mers. I thought their bathing costumes both seemly & becoming – which is
not always the case! After dinner we all went out – except the Ambassador
who had providentially caught a slight chill – in two boats on the river in the
dark. The Princess lay prone and silent on the floor of the punt. It was very
placid and deliciously warm, with a suggestion of moon & not too many
stars. I wished you were there. I motored up alone this morning, the others
having left at cockcrow, and during my solitary journey thought of many
things and one person.

When I had settled my questions I went to Eccleston Square[3] to Edward
Grey's to luncheon to meet Roosevelt. The other guests were Ll. George,
Harcourt, Bryce & Spring-Rice, his successor at Washington. Roosevelt
held the floor practically the whole time, and talked to & at us as tho' we had
been a public meeting or (occasionally) a Sunday school. What is it that
makes all Americans so intolerably long-winded, & so prone to platitude?
He is a second-rate man with overflowing vitality, and now & then quite a
passable sense of humour – full of egotism, but *au fond* (I should think) a
good fellow.[4] After questions, I had to battle with a deputation of Liberal
malcontent MP's over L.G.'s Budget – the Impeccable, the Infant Samuel, &
the Assyrian being in grim & silent attendance.[5] I am going to have a talk
·here in the morning over the Amending Bill with Simon & Crewe & 1 or 2
others. I dine at Grillions to-night – but I am always thinking my darling of
you. *All* love

[1] Her husband was uncle to Lady Diana Manners and owner of the Manor House, Sutton
Courtney.
[2] Angela, daughter of Lord Manners and a distant connection of Lady Diana's. For the
latter's aquatic feats see her account in *The Rainbow Comes and Goes* (1958), pp. 86–7.
[3] No. 33: Churchill's house, rented by Grey, the Churchills being in Admiralty House.
[4] At this meeting (not his first with Theodore Roosevelt) Asquith's intellectual fastidious-
ness seems to have become a little too noticeable. 'When R. declaimed trite statements,' Lloyd
George told Riddell, 'such as "I believe in liberty but liberty with order", the P.M. glowered at
him with a look of curiosity. I think Roosevelt saw it' (*More Pages From My Diary*, p. 217).
In *War Memoirs*, ch. 9, Lloyd George gives a more highly coloured version. Roosevelt later
told a critical Conservative that Asquith was '"able" only in the sense that Wilson and Taft are
able. . . . I felt that . . . [his] real concern . . . [lay] in the ordinary party success achieved in
the ordinary political way' (to A. H. Lee, 17 June 1915). For Asquith on American statesmen
see also Letter 97, text and n. 2.
[5] According to *The Times* (16 June, 8d) it included 30 to 40 Liberal M.P.s.

81

17 June 14 [i]

I am sending with this *Shallow Soil* wh. I finished last night. It is a
disagreeable book but worth your reading – for, if the thing *had* to be done,

it is well done. Why these sort of writers shd. be called Realists passes my comprehension: there is much more 'realism' in Shakespeare or even in Dickens than in these more or less morbid studies of Scandinavian & Russian putrescence. However I shall be interested to know what you think.[1]

I have made a discovery this morning wh. may amuse you about our evanescent friend V—s. He turns out to be a baronet! created such by me! (unwittingly I need not say). I find also that he is of mature years and cannot look for a long span of enjoyment either in the Cloisters, or in his White Cottage (with which you were no doubt once familiar) in the County of Sussex. He is gradually being stripped of his cloak of mystery.[2]

I got no dinner last night till after 10 when Bongie & I had a scratch meal in my room. I sat through the speeches till then (except Amery's – at whom I draw the line)[3]. . . .

. . . Yesterday was a particularly dreary day – except for our divine time together, for wh. I bless you. I shall see you to-night?   All love.

[1] *Ny Jord* (*Shallow Soil*) by Knut Hamsun (1859–1952), the Norwegian novelist, first published in Copenhagen, 1893. The English translation by C. C. Hyllested appeared in 1914. The novel contrasts the rottenness of the artistic set in Oslo with the sterling merit of the business community.

[2] Asquith had given the nickname 'Venetius' to Sir Boverton Redwood, then aged 68, a distinguished petrochemical engineer who had received a baronetcy in 1911. Venetia had presumably met him some years earlier; but the origin of the nickname and of the joke which it enshrined is not clear. The Cloisters was in Avenue Road, Regent's Park; the White Cottage at Cooden Down, near Bexhill, Sussex.

[3] Lord Robert Cecil moved the adjournment to call attention to the growth of private armies in Ireland. The Government, Bonar Law said, knew that 'the people . . . were not behind them': hence their inability to put down the two sets of Volunteers. Amery had been rebuked by the Speaker on 22 Apr. 1914 for accusing Asquith of telling lies.

82

17 June 14 [ii]

. . . I am beginning to receive letters of thanks from the recipients of honours.

Henschel is strongly backed by Charles Stuart Wortley who knows a good deal about music.[1] I am sorry about Parky.[2] We are going to make Beauchamp a KG: he has done pretty well out of changing his party. . . .

[1] George Henschel – singer, conductor, and composer – was knighted. Stuart-Wortley, who had been a Conservative M.P. since 1880, was an accomplished amateur musician.

[2] 'I shall try', Asquith wrote to Margot on 4 June, 'to smuggle in Parky among the knights.' It is not clear why this attempt was abandoned. Both Balfour and Campbell-Bannerman had obtained knighthoods for their family doctors. Parkinson was knighted in 1916.

83

I have not heard how you fared at the House last night or what you are doing to-day. I did not go back, as there was no real fight over the Oil business.[1] Winston & Clemmie dined with us: also the Derenburgs, & Drummond & E. Blackwell. We played a little bridge. Illingworth arrived after the House rose in a state of some perturbation over the manifesto of the Anti-Budget mutineers which appears in this morning's papers. It is (I think) a very able document, and to most of its arguments there is no real answer. If we could put off the last stage of the Finance Bill (as we thought we could) till Sept, we shd. have time to do something; but as it has to be passed by Aug 5th it is quite impossible to get both it & the Revenue Bill[2] by that date, and we should be in the absurd position of having imposed a lot of unnecessary taxes, with the chance (if there is an election & it goes wrong) of the Tories coming in & spending the money. (Is this clear, I wonder?)

The rational course is to drop the whole thing – except so much as is necessary to pay for the Navy &c this year. Simon & McKenna both agree about this, but of course it would be very nauseous & even humiliating to Ll. G, who attributes all the trouble to the 'Radical millionaires' i.e. Mond, Molteno, de Forest & Co.[3] He will probably threaten to resign, tho' your friend at the Home Office[4] – with whom I had a talk this morning – thinks (as he says) that he (Ll. G) will not 'adhere' to it. We are going to have a Cabinet on Monday after the 'Trooping' to deal with the situation, which is quite as embrangled as in the early days of the year, when the Beagles were in full cry.

Another small complication is that Sylvia Pankhurst, whom M^cK is letting to-day out of prison – she has been *8* days without food or drink – proposes to continue her 'strike' to the point of suicide, either at her own home or perhaps on a stretcher in Downing St, until I receive a deputation of East End suffragists! I don't want, if I can help, to secure her the martyr's crown, but *que faire*?[5]

I suppose you are playing tennis placidly all the time.

We have had, after all, to give up Dunn for this honours list. Bongie went to see Sir F. Schuster about it, and his report – tho' not adverse to Dunn personally – was very unfavourable to his being singled out at the moment, when all his adventures are in rather stormy water, and the whole of the City would say that he was being rewarded for a huge donation to our party fund – to which, so far as I know, he has not given or promised ½d. So he has had to be postponed. The poor Barkers are in despair.[6] Edgar Vincent's case is I think all right.

We are going to dine with the Islingtons at Putney. Where do you lunch to-morrow? I will come for you after lunch; there are lots of things to say.

You will wonder when I am going to bring this to an end! Does it bore you my darling? You know how I love sharing things with you.

All love.

Write

¹ The Government planned to acquire shares in the Anglo-Persian Oil Company to safeguard naval fuel supplies. The Commons resolution authorizing this was accepted by 254 votes to 18. The company's title was changed to Anglo-Iranian in 1935 and to British Petroleum in 1954.

² The Government was pledged not to pay any grants to local authorities until the Revenue Bill to alter the valuation system had become law.

³ Sir Alfred Mond had succeeded his father as the chief figure in Brunner, Mond, the great chemical firm which was later (1926) the main component in Imperial Chemical Industries Ltd.; cr. Lord Melchett, 1928. Percy Molteno was a barrister and shipowner; Maurice de Forest (later Count de Bendern) the natural son, and heir, of the financier Baron Hirsch. The 'mutineers' were led by R. D. Holt (1868–1941), the Liverpool shipowner. They agreed in their manifesto that 'the heaviest burdens should be laid on the broadest backs'.

⁴ McKenna.

⁵ She returned home when Asquith agreed, through the intervention of George Lansbury, to receive the deputation.

⁶ Sir Felix Schuster was a well-known Liberal banker. Lord Beaverbrook recorded the ups and downs of James Dunn's career in a biographical study, *Courage* (1962). Dunn and Louis Fischer had founded a merchant bank in 1907. When the latter defaulted and fled the country in 1913 Dunn became liable for debts to an unknown amount. He survived these troubles, became a baronet in 1921, and was worth $65m. when he died in 1956. Granville-Barker was much involved in the plans to build a national theatre in time for the tercentenary of Shakespeare's death in 1916. If honoured, Dunn would presumably have become the benefactor for this 'repertory theatre business', as Asquith called it. The Liberals' needs both for peers and for money were notorious. In the aftermath of the Marconi scandal a Liberal premier was wise to tread carefully.

84

Wed 24 June 14

I began the day yesterday in a good deal of depression – for various reasons. But between 6 & 7 every cloud was lifted (you were never more dear) and later on at the Opera, amid all the indecency and glare & noise of Strauss's worst moments, I felt more than happy. This time at any rate I loved your dress, and even my most critical scrutiny (in other respects) was more than satisfied. I wish I were going to be with you again this evening; I am sure I should like the *Coq* more than *Joseph*,¹ – especially as I fear very much I shall not get to the Speyers, where (after all) what should I see of you?

I never talked to you yesterday (nor you to me) of political things: I wanted to show you a letter of the Speaker's to whom I have suggested an attempt to bring C & R into the same room. I am going to speak to him about it now. The performance in the H. of Lords yesterday leaves things much as they were. I am beginning to form ideas – nebulous but growing crystallised – about the future, which I must share with you. Talking with no one else does me so much good. But when?

We had a Cabinet this morning – mainly about the new Education Bill. Incidentally we agreed that the Liberal Peers on the Committee for antiquarian research with wh. the Lords are going to delay the Welsh Ch. Bill, should be Lords Bryce & Sheffield. Don't you think that is a good choice?[2]. . . .

[1] *Le Coq d'Or* by Rimsky-Korsakov, with choreography by Fokine for Diaghilev, and *La Légende de Joseph*, Richard Strauss's ballet, were first performed in Diaghilev's productions at the Paris Opéra in May 1914. At Drury Lane *Joseph*, which had opened the previous evening, was performed on 23 June, *Coq d'Or* on 24 June. Massine made his London début in *Joseph*; the costumes were by Léon Bakst, the scenery by the Spanish artist J. M. Sert.

[2] On 25 June the Lords established a Select Committee to report 'whether the constitution of the Convocations of the Church of England has ever been altered by Act of Parliament . . . against the protest of Convocation'. Asquith thought that the cabinet 'ought not to ignore their [the Conservative peers'] committee but should put Lord Bryce and Sheffield on it, for no one on their side could know so much or talk so long as both of them and so they might confuse the others' (Hobhouse *Diaries*, p. 173). The committee, which was chaired by Lord St Aldwyn, had not reported by the outbreak of war.

85

25 June 1914

I am just off to the House to make what I can of my dull speech.[1] I confess it was rather a blow (what you said) – not God knows from vanity, but from what I thought you cared about things & their values. Don't think I am vexed: it is silly to mind, and I dare say, if any proper calculus were applied, you measured rightly –   All love.[2]

[1] On the second reading of the Finance Bill.
[2] Presumably Venetia had preferred another engagement to listening to the speech from the gallery.

Sarajevo: 'An "obituary" on the Austrian royalties' (Letter 86)

THE Archduke Franz Ferdinand and his wife were shot and killed in Sarajevo by a Bosnian student on 28 June. Asquith mentioned this two days later in Letter 86 to Venetia without expressing fears about the international complications which might follow. There is no further reference to the assassination in the Letters until 24 July (Letter 103), by which date, with the delivery of the Austrian ultimatum to Serbia, the affair had moved into a more serious phase. The Letters might thus seem to support the views of Colonel House, President Wilson's special envoy, who arrived in England on 9 June from Germany and stayed until 21 July. He brought a horrific account of war fever in Berlin, and was dismayed to find the British Prime Minister apparently unworried by the state of the European powder barrel.[1]

On the other hand, Asquith himself, writing after the war, suggested that the danger to peace early in July increased his anxiety to settle the Ulster question and so 'reconcile our domestic dissensions'. Even now it is not easy to say what attention he gave before 24 July to the incipient European crisis.

On 6 July the *Morning Post* warned that Austrian reactions to the assassination might lead to a 'European war'; but no general alarm was felt in Britain at this stage. On the same day Sir Arthur Nicolson gave a Foreign Office view to an ambassador, when he expressed the hope that Sarajevo 'would have no serious political consequences at any rate outside of Austria-Hungary'. Grey knew by then, however, that the crisis could be serious. Lichnowsky, the German Ambassador, had returned from Berlin with the warning that the Germans could not always be restraining their Austrian ally. He saw Haldane on 4 July and Grey two days later. 'There was some feeling in Germany', Lichnowsky said, 'that trouble was bound to come and . . . better . . . now rather than later.' Grey concluded that Germany might well 'bring on a conflict with Russia . . . before the increases in the Russian army have their full effect and before the completion of the Russian strategic railways'. He had his dispatch recording this view, and all the principal dispatches on the crisis which he issued thereafter, circulated to the King and the cabinet;[2] and Beauchamp told Lichnowsky that Grey had spoken to the cabinet on the matter. There was no mention of it yet in Asquith's cabinet letters to the King; but George V made 'a very blood-curdling reference to foreign affairs' when opening the Buckingham Palace Conference on the Ulster problem (21 July), this being omitted from the official report.[3]

Some members of the cabinet probably paid no great attention to Grey's warnings. They may have taken Lichnowsky's remarks to be just an attempt to persuade Grey into restraining St Petersburg, and so helping the Austrians to deal with Serbia. They shared in the optimism about international affairs which was described earlier (p. 36). They may well have held the view expressed by *The Times* leader-writer on 16 July. An Austrian attempt to bully the Serbs, *The Times* pronounced, 'would constitute a fresh peril to European peace, and that, we are confident, the [Austrian] Emperor and his most sagacious advisers very clearly perceive'. Lloyd George said at the Mansion House on 17 July that, while there was never 'a perfectly blue sky in foreign affairs', he remained confident, despite the clouds, of overcoming the current difficulties. On the day of the Austrian ultimatum to Serbia (23 July) he told the Commons that relations with Germany were 'very much better' than they had been 'a few years ago'.

Asquith was almost certainly better informed than his Chancellor of the Exchequer. Despite his all-absorbing Irish preoccupations he could well have discussed the European crisis with Grey before 24 July. Constantine Benckendorff, the Russian Ambassador's son, described a conversation at The Wharf early in July. According to his memoirs he contended that an Austro-Serb quarrel would find 'Russia not only united but entirely intractable'. Asquith 'kept his counsel' at these remarks, while the rest of the company jumped down Constantine's throat.[4] None the less the Austrian ultimatum and all that followed from it were an enormous shock to Asquith. It took more than Grey's warnings to shake his assumption that the statesmen of Berlin and Vienna were as pacific, and as fully in control of their countries' armed forces, as he was himself.

[1] House's account necessarily reflects the nature of his mission. Asquith and Grey were bound to be reserved about American suggestions for a *rapprochement* with Germany in view of the nervousness of Britain's Triple Entente partners.

[2] See *Brit. Docs. War*, xi. 24–5 (No. 32), Grey to Rumbold, 6 July. In vol. xi there are no indications about the circulation of the dispatches. For Grey's instruction on circulation see FO 371/1899, file 30742. This document is filed misleadingly under Austria-Hungary.

[3] G. H. Mair to C. P. Scott, 23 July: Add. MSS 50908, f. 22.

[4] C. Benckendorff, *Half a Life* (1954), p. 94.

86

30 June 14

. . . I have had myself rather a busy day – at the War Office, Army Council &c all morning, then to lunch at the Mansion House with the Elder Brethren – rather a dreary function:[1] thence here for an 'obituary' on the Austrian royalties;[2] and after a ridiculous debate, nominally on my salary, but in reality an attempt to rake up the ashes of Marconi,[3] I shall dine at home with the family, and then perhaps go on with them for a short time to Fanny Mounsey's dance in Melbury Road. She has a good sized garden & it may be cool.

To-morrow we have a Cabinet & I lunch with E. Grey & Kitchener.[4] I will tell you of the queer things that are going on about Ulster &c. I wonder if you have thought out any of the problems we discussed on Saturday? I wonder also if you want to talk to me as much as I want to talk to you? Bless you my darling – think of me & write.

[1] The Elder Brethren of Trinity House were (and are) the lighthouse and pilotage authority for England and Wales.

[2] 'Royalties' is here used loosely. As the Archduke had married morganatically, his wife, the Duchess of Hohenberg, was not royal.
[3] The Prime Minister refused to issue a Treasury minute forbidding civil servants from speculating. The motion to reduce his salary by £1,000 was defeated by 274 to 122.
[4] Kitchener had been British Agent and Consul-General in Egypt since Sept. 1911 and had recently been made an earl. He was home on leave.

87

2 July 14 [i]

I am in rather better spirits this morning – thanks mainly to you. I hope I did not depress you unduly yesterday. You were very dear and sympathetic, and helped me as you always do. I am truly grateful in my heart of hearts.

I suppose at this moment you are plunging in the water somewhere in the company of Lady Scott. I have rather a drab day before me, including an interview with the King at 4.30. I hope before then to have a further report from the 'negotiators'.[1] Lansdowne's speech last night gives one the impression that he is in an expectant attitude. At any rate there was nothing truculent in it.

Ottoline asked me to dine there to-night: so it is possible I may have a glimpse of you. I gather from what you said yesterday that you will be away in the North all the end of next week: so to-morrow is positively our last Friday, or at best last but one, this year![2] It is not merely my 'affection' that makes me look back upon them, and treasure their memory as I do.

Bless you darling.

[1] Asquith told the King that Tyrone was 'the crux' of the negotiation conducted by Lord Murray of Elibank and Lord Rothermere; the time-limit would 'present no difficulty'. 'The P.M. hopes', Stamfordham recorded, 'that an agreement may be reached before the Amending Bill leaves the . . . Lords': R A GV K 2553 (5) 76.
[2] Venetia was to sail shortly for India and Australia: see Letter 93 and n. 4.

88

4.15 p.m. 2 July 1914 [ii]

Don't if you can avoid it beloved go on this infernal river trip, but *do* come to Ottoline's. Couldn't you even manage dinner there? it would be so nice. But if that is impossible I look forward to seeing you there later on. *Do try.*

Your own.

89

5.30 3 July 14

I hear the Islington ball is put off on account of the river tragedy. I forgot to tell you that when I wrote to you asking you not to go & to come to O's instead, I had a kind of uneasy presentiment, and that after I got to bed I dreamt that Edward's launch was wrecked. Isn't that rather strange.[1]

As all the family here are dining in bed, I am going to join Bongie's party at Queen Anne's Gate.

We had a most heavenly talk, and there can never any more be any misunderstanding between us, my darling.

Dearest love.

[1] Constantine Benckendorff, son of the Russian Ambassador, and Edward Horner entertained their friends of the Coterie (p. 117) to a Thames cruise on the evening of 2 July. Raymond and Katharine Asquith were among the guests, as was Sir Denis Anson, who had succeeded to his uncle's baronetcy a few weeks earlier (Letter 77). Venetia was invited, and came to Westminster Bridge steps, but did not embark. Late in the evening swimming was suggested. Not knowing the force of the tide Anson dived in. When the alarm was given, one of the musicians, and then Constantine Benckendorff, dived in as rescuers. Anson and the musician were drowned. Benckendorff was rescued, utterly exhausted. In *The Rainbow Comes and Goes* (1958), pp. 109–12, Lady Diana Cooper gave the account of an eyewitness and further details have been provided in P. Ziegler, *Diana Cooper* (1981). pp. 43–5. Anson had been well known among his friends for feats of daring. See O. Sitwell, *Great Morning* (1948), p. 258.

90

Sat 4 July 14

I just caught a glimpse of you as we were leaving the Silken Tent last night for a rather garish affair in the way of a supper party. I have never experienced such a glare of lights as when we were all 'cinema'd' (if that is the right word) for Barrie's play. I sat between or among Lillah, Miss Gladys Cooper, & Lady Howard de Walden. I did not find the company very amusing, nor the little plays that followed,[1] but that did not matter as I had lots to think about, and my thoughts for once were almost wholly pleasant. Perhaps you can guess the principal reason.

This morning we have been at St Margaret's at the funeral service for Ld Wemyss. There is another at the same place on Monday for poor Chamberlain.[2] I sat next old Benck who told me Constantine was none the worse, but has had to postpone his return to Russia[3]. . . .

[1] A supper during which the guests were filmed was followed by six of J. M. Barrie's sketches played by stars of the London theatre. Shots from the 'cinema supper' were to be used to introduce a scene in Barrie's forthcoming revue. The guests seem scarcely to have realized

how extensive the film was and how it was to be used. 'Some', G. K. Chesterton wrote, 'were throwing bread about and showing marked relaxation from the cares of state.' Asquith is said to have written to Barrie afterwards protesting at the use proposed. It was announced in Sept. 1914 that the revue had been abandoned; but the film was shown privately in 1916:Cynthia Asquith, *Diaries, 1915–18* (1968), pp. 153–4.
    [2] Memorial services in both cases. The funeral of the first named was in Aberlady, East Lothian, and of the second, Joseph Chamberlain, in Birmingham.
    [3] Constantine Benckendorff gave evidence at the Anson inquest on 8 July. Count Benckendorff was three years older than Asquith.

91

War Office,
Whitehall,
S.W.

6 July 14

    . . . We too had a very wet Sunday & it was not very amusing: tho' Viola who was there with her husband is always nice. It was impossible either to golf or to go on the river. I began another Dickens – this time *Our Mutual Friend*. It was quite pleasant driving up this morning, but I have been assailed since I arrived by a succession of small & middle-sized worries. Edward Grey's eyes are not satisfactory, and he thinks of returning to the country with perhaps a fortnightly visit to London.[1] Then poor Mrs Birrell has had some fresh sort of attack which makes him anxious, and he would like to resign his office! – at this moment of all others. Finally we have a very serious strike going on at Woolwich which threatens to spread, and after the best part of 2 hours of confabulating with Bluey & the soldiers, I don't see my way for the moment out of the mess.[2] On reflection I thought it better (why didn't you give your opinion?) not to open out to-day to B. Law on Ireland. I feel that we might both have been tempted to say things which we should afterwards wish unsaid.[3] But I may very likely have a secret talk with Carson to-morrow or Wed. I believe we are dining with R & Kath. I wonder what you are doing to-night? & to-morrow? let me know. Winston is better & says he starts Wed: so I fear you will go then too.[4] My darling you don't know how I miss you.   All my love.

    [1] Grey had grown anxious about his sight some months earlier. He was finding it difficult to follow the ball when playing squash and he could no longer pick out his favourite star. He gave up smoking on his oculist's advice, but without effect on his eyes. On 26 May two consultants examined him and found a serious infection. 'The sight of both eyes is affected,' he reported to Glenconner; 'they think its progress will be slow and that the worst that could happen in the long run would be not blindness but loss of ability to read. They would like me to stop work and go away for six months; but they dont think that necessary yet.'
    [2] A workman at the Arsenal had been dismissed for refusing to erect a machine on foundations laid by non-union labour. Work was resumed on 9 July after the Government had promised an immediate court of inquiry, the reinstatement of the man concerned pending its findings, and no victimization of the strikers.

³ Asquith's conversation with Bonar Law on 6 Nov. 1913 had led to a serious misunder-standing. Asquith undertook to report the Conservatives' exclusion scheme to the cabinet. He did not press it on the cabinet, or on the Irish Nationalists, as Bonar Law thought him pledged to do.
⁴ To Scotland in the *Enchantress*.

92

8 July 14

It was a rare piece of luck to see you last night, even tho' the conditions were not all that one might have desired. But it is always a joy (I won't say to repaint) but to revive and keep alive a much loved picture. And I hope you won't forget what I said about your letters. The one I got this morning was in every way delightful, and a pretty complete refutation of what you allege as to your 'inadequate' powers of expression. But I *do* miss what (until quite lately) you always gave me, & that is the message at the end. . . .

I had rather an interesting talk yesterday with Carson at No 24.¹ It showed me how much the Master & Rothermere had taken for granted & how little real progress they had made.² The most striking thing was that as between the exclusion of the 6 counties only & of the whole of Ulster he evidently thought that his more extreme followers would prefer the former. They are apparently afraid that a big entire Ulster would gravitate towards a United Ireland.³ C is quite anxious to settle but makes much (I dare say honestly) of his difficulties with his own friends.

We had a long & rather dreary Cabinet this morning, trying to solve the old problem of how to get a quart into a pint pot; I am writing from the House where we are still debating this tiresome guillotine.⁴ Later on I have to take the chair at a dinner at the Reform Club to old Bryce: not a very lively prospect, is it? I shall dine with the Burnses on Friday & go to the Wharf for Sunday. When you get this you will be in sight of the coast of Fife. My darling – you are dearer to me than I can tell you.

Write – all love.

¹ Montagu's house in Queen Anne's Gate.
² On 2 July Bonar Law and Carson told Lord Murray that if an area which included four complete Ulster counties, and parts of two more, were excluded without time-limit they would support Home Rule for the rest of Ireland and would not repeal it should the Conservatives gain power. Redmond refused 'even [to] discuss . . . the time limit, unless the plebiscite by counties were accepted'. Carson's speech at Herne Hill on 4 July included an uncompromising statement of the Conservative demands (see pp. 83–4). Lord Murray seems to have been over-impressed by the apparent willingness of the Conservative leaders to abandon their followers in southern Ireland.
³ Carson was to reiterate this preference on 21 July at the Buckingham Palace Conference.
⁴ For the Finance Bill. Government business in the Commons was greatly in arrears.

93

Th. 9 July 14

I wrote yesterday (Wed.) to you as at Dundee: I hope you have got it. It was a real delight to get your little letter written on the eve of your journey, but it is sad to think how long it will be before I see you again. I am pleased that you liked my speech on J. C.: as you know, no praise is so sweet to me.[1] Why didn't you come? . . . I should have been still more interested if you had sent me a few specimens of your 'meagre & reluctant' adjectives – most beloved (& feared) of critics! We got through our 'guillotine' yesterday by ¼ past 8 & I went on to the Reform Club to preside over a dinner to Ld. Bryce. . . .

The inquest on poor Denis Anson went off very well, and Iris Tree who volunteered to step into the breach, distinguished herself (they say) both by the matter & the manner of her evidence. . . . Anyhow they are all now in a pretty sober mood, & Edward Horner & Constantine Benck. are coming to us at the Wharf for Sunday. Violet reports an amusing interview she had with the Assyrian last night: full of *schadenfreude* at our majority being reduced to 23 &c &c.[2]

It is a lovely afternoon, and I wish more than I can tell you that I was on board the *Enchantress*, tho' I don't envy you to-morrow's functions. I had a long call from Stamfordham this morning, who wanted to report to the King about Ulster prospects &c. He is, of course, very one-sided, and I had to point out to him that the Lords by omitting plebiscite &c, and cutting up Ireland as if it were a butcher's joint to suit their own palate, were not helping towards peace.[3] It is as dull as can be here (at the House) to-day – John Burns's salary in Supply: and if only you were in London I would come and take you for a drive into space. Alas! Your Mother told me gleefully at the Americans' the other night how she had secured passages in a P & O boat.[4] I felt as if a knife was going straight into my heart. Another symptom of 'folly'? Now I must go to the War Office, with the prospect of dinner at Jack Tennant's to meet the S. Buxtons! I will write to-morrow (Fr) to S. Queensferry, & Saturday to Overstrand. To-morrow will be a wasted Friday. . . .

---

[1] On 6 July Asquith had moved the adjournment of the House in tribute to Joseph Chamberlain. His obituary speeches in the Commons were much admired. He was apt to compose one for any colleague who bored or annoyed him. 'It is highly uncomfortable', Birrell remarked, 'when, after circling round the table, the Prime Minister's *obituary eye* rests meditatively upon oneself.' Some obituaries were thus made virtually without special preparation. The one for Kitchener in 1916 was said to have been in this category.

[2] In the first division on the Finance Bill guillotine.

[3] Asquith appeared 'placid and contented' to Stamfordham. He struck Bryce at this time as 'very sanguine', and the Archbishop of Canterbury as 'pulseless', according to Stamfordham's report to the King: R A GV K2553 (5) 111. No doubt he was concerned to keep up a confident front; but the evidence suggests that he did not become really alarmed about Ulster until he had seen Northcliffe, and Redmond and Dillon, on 13 July (Letter 95).

[4] Lady Sheffield planned that she and Venetia should travel to India and then visit the Arthur Stanleys in Australia (p. 119 and Letter 25, n. 5).

94

10 July 14

. . . Did you see Sir H. Tree's speech about poor Anson & the Heavenly Schoolmaster – at some prize giving yesterday? Some of the evening papers had for placards 'Diana's Love' – I suppose in allusion to her wreath at the funeral. Nothing can exceed the blackguardism of the press, but by misfortune or design some people are always in the limelight. I am thankful that you are not one of them. . . .

. . . Jack Tennant's dinner last night was a farewell to the S. Buxtons: it was not a lively affair & was followed by a rather draggling & protracted 'drum'[1] which involved my standing at the top of the stairs & shaking occasional hands for the best part of 2 hours. The company was mostly politicians & such, and I was glad when the 'clock struck the hour for retiring'. Before going to bed I started on the first vol. of Chamberlain's (the German) *Kant* translated by old Redesdale who gave it to me the other day.[2] It is quite well written.

This morning besides my usual visits from Illingworth & Ll. George & the Assyrian, I had one from Gen[l] Paget. He has had a row with the Court & tendered his resignation. It all arose out of the old incident at the Curragh where the King has been led to believe that he made an improper use of his name. Paget denies this & is backed up by his Generals. I refused of course to allow him to resign & shall try to get Stamfordham to write him some adequate *amende*. The last thing one wants is to have that wretched business dug up again from its grave. (I wonder if it alarms you to see that I have started on another sheet?)

The Assyrian reports that Northcliffe, who has been spending a week in Ulster, and has been well fed up by the Orangemen with every species of lurid lie, has come back in a state of panic. The Master who is again taking a hand is anxious that I should see him (N). I hate & distrust the fellow & all his works,[3] and will never make any overture to him: so I said merely that if he chose to ask me directly to see him, & had anything really new to communicate, I would not refuse. I know of few men in this world who are

responsible for more mischief, and deserve a longer punishment in the next:
but it doesn't do to say this to Winston.[4]. . .

I go to the Wharf to-morrow, after whiling away an hour over the Budget
with Simon & Montagu. Margot goes to-day, as the Burnses cannot thro'
illness give their dinner. I am bidden to dine at 18 Mansfield St, which is
very nice, but without you will seem more than strange. Have I worn out
your patience beloved? You told me to tell you everything: there is one
thing I can never tell you, but you know it.

[1] A 'drum' occurred when a dinner party were joined after the end of the meal by a larger
number of guests.
[2] Houston Stewart Chamberlain had spent most of his life in Germany and Austria. He was
not, however, naturalized as a German until Aug. 1916. He had married Wagner's daughter,
Eva, as his second wife, in 1908. His *Kant* appeared in German in 1905. Redesdale's
translation was published in 1914.
[3] The Master of Elibank, lately Asquith's Chief Whip, had been created Lord Murray of
Elibank in 1912. He knew Northcliffe's brother Rothermere well. Asquith's distrust of
Northcliffe was shared at this time with many Liberals, who held as an article of faith that
Northcliffe fomented war scares, and the armed resistance of Ulster, in order to increase the
circulation of his papers.
[4] Northcliffe liked Churchill's strong navy policy. Early in 1913 Churchill had persuaded
him not to persecute 'the Marconi ministers' (Letter 7).

95

13 July 1914

I am extremely glad that I didn't know beforehand that you were going to
take to yourself wings & fly: even Winston was shamefaced & apologetic
when he mentioned your exploit to me on the bench. Thank God you are
safely down again, and I earnestly hope you won't be in a hurry to repeat the
experiment.

It was a delight to get your letter from Overstrand this morning: on the
whole the cruise must have been a pleasant & placid interlude. If only I
could have shared it!

We had a very uneventful Sunday, but for a freak of the Bud's, who got
out of the side of the boat in her hat & full clothing & began to swim.
Happily there were lots of swimmers & punts around & about, and with the
aid of the champion rescuer Constantine Benckendorff[1] she was hauled out
dripping & draggled on the river bank. I thought her nice & far from bad
company, but she doesn't carry one far. Edward Horner is still in rather a
low key . . .

I have had two interesting if not very enlivening interviews. The first
(which is most secret) was with Lord Northcliffe – of all people – at the

Master's flat in Ennismore Gardens. He has been 'doing' Ulster, & is much struck with the Covenanters, whom he regards (what with fanaticism & whisky) as a very formidable tho' most unattractive crew.[2] I talked over the question of areas &c with him, & tried to impress upon him the importance of making *The Times* a responsible newspaper.[3] After I got back to the House I had half an hour with Redmond & Dillon – also mainly about areas. I found them in a decidedly impracticable mood,[4] and I foresee great difficulties in the coming week wh. will practically decide whether we can come to an agreement. I long to talk over this & other things with my most darling counsellor. The choice is I think between to-morrow (Tues) & Wed. (when there is a singing party at our house in the afternoon). Which wd. suit you best? We might take from 5 oclock to 10 minutes to 7. Please let me know as soon as you can. I dine at Grillions. Write to me beloved. I love you.

[1] For Constantine Benckendorff's visit see p. 93.

[2] Northcliffe was making elaborate preparations to cover 'the war' in Ulster (Norman Angell, *After All* (1951), p. 179). He had been born near Dublin. Until this conversation virtually all Asquith's information about the Ulster Volunteers had come from committed Liberals and Irish Nationalists, or from professional soldiers – that is, from people with an inclination to play down the capabilities of the Volunteers. Carson and his friends had signed the Ulster Covenant on 28 Sept. 1912. It was eventually signed by more than 470,000 Ulster people.

[3] Northcliffe had gained control of *The Times* in Mar. 1908 and had reduced its price to 1d. in Mar. 1914.

[4] They reminded Asquith that, even if agreement could be reached on the areas to be excluded, the time-limit difficulty would remain. See, however, Letter 96a, n. 4.

96

14 July 14 10.30 p.m.

As I want you to keep au courant with what is going on step by step in these anxious days, I send you the enclosed. The important one is Spender's letter, which is the result of what I said to him at lunch to-day. You needn't return it, but don't destroy it lest I shld. want it hereafter.

We had a heavenly drive, and you were never more wonderful. Do keep close to me beloved in this most critical time of my life.[1] I know you will not fail. *Write.* – dearest love.

96a

45 Sloane Street,
S.W.
                                        July 14, 1914 [enclosure (i)]

My dear Prime Minister,

I saw Dillon this afternoon & we talked very freely about the whole situation. There are undoubtedly some injured feelings. He said that the Irish party had been opposed to any concessions being made before the final stage, that they had reluctantly consented to the offer of Mar. 9, but in doing so had made it clear that this was utmost they could do; that they were now asked to make further large concessions without any certainty that it would settle the question & with high probability that it would be the beginning of further demands; that the yielding of Tyrone would be their destruction in Ireland & the handing over of Nationalism to the physical force party[2] etc. etc. all arguments with which you are familiar. There was also a suspicion that the question might be settled behind their backs by some deal between the Government & the Opposition.

I answered that this suspicion was groundless, that your whole effort was to carry Liberals & Irish together to a settlement, that if you had had dealings with the other side it was simply because you know the Irish view, but had necessarily to discover the view of the other side before you could have anything to put before them. Without at all professing to speak for you, I said that you would not have approached them, unless you had the best reason for thinking that you could get a settlement on the terms proposed, but that in any case all the suggested concessions would be conditional on a settlement being reached, & would fall to the ground if it were not reached.

I think the first most important thing is to convince them that a settlement can be reached on the lines suggested. At present they are very sceptical & think that Carson is setting a trap.

I cannot report that I made much impression so far, but I seemed to make rather more impression in another line which was wholly on my own responsibility.

I asked D. to consider what would happen if the Amending Bill broke down. He said full steam ahead. 'Put the Home Rule Bill on the statute book & nothing will happen'. I asked did he think it quite easy in the supposed circumstances to get the H.R. Bill on the Statute Book, and briefly sketched two possible alternatives: 1) that the King would say that he couldn't sign the H.R. bill alone & drive us to an election – rather difficult in the circumstances – which, even if won, might require the H.R. question to be begun again *de novo*, 2) more probable, that the Royal assent would be got on the condition that a dissolution followed immediately, or that the situation in Ulster would require such a dissolution. I asked him to consider these possibilities, or rather the extreme probability that everything would make shipwreck on one or other of these rocks, if Irish & Liberals were supposed by the public to have been unreasonable, & I appealed to him to weigh them against the advantages of an agreed settlement safe against tory reaction.

Much of this seemed really to be new to him[3] & I think it made some impression.

I said further that though Irish opinion was naturally all important to them, *you* had necessarily to consider British opinion as well, & that it would be impossible to convince the British public that either of us had acted sanely or reasonably in making Tyrone paramount, when offered peace & an agreed settlement for the rest of Ireland.

The Irish seem really very ignorant of British politics & I think it might do good, if you could enlarge a little on the British aspect of the case.

It struck me in talking how much sentiment counts. D. said that the language used in the House of Lords about the need of a United Ireland had reconciled them to the loss of the time limit.[4] He admitted that many things which now looked impossible would become possible, if Carson & Redmond could get on to really generous terms. From this point of view the 'last card' did not seem unpromising (I said nothing about it).[5]

I am afraid this is a rather rambling letter & you may think it contains a preposterous deal of what *I* said, but I put this in to give you the impression. D. seemed susceptible to an appeal to consider your difficulties.

Yours ever,
J. A. Spender

96b

69 Ennismore Gardens,
S.W.

July 14/14. [enclosure (ii)]

Dear Prime Minister,

Thank you for your letter. I was annoyed with *The Times* this morning and threw Rothermere unto his brother.[6] I enclose his reply.

I hear tonight that Dillon has stated 'outside' that in his opinion there will be a settlement on a six County basis . . .

Yours ever,
Murray of E

96c

Claridge's Hotel,
Brook Street, W.

14 July 1914 [enclosure (iii)]

My dear Alick,

Since our conversation I have seen N and the Editor and strongly pressed our view on them that today's leader was not helpful.[7] They replied that so great were the internal difficulties in regard to Ireland particularly with Robert Cecil that great caution must be exercised not too markedly to alter their attitude.[8] On the whole you and I were not to mind if the paper for tactical reasons pursued its present policy and that we could count on their doing the right thing by the Prime Minister at the proper moment.

I am as you know in constant touch with N on the subject. The Prime Minister made a very profound impression on him personally yesterday.

Always yours faithfully
Rothermere.

[1] This almost certainly referred to the Ulster problem alone. It is improbable that by 14 July Asquith regarded the European situation as especially critical. See pp. 92–3.

[2] Dillon was better informed than Redmond on such semi-secret organizations as the Irish Republic Brotherhood, and Sinn Fein (founded 1905). The Irish Nationalists in the Commons had been weakened by the collapse of the Irish Transport Workers' Union in Jan. 1914 after a long lock-out. As a result of this failure many Dublin workers joined Sinn Fein.

[3] Even Spender could not tell Dillon the truth, namely that if the Liberals wanted a future they could not (in Carson's phrase) 'coerce a people for being loyal'. For the King's intentions over the Royal Assent see Letter 105, n. 2.

[4] Asquith was to tell Bonar Law on 17 July that he was willing to give up the time-limit. On the need for a united Ireland see Curzon, 6 July: *Parl. Deb.* Lords xvi.747.

[5] This refers to migration from (and to) the excluded areas at state expense. Asquith noted against Spender's remark 'i.e. [£]11m'. See Letter 97.

[6] I.e., sent Rothermere to remonstrate with Northcliffe.

[7] The leader ended: 'Mr. Asquith is either at his wits' end or is hoping and waiting for some favourable turn of affairs. He may wait too long.'

[8] Lord Robert Cecil had no time for the Ulster Volunteer Force (see Letter 81, n. 3).

97

15 July 14

I didn't of course expect to get any talk with you this afternoon: it would in any case have been impossible with all those prying Jewesses about. I am afraid it was a stifling and rather boring entertainment.[1]

I had a dull evening, dining at home & then to the House to divide, & afterwards a course of Chamberlain's *Kant*, which is much too diffuse; and then bed with rather broken slumbers.

There has been nothing of interest to-day (for poor Lady Hardinge's memorial service can hardly be so described – nor can a lunch at Edward Grey's with an American Senator Lodge)[2] until I went to the House & had a short talk with B. Law before questions. I pointed out to him that a failure to settle would mean a general election, with a very difficult situation at the end of it, for whoever was victorious: therefore a thing to be avoided on both sides, if any arrangement were possible.[3] He told me that the Master was then in confabulation with Carson, and later on (just when you disappeared) the former arrived with his friend Rothermere, and a large supply of maps. They had had long discussions & arguments with Carson, and in the end I asked them to find out whether C & his friends would *definitely* treat, if I made them an offer to exclude Antrim, Derry, Down (except the Catholic parts of the South) Armagh (except South) North Fermanagh, with the possibility of a split Tyrone: provision to be made on both sides for the migration at State expense of Protestants & Catholics into & out of the excluded area. They have gone to see what his reply is. Of course I said I could not *guarantee* that Redmond wd. assent, but if C. falls in, I shall have to put on the screw to R. I thought you wd. like to know that at once – so I send it you, with all my blessings & love.

[1] Lady Sheffield and Venetia had attended Margot's musical 'at home' at which Steuart Wilson sang.

[2] Grey was far more sensitive than Asquith to American opinion. If any American politician could have been congenial to Asquith it should have been Lodge, who was a lawyer, a scholar and a patrician.

[3] The Conservatives had all along demanded that the Home Rule Bill should be 'referred to the people'; but by mid-July their leader no doubt knew how hard he would find it, if he won at the polls, to govern Ireland on any basis other than Home Rule. The situation had been greatly altered during 1914 by the rise of the National Volunteers: see p. 69. Moreover, some Conservatives did not want to fight an election in which they might be made to look like irresponsible diehards, who preferred relying on a private army to accepting the Parliament Act and the fair terms offered to the Ulster Protestants.

98

17 July 14 midnight

. . . I found the royal person in a tent in the garden and had nearly ½ an hour with him.[1] He was full of interest & excitement about the Conference – and made one really good suggestion – namely that the Speaker should preside.

We arranged that I should write a Memorandum for the King, advising a Conference and that the King should send a cordial reply amounting to an invitation. He was anxious that Arthur Balfour shd. come in, but I objected to this strongly, as A.B. is in this matter a real wrecker.[2] As between Crewe & Ll.G. – the K. was (with me) in favour of the latter.[3]

Subsequent reflection has led me to think that to make the thing really complete we ought to include Ramsay Macdonald (for Labour) & W[m] O'Brien (who holds 9 seats in Ireland).[4]

It was a great satisfaction to me that you were so clear that this is the right course, my darling counsellor: and I will tell you everything as it develops. I probably go with the King about *3.30* Sat. aft. to Portsmouth.[5] Do write to me so that I get it before I leave, & tell me your Godley address. It was heavenly to have 2 hours respite and real companionship with you to-day. May this never fail me! *All my love.*

[1] At an audience on 17 July (not at a State Ball, despite Jenkins, *Asquith*, p. 319).

[2] After the failure of Gladstone's first Home Rule Bill Balfour had proved, during the Chief Secretaryship which established his reputation (1887–91), that Ireland could be governed without home rule. See also Letter 67.

[3] Asquith told Crewe that the Irish were 'very insistent' on Lloyd George as the Government's second man.

[4] These suggestions were not pursued. Eight assembled under the Speaker – Asquith and Lloyd George; Bonar Law and Lansdowne; Redmond and Dillon; Carson and Craig (afterwards Viscount Craigavon).

[5] As a gesture of economy a test mobilization of the navy had been substituted for the usual naval manoeuvres. This was to include a review of the fleet by the King at Spithead.

99

H. M. Yacht Victoria & Albert

Sat. 18 July 14 [ii]

. . . I came down in the train from Victoria with the King and the P of Wales. The latter told me he had not been in bed more than 4 hours any night this week. He dances assiduously & is obliged to be at his riding school at 9 every morning. I suppose he is practising for life in the R. Horse Art[y], which is to be the first phase of his military career. There doesn't seem to be anyone else on board except the young Prince Albert,[1] who is a bit better than his brother, & the usual lot of equerries &c &c, and as we are moored up against a jetty in Portsmouth harbour, out of sight of all the war ships, & are apparently destined to remain so tho' it is a lovely evening for a cruise, the immediate surroundings are not very lively. This so-called 'yacht' is a huge spick & span structure ('span' is really a good epithet for the Mascot-tamer), much bigger than the *Enchantress* and redolent of comfort. Whether she sails well I shall be better able to tell you to-morrow. I suppose we shall have a lot of Admirals to dinner, but I am afraid not Winston. There is at present no sign of the *Enchantress* which has no doubt gone off (as I wish we had) in search of adventures.[2]

Stamfordham came to see me just before I started to settle the form of his 'invitations' which will go out tomorrow for *Tuesday* – the earliest possible date. The King is for Ll. G. in preference to Crewe. It is a curious whirligig – isn't it? since this time last week, and one can't help wondering where the wheel will have turned this time next week, or a week later when I come to you. Do you remember the Potter's Wheel metaphor in 'Rabbi ben Ezra'?

> 'What tho, about thy rim,
> Skull things, in order grim
> Grow out, in graver mood, obey the sterner stress?'[3]

But I have felt ever so much happier & more hopeful since our talk yesterday. Blessed are the life-givers, of whom there is none to equal you.

I am going to stop now, and take a little walking exercise on the upper deck.[4]

1 Afterwards King George VI.
2 Asquith enjoyed visits to the fleet. Churchill reported to his wife from Spithead in July 1912: 'The P.M. is quite indefatigable and has been on his legs all day. He loves this sort of life and is well suited to it. He would make a much better admiral than most I have to get along with.'
3 From stanza xxix of Browning's poem.
4 The continuation to this letter, written on the following day, has not been selected for publication.

100

20 July 1914 [i]

. . . Both the King & I were pluming ourselves on the admirable manner in wh. a secret known to so many had been kept for over 48 hours. The first thing I saw when I started back soon after 7 on my early journey this morning was the disclosure in the two Northcliffe organs.[1] It is impossible as yet to say who is the guilty party. I suspected Rothermere but the Master[2] has hastened to assert that he had nothing to do with it. It must I think be one of Bonar Law's lot, for no one else but he knew that Ll. George & not Crewe was to go with me. I told it to Winston for the first time on the yacht yesterday.[3] It is annoying on every ground, & puts the whole Liberal press in the worst of tempers: they are as jealous as cats & naturally resent the notion that *The Times* has been preferred to them[4]. . . .

1 *The Times* and the *Daily Mail*.
2 The Master of Elibank, since 1912 Lord Murray of Elibank.
3 Lloyd George was suspected by Riddell (*More Pages from My Diary*, p. 216) of having passed the information during a talk with Northcliffe at the Mansion House on the evening of 17 July. Riddell, being a newspaper magnate himself, was well placed to judge the probabilities.

[4] For the annoyance of the Liberal editors in March when Asquith gave his statement about the Curragh exclusively to *The Times* see Letter 50, n. 2. Northcliffe and his men answered Liberal charges of their preparations to cover an Irish civil war being provocative, by accusing the Liberal press of suppressing news about the Ulster crisis. They made all they could of their Conference coup. The *Daily Mail* (22 July) called the ignorance of the Liberal papers about the Conference 'part and parcel of the inertia of the Liberal party'.

101

20 July 14 [iii]

I exercised real self-denial darling in regard to your suggestion that I should join you at dinner. I hate even the possibility of gossip about us. It was heavenly to be with you for half an hour. I will come to-morrow at or soon after 5.30, and will tell you all that has happened. I hope you weren't oppressed by getting 2 days' letters in one.

The Labour party have passed a rather furious resolution denouncing the 'undue interference of the Crown', and the presence in the Conference of '2 rebels in arms against constituted authority'. This doesn't amount to much, but more serious is the wide-spread feeling among our own rank & file (so Illingworth reports) that the whole thing is a prelude to an immediate General Election – which they think would be a practical negation of the Parliament Act.[1]

I confess to being a little anxious as to how we are to get the thing on walking legs to-morrow. I shall be able to tell you exactly how this stands when we meet.

It is to me a great stroke of luck that you are still here & near: for (as the hymn says) 'I need thy presence every passing hour'.[2] All my love.

[1] The prospect of the majority in the Commons being thwarted despite the Parliament Act enraged committed Liberals. 'You must suppress Carson, if it becomes necessary, *without an election*' was the message from the party's Yorkshire stalwarts (Trevelyan to Runciman, 25 July: C. Hazlehurst, *Politicians at War* (1971), p. 27). Moderates and floating voters, on the other hand, were intent on an agreed settlement.

[2] 'Abide with me', by Henry Francis Lyte.

102

Wed 22 July 1914 4.30

I am afraid I was rather a 'grumpy' companion yesterday, but as always happens your comradeship & counsel and understanding were worth more than a King's ransom. I dined with the Dss. at Roehampton – no one there but Bron & Nan & Maurice and the novelist Mason, & of course Rosemary.[1]

It is a charming place & it was nice out in the garden in the starlight after dinner. I drove home alone & thought about things.

You would see the rumpus in the morning papers over the King's speech: one sentence, not very happily worded, in that truly artless performance (wh. I purposely did not revise) has been seized upon & twisted about in a very unfair way. So I felt bound to-day at question time to take the responsibility for the whole thing, & to let it be known that it was not the King but the Conference (Dillon among the most urgent) who decided upon the publication.[2]

We sat again this morning for an hour & a half, discussing maps & figures, and always getting back to that most damnable creation of the perverted ingenuity of man – the County of Tyrone. The extraordinary feature of the discussion was the complete agreement (in principle) of Redmond & Carson. Each said 'I must have the whole of Tyrone, or die; but I quite understand why you say the same'. The Speaker who incarnates bluff unimaginative English sense, of course cut in: 'When each of two people say they must have the whole, why not cut it in half?' They wd. neither of them look at such a suggestion. L.G. & I worked hard to get rid of the county areas altogether & proceed on Poor Law Unions, wh. afford a good basis of give & take. But again both Irish lots would have none of it. Nothing could have been more amicable in tone, or more desperately fruitless in result. We agreed to meet once more to-morrow, when we shall make a final – tho' I fear futile – effort to carve out a 'block'.[3] I have rarely felt more hopeless in any practical affair: an impasse, with unspeakable consequences, upon a matter which to English eyes seems inconceivably small, & to Irish eyes immeasurably big.[4] Isn't it a real tragedy?

I feel rather at sea about you & your doings. I may possibly be able to see a little of the *Coq* to-night, but I doubt it. And what of to-morrow? You will come to the Garden party, & if it is fine we mt. slip away.[5] What about dinner? Do come if you can. And then?

We had a curious lunch party even for us – Cambon, Comte d'Hausson-ville, Chaliapine, Diana Manners, Lady Paget, Raymond, Mrs Lyall, Count Kessler[6] – were a few of the figures that I found seated at the table. I was rather preoccupied, and did not get much out of this rarely mixed lot. Just going to have a Cabinet. One thing is certain – that I love you my darling.

[1] The 4th Duke of Sutherland had died in 1913. His widow, and her daughter Lady Rosemary Leveson-Gower, were at Saint Serf's House, Priory Lane, Roehampton. 'Bron and Nan' were Auberon Herbert, Lord Lucas, then Parliamentary Secretary, Board of Agriculture, and his sister. He was a close friend of the writer Maurice Baring. A. E. W. Mason, the novelist, had been a Liberal M.P., 1906–10.

[2] 'Today', the King had said, 'the cry of civil war is on the lips of the most responsible and sober-minded of my people.' Most Liberals reacted angrily to this phrasing, since it implied that the Ulster preparations for armed resistance were legitimate. Asquith pointed out that he

himself had referred in March to the prospect of 'civil strife' in Ulster. The Prime Minister 'knows perfectly well', the *Daily Chronicle* replied, 'that . . . the inexcusable words were published . . . , not because they were innocent, but because he was careless.' While the phrase, and Asquith's defence of it, brought his relations with his party momentarily to a low point, he gained the lasting gratitude of the King (Letter 105).

³ Asquith had gone beyond county option (p. 83) and was prepared to exclude 'the Protestant area' as a whole (Letter 97).

⁴ See p. 16. Apart from the fact that the time-limit problem had barely been discussed, this paragraph shows how far Asquith was from a realistic appraisal. The conference failed because neither Ulstermen nor Nationalists wanted a compromise settlement. Both sides believed that they would gain the best terms by maintaining their positions to the end. For both, therefore, Tyrone had symbolic, as well as intrinsic, importance.

⁵ As Margot had invited 1,600 guests to her garden party, 'slipping away' cannot have been too easy.

⁶ Wrote, with von Hofmannstahl, the book of Strauss's ballet *La Légende de Joseph* (Letter 84).

PART 2

The Admired War Leader

THE war crisis brought Asquith within a matter of days from the brink of political disaster to a pinnacle of prestige. By 1 August he was being praised by Northcliffe's *Daily Mail* for his admirable answers and statements in the Commons. His speech on 6 August vindicating British intervention in the war was judged unanswerable. Three weeks later when he expressed the 'sympathy and admiration' of the Commons for the Belgian resistance a correspondent to *The Times* suggested that his words should be posted up 'in every town and village in these islands'. The extent of the premier's apotheosis, and of the chagrin it aroused, is clear from the letters of his enemies. Henry Wilson told Leo Maxse in September that he was made 'positively sick' by 'Squiff's sham patriotism'.[1] Asquith's reputation stayed high throughout the early months of the war. To Hankey, who was well placed to judge, he seemed 'an admirable chairman'[2] during this period. In November H. W. Massingham, who had been critical of Asquith for some years, wrote in the Liberal *Nation*:

If you want a tonic . . . have a look at the Prime Minister. Unquestionably, Mr Asquith is carrying his burden with great courage; with a steady, massive, self-reliant, and unswerving confidence which is in itself a moral asset of no slight value.[3]

While neither Asquith nor any other statesman could foresee all the horrors ahead, he hated war and was more sensitive than many to the suffering which it would entail. But Venetia was not the only one to whom he expressed his relief that the war crisis had put Ulster into the shade. 'The one bright spot', he told Pease on 3 August, 'was the settlement of Irish strife. . . . God moves in a mysterious way his wonders to perform.'[4] In March 1915 he told Venetia that 'the sudden outburst of the Great War' had been the greatest stroke of luck in his political career (Letter 342). He may have owed this chance to mend his political fortunes to luck; but he seized it with skill. His friendship with Venetia, together with his elation at having escaped from the Ulster impasse, kept him during these months at the top of his form. 'Without you' he told her on 1 August (Letter 112), 'I tremble to think what would have happened to me.' Grey, he wrote on 9 August (Letter 119), was 'much overstrained. So should I be', he added, 'if it were not for you.'

Contemporaries regarded it as Asquith's greatest achievement that he led a united country into the war. If he had swerved during the haggard days which preceded the British ultimatum to Germany, either towards a premature intervention or in the direction of a declaration of neutrality, he would have broken up his Government and split his party. Asquith wrote after the war:

> In a long succession of critical . . . situations Sir Edward Grey had trodden, without losing head or foothold, the narrow path between two abysses; like one of those duckboards by which, later on, our soldiers used to find their way across the craters and morasses dug out by shell and mine in Flanders.[5]

A swerve one way off the centre line would have meant coming quickly to the help of France and Russia, Britain's partners in the Triple Entente. The temptation to do this was implicit in Asquith's fourth principle (Letter 113), in which it was held to be 'against British interests that France should be wiped out as a Great Power'. Timely help might deter Berlin; and without it the French might be overwhelmed before the Russian armies came into action. Moreover letters exchanged between Grey and Cambon, the French Ambassador, in November 1912 referred to the arrangement whereby the French fleet was in the Mediterranean, the Channel and Atlantic coasts of France being guarded by the British Navy. By this exchange the British Government was pledged to discuss with the French what 'common measures' should be taken in a war crisis such as this. The Grey–Cambon letters were known only to the cabinet; but plainly they could not be kept secret much longer.

The case for a British declaration of neutrality is harder to describe. The isolationists had little difficulty with the letters of November 1912.[6] These specifically stated that the Anglo-French staff talks did not

> restrict the freedom of either government to decide at any future time whether or not to assist the other with armed force. . . . The disposition . . . of the French and British fleets respectively at the present moment is not based on an engagement to co-operate in war.

The isolationists' central tenet was that Britain's undertaking to maintain the neutrality of Belgium did not involve making war to prevent 'a strategic passage of German troops through that country'.[7]

The 1839 treaty on Belgian neutrality gave each of the signatories not the duty, but the right, to intervene if Belgium were invaded. This right existed in law whether or not the Belgians resisted the invasion themselves or called for the help of the guarantor powers. In practice, however, there would not be a conclusively strong case for trying to defend the Belgians unless they themselves put up a resistance and asked for help.[8] No one in the cabinet had much doubt that the German army would invade France via Belgium on the outbreak of war.[9] The question was how the Belgians would react. It was generally thought in Whitehall that they would neither resist nor call on Britain for help. In 1912 they had rebuffed a British proposal for a resumption of Anglo-Belgian staff talks. Their army was deployed, not against a German invasion, but to resist attack from any direction. They had ceased to think of Britain as a reliable and disinterested protector once the Anglo-French Entente had been formed.[10] They now saw the British as aligned with one of the warlike combinations which cared everything for victory and nothing for Belgium. When caught between the great armies in war they would be concerned to limit their sufferings during the struggle and to emerge from it as an independent state. It was doubtful whether an appeal to Britain would promote either object. It would not prevent the invasion, since it could not be made until the frontier had actually been crossed and the British army was far too small, and too distant, to deter the invader; and it would prove Belgium's undoing if Germany should win the war. The most probable course for the Belgian Government, when its eastern frontier was crossed, was therefore the one outlined by Churchill:

I thought, and Lord Kitchener, who lunched with me on the Tuesday (28 July), agreed, that Belgium would make some formal protest and submit. A few shots might be fired outside Liège or Namur, and then this unfortunate state would bow its head before overwhelming might.[11]

The expectation that the Belgian troops would 'line the route'[12] as the German columns passed was underpinned by a prediction of where that route would be. The scheme for a great wheel into France from the north-east, called the Schlieffen Plan after its originator, had been much modified over the years. The Committee of Imperial Defence were aware that, while it had once included the invasion of the Netherlands, the current version was greatly curtailed. They had been advised that the German armies were likely to remain south and east of the line formed by the River Sambre and by the Meuse after its junction with the Sambre.[13] There were several reasons for supposing the curtailment to be as large as this. First, calculations suggested that the Germans could not deploy enough front-line troops to extend their right wing into northern Belgium without a dangerous weakening of their centre and left. Secondly, it was argued that the Germans could not move through central Belgium in strength unless they could take the Meuse fortresses of Liège and Namur very quickly. Both fortresses seemed proof against an early assault, given determined Belgian resistance;

yet it was precisely the attempt to move large forces north of the Meuse which would provoke such resistance. Asquith's reference on 29 July (Letter 109) to Belgium as the German army's 'shortest route' suggests that he had accepted the view of his defence advisers that the Ardennes route was the most likely one.

The expectation that the German army would take 'the shortest route' by keeping south of the Sambre–Meuse line was even more important in its strategic than in its diplomatic effects and more will be said of it later (pp. 154–6). The Belgian Government could hardly be expected to take immense risks in order to prevent a German passage through the Ardennes, which represented no more than a third of their country in area and much less in population.[14] Moreover, if an invasion by this route were made the ground of an appeal to London, the British would have little moral obligation to answer it in arms and no strategic reason for doing so[15]: their strategic concerns lay entirely in north Belgium, and specifically in Antwerp and the mouth of the Schelde. It seemed possible that there was some secret agreement or understanding between Berlin and Brussels by which the German troops would be allowed free use of the Ardennes route.[16]

At the start of the crisis Asquith accepted large parts of the isolationist argument. He told Venetia on 24 July that there seemed no reason why the British should be anything more than spectators of Armageddon (Letter 103).[17] He had no partiality for the conservative and clerical administration in Brussels: they were thought to be pro-German.[18] Ottoline Morrell recorded after her visit to The Wharf on 26 July (Letter 106) that someone had mentioned Belgium, but that Montagu

and Asquith seemed to think we were under no obligation to assist them. And amongst themselves they said, 'We have made no pledge to help them.'[19]

Ottoline Morrell was not the most reliable of diarists; but her note is supported by something which Asquith himself wrote a few days later. During the opening phase of the crisis the cabinet were concerned primarily with Grey's attempts to promote a settlement, so that their first serious discussion of the Belgian problem was not held until 29 July. It was assumed that any Belgian appeal for help would be addressed solely to Britain, since the French were likely to be too busy defending themselves to defend Belgian neutrality. Indeed there were some fears in London that the French forces might be tempted by a German feint into being the first to cross the Belgian frontier.[20] After the 29 July cabinet Asquith reported to the King:

It is doubtful how far a single guaranteeing state is bound under the Treaty of 1839 to maintain Belgian neutrality if the remainder abstain or refuse. The cabinet consider that the matter if it arises will be rather one of policy than of legal obligation.[21]

Despite the strong points in the isolationist case, and his profoundly pacific inclinations, Asquith was never tempted to swerve off the centre line in the direction of staying-out-at-all-costs. This was not because he could assess all the forces at work or foresee the outcome of the crisis. He did not realize that the inflexible neutrality of King Albert and the Belgian ministers represented, not a covert intention to help Germany, but their determination to uphold before the world their status and claims under the treaty. In the early stages of the crisis he probably did not know that a pre-emptive advance into Belgium found no place in the French Army's Plan 17.[22] It is unlikely that he foresaw how quickly British opinion would move towards intervention, once the centre of interest had shifted from eastern Europe to the threat to France. He knew no more than anyone else how it would all end. He simply used all his experience and authority to keep the options open until he and his colleagues could see their way; and after ten days the German General Staff, and their nominal masters, solved his problems for him. Instead of a secret negotiation between Berlin and Brussels, or an offer to confine the German march to the Ardennes, there was what Asquith termed a piece of 'almost Austrian crassness' (Letter 114), that is, an ultimatum demanding, at twelve hours' notice, the submission of the Belgians to a total invasion. This blew away the distinctions between an attack on Belgium and a strategic passage through that country, and convinced everyone in Brussels, and almost everyone in London, that only one option was left.[23]

*   *   *

No rivals threatened Asquith's ascendancy during the early months of the war. Lloyd George had not yet recovered from the Marconi scandal and the fiasco of his 1914 budget. Grey was threatened with partial blindness. Crewe was a peer with no popular following. Neither of the ministers with direct responsibility for the operations of war could be any sort of rival. Kitchener did not count as a politician at all. Churchill soon alienated what Liberal friends he had by his yearning for a wartime coalition; and he achieved no significant *rapprochement* with the Conservatives.[24] The latter took his determination to have a directing hand in naval movements as yet further evidence that he was bent on self-aggrandisement. An ascendancy such as this was dangerous for a Prime Minister prone to over-confidence. Praising Attlee's modesty, Churchill once said: 'Plenty to be modest about.' By the end of 1914 Asquith had 'plenty to be arrogant about'. Neither then nor at any other time did he become arrogant in bearing. But he suffered from the arrogance of judgement which is apt to afflict the ablest people if they are not imaginative enough to foresee the shifts in the scene;[25] and in war this told against him. He was slow to adapt the machinery of government to wartime needs. He had no thought of altering his personal style. He continued to regard 'energy under the guise of lethargy' as one of his greatest qualities (Letter 342). It does not seem to have struck him that, however serviceable the guise may have been in peace, it was damaging in war. The patience which had so often preserved the unity of the Government and the party had lost some of its efficacy in a war in which events and the public mood moved so quickly. It was of little use being the master of debate when party battles were suspended; and distant relations with the press[26] were dangerous when the appetite for war news made the press ever more powerful.

The Liberal Government shared in the premier's brief triumph and was equally vulnerable. Though the Conservatives observed the party truce many of them seethed with rancour.[27] Having lost the last three general elections they had at last found what promised to be a winner in the Ulster question, only to be halted in sight of victory by a sign marked 'national unity in war'. The Liberals had started to steal a major Conservative asset by showing that when it came to patriotism and national defence they were at least as effective as their true blue opponents. By appropriating in Kitchener the only recruiting sergeant capable of raising a vast volunteer army, they had sidestepped conscription, the wartime issue which threatened to be their worst political problem; and Kitchener had put the finishing touch to the coup by allowing it to be known that he found his Liberal colleagues 'a capable lot'.[28] Asquith and Lloyd George spoke to cheering audiences as national leaders a day or two after they had put Home Rule on the statute-book by what the Conservatives thought a piece of partisan trickery (pp. 173–5). The Opposition were consoled only by the conviction that it could not last: the wretched radicals might be able to take Britain into a war but a few months of fighting would show them up as faint-hearts.

The prediction that it could not last was in a sense entirely correct. Although few politicians yet favoured a coalition, a single-party government was not a suitable instrument for conducting a long war: 'The political truce is very thin,' Runciman wrote in February 1915; 'if things go wrong we shall be flayed.'[29] There was no way of preventing things from 'going wrong' in a war such as this.

*   *   *

One dangerous feature of his lack of watchful prescience was Asquith's unimaginative rigidity of habit: he hardly curtailed his social activities during wartime. His vulnerability in this area was of long standing. He had entered politics determined to avoid the 'aristocratic embrace';[30] but over the years his need for intellectual stimulus, and for an escape from family tensions, altered his attitude. He was never, in any simple sense, a snob:

high rank did not impress him. In the 1890s he had thought very little of the set who revolved round the then Prince of Wales. 'I dined last night at a very "smart" party at the Randolph Churchills',' he told Mrs. Horner in June 1893,

the P. of Wales, Lady de Grey, Lady Brooke . . . etc., etc. . . . . If I kept a diary I think I should enter in it, as Louis XVI did on the day of the taking of the Bastille, 'Rien.'[31]

Asquith sought in his acquaintances, not coronets, but intellectual distinction, style, and a command of life's good things. Unfortunately these legitimate preferences were not thought suitable in a Liberal premier.

By 1914 Bagehot's dictum, that a prime minister was expected to 'combine the vivacity of an idle man with the assiduity of a very laborious one' had been long outmoded, for the Liberals at least. From the 1880s the division between the parties had begun to follow class lines. London society was thus predominantly Conservative and many Liberals preferred their leaders to steer clear of it. That Asquith's active social life did him no good was one of the few points on which Rosebery's opinions coincided with Campbell-Bannerman's.[32] From 1912 or thereabouts Asquith was not helped in this by the activities of his eldest son. Raymond headed a youthful group known by their elders as 'the Corrupt Coterie'. The Coterie's pride, wrote Lady Diana Cooper, 'was to be unafraid of words, unshocked by drink, and unashamed of "decadence" and gambling – Unlike-Other-People, I'm afraid. Our peak of unpopularity was certainly 1914 and 1915.'[33]

Asquith and his family had a distaste, which they made little attempt to conceal, for the less interesting and decorative members of their party. As Violet Asquith wrote to a friend in January 1912, she could not imagine any hotel companions 'more undesirable [in bad weather] than the small fry, the *whitebait*, of the Liberal party'.[34] The people to whom she was referring so disparagingly included Masterman, who was, by any standards, a man of exceptional ability. When Christopher Addison became a junior minister on the outbreak of war, he received a particularly warm welcome in the Whips' Office 'because I was not the first-cousin-once-removed of a Countess, nor had I been private secretary to any minister'.[35] The disapproval which Asquith's social engagements aroused did not originate solely in small-minded resentment against those of outstanding distinction. It was clear that his outlook had altered; and his social habits had helped to bring this about. The social reformer of the 1890s who told his young daughter what he would do to lessen the miseries of the factory girls[36] had turned by 1914 into a Prime Minister so unradical in style that he wrote of Mary Macarthur as a stranger and of Lady Bell as a bore (Letters 160 and 20). Yet the first was an outstanding trade-unionist and the second a notable authority on factory conditions as they affected women.

Radical disapproval of the company which the Prime Minister kept was not offset by increased standing among the aristocracy. In 1909 Wilfrid Scawen Blunt found the 'evolution of the square-toed Asquith . . . into the "gay dog" of London society . . . irresistibly funny'.[37] Earl Grey was another who detected middle-class traits in the premier below the knee: in 1913 he talked to Lady Scott of 'old Squiffy and his little bourgeois legs'.[38] Edward VII and George V were both uncertain whether Asquith was a gentleman.[39]

Social activities which had merely been thought unsuitable in peacetime were condemned far more strongly amid the deprivations and sufferings of war. 'In war it is necessary', Bonar Law wrote to Asquith in February 1916, 'not only to be active but to seem active.'[40] The advice came too late and was not heeded. Few people appreciated how rapidly and inconspicuously Asquith worked. The wives and parents who waited in dread for the War Office telegram saw a Prime Minister immersed in luncheon and bridge parties, and judged this style of life frivolous and heartless in the nation's war leader.[41] In this matter, as in others, Asquith failed to see where he had become vulnerable or had laid himself open to criticism. With all his gifts he lacked the highest quality of percipience. 'The Almighty', as Margot put it, 'is a wonderful handicapper. He will not give us everything.'[42]

*   *   *

The strange alarms and demands of war confirmed and deepened Asquith's dependence on Venetia. He sent her the most secret war news,[43] and begged her to provide 'ideas or phrases' for his speeches. He wrote to her from the Treasury Bench in the House, and occasionally when presiding over the cabinet.[44] He always reread the latest letter from her last thing at night. His cries for her love and help were by now far from the practised flatteries of a philanderer. He knew that such dependence showed him as far from heroic. On 4 December 1914 he wrote:

I sometimes think how much . . . higher you might possibly rate me, if I were not so fond of you.

And on 8 December:

I can see you smile and say to yourself 'The poor man, whom mankind thinks sane and strong, has a touch of fantasy.' . . . Perhaps! Anyhow, I hug my chains, if chains they are.

At least one close colleague smiled on a friendship which kept the Prime Minister in trim. In October 1914, when Violet proposed to train as a nurse, she was lectured by Winston Churchill on 'the duties of women to those . . . at the "apex" of responsibility':

No, my dear, . . . you must remain here at your father's side – and mine. . . . We who are directing these immense and complicated operations . . . need every comfort, care and cosseting. . . . *We* are your duty. This is your war-station.[45]

Venetia passed these views to Asquith, who naturally approved of them (Letter 194). Probably they were not meant to apply to Violet alone.

Lady Sheffield was less approving than this. She seems to have become worried during the summer at the Prime Minister's interest in her youngest daughter. She had planned, before the war intervened, to travel with Venetia to India and Australia. By the autumn she was being implored by Margot to put a stop to the romance.[46] The threat to it came less from these pleas, however, than from a change in Venetia's life. Early in January 1915 she started on a nursing course at the London Hospital, and so shed some of the attributes of a society girl. She lost, not only the leisure needed by the Prime Minister's friend, but the inhibitions which had kept her from Edwin Montagu.

Notes to the Introduction to Part 2

1. Leo Maxse MSS, vol 469 f.549. It was the combination of 'sham patriotism' with 'Home Rule trickery' to which Wilson objected so strongly.
2. Hankey, *The Supreme Command*, i. 255. Hankey judged, however, entirely from War Council and committee meetings: he did not see Asquith in cabinet.
3. 31 Nov: see also *British Weekly*, 3 Sept. 1914.
4. Pease's diary, 3 Aug.; C. Hazlehurst, *Politicians at War* (1971), p. 32. Pease's entry for 2 Aug. shows how impressed a colleague was by Asquith's calm demeanour during this crisis.
5. *The Genesis of the War* (1923), p. 218.
6. A naval attack on the French coasts was in no way essential to German war plans in 1914.
7. H. W. Massingham's letter in *The Times*, 4 Aug. 1914.
8. For British pre-war policy on Belgian neutrality see *Brit. Docs. War*, viii. ch. 67. This ch. includes extracts from the minutes of the 114th and 116th C.I.D. meetings. The account in Tom Bridges, *Alarms and Excursions* (1938), pp. 62–3, is inadequate. For doubts on 3 Aug. whether the Belgians would call for Britain's help see *Churchill: Companion Docs., 1901–14*, p. 1996.
9. See, for instance, the account given in *Spectator*, 26 Dec. 1914.
10. See H. Nicolson, *Lord Carnock* (1930), pp. 399–400.
11. *World Crisis*, 1914 (1923), p. 202:
12. The phrase is taken from the remarks of a German diplomat in 1911.
13. See *Brit. Docs. War*, viii. 381 (Henry Wilson to C.I.D., 23 Aug. 1911); *National Review* LV.753 (Earl Percy, 1910), LXII.55. For a different view see Hilaire Belloc, *London Magazine*, XXVIII. 279–90 (May 1912). For Wilson's adoption, early in 1911, of the view that the German advance would stay south of the Sambre-Meuse see S. R. Williamson, *The Politics of Grand Strategy* (1969), p. 169; for the popularity of this view in France, ibid, pp. 218–19. See also Hazlehurst, op. cit., pp. 315 (Wilson, Sept. 1911), 322 (Ollivant, 1 Aug. 1914). This Wilson memo was seen by Haldane, Ollivant's by Churchill and Lloyd George. While Wilson stuck to the view that an advance north and west of the

Sambre-Meuse line was unlikely, he did not rule it out as a possibility (Wilson, diary, 7 Apr. 1912: Imperial War Museum).

The Germans' strategic railways near their Belgian frontier did not indicate a movement N. of the Meuse. A wedge of Dutch territory, the Maastricht Appendix, lies between Germany and north Belgium. The preparations near the frontier were thus compatible with an advance by the Ardennes route. This question has been obscured by statements made after the war. Compare, for instance, C. à Court Repington's article in *The Times*, 23 Jan. 1911, with his account of it in *Vestigia* (1919), pp. 304–5. A film script by Churchill (Jan. 1935) depicted Henry Wilson as telling the C.I.D. in 1911 that, if the Germans were to attack 'in three years' time', they would move N. of the Meuse; *Churchill: Companion Docs., 1929–35, p. 998.* In fact, Wilson said 'in ten years' time'.

14. See J. E. Helmreich, *Journal of Modern History*, xxxvi (Dec. 1964), 416–27, and S. R. Williamson, op. cit., p. 221, n. 49. An unsigned note by the Political Director of the Belgian Foreign Office, 28 Feb. 1914, suggests that, if the German army had kept south of the Meuse, Belgium might well have remained neutral. King Albert never suggested that his country had been inclined to make a heroic stand. 'We were cornered into it,' he said after the war: Barbara W. Tuchman, *The Guns of August* (1962), p. 179. See also n. 16 below.

15. See *Parl. Deb.* lxv. 1835 (P. Morrell). Lloyd George made much to C. P. Scott of how unwilling he would have been to go to war if the invasion of Belgium had been confined to the Ardennes: Trevor Wilson (ed.), *Political Diaries of C. P. Scott, (1970)*, pp. 96–7 and 104. See also Beaverbrook, *Politicians and the War, 1914–1916* (1928), i. 29; Grey, *Twenty-Five Years* (1925), ii. 13; Hazlehurst, op. cit., pp. 66 (Pease on 'the invasion wholesale of Belgium') and 70 (C. P. Trevelyan distinguishing between 'marching through Belgium' and 'seizing Antwerp and the whole of Belgium').

16. See Churchill to Lloyd George, 31 Aug. 1911: *Churchill: Companion Docs., 1901–1914*, p. 1119. It was realized in the British Foreign Office, however, that a secret agreement would be extremely risky for any Belgian government. A far more likely hypothesis was that the German army would take the Ardennes route, not as a result of a secret agreement, but simply in the confidence that the Belgians would not offer serious resistance to that kind of limited invasion. See *Brit. Docs. War*, viii. 386; Hazlehurst, op. cit., p. 309; John Gooch, *Plans of War* (1974), p. 292.

17. This remark is not included in the passages from the letter reproduced in *Memories and Reflections*, ii. 5.

18. See *Brit. Docs. War*, xi. 350. The Congo did not come under Belgian rule, in the strict sense, until 1908. But the atrocities committed there when it had been the personal fief of Leopold II had done much to tarnish Belgium's reputation in London. The Brussels Government did not much like 'atheistical' and republican France.

19. R. Gathorne-Hardy (ed.), *Ottoline* (1963), p. 258.

20. *Brit. Docs. War*, viii. 380; J. W. Headlam, *History of Twelve Days* (1915), p. 377; Tuchman, op. cit., pp. 34, 64, and 127. See also n. 23 below.

21. Spender and Asquith, ii. 81.

22. For the disclosure of the French Plan to the cabinet see *Political Diaries of C. P. Scott*, p. 99. The determination of French politicians not to violate Belgian neutrality had done much to shape Plan 17: see p. 194, n. 1.

23. The King asked the American Ambassador: 'What else could we do?' (B. J. Hendrick, *Walter H. Page* (1923), i. 309). See also the interview with Lloyd George in *Pearson's Magazine*, Mar. 1915, p. 264. On 18 June 1910 the Liberal *Nation* had implied that it would be justifiable to 'risk war in defence of the integrity of Belgium against a Franco-Prussian encroachment'.

24. See pp. 420–1. When they looked back Conservatives were apt to disparage Churchill's patriotism as a somewhat recent phenomenon. They did not forget that he had been a Little Navy man in 1909.

25. For his tendency to criticize people without making allowances for their difficulties or background see Letters 80 (Roosevelt), 105 (the Austrians), 207 (pensions), and 281 (Samuel).

26. See R. D. Blumenfeld, *R. D. B.'s Procession* (1935), pp. 121–3, for Asquith's tendency to mistake the Editor of the *Daily Express* for the Chilean Naval Attaché; but the *Express* was not then a very important paper.

27. See Grey, *Twenty-Five Years*, ii. 236.

28. Runciman to Sir Robert Chalmers, 7 Feb. 1915: Runciman of Doxford MSS.

29. Ibid.

30. See R. B. Haldane, *Autobiography* (1929), pp. 103–4.

31. Earl of Oxford's MSS.

32. R. Rhodes James, *Rosebery* (1963), p. 438 n. 2; John Wilson, *Campbell-Bannerman* (1973), p. 127. For two of Asquith's imprudent acquaintanceships see pp. 11–12 (Maud Allan) and Letter 15, n. 2 (Robert Ross).

33. *The Rainbow Comes and Goes* (1958), p. 82. Raymond Asquith's *Letters*, ed. John Jolliffe (1980), show that the Coterie represented only one side of his life.

34. 3 Jan. 1912, to Hugh Godley, who was in a hotel at Mürren with the people described.

35. C. Addison, *Four and a Half Years* (2 vols., 1934), i. 36–7.

36. Violet Bonham Carter, unpublished autobiographical fragment.

37. W. S. Blunt, *Diaries* ii (1920), 289.

38. Lady Scott's diary, 10 Dec. 1913: Kennet MSS, Cambridge University Library. Other parts of this entry are reproduced in *Self-Portrait of an Artist*, pp. 125–6.

39. Jenkins, *Asquith*, pp. 186–7; G. St. Aubyn, *Edward VII* (1979), p. 409; M. Gilbert, *Churchill, 1914–1916* (1971), p. 87.

40. Spender and Asquith, ii. 230.

41. See A. J. P. Taylor (ed.), *Frances Stevenson's Diary* (1971), p. 97; Hankey, diary, 12 Nov. 1916. For the practice among rich women of dressing shabbily during the war see Mrs C. S. Peel, *How We Lived Then* (1929), p. 52. It was often remarked that Bonar Law's life-style was far simpler than Asquith's.

42. *Off the Record* (1943), p. 44.

43. See pp. 419–20.

44. See Appendix 1, n. 7.

45. Violet Bonham Carter, *Winston Churchill as I Knew Him* (1965), p. 384.

46. For the letters on this which passed between Lady Sheffield and her daughter-in-law, Lady Stanley, see Adelaide Lubbock, *People in Glass Houses* (1977), pp. 81–3. The letter by Lady Stanley from Melbourne quoted on p. 82 was written on 15 Nov. 1914 (State Library of Victoria).

103

Fr. 24 July 1914

This is a black letter day in my Calendar – first & foremost because the 'light has failed', which as you know means that what I have come to rely upon most is removed far away, and that I feel like a man who is being sucked away from his life-buoy.[1] This is no fault of yours, but my bad luck. But then I have the infinite & abiding consolation that, whether far or near in space, you are always really close. Wednesday night & yest. afternoon are memories that will never fade.

The other cause of 'blackness' is that, as I told you was pretty certain, the Conference broke down, and as you will see by the papers I announced to the House the terms of the Speaker's rather bald & jejune report. The last meeting this morning was in some ways dramatic, tho' the actual business consisted merely in settling the words to be publicly used. At the end the King came in, rather *émotionné*, & said in two sentences (thank God! there was not another speech) farewell, I am sorry, & I thank you. He then very wisely had the different members brought to him privately, and saw each in turn. Redmond was a good deal impressed by his interview, especially as the King told him that he was convinced of the necessity of Home Rule.

We then had a meeting at Downing St – Redmond & Dillon, Ll George, Birrell & I. I told them that I must now go on with the Amending Bill – *without* the time limit:[2] to which after a good deal of demur they reluctantly agreed to try & persuade their party to assent. It will come on on Tuesday – not Monday: so that I have a little breathing space to collect my ideas – and yours.

I lunched with the Arch-Colonel & a company of airmen, Naval & Military, at the Marlborough Club. Happily I was next David Henderson[3] who is really good company: the Colonel himself was in his most characteristic form & you would have been amused at his views of the Hebrew race.

By the way I forgot to say – about the 'dramatic' side of the close of the Conference, that Redmond assured us that when he said good-bye to Carson the latter was in tears, and that Captain Craig who has never spoken to Dillon in his life came up to him & said: 'Mr Dillon will you shake my hand? I should be glad to think that I had been able to give as many years to Ulster as you have to the service of Ireland'. Aren't they a remarkable people? And the folly of thinking that we can ever understand, let alone govern them!

At 3.15 we had a Cabinet where there was a lot of vague & not very fruitful talk about Ulster, the provisional government &c; but the real interest was Grey's statement of the European situation,[4] which is about as bad as it can possibly be. Austria has sent a bullying and humiliating

Ultimatum to Servia, who cannot possibly comply with it,[5] and demanded an answer within 48 hours – failing which she will march. This means, almost invevitably, that Russia will come on the scene in defence of Servia & in defiance of Austria; and if so, it is difficult both for Germany & France to refrain from lending a hand to one side or the other. So that we are within measurable, or imaginable, distance of a real Armageddon, which would dwarf the Ulster & Nationalist Volunteers to their true proportion. Happily there seems to be no reason why we should be anything more than spectators. But it is a blood-curdling prospect – is it not?

I made my statement in the House at 5 in the most commonplace fashion, & as B. Law followed suit, the whole thing was over in 4 minutes.

I don't know what I shall do this evening: I missed you terribly last night & I think you would have enjoyed it. To-morrow I go to the Wharf, where I find we shall have Kitty Somerset & Ottoline. Most beloved, I wish I could tell you what a stay you have been & are & will be to me. After all we both said on Wed. night there is no room for misunderstanding & doubt. I wonder what sort of a journey you had? & whether you found Huck & the Penguin?[6] & what dress you are going to wear this evening? & – heaps of things. *Write fully.* Bless you my love.

[1] Venetia had left London for Penrhos.

[2] Asquith meant to restore 'county option', however.

[3] Director-General of Military Aeronautics. He was shortly to command the four squadrons of the Royal Flying Corps which went to France with the B.E.F.

[4] The ministers had 'toiled around the muddy byways of Fermanagh and Tyrone', Churchill wrote, and were exhausted. Grey 'had been . . . speaking for several minutes before I could disengage my mind from the tedious and bewildering debate which had just closed': *The World Crisis, 1914* (1923), p. 193. Bonar Law and Lansdowne learned of the Austrian ultimatum when they were waiting with the Speaker for their audiences at the end of the Conference; the Speaker 'happened to pick up *The Times* and there saw the telegram': Lord Ullswater, *A Speaker's Commentaries* (1925), ii. 164.

[5] This was not the general reaction in the British press, which had been much wooed during July by the German and Austrian embassies. Most of the London papers regarded the ultimatum as justified, but the measures demanded excessive in scope. The *Standard, Manchester Guardian, Daily News,* and *Daily Chronicle* thought the ultimatum entirely justified. The press did not begin to swing against Austria until 27 July.

[6] The penguin was one of Venetia's unusual pets. At one period she also kept a bear cub. 'I have been seized with the desire to own two penguins,' she wrote to Edwin Montagu in October 1912; 'and consequently went off to Liverpool yesterday . . . to buy a couple. Unfortunately there were none at the moment. I . . . consoled myself, after resisting the charms of a huge square brown owl, . . . with a young fox. He is moderately nice only, but still very shy.'

104

It was heavenly to get your most delicious letter this morning: it will be 'all the light of all my day'.[1] If you knew my darling how much I prefer your 'dumbness' to other people's speech! What you say about these last months touches me deeply; our lives and interests are so mingled together that any *real* separation is to me an unthinkable tragedy. Every hour I think of you & refer things, big & little, to the unseen tribunal of your wise and loving judgment.

After I wrote to you yesterday I finished up a few things at the House, and then (you will be glad to hear) went & had my hair cut! I hope the result will commend itself to your critical eye. There was a curious lack of excitement in the political atmosphere: the only agitated person seemed to be Winston, who is meditating either a speech or a letter (I don't know which) on the situation.

As Margot was tired & in bed, I improvised a little dinner here, consisting of the 2 McKennae, Masterton Smith & myself. We played some really amusing Bridge – tho' in the end not much money changed hands. My partner went 6 hearts agst 5 royals & only lost by one trick. Afterwards I went on with Pamela to supper at the Assyrian's who had been doing an evening with his constituents in the company of Birrell. Their respective accounts of one another's speeches were quite entertaining. Violet & Bongie came in, but we did not stay late.

This morning tho' there is lots of wind we have a little more sun, and after seeing Stamfordham & Morley (who is in some political perturbation – I don't know exactly why) I shall motor with Oc via Skindles to Huntercombe & golf there with him & the McKennae. Violet is going for Sunday to the Curries[2] in Wilts.

I am delighted to have the little bit of sweet smelling green you sent me. It brings back Penrhos to me – and you. I like to think of you in your placid surroundings – away for the moment from Life A,[3] reading Pepys, ambling with the Penguin, and 'making your soul', while I am still tossing in the open much broken sea. The usual weekly 'crisis' is this time (as you see) postponed from Monday to Tuesday.[4] I will write more about it to-morrow (Sunday) tho' I fear the posts are bad. My own loved & treasured, I always think of you.

---

[1] That and the Child's unheeded dream
Is all the light of all their day.

Coventry Patmore, *The Angel in the House*, I. viii, Prelude 2.

[2] James and Hilda Currie of Upham House, Aldbourne. Arthur Asquith had served in the

Sudan, where James Currie was Director of Education, and Principal of Gordon College, Khartoum, 1900–1914.
³ The 'pleasure-hunt': see Letter 75.
⁴ The Commons were to discuss the Amending Bill on Tuesday, 28 July (see Letter 103).

105

The Wharf,
Sutton Courtney,
Berks.

Sunday 26 July 1914

My darling before I left London yesterday I had a visit from Stamford-ham. His main object was to assure me that there is no truth in the story, which has been going the rounds this last week, that he (S.) had told Arthur Ponsonby[1] that the King would not give his assent to the Home Rule Bill unless it was accompanied by an Amending Bill. I told him that I had heard the story from Lulu, but had said at once that I didn't believe it. He said he thought the King, so far, had no fixed intentions, and that he was much touched by the way I had defended him in the whole matter of the Conference.

They have got hold (I believe) of a rather ingenious notion that the introduction, or at any rate the passing, of the Amending Bill would make the Home Rule Bill – which it amends – not the 'same' measure as that passed in the two previous Sessions, & therefore not entitled to the benefit of the Parliament Act. There is some plausibility in this, tho' I do not think it is really sound. I doubt whether an Amending Bill in any shape will get thro' both Houses, tho' of course the pressure to settle is bound to become more & more severe. If it doesn't, it is quite on the cards that the King may say he will assent to the Home Rule Bill, provided an immediate dissolution follows,[2] and that if we are unable to agree to this (as you know, our party loathes the idea of a dissolution until after Plural voting is gone) he will politely dismiss us & send for Ministers who will agree. A general election under such conditions would be one of the worst things that cd. happen to the country, or (I suspect) to the Liberal party.

Meanwhile, no one can say what is going to happen in the East of Europe. The enclosed telegram from our Ambassador at Petersburg wh. came on Friday night[3] will interest you, because it shows the Russian view, & how even at this stage Russia is trying to drag us in. The news this morning is that Servia has capitulated on the main points, but it is very doubtful if any reservations will be accepted by Austria, who is resolved upon a complete & final humiliation. The curious thing is that on many, if not most, of the points Austria has a good & Servia a very bad case. But the Austrians are

quite the stupidest people in Europe[4] (as the Italians are the most perfidious), and there is a brutality about their mode of procedure which will
make most people think that it is a case of a big Power wantonly bullying a
little one. Anyhow it is the most dangerous situation of the last 40 years,
and may have incidentally the good effect of throwing into the background
the lurid pictures of 'civil war' in Ulster.[5]

What a screed about politics! Poor darling – but you are very patient, and,
what is even more to the point, *really* interested – aren't you?

Do you follow the triangular duel between Caillaux and his two wives? A
French Criminal trial is a masterpiece of irrelevance & indecency. I see the
latest 'incident' is that the presiding judge has sent a challenge to one of his
colleagues on the Bench.[6]

I motored with Oc to Skindles where we met the McKennae, & proceeded
with them to Huntercombe to engage in a family foursome. I am glad to say
that we beat them by 2 & 1: Pamela has certainly improved wonderfully, &
did 2 or 3 quite excellent drives. . . .

. . . Between now & Tues. I have to think out something to say about the
Amending Bill, and I contemplate with horror returning to London to-
morrow without a chance of seeing & talking to you, most beloved, till the
end of the week. I am not at the moment very fond of my fellow creatures,
tho' I don't go quite so far as a line of Clough's wh. I saw yesterday: 'The
wise are bad, the good are fools'. Write to me & tell me you are thinking &
wishing of & for me, and that will do more than anything to make me happy
& strong. *All* love.

[1] Liberal M.P. (see Letters 59, n. 1, and 74a, n. 10). His brother, Frederick, was Assistant
Private Secretary to George V.
[2] On 31 July the King drafted a letter, in consultation with Earl Loreburn, which made clear
that the Royal Assent would be given to the Home Rule Bill on the sole condition that the
cabinet should provide a written 'statement of [their] full and considered reasons' for
requiring it (Nicolson, *George V* (1952), p. 234, n. 1).
[3] The Ambassador had been told by the Russian Foreign Minister that 'if war did break out,
we would sooner or later be dragged into it; but if we did not make common cause with France
and Russia from the outset we should have rendered war more likely, and should not have
played a "beau rôle" ' (*Brit. Docs. War*, xi. 81, No. 101).
[4] It was characteristic of Asquith to attribute the recklessness of Austrian statesmen, not to
the almost insuperable difficulties of the Dual Monarchy, but simply to stupidity.
[5] Asquith spoke like this to several people. See p. 111 and Lady Ottoline Morrell's diary,
R. Gathorne-Hardy (ed.), *Ottoline*, (1963), p. 258. Other Liberals thought the same: see
Mrs Drew's remark to Asquith in L. Masterman (ed.), *Mary Gladstone*, (1930), p. 477.
[6] Caillaux, when Minister of Finance, was attacked in the *Figaro*, which published a letter
written to him during his first marriage by the lady who had become his second wife. It had
come to the paper from his first wife who had purloined it. The second wife, fearing the
publication of other letters, shot the *Figaro*'s editor, Calmette. Caillaux resigned his office and
at his wife's trial testified forcefully on her behalf. She was acquitted. The quarrel between the
two judges concerned the wish of the defence to read the 'other letters' to the court. Each of the

judges trying the case was liable to be accused of political bias. See Peter Shankland, *Death of an Editor* (1981).

106

Mond. 27 July 14

11 a.m. It was a great joy to get your little Sunday letter. No – I'm not going to 'stop writing'; nor did I find your letter at all 'dull' (tho' I wish you would *never* doubt that you have a soul!): indeed I wd. very gladly have had more of it. Expression (whether by speech or writing or other less articulate ways) comes more easily – as the French say – to the person 'qui baise' than to the person 'qui tend la joue'. And though I trust that is not our case, yet I know that (most naturally) I feel more than you the actual *need* of sharing everything. Not that you keep things back, any more than you give them away, and I love to think that you write just as much or as little as comes into your mind for the moment. I should hate to feel that you were ever forcing the pace – just as I should hate to believe that there was some side of your heart & life that you kept a sealed book from me. I don't want any change in you my darling.

I admit too that there is more happening here just now than at Penrhos. We have indeed a surfeit of problems and worries. We were placidly playing Bridge at the Wharf last night when a telephone message came in reporting the shocking news from Dublin. I at once came up with Bongie in his new motor, & we arrived here about 1 a.m., but there was nothing fresh. I am now waiting for Birrell & for fuller news from the War Office. The malignity of fortune could hardly have devised a more inopportune coup, and how the devil the soldiers came to be mixed up in it at all, still more to fire their volleys, at this moment passes my comprehension. The Nationalists of course are furious & not without reason, and the whole thing in any case must react most unfavourably on the chances of peace & settlement.[1] The Eastern 'crisis' seems to be still hanging in the balance: we are to have a Cabinet about it this afternoon.

I will write more about all this later in the day. We had a fine Sunday & I played golf with Lady Kitty (who is pretty good) in the afternoon. Ottoline only arrived just before dinner: you should have seen her in her evening war-paint: blackened eyes, green silk trousers, and a turban with a long protruding feather: as you say, a little above life-size in every way for a place like the Wharf.

Later. I have just had a confabulation here with Birrell, Ll George & Winston. The summoning of the military – a most improper proceeding – was the act of an Ass^t Police Commissioner called Harrel, whom we have at once suspended.[2] The firing wh. led to the loss of life was the act of some exasperated soldiers in the rear ranks who were being mauled with missiles; it was not ordered by the officers, who stopped it. But of course it has left enormous exasperation behind in the minds of the Dublin populace. Irish history is a long chapter of untoward & impish accidents. The Irish party are now meeting, ostensibly to discuss the Amending Bill! and we shall soon hear what their temper is.

4 p.m. I've just got your Saturday letter, wh. came on from the Wharf, it gave me much delight – tho' you may think I am a 'prejudiced' reader. What a shock over the King's letter! I was calculating in bed last night that, roughly speaking, since the first week in December I must have written you not less than *170* letters. I have never in the same space of time written nearly so many to any human being, and never come within 1000 miles of revealing so much that was my own secret property. Isn't it strange? How do you account for it? I often have a misgiving that *some* at any rate of the things wh. I tell you, because they interest me, can't *really* interest you. But I have faith in your word.

I enclose 2 or 3 little extracts from the foreign telegrams, because they are not in the newspapers. We seem to be on the *very brink.*

We have just got thro' questions, & Grey has made his statement about the Eastern situation, wh. you will see in the papers.[3] At 8.15 we are going to have a debate on the Dublin business, and as the Irish are still much perturbed we have put off the Amending Bill from to-morrow. We are now just about to have a Cabinet, & I must stop. I will tell you more to-morrow about other things. *Do write* – anything, everything, nothing – so long as it is part of your life, I wish for nothing more interesting. If you were only nearer! – but near or far, you are my beloved & fill my thoughts & heart. *All love.*

¹ For the gun-running at Howth see p. 84. Asquith and Birrell no doubt assumed that, now one side was armed, the other would be allowed to arm as well. But they had not removed the ban on importing arms. The Assistant Commissioner of Police called on a battalion of the King's Own Scottish Borderers, as well as on police, to prevent this arms distribution. After a scuffle the Volunteers succeeded in making away with most of the rifles. Dubliners were furious at the apparent discrimination; and as the troops were marching back into the city along Bachelor's Walk they were heavily stoned. They turned and fired on the crowd, killing 3 and injuring 38.

² A committee of inquiry under Lord Shaw of Dunfermline censured Harrel. His action in calling out the troops was 'not in accordance with law' and there had been 'no case warranting military intervention'. He was dismissed, but quickly secured a good appointment.

³ Grey told the House that he had proposed a conference in London between the French, German, and Italian ambassadors and himself 'to endeavour to find a means of arranging the present difficulties'. The four powers – those not directly concerned in the aftermath of Sarajevo – were to ask Vienna, St Petersburg, and Belgrade 'to suspend all active military operations pending the result of the conference'. Grey had authorized the telegrams from Itchen Abbas, where he had a fishing lodge, at 2 p.m. on Sunday, 26 July.

107

Tu 28 July 14 [i]

Thank you darling so much for your letter from the rocks; it brought with it a breath of sea air & what is much better a vivid glimpse of yourself. I am glad you think I am a good correspondent. Writing to you & reading over your letters are the only refreshment in my life in these bad days. It is a blessed thing to have such food for the 'inward eye'. I don't believe I could get on without it.

What you say à propos of the War of cutting off one's head to get rid of a headache is very good. Winston on the other hand is all for this way of escape from Irish troubles, and when things looked rather better last night,[1] he exclaimed moodily that it looked after all as if we were in for a 'bloody peace'!![2]

Lady Frances Balfour recalls a saying of mine to her some years ago which I had forgotten, & wh. is rather appropriate to last week's proceedings: 'A Conference is either a bear-garden or a tea-party'. This one was of the tea-party kind – amiable & futile.

We had a Cabinet yesterday after I wrote to you: mainly to talk about war & peace. I am afraid that Grey's experiment of a Conference à quatre won't come off, as the Germans refuse to take a hand. The only real hope is that Austria & Russia may come to a deal between themselves.[3] But at this moment things don't look well, & Winston's spirits are probably rising.

As you would see, we had a real rough and tumble debate in the evening. Birrell was very ineffective, and I have never known B. Law more offensive or the Tory rank & file more ill-mannered & irritating. I had to make the best of an unpleasant situation, and got through fairly well. The state of things in Dublin is still far from agreeable, and I am tempted to regret that I didn't take the 'clean cut'[4] 6 months ago, and insist upon the booting out of Aberdeen, Dougherty, Ross, Chamberlain[5] & the whole crew. A weaker & more incompetent lot were never in charge of a leaky ship in stormy weather,[6] and poor old Birrell's occasional & fitful appearances at the wheel[7] do not greatly improve matters.

(Here comes Mr Creedy with W.O. papers).

He has gone, and in the meantime I have incidentally settled 2 matters wh. will show you the variety of my day's work – the removal of the Scottish Borderers from Ireland,[8] & the appointment of Sir John French as Inspector Genl of the Forces.[9]

[1] Lichnowsky told Grey on the afternoon of 27 July that the 'German government accept in principle mediation between Austria and Russia by the four powers, reserving, of course, their

right as an ally to help Austria if attacked'. France and Italy also accepted the conference proposal.

² Churchill was troubled by the fascination which war held for him. He wrote to his wife:

Admiralty
28 July midnight

My darling one and beautiful,

Everything tends towards catastrophe and collapse. I am interested, geared up and happy. Is it not horrible to be built like that? The preparations have a hideous fascination for me. I pray to God to forgive me for such fearful moods of levity. Yet I wd do my best for peace, and nothing would induce me wrongfully to strike the blow. . . . I wondered whether those stupid Kings and Emperors cd not assemble together and revivify kingship by saving the nations from hell but we all drift on in a kind of dull cataleptic trance. . . .

Churchill took the view, as he explained to Beaverbrook in 1925, that 'if war was inevitable this was by far the most favourable opportunity and the only one that would bring France, Russia, and ourselves together': *Companion Docs., 1922–1929*, p. 560. See also Letter 115; Margot Asquith, *Autobiography*, ii, end of ch. 7; Moran, *Churchill* (1966), p. 697 ('this delicious war'); Churchill, *History of the English Speaking Peoples*, iv (1958), 136 (attitude to war of Lee and Jackson).

³ On the evening of 27 July the Ambassador in Berlin telegraphed:

Secretary of State for Foreign Affairs says that conference you suggest would practically amount to a court of arbitration and could not, in his opinion, be called together except at the request of Austria and Russia. .

This reversal seems to have resulted from Bethmann-Hollweg's belief, which the Kaiser did not share, that Russia would not intervene to save Serbia if this were known to risk war with Germany.

⁴ Asquith uses the phrase ironically. Carson had used it to denote the unconditional exclusion of Ulster as a whole, as opposed to county option with a time-limit. See p. 83.

⁵ The Lord-Lieutenant; Under-Secretary; Chief Commissioner of Dublin Police; and Inspector-General of the Royal Irish Constabulary.

⁶ The Earl of Aberdeen and Sir John Ross of Bladensburg were 66. Sir James Dougherty, who was 69, had started his career as a presbyterian minister and had joined the 'crew' after 16 years as a professor at Magee College, Londonderry; Ross had been a Conservative M.P.; Hobhouse thought Sir Neville Chamberlain 'incompetent and disloyal' (Hobhouse, *Diaries*, p. 169: 1 May 1914). Ross resigned at once; Dougherty, and then Aberdeen, retired soon afterwards. Chamberlain and Ross owed their appointments to the Conservatives. Campbell-Bannerman had appointed Aberdeen. Dougherty had become Under-Secretary early in Asquith's premiership on 'Buggins's turn' principles.

⁷ According to Hobhouse (*Diaries*, p. 193), Birrell's stay at Chief Secretary's Lodge, Dublin, in Sept. 1914 was his first for two years. Hobhouse was wrong; but Birrell's appearances there were certainly 'occasional'.

⁸ It was a unit of this regiment which had fired into the crowd in Bachelor's Walk.

⁹ French was to hold his post for only a week before being appointed to command the B.E.F.

108

[28 July 1914 (ii)] H of C 5. 30 p.m.

I have just sent you a telegram to say that I seem to see my way clear to come at the end of the week.¹ I hope the prospect gives you half the joy it does me.

We had at lunch Admiral Burney – a good resourceful sailor who did so well at Scutari commanding the international force last year,[2] & Mrs Drew & her daughter,[3] with the usual tail.

I had a struggle with Illingworth over the Amending Bill, which at the instance of Redmond he implored me to postpone till Monday – in my judgment an idiotic proposal wh. wd have made everyone say that we were drifting on, not having yet made up our own minds, & waiting for our Irish 'Master' to make them up for us. So I was quite obdurate, & announced at question time that we would take it this next Thursday. I am sure this was right: don't you agree?

My room here has seen a curious medley of visitors since then. First, I had Redmond & Dillon with Ll. George & Birrell, to talk over things in Ireland & especially in Dublin. I pointed out how the debate last night had illustrated the need of overhauling Dublin Castle, & especially of replacing old Dougherty the Under Sec. who is over 70 by a younger man. We canvassed names, among wh. Sir M. Nathan found the most favour, & I am going to sound him to-night as to his willingness to go. If he does, there will be yearnings at many London tea tables for 'the sound of a purr that is still'.[4] Then came Lord Rothschild[5] to tell me that he had received an order from his Paris house to sell a vast quantity of Consols here for the French Gov[t] & Savings banks, which he had refused to do. It looks ominous. Finally, there appeared the Adjutant General to discuss what was to be done with the Scottish Borderers &c – a telegram meanwhile arriving that Austria had ordered war![6] You say in your dear letter to-day that there are few moments in our lives when you wouldn't like to exchange places with me. I wonder how you would like it, tho' I am sure you would do it well.

It is a slack evening of Supply at the House, so I am getting Violet to beat up one or two people to dine at home & play Bridge: perhaps the Herbert Gladstones may come – they arrived from S. Africa this morning. We have a Cabinet to-morrow. There – I must stop now, having given you more than enough to read at one stretch. Bless you – own beloved.

[1] Asquith had an engagement in Chester to inspect the local Red Cross Society detachments at the end of their training week. He was also to see the Cheshire Territorial Brigade complete an anti-invasion exercise. He planned, after staying the night with the G.O.C. Western Command, to go on to Penrhos.

[2] In April 1913 Montenegro seized Scutari (now Shkodër) despite a decision by the Ambassadors' Conference in London that it should go to Albania. The Conference agreed on a naval demonstration against Montenegro and this was successful. The King of Montenegro gave way (after making large sums on the Stock Exchange by stirring up rumours of war).

[3] Mrs Dorothy Parish, a granddaughter of W. E. Gladstone.

[4] Chairman of the Board of Inland Revenue; aged 52. He accepted the Under-Secretaryship, but returned to England after the 1916 Easter rising in Dublin, over which he was much criticized.

[5] Lord Rothschild no doubt objected to increasing the outflow of funds from London; but he may also have had political reasons for refusing to help in France's financial preparations for

war. He was a strong opponent of British action against Germany. On 31 July he tried to influence the financial editor of *The Times* against intervention, much to the latter's fury: H. Wickham Steed, *Through Thirty Years* (1924), ii. 8–9. The pogroms had made him particularly hostile to association with Russia.

⁶ The Austrian declaration of war against Serbia – the first issued by a great power against another European country since 1870 – had reached Belgrade a few hours earlier. The Austrian Foreign Minister, Berchtold, had been prodded into action by warnings from Berlin that Grey's conference proposal could not be resisted for much longer: Austria must produce a *fait accompli*. It was generally assumed that Austrian forces would move quickly on Belgrade, and halt there while an effort was made, in Grey's words, 'to bring some mediation into existence'. The Austrian General Staff would not attempt this swift movement. They were not willing to move on Belgrade until their mobilization was complete on 12 Aug. They did not know that the Serbs meant to leave the city undefended. By his declaration of war Berchtold thus succeeded in enhancing, not his own bargaining position, but the risk of a general conflagration.

109

Wed 29 July 14

Thank you so much for this morning's letter: you have been *most* good in being so regular, & you don't know what it means to me. I was more touched than I can say by the little piece of white heather & what you wrote about it. I know you thought it wd. just come in time for my speech on the Amending Bill. I shall keep it for that to-morrow & long afterwards. Like you I count the hours till Saturday, and picture myself joining you & the dogs & the penguin on the rocks, and telling you all that I have left unsaid since we parted.

The Amending Bill & the whole Irish business are of course put into the shade by the coming war – 'coming' for it seems now as if nothing but a miracle cd. avert it. After dinner & a little Bridge last night (we had the Bencks & Winston & Eddie Marsh & Bluey) I went across to E. Grey & sat with him & Haldane till 1 a.m. talking over the situation, and trying to discover bridges & outlets. It is one of the ironies of the case that we being the only Power who has made so much as a constructive suggestion in the direction of peace, are blamed by both Germany & Russia for causing the outbreak of war. Germany says: 'if you say you will be neutral, France & Russia wouldn't dare to fight'; and Russia says: 'if you boldly declare that you will side with us, Germany & Austria will at once draw in their horns'. Neither of course is true.[1] We have just had a long Cabinet (it is now lunch time) on the subject. On the whole it was a very satisfactory discussion: the acute point will arise if & when Germany proposes to invade France by way of Belgium – her shortest route – we having with other Powers guaranteed the neutrality of Belgian territory. The main conclusion to which we came was to issue this afternoon what is called in official language the 'warning telegram' – which requires the Army & Navy & all other departments to put themselves at once in a state of readiness for the 'precautionary period' which precedes any possible outbreak of hostilities.[2] Of course we want to keep out of it, but the worst thing we could do would be to announce to the world at the present moment that in *no circumstances* would we intervene.[3]

John Morley & the Harcourts & Mme de Greffulhe[4] came to lunch. Violet had a little operation on her cheek this morning – performed by Cheyne with the assistance of Malcolm Morris, Parkie, & others. It was of course in itself a small affair, but they seem to think that she has some microbe in her blood, of which after the modern fashion they are going to make 'cultures', with the object of anti-toxin injections afterwards. It is a great nuisance, but it is high time that she expelled the virus from her constitution.

I have been reading over again your account of your daily life and begin to feel almost guilty at the thought that I shall introduce an alien element into such a perfect Arcadia. But I long more than any words can say to see & be near you again. It seems a whole century since our last broken half-hour on Thursday, but I shall never forget a week ago to-night.

I am just off to the War Office to see that the 'Warning' is in full force, & to take part in an Army Council.

6 p.m. I have just finished an Army Council – concerned entirely with arrangements during the 'precautionary period'.[5] Rather interesting because it enables one to realise what are the first steps in an actual war.

You will think of me to-morrow darling won't you? and I shall have your white heather very near my heart. Post just going – tho' I have still lots to say to you. *All my love always.*

[1] This characteristically confident judgement was almost certainly correct. Germany decided on war without counting on British neutrality, France and Russia without the assurance of British support. Bethmann wanted a British declaration of neutrality because he believed mistakenly that it might deter France and Russia. Once he knew that it would not, he was as ready as the German General Staff for British intervention. The German ultimatum to Belgium, which carried a high risk of British intervention, had been drafted on 26 July. See A. J. P. Taylor, *The Struggle for Mastery in Europe, 1848–1918* (1954), pp. 525–6.

[2] Naval precautions had begun three days earlier. On the afternoon of Sunday 26 July the First Sea Lord (Prince Louis of Battenberg) had signalled to Portland to prevent the dispersal of the Home Fleets which had been due to start at 7 a.m., 27 June, when the test mobilization ended (Letter 98, n. 5). On 28 July Asquith, without consulting the cabinet, had authorized the move of the First Fleet to Scapa Flow. This was carried out on 29–30 July, the fleet passing through the Straits of Dover in darkness, with lights extinguished. 'I persuaded Mr. Asquith', Churchill told Neville Chamberlain in Mar. 1939, 'to let me send the Fleet to the North Sea . . . *before* the diplomatic situation had become hopeless.' For the final mobilization of the Fleet see below, Letter 112, n. 3.

[3] The Government had a good press during this week. See, for instance, *Daily Mail*, 1 Aug.: 'The Prime Minister's answers and statements in Parliament throughout this grave crisis have been admirable.' Press criticisms tended to cancel each other out. The Liberal *Nation* would have welcomed a non-intervention announcement. Its editor (H. W. Massingham) referred (1 Aug.) to the Government's 'needless, dangerous, and ill-advised' naval precautions. The *Daily Express*, by contrast, wanted the Government to announce (31 July)

that 'an invasion of Belgium or of France would mean the instant blockade of the North Sea ports and the closing of the Baltic'.

⁴ She is supposed to have been one of Proust's 'models' for the Duchesse de Guermantes. There were, however, according to Proust's account to Lucien Daudet, so many keys to each door that in reality there was no key.

⁵ The 'precautionary period' did not start smoothly although the War Book had been recently revised. The Prime Minister's Private Secretary rang Hankey, who was at lunch at the United Services Club, to say that the precautionary measures were to be taken, 'but that no one had the slightest idea how to start the ball rolling'. Hankey answered that each minister should tell his department to put its section of the instructions in the War Book into effect. One minister told his officials that the 'precautionary period' started 'next Monday'; he then left London. Another was so engrossed in a forthcoming parliamentary speech that he told his department nothing until late in the evening. An instruction to the War Office to send confirmatory information to all departments had, however, been inserted in the latest edition of the War Book. With some justice Hankey thought that these episodes established the need for a cabinet secretariat: *The Supreme Command*, i. 154–8.

Ulster V: The Amending Bill Postponed (Letter 110)

WHEN war threatened, both sides in Ireland became anxious to prove their patriotism. Redmond's Nationalists were apt to be reminded that they had cheered a British defeat in the Boer War. Carson's followers were on record as preferring the Kaiser's rule to that of Dublin.¹ An offer to postpone the Home Rule question would be 'most patriotic', Craig wrote to Carson on 30 July; and 'it may greatly disconcert . . . the Nationalists. They would find it extremely difficult to follow on with a similar offer from their side; and surely the country would . . . store up that much to our credit when the issue is finally fought out.'²

There were no obvious drawbacks to the scheme. The Ulster Volunteers were well enough disciplined to wait; and every day's delay in the enactment of the Government's Home Rule programme seemed to the Ulstermen's advantage. Bonar Law and Carson took the same line as Craig and it was agreed, as Asquith describes in the next letter, to postpone the Amending Bill (for which see pp. 69 and 83–4).

Patriotism and the advantage of the Conservative party were not easily combined, however, where an antagonist of Redmond's calibre was concerned. He had not only himself wanted the Amending Bill postponed (Letter 108); but, as Letter 110 shows, he was quick to see a chance of having the Home Rule measure put at once on to the statute-book. Its operation would, of course, be suspended until the party battle was resumed; but in the meanwhile it would be the law, and the risk of a last-minute hitch in enacting it would have been eliminated.

Asquith's undertakings at the end of July became the subject of controversy. He said in the House that the second reading of the Amending Bill was being postponed by agreement 'in the hope that . . . the patriotism of all parties will contribute . . . , if not to avert, at least to circumscribe, the calamities which threaten the world. In the meantime the business which we shall take will be confined to necessary matters and will not be . . . controversial.'[3] He assented to the publication of a resolution by Carson's followers in Ulster in which they agreed to 'the adjournment of the debate on the Amending Bill until such date as the Government and the leaders of the Opposition may . . . determine'. Finally, he told Bonar Law and Carson at Pembroke Lodge, according to their account, that 'until we again resumed discussion of the Amending Bill no controversial legislation should be taken, and . . . that by the adjournment no party to the controversy would be placed in a worse position'.[4]

These promises were made in the light of the Prime Minister's earlier expression of hope that the Home Rule and Amending Bills would 'become law practically at the same time'. They were open to more than one interpretation. The Home Rule Bill had left the Commons altogether, having passed through all the stages prescribed in the Parliament Act; it awaited the Speaker's Certificate and the Royal Assent. To Redmond and the Government 'taking controversial legislation' referred to putting the Home Rule Act into effect in the absence of agreement between the parties, whereas to the Opposition putting that measure on the statute-book, even if its operation were suspended, would be intensely controversial. The political gains on 30 July went to Redmond; and four days later he made a brave and astute move to consolidate them (Letter 114).

[1] See p. 38, n. 4.
[2] I. Colvin, *Carson*, ii (1934), 422.
[3] *Parl. Deb.* lxv. 1601–2.
[4] Ibid., lxvi. 896–7.

110

Th. 30 July 14

Thank you so much darling for your dear letter. I believe with a little practice you could 'take on the job' & do it as well as anyone. But fate & nature have ordained that you should not have the chance! However you know more than anyone about how it is done, and what are the shifting & baffling phases which the would-be doer has to encounter.

We had another turn of the Kaleidoscope to-day. I was sitting in the Cabinet room with a map of Ulster, & a lot of statistics about populations & religions, and some choice extracts from Hansard (with occasional glances at this morning's letter from Penrhos), endeavouring to get into something like shape my speech on the Amending Bill, when a telephone message came from (of all people in the world) Bonar Law, to ask me to come & see him & Carson at his Kensington abode – Pembroke Lodge. He had sent his motor, which I boarded, and in due time arrived at my destination: a rather suburban looking detached villa in a Bayswater street, with a small garden, and furnished & decorated itself after the familiar fashion of Glasgow or Bradford or Altrincham.[1] It was quite an adventure, for I might easily have been kidnapped by a section of Ulster Volunteers.

I found the two gentlemen there, & B Law proceeded to propose in the interest of the international situation, that we should postpone for the time being the 2nd reading of the Amending Bill. He thought that to advertise our domestic dissensions at this moment wd. weaken our influence in the world for peace &c.[2] Carson said that at first he had thought it impossible to agree, as it wd. strain still further the well-known & much tried 'tension' of his Ulstermen, but that now he had come to see that it was a patriotic duty &c. I of course welcomed their attitude, but said I wd. consult some colleagues before giving a definite answer. Carson told me a curious thing – which I am loth to believe: that if there was a mobilisation of the Army a number of old officers & reservists among his volunteers would refuse to join the colours & stay to defend Ulster![3] I pointed out that there were at least as many of the same class among the National Volunteers.[4]

When I got back I saw Ll. George & Grey, & we agreed that it was right to close with the offer. Redmond, whom I saw afterwards, thought it an excellent chance of putting off the Amending Bill, & for the first time in my experience of him made a really useful suggestion: namely, that if we wd. put off the Amending Bill till next session, he would agree that the operation of the Home Rule Bill (to be put of course on the Statute book now) should be suspended until the Amending Bill became law. He said that under those conditions he could make much larger concessions than he can now.

E. Grey came to lunch: also Ld. Knollys, the H. Gladstones, Ettie, & Waldorf Astor.[5] The European situation is at least one degree worse than it was yesterday, and has not been improved by a rather shameless attempt on the part of Germany to buy our neutrality during the war by promises that she will not annexe French territory (except Colonies) or Holland & Belgium.[6] There is something very crude & almost childlike about German diplomacy. Meanwhile the French are beginning to press in the opposite sense,[7] as the Russians have been doing for some time. The City, wh. is in a terrible state of depression and paralysis, is for the time being all against English intervention.[8] I think the prospect very black to-day.

We are going to have another Cabinet at 11 to-morrow morning. It will depend a good deal on the state of things then whether I can fulfil my

Chester engagement[9] (about wh., except as a means to an end, I am not very keen). But unless Fate is very unkind I shall all the same hope to come to you Saturday, and see you – perhaps in your new striped dress, not the 'yellow peril' – You say you wd. be 'really disappointed' if I didn't come. I wish I cd. tell you how *I* should feel! All my dearest love beloved.

[1] Pembroke Lodge, Bonar Law's home from 1909 to Dec. 1916, is off Edwardes Square – in Kensington, not Bayswater.

[2] 'I agreed', Asquith reported to Stamfordham, 'and read to them the latest telegrams from Berlin which, in my judgement, assume that the German government are calculating upon internal weaknesses to affect our foreign policy': R A GV K 2553 (6) 55. It was thought in Berlin, the Belgian Ambassador had reported to his Government on 26 July, that Britain was 'paralysed by internal dissensions and her Irish quarrels': J. B. Scott (ed.), *Diplomatic Documents . . . Outbreak of . . . War* (Carnegie, 2 vols., 1916), i. 429. The most important of the telegrams which Asquith read was the one reporting the German attempt to 'buy Britain's neutrality': see n. 6 below. Asquith no doubt inferred that the German Chancellor would scarcely have made this overture had he believed Britain to be in a condition to intervene in the European crisis. Carson described the impression which this telegram had made on him when he spoke to the Conservatives at the Carlton Club on 14 Sept.

[3] On 30 or 31 July Carson, advised by Craig, telegraphed to HQ Ulster Volunteers: 'All officers, N.C.O.s, and men who are enrolled in the Ulster Volunteer Force, and who are liable to be called out by His Majesty for service in the present crisis, are requested to answer immediately to His Majesty's call.' According to *The Times* of 1 Aug. many members of Carson's force were offering to volunteer for war service. One officer was reported to have added, when making this offer: 'I will take every man of my company with me.'

[4] An apposite reply. On 31 July Colonel Moore, 'Inspector-General' of the National Volunteers, wrote to Redmond: 'If there is any hesitation . . . in getting the King to sign the Home Rule Bill immediately, the Irish Reservists ought to be told not to join.' Moore estimated that there were 25,000 of them.

[5] Son of the owner of the *Pall Mall Gazette* and *Observer*; but he probably owed his invitation to Margot's affection for his wife, Nancy. Margot did not behave to the pair as if she needed to conciliate a press magnate: see C. Sykes, *Nancy* (1972), pp. 118–23 and 164–5. Astor was a Conservative M.P., but belonged to the most moderate section of the party.

[6] A promise not to annex Belgian territory was far from one to respect Belgian neutrality. Asquith dissected 'this infamous proposal' in his speech on 6 Aug.; it aroused Grey to 'a white heat of passion' never before seen in him: K. Robbins, *Grey* (1971), p. 294. The British Government, he replied that afternoon, would neither desert France nor 'bargain away whatever interest we have as regards the neutrality of Belgium'. This reply was given to the German Chancellor on the morning of 31 July.

[7] See *Brit. Docs. War*, xi. 200–1 (Nos. 318 and 319): conversations between (a) President Poincaré and the British Ambassador, (b) Grey and Cambon. The latter referred to the obligation specified in the letters of Nov. 1912 (p. 112) to 'consult' on possible measures to be taken 'in common'.

[8] Sir Eyre Crow (Assistant Under-Secretary, Foreign Office) wrote (31 July): 'The panic in the City has been largely influenced by the deliberate acts of German financial houses, who are in at least as close touch with the German as with the British government, and who are notoriously in daily communication with the German Embassy.' It was also suggested later that the German houses knew, from 23 July or earlier, that war was coming and that they would be well advised in their own interests to sell some of their foreign holdings (article by Morgenthau in *Land and Water*, 13 June 1918; A. J. P. Taylor, *Beaverbrook* (1972), p. 83). While there may be truth in these explanations the alarm in the City is wholly explicable without them. The Berlin Bourse had been just as panic-stricken during the 1911 Agadir crisis; and this would have repeated itself in 1914 but for the precautions of the German

authorities (*Brit. Docs. War*, xi. 205–7: Sir F. Oppenheimer). The London Stock Exchange was the last important European bourse to remain open. It was closed at 10 a.m. on 31 July.
⁹ See Letter 108, n. 1.

111

31 July 1914

This has been a most disappointing·day. You sent me a very nice letter (altho' you forgot for once to send me your usual & much treasured message!). Things in the early morning looked a little better in the East, as we were told that Austria & Russia had begun 'talking' again. We had a Cabinet at 11, and I soon saw that Chester would be impossible to-day. This I didn't much mind if to-morrow & Sunday could be saved out of the wreckage. We had a very interesting discussion – especially about the neutrality of Belgium, and the point upon which everything will ultimately turn: are we going to go in or to stand aside? Of course, everybody longs to stand aside, but I need not say that France thro' Cambon is pressing strongly for a reassuring declaration. E. Grey had an interview with him this afternoon wh. he told me was rather painful. He had of course to tell Cambon (for we are under no obligation) that we could give no pledges, and that our action must depend upon the course of events – including the Belgian question, and the direction of public opinion here.[1]

Kitchener whom I met at lunch at Winston's is very strong that if we don't back up France when she is in real danger, we shall never be regarded or exercise real power again.[2] But the general opinion at present – particularly strong in the City – is to keep out at almost all costs.[3] They have been having a black day there, and the Governor of the Bank is now waiting here to get our consent to the suspension of gold payments! – a thing that has not happened for nearly 100 years.[4] I had an interview with the King in the afternoon: he had just received a most depressing telegram from 'William' deploring the perfidy of 'Nikky' in mobilising,[5] while the 'talking' was still going on. Things look almost as bad as can be, & I fear much about to-morrow, to which I have looked forward day by day as the one oasis in my desert pilgrimage. I still hope: but 'our hope is too much like despair'; I will wire in the morning. If I come, it will be by train wh. gets to Holyhead 6.45 p.m. If I can't, do telegraph & write to me most beloved, and give me your love, & tell me your plans. I *must* see you. *All my dearest love.*

[1] Grey also told Cambon that 'our standing aside might be the only means of preventing a complete collapse of European credit'.
[2] Grey was to use this argument in the Commons on 3 Aug. 'If we stood aside', he said, 'our moral position would be such as to have lost us all respect.' Though Kitchener's view of French

military strength seems to have fluctuated, he doubted whether France could repel a German invasion without British help. 'Germany', he predicted in Sept. 1911, could 'walk through the French army like partridges.' He praised the endurance of French troops, but thought that German organization and generalship outweighed this: Lloyd George, *War Memoirs*, pp. 38, 451; J. S. Sandars to Balfour [*c*.17 Sept. 1911], B L Add. MSS 49767, ff. 182–3; *Churchill: Companion Docs., 1901–1914*, p. 1125.

³ See Letter 110, n. 8. Asquith told Margot at this time that the City's leaders were 'the greatest ninnies . . . all in a state of funk, like old women chattering over tea cups in a cathedral town'.

⁴ Bank rate was raised to 8 per cent on 31 July, and to 10 per cent on 1 Aug. It was thus moved in two days from a 'normal' 4 per cent to the highest rate known since the financial panic of 1866. Gold payments for notes had been suspended by the Bank of England between Feb. 1797 and 1 May 1821.

⁵ The Kaiser and the Tsarina Alexandra, wife of Nicholas II, were first cousins of George V. The Russian Foreign Minister, Sazonov, had wanted a partial mobilization directed against Austria-Hungary; but the Russian generals objected that putting this into effect would slow down the further moves which might be needed against Germany. After the question had been debated before the Tsar throughout 29 July it was decided that general mobilization should begin the next day. This did not commit Russia to war; but it gave the German General Staff a reason, or at least an excuse, to demand counter-measures, since they could not afford to be caught unprepared on their eastern front. On 31 July *Kriegesgefahr* (danger of war) was declared in Germany, an ultimatum being sent to St Petersburg requiring a promise of demobilization within 12 hours. On 1 Aug. as soon as the ultimatum expired, Germany declared war on Russia and mobilized.

112

Sat 1 Aug 14

I can honestly say that I have never had a more bitter disappointment. All these days – ever since Thursday in last week – full of incident & for the most part anxious & worrying – I have been sustained by the thought that when to-day came I should once more see your darling face, & be with you, and share everything and get from you what I value most, & what is to me the best of all things in the world – your counsel & your understanding & your sympathy and your love. All that has been shattered by a truly devastating succession of the blows of fortune. I should be desolate, if it were not for your sweetest of all letters this morning – the best, or nearly, if not quite, the best, that you have ever sent me – which gives me a new fund of courage & hope. My darling – can I ever thank you enough? Without you, I tremble to think what wd. have happened to me.

After I wrote yesterday, I came back here & grappled with Ll. George & the Bank directors. We dined *en petit comité* – the Assyrian & a few others, reinforced later by Winston & E. Grey. When most of them had left Tyrrell arrived with a long message from Berlin, to the effect that the German Emperor's efforts for peace had been suddenly arrested & frustrated by the Czar's decree for a complete Russian mobilisation.¹ We all set to work –

Tyrrell, Bongie, Drummond & myself – to draft a direct personal appeal from the King to the Czar, & when we had settled it I called a taxi & in company with Tyrrell drove to Buckingham Palace at about 1.30 a.m. The poor King was hauled out of his bed, & one of my strangest experiences (& as you know I have had a good lot) was sitting with him – he in a brown dressing gown over his night shirt & with copious signs of having been aroused from his first 'beauty sleep' – while I read the message & the proposed answer. All we did was to suggest that it should be made more personal & direct – by the insertion of the words 'My dear Nicky' – and the addition at the end of the signature 'Georgie'![2] I got home again about 2 a.m. and tossed about for a little on my couch – (as the novelists say) – but really I didn't sleep badly, and in that betwixt & between of sleeping & waking, thank God the vision of you kept floating about me and brought me rest & peace.

You see I can't expel you, if I would – and wouldn't if I could.

There was really no fresh news this morning. We had a Cabinet wh. lasted from 11 to ½ past 1. It is no exaggeration to say that Winston occupied at least half of the time.[3] We came, every now & again, near to the parting of the ways: Morley & I think the Impeccable are on what may be called the *Manchester Guardian* tack[4] – that we shd. declare now & at once that *in no circumstances* will we take a hand. This no doubt is the view for the moment of the bulk of the party. Ll. George – all for peace – is more sensible & statesmanlike, for keeping the position still open. Grey, of course, declares that if an out & out & uncompromising policy of non-intervention at all costs is adopted, he will go. Winston very bellicose & demanding immediate mobilisation. Haldane diffuse (how clever of you to retrieve the second 'f') and nebulous. The main controversy pivots upon Belgium & its neutrality. We parted in a fairly amicable mood, & are to sit again at 11 to-morrow (Sunday) an almost unprecedented event.

I am still *not quite* hopeless about peace, tho' far from hopeful. But if it comes to war I feel sure (this is entirely between you & me) that we shall have *some* split in the Cabinet. Of course, if Grey went I should go, & the whole thing would break up. On the other hand, we may have to contemplate with such equanimity as we can command the loss of Morley, and possibly (tho' I don't think it) of the Impeccable.

I am writing this in the midst of a conversation with Haldane & Crewe about the 'Moratorium'![5] The number of new questions that come forward every hour is almost inconceivable. I will write again to-night & to-morrow, my beloved. Violet has only sent part of her bags to Lulworth. The others may follow on Monday or Tues. I bless and love you with all my heart.

---

[1] *Brit. Docs. War*, xi. 229–30.
[2] *Brit. Docs. War*, xi. 235. It was published on 5 Aug.

H. H. Asquith and Edwin Montagu *en route* for Sicily, January 1912

H. H. and Margot Asquith at Penrhos, July 1912 (Maurice Bonham Carter behind)

Hurstly, near Lymington: lent to the Asquiths, Spring 1912

The Wharf, Sutton Courtney

3 The cabinet refused Churchill permission to complete the naval mobilization. Late that evening, however, having learned that Germany had declared war on Russia, he received from Asquith the assent refused earlier in the day.

4 The *Daily Chronicle* and *Daily News*, the leading Liberal dailies in London, were as vehement for non-intervention as the *Manchester Guardian*; but, unlike the *M.G.*, they showed some caution on questions such as Belgian neutrality, and did not call for an immediate pledge of non-intervention. See *Daily News*, 31 July, 2b; 1 Aug., 2b; *Daily Chronicle*, 1 Aug., 4c. Speaking at Manchester on 25 July Simon had called for a 'resolve that . . . the part which this country plays shall from beginning to end be the part of a mediator'. As for Austria's punishment of the Serbs, he thought that 'the occupation of Belgrade should suffice'.

5 On 2 Aug. it was announced that payments on bills of exchange now falling due could be postponed for one month.

The Decision for War

WHEN Grey looked back, some months later, on the war crisis, he ridiculed 'the idea that one individual . . . in the Foreign Office could pledge a great democracy . . . , in advance, either to take part in a great war or to abstain'.[1] 'One of his strongest feelings' had been, he said, 'that he himself had no power to decide policy and was only the mouthpiece of England.'[2] During the first week after the Austrian ultimatum there was no decisive movement of British opinion. When Cambon was warned on 31 July (Letter 111) that decisions in London would 'depend on the course of events – including the Belgian question, and the direction of public opinion here', Asquith may have overestimated the degree to which that opinion was still non-interventionist. He had been hearing about the war panic in the City; and he could not neglect the views of the leading Liberal editors and back-benchers, however much they irritated him.

None the less, what Asquith told Venetia on 31 July was broadly true. On that Friday there was no overwhelming movement for intervention; even Conservative opinion was not uniformly interventionist. On 29 July, or thereabouts, Bonar Law had told Grey that he doubted whether his party 'would be unanimous or overwhelmingly in favour of war, unless Belgian neutrality were invaded (*sic*); in that event, he said, it would be unanimous'.[3] The Conservative newspapers, including the Northcliffe press, had urged intervention from an early stage; but, with the prospect of war terrifying the Conservatives in the City, Bonar Law's assessment of opinion in the parliamentary party would still have been reasonably accurate on 31 July. Many Liberal back-benchers refused even to envisage the possibility that the German army might march through Belgium. 'Suppose Germany violates the neutrality of Belgium?' Grey asked a 'very active Liberal M.P.'. 'She won't do it,' the non-interventionist replied.[4]

Two days later the shift of opinion towards intervention was unmistakable. Now that the threat to France had developed, Asquith's fourth principle loomed large for the governing class: it was 'against British interests that France shld. be wiped out as a Great Power' (Letter 113). Among Conservatives John Bright's 'foul idol', the balance of power, was worshipped urgently. But most of the pro-French feeling was less calculating than this. The tenth anniversary of the Anglo-French Entente had just been celebrated. In 1914 most British people were not sophisticated, nor by modern standards well informed. They moved in a world of simple principles. One of these was to stand by friends when they were in trouble. Approve of the French or not, France ranked as Britain's friend. By 2 August that had begun to tell; and at its morning meeting the cabinet authorized Grey to assure Cambon that the British 'fleet would not allow the German fleet to make the Channel the base of hostile operations' (Letter 113). Asquith and Grey had secured agreement to this pledge from all their colleagues except Burns because it meant one thing to the interventionists, and another to the 'peace party'. It was a move towards supporting the French; but it had warlike implications only in so far as the Germans intended to use their fleet against the northern coast of France. The intervention towards which it edged Britain was a limited naval affair. 'The naval war will be cheap,' Churchill told Lloyd George in a note passed during cabinet.[5]

The cabinet was not ready to send the expeditionary force to France. Henry Wilson himself had abandoned the theory which he had propounded in 1911 that a British Expeditionary Force consisting of six divisions of infantry and one of cavalry might tip the balance of numbers between France and Germany.[6] The Liberals who were doubtful on that Sunday* morning about intervening in the war were insistent against hurrying the expeditionary force across the Channel. The *Westminster Gazette*, which was the only Liberal paper not to take an entirely non-interventionist line, pronounced on 3 August: 'We cannot throw this army into the seething cauldron of the European struggle.'

This notion of a solely 'naval war' was made easier by the strategic views of a powerful 'navalist' group, who had never accepted the idea of a British army extending the French left wing.[7] They wanted the expeditionary force used for amphibious operations. They had exploited the new menace of the torpedo to battle fleets to revive invasion fears. The resulting invasion inquiry – the third in eleven years – confirmed that it might be necessary to hold back two of the six divisions for home defence until some of the Territorial units had been trained up to standard. Nearly half of the men available for the expeditionary force would be reservists; and if the whole

* 2 Aug.

force was to be sent abroad at the start of a war, Britain would have virtually no trained troops left available for other overseas operations, the obligations of Haldane's Territorials being confined to home service. There was some resistance at a more popular level to the dispatch of the expeditionary force. A series of 'best sellers' had depicted 'the next war' in terms of the invasion of Britain.[8] The movement for conscription had been directed entirely towards the defence of Britain itself. Northcliffe, who had clamoured for compulsory service for home defence, opposed sending a single British soldier to the Continent.[9] The second of Asquith's six principles in his Letter 113 would have read, in a more candid version, that he believed the dispatch of the B.E.F. to France to be strategically pointless, and knew it to be politically unacceptable.

A solely 'naval war' had no sooner been envisaged than events made it impossible. Public attention during Sunday* was still fixed on France; but by that afternoon the members of the cabinet had another preoccupation: they waited, as Asquith wrote in Letter 113, to see whether the German army would cross into Belgium. When a message reached the Foreign Office at 1.25 p.m. that the Belgian Foreign Minister had 'no reason whatever to suspect Germany of an intention to violate neutrality', an official minuted:

It is impossible for the German troops to get out of Luxemburg without crossing Belgian territory except through a narrow bottleneck into France.

The cabinet, reassembled at 6.30 p.m., could postpone a statement of their position on Belgian neutrality no longer: Grey's speech in the Commons was due the next day. The notion that the Belgians would merely line the route of the German invaders had faded. On 1 August the Brussels Government had stated without reservations that Belgium would 'defend its neutrality'.[10] Nor was it possible still to think of the British as the only guarantors to whom Belgium would appeal. When Grey had asked for an engagement to respect Belgian neutrality he had been given it from Paris, but had received no answer from Berlin. He was now authorized to tell the Commons 'as regards Belgium', as Crewe reported to the King, 'that a substantial violation of the neutrality of that country would . . . compel us to take action'.[11] Before the King read the report the German ultimatum had been delivered in Brussels.

The pressure to enter the war was increasing with every hour. The anti-war demonstration in Trafalgar Square on Sunday afternoon 'proved', in J. A. Spender's words, 'but a feeble effort'. The story was no different in the provinces. Lloyd George dined that evening with Masterman and Simon. The latter was drafting his resignation letter. Masterman, begging

---

* 2 Aug.

him not to send it, said, 'You ought to think of public opinion.'[12] By that evening resignation might be all very well for a septuagenarian such as Morley, or for Burns, who was the cabinet's oddity: it was not a wise move for the rising and ambitious Simon. The only effect of splitting the cabinet by holding out against intervention would be to give the Tories, with all their warlike propensities, at least a share of power.

On the following day, Monday 3 August, the imminent prospect of a German invasion of Belgium finally overwhelmed the 'peace party'. When Bonar Law and Lansdowne saw Asquith that morning they 'laid great stress on Belgian neutrality', whereas in their letter of the previous day they had not even mentioned Belgium (Letters 113, 114). The news which arrived from Brussels on 3 August was incomplete and unreliable. Delivery of the German ultimatum was not announced in the British morning papers until Tuesday, 4 August. The *Daily Telegraph* carried a story on 3 August that German motor-cycle detachments had been sighted in eastern Belgium and an Exchange Company telegram reported German troops 'in operation to the north of Liège'. Both reports were of doubtful authenticity,[13] although Asquith seems to have accepted at least one of them (Letter 114). The German army did not cross the frontier in any force until the morning of 4 August. These uncertainties were of no consequence. The German decision to invade Belgium was already irreversible. The trainloads of German troops were moving, with their supplies, to their battle positions in the West. The international crime which was to put an end to all ideas of limiting the British war effort, was patently under way. As Asquith told Venetia (Letter 115), the German invasion of Belgium 'simplified matters'.

*   *   *

The 'crassness' of the ultimatum to Belgium originated, not in sheer stupidity as Asquith thought (Letter 114), but in a gamble by the German General Staff. The Kaiser and the Chancellor had neither the prestige nor the grip on events needed to veto a measure on which the General Staff's strategy depended. The Kaiser's last-minute attempt to turn the German armies eastwards was ineffective; the Chancellor wanted British neutrality only as long as he hoped to use it to intimidate the French.[14] The strategy precluded any secret agreement or understanding with the Belgian Government; it depended on an advance in force through central Belgium. As will be related (p. 155), a solution had been found for the problem of a rapid movement north and west of the Sambre-Meuse line. The General Staff were convinced that this great wheel through central Belgium would enable them to knock France out of the war in forty days, and then turn on the Russians in overwhelming strength. In order to pursue this strategy they were willing to risk Belgian resistance and British intervention.

In Berlin, and still more perhaps in Vienna, some hope was cherished during July 1914 that the Irish troubles would dissuade Britain from intervening on the Continent; but this was not essential to the calculation.[15] British intervention would be dangerous only in a long war. If the strategy worked the war would be very short. Should the little British Expeditionary Force arrive on the battlefield it would share the fate of the French army. This final version of the Schlieffen Plan was one of the wildest military schemes ever undertaken. In 1914 the attacking armies, once past their railheads, moved only at the speed of a marching man; and all the available evidence suggested that once battle was joined, the advantage would lie, not with them, but with the defence. Yet this reckless plan almost succeeded.

[1] Memo., Apr. 1915: G. M. Trevelyan, *Grey* (1937), p. 250.

[2] Hazlehurst, op. cit., p. 52.

[3] Grey, *Twenty-Five Years*, i. 337.   [4] Ibid., i. 338.

[5] Churchill: *Companion Docs.*, *1901–1914*, p. 1997. See also Hankey, *Supreme Command*, i. 173; Hazlehurst, op. cit., p. 82 n. 2. (Nicolson, Apr. 1914); *Brit. Docs. War*, xi. 253, 275; C. E. Callwell, *Sir Henry Wilson* (1927), i. 154; *Parl. Deb.* lxv. 1824 (Grey).

[6] Hazlehurst, op. cit., p. 319 n. (Wilson's note, 17 Oct. 1912).

[7] See Hobhouse, *Diaries*, p. 179 (McKenna). Hankey seems to have taken a 'navalist' view until the end of July 1914.

[8] I. F. Clarke, *Voices Prophesying War* (1966), chs. 2, 3 and 4. See also P. G. Wodehouse, *The Swoop, or How Clarence Saved England: a Tale of the Great Invasion* (1909).

[9] Tom Clarke, *My Northcliffe Diary* (1931), pp. 65–7.

[10] Grey, op. cit., ii. 9. Mobilization had been ordered in Belgium on 31 July.

[11] Spender and Asquith, ii. 82. Crewe had in mind Gladstone's position in 1870. He and his colleagues may have regarded a march through the Belgian Ardennes as falling short of a 'substantial violation': see A. J. P. Taylor, *Politics in Wartime* (1964), pp. 87–8.

[12] G. A. Riddell, *War Diary* (1933), pp. 3–5. Ramsay MacDonald was also present and told the same story to Hankey in 1931: *Supreme Command*, i. 161. See also *Parl. Deb.*, lxv. 1841 (Ponsonby).

[13] See *The Times*, 1 June 1915, 6c, for an early discussion of this.

[14] For Asquith's belief that uncertainty about British intervention might act as a restraint in Berlin see G. K. A. Bell, *Randall Davidson* (3rd. edn., 1952), pp. 733–5. The Archbishop saw the Premier on 31 July, and at once made a record of the conversation. See also Letter 109, n. 1.

[15] See D. C. Watt, *European Studies Review* iii (1971). 238–9. Germany had received encouragement from both sides in Ireland: see p. 38 n. 4; *National Review*, lxii. 209, 377; *Sinn Fein*, 20 June 1914. Contemporary British and American statements about the effect of this should be received with reserve. See, for instance, Theodore Roosevelt to G. W. Russell, 6 Aug. 1917, 'Carson, Smith and Company, and the English Tories who backed them, are more responsible for this war than any other . . . men in the world except the German General Staff:' E. E. Morison (ed.), *Letters of Theodore Roosevelt*, viii (1954). 1220–1.

113

Sunday 2 Aug 1914

After all there was not as I thought & hoped a Sunday delivery: so I got no letter from you this morning, which is the saddest blank in my day. Apart from that, it has been pretty black. Germany is now in active war with both Russia & France,[1] and the Germans have violated the neutrality of Luxemburg: we are waiting to know whether they are going to do the same with Belgium.[2]

I had a visit at breakfast time from Lichnowsky, who was very *émotionné*, and implored me not to side with France. He said that Germany, with her army cut in two between France & Russia, was far more likely to be 'crushed' than France. He was very agitated poor man & wept. I told him that we had no desire to intervene, and that it rested largely with Germany to make intervention impossible, if she would (1) not invade Belgium, and (2) not send her fleet into the Channel to attack the unprotected North Coast of France. He was bitter about the policy of his Government in not restraining Austria, & seemed quite heartbroken.

Then we had a long Cabinet from 11 to nearly 2,[3] which very soon revealed that we are on the brink of a split. We agreed at last (with much difficulty) that Grey should be authorised to tell Cambon that our fleet would not allow the German fleet to make the Channel the base of hostile operations. John Burns at once resigned, but was persuaded to hold on at any rate till this evening when we meet again. There is a strong party including all the 'Beagles' and reinforced by Ll George Morley & Harcourt who are against any kind of intervention in any event.[4] Grey of course will never consent to this, & I shall not separate myself from him.[5] Crewe, McKenna, & Samuel are a moderating intermediate body. B Law writes that the Opposition will back us up in any measures we may take for 'the support of France & Russia'.[6] I suppose a good ¾ of our own party in the H. of Commons are for absolute non-interference at any price. It will be a shocking thing if at such a moment we break up – with no one to take our place.[7]

Happily I am quite clear in my own mind as to what is right & wrong. I put it down for you in a few sentences.

(1) We have no obligation of any kind either to France or Russia to give them military or naval help.

(2) The despatch of the Expeditionary force to help France at this moment is out of the question & wd. serve no object.

(3) We mustn't forget the ties created by our long-standing & intimate friendship with France.

(4) It is against British interests that France shd. be wiped out as a Great Power.

(5) We cannot allow Germany to use the Channel as a hostile base.

(6) We have obligations to Belgium to prevent her being utilised & absorbed by Germany.[8]

That is all I can say for the moment. If only you were here my

beloved! How I miss you – in this most critical of crises. Think of me
& love me & *write*. Every day I bless & love you more.

[1] Germany did not declare war on France until 3 Aug.; but the invasion of France had been set in train two days before that.

[2] At 7 p.m. on 1 Aug. a German infantry company, using motor vehicles, had seized the railway station and telegraph office at Trois Vierges (Ulflingen) in Luxemburg. At 7.30 p.m. a second detachment arrived at the station, declaring the invasion to have been a mistake. This reversal resulted from the Kaiser's short lived attempt to rearrange the German mobilization and to direct the invading armies against Russia. By midnight the seizure of Trois Vierges had been confirmed, the rest of the Grand Duchy being occupied during Sunday. See p. 143.

[3] Asquith wrote before the cabinet reassembled at 6.30 p.m. During this second session, as we now know, the German ultimatum was being delivered in Brussels.

[4] This oversimplifies the 'non-interventionists' ' position as it was by 2 p.m. on 2 Aug.: see Hazlehurst, *Politicians at War* (1971), ch. 5. The decision which the cabinet had made with such difficulty (Burns dissenting), to intervene should the French Channel coast be bombarded, related to a move which the German leaders did not intend to make. The German Embassy in London stated on 3 Aug.: 'Germany would be disposed to give an undertaking that she will not attack France by sea in the north, or make any warlike use of the sea coast of Belgium or Holland' if Britain would remain neutral 'for the time being' (*Westminster Gazette*, 3 Aug., 6c). For 'the Beagles' see Letter 27, n. 3.

[5] Samuel wrote to his wife that night, 'Had the matter come to an issue Asquith would have stood by Grey.'

[6] The sending of this letter became known within a few weeks, and on 14 Dec. 1914 Bonar Law gave its text to a Conservative meeting. Writing to St Loe Strachey (11 Aug. 1918) Asquith denied that it had influenced the cabinet. This denial, which Grey later confirmed, is accepted by Bonar Law's biographer: Robert Blake, *The Unknown Prime Minister* (1955), p. 223. See, however, K. M. Wilson, *Br. Journal of International Studies*, 1 (1975), 148–59.

[7] Asquith referred disparagingly at this time to the capacities of the Conservative leaders and the viability of a coalition. Some Liberals disliked coalition proposals because Churchill favoured them. If the Government had broken up, however, a coalition would almost certainly have been attempted. Balfour was prepared for one, but thought it 'would be a very great misfortune'.

[8] Asquith read a version of this six-point summary to the Sunday morning cabinet. The six points are also reflected in the reply which he sent later in the day to the Conservative leaders.

114

Monday 3 Aug 14

I had a great treat this morning in the shape of 2 delightful letters from you – Saturday's & Sunday's. I can see that you are chafing rather in your present isolation from the main stream, tho' I do my best (as you most dearly acknowledge) to keep you in touch with its ever shifting currents. It is the next best thing to having you close at hand to write everything (both of us), and during this week of worries & sensations & horrors your regular daily letter has been my standby and help. You don't know what a world of difference it has made.

The clouds tend rather to thicken than to disperse. We had another Cabinet yesterday before dinner 6.30 to 8, the most notable feature of which was Burns's repetition of his unalterable determination to go. We i.e. Violet Eliz Cys the Assyrian & I, dined with the McKennae. There were large crowds perambulating the streets and cheering the King at Buckingham Palace, & one could hear this distant roaring as late as 1 or 1.30 in the morning. War or anything that seems likely to lead to war is always popular with the London mob. You remember Sir R. Walpole's remark: 'Now they are ringing their bells; in a few weeks they'll be wringing their hands'.[1] How one loathes such levity.

This morning two letters arrived for me – one from J. Morley, the other from the Impeccable – announcing that they must follow J. Burns's example. They are both characteristic productions wh. I would send you but that I am rather afraid about your address to-morrow: anyhow you shall have them later. At the Cabinet later in the morning Beauchamp ('Sweetheart') declared that he must do likewise. That is 4 gone! We had a rather moving scene in which everyone all round said something – Ll. George making a strong appeal to them not to go, or at least to delay it. In the end, they all agreed to say nothing to-day and to sit in their accustomed places in the House. (I must stop for luncheon.)

I ought to have said that B. Law & Lansdowne came to see me early this morning: they were in general agreement, but laid great stress upon Belgian neutrality. The Germans, with almost Austrian crassness, have delivered an ultimatum to Belgium & forced themselves on to their territory, and the Belgian King has made an appeal to ours.[2]

Edgar Vincent & Barbara Wilson & the Percy Wyndhams came to lunch, & then we all went to the House wh. was crammed to such an extent that all the middle part of it was occupied by chairs. Grey made a most remarkable speech – about an hour long – for the most part almost conversational in tone & with some of his usual ragged ends; but extraordinarily well reasoned & tactful & really *cogent* – so much so that our extreme peace-lovers were for the moment reduced to silence; tho' they will soon find their tongues again.[3] Redmond cut in very effectively with the suggestion that all our troops shd. be withdrawn from Ireland, wh. shd be left for defensive purposes to the joint efforts of the two sets of Volunteers.[4]

After Ramsay had put in the inevitable Labour protest,[5] the sitting was suspended till 7. The streets are full of cheering crowds.

We are mobilising the Army as well as the Navy – so as to be well prepared.[6] After to-morrow Haldane is going to help me every day at the W.O. and we have kept back Kitchener in case of need.[7]

I am sorry to hear of the Penguin's sad case: mainly (to tell the truth) because I fear it will cause you pain. I have just been arguing his case with the Impeccable, & I have some hope that he may still remain. . .[8]

I suppose you will now stay on till Friday: thank God, I shall see you then or Sat. at latest my own beloved. How I long for a sight of you! Please go on writing: it is my life-breath. *All love always.*

1 John Morley's *Walpole*, in which this remark is quoted, first published in 1889, was for many years one of the best known volumes in Macmillan's series, 'Twelve English Statesmen'.

2 This was an appeal for diplomatic action. King Albert of the Belgians did not ask for military intervention until German troops were known to have crossed the frontier in force, that is, until noon on 4 Aug.

3 Lord Hugh Cecil, a Conservative who had opposed intervention, thought the speech 'very wonderful – . . . the greatest . . . delivered in our time or for a very long period' (to Wilfrid Ward, 6 Aug.: copy in Glenconner MSS).

4 Redmond was not unprompted in making this offer: see *The Times*, 1 Aug. 6c, and Margot Asquith, *Autobiography*, ii. 164. He is thought to have seen Asquith just before Grey spoke; but he could not consult his principal colleagues, Dillon being in Dublin and Devlin in Belfast. T. P. O'Connor, who was more sympathetic to the cabinet than most Nationalists, advised in the House against any offer. The inquest on those killed at Bachelor's Walk was being held as Redmond spoke. As he finished speaking many Conservatives rose and cheered him. For the sad sequel see pp. 236–7.

5 MacDonald spoke nominally as leader of the Labour party, but in fact for a small, though distinguished, minority of his colleagues.

6 Asquith wrote out the authority to mobilize the army in the small hours of 3 Aug. and Haldane brought this to the War Office at 11.0 a.m. on that day. The actual mobilization order reached the army commands on the afternoon of 4 Aug. It did not authorize embarkation of an expeditionary force.

7 Kitchener was recalled to London as he was returning to Egypt. A telephone message reached his house at Broome, on the Canterbury–Dover road, about noon on 3 Aug. soon after he had left. He had boarded the 12.55 p.m. Channel steamer for Calais, and his aides were urging the captain not to wait any longer for the overdue London boat train, when the Prime Minister's message reached him. He needed some persuading before he would disembark. See pp. 152–4.

8 Simon withdrew his resignation.

115

4 Aug 14

I am really rather in doubt where to address this. All through your letter to-day you assume that you will be in the train, having moved your tent from Penrhos, and as you indicate no other destination I infer that you were intending to make for Lulworth. But the camp there is broken up (Oc appeared at Downing St at luncheon to-day), and they assure me that you were informed of this. I thought of telegraphing but if you were away that wd. be of no use: so I am sending this to Penrhos in the hope & belief that you are still there. I can well understand your restless feeling in present circumstances, and you don't need to be told how I long for you here. I am still hoping to see you Friday or Saturday, and if fate is kinder than I have any reason to expect or even hope, I might put myself on for Mells this Sunday. Would you like that? or rather wait for the next? I am afraid it is the dimmest glimmer of a most fitful & flickering ray of hope – for, if things develop as they threaten, it is doubtful whether I shall be able to be away for 24 hours so far from here. But we have both been through so much since we parted, and with all my 'copious' daily outpourings there is so much that I have left unsaid, and the longing to see & hear you & be near & with you is so keen & ever growing, that I grasp at the skirts of chance, & as Tennyson (whom you won't read) aptly says 'I faintly trust the larger hope'.[1]

I am rather alarmed at the family curiosity as to the contents of my letters, & I am sure you were judicious in what you read to them (& didn't read): I suppose (& hope) that it was an exceptional case, due to the lateness of the Bank Holiday post. You feared, did you? that I should forget the extra stamp! You don't quite know me – even now.

I think the effect produced by Grey's speech has not died down. It is curious how, going to or from the House, we are now always surrounded and escorted by cheering crowds of loafers & holiday makers. We had a sort of scratch dinner party last night – Jack Pease, Mrs Keppel & girl,[2] Anne Islington & Pauline,[3] Harry Wilson & Barbara[4] &c &c. In the course of the evening I had a call from Bonar Law who is afraid (or says his followers are) that we shall make use of the 'truce' to spring a trick on them, by suddenly proroguing & putting our Home Rule & Welsh Church Bills on the Statute book as *faits accomplis* before they can say knife. I assured him that there wd. be no thimble-rigging, but it is not easy at the moment to decide exactly how to deal with the Bills. The best thing of course wd. be a deal between Carson & Redmond, wh. is far from impossible.[5]

You will be relieved to hear that there is a slump in resignations. I wrote last night a strong appeal to the Impeccable, with the result that he & Beauchamp have returned to the fold, & attended the Cabinet this morning. J. M. remains obdurate & I fear must go: he wrote me a particularly nice letter wh. I will show you. Master C. Trevelyan also persists in his determination: happily, *il n'y a pas d'homme nécessaire*.[6] I am putting Runciman to the Board of Trade, & think of making Bron his successor at Agriculture, and Emmott J.M's at the Privy Council.[7]

We had an interesting Cabinet, as we got the news that the Germans had entered Belgium, & had announced to 'les braves Belges' that if necessary they wd. push their way through by force of arms. This simplifies matters, so we sent the Germans an ultimatum[8] to expire at midnight,[9] requesting them to give a like assurance with the French that they wd. respect Belgian neutrality. They have invented a story that the French were meditating an invasion of Belgium, & that they were only acting in self-defence: a manifest and transparent lie.[10]

Winston, who has got on all his war-paint, is longing for a sea-fight in the early hours of to-morrow morning, resulting in the sinking of the *Goeben*.[11] The whole thing fills me with sadness.

The House took the fresh news to-day very calmly & with a good deal of dignity and we got through all the business by ½ past 4.[12] I am now going for a little drive – perhaps past the pleasance of the widowed Venetius.[13] We are on the eve of horrible things. I wish you were nearer my darling: wouldn't it be a joy if we cd spend Sunday together? I love you more than I can say.

[1] *In Memoriam*, 55. Sir John Horner's house at Mells, Somerset, was more than 110 miles from London. See Appendix 3.

[2] Probably her elder daughter, Violet (b. 1894), who married, 1919, Denys Trefusis.

[3] Pauline Stapleton-Cotton.

[4] Sir Mathew Richard Henry Wilson (nicknamed 'Scatters') and his wife, Margot's niece, née Lister. He had succeeded as 4th Baronet in Jan. 1914, and had won South West Bethnal Green for the Conservatives, defeating Masterman (Letter 38, n. 2) in Feb.

[5] Redmond and Carson met on 5 Aug. with the Speaker present. 'I found Sir Edward Carson', Redmond reported to Asquith, 'in an absolutely irreconcilable mood about everything.'

[6] He was 43 and had been Under-Secretary, Board of Education, since Oct. 1908. Venetia was first cousin to his wife.

[7] Beauchamp succeeded Morley as Lord President, Runciman replacing Burns at the Board of Trade. 'Bron' (Auberon Herbert, Lord Lucas) joined the cabinet as Minister of Agriculture, and Lord Emmott as First Commissioner of Works.

[8] See p. 144. The actual invasion of Belgium did not begin until the morning of 4 Aug., by which time the Grand Duchy of Luxemburg had been in German hands for more than a day. The British ultimatum was timed to avoid a risk of hostilities starting before the navy was ready: Pease, diary, 3 Aug.; S. R. Williamson, *Politics of Grand Strategy* (1969), pp. 360–61.

[9] Grey's telegrams to the Ambassador at Berlin required that a satisfactory answer 'be received here by twelve o'clock tonight'. The Ambassador took this to mean that the German Government had until midnight by Central European Time, which corresponded to 11 p.m. by Greenwich Mean Time. It was decided in the cabinet room that the ultimatum expired as Big Ben struck 11 p.m. A report which reached the Foreign Office during the evening that Germany had already declared war on England caused the German Ambassador to receive an inappropriately phrased declaration of war. This was recovered just after 11 p.m., a corrected declaration being substituted.

[10] It was a cardinal principle of French policy to be extremely scrupulous about Belgian neutrality, since by infringing it France might forfeit British help. The French were almost equally careful about their own border with Germany. On 30 July French troops were withdrawn ten km. from the frontier.

[11] The *Goeben*, a fast German battle-cruiser, flew a Russian flag and bombarded Philippeville (now Skikda), the port of Constantine in French Algeria, early on 4 Aug. in order to disrupt the embarkation of troops for France. She then set course for Constantinople, where her commander was meant to help in persuading the Turks to declare war on Russia. She was sighted off Bône (now Annaba) by two British battle-cruisers at 9.30 a.m. on 4 Aug. Churchill, thinking that she was still operating against French troop transports, at once sought approval to engage her, even before the ultimatum expired, should she fire on the transports; but the cabinet were unwilling to allow any act of war until the time of expiry.

[12] The *Daily Graphic*, a Conservative paper, commented on the Prime Minister's 'dignity and composure' when telling the House of the ultimatum to Germany. Hankey, who was with him in 10 Downing Street, wrote: 'All day telegrams were pouring in, not arranging themselves in an easy and clear sequence but confused by a medley of rumours and reports from every quarter. During these events I was for the first time in close personal touch with Asquith; and I was very much impressed by his clear, orderly mind, his coolness, courage, and

decision, and his amazing power of seizing on essentials. He inspired me': *Supreme Command*, i. 159–60.

[13] See Letter 81, n. 2.

The First Days of War (Letter 116)

A. 'Kitchener . . . a hazardous experiment'

THE suggestion that Kitchener should be appointed Secretary of State for War had been made by Lord Rosebery in 1903 and in Horatio Bottomley's *John Bull* in April 1914; but it was not widely taken up until, with war imminent, the impossibility of the Prime Minister's continuing at the War Office became plain. Churchill, prodded by Balfour, suggested the appointment of Kitchener to his chief on the morning of 3 August: 'I could see', he wrote, 'from Mr Asquith's reception of my remarks that his mind was moving, or had already moved, along the same path.' On that morning *The Times* carried an article by its military correspondent making the same suggestion.[1]

Other papers were stimulated to follow the lead of *The Times* by the news that Haldane had been installed in the War Office as Asquith's deputy (Letter 114, n. 6). It was at once suspected among the Opposition that this might be the prelude to some more permanent arrangement.[2] It is not clear whether there was any ground for these suspicions. Asquith told the Commons in 1917: 'The only person . . . whom I ever thought of as my successor [in the War Office] was Lord Kitchener,' while Grey wrote: 'A new appointment was necessary. Asquith's first thought was naturally to send Haldane back to the War Office.'[3] Haldane confided to Ian Hamilton that he had come to keep out Kitchener; yet he advised Asquith to appoint Kitchener. The latter told the Prime Minister on the evening of 4 Aug. that, if his services were needed in England, he would not accept less than the Secretaryship of State.[4]

Whatever Asquith's first thoughts may have been, he decided on Kitchener at an early stage. He had then to reconcile his leading colleagues to the idea of a Field Marshal in the cabinet, and to persuade the Foreign Office that Egypt could be left in other hands. His appeals were aided by a press demand for Kitchener's appointment which had grown overwhelming. Even the *Westminster Gazette*, the Liberal paper closest to the Government, joined in the chorus. The Northcliffe papers and the *Daily Express* protested that Haldane must not stay at the War Office, chiefly on the ground that his well-known sympathy for Germany was bound to make him unacceptable as a war leader to the French. These reasoned protests heralded far worse things.[5]

This decision bound Asquith's fortunes closely to Kitchener's; and something must be said, however inadequately, of the qualifications which 'K. of K.' brought to the post. He had an unequalled power of galvanizing an institution into emergency action; and his 'outsider's' vision was unclouded by the fashionable illusions. He did not expect the war to be short and he saw quickly that the Germans were advancing in force north and west of the Sambre-Meuse line (pp. 154–6, 177–8; Letter 125). To flout conventional wisdom by training a great army from scratch during the war needed standing and courage. Kitchener's immense prestige with the public greatly helped recruiting; he made, in Margot's phrase, 'a great poster'. As the British lacked any substantial reserve trained for overseas service, and were unready to accept conscription, this recruiting achievement was of crucial importance.[6]

The Empire-building which gave Kitchener such an impressive aura had left large gaps in his qualifications, however. He lit the scene with 'flashes of greatness' in Lloyd George's phrase;[7] but these were succeeded by total darkness. Knowing little of European warfare[8] he was extremely slow to realize what enormous supplies of artillery ammunition would be needed. He understood still less about the psychology of his countrymen[9] and, as he distrusted most politicians, he was ill-placed to correct this. He had gained his Imperial reputation by winning campaigns on the cheap; planning for prodigal expenditure was abhorrent to him. He was too old to change and he had gone a little to seed. The strong, silent Empire-builder could be very talkative.[10] The fixity of his gaze, thought to betoken resolve, resulted in fact from an eye injury suffered in the desert. 'A fatted pharoah in spurs . . . garrulously intoxicated with power' was Rudyard Kipling's judgement after a visit to Cairo in 1913.[11]

Kitchener's dictatorial and secretive methods as Secretary of State were made more dangerous by the absence of an effective organization in either the War Office or the cabinet. Nearly all the ablest staff officers in the War Office were leaving for the Expeditionary Force; and Asquith did not even start to adapt the cabinet for war. Kitchener tried to direct everything in the War Office himself, from recruiting to planning strategy. He would neither organize munitions supply on a large scale nor give up responsibility for doing so. Meanwhile Asquith and his colleagues knew a certain amount, and Venetia and other ladies too much; but there was, as Hankey wrote in May 1915, 'literally no one in this country who knows, or has access to, all the information, naval, military, and political on which future plans must be based'.[12]

[1] Repington says that he wrote 'with the approval of the editor': *First World War* (1920), i. 20.

[2] L. S. Amery, *Diaries* i (1980). 107–8.

[3] *Parl. Deb.* xci. 1758; *Twenty-Five Years*, ii. 67.

[4] G. H. Cassar, *Kitchener* (1977), pp. 172–7; Haldane, *Autobiography* (1929) p. 278; M. I. Cole (ed.), *Beatrice Webb's Diaries, 1912–24* (1952), p. 27.

[5] See pp. 322–3.

[6] See Churchill, *World Crisis, 1914* (1923), p. 282.

[7] *War Memoirs*, i. 450. Grey and Balfour echoed this: *Twenty-Five Years*, ii. 69; Max Egremont, *Balfour* (1980), p. 262.

[8] See p. 345 and E. L. Woodward, *Great Britain and the War of 1914–18* (1967), p. 54 (Haig's diary, 14 July 1915).

[9] See I. Colvin, *Carson*, iii (1936). 79; Letters 145 and 149.

[10] O. Sitwell, *Great Morning* (1948), p. 263; Esher, *The Tragedy of Lord Kitchener* (1921), pp. 26, 30–1. Esher's book was, however, inaccurate and perhaps not free from malice.

[11] Charles Carrington, *Rudyard Kipling* (1955), p. 419.

[12] *Supreme Command*, i. 326.

B. 'What to do with the Expeditionary Force'

WHILE peace lasted, the role of the Expeditionary Force was an unmentionable subject in Liberal circles, since many Liberals had been unwilling to admit that it would have any role at all in a Continental war.[1] The distinguished group who met as a 'War Council' on 5 and 6 August were not constrained, therefore, by pre-war plans and they ranged widely over the possibilities. It was soon clear, however, that the only feasible option was to despatch the British Expeditionary Force immediately to a concentration area on the French left. A landing at Antwerp would involve a sea crossing which the navy could not guarantee; and it would infringe Dutch neutrality. Holding the B.E.F. back until it could hand over all coast defence to the Territorials, and cross at full strength, meant infuriating the French and taking no part in the opening battles which were expected to be decisive. The choice was narrowed to Maubeuge or Amiens. The first was the area designated in the plans which Wilson had made before the crisis. It stood about midway along the Franco-Belgian border on the French side, and had been chosen on the assumption that the B.E.F. would be ordered to mobilize and embark on the day on which French mobilization began. In the event the German advance, and the French mobilization, had started some days before embarkation orders for the B.E.F. became the subject of discussion. This gave the more cautious plan of concentrating at Amiens, due north of Paris, obvious attractions. 'A month ago', Wilson told the Council, his staff

had worked out an alternative scheme in co-operation with the French general staff, according to which the British force might concentrate at Amiens, whence they could very easily be despatched in any direction, according as the situation might develop.[2]

Concentration at Amiens was strongly favoured by Kitchener. It was agreed to defer a decision until the representatives of the French staff had been consulted. In the final discussions on 12 August Asquith ruled for Maubeuge.

This decision put the B.E.F. in great peril. The danger that they would be overrun in the concentration area before they were even deployed never materialized; the Belgian resistance slowed the German advance just enough to compensate for the delay in the embarkation orders. The plan to concentrate at Maubeuge was dangerous because it was based on the prediction that no strong German attack would develop north of the Sambre–Meuse line (see pp. 113–14). On 10 August the French high command felt 'confirmed in the impression that the principal German manoeuvre would not take place in Belgium'.[3] Sir John French held much the same view, as his remarks to Asquith on 12 August show (Letter 121).[4] It was argued that, now the Germans had to reckon with determined Belgian resistance, they could not count on taking Liège and Namur quickly enough to make an advance through central and northern Belgium feasible.

It was conceded that the German General Staff might not behave in the way expected. This possibility did not worry the French high command. According to the French theory the Germans could extend their right wing north of the Sambre–Meuse line only by weakening their centre and left, and so making themselves highly vulnerable to the French attacks planned for the Ardennes and Lorraine.[5] Thus it was supposed that no strong German forces would debouch into France from central Belgium; the German army would either not take the northern route, or would be obliged to abandon it because of successful French attacks farther south.

This picture did not accord with the facts. The forts at Liège and Namur had been built in the 1880s. The German army had obtained some 305 mm. howitzers from the Austrian Skoda works, and a few of 420 mm. which Krupps' had begun to produce. With these they could batter Liège and Namur into submission in a matter of days. Moreover the German General Staff had devised a scheme for including reserve formations in the front line. Enough fighting troops could thus be deployed in the West to extend the right wing northwards without denuding the centre and left.[6]

The ineptitude of French military planning in 1914 stemmed less from incompetence than from obsession. The will to attack lay at the heart of French military theory. The French commanders and staffs believed that it was the absence of the offensive spirit which had led to their defeat in the war of 1870. They were determined, while showing scrupulous respect for Belgian neutrality, to start their campaign with a general offensive. Indeed their latest military agreement with Russia pledged both powers to start their operations in this way. As they were outnumbered by the German forces, they could not station enough troops to attack along the Franco-German frontier without leaving the northern half of their border with Belgium virtually undefended. They were bent on persuading themselves that this gap in their defences would not prove dangerous.

In trying to send the B.E.F. to a safer and less advanced concentration area than Maubeuge Kitchener encountered obstacles which even his immense authority could not remove. The French staff officers were insistent for Maubeuge. They wanted the B.E.F. to concentrate where they could be sure that it would take part in the crucial opening battles, and where disengagement from the French armies would be almost impossible. They were supported by Wilson, who, once he had the cabinet's decision of 6 August to send the B.E.F. to France (Letter 117), grew much less accommodating about changing his plans and displeasing the French. 'We wrangled with K for three hours,' Wilson noted in his diary for 12 August:

> K wanted to go to Amiens; and he was incapable of understanding the delays and difficulties of making such a change, nor the cowardice of it, nor the fact that either in French victory or defeat we would be equally useless. He still thinks the Germans are coming north of the Meuse in great force, and will swamp us before we concentrate.[7]

Kitchener showed fine strategical insight in these discussions; but this is unlikely to have been matched by his presentation of his case. Moreover, while he was sure that the plans of the French command were mistaken (p. 177; Letter 125), he did not know how disastrous their intended offensives would be, nor the extent to which Joffre would persist in them until the left wing was in extreme danger. Above all, he had no idea that Namur would surrender after no more than a few days of bombardment (Letter 131). So the B.E.F. concentrated near Maubeuge, with 700,000 Germans moving against them through central Belgium, and no French first-line infantry division north of the Sambre.

[1] See Crewe's careful remarks in Apr. 1913: *Parl. Deb.*, Lords, xiv. 136–7.

[2] A. J. P. Taylor, (*English History, 1914–1945* (1965) pp. 6–7) gives an inaccurate account of the War Council meeting, Wilson's part in it being notably misinterpreted.

[3] Barbara W. Tuchman, *The Guns of August* (1962) p. 189.

[4] In view of Letter 121 French's statement (in *1914* (1919), pp. 10–11), that he had always expected the Germans 'to pour over the whole' of Belgium 'and outflank the allies', is hard to accept.

[5] On 20 Aug. Wilson wrote in his diary: 'we think . . . the enemy has 3 cavalry divisions and 6 corps over the river. The more the better, as it will weaken their centre:' C. E. Callwell, *Wilson*, i. 165.

[6] For Moltke's analysis of the problem, in a paper of 1911 or earlier, see G. Ritter (trans. A. and E. Wilson), *The Schlieffen Plan* (1958), pp. 166–7. Repington published a fairly accurate summary of the German western armies in *The Times*, 12 Aug., 4a, b; but he expected the main advance to come 'through the Belgian Ardennes'. For the discovery by Joffre's HQ, 24 Aug., about the German use of reserve formations see Tuchman, op. cit., p. 282. It has been argued recently that to move N. of the Meuse without invading the Netherlands was strategically unsound: see L. F. C. Turner in P. M. Kennedy (ed.), *The War Plans of the Great Powers* (1979), p. 213.

[7] Callwell, op. cit., i. 162–3. See also C. E. Huguet (trans. Minchin), *Britain and the War* (1928), p. 41.

116

5 Aug 14.

. . . It is difficult . . . to be away from London even for an hour in these anxious times: the telegrams that come in, & the 1000 & 1 people who are perpetually asking to see one, and the nervous condition to which some people are reduced if one is not always at hand, make it hard to get away. Still there may be a lull, and I picture to myself the delight of a few hours by your side.

I have taken an important decision to-day to give up the War Office and instal Kitchener there as an emergency man, until the War comes to an end. It was quite impossible for me to go on, now that war is actually in being: it requires the undivided time & thought of any man to do the job properly, and as you know I hate scamped work. As you will agree, there was none of my colleagues that I could put in my place: impeccables, sweethearts, trays &c all very well each in his own kennel, or in pursuit of his own particular quarry; but it is all-important to avoid a repetition of the Arch-Colonel fiasco.[1] K. was (to do him justice) not at all anxious to come in, but when it was presented to him as a duty he agreed. It is clearly understood that he has no politics, & that his place at Cairo is kept open – so that he can return to it when peace comes back. It is a hazardous experiment, but the best in the circumstances, I think. What do you say? The person I feel rather uneasy about is Anthony Henley, whom I decoyed from a congenial post, and who has been most useful & helpful.[2] So I spoke to French about him to-day, and I have good reason to think that, if the expeditionary force goes abroad, he will find him very soon a place on the staff.

We had a longish Cabinet at which we decided to ask to-morrow for a stiff vote of credit – 100 millions – which will carry us on for a long time & produce a good immediate impression. Oddly enough, there is no authentic war news – either by land or by sea: all that appears in the papers is invention. Winston's mouth waters for the *Goeben*, but so far she is still at large. . . .

After the Cabinet I went to see the King. He is really a good deal relieved that war has come: he could not stand the tension of last week. As you might expect he is becoming very anti-German. I am truly sorry for the poor Lichnowskys: they are broken-hearted,[3] and she spends her days in tears.

After the House, I had a War Council here – a rather motley gathering: Ld Roberts, Kitchener, Ian Hamilton, French, Douglas Haig &c with Haldane Grey Winston & myself. We discussed the strategic situation, and what to do with the expeditionary force, and adjourned till to-morrow, when we shall see a representative of the French General Staff.[4]

I am very well, tho' at times I feel rather tired, and always miss you terribly. The only really happy times in the day are when I am reading your letter & writing to you. Isn't it a wonderful thing that we – you & I – should be like that? I never could have counted on it, or even dreamt of it; but it is my joy & stay. My darling – I shall see you Saturday – and am always & everywhere *Yours*

[1] See pp. 57–8. For 'sweethearts, trays' see Letter 27, n. 3.
[2] See Letter 59, n. 2.
[3] See Letter 79, n. 1.
[4] Asquith had asked Haldane on 3 Aug. 'to select those who should attend'. The minutes are in P.R.O. CAB 22/1/1. Churchill, French, Grey, Haig, Haldane, and Hankey all recorded their memories of this meeting. For the later War Council, which was differently constituted and met first on 25 Nov. 1914, see p. 184.

117

Thurs. 6 Aug 14

. . . As you say, it is all incredibly sad, and will become worse day by day. The latest authentic news is that the cruiser *Amphion* wh. did so well yesterday, has been blown up by mines to-day, & apparently no one saved.[1] Mines are a hellish device wh. every civilised nation except the Germans wanted to abolish at the Hague years ago.[2]

We had our usual Cabinet this morning, and decided with much less demur than I expected to sanction the despatch of an Expeditionary force of four divisions.[3] We also discussed a number of smaller schemes for taking German ports & wireless stations in E & W Africa & the China Seas were discussed with some gusto:[4] indeed I had to remark that we looked more like a gang of Elizabethan buccaneers than a meek collection of black-coated Liberal Ministers.

. . . K. is already throwing great energy into his job; already to-day he has undertaken to raise another 100,000 Regulars![5] It will be amusing to see how he gets on in the Cabinet.

I had to introduce the Vote of Credit, & tho' I had not had more than about 5 minutes to prepare, I think I made a fairly successful speech.[6] B Law was very Bonar-ish, but the House was in a good mood & the whole thing went off well. I wished you had been there beloved. Since then we have had another War Council – with Ld. Roberts & Comp^y – and settled the details of the Expeditionary force, wh. I hope will start on Sunday morning. Troops are terribly slow moving things.[7]

As if we hadn't enough on hand, Redmond has started a row of his own. We are proposing a short adjournment to-morrow or Monday, instead of proroguing: & he is full of suspicion as to what may happen to his Bill, wh. naturally enough he wants to see on the Statute book.[8] Bonar Law & Carson are equally suspicious, lest we shd. play tricks against them with the truce. Altogether it is rather a difficult Parliamentary situation, and I shall have to try to-morrow to steer through it . . .

[1] The *Amphion*, with a flotilla of destroyers, chased and sank the *Königin Luise*, a Hamburg-Amerika vessel fitted as a minelayer, which had laid 180 mines off Harwich and Southwold. Returning from the action the *Amphion* ran on to one of the mines and was sunk. Her captain, 16 officers, and 135 men were saved.

[2] Under the Hague Convention of 1907 minelaying was allowed only in the enemy's territorial waters, that is, within 3 miles of his coasts. The German authorities did not regard themselves as being bound by the Convention since it had not been ratified by Russia. The Germans laid 43,000 mines during the war, 25,000 of them in the North Sea and round the British Isles.

[3] See pp. 142 and 154. The fleet was completely mobilized and at its battle stations (Letter 112, n. 3). It was known everywhere that the Belgians were resisting the invader and that they had appealed for military help. It was thus feasible to send the B.E.F. across the Channel and there was immense popular pressure to do so. According to Henry Wilson, when Asquith backed Kitchener in withholding two divisions he was thinking of disorder rather than invasion: he said that 'the domestic situation might be grave; and colonial troops and territorials could not be called on to aid the civil power'. The decision to hold two back probably proved fortunate. Their presence at Maubeuge 'might easily have impelled [French's] G.H.Q. into further rashness, which might have smashed up the whole army' (John Terraine, *Mons* (1960), p. 88). Kitchener seems to have insinuated later that he had been prevented by his cabinet colleagues from sending all six divisions. The minutes of the short War Council meeting on 6 Aug. establish, however, that he wanted to send only four (P.R.O. CAB 22/1/2; Hobhouse *Diaries*, pp. 188–9). Asquith mentions only the infantry divisions. The B.E.F. also included a cavalry division.

[4] A sub-committee of the Committee of Imperial Defence had made recommendations on 5 Aug. for 'offensive operations against German colonies'. These were intended, by depriving Germany of coaling ports and wireless stations, to help in driving her shipping from the seas. The port and wireless station at Dar es Salaam were put out of action on 8 Aug.; Togoland surrendered on 26 Aug.; and the Australians and New Zealanders dealt with the German possessions in the South Pacific during Aug. and Sept.

[5] Asquith uses 'regulars' to denote troops liable for overseas service, as opposed to the Territorials of 1914 whose obligations were normally limited to home defence.

[6] This was one of Asquith's most admired parliamentary speeches. He 'rose to a height of eloquence, and also of convincing persuasiveness, never surpassed' (*Spectator*); '. . . to heights which oratory is seldom competent to gain' (Daily Mail); 'one of those marvellously concise speeches for which the Prime Minister is famous' (*Daily Graphic*). None of these journals had lately been supporting the Liberal Government.

[7] For the delay in issuing embarkation orders to the B.E.F. see p. 154 above. On 31 July Asquith had refused to protect the railway schedules for mobilization by stopping the movement of Territorials to their summer camps. The Bank Holiday on 3 Aug., the fact that further rail track had to be laid into Southampton Docks, and a three-day fog in the Channel, were further complicating factors. Apart from all this, the reservists had to travel from where they lived to rejoin their units before the latter could start moving to the docks. The B.E.F. arrived 'in time' because of the excellence of the movement plans originated by Haldane, and perfected under Wilson, and because (unexpectedly: see p. 155) the Belgians fought the invader and disrupted his communications.

[8] For this correspondence (5 and 6 Aug.) see D. Gwynn, *Redmond* (1932), pp. 363–4. The question is discussed on pp. 173–4.

118

8 Aug 14

My darling it was the greatest of joys to be with you again & see you & hear you talk & feel that you were near & the same. Only it was all too short. I wish you hadn't torn up your letter. I wonder if you were as glad to see me again? Please write to me to-morrow & tell me exactly where you will be. I like to know every hour.

I have had further correspondence with B Law who has written to-day almost every 2 hours.[1] He & Lansdowne propose to issue a manifesto in Monday morning's paper denouncing us for proceeding with controversial things like Home Rule – when 90 Members of the H of C (70 Unionists & 20 Liberals) have already gone to the colours, with more to follow &c. I told him that all this did not, & could not apply, to any proposal, by a one clause Bill, to suspend the operation of a Home Rule Act until in another Session an Amending Bill had been disposed of. McKenna & the Assyrian who have been with me & to whom I read the correspondence thought that I was quite right. Since then I have had Kitchener & read his instructions to Sir John French as Commander of the Expeditionary force: they are quite good.[2] I have told him to send me a full statement of the composition of the force – regiments &c: & this I will show you or send to you. To-morrow I will write to *Mansfield St*: tell me how long you will be in London on Monday.

I love & prize you with all my heart.

We are making Islington Under Sec. for Colonies.[3]

[1] See three letters in Asquith MSS, vol. 13 ff. 195–200.
[2] Displayed in Imperial War Museum. See J. E. Edmonds, *Military Operations, France and Belgium, 1914*, i (1922). 442–3; French, *1914*, pp. 13–15. The crucial passage read: 'The . . . strength of the British force and its contingent reinforcement is strictly limited . . . ; therefore, while every effort must be made to coincide most sympathetically with the plans and wishes of our ally, the gravest consideration will devolve upon you as to participation in forward movements where large bodies of French troops are not engaged and where your force may be unduly exposed to attack.'
[3] He replaced Lord Emmott. See Letters 12, n. 6, and 115, n. 7.

119

Sunday 9 Aug Midnight

It was no use my darling writing you a letter to-day tho' I have thought much of yesterday & our delightful hour. We had Cambon to dinner last night & he gave me his 'felicitations' on my 'discours magnifique' &c.[1] I have also rather a pathetic tho' somewhat rhetorical letter from M. de Broqueville – the Belgian Prime Minister – which I will give you if you care to have it. I felt really tired this morning & lay in bed like a log till quite late. Winston has been very tiresome about Ivor Guest whom he wishes to have at the Admiralty as Civil Lord in place of Lambert. L. is not very competent but to boot him out at this moment wd. be cruel, & the place is one wh. no peer has ever held: let alone the fact that Ivor Guest is very unpopular, & the whole thing wd. be denounced as a Churchill job.[2] I thought & still think it inconsiderate of Winston to raise & press such a point at such a time.

A much more serious matter is what we are to say to-morrow about the future of the Session. The King is fussing in his usual nervous way,[3] and both parties (our own & the Unionists) are very suspicious lest advantage should be taken of the 'truce of God' to dish & betray them. We have a Cabinet in the morning, & I shall try (as usual) to devise some saving formula.

I wonder what you have been doing all day at Mells – Couldn't you come to lunch to-morrow? We could send you in a Dunn[4] motor to Aldershot. As I have the Cabinet I can't possibly come to Mansfield St in the morning – and it makes such a difference to have even an unsatisfying glimpse of you.

The only *authentic* news we have to-day (wh. you must not breathe to anyone) is that one of our best & biggest battleships – the *Monarch* – was very nearly torpedoed this morning at Scapa Flow[5] (Orkneys) by a surreptitious German submarine. Of this 'battle in Alsace' we have so far no real confirmation.[6]

I lunched with Haldane & E Grey & we talked about Japan & other incidental things. Grey went afterwards with the Assyrian to the Zoo to look at beasts & birds, but I gather from the latter – with whom I dined to-night – that he (E.G.) was very distrait & full of preoccupations. I am afraid – like Winston & others – that he is much overstrained. So should I be – if it were not for you. Violet & I & Bongie & Oc & Jack Tennant drove after lunch to Swinley Forest to get some fresh air & golf. V. Oc & I played a few holes, & then she & I came back in Geoffrey's motor. I went alone afterwards to the 7 o'clock service (very short) at Westminster Abbey, where I liked the music & the hymns and quite a good sensible sermon from young Sheppard – the son of the rather oily Court Chaplain. As I came out I knocked up against the Arch-Colonel Seely, & walked to Downing St with him. He is going out on French's staff to-morrow or next day: 'a good thing to set an example' &c as he told me rather unctuously.[7] There were great crowds in the streets, and as we turned the corner from Whitehall I was recognised by some casual loafer, & was followed to the front door by an enthusiastic & cheering crowd! I have never before been a popular character with the 'man in the street' and in all this dark & dangerous business it gives me scant pleasure. We played Bridge at the Assyrian's with Rufus Isaacs & McKenna – not very amusing.

Now (1.15 a.m) I am going to bed – to try to get to sleep. I shall think of you – in the moments when you have been most dear & responsive & inspiring. Sometimes – now for instance – I feel rather weary & hopeless – like the men in Tennyson's poem 'ever climbing up the climbing wave'.[8] You must help me – & you *will*.

All my love.

[1] Speech on 6 Aug.: see Letter 117, n. 6.

[2] Guest (who had been cr. Lord Ashby St Ledgers, 1910, and had succ. as Lord Wimborne, 1914) was Churchill's first cousin. 'One must suppose that God knew best/When He created Ivor Guest' indicates the consensus about him in social and political circles. Haldane wrote: 'Have a room for Wimborne in the Admiralty by all means. . . . But don't let it be said that you expelled Lambert.' 'I often told him [Churchill],' wrote Violet Asquith, 'that one quality he shared with his great hero Napoleon was nepotism.'

[3] See Lord Esher's account (*Journals and Letters*, iii (1938), 155; 21 Jan. 1914) of one of his conversations with the King on Home Rule: 'I said that it was impossible to come to any decision yet . . . and that he ought not to worry himself to death but put the matter aside.'

[4] For James Dunn see Letter 83, n. 6.

[5] This was a scare. No German submarine entered Scapa Flow during the 1914–18 war, though one was destroyed in the outer approaches in Nov. 1914. A more serious scare at Scapa on 17 Oct. made the fleet put to sea.

[6] The French 7th Corps had crossed the frontier into Alsace at dawn on 7 Aug., and had occupied Mulhouse without resistance on the following day. This re-occupation of one of the provinces lost to France in 1871 generated great emotion. The advance was short lived. German reinforcements were sent from Strasbourg; and the French evacuated Mulhouse at 7 a.m., 10 Aug. At this stage Joffre issued little news from the battle zone even to his own Government.

[7] Seely recounted some of his early war experiences in *Fear, and be Slain* (1931), chs. 9 and 10.

[8] 'The Lotos-eaters', Choric Song st. iv.

120

Monday 10 Aug 14

Do darling send me *at once* one or more of the photographs. I delighted in your letter from Mells.[1] . . .

Edward was here at lunch to-day: he is full of zeal but poor fellow, rather

feckless. No wonder: he has never had any plan of life, with all his attractive
& genuine qualities. I think it is rather a good idea of his that Raymond shd.
go out now as a *Times* correspondent. He is a friend of Geoffrey Robinson,[2]
who wd. no doubt try to get him the job. I was amused at your picture of
Katharine & her mother: that kind of strained strenuousness which Frances
shows in emergencies (and which is quite effective) does not appeal to
Katharine's rather pulseless, tho' not superficial, temperament. . . .

We had a long & rather critical Cabinet this morning: the main question
being (as I told you) what I was to say on the Adjournment about the Home
Rule & Welsh Church Bills. Redmond was pressing for prorogation &
immediate placing on the Statute Book. Carson sent in a rather threatening
letter in the opposite sense.[3] We had a very animated debate, Winston all for
'settlement', Lord K. very strong as to the danger from a military point of
view of the setting up of a provisional Gov^t in Belfast, & E. Grey declaring
that he could not remain if in existing circumstances the Home Rule
controversy was once more made acute. There was also a long screed from
the Abp. of Canterbury as to the wickedness & meanness of proceeding with
the Welsh Bill, when all 'Church folk' were pouring out their money to
relieve distress & promote the war.[4] McKenna & Ll. George (quite properly
& with good temper) took up the Nationalist & Welsh cudgels, and for a
time it seemed as tho' we shd. come to a deadlock. Happily, not for the first
(or perhaps the last) time I was able to devise a form of face-saving words
wh. pleased everybody, and wh. I have just (5.15) read to the House with
the benediction of Bonar Law, & not a single question from any quarter.[5] As
this turns a really difficult corner, I think you might like to have the thing I
drafted at the Cabinet & afterwards read out here: tho' it increases the bulk
of my letter. . . .

We had the usual strange assortment at lunch – if only you had been
there! – Waxworks, Harry Wilson & Barbara (who are now almost inmates
of our house), and Laura came in. She has shown wonderful resource – put
up 200 beds at Beaufort & laid in a copious supply of nurses drugs medical
appliances &c, all off her own bat.[6] I wrote a strong letter this morning to
French about Anthony[7] and I enclose his reply. You see he is coming to see
me at 11 to-morrow morning before he starts. I know he will be as good as
his word, for he feels himself under strong obligations to me. The Expeditionary force (entre nous) is moving on oiled castors: a considerable part of
it is now in France,[8] and there is not a whisper in the newspapers. I think we
may fairly claim to have managed well so far. My darling I wish you were
nearer me; but you will write *every* day. Do you know how much I love
you?

¹ See Letter 115, n. 1.
² Robinson and Raymond Asquith were Fellows of All Souls.
³ See p. 174.
⁴ By the disestablishment measure the Welsh Church was to lose part of its endowments and the Church leaders planned to replace these by a major fund-raising effort. The Government scheme, as Asquith was to outline it on 15 Sept. 1914, while putting the measure on the statute-book, suspended its operation for 12 months or, if the war had not ended by then, 'for the duration'. The Welsh Church Act finally came into operation on 31 Mar. 1920.
⁵ Asquith repeated his pledge of 30 July that postponing the Amending Bill 'must be without prejudice to the domestic and political position of any party' (see pp. 134–5), and announced an adjournment until 25 Aug., the Government being 'not without hope that in the interval we may be able to make proposals . . . which may meet with something like general acquiescence'.
⁶ Beaufort was accepted by the Admiralty, but was never actually used as a hospital, since no naval engagement took place in northern waters. It is on the Beauly River, Inverness-shire (Grampian Region).
⁷ Henley: see Letter 59, n. 2, and 116.
⁸ A pardonable exaggeration. Most of the B.E.F. crossed between 12 and 17 Aug.

Sir John French: 'I am sure he is our best man' (Letter 121)

THE British Army of 1914 did not include many men of the highest ability. Asquith may well have been right in choosing Sir John French to command the B.E.F.; indeed any other choice would have presented great difficulties. French had some of the qualities needed for high command. He made a very good impression, for instance, when in personal contact with his troops. His intellectual grasp was mediocre, however. He had gained considerable 'battle experience' in the Boer War; but it was mostly of a rather inappropriate kind, since, like the commander of his First Corps, Douglas Haig, he was a cavalryman. His worst defects were a hot temper and, in the words of a standard war history, 'that mercurial temperament commonly associated with Irishmen and cavalry soldiers'.[1] He was 61 and it has been suggested that he had recently 'suffered from a severe heart attack'.[2] The suggestion rests on doubtful evidence; but French's steadiness and equanimity, even if unimpaired, were not great.

¹ C. R. M. F. Cruttwell, *The Great War* (2nd edn., 1936), p. 23.
² B. H. Liddell-Hart, *First World War* (1970 edn.), p. 93 n. Haig noted in his Diary (National Library of Scotland), 21 Nov. 1914: 'Sir John . . . told me that he had had a severe attack of heart and Drs. ordered him to take things easier. He looked rather pulled down.' This passage would refer most naturally to a heart attack in Oct./Nov. 1914. By the time he resigned as Commander-in-Chief (4 Dec. 1915) French's health had become uncertain: see Robert Blake (ed.), *The Private Papers of Douglas Haig* (1952), p. 111; Esher (ed.), *Journals and Letters of Reginald, Viscount Esher*, iii (1938), 287–8.

121

. . . Of course I will remember what you say about Oliver:[1] there is nothing I shd. like better than to do a 'job' for you. Very soon they will want all the trained & competent men they can lay hands on at the front.

I drove with Violet in Richmond Park & thought of drives with you. We had our usual dinner: E. Grey came in afterwards & we played some indifferent Bridge. Poor Edward Horner (as you say) is not likely to get nearer the front than Winchester. Raymond might do worse than try his luck as a correspondent, tho' the rôle of war correspondent is not what it used to be.

There has never been anything more wonderful than the persistent & impenetrable secrecy in which everything both on sea & land continues to be enveloped. Imagine the Channel between Southampton & Havre & between Newhaven & Dieppe swarming now for nearly 3 days with transports carrying troops: the troops arriving on French soil with no doubt a lot of popular acclamation: whole regiments of khaki-clad guards & Highlanders, marching as they have been to-day, thro' the streets of London, with bands playing the Marseillaise, & apparently disappearing into space: and not a word in any newspaper to indicate what is going on. And the same thing is to be seen – or not seen – in Germany & France. It enables one to realise how easily & how soon any part of the world might be isolated from the rest.[2]

Sir John French came to pay me a farewell visit this morning, & I clinched Anthony's affair. He gave me an interesting *aperçu* of the military situation. He thinks that just South of Luxemburg will be the real 'theatre',[3] when each side has collected & concentrated its forces. He starts (this is *secret*) on Friday morning in a torpedo destroyer for Boulogne; thence to Paris where he will show himself: then back to Amiens where by that time there will be a large concentration of our troops; and after that in a little less than a fortnight from now the striking force will be in its proper place. It takes a long time – doesn't it? – to move these vast modern machines, & yet so far there hasn't been a hitch, & everything & everybody is slightly in advance of the appointed time. French was very composed & (like you) 'un-vain', and I am sure he is our best man.

We had a long Cabinet, in which a huge part of the talking was done by Winston & Kitchener: the former posing as an expert on strategy, and the latter as an expert on Irish politics![4] The Japs are coming into action,[5] and Venizelos, the Greek Prime Minister, who is much the most capable man in Eastern Europe, has a great scheme on foot for a federation of Balkan States against Germany & Austria: to be rewarded by slices of Austrian territory. If they can get this on to its legs we will help them with any amount of money.

At lunch we had Cassel & Sir E. Goschen, just returned from Berlin. He gave a lot of interesting particulars about his last days there.[6] At the end his footmen took off their liveries & spat on them & refused to carry down his boxes &c. . . .

. . . I pine for you – but your letters are the next best thing in the world to your own dear self. Am I a fool? What do you *really* think? Anyhow I *love* you.

[1] Lord Sheffield's third son.

[2] The foreign press had naturally not been as restrained as the British. The presence of British forces in France was announced in the *New York Herald* on 8 Aug., and in its Paris edition two days later; but the German high command did not know the whereabouts of the B.E.F. when the Kaiser ordered von Kluck on 19 Aug. to 'walk over General French's contemptible little army'. On 12 Aug. the *Westminster Gazette* inferred from an official statement 'that the British army was co-operating with the forces of the allied nations in the theatre of war'. An authorized statement that the British were across the Channel appeared in the London press on 18 Aug. and von Kluck read this two days later in a Belgian paper. On the evening of 21 Aug., however, he was told by the high command: 'It is believed that no landing of British troops on a big scale has yet taken place.' On the following day some of his cavalry ran into part of a British squadron. On 23 Aug. the various corps of his First Army came on the British in strength at Mons.

[3] See p. 155. On 12 Aug. the *Westminster Gazette* followed *The Times* in predicting that the main attack would come through the Belgian Ardennes.

[4] Kitchener wanted to make recognition of the National Volunteers the lever for postponing the passage of Home Rule (pp. 173–5). He had lived in Ireland until he was 14, his father being a Protestant landlord in Kerry and Limerick. His first discussion in the War Office with Carson started as badly as his political début in the cabinet. 'Surely you're not going to hold out for Tyrone and Fermanagh?' he asked. 'You're a damned clever fellow,' Carson answered, 'telling me what I ought to be doing.' Kitchener's garrulity in cabinet must have become a subject of gossip in Asquith's family. 'K of Chaos . . . seems to be a sad mixture of gloom, loquacity, and ignorance,' Raymond Asquith wrote to Conrad Russell on 18 Aug.; he 'cannot be persuaded in the cabinet to give his mind to anything but Welsh Disestablishment, on which he descants at inordinate length'. Earl Kitchener of Khartoum was often shortened to 'K. of K.' The 'K of Chaos' joke seems to have originated in Egypt: Elizabeth Longford, *A Pilgrimage of Passion* (1979), p. 385.

[5] On 15 Aug. the Japanese sent an ultimatum to Germany demanding the restoration of Tsingtao, a Chinese port leased to Germany since 1898.

[6] Goschen had been British Ambassador at Berlin since 1908. His final dispatch, 6 Aug., is given in *Brit. Docs. War* xi. 350–54.

Kitchener's 'indifference to the Territorials' (Letter 122)

WHETHER Kitchener could have made more use of the Territorial Army in his recruiting campaign has been much debated. He seems to have had an unnecessarily low opinion of the Territorials. He was better fitted by temperament to build his own system than to adapt what others had created. His experiences as a young volunteer in Chanzy's army in 1871, and later with Boer War units raised by patriotic notables, had left him distrustful of 'citizen armies', and of those with which civilians were liable to interfere. In urban areas the Territorials looked to Kitchener like 'a town clerk's army';[1] elsewhere their County Associations were controlled by local magnates.

The most substantial argument against basing army expansion on the Territorials was that it would involve converting a home defence organization into one for overseas service. Moreover the Territorial Army did not enjoy high enough prestige in 1914 to attract recruits in enormous numbers; a Kitchener army was a better magnet. The Territorials were a Liberal creation; and there may have been bias in some Liberal criticisms of Kitchener's methods. But there was substance too; and not all of those who wanted to base the wartime system on the Territorial Army were Liberals.[2]

In the first eighteen months of the war 1,741,000 volunteers joined the Kitchener armies, and 726,000 the Territorials.

[1] Grey, *Twenty-Five Years* (1925), ii. 68.
[2] For the most recent discussion of this problem see George H. Cassar, *Kitchener* (1977), pp. 197–201.

122

Wed 12 Aug. 14

. . . Margot & I drove yesterday afternoon to Stanmore to see the Benckendorffs, who have taken Barbara Wilson's house. I saw her off at Kings Cross before dinner; it is a terribly long journey to Hopeman and the trains are sure to be late. E. Grey (by the way) spoke to me quite seriously this morning about Fraü remaining in the house. He said it was much commented on; that everyone knew that we spoke freely among ourselves about what was going on; and that it was her duty as a patriotic German to report every scrap of information she could pick up. This of course is quite true, and I have asked the efficient Way[1] to approach her tactfully on the subject, and suggest that perhaps . . . some . . . semi-German abode would be a more appropriate shelter for her just now. I hate even the appearance of cruelty, but I don't see how I could do otherwise – do you?

We had a small scratch dinner last night which was 'graced' (as the papers would say) by the presence of the 2 sisters Osborne, who certainly have a good share of real distinction and charm. At Bridge afterwards Francis McLaren & I made a rather remarkable score against Raymond & Bongie:

1450 points, with only three rounds, and trumps twice re-doubled success-fully. Francis is quite a dashing player.[2]

I see that the *Birmingham* which sank the German submarine belongs to Bill Goodenough's[3] Light Cruiser Squadron.

We had a Cabinet this morning as usual. The only interesting thing is the arrival of the *Goeben* in the Dardanelles & her sale to Turkey! The Turks are very angry – not unnaturally – at Winston's seizure of their battleships here.[4] As we shall insist that the *Goeben* should be manned by a Turkish instead of a German crew, it doesn't much matter: as the Turkish sailors cannot navigate her – except on to rocks or mines.[5]

Lord K has rather demoralised the War Office with his bull in the china shop manners and methods,[6] and particularly his ignorance of & indif-ference to the Territorials. I set Haldane on to him yesterday, and to-day there is a perceptible lowering of the temperature. Meanwhile the embarka-tion of the Exped^y Force goes smoothly & steadily on, and so far there has not been the slightest hitch – which is very gratifying.[7]

I miss you so much: if only you were nearer, & I could see you, even for a quarter of an hour, each day it wd. make such a difference. Frances Horner has been here to lunch, & I told her I *hoped* for Mells on Sat (not mentioning you). I long to hear your plans. Never mind about Friday if you can be here by lunch on Sat, & we can drive there together.

Meanwhile, in the midst of these distractions, I am trying to get the Irish & Welsh Bills on to a 'peace' footing. Ld St. Aldwyn & Bob Cecil came to see me after the Cabinet about the latter, & I have been consulting with Birrell who came to lunch how best to put an effective pistol at the head of Redmond.

I am now going out for a little drive with Katharine & Violet. Alas for our Fridays! Shall we ever forget them? And the future, when I dare to peer into it, seems full of clouds & 'darkness visible'.[8] The whole world is in the melting pot – including you & me? I wish I knew, my own darling. Write to me & send me your *real* love.

[1] Miss Way was the Asquiths' personal secretary.

[2] Lady Guendolen and Lady Moira Osborne were daughters of the Duke of Leeds; Francis McLaren, the brother-in-law of Pamela McKenna (killed in action, 1917).

[3] The Germans had lost two submarines from a flotilla cruising in the North Sea, one of them being rammed by the *Birmingham*. Goodenough had married Venetia's eldest sister, Henrietta Margaret.

[4] The *Sultan Osman* and the *Reshadieh*, just completed on the Tyne. The money for them had been raised by public subscriptions in Turkey, and the first instalment on one of them had been paid. The British Government promised that the financial and other loss to Turkey would be given 'due consideration'.

[5] An over-optimistic forecast. German 'experts' remained on board the *Goeben*. On 29 and 30 Oct. 1914, with the *Breslau* and a Turkish squadron, she made an extremely destructive raid against Russian shipping and installations in the Black Sea.

[6] The Financial Director at the War Office (Sir Charles Harris) described the first Army

Council meeting with Kitchener in the chair as 'Hell with the lid off': Eleanor Acland, diary [8 Aug]; Acland MSS.

⁷ During the first 24 hours of embarkation a train arrived in Southampton Docks every 10 minutes. For the next 19 days trains arrived at the rate of about 90 a day. At one point the Channel fog produced a serious complication: see Letter 117, n. 7. See D. Chapman-Huston and O. Rutter, *General Sir John Cowans* (2 vols., 1924), i. ch. 8.

⁸ Milton, *Paradise Lost*, i. 63.

'The "strangulation" of Germany' (Letters 123, 125, 126, 168, 199 and 241)

IT was impracticable in 1914 to cut off Germany's sea-borne trade by an old-fashioned blockade of her ports. Mines and torpedo-firing submarines had made patrolling along the enemy's coasts impossibly dangerous; and in 1912 the Admiralty had changed its plans from 'close' to 'distant' blockade. Moreover the Germans might well obtain as much war material through Dutch and Danish ports as through their own. On the other hand, the British controlled the exits from the North Sea to the sea lanes of the world. By checking shipping in the Channel, and between the north of Scotland and Norway, and searching cargoes, they could greatly reduce the volume of contraband reaching Germany.

The problem was to compile contraband lists, and to exercise the right of search, without enraging the United States and the other neutrals. According to most of the naval officers concerned, Grey was far too sensitive to neutral, and above all to American, reactions; it was argued that, however much neutral traders and shippers might complain, they were doing far too well out of their trade with Britain to allow their Governments to retaliate against her. This view was too simple. Reasonable relations with the Dutch and Scandinavian Governments were a pre-condition of making useful agreements with them: they arranged to prevent contraband from reaching Germany in return for unmolested sea passage to and from their ports. Their merchants naturally preferred being obliged to redirect their trade to having their ships and cargoes seized. By abstaining from unnecessary provocation the British Government allowed this preference to take effect.

Where the United States were concerned the case for moderation was even stronger. In the first place, to have allowed the disputes about contraband to grow bitter would have meant throwing the field open to demagogues. Americans would have been reminded that they had fought the war of 1812 on this very issue of 'the freedom of the seas', and that the British had burned the White House in that war. The commercial men who had started the American protest might not have remained in control of it; there were many Americans of German and Irish descent waiting to take it over.

Secondly, Britain's enormous dependence on sea-borne food and supplies increased with every week of war; and in the munition field the French were soon almost equally dependent on the United States, since most of their steel production lay in areas occupied by the Germans. Thus an American denial of supplies, even if limited to a few crucial commodities, might have been fatal to Britain and France. Moreover the moderation with which contraband control was exercised did not make it an ineffective method of warfare. The Germans had depended heavily on imported fertilizers, for instance; and their harvests suffered from the lack of these from 1915 onwards. The object of Grey's diplomacy therefore was, as he later wrote, 'to secure the maximum of blockade that could be enforced without a rupture with the United States'.

The Letters hint how this objective was attained. The contraband lists were drawn up and revised with care. They did not include copper and rubber until late in September 1914, or cotton – politically the most important commodity of all – until August 1915. In these problems Grey was greatly helped by the American Ambassador, Walter H. Page, who supported Britain to the limits of neutrality. 'A government can be neutral,' Page wrote; 'but no *man* can be.'[1]

[1] B. J. Hendrick, *Walter H. Page* (1923), i. 361.

123

Monday 17 Aug 14

My darling – I hope you got a little farewell message I wrote near midnight from Munstead[1] & entrusted to F. McLaren. It was so blank and disheartening to think that I should not be near you again for such an indefinite time. And, tho' yesterday was rather broken up, Saturday was a golden day & I shall never forget (will you?) the hours we spent together under the leaden sky & dripping rain, with the glimpses of heather, & the constant change of pine & oak, and (what was worth more than everything outside) the close real deep understanding & love, which in these moving times is to me more than anything in the world. Be sure, whatever happens, that it has made to me all the difference between what I might have been (but for you) and what (with you) I am & hope to be.

I wonder how you are faring in your long journey. Here it is bright & sunny: and you carry with you every inch of your journey the best head & strongest heart, and (I trust) the most undimmed confidence of any woman in these islands. Thank God that I can always count on you.

We had a dullish dinner, and played Bridge, with the result that F. M^cL &

I took about 117/- out of the McKennae. Then about 11.30 the Assyrian & I drove back to London with a beautiful crescent moon lighting up the edge of the horizon. I thought of you.

We had a Cabinet at noon: Ll. George has got neuralgia & could not come. Turkey has come into the foreground, threatens vaguely enterprises against Egypt, and seems disposed to play a double game about the *Goeben* & the *Breslau*. Winston, in his most bellicose mood, is all for sending a torpedo flotilla thro' the Dardanelles – to threaten & if necessary to sink the *Goeben* & her consort. Crewe & Kitchener very much against (in the interest of the Moslems in India & Egypt) our doing anything wh. could be interpreted as meaning that we were taking the initiative agst Turkey. She ought to be compelled to strike the first blow. I agreed to this. But the Turks must be obliged to come out & tell us whether they are going at once to dismiss the German crews.

We then resumed the topic (now so familiar to you) of the 'strangulation' of Germany. The Americans protest, in the interest of neutral shipping, against our following the German example & laying down mines in the North Sea.[2] As you know, I am all against this provocative & rather barbarous mode of procedure, and I strongly urged the development of the Runciman plan of taking up all the carrying ships we can get, and so diverting the trade from Rotterdam.[3] There was a lot of talk about international law & its niceties (in wh. the Impeccable took quite a good part) and Runciman is going to present us to-morrow with the flesh & blood on his skeleton.

I brought up the question of the sale of the Ulster rifles to the Belgians.[4] Happily Kitchener has some 4000 Mannlichers in stock, wh. he will sell at once to the Belgians, & this gives one a day or two's breathing space. Meanwhile Winston was able to push through a new little scheme of his for getting us this year 12 more destroyers & 12 submarines.

Kitchener showed me a letter from French describing his visit to Paris &c. He has now gone to his headquarters (Cateau, about 30 or 40 miles S.W. of Maubeuge): 3 divisions are already there & the rest will follow in 2 or 3 days. There is no news except that I hear just now that our 2nd General Grierson – a good but rather apoplectic man – has suddenly died in the train between Havre & Amiens. I haven't spoken to Kitchener yet, but I think Smith Dorrien is the best man to fill his place.[5]

Elizabeth, who is back here to lunch, on her way to Stanway,[6] yesterday went over the naval hospital at Harwich – full of naval men (mostly Germans) terribly wounded in the mine-laying[7] affair in the North Sea. One of the Germans had 60 wounds, & they were almost all maimed, blinded, or terribly disfigured. They are delighted with their treatment, and dread the time when they will be discharged from the hospital.

It looks as if the big battle would not begin for another 48 hours. If so, our force will be in the thick of it near the end.[8]

I acted on your suggestion & told Birrell to summon Redmond back by telegraph. He will be here Wed. morning, and we must then go hard at it to get the two Bills on the shelf.

Darling I tell you everything, but it makes *such* a difference not having you close by. Do you realise? Be dear and *write*, and above all think & advise, – & love.

I bless you & love you with all my heart & soul.

[1] Munstead House (see Appendix 3) was the home of Sir Herbert and Lady Jekyll. Their elder daughter, Barbara, was married to Francis McLaren, then a Liberal M.P., the younger, Pamela, to Reginald McKenna. Venetia was going to Penrhos.

[2] On 6 Aug. the American Secretary of State invited the belligerent Governments to declare their adherence to the Declaration of London, 1909. The British refused. They had never ratified the Declaration and to have accepted it now would have restricted their ability to stop supplies reaching their enemies. On 7 Aug. the Germans, having laid an 'ambush' minefield off Harwich (Letter 117, n. 1), announced that the 'necessity would arise . . . of blockading with mines the points of departure . . . of hostile fleets against Germany, and the ports . . . of troop transports'. This announcement reached Washington, however, in a hopelessly garbled form. Grey told the American Government on 11 Aug.: 'In view of the measures adopted by Germany, the British Admiralty must hold themselves fully at liberty to adopt similar measures in self-defence.' The Secretary of State answered (13 Aug.) that the German minelaying provided no reason 'for His Majesty's Government adopting a similar course'. He was assured (14 Aug.) that neutral shipping would be shown a safe way into Antwerp (though not into Rotterdam); but five days later the British Chargé d'Affaires in Washington reiterated that the British could not renounce a method of war which their enemies were using (*Foreign Relations of the U.S., 1914 Supplement* (1928), pp. 454–8). For the change in Asquith's views on mining after eight weeks of war see Letter 168.

[3] By 31 Dec. the additions to British shipping by capture, purchase, and new building, far outweighed the losses, the gross steam tonnage on the British Register being 462,000 tons higher than a year earlier.

[4] At this stage James Craig 'refused to part with one rifle'. The Government apparently gave the Belgians the rifles captured from the Nationalist Volunteers (Letter 106, n. 1) during the Howth gun-running (Colvin, *Carson*, iii (1936), 35; Hobhouse, *Diaries*, p. 183).

[5] Grierson had been one of French's two corps commanders, Haig being the other. French asked for Plumer as the replacement; but Kitchener wired: 'King and government decide for Smith-Dorrien. Plumer can hardly be spared at present, but will be available later.'

[6] See Appendix 3.

[7] See Letter 117, n. 1.

[8] 'Near the end': Asquith probably meant by this 'during the later part of the battle'. He would have known that the B.E.F. could not be ready for action in two days' time, that is, by 19 Aug. If the phrase referred, not to time, but to the position of the B.E.F., it was optimistic: they were not 'near', but *at* 'the end'. There were practically no French infantry on their left until Joffre started to switch divisions to the left wing on 25 Aug.

Bust of H. H. Asquith, by Lady
Scott, 1913

Cartoon by Max
Beerbohm, 1913: see p.
11. The caption reads:

Come one, come all,
    this rock shall fly
From its firm base
    as soon as I
(Scott, *Lady of the
    Lake*, v.x)

Handwriting of Venetia Stanley: Letter to Edwin Montagu, November 1912

Handwriting of H. H. Asquith: from Letter 115, 4 August 1914

Ulster VI: 'A really great achievement?' (Letters 114–28, 131–4, 136, 139–41, 146, 148, 150–2, 154–9, and 161–2)

THERE were four ways of dealing with Home Rule once Britain was at war. All were based on suspending any action under the measure during wartime. The first was to seek an agreement between Carson and Redmond, in the hope that war conditions would elicit the compromise which had eluded the Buckingham Palace Conference (Letters 115 and 124). In fact the war had done nothing to decrease the difficulty of a negotiation between the two. Redmond could not fulfil his pledge of Irish help for the war effort (Letter 114) unless Home Rule went on to the statute-book. Carson was not going to yield anything at a moment when Ulster could not be coerced nor the Home Rule measure brought into effect. The second possibility was for the Government to bring forward a compromise solution and to impose it despite the protests of the extremists (Letter 128). Asquith adopted a formula which would have put Home Rule on the statute-book, while first keeping the six counties out of the Home Rule area for three years, and then giving each county the chance to opt out for good. The enactment of the measure and the 'county option' element were designed to favour Redmond, the chance of permanent exclusion being the attraction for Carson. Bonar Law promised his personal backing for the scheme (Letter 133) and seems to have persuaded his party to take the same view:[1] it foundered on Liberal and Nationalist objections (Letter 134). Redmond's speech on 3 August (Letter 114) had won him much sympathy:[2] some prominent southern Irish Conservatives now supported him. Many Liberals refused to requite him by conceding the principle of permanent exclusion.

The third and fourth possibilities entailed acknowledging that no agreement could be found. Both were based on fighting the battle of the Amending Bill at the end of the war and meanwhile 'freezing' the position. Under the third the Bill would be passed, but not put into operation. Under the fourth it would not reach the statute-book at all, but would be kept to the end of the war just as it had been at the beginning, retaining full protection under the Parliament Act. Redmond was safeguarded against accidents by the third, the Conservatives by the fourth (Letter 124*). There was no way of protecting Redmond without passing the Bill because this would have entailed a promise by the Government that there would be no wartime election. While the Conservatives were willing to forgo an election during

---

* Asquith lists only three possibilities in Letter 124. His third course is identical to the fourth in the fuller list given above.

wartime as far as Home Rule was concerned, one might become necessary for quite different reasons.

Asquith regarded the fourth solution, of preserving the position exactly as it had been on 30 July, as the fairer of the two (Letter 124): it was certainly the one most clearly corresponding to the pledges which he had given. Like the second possibility outlined above, however, it was subject to the insuperable objection of being unacceptable to Redmond. By coming out in support of the British war effort the Nationalist leader had both established a claim to have Home Rule enacted at once, and exposed his party to ruin if it were not. War had turned the tables, Redmond being now in a stronger bargaining position than Carson. A wartime government could not afford a disaffected Ireland, to say nothing of Irish anger in the Dominions and the United States. Redmond's hold on the National Volunteers had always been precarious. Unless Home Rule became law there would be no Irish recruits outside Ulster. Carson could not match Redmond's threats, though in the first week of the war he tried hard to achieve this. Were Home Rule to be enacted, he wrote (Letter 120), 'I must either resign the leadership of Ulster, or go over to Belfast and throw in my lot with my people there in any action they feel bound to take, however distasteful it might be to me and however much it might be disliked in England . . . If [the controversy] were postponed Captain Craig . . . is in a position to offer Kitchener at once two divisions of trained men (about 20,000) with all their equipment for immediate active service abroad; and in addition a similar number for home service in Ulster. If the controversy goes on, of course none of these men will be available, much to my regret.' This soon turned into a bluff. By the time the B.E.F. reached France Carson was neither able nor willing to stop his Ulster loyalists from enlisting. 'Dear Sir Edward,' a Tyrone man wrote on 18 August, 'We decided today . . . to hold all we can back till 26th . . . ; but, Home Rule won or lost, we must go in then for King and country.' 'However much we curse and damn the P.M. in the House,' Craig told Carson on 20 August, 'we must say all the same that we will do our best . . . for the army and for the country.' In the last week of August Carson and Craig offered to recruit all the Ulster Volunteers they could for active service: they secured very good terms for their Ulster Division from the War Office (p. 236), but made no conditions about Home Rule.

Having chosen the fourth solution, of putting the Bill on the statute-book, Asquith conducted the parliamentary business with his usual skill. By the tone of his speech on 15 September (Letter 157) he indicated how unseemly extreme partisanship was in war. 'Under the conditions which now exist,' he said, 'the employment of force . . . for the coercion of Ulster is . . . absolutely unthinkable.' His role as the nation's leader in war was

made more convincing by the overpitched bitterness of Bonar Law's reply.
This repelled even the faithful Max Aitken, while a moderate Conservative
hoped that F. E. Smith could use his powers in the Press Bureau to censor
his leader's outburst.[3]

1 Asquith made clear in his letter that the suggestion was not an offer.
2 Carson's anger at this showed in his Carlton Club speech, 14 Sept., when he referred to
speeches by Irish Nationalists as 'calculated to humbug and deceive'.
3 A. J. P. Taylor, *Beaverbrook* (1972), p. 87; *Nation*, 19 Sept., p. 862.

124

Tue. 18 Aug 14

My darling – of course there was no letter from you this morning: how
could there be when you were in the motor all day? (Beb reported having
seen you at Stanway). All the same its absence left a blank feeling, and I look
forward eagerly to to-morrow.

After I wrote I had a lot of bother over the Prince of Wales's Relief Fund.
It is over a million now & no one seems to have the least idea what exactly it
is for, or how or by whom it is going to be spent! I have asked A.J.B. and Sir
G. Murray to join the Committee, which seems to be rather a rudderless
affair,[1] and after all it is none of my business. I haven't even sent my
subscription yet. Among my callers on the subject was the Abp. of Canterbury, and I took the opportunity of opening up with him the proposed
moratorium for Welsh disendowment.[2] I think he was rather agreeably
surprised, but I don't know what his second thoughts will be.

Redmond is I hope coming over to-night, and I have told Birrell to see him
first thing to-morrow, & to impress upon him that *some modus vivendi* is,
in existing circumstances, absolutely imperative. The choice is between 3
courses (1) agreement upon the basis of provisional exclusion of 6 counties
or thereabouts (2) passing the Bill as it stands with a suspensory clause, say
for 1 year, capable of renewal (3) hanging up the Bill to next Session, with a
provision that it shd then be in precisely the same position (i.e. deemed to
have passed the H of Commons & gone to the Lords) as it is now, & entitled
to full benefit of Parliament Act.

(1) with all its logical drawbacks is the best – for so far as G. Britain is
concerned it clears the whole damned business out of the way.

(2) I doubt whether the Tories wd. accept: they wd. say it left them too
much at the mercy of the chapter of accidents.

(3) is really the fairest in the circumstances: for it leaves both parties in
their present position when next Session comes. I expect Redmond will jib

at it, because it does not give him his Bill on the Statute book now, & leaves *him* more or less to the mercies of fortune.

Rather interesting isn't it? Of course (3) cd. be applied to the Welsh Bill also, if there are difficulties about agreement there.

Violet & I drove out to Stanmore to dine with the Bencks. Only the Count and Countess & Nathalie were at dinner; Bron & Nan came in afterwards. We played some rather moderate Bridge & came home with a fair sum out of the Ambassador's pocket: he & 'Sophie', hate playing as partners, and never get to better terms than a kind of armed neutrality. I am very fond of them both.

There was a rumour all over London yesterday, wh. was universally believed, that Fraü had at last been arrested & cast into prison, no less than 4 documents of the most incriminating kind being found upon her! Of course it was only a 'well-invented para.' . . . but every one was prepared to accept it as gospel – including the Bencks.

Do you remember remonstrating with me for throwing out of the window that little rolled up ball of 'flimsy' as we drove thro' Roehampton lane on Sat? The only people – except E Grey – who get these secret flimsies are myself, Winston, Kitchener & Harcourt. It appears that the police have discovered fragments of them in St. James' Park, in Oxfordshire near Goring, & one or two other places in the country. These they have laboriously collected and the pieces came round in a box this morning with a severe admonition from E Grey as to the dangers to wh. the Foreign Office cypher was exposed from such loose handling of secret matters! My conscience was quite clear as to St. Jas's Park & Goring: so I simply wrote 'not guilty' – nor was our little ball among the *pièces de conviction*: but what damning evidence you might have given!

We had a Cabinet this morning, but there was nothing very interesting. Poor old Grierson seems to have died of apoplexy & excitement, & is to be succeeded by Smith Dorrien. Everyone is very pleased with the smoothness & secrecy of the Exped^y Force. Winston is engaged in chasing a German cruiser about the North Sea with 2 of his flotillas, & hopes to run her down before nightfall.

Since I began this I have been out to luncheon at the French Embassy to meet Jules Cambon, late of Berlin. E. Grey, Benck, Tyrrell & a lot of Frenchmen were there. Paul Cambon said rather a good thing to me about Jaurès who was assassinated the other day: 'He was by nature an orator, & he took up all the ideas, creeds &c – such as Socialism, fraternity of nations & the rest – wh. most readily lead themselves to oratory'. I had a really interesting talk after lunch with the other brother Jules, who is the quicker & brighter of the two. He says Bethmann-Hollweg is a man 'très médiocre'

– 'bourgeois et courtisan' – wh. as I said is a combinaison mauvaise. At his final interview with Jagow, the German Foreign Sec^y, he (Jules) said to him: 'you will be conquered in this war by the same forces wh. conquered Napoleon – les deux Puissances intangibles' – England & Russia.[3] One you cannot reach by water, nor the other by land, &c. He thinks rather meanly of the Kaiser 'vaniteux & poseur', and says that he was drawn into the war by the military party, by the junkers who want to destroy Parliamentarism & reestablish the Bismarckian régime, and by jealousy of the Crown Prince who is the idol of the mob.[4]

Good Heavens! the best part of 3 sheets. You will I am afraid think that I am getting garrulous, and I have not time to cut out the dull parts. I dine with Cassel to-night. Think of me always my darling, and tell me your thoughts, and be my stay & joy. I love you.

[1] The Prince of Wales had appealed on 6 Aug. for funds to relieve the distress which the war was sure to entail. Queen Mary added a special appeal to women, while Queen Alexandra appealed for the Soldiers' and Sailors' Families Association. On 11 Aug., it was announced that these funds would be fused and would 'embrace . . . the relief of all hardship, whether arising directly from war casualties or through unemployment caused by the inevitable dislocation of trade'. Wedgwood Benn (see Letter 74, n. 11) was the first chairman, being succeeded, when he took an army commission, by Sir George Murray. By 31 Mar. 1915 £4,907,000 had been subscribed, and £1,960,000 allocated.

[2] See Letter 120, n. 4.

[3] Cambon's description of Bethmann-Hollweg as 'a bourgeois and a courtier' was apt. The German Chancellor did not have the political weight to keep either the Kaiser or the generals under control. Russian military strength was generally overestimated in Britain and France. It was not realized how far corruption and inefficiency in St Petersburg had slowed the military recovery after the Russo-Japanese war. Sukhomlinov, Minister of War, 1908–14, was pleasure-loving, venal, and involved with the spies and agents of both Germany and Austria, his only military exertions being aimed at obstructing all modernization. Russia started the war with 60 batteries of heavy artillery to Germany's 381, and with a supply of shells per gun about one-third as large as in the Western armies.

[4] Asquith's assiduity as a correspondent is illustrated by the appearance of this passage, with only the most minor variations, in his letter of the same day to Margot. See Spender and Asquith, ii. 107.

'The Germans are coming round in a big enveloping movement' (Letter 125)

WHEN Kitchener told the French staff officers on 12 August that the Germans would advance north and west of the Sambre–Meuse line in great strength they pronounced such a movement to be 'impossible' (pp. 154–6).[1] By 19 August he was sure that it was happening; and he did all he could to warn Sir John French, wiring on 19 August: 'The movement of the German right flank, north of the Meuse, which . . . I mentioned as likely . . . seems to be definitely developing'; and on 21 August: 'Minister

Antwerp says 2nd, 4th, 10th, 7th and 9th German army corps north of Meuse'. Yet on the afternoon of 23 August, while the Mons Battle was being fought, Wilson persuaded French 'that we had only one corps and one cavalry division (possibly two corps) opposite to us'. As the presence of two German corps and a cavalry division had been established from prisoners and uniforms early that morning, and a third joined the attack in the afternoon, this was a notably optimistic assessment. Fortunately Wilson received a warning at 8 p.m. which even he could not disregard: 'A wire came from Joffre', he recorded, 'to say we had two and a half corps opposite us. This stopped our attack.'

If Letter 125 can be assumed to reproduce Kitchener's views with reasonable accuracy,[2] it shows that, though he knew enough to be very critical of Joffre's strategy, he was imperfectly informed about the disposition of the French left wing. At Mons on 23 August the B.E.F. were far from being 'in the rear of some five French army corps'. Apart from that, an assessment of the danger to the B.E.F., made on 19 August, necessarily turned on the resistance of Namur: Kitchener assumed that it would hold out for some days at least (p. 156). While it did so, there was a chance of striking at the German right wing on its inner flank – 'a thrust at the shoulder . . . of the long, straining, encircling arm', in Churchill's phrase, 'which should lop it off or cripple it fatally'.

[1] Asquith to Margot, 19 August. Kitchener, Asquith added, 'is very good on these things'. On this subject, if on no other, Kitchener told the cabinet all he knew: Lloyd George, *War Memoirs*, p. 455; Lucy Masterman, *C. F. G. Masterman* (1939), p. 269.

[2] Kitchener can hardly have regarded this version of the Schlieffen Plan as 'new'.

125

Wed 19 Aug 1914

My darling – it was heavenly to get your dear long letter this morning: just what I want & like, because it tells me what you are doing every hour of the day. . . .

I only hope that dear old Haldane may get the credit he deserves for the ease & efficiency of all the arrangements [for the B.E.F.]. . . .

. . . I dined with Cassel – Winston & Clemmie were there, and a pack of the women one cares for least – Lady S. Wilson, Mrs Keppel, Julia Maguire, Lady Randolph.[1] So different from our interesting lunch at Cambon's. . . .

I read before going to bed a new novel by the author of 'Queed'[2] sent me by Pamela McKenna, with the ridiculous title 'Captivating Mary Carstairs'. It is more of a farce than anything else, but quite readable & clever.

I was very disappointed to hear from Birrell this morning that Redmond wd. not return till to-morrow (Thurs) night. It is wrong of him, because it makes the time for arrangement so short, and so far blocks the road. I told Birrell to write to him at once pointing out the 3 possible roads, as I described them to you yesterday, and preparing him to take his choice.

Weren't you amused at the Press bureau notice, that there was a certain 'liveliness' in the Southern part of the North Sea? A coin that cd. only come from the Winston mint.

I didn't feel very comfortable this morning about the military situation, & got Kitchener to go into it thoroughly. He thinks that the Germans are coming round in a big enveloping movement, & will try to break through into France over the frontier between Maubeuge & Lille. Have you got a good map? If this is their new plan of campaign it may be a good many days yet before the big fighting begins and our force will be in the rear of some 5 French Army Corps, and ought to give effective support.

We had the usual Cabinet. The situation as regards Turkey is decidedly better (happily Louis Mallet is now back again at Constantinople), and will be further improved if we offer them to return their two seized battleships[3] at the end of the war, meanwhile paying them £1000 a day for the use of the ships from the moment the last of the German crews of the *Goeben* & *Breslau* have cleared out of Turkish territory.

Nothing much came out of the alarums & excursions in the North Sea yesterday. In the 10 or 12 days that the war has so far lasted, we have captured 35 German ships on the high seas as prizes, & they none of ours.[4] That is not a bad state of the account.

We had a good deal of further talk about 'strangulation'. The first thing is to secure that the 12 Hamburg-Amerika ships in New York shall either be bottled up where they are, or transferred to the British flag.[5] The men who are really useful in these discussions are Grey (of course) Runciman Lloyd George Winston, & (with reservations) Kitchener & the Impeccable. The others rarely intervene.

The trouble about the Prince of Wales's fund still goes on simmering and is really a nuisance. I send you (to add to your collection of oddities) the first letter I have ever received from our 'Gracious Queen Mary'. I know you will keep it in safety, perhaps wrapped up in lavender! Tell me what you think of it? It is quite business-like to my thinking, & don't you like the thin-spun mid-Victorian handwriting? . . .

Violet & I have just lunched with Winston & Clementine at the Admiralty. He is in quite undefeated form, and the particular 'swine' at whom he would now like to have a fling are his kinsmen in the United States.

I feel so solitary, & so far away from you, my own darling. So I take my revenge, & such consolation as I can get, by pouring out everything into your lap. The touch of your hand would be worth far more than a King's ransom – while the whole world goes whirling on in what Carlyle wd. call this 'devil's dance'. I bless you every hour: without you, I tremble to think where I, & everything that depends on me, would have been. Do you understand & realise this?

All my love.

125a

Buckingham Palace   Ansd [Endorsement by H.H.A.]

Augst 19th 1914

Dear Mr Asquith,

Lady Crewe tells me that she has outlined to you my proposal for giving work to unemployed women, & that you listened to her with a sympathetic ear! I am very anxious that it should not in any way interfere with the National Relief Fund, & therefore the ladies on my Executive Committee will collect for that Fund, and in return I want to ask the N.R.F. for a grant of money towards the expenses of my scheme which I fear will be very large. On every point I wish to consult the Local Government Board & other authorities & the scheme which my advisory committee is drawing up will be submitted at once to Mr Samuel for approval. On my advisory committee I have secured the services of 4 women experts on the Labour question, besides other ladies experienced in industrial matters. I feel very strongly that the subject is an urgent one & needs immediate attention as every day small schemes are starting which ought to be coordinated with mine. As a woman I feel deeply for my fellow women who are already beginning to suffer acutely from the effects of the War on their various trades, and I know I can count on the support of other women all over the country. I am quite aware of the enormous difficulties, both economic & industrial, which confront us, still I hope we may find some way out which will not clash with trade interests.

May I show you the scheme after it has been put before Mr Samuel?[6] Believe me

Yours very sincerely

Mary

---

[1] For Mrs Keppel and Mrs Maguire see Letter 39, n. 2. Lady Sarah Wilson, a daughter of the 7th Duke of Marlborough, was to be associated with Mrs Keppel in running a wartime hospital in France. Lord Randolph Churchill's widow had divorced her second husband,

George Cornwallis-West, in 1913, and was usually known by the Christian name of her famous first husband (d. 1895).

2 Henry Sydnor Harrison.

3 See Letter 122, n. 4.

4 By Art. 3 of the Sixth Hague Convention, 1907, a ship which was encountered at sea while still ignorant of the outbreak of war was not to be confiscated as a prize but merely to be detained during the war or requisitioned on payment of compensation. Germany had not ratified this article, however, so that it did not apply to German ships.

5 A quarter of a million tons of German shipping lay in New York. A Ship Registry Act, designed to facilitate its transfer to the American flag, had been signed by President Wilson on 18 Aug. Grey told the American Ambassador that Britain was determined not to allow these ships to supply Germany, whoever their owners and whatever their flag. American would-be purchasers were thus scared off; and the Hamburg-Amerika Line's negotiations for sale languished. There would be no objection, Grey added, if the American Government bought the ships, and promised not to use them against the Allied Powers: his own Government had been thinking of buying them; but, granted these conditions, it would gladly give place to the Washington authorities. The Wilson administration's Ship Purchase Bill did not pass, however; and the ships remained in New York harbour. They included the *Vaterland* (54,000 tons), the largest merchantman afloat, and three Norddeutscher Lloyd liners. The slowest of these four could steam at nineteen knots. There was also a Hamburg-Amerika liner in Boston. It was particularly important to the British that these five should be 'bottled up', or transferred into sympathetic hands, since, if taken to sea, they could be used as armed merchant cruisers. Even if they did not have guns on board already, the German navy might contrive to arm them at a sea rendezvous.

6 The scheme was organized under the umbrella of the National Relief Fund, the central committee consisting of thirteen women drawn from all three parties. It was chaired by Lady Crewe (Letter 127) and had Mary Macarthur (Mrs W. C. Anderson) as secretary (Letter 160).

126

Thur 20 Aug 14

Beloved – you sent me a most delicious letter this morning. I like to have the picture of your daily life – prawning up to the waist all the morning, riding your unbroken horse in the afternoon, sitting in the little square garden, wh. I know so well & love so much, writing your letters (one, at any rate, to me, & I try not to be jealous of the others), and now & again reading over my letters, & not finding them too long! One ought not to complain, in times like these, that life is imperfectly arranged. Sometimes, at odd moments, I dream dreams & draw pictures, & fancy imaginary conditions, which, if they cd. only be realised, would make everything so much easier, remove grim barriers of time and space, annihilate distance, give a new shape & colour both to one's working & resting hours, and – but you know what I mean, and can finish & round off my ideal. My darling. You will forgive me, won't you? Five minutes of reverie – the 'bliss of solitude'. There is no one else in the world who even suspects where my thoughts and aspirations (hopes, I may not & cannot say) are always centred. You understand – you only – and *tout comprendre, c'est tout pardonner*. And perhaps even more than that. . . .

I wish with all my heart – every day, all day, & most of the night – that Penrhos was 200 miles nearer London. I am more glad than I can tell you that I can look back upon & re-create our far-off Whitsuntide. You saved me then from something very like despair – and you will do the same again. . . .

The poor Belgians have been having a bad hammering, & are now driven back to Antwerp, and Brussels is in the hands of the Germans. For the real purposes & fortunes of the campaign, this is all to the good – for it means that the Germans have to spend 2 or possibly even 3 days more (to the disarrangement of their time table) before the real fighting on the great scale begins. It looks as if our troops (whose headquarters is Le Cateau S.W. of Maubeuge) may be in the thick of it before long. We are sending off another Division – the 5th – on Saturday to the front.[1] This will practically denude Ireland of regulars, & Paget[2] is about to retire. It is in some ways a pity, for he is a man of war, but he had completely lost the confidence of the Army.

We had rather a long Cabinet this morning. All sorts of odds & ends about coal[3] & contraband & 'continuous voyages'[4] & such like technicalities. The main question was as to what answer we should give to Venizelos's offer of a Greek alliance, not only against Turkey, but possibly also against Bulgaria if she should attack Servia. I am all against interfering in the Balkans among these small States: on the other hand, one does not want to snub Greece; & it took some time to hammer out a cordial yet not too-committal reply.[5]

I had a very slippery & characteristic reply from the Abp. of Canterbury to my proposal for a 'moratorium' in the matter of Welsh Disendowment.[6] The 'children of light' are more than a match for the 'children of this world', when it is a question of appropriating flesh-pots & dividing spoils. Redmond comes back to-day, & Birrell is to see him this evening, by way of preparation for an interview between him & me to-morrow morning. I expect I shall find him difficult & disposed to be exorbitant. But (as you know) it is essential not at the moment to have a domestic 'crisis'. I can't tell you beloved how much I wish you were to be here to-morrow to talk to, and to give me understanding & sympathy. . . .

. . . I wd. give more than I can put down on paper to be able to – some sentences are best left unfinished.

---

[1] The fifth infantry division to land. In designation it was the 4th Division. They came into action on 24 Aug. covering the retreat to Le Cateau, and were heavily engaged on 26 Aug., though many of their supporting services had not yet arrived at the front. See Letter 136.

² See p. 57 and Letters 49 and 51.

³ Germany normally imported large quantities of British coal. It was feared that she might continue to receive these indirectly through the three Scandinavian countries; but the returns for coal shipments to them soon showed that this was not happening.

⁴ By the doctrine of 'continuous voyage' a cargo was judged contraband in the light, not of the port to which it was consigned, but of its final destination. Since the Declaration of London all contraband lists had been divided into 'absolute contraband' (munitions, etc.) and 'conditional contraband' (food, forage, military clothing, etc.). The extension of the continuous voyage doctrine to conditional contraband was controversial.

⁵ Apart from bringing Turkey and Bulgaria into the war against the Allies, acceptance of the Greek offer would, in Grey's view, have led to 'the unsettlement of Russia's wholeheartedness in the war'.

⁶ See Letter 120, n. 4.

Directing the War Effort:
'a united and <u>most</u> efficient cabinet'

LIKE all his predecessors Asquith ran cabinet meetings with no secretary in attendance. The letter which he wrote in longhand to the King constituted the only record of the decisions taken. He thus maintained the tradition by which ministers were protected against any hostile reminder of the views which they had previously expressed in the cabinet room, note-taking being discouraged.

It was immensely difficult to adapt this system to the exigencies of war. The Committee of Imperial Defence, though served by a highly efficient secretariat, was unpopular with those ministers who had only yesterday been non-interventionists. It was also too large, and too full of retired grandees, to be convertible into an effective war committee. The War Council which had been summoned to discuss the despatch of the Expeditionary Force (Letter 116) would have been equally unsuitable as a continuing body. Moreover, the conviction that in a parliamentary régime all decisions should be taken by the cabinet went deep.

It was soon clear that this conviction did not accord with the realities of a war which was far outrunning pre-war plans. Crucial decisions had to be made by little groups of ministers. The group which despatched Kitchener to Paris in the small hours of 1 September (Letter 141) included McKenna and 'Jack' Pease simply because they had been dining at 10 Downing Street that evening. Effective direction in war depends on complete information and on the means to plan ahead and to co-ordinate. Even if Kitchener had been willing to entrust his cabinet colleagues with the information, they possessed no such means. Nothing was done during September to help in defending Antwerp, though the threat to it had been clear to Churchill and Hankey throughout the month (Letter 170, n. 7).

Asquith's ingrained habits added to these difficulties. During the early months of the war he did not press his colleagues to accept a change of system because he was slow to see the need for this himself. His cabinet methods were, in Hankey's words, 'slightly Gladstonian'.[1] Towards the end of November 1914 he established a War Council of eight – Prime Minister; Chancellor of the Exchequer; Foreign Secretary; First Lord of the Admiralty and First Sea Lord; War Secretary and C.I.G.S.; and Balfour. No public announcement was made. As late as May 1915, after one of the Council's meetings, *The Times* reported that 'a meeting of a sub-committee of the Committee of Imperial Defence was held at 10 Downing Street'.

The War Council, like its successors during Asquith's wartime premiership, grew steadily. By 10 March 1915 its membership stood at thirteen. Though served with great efficiency by the Committee of Imperial Defence secretariat under Hankey, it never became the body for daily planning and co-ordination which was needed. Edwin Montagu (who had joined the cabinet some weeks earlier) wrote to Hankey on 22 March 1915:

You do not get discussions in the War Council differing materially from those in the cabinet; you have the same protagonists in both; and all you do is to substitute a different set of spectators. The War Council should be used by its political members to get a frank opinion of the military experts; but . . . this is not done and will not be done unless the Council is reconstituted or unless the president lays down this as its specific duty.[2]

As the 1915 Letters will show, there was force in Montagu's criticism. To have secured by the end of 1914 a directing body of a sort, the conclusions of which were circulated in minutes, was something, but not enough.

[1] On the need for a cabinet secretariat see *Parl. Deb.*, Lords, xxx. 265 (Curzon, 19 June 1918), clv. 219, 224 (Austen Chamberlain, 13 June 1922); Machinery of Government Report, para. 10: *Parl. Papers* 1918, CD9230, xii. 6. The institution of a small war cabinet, served by a secretariat, was not a recipe for instant efficiency, however. 'The war cabinet', Hankey noted in Mar. 1917, 'never discuss their Agenda paper at all. . . . Consequently all the work is dreadfully congested – far worse than it ever was under the so-called "Wait and See" Government': Stephen Roskill, *Hankey*, i (1970), 371. In Mar. 1910 Asquith had told those enquiring about the reintroduction of the budget to 'wait and see'. The phrase was later used against him in accusations of dilatoriness.

[2] Roskill, *Hankey*, i. 172. See also p. 375, n. 8.

127

Fr. 21 Aug 14

My darling – it was a great blow to get no letter this morning: the first time it has missed. I was afraid you might perhaps not be well – so I wired: but I trust it is no more than a delay in the post. I wrote to you, carrying out to the letter your injunction not to spare you a single word!

It will be 27 years to-morrow since you opened your eyes on this sinful world, and it is not yet quite 3 since I made my great discovery of the *real* you. I sometimes wonder, looking back, whether you would rather that I had *not* made it, and that things had continued between us as they were in the early days of the Venetiad.[1] I believe – indeed I know from what you have told me, and you never lie – that it has made a difference to the interests & pleasures (perhaps also at times to the anxieties) of your life. I cannot tell you, for you might think I was exaggerating – the length & breadth & depth of the difference it has made to mine. It has been given I suppose to few men to go through such a succession of 'crises' in the same space of time; you have been a stay and refreshment to me in them all; and during this last 12 months with its almost miraculous series of emergencies I have come more & more to rely and rest upon you, and you have never failed me either in counsel or in love. So I bless you darling with all my heart, and pray for you every boon that the years can bring.

———

Since I broke off your dear letter has come: I suppose the trains were late; you are leading an ideally peaceful life – if only I could share it for 24 hours! I went to Bumpus's yesterday and searched high & low for a birthday present for you. In the end, I got one or two books that I thought you might really like to have – all first editions (which personally I always like to have). I wrote your name in only one – the *Critic* – but if you like I will do the same in the others. The *Oliver Twist* is remarkable because it has a plate of Cruikshank's about p 330 of the 3rd vol (called by the critics the 'Family Plate') wh. for some reason or other was never reproduced in the later editions. I hope, darling, you will like them: no books since the world began, or at any rate since people took to printing, ever took with them a deeper & truer message of love.

V & I dined with Hugh last night in his rather frost-bitten little house. The other guests were Mr & Mrs Lyell, Sir A. Thring, Lady Brassey (!) & Viola. We had quite a nice evening – with great difficulty persuading Hugh in the end to scrape his viola with a bow. There were *no* symptoms,[2] & notwithstanding his signs of assiduity I feel sure that *that* book is closed.

Redmond came (at last) to see me this morning with Birrell. Of course he rules out my No 3, would prefer the 'moratorium'[3] (No 2), but agreed (as I am glad to see that you do) that No 1 (agreement, with an area of exclusion) would if practicable be the best. The old bother about Tyrone & those infernal snippets of Fermanagh Derry &c popped up again, and he doesn't see how he & Carson can be brought nearer, in regard to all this, than they were at Buck^m Palace 3 weeks ago. I have since seen Bonar Law, who won't have No 2 at any price, & says that his party would regard themselves in that case as jockeyed & cheated &c &c. He would agree to No 1, provided we could give him the 6 counties, and would then concede a 3 years time limit.

I shall try to work to some concordat on these lines, but it is difficult (if possible) to get it through in the next 2 or 3 days, and rather than have a smash next week I should be disposed to a further adjournment of the House – for a short time. Oddly enough Crewe was seeing Lansdowne at the same time, & I shall be curious to hear his report.

We had a long Cabinet this morning, mostly about rather boring details connected with the war. The real centre of interest (political, not military) at the moment is Turkey – & the two darkest horses in the European stable, Italy & Roumania. The different points of view of different people are rather amusing – Winston violently anti-Turk, Kitchener strong that Roumania is the real pivot of the situation, Masterman eagerly pro-Bulgarian, I very much against any aggressive action *vis-à-vis* Turkey wh. wd. excite our Mussulmans in India & Egypt, Ll. George keen for Balkan confederation, Grey judicious & critical all round, Haldane misty & imprecise, Simon precise & uninspiring, Hobhouse assertive & irrelevant, Runciman instructive & juiceless, and the Beagles & Bobtails silent & bewildered.[4] There's a picture for you of a united & *most* efficient Cabinet! What a pity you are not there – with Huck & the Penguin under the table.

In the midst of the last sentence but one I was interrupted by a call from Peggy Crewe, who is suffering from the unbusinesslike habits of her fellow women on the Queen's Committee. As she says of herself, it is something to be both a Semite & a Scot.[5]

Darling I must stop now, as I have to go & see the King. Perhaps you had better write to-morrow & Sunday to London, as I fear it would not get to me at Lympne, whence I shall probably return on Sunday night. You might send me a telegram *here* to-morrow (Sat) morning before lunch to say if the books have arrived. I see the Abp. & the Mascot-tamer at 11.0. I am afraid this is a ragged letter – hardly worthy of your birthday. But no one will ever love you more – or so much. *Never.*

[1] See Pamela Jekyll to Asquith, 3 Nov. [1907]: '. . . Venetia and I had several heated disputes concerning our rival claims to your affection. She hinted darkly to me of some communications you had addressed to her in verse known as the Venetiad – and even went as far as showing me a few choice couplets.'

[2] See Letter 74, n. 2.

[3] For the three schemes see Letter 124.

[4] For the use of this passage in Asquith's *Memories and Reflections*, and in Beaverbrook, *Politicians and the War*, see Appendix 1.

[5] Lady Rosebery, Lady Crewe's mother, was a Rothschild. Dalmeny, the principal seat of the Rosebery family, lies on the Forth, near South Queensferry.

128

My darling – this is your birthday. How I wish I could spend it with you! I was much touched by the beautiful lines you quote in your letter to-day from the Sonnet. As we cannot escape the limitations of the 'dull substance', we must make the best use we can of the post, and you have been adorably good in the regularity and interest of your letters. It is because I have got so used to one every morning (which I re-read at intervals through the day) that I was impatient yesterday and could not wait (as I ought to have done) for the second post . . .

. . . I was thinking all this morning – in the back of my mind – in the midst of almost countless & rather exacting interviews – what a distance you & I have travelled in the course of a *calendar* year. There are some things, wh. as I look back upon them, seem quite incredible now: missed opportunities; half-spoken words; still worse, words that only told half – or a hundredth part of – the truth. This is the débris of life, and it would not be nearly so interesting, or so real, or so well worth living, if the plan were sketched out from the first (like your embroidery, with rhinoceroses, and palm trees, and orange groves & the rest) and all one had to do, or to expect, was to fill in with careful stitches, & well chosen silks, the vacant spaces. Poor old B.J.[1] used to say: 'I praise Allah for the variety of his creatures'. I am getting rather sated with the infinite chaos of his varieties, and I cling more & more to *the One*, who gives me *all* that I need. If only I could feel that I can make any real return: but (one of my favourite lines) 'High Heaven rejects the lore of nicely calculated less or more'.[2]

We (i.e. Violet & I and Hugh as a fellow passenger) dined last night with the Bencks at Stanmore. He & his wife had almost a quarrel across the dinner table about some Russian lady who on her way from France had been stranded in a coal-vessel at Cardiff. Violet declares that when the ladies left she heard the Countess say to the footman (an old servant of ours) in her curious brogue: 'Take – quick – coffee to the Count. He is cross with me: without his coffee, he will not telephone'! The poor old boy was glued to the telephone afterwards for half an hour, exchanging messages with the Home Office about the distressed lady. . . .

. . . Interviews: first with Crewe, McKenna & the Archbishop about the Welsh Church, which I think will now go through. Then with Birrell, Redmond & Dillon, about Home Rule. I told them of my conversation yesterday with Bonar Law, & afterwards with the King. (That last by the way, was after I wrote to you: he was full of admiration & appreciation of his Ministry & of flattery for me: 'You can if you like, by the exercise of *your* authority settle the whole question'. Of course I did not repeat this to D & R.) We went over a lot of the whole ground – without much profit: & I am coming to think (but I want *your* advice about this) that in 2 or 3 days I may have to come forward myself, & risking everything, declare that they *must all* take (1) H. R. Bill on statute book (2) exclusion of 6 Counties for perhaps 3 years (3) at the end of the 3 years, each of the counties to opt itself in or out. A sort of ultimatum. Darling, tell me (for I rate your opinion above every other) do you counsel me to do this? I *must* stop, tho' I have thousands of things to say. I love you more every day – with all that I am or ever hope to be. *Write*

Just off to Lympne – back by motor Sunday midnight

¹ One of Asquith's letters to Mrs Henley reveals that 'B.J.' was Sir Edward Burne-Jones, the painter and designer. The saying is from the *Arabian Nights*. Asquith's friend Lady Horner had known Burne-Jones.
² Wordsworth, *Ecclesiastical Sonnets*, iii. 43.

129

Lympne Castle,
Lympne,
Kent.
                                            22 August 1914[ii] Midnight

. . .At last (about ¼ to 4) we managed to mobilise our forces, and started in the Napier from Downing St to drive here – Violet Bongie Oc & I. We got to Littlestone at ½ past 6 – and while Violet drove on to Lympne Oc Bongie & I played 7 holes on the links. I hope you haven't abandoned golf for good & all: it would be so delicious if we were able from time to time to play together. We drove on here in the gloaming, arriving at 8 in time for dinner. There is no one here but the family – Frank & Annie, Guy & Frances, Dinah & Kakoo – both the last two in the best of good looks. They are by way of turning this house into a hospital or convalescent home – for which latter purpose it is well fitted. Annie tells me she wants to sell it, or give it away, now that they are committed to their large Scottish adventure at Innes¹ – a place (as little Michael² says) without grouse or heather, or even a view of the sea. . .

¹ Near Elgin. See Appendix 3.
² Probably Francis Michael Tennant (b. 1899), youngest child of 'Frank and Annie'.

130

Lympne Castle,
Lympne,
Kent.

Sunday morning 23rd [August 1914]

. . . I was not disappointed. Your darling little letter came just as I awoke: it was most considerate of you to write so early. . . .

It is rather a windy day with beautiful lights & shadows over the whole extent of the marsh. Out at sea but quite near we can see a squadron of 8 battle-ships and 2 cruisers creeping slowly along. I don't know why they are so far up the Channel: there is another Division (making 5) of our troops being transported across to-day: I suppose from Southampton & Newhaven, as we see nothing of them here. I wrote to Kitchener that I wished to be kept informed well in advance of any movements to the front, and you may like to see his answer. The message from French is re-assuring. It looks as tho' the Germans intended to try to force their way through the *trouée* between Lille & Maubeuge: if so they ought to get a heavy hammering,[1] but everything that we know or hear points to their army being of the best quality and well led.

130a

SECRETARY OF STATE FOR WAR

War Office,
Whitehall,
S.W.

22nd August

My dear Prime Minister

You know the 4th Division is now crossing that is the 5th in France.[2]

I may speak to you on Monday about the 6th Division going, but am not sure until I get a letter from French which I expect. I have just had a wire from French in which he says

"I am quite satisfied with the situation – Concentration complete"

I will always let you know about any movements of importance. I presume you do not mean small detachments joining units in the field.

Yours very truly
Kitchener

---

[1] The B.E.F. were fighting off attacks from greatly superior German forces at Mons as Asquith wrote. He may not have known that, though Maubeuge was fortified and provisioned,

the French General Staff had abandoned the fortifications of Lille in 1913. More important was his belief, which he shared with all other British observers, that Namur would hold out for some days.

[2] Like Asquith (Letter 117), Kitchener counted only infantry divisions. The B.E.F. also included a cavalry division.

'A lasting business which will try all our mettle' (Letter 131)

MOST of the British public expected the war to consist of decisive sea battles from which the Royal Navy would emerge victorious, together with a short Continental campaign in which the German armies, held by the French in the West, would be overcome from the East by the Russian steamroller. They were to learn that the mine and the submarine had precluded naval victories against an enemy who failed to come out and fight, and that steamrollers, as a witty lady remarked in 1915, are designed to go quickly into reverse (see Letter 124, n. 3).

British naval supremacy meant that Germany and Austria would be subjected to an increasingly rigorous blockade. But long before that weapon had taken full effect the British Government would be faced with the need to organize manpower and war production. This was a task beyond the experience of any British statesman. The cabinet's directing triumvirate had made a good start. But neither Kitchener nor Churchill found teamwork congenial; and the dynamic and imaginative leadership required in war was not wholly within the scope of Asquith's gifts, transcendent though these were.

131

Monday 24 Aug 14.

. . . You are *most* wise in what you say about Redmond & the 'ultimatum': I wanted (as I always do) when I am on the road to a decision, to be quite sure that your judgment goes with mine. Nor is it an easy matter – anyway. We i.e. Bongie Oc & I drove up in the motor after dinner from Lympne in a dense sea fog, and after many challenges from the Kent Constabulary – who scrutinise every motor with as much of the Sherlock Holmes manner as they can assume – we arrived here about 1.30 a.m. Margot had come up from Hopeman on Sat. night & greeted us.

Early this morning I was aroused by Kitchener[1] bringing French's telegram, which I enclose. Very bad news. For we all assumed that Namur was safe, if not for a fortnight, at least for 2 or 3 days.[2] And (tho' our soldiers seem to have held their own) its fall, of course, takes out the pivot from the movement which was in contemplation. . . . It is a bad check, to say the least. French has since telegraphed that he wants reinforcements to the extent of 10 per cent – wh. implies fairly heavy losses;[3] tho' Gen[l] Cowans (the Quartermaster General who lunched here) says that we had calculated on not less than 25 per cent. The casualty list has not yet come in, and one trembles to think what names it may contain. I will, of course, wire you at once, if there are any we know & care for. You say you were waiting for the battle; but when it comes, what a terrible reality it is! I can't help feeling anxious lest the Germans shd. now come right round beyond our left, & finding little resistance – for the main body of the French is a good deal to the East – get through Lille to Dunkirk & the coast.[4] The last thing French said to me, when we took farewell in this room, was that we must be prepared for a reverse or two at the first. And you know how disgusted I have been with the silly optimism of our press, their contempt for German quality & tactics, & all the rest of it. Uncle Hugh is of course an almost professional pessimist; but I feel that this is going to be a lasting business which will try all our mettle. Kitchener outlined at the Cabinet to-day his plans, which if they come off will give us some 600,000 or 700,000 men by April in next year. He is not at all downcast: nor am I.

Meanwhile it seems trivial & futile to be haggling about the boundaries of the 6 counties, the precise terms of a time limit, and all the other 'sticking points', as you so well describe them. So I have sent Birrell to the Irish to say that these are not the urgent matters of the moment and, if the situation abroad does not mend, they must be content with further delay. Don't you think this is right? If I could only talk with you! It is cruel that I can't, but you are quite right to stay with Sylvia, and I will tell you everything almost as soon as if you were here. . . .

I wish we had something like a code that we cd. use by the telegraph. This morning for instance I longed to let you know before anyone else what had happened & was happening. Do you think it is impossible to invent something of the kind? You might think of it, & even elaborate it, in the intervals of prawn-hunting. There are many occasions on which it might save us both anxiety, and convey our real thoughts & wishes.

Darling I love you: how much I cannot put into words, but *some day* you will know.

131a

SECRET

[Deciphered Telegram]
From Sir John French
To Lord Kitchener

F26. August 24th

24/8/14

My troops have been engaged all day with the enemy on a line roughly east and west through Mons. The attack was renewed after dark but we held our ground tenaciously. I have just received message from General commanding 5th French Army that his troops have been driven back, that NAMUR has fallen, and that he is taking up a line from MAUBEUGE to ROCROY. I have therefore ordered a retirement to the line VALENCIENNES to LONGUEVILLE-MAUBEUGE which is being carried out now. It will prove a difficult operation if the enemy remain in contact. I remember your precise instructions as to method and direction of retirement if necessity arises. I think that immediate attention should be directed to defence HAVRE. Will keep you fully informed.

[1] Kitchener aroused the First Lord also with this news. 'The apparition of Kitchener *Agonistes* in my doorway', Churchill wrote, 'will dwell with me as long as I live.'

[2] At Namur, as at Liège, the forts built in the 1880s had been battered into submission by the 305 mm. and 420 mm. calibre German howitzers (pp. 155–6). On the morning on which Asquith wrote, *The Times* pronounced Namur to be 'perfectly capable of taking care of itself for the next three months'. The Dowager Duchess of Sutherland was in the city with a nursing team during the bombardment (Letter 164).

[3] The B.E.F. suffered 1,600 casualties at Mons, all but 42 of them in Smith-Dorrien's 2nd Corps, and about half of them in two battalions of one of his brigades. In the four days 20–23 Aug. the French suffered 140,000 casualties.

[4] For von Kluck's obsession with reaching 'right round beyond the British left', which helped to save the B.E.F. from the German pursuit during the retreat from Mons, see p. 207. French's first thoughts on 24 Aug. had been to retreat westwards 'on his lines of communication'; but he was quickly persuaded by Joffre to move southwards instead, and so to stay in contact with the 5th French Army. He resisted the temptation to take refuge in the fortress of Maubeuge, though this lay near his line of retreat.

132

Monday 24 Aug 14 nearly midnight[ii]

My darling – in these anxious hours everything is out of gear. We have been dining here – what you might call a regular scratch party – Margot & I & Oc Eric Drummond, Sir C. Mathews, & the 2 Harcourts – and playing Bridge in the conventional way, with a lot of preoccupation & mental reserves. And then about 10.30 we hear that a cypher telegram from French has come to the War Office, and as always happens it takes almost an eternity to decypher. And meanwhile we are all on tenterhooks, not knowing whether it is going to bring the news of a victory or a defeat, or, worse than all, the names on the casualty list. And everybody tries to be placid & polite & unconcerned, & to make conversation, and preserve the habitual social pose. But all the time there is an undercurrent of hope & fear, which makes it all seem profoundly unreal[1]. . . .

We i.e. Margot Nan & I went for a long drive by Hatfield & all the places that you & I know so well, and you don't need to be told how I miss'd the 'vanish'd hand'. Bongie has gone off to Lympne to bring back Violet in his motor. And here I sit in the Cabinet room alone, trying to summon up your picture and to realise your thoughts. War makes a strange jumble of everything, alters perspectives, reverses values, readjusts one's estimates both of people & things: and it is a supreme blessing to feel, in the midst of it all, that, between you & me, all is, and will be, essentially & always *the same*. Isn't that true?

I was greatly strengthened by what you wrote to me to-day. It braced me up to my contemplated *coup d'état*.[2] The more I think of the situation & its ghastly possibilities, the less I see any other outlet or real way of escape. But it makes a really enormous difference to know that *your* judgment goes with mine. . . .

[1] A more highly coloured version of the evening is given in Margot Asquith's *Autobiography*, ii. ch. 8. French's telegram reported: 'The retirement is progressing well . . . casualties . . . considering the nature of the attack . . . not heavy.'

[2] Asquith refers to the idea of imposing his own Home Rule solution on both Irish parties (pp. 173–4 and Letter 128).

'The French plan of campaign has been badly bungled' (Letters 133–136)

ASQUITH's complaints about the French army read oddly, since he was apt to write as if repelling the German invasion was falling almost entirely on the B.E.F., who could have done the job better had they not been hampered by an ever-retreating ally. In fact, the casualties suffered by the French between 20 and 23 August amounted to almost twice the B.E.F.'s total strength. Very little news of this huge and tragic French effort came to Kitchener, on whom the Prime Minister depended for his information; still less reached the British, or indeed the French, newspapers. Even so, whatever the distortions in his account, Asquith's criticisms of French planning were, in essence, justified, as the outline of the B.E.F.'s problems given earlier shows (pp. 154–6).

The mystique of attack, implanted in the French officer corps by the defeats of 1870, ran counter to the whole trend of military development since that day. The improvements in fire-power in these forty years favoured the defence; but any French staff officer who stressed that was judged deficient in attacking spirit. The French neglected heavy artillery, machine-guns, and entrenching equipment because these belonged to the defence. Little value was placed on reserve divisions because they were thought to have no *élan* in attack.

Nothing illustrates the potency of this mystique more vividly than the fact that it had captivated a commander as cautious and sensible as Joffre.[1] Once he and his generals and staff had begun to see the campaign as it was, his steady will-power, and the fighting quality of the French troops, came into play. In 1914 the French commanded what they were to lack in May 1940 – time in which to regroup and strike back. On the day on which Asquith wrote Letter 133 Joffre began to regroup for an effective stroke at the German right wing.

[1] Not all French generals believed in the attacking strategy of Plan 17; but the defensive school did not occupy key positions in 1914. In 1911 General Michel had been ousted, and superseded by Joffre, for proposing a defensive war plan. Joffre had considered making his initial attack, not along the Franco-German border, but in the Ardennes. He had been dissuaded by the politicians who were determined not to alienate Britain by a French violation of Belgian neutrality: see S. R. Williamson, *The Politics of Grand Strategy* (1969), pp. 209–218.

133

Tu. 25th [Aug 14]

Delicious to get your letter this morning. . . . We got news after midnight from French who had been fighting all day but had got back to his new position. This morning there is another message from him, which is pretty bad.[1] The Germans harassed him all the way but were shaken off – not without considerable losses to the 2nd Army Corps (Smith Dorrien's) & the Cavalry: over 2000 in all.[2] De Lisle's Cavalry Brigade, of which Anthony used to be Brigade Major, in charging some infantry got entangled in wire & were 'severely handled'.[3] No names as yet of killed or wounded. French's troops were in the best of spirits & 'quite ready to take the offensive', but the French resolved on a further retirement, & so our men have had to follow suit & are falling back on their original lines at Cambrai–Cateau.[4] Kitchener is furious with the French who (he says) put their worst troops in the post of danger where they were annihilated by the Prussian Guards.[5] So far the

ANOTHER "SCRAP OF PAPER".
K. OF K.
(Kitchener in the Lords, 25 August 1914, *Punch*)

French plan of campaign has been badly bungled. To make things more mysterious, I have just seen a furious telegram from the Belgian Foreign Minister, who denies indignantly that Namur has fallen: 'Les forts resistent & resisteront au bout'. This (if true) makes the French retirement very difficult to understand.[6]

Later He of C. 4.0 p.m. The House met in large numbers, and we introduced another dozen Emergency War Bills. I made a guarded and not very 'luciferous' statement as to French's position. The Belgians who are really gallant fellows – and so far compare very favourably with the French – are now re-collecting their forces, and moving out of Antwerp with the King at their head, to try & cut the German lines of communication. I have just sent for Bonar Law to propose that we should pass an Address in the House of sympathy & laudation to the Belgian Army & people. They certainly deserve it.

Kitchener is making his maiden speech in the Lords this afternoon. It is carefully type-written, and Winston & I have gone over it with him. He is quite nervous, but I think it will do very well. Bonar Law has now come & gone. (I don't know whether you like this sort of hour-by-hour diary. But you say to-day that I am to give you *all* my news – 'especially personal'. If that means *my very own*, you know well my darling how every hour you are with me.) He is disposed to agree about Belgium, and I went on to tell him in outline of my 'ultimatum'. He says that personally he would back it up, but he is going to impart it in confidence to Carson. The poor King wrote

me a letter this morning strongly urging immediate settlement (I have lent
it to Birrell, or I think I would have sent it you) and enclosing another in the
same sense which he would evidently like me to publish. I have however got
into enough hot water through giving constructive authority to his effu-
sions and I am not going to repeat that experiment.[7] Moreover, it is *entre
nous* a rather *banal* & unimpressive document. I have let Birrell have the
letter to me to use as a fly for Redmond & Dillon: the royal handwriting &
his expression of willingness to see R. again may have some effect. I won't
brusquer things for a day or two at any rate.

I ought to stop now – for I have a lot to do – tho' happily I have ceased to
fear that I shall weary you. Talking with you in this way is the one
alleviation of my days – especially when one feels anxious as to what is
going to happen. Write to me my own darling a *dear* letter – such as you
can; and it will be worth all the world to me. I *love* you.

[1] The B.E.F. had fought extremely well on 24 Aug., the average advance of the German 1st
Army units on that day being only three and a half miles. These hold-ups meant, however,
that von Kluck had one more corps in line against the British left, and another approaching it.

[2] Again largely in the 2nd Corps. No guns had been lost, nor transport abandoned.

[3] This was not a barbed-wire entanglement erected for war purposes, but simply a double
wire fence beside a sugar factory.

[4] Asquith accounts for the decision to retreat farther as French did in his telegram (P.R.O.,
W.O., Secret Telegrams Series A, vol. 1, No. 77). Apart from the renewed retirement of the
5th French Army there were ominous reports from the Royal Flying Corps of German
movements to the west of the B.E.F.

[5] Kitchener probably referred to the failure of the 5th Army to hold the line of the Sambre
on 21 Aug. It seems, however, to have been the commander of the French 19th Division,
rather than his troops, who became so frightened at the presence of the Prussian Guard.

[6] It was not true. The Germans had taken the northern forts and entered the city of Namur
on 23 Aug.; they announced the capture on 25 Aug.

[7] See Letter 102.

134

Wed 26 Aug 1914 1.30 p.m.

My darling – I have just now (at the end of the Cabinet) got your dear letter
wh. came by the 2nd post. As I wired you there is no news yet of names.
French telegraphs that it is difficult to compile the lists over such an
extended front, and that there are among the casualties a large proportion of
'missing', which of course may mean killed or wounded, or taken prisoner –
tho' I fancy the last category is very small. The moment I hear anything I
will wire to you. You were *quite* right to write yesterday morning, and you
know well that you cannot give me a greater pleasure in the world than to do
anything for you. I only wish I could do more.

After writing to you yesterday I went for a little drive with Violet . . . &

when I came back here I had a long visit from Winston & Kitchener, and we summoned Edward Grey into our counsels. They were bitten by an idea of Hankey's: to despatch a brigade of marines (about 3000) conveyed & escorted in battleships to Ostend, to land there, & take possession of the town, & scout about in the neighbourhood. This wd. please the Belgians, and annoy & harass the Germans who would certainly take it to be the pioneer of a larger force: and would further be quite a safe operation, as the Marines cd. at any moment re-embark. Grey & I consented, and the little force is probably at this moment disembarking at Ostend. I don't think it would be advisable in present circumstances to follow it up with anything like a Division of regular troops. Until we get the two Divisions from India & the Egypt & Mediterranean garrisons back here, we ought not except in a great emergency to send another Division away from home. It might at any moment be needed to send to Dunkirk or Calais or some such place to help French and secure his communications. Winston, I need not say, was full of ardour about his Marines, & takes the whole adventure (of wh. the Cabinet only heard for the 1st time an hour ago) very seriously.[1]

We had a few people to dinner as usual including the Assyrian, and such strange figures as the Maguires & Mrs Greville & Ruby Peto (who was looking wonderfully well). She spends her time in a cottage near Canterbury keeping house for her husband & 2 brother officers in the Yeomanry. About ½ of them volunteered for the war, but the remainder – including Philip Sassoon[2] – preferred to remain at home. I played some mild Bridge and then about 11 got French's telegram, announcing that (much against his will) he was falling back on Péronne, which you will see on the map between St Quentin & Amiens. His men were in excellent condition and most anxious to take the offensive, but the French Commanders seem to be stricken with hesitation & something very like funk, and were persisting in further retirement. We all think that they have been very wrong in not taking us more into their confidence, and we have sent a pretty strong message for more precise knowledge of their plans & intentions. Happily the telegram this morning is more reassuring: they seem to be regaining confidence & are even taking the aggressive in Belgian Luxemburg.[3] French's situation is not a very pleasant one – in command of an unbeaten army full of fight yet compelled always to go back. I hope it is only a passing phase: as you wisely say to-day. One is apt to exaggerate the importance of what may be temporary set-backs.

There was practically nothing else of much interest at the Cabinet to-day: a lot of details. Birrell tells me that Redmond & Dillon are not greatly impressed by the King's letters: they think he might very well see *Carson* & put pressure on him, but are not inclined to expose their own icy fronts to the thawing influences of Court sunshine. Birrell himself thinks that my 'ultimatum' goes too far in the way of concession to Carson, & McKenna, to whom I spoke of it to-day, tho' strongly of opinion that Redmond ought & wd. be well advised to accept it, is sure that if he demurs & protests he will carry the bulk of our party with him. The war has not softened them, and they look upon Nationalist Ireland & its cause & claims as a second Belgium. . . .

I was amused by your account of the irritation caused to you by your Aunt, & her 'strings of foolish questions' to which neither you, nor anyone else, can give an answer. . . . You are the only woman who *never* asks a stupid question, and *always* understands. Is that a tribute you care for? Yes – I was quite interested in the cholera belt & the pair of socks. You can always safely tell me these things.

I was amused with what your soldier guests said about Kitchener & conscription. Winston indulged at the Cabinet yesterday in a long and rhetorical diatribe on the subject.[4] He has of course always had a twist in the direction of compulsory service. But he got very little help from K. who is all for proceeding upon our present lines, until (if ever) their failure is demonstrated & complete. . . .

I am anxious now to get all the party machinery on both sides to work – first, to stir people up about the war, for there is great & I fear in some places growing apathy; and next, to bring the multitude of idle able-bodied loafers & indifferents into the recruiting net. I believe it can be done, but it requires both time & tact.

I have just had a visit here (H. of Commons) from Lord Roberts. He is particularly keen for the moment about 2 things – the bringing over of the Indian troops,[5] and the enlistment & training of *both sets* of Irish volunteers.[6] He has been interviewing both Carson & Redmond, and believes that he can form two big camps there wh. he is prepared himself to inspect & more or less train. Poor old boy! he was rather *émotionné*, and asked me to 'forget the past' (I suppose the Curragh business &c) and assured me that he was now entirely on my side! A lot of whirligigging we have seen – haven't we darling? If only I can knock together the heads of these damned Irish politicians, I shd. feel that we cd. go full steam ahead. Is this too long, sweetest? I love you & think of you & treasure you all day & every day.

[1] Three battalions of Royal Marines were landed at Ostend on 27 and 28 Aug. Apart from giving rise to rumours which alarmed German Headquarters they effected nothing, since the retreat was taking the B.E.F. farther each day from that part of the coast. They were re-embarked on 31 Aug.

[2] He served overseas later, on Haig's staff.

[3] The Belgian Province of Luxemburg lies west of the Grand Duchy. The 3rd and 4th French Armies were back on French soil, fighting savage holding actions after the débâcle of

their Ardennes attacks. Joffre's General Order No. 2, 25 Aug., required 'short and violent counter-attacks' during the retreat. In Asquith's *Memories and Reflections* 'Belgian Luxemburg' was altered to 'Belgium and Luxemburg'.

⁴ Pease and Emmott wrote critically of Churchill in their diaries, Hobhouse less critically. 'The P.M.', according to Pease, 'asked how many of our own men in the H. of C. would now assent [to conscription]: such a proposal would divide the country from one end to the other.' The *Observer*, which had campaigned for conscription before the war, refused to agitate for it now. Its Editor, J. L. Garvin, pronounced: 'We must keep the country together at all costs. . . . The war is being conducted by a Liberal Government and it is essential that it should carry Liberals with them.'

⁵ On 14 Jan. 1915 Asquith told Venetia (Letter 260) that, at the War Council on 5 Aug., Roberts had 'strongly deprecated the sending of Indian troops to Europe', but had later recanted on this.

⁶ Roberts pursued this idea for some weeks, but gave it up 'most reluctantly' at the end of Oct. 1914.

135

27 Aug 1914

My darling – you sent me a most delightful letter – just what I wanted. It is strange that we are still without any list of the casualties, but at latest we must get it to-morrow morning. Kitchener got a mutilated telegram from some unknown source yesterday, but it only contained 6 or 7 names & may be quite unauthentic. Among them, so far as he remembered, was only 1 killed – a boy called Vereker who I see was in the same battalion of the Grenadiers as John Manners, & only joined a year ago. French was fighting all day yesterday against no less than 4½ German Corps & 3 Cavalry divisions, and all the time making his way to his new position between St Quentin & Amiens. He has now the support of 3 French Cavalry divisions on his left, and a fresh French Army Corps is coming from the South to Amiens.¹ He has not been well treated by the French who ought to have been much more active in protecting his retreat, but he speaks handsomely of their Regulars: says their spirit is high, that they are very good troops and well led by their officers. The new line of the whole Allied army (this is *quite secret*) will be from Amiens to Rheims, and as they will have 17 Army Corps & 9 Cavalry divisions they ought to be able to hold their own. Joffre's first plan miscarried, apparently because he hadn't sufficiently realised the difficult character of the country in the Ardennes: one wd. have thought that after 40 years of study the French staff ought to have been sufficiently alive to this!² He (French) was still fighting when he telegraphed last night, but hoped to 'shake off' the enemy to-day. He has certainly had to bear the brunt of more than his share of the fighting so far, but he seems to be in quite good heart & spirit: very anxious, of course, as are all Generals in the field, for reinforcements. We have filled up all his gaps, but are loth to send out a fresh division until the course of things is more decided.[3] I am afraid he must have had a lot of further casualties, but in any case the Germans have lost tremendously. With the Russian wave moving slowly towards them on the East, every day is to them of vital importance,[4] and they are prepared to sacrifice almost any number of men to break through the French line. Of course I will telegraph to you at once as soon as I hear anything.

Meanwhile Winston has been scoring some small but not unimportant points. His 3000 Marines have taken Ostend & are scouting about the country in that region, and the *Kaiser Wilhelm* – a huge armed German liner which was pirating about off the coast of W. Africa – has been sunk by the *Highflyer*, a rather venerable specimen of the light cruiser type.[5]

I am writing from the House in a brief breathing space before I receive a Trade Union deputation. Our main business was to pass an address in honour of the Belgians, and you will read what I said. I hope you will like & approve: you know that is the verdict for which I care far the most. The House was quite appreciative.

Violet has gone to-day to Stanway whence Elizabeth has just returned. We are intending to go again to Lympne for Sunday. We are going to dine with the Islingtons to-morrow night. The House will probably rise on Monday for 10 days or a fortnight: so the 'crisis' is once more put off – for the last time I suspect. I still have a feeling that we shall round that corner: I dare say you think I am rather a gross & purblind optimist!

The Impeccable is, I am told, in a very disgruntled mood: in trouble about his soul; and talks moodily to his familiars about shouldering a musket & going to the front!

I have strange visitors in these days – I told you of Ld. Roberts, who was followed by F. E. Smith & Harry Cust,[6] both profuse in offers of service. I wish I had something to read at nights. I always finish off with your letter: can you suggest anything for the preceding $\frac{1}{2}$ hour? The Bud & her lot are apparently still at Brussels. I am well, except for a bloodshot eye, the result of motoring *en plein air* from Lympne in the small hours of Monday morning. I wonder sometimes what you are wearing: I suppose the stripes are abjured.

I have just received the deputation & listened & talked to them for the best part of an hour. They were quite sensible Trade Unionists of the old fashioned Lancashire type, & I soothed them with soft words.[7]

This is a very poor letter, but I have been rather hard pressed to-day & have only time to save the post. But that hasn't prevented me from thinking often of you my darling, and the thought of you to-day as always lightens the burdens of my life. Bless you, and believe always in my never ceasing & ever growing love.

[1] Joffre had decided on 25 Aug. to withdraw troops from his right in Alsace, from his centre, and from Paris, in order to 'create on the outer wing of the enemy a mass capable, in its turn, of enveloping his marching flank'. This proved one of the most important strategical decisions of the war.

[2] In this comment Asquith took no account of the difficulty which the French had encountered in making staff studies on Belgian territory. The French General Staff had persuaded themselves that battle in the hilly, thickly wooded Ardennes would be 'rather favourable', in Joffre's words, 'to the side which, like ourselves, had inferiority of heavy artillery but superiority of field guns'. This overlooked the impossibility of searching steep ground with guns of relatively flat trajectory such as the French seventy fives. The French horse transport, manned largely by reservists, was inefficient in bad country. A more basic fact had, however, doomed the Ardennes offensive like those farther south: all were based on the mistaken presumption that by reinforcing their right wing the Germans had left a dangerous weakness in their left and centre.

[3] See Letter 143.

[4] On 25 Aug. von Moltke had decided to send the two corps released by the fall of Namur to the Russian front (where they arrived only after the Germans had won the Battle of Tannenberg). He admitted afterwards that taking these troops from the right wing 'was a mistake and one . . . fully paid for on the Marne': see p. 207. By advancing through East Prussia before their mobilization was complete the Russians were rendering the Allies an enormous service, even though the advance ended in a shattering defeat.

[5] The *Kaiser Wilhelm* was caught when sheltering illegally in Spanish territorial waters. Her captain put the prisoners from the ships he had sunk in safety on neighbouring colliers before the firing began. One man was killed on the *Highflyer* and 5 slightly wounded. This action eliminated the largest of the only five armed merchantmen which the German navy managed to send to sea as commerce raiders. The *Cap Trafalgar* was sunk on 14 Sept. by a British armed merchantman. The three others eventually took refuge in neutral harbours and were interned.

[6] Cust became Chairman of the Central Committee for National Patriotic Organizations.

[7] See the account in Asquith MSS, vol. 89, f. 156. The delegation were concerned at the drain on trade union funds from the unemployment which the war had brought. Secondly, they contended, as many others were to do during the following three months, that the Government's munitions contracts were not being spread over enough factories.

136

Fri. 28 Aug 14 [i]

My darling – I loved your 'grousing' letter. . . .

Did you like my speech?[1] You complain that I've spoken too little lately. What will you say when you read in the papers to-morrow my letter – composed after I went to bed last night – if I had thought of it earlier I wd. have consulted you – to the 4 Lord Mayors offering to speak in London Edinburgh Dublin & Cardiff? If it comes off, I can at any rate stay at Penrhos for a night on my way to or from Dublin: fancy the joy of being with you there even for a few short hours! Do you think it is a good idea? . . . It is not perhaps precisely my role to carry round the fiery cross, but things being as they are I must do my best to look & act as a crusader. . . .

We got a telegram from French this morning describing Wednesday's fighting, of which I gave a rather bald summary to the House. They fought for a whole day against odds of more than 2 to 1 without the slightest assistance from the French army![2] Indeed all this week our men have borne the whole brunt of the German attack.[3] The casualties are mainly in the 2nd Army Corps (Smith Dorrien's) & the 4th Division (wh. came from the Eastern Command) 'owing' (as Sir J.F. says) 'to the necessity of withdrawing them under a terrific artillery fire'. He says the casualties are very heavy, probably 'amounting to several thousands & 18 or 20 guns'. The 1st Army Corps (Haig's) on the other hand inflicted heavy losses on the Germans.[4] At last the French have been induced to move up on both their flanks, and 'take the pressure off his'. Today & to-morrow he ought to be safe in a strong position behind the river Oise near Noyon – *Secret*.

The French have so far played a poor part, and it is time that they began to draw the German fire. Kitchener has sent a strong telegram to Joffre urging him now to make a determined stand. Our men have never been defeated & have retired against their will. We are going to send all the Egyptian & Mediterranean garrison & the 2 Indian divisions as soon as they can be got to Marseilles to support them.

There darling is all the war news – not very exhilarating for the moment but there is nothing in it to excuse despondency.

We are going to adjourn on Monday till Wed. week. The Irish are very jumpy & intractable, fearing for their Bill, & the Unionists (as B. Law told me to-day) equally so, fearing that they are going to be cheated – after Carson has offered (as he did this week) the flower of his volunteers to Kitchener to enlist as Regulars – unconditionally![5] I am now getting Birrell to try & persuade Redmond to agree, if he can get his Bill on the Statute book, that it shall not operate (1) for 12 months, nor (2) till an Amending Bill receives the Royal Assent.[6] This wd. I think satisfy Law Carson & Co, and it is really a small concession for R to make. The best thing about it is that it wd. get rid of exclusion, & the 6 counties, & all (what you call) the B. Palace 'sticking points'. . . . Be an angel, & write me a line . . . by the early post to-morrow. It makes *such a difference*.

I have a lot to do yet and fear I cannot write more before the post. I will begin a letter later on this evening. My own darling *I love you*.

[1] Moving a Humble Address praying the King to convey to the King of the Belgians 'the sympathy and admiration of the House'. For the admiration which this speech aroused see p. 111.

[2] The battles of Landrecies and Le Cateau.

[3] Like almost everyone else Asquith had no authentic news from Joffre. He did not know that in the sector farthest from the B.E.F. two French armies were resisting a prolonged and furious attack by the German left wing under Prince Rupprecht.

[4] French almost certainly exaggerated the German losses against the 1st Corps at Landrecies, putting them at '800 to 900 dead and wounded'. The German official lists reduced this to 127 casualties.

⁵ 'As regulars', i.e. for overseas service.
⁶ This represented a greater concession to the Conservatives than was eventually made on 15 Sept., when Asquith merely promised that the Home Rule measure would not come into operation 'until Parliament has had the fullest opportunity by an Amending Bill of altering, modifying, or qualifying its provisions'.

137

Fr. 28 Aug 14 midnight [ii]

My darling – I think I told you this morning (or did I forget?) that Winston had a little scheme on foot. It has come off very well – 3 German cruisers sunk (in addition to the *Kaiser Wilhelm* & the *Magdeburg* yesterday) is a good haul – & some set-off to our sad losses on land. I am delighted that Bill Goodenough had a share & a good one in this notable enterprise. It will hearten up everybody – apart from its real & intrinsic merits.¹

We dined at the Islingtons – where were Winston & Clemmie, Wolkopf the Russian, & Sommie Somerset. Winston read with natural complacency his carefully composed bulletin – with the alliteration 'fortunate & fruitful' &c – and we all congratulated him. Kitchener sent in just before dinner for my approval a message he was sending to General Joffre, with a well-deserved hit at the French for their want of co-operation hitherto. He proposed to send it in French, but we all agreed that the French was so indifferent, that it wd. be better – as well as more dignified – to send it in English.

Fraü, who is at Hopeman with Puffin, has got a telegram from her Rolf urging her to go *zurück*² & as the coast seems to be clear (he is at Regensburg) she will probably start to rejoin him on Monday.

Margot & Elizabeth & the Assyrian & I go to Lympne to-morrow for Sunday. I shall motor there after lunch & perhaps get a few holes of golf. Dinah & Frances are there: the rest have gone to Scotland.

We haven't even now got the casualty list – which I fear after Wednesday's fighting will be long & terrible. A few names are already trickling in – amongst them the Plymouths' son, Archer Clive, 'dangerously wounded'.³ The Coldstream are said to have suffered a lot. I will wire you of course as soon as I know. I think this particular & very important thing has been terribly mismanaged. Did you happen to see Rosebery's allocution to his local regiment: to describe Belgium at this moment as a 'third rate Power' doesn't seem very felicitous.⁴

I wonder if you will like my letter to the Lord Mayors? You must really try to come with me to Dublin. Do you remember last time? I can see you now in the box at the theatre. My eyes were still not fully unscaled – but they were beginning to realise true values.[5] Darling send me a book to read – I don't care what it is – so long as it comes from you. I must go to bed. Bless you my guardian angel.

[1] In the Heligoland Bight action the Germans also had a destroyer sunk and 3 cruisers damaged. Their smaller ships were attacked when the state of the tide at the bar of the River Jade prevented the battleships and battle-cruisers from coming to the rescue. The attacking force was lucky to survive at least one failure in communications without mishap. This action in the home waters of the Kaiser's navy damaged the morale of his fleet and made him resolve to avoid further naval losses. The *Magdeburg* was wrecked in the Baltic. On the body of one of the under-officers recovered by the Russians were the cipher and signal books of the German navy. These were handed to the British and reached the Admiralty late in Oct.

[2] *Zurück*: back.

[3] He died of the wounds received on 26 Aug. when the 3rd Coldstream were attacked at Landrecies.

[4] Rosebery was reported to have said 'that he would rather see Britain wiped out than one third-rate power extinguished'. He explained on 5 Sept. that he had been misreported. He had referred, not to Belgium, but to Britain; he had rather that the British people 'were to pass into exile and . . . death' than that they should sink to be a third-rate power through failing to uphold the public law of Europe and the sanctity of treaties.

[5] Asquith visited Dublin in July 1912, staying the night at Penrhos and crossing from Holyhead. He was accompanied by Margot, both his daughters, Venetia, and a large party. The visit occurred some months after 'the scales had dropped from his eyes' during the weekend near Lymington (p. 2).

138

Sat. 29th Aug

So many thanks for darling letter. I am more than glad that you liked my speech.[1] It is cruel that you are never there on these occasions – neither your fault nor mine, but the worst of bad luck – for me. . . .

Still no names. French as you will see from enclosed telegram wh. came this morning knows of our anxiety. As they were constantly retiring they must have left many wounded behind and could not go back to collect them. There are horrible stories of the Germans killing them, which one prefers not to believe. The burning of Louvain is the worst thing they have yet done. It reminds one of the Thirty Years War (did you in your early youth as I did read that extremely dull book, Schiller's *History of the 30 years war*?) & the achievements of Tilly & Wallenstein. I believe the library was one of the best in Europe, and some of the buildings & churches were almost unique.[2] French, as you see, is getting a rest at last, wh. he must sorely need.[3] When the details come in I believe his day's fighting will be found to be one of our best military feats. We hope & believe that at last the French have linked up & are giving him proper support. My letter to the Mayors seems to be well received.

We had a Cabinet this morning wh. lasted for 2 hours and did an enormous lot of miscellaneous business. There were 2 things that will interest you. One was a proposal to be made to the Russian Gov^t to send 3 or 4 Siberian Army Corps, wh. are difficult to move South, to Archangel on the White Sea. We would then transport them in 5 or 6 days to Ostend or some other port, where they would either join Sir J. French, or harass & cut the German communications. Don't you think this is rather a good idea?[4] (Of course, *very* secret.) The other thing was the news that about 16,000 Belgian troops from Namur & the neighbourhood escaped & accompanied the French armies, and are now at or about Havre. We are going to transport & land them at Ostend, where they can relieve Winston's little brigade of Marines.

Winston estimates our loss on the sea yesterday at near 200, killed & wounded (mostly of course the latter) and the German loss – mostly drowned – at not less than 1500. Curiously enough the ship of ours that suffered the most was the *Arethusa*[5] – the first of Winston's own ships to take the water: all the rest are McKenna's or pre-McKenna's – a beautiful light cruiser of 30 knots, which only came out of the dock a day or two ago & was making her first voyage.

Among the other subjects wh. came up – they range in these days from the infinitely great to the infinitely small – was that of Carrier Pigeons! Both Winston & Kitchener are rather suspicious of them, and the task of securing the speedy liberation of the whole tribe from captivity was left in the deft hands of the Home Secretary: just the man for such a job – don't you agree? The Impeccable & Lord K. are coming to lunch.

[1] Moving the Address in honour of the Belgians (Letter 135).

[2] The burning was begun on 25 Aug. and lasted for six days before it was called off. It was occasioned by an exchange of shots in the city following a successful sortie by the Belgian army from Malines, on the edge of the Antwerp entrenchments. It was entirely deliberate and did more to turn American opinion against Germany than any other event during the first month of the war.

[3] French's telegram reported: 'No fighting today, and yesterday . . . only a very slight rearguard affair. I am nearly sure of securing two or three days rest.'

[4] It had originated with Churchill. See the end of Letter 140.

[5] Casualties were fewer than this on both sides. For the British there were 35 killed and about 40 wounded; for the Germans something over 1,200 in all. One of the *Arethusa*'s feed-pipes had been smashed, her speed being reduced to 7 or 8 knots.

139

Lympne Castle,
Lympne,
Kent.

Sunday 30 Aug 14

My darling – it was a great joy to get your nice long letter this morning. I am glad you like the idea of the Recruiting Crusade . . . and think me not unsuited for the part. I hope Dublin will be all right: he is the only one of the Lord Mayors who has not yet replied. I trust there will be no Carson–Redmond *tracasseries*[1] to spoil the prospect. I frankly own that its chief attraction to me is to be found en route. I was amused by your account of your experiences at the local Hippodrome. It is perhaps as well that my countenance is 'screened' with the grim expression of a man of wrath. You, at any rate, have no cause for alarm. I can honestly say that all this time, tho' I may at moments have been anxious, and perhaps even rather jealous, you have never made me angry. But then you have the sweetest temper as well as the best head of your sex.

I drove down yesterday with Elizabeth & Nan Tennant: a most lovely day followed this morning by another. I always think the view here across the Marsh when there is a real play of light & shade one of the most fascinating in England. Frank & Annie & Kakoo are all in Scotland, and we are entertained by Dinah with Frances & Guy. Margot & Lucy came down by train & the Assyrian rather late in his motor. We had some quite good Bridge last night.

I took to bed with me Sir Walter Scott's Journal which I found in the Library. Have you ever read it? It only begins in 1825 when he was on the brink of ruin, and spreads over the last 7 years, which were the saddest tho' by far the most heroic of his life. He was singularly un-vain (a word, wh. tho' not good English, you will perhaps recognise), and his actual daily output of work I should think exceeded that of any modern man (I don't include St Thomas Aquinas, & Schoolmen who never saw the world) yet he seems always to have leisure for walking & conversation & conviviality. He wrote his poetry 2 or 3 times over, but his prose flowed along spontaneously as fast as his pen cd. write. He says that whenever he was in a difficult situation in one of the novels &c he pulled up, & the solution always came to him in bed in the morning between waking & getting up. I wish I could say the same! In one point I try to think I can detect a faint resemblance between him & *both you & me*: 'Worked at *Pepys* in the evening. . . . Few men . . . have seen more variety of society than I – few have enjoyed it more, or been *bored* (as it is *called*) less by the company of tiresome people.' (Apparently *bore* was a new word in those days.). . . .

That is enough for one day of Sir Walter, but I am sure I shall get a lot of good stuff out of him before I have finished.

Dinah has just gone off with her Scouts to Church. She is in very good looks just now, and in her Scout dress presented a very smart appearance. I had a curious talk with her last night about her affairs of the heart. I think men are very silly not to want to marry her. Don't you?. . . .

We are thinking of motoring this afternoon to Folkestone & Shorncliffe & Dover, where we may see some of the Belgians & perhaps some of our own wounded in the hospitals. Not a word yet of the *names*: isn't it strange? I fear that Tues. & Wed. were far more destructive than Sunday.[2]

I shall have a *mauvais quart d'heure* in the House to-morrow over the adjournment, steering between Scylla Law & Charybdis Redmond. I will write to you about it. My beloved you are not really absent from me – and I bless you always & everywhere.

[1] *Tracasseries*: fusses; ill-natured interference.
[2] Asquith was right. The 2nd Corps had 7,812 casualties at Le Cateau on Wed. 26 Aug., and lost 38 guns.

'Bad news . . . from French' (Letter 140)

How did the British Expeditionary Force escape intact from an appallingly exposed position? First, the ponderous enveloping manoeuvre of the Schlieffen Plan could not succeed unless the right wing of the German advance was kept at maximum strength regardless of the costs elsewhere. The German statesmen and commanders did not meet this requirement. They allowed large-scale attacks to be mounted in the south on the Franco-German frontier; and on 25 August, when the unexpectedly early Russian offensive looked threatening in East Prussia, it was decided to transfer troops from West to East. Secondly, the German commander on the right wing, von Kluck, was over-intent on the movement which Asquith feared (Letter 131): he aimed to seize the ground between the B.E.F. and its Channel base. He was so concerned to feel round the British left flank that he neglected to keep in constant contact with the bulk of French's force. He gave the British more than one chance to disengage without heavy loss.

Thirdly, the B.E.F. were the most skilful of the armies engaged and the only one containing a substantial proportion of battle-experienced troops. There was much that was misleading in the lessons taught by the Boer War, as Asquith later wrote (pp. 263–4 and Letter 175); but in August 1914 any battle experience was at a premium. The B.E.F. had a better rifle than the other armies and they used it better. Their rapid rifle fire was so devastating that each British infantry battalion was credited in German reports with 28 machine-guns. The correct figure was two.[1]

[1] A proposal for 6 machine-guns per battalion had been rejected in 1909 on grounds of expense. Special training in rapid rifle fire had then been instituted.

140

Mond. 31 Aug 14

My darling – thank you so much for your letter. It is sad to think that in these soul-stirring days you are reduced to running a crèche. And you have even taken to Church-going! I went alone last night to the evening service at the little Church at Lympne – not much life about it, and a poor sermon. I thought the special ('intercession') prayers compiled by the Archbishop, and now said or sung in all Churches, rather poor stuff, and both in tone & language much inferior to what one might have expected, or at any rate hoped. The Prayer-book prose – mainly Cranmer's – is in the very best early Tudor, pre-Elizabethan, style. In comparison even the best of the Caroline compositions – such e.g. as the General Thanksgiving – are verbose, artificial, & teeming with 'conceits'. And the modern hymns – such as the popular jingle wh. was sung there last night – Faber's 'Pilgrims of the Night'[1] – have all the false notes of the tinkling cymbal.

We had rather an interesting afternoon, as we drove first to Dover Castle where we saw in a fine *coup d'oeil* one of Winston's torpedo-destroyer flotillas, & 2 or 3 submarines, lying in the harbour, & prepared for the worst. It was a gorgeous day, with a light haze over the Channel. Thence we went to Folkestone to see the Ostend packet arrive, with a cargo of Belgians civil & military. We talked to some of the soldiers & gave them cigarettes. We then drove on to the military hospital at Shorncliffe, where there were from 50–100 of our wounded soldiers, mostly of course light cases, as all the serious ones are still in the field hospitals. The first I saw was Col. Parker of the 5th Lancers[2] (with a bullet wound in the calf, and attended by a wizened & rather acidulated wife). He, by the way, was one of those who behaved worst in the Curragh incident. He seemed a nice soldierly sort of man, & was able to give me reassuring news about Anthony. I at once wired to Sylvia & I hope she got my message. I thought it wd. save her from further suspense, but Sunday telegraphing is always hazardous. There was a young Lieutenant in the next room from the South Lanc. regiment, who gave me a vivid account of the German machine guns, which enfiladed the trench in wh. they were lying, & swept it from end to end. The private soldiers in the general ward were really more interesting. They had all the greatest contempt for the German rifle-firing, & for their cavalry; but all agreed that their artillery directed by a whole flight of aero-planes, & their machine guns were serious business. One of them – a private in the Dublin Fusiliers – assured me, & stuck to it in cross-examination, that he had seen with his own eyes after Mons the Germans advancing with a screen of women & children in front of them, & when any of these were wounded throwing them aside & putting others in their places.[3] Pretty bad! They are none of them the least afraid of the Germans & all most anxious to go & fight them again. As I dare say you saw, *The Times* published a most wicked telegram on Sunday from a supposed correspondent at Amiens, describing the rout & desperation of our army.[4] Winston replied in the full official communiqué which you read in the paper this morning. F. E. Smith, who seems to have passed it as Censor, is going to be hauled over the coals about it in the House this afternoon.[5] I had a furious letter on the subject from one Gwynne, who is the Editor of the *Morning Post*. A casualty list (of about 800) came in this morning: about 30 officers, & the wounds mostly not serious. It is curious & indeed incredible that even now they can't send us a list of the dead.

The Assyrian & I motored up at midnight, & soon after Maidstone had to take a derelict motor in tow, with a rope, as far as Wrotham. It was a family party coming from Margate after their holiday, and as their motor cd. go no further, we took in the 2 children & deposited them at their home – a shop at Lewisham. The little girl, who sat on my knee, told us her name was 'Milborough Cabeldu', wh. I shd. think is a baptismal record.

We had bad news this morning from French. Joffre was in favour of a further retirement of the French armies, & wished French to remain practically where he is. French took umbrage at this, and proposes himself to retire behind the Seine, basing himself on La Rochelle. We all think this quite wrong (all this is *most secret*): because he wd. be leaving the front line, and give our allies hereafter some pretext for saying that, at the pinch, the English had deserted them. The matter was rather hotly debated at the Cabinet this morning, but there was in the end practical unanimity.[6]

The Irish (both sets) are giving me a lot of trouble, just at a difficult moment. I sometimes wish we could submerge the whole lot of them, & their island, for say 10 years, under the waves of the Atlantic. When the tide receded & a new race had to take their place, it would not be more unmanageable, or less amenable to reason & common sense, tho' in other ways it might easily be less attractive & appealing. I have had interviews to-day – in the intervals of what are equally serious & more urgent things – with Redmond & with Bonar Law (inspired by Carson); and they almost fill one with despair.

It is dear of you to send me a book – I am sure I shall like it. I shall finish my Scott journal, which has occasional reaches of dullness.

(*Secret*: The Russians *can't* come – it wd take them about 6 weeks to get to Archangel!) My darling I love you always.

¹ Although F. W. Faber was converted to Roman Catholicism in 1845 when he was 31, his hymns, like Newman's,have often been selected for Anglican hymnals. 'The Pilgrims of the Night' is in *Hymns Ancient and Modern.*
² He had been wounded at Angre on 24 Aug., but returned to the front and commanded the regiment until 1917.
³ According to the Bryce Report 'on alleged German outrages' published in May 1915 (*Parl. Papers, 1914–16*, xxiii. 39, 165–7), 'the progress of the Germans through Mons was marked by many incidents' in which German units forced Belgian civilians into screening their advance. One of the most detailed pieces of evidence cited in the Report (ibid., 167: quotation g 11) related to 24 Aug., the first day of the British retreat. As the Bryce Committee remarked, it was hard to distinguish between the occasions when German troops had coerced the inhabitants in this way, and those in which they had simply taken advantage of civilian movements between the lines. Thus it is not clear whether the party of Belgian schoolgirls whose presence masked the advance of the German 6th Division at Mariette on 23 Aug. was sent forward deliberately, or consisted simply of people caught between the lines who had decided to make a dash for it. This incident was witnessed by the machine-gun section of the Royal Irish Regiment, but not by the Dublin Fusiliers.
⁴ There were two such reports, one in Northcliffe's popular Sunday paper, the *Weekly Dispatch*, the other in a special Sunday edition of *The Times*. The first was by Hamilton Fyfe, the second from Arthur Moore. They were not entirely pessimistic, the conclusion being, 'While the first great German effort has succeeded, it is possible that its limits have been reached'; but a reference to 'the broken bits of many regiments' was extremely disturbing to a public which knew little about the retreat. As British G.H.Q. was allowing no war correspondents at the front, in deference to French wishes and practice, it was impossible for any journalist to give an undistorted account of the fighting. On 31 Aug. the Press Bureau issued a corrective reassurance and in the Commons Asquith condemned a 'very regrettable lapse' by the papers concerned. This statement, which was made in the knowledge that the censor had passed the dispatches, but in ignorance that he had encouraged and added to them, naturally enraged Northcliffe; but Asquith seldom tried to appease newspaper magnates. He did not correct his remark.
⁵ F. E. Smith, who had been in charge of the Press Bureau since its formation on 8 Aug., not only encouraged publication, but added a sentence or two at the end to point the recruiting moral, 'We want reinforcements and we want them now.' He revealed this in a long speech in the House on 31 Aug. (Letter 141); and on 1 Sept. his final paragraph and covering note to the despatch were reproduced in facsimile in the *Daily Mail.*
⁶ French wired (Secret Telegrams, No. 162): 'I have let him [Joffre] know plainly that in the present condition of my troops I shall be absolutely unable to remain in the front line, as he has now begun his retirement.' Kitchener replied at once: 'I am surprised at your decision to retire behind the Seine. Please let me know, if you can, all your reasons.' After the cabinet meeting Kitchener wired: 'The government are exceedingly anxious lest your force . . . should, owing to your retirement so far from the line, not be able to co-operate closely with our allies and render them continuous support.' Significantly, Seely, the only senior politician at G.H.Q., 'bitterly protested' at French's decision: Seely, *Fear, and be Slain* (1937), p. 218.

*The B.E.F. in Retreat: 'The only thing . . . was for Kitchener to
go there' (Letters 140–43 and 148)*

IT was no wonder that the cabinet became 'mystified and perturbed' by
French's telegrams on 31 August. On 29 August he had told them that the
spirit of his troops was 'quite wonderful': on 31 August they learned that,
while he would 'like to have assumed a vigorous offensive at once', his force
(and especially the Second Corps) was 'shattered'. In reply to the cabinet's
remonstrances he sent the most disturbing telegram of all. 'If the French go
on with their present tactics,' he wired, 'the consequences must be borne by
them. . . . I do not see why I should . . . again run the risk of absolute
disaster in order a second time to save them.'

No ministers with any grip on events could have accepted without a
demur a decision to leave an ally in the lurch, when the reasons for it were
given so confusedly and with such pique. If Asquith and his colleagues had
known the full facts they would have been confirmed in their resolve to
intervene; for, on one occasion at least, French had behaved as badly to his
allies as they had ever behaved to him. On 28 August he had refused Haig's
plea to be allowed to help the 5th French Army by a concerted attack on the
open flank of the German advance. French had a terrible responsibility in
ensuring, during a long retreat, that Britain's only army was not 'unduly
exposed to attack'; by 31 August it had weighed him down. The B.E.F.,
though battered, was still full of fight; but its commander, and some of his
staff, had become somewhat unnerved.[1]

As Asquith says in the following letters, Kitchener succeeded in his
mission. He wired to the cabinet: 'French's troops are now engaged in the
fighting line, where he will remain, conforming to the movements of the
French army, though . . . acting with caution to avoid being . . . unsupported on his flanks.' This was copied to French, with the note: 'I feel sure
you will agree that the above represents the conclusions we came to; but in
any case . . . please consider it as an instruction.'

Two features of the mission were unfortunate, however, and damaged
Kitchener's relationship with the Commander-in-Chief. He travelled in
uniform; and he proposed, apparently at the cabinet's wish, to visit and
inspect the troops. French represented that such an inspection by a Field
Marshal senior to himself would impair his authority and the proposal was
dropped. He may have had his own reasons for preventing Kitchener from
seeing how unshattered his troops, especially in the First Corps, actually
were, or for giving K. of K. no chance to listen to the two corps commanders; but, faced with a proud and hard pressed man, Kitchener did not show
all the sensitivity and caution needed in a Secretary of State who was also his

country's greatest soldier. This meeting in Paris was bound to make French feel insecure and 'on probation'. His unease was increased when he heard rumours (which were far from baseless) that Kitchener was thinking of becoming Supreme Military Commander as well as Secretary of State. This rumour naturally led to another, for which there was no foundation, but which was even more disturbing to the Commander-in-Chief. Kitchener, it was said, meant to take command on the Western Front as soon as victory was in sight.

¹ See John Terraine, *Mons* (1960), ch. 9. In one hurried retreat by G.H.Q. on 1 Sept. the Adjutant-General and his staff were inadvertently left behind.

141

Tu 1 Sept 14

My darling – I am glad that my telegram on Sunday brought relief & pleasure. I have a very nice letter from Sylvia, to whom give my love. Your Mother & Blanche were here at lunch to-day and I was able to reassure them about Eric Serocold. We have a real casualty list at last to-day, giving dead wounded & missing up to Friday, but for not much more than half the force. But it seems to include his battalion, in which apparently there were few casualties. The whole thing is very capricious; in the Guards' brigade there were only 2 deaths of officers – young Vereker (aged 18 or 19) and Archer Clive, Lady Windsor's¹ son – the second who has died quite young. Happily – so far as I was concerned, there were only a few familiar names. The extraordinary feature is the enormous proportion of 'missing' (over 4000), of whom the large majority must be either killed wounded or prisoners. The 1ˢᵗ battalion of the Cheshire regiment – which was in the Fifth division – records Colonel Major 4 or 5 Captains, and some 8 Lieutenants all 'missing'. It must have met with some strange disaster:² I don't know whether any of them are friends or neighbours of yours. The returns are still to come in of some of the units which were most heavily hit – for instance the 2ⁿᵈ Brigade (De Lisle's) of Cavalry. I am certain it will be found that French has greatly underestimated his total losses, which are much more likely to work out at 10,000 than 5,000.³ In fact if it were otherwise, it is impossible to account for his telegrams, in which (*Secret*) he speaks of his force as 'shattered' & quite unable to take a place for the time being in the forefront.

I told you yesterday that we were a good deal mystified & perturbed by all this, & particularly by his determination to retire beyond the Seine: wh. wd. mean that for at least a week to come he would be of no effective use to the French in withstanding the further German advance. A telegram in this sense (in reply to our remonstrance earlier in the day) came in just before midnight, and I had a conference after 12 p.m. downstairs with Kitchener &

Winston, McKenna & Jack Pease (who had dined with us) being also there, & later Lloyd George. We came to the decided conclusion that the only thing to be done was for Kitchener to go there without delay, & unravel the situation, & if necessary put the fear of God into them all. He is a real sportsman when an emergency appears, & went straight home to change his clothes & collect his kit, & started by special train from Charing Cross about 1.30 a.m. this morning. Winston provided him with a fast cruiser at Dover, whence he was to make his way to Havre & Paris. He ought to have arrived in Paris about lunch time & wd. go on from there to join French & his army & look round & take or give counsel. Hardly a dozen human beings realise that he is not at the War Office to-day, and tho' he is a difficult person to keep incognito, I shd. not be surprised if he got back here before the world suspected his absence. Don't you think it was a bold & wise step? Unless it has leaked out in the papers, you had better keep it quiet for the time. I have just come back from seeing the King who knew nothing until he heard from me this morning, & informed me that he had not told the Queen! Their second boy Prince Albert, who was in the *Collingwood* was attacked by appendicitis, & is now in a nursing home at Aberdeen waiting to be operated upon which is very bad luck for the poor boy. I met him on the yacht at Portsmouth, and thought him quite nice & attractive.[4]

You would see that I got fairly well between Scylla & Charybdis in the House yesterday, but A.J.B. flogged the placid waters into a storm by a singularly foolish speech, and there were all the signs of a growing tornado, when I intervened & was able to say 'Peace, be still'.[5] After that it was tepid & featureless, and I am told that F.E. spoke for 1½ hours in defence of the Press bureau. We had a Cabinet this morning – mainly about finance & moratoria & bills of exchange – which I will not inflict upon you. My meeting at the Guildhall is to be at noon on Friday. I think Dublin will be all right now – so after all I hope & *long* to find a haven at Penrhos. I must stop now. Write me a *dear* letter. As the hymn says "'Tis manna to the hungry soul, And to the weary rest'. I don't think you know at all how much I love you! Do you?

[1] See Letter 137, n. 3. Lord Windsor had been cr. Earl of Plymouth, 1905.

[2] At Audregnies on 24 Aug. the order to retire did not reach the 1st Cheshires. Of the battalion's 25 officers and 952 other ranks present that morning, only 7 officers and 200 other ranks remained by nightfall.

[3] Asquith made a good guess here; but the higher total of casualties did not j·· stify French's reports.

[4] Later King George VI. See Letter 99.

[5] Asquith moved the adjournment of the House until 9 Sept., and declared his hope that the question of Home-Rule-in-wartime would be settled 'at any rate without any revival of acute controversy'. Redmond stated it to be his understanding that, if the settlement proposal should not command 'general assent', the Government would none the less place Home Rule on the statute-book. Balfour protested at Redmond's remarks.

142

Wed 2 Sept 1914

My darling – this is the anniversary of Sedan in 1870 – a date of ill omen: and we hear this morning that this evening the President & Government of France leave Paris for Bordeaux. I have no doubt they are right to do so, but it will give the world a shock; and it is to me even now inconceivable that the hundreds of thousands of French soldiers who are between the Belgian frontier and Paris should not have been able to interpose a more dogged & effective resistance. But this is the kind of war in which endurance & time will prove in the long run to be the determining factors. So we ought to take long views, and above all never be either exalted or depressed because we are for the moment on the crest or in the trough of the waves.

It gave me a momentary pang of disappointment in my bedroom this morning when I eagerly turned over my small heap of letters not to find the only one to which I look forward, upon which I count as my stand-by during the day. It came however by the second post, and since then has been often read. I am rather alarmed by your description of the photographs. Why do you face the 'semitic' as a fact? I would take many oaths to the contrary. At any rate, *coûte que coûte*, send me what you think the best; for tho' I cd. live for a long time – perhaps always, on memory, I should love to have a visible & tangible reminder of what is so dear to me. Thank you so much for Rhoda's[1] book, which will be a welcome substitute for *Our Mutual Friend*.

Poor Fraü left at last this morning. They saw her off at Charing Cross, bound in the first instance for Goch, the Dutch-German frontier town, & hoping thence to find her way to Munich, where Frank Lawson's son has kindly made over to her his flat. He is enlisting in the Kitchener army. By the way, recruiting is going on so fast & furiously (no less than 28,000 came in yesterday) that it is becoming a question whether we should not rather try for the moment to damp it down. It will be very difficult, if possible, to find an adequate supply of instructors,[2] clothing, rifles, guns &c for such a huge number if they continue to increase at their present rate. I need not say how much I wish you could be at the Guildhall meeting on Friday, tho' I have always known that that was impossible. Meanwhile you must hope & pray that I may make a good speech, & for God's sake send me any ideas or phrases that occur to you. If only you were within range!

Apart from Paris, the war news to-day is far from good. The Russians seem to have met with a severe check in East Prussia.[3] The successes wh. so far the Germans have gained are not due to the superior excellence of their troops, either in shooting or in riding or in other ways, but to intelligent leading, and careful observance of Napoleon's maxim always to be in preponderating numbers & force wherever they deliver the attack. French says that the French Generals (with one or two exceptions) are not good, many of them owing their commands to political influence.[4] I don't honestly think that *we* have anything to complain of, as regards either the ability of the leaders or the fighting quality of the rank & file. Ours is unquestionably *far* the best army now in the field: but there is so little of it. If the French had been able to confront the Germans on anything like equal terms, we should (as was intended)[5] have completely turned the scale.

I should have liked to be at your sand pic-nic. They think now that we must not hurry on either the Edinburgh or Dublin meetings, lest we should over-fill the cup. But (as is the case with you) it is the Dublin one to wh. I really look forward. (I expect, in your heart of hearts, you are inclined to smile at my weakness – at such a time – but I am sure you don't despise, & I *hope* you welcome it.) E. Grey, Tyrrell, & one or two others came to dinner last night. Mrs Lyell was the only woman outside the family. I find her sensible & rather attractive, and she seemed to commend herself to our two connoisseurs – Bluey & the Assyrian. After dinner telegrams came in from Bertie[6] & Kitchener. K. had straightened out French's position, and thought he had better return at once, and as Grey & I concurred he left Paris at 6 this morning. Rather to my relief – for you never know how far the German cavalry may have penetrated, and he would be the best 'bag' they could secure – we find that he took ship at Havre at 11.30 & will be at Portsmouth at 4 this afternoon. So we are going to have a Cabinet at $\frac{1}{4}$ to 7 to hear his report on the situation. I am very glad he made the journey. It will be too late for me to tell you his impressions & our decisions.

We had our regular Cabinet in his absence this morning, and you can judge of the kind of thing that comes up day by day by this short synopsis of topics (1) Naval air reconnoitring at Dunkirk (2) protection of London against bomb throwing from Zeppelins (3) Greece & Turkey (on the verge of war) – we to sink Turkish ships if they issue from the Dardanelles[7] (4) Proposed offer of financial help to Roumania[8] & Servia (5) Japan – can she help with her fleet, or army, or both in the European theatre.[9] (6) Scheme for pledging State Credit to deal with the discounting of 'post-moratorium' Bills (!) &c &c.

It is a lovely day & I hope you have enjoyed your holiday from the crèche, & found Prestatyn a repaying change. I lunched with Winston & Clemmie: Goonie,[10] whom I had not seen for ages, was there: also Admiral Burney & F.E. The latest story is that Speyer has been arrested as a German spy.[11] I must not (tho' tempted) begain a fresh sheet. My own darling – send me a sweet encouraging letter. *All my love.*

---

[1] Rhoda Broughton.

[2] Kitchener used as instructors 500 Indian Army officers who had been on leave in Britain at

the declaration of war, and retired officers and N.C.O.s whom he recalled ('dug-outs'). He also kept back some officers and N.C.O.s from the B.E.F. to help in training the new armies. This latter policy (thought 'scandalous' by Wilson in Sept. 1914) was later judged by Churchill 'the greatest of the services which Lord Kitchener rendered . . . at this time, . . . a service which no one of lesser authority than he could have performed'.

³ After nearly a week of fighting, the Battle of Tannenberg had ended in the virtual destruction of Samsonov's 2nd Army. The Russians had lost about 30,000 in dead and missing, 92,000 prisoners, and between 300 and 500 guns.

⁴ Joffre was then engaged in weeding out his incompetent generals on a scale which gives substance to this comment; but French's views were coloured by snobbery. 'One has always to remember the class these French generals mostly come from,' he told Kitchener in Nov. 1914; '*au fond* they are a low lot.'

⁵ By Oct. 1912 Henry Wilson had abandoned the doctrine, which he had propounded earlier, that the B.E.F. could 'turn the scale' in the West, in the sense of preventing the Germans from achieving numerical superiority there: Hazlehurst, *Politicians at War*, p. 319 n. His change of view seems to have been unknown to Asquith.

⁶ British Ambassador, Paris.

⁷ Greece was to receive an assurance to this effect.

⁸ Romania was to receive this help 'if she agreed to join the allies' (Asquith's Cabinet Letter to the King, 2 Sept.: Asquith MSS vol. 7, f. 187).

⁹ The whole question of enlisting Japan in the Allied war effort without offending the U.S. (or indeed Australia and New Zealand) was most delicate.

¹⁰ This name cannot be deciphered with certainty. Asquith may have written 'Sonnie', the nickname of the 9th Duke of Marlborough (usually given as 'Sunny').

¹¹ Sir Edgar Speyer had been born in New York, educated in Frankfurt, and naturalized as a British subject in 1892. His brother James in New York was known to be pro-German. See pp. 292–3.

143

Thurs. 3 Sept 14

My darling – you sent me a delicious letter, and contrary to my fears it came by the first post. It is tantalising to think that you might have been here to-morrow, but I dare say it would have been unsatisfactory: for I doubt whether it would have been possible to drive you to Blackdown. So far as you & I are concerned I live on memory and – on hope: but your daily letter, which never fails, is the prop & joy of my life.

I think, considering the succession of anxieties & surprises, and new things that have to be decided, and the fuss & folly of some of our friends, I maintain a fairly solid average of equanimity. I am ashamed, now & again, how, for the moment, excellent & well-meaning people get on one's nerves. Do you remember that morning at Alderley when you threw your box of beads in poor Bongie's face? He is the best of men, tireless & devoted, & efficient: but sometimes when he pursues me like a shadow, and says things in a half-articulate & barely audible way, I feel a wicked impulse to lose my temper & swear. Happily it does not last long. Miss Way again – how would you like to live with her? With her copious explanations of her elaborate &

well-thought out schemes for dealing with the infinitely little. She now &
again provokes all the primaeval passions which slumber, & perhaps smoul-
der, in the old Adam! Now I have I hope let off my superfluous steam. It is
rather a shame that undeserving you should be the victim; but, as you
know, it is because I love & trust you, and instinctively make my appeal to
you.

K. successfully accomplished his return journey & reappeared here soon
after 7 last evening, when we had a second Cabinet. He went to Paris, saw
French[1] & his staff there, and the French Minister for War, Millerand,
whom I used to know, & who is a capable & level-headed man.[2] I asked K if
he (M) was at all optimistic about the situation. He said No, but on the other
hand he was not at all dejected, indeed quite composed – tho' they were on
the eve of moving bag & baggage out of Paris. It is plain from K's account
that there has been a good deal of misunderstanding & something
approaching to friction between French & Joffre: each, I suppose, thinking
that the other was not giving him in full measure the right kind of support.
Moreover, altho' we have sent French all & more than all that he needed to
refit his army, & replenish his supplies & equipment, there has been a lot of
disorganisation on the lines of communication, and he had not received his
proper reinforcement either of men or things. K. did his best to put all this
right, and we are going as soon as possible to send French the 6th Division –
fresh men who have seen no fighting so far, and are intact & unfatigued.[3]
The 2 Indian Divisions, the first of which is now well on this side of Aden,
will be halted for a few days in Egypt, before proceeding to Marseilles. This
is desirable, both as a warning to the Turks to keep quiet, and because the
actual situation in France will then be much more clear. There is no doubt
from what K reports that French's troops, always fighting & always retiring,
have been a good deal battered (tho' never beaten) and that they need a few
days' rest. He estimated his casualties up to yesterday at about 8000, of
whom a large proportion are 'missing': he thinks that in a few days some
2000 of these will have returned to the colours. When it comes – if it does –
to anything like an investment of Paris, I am disposed to believe that the
Germans with their immense line of communications, and the heavy losses
they have suffered, may yet have a very bad time.[4] Meanwhile it is satisfactory that the Russians have given the Austrians a really tremendous beating
at Lemberg, – capturing no less than 150 guns.[5]

The recruiting is going now at such a tremendous pace – 30,000 men a day
– that (as I told you) it will very soon become impossible to digest the new
material & provide it with clothing & arms. All the same it is not desirable to
damp it down, while the wave of enthusiasm is running high; and I have to
be careful about this when I speak to-morrow. We have got now nearly
300,000 – since Kitchener's first appeal. The best plan, I think, is to take

them all (subject to medical inspection &c) – particularly as the new-comers are of much better quality than the first; and to give those who cannot be immediately enrolled & trained cards or tickets, wh. will bind them to come up as soon as they are called upon.

The mines sown by the Germans in the North Sea continue to give a lot of trouble – mostly to our own & neutral trawlers, some of which are sunk almost every day. We have actually 400 vessels constantly engaged in sweeping & scouting for mines; but the area is so vast that it is impossible to make sure that it is clear.

We dined last night with the Assyrian; much the usual lot – Harcourts, McKennae, Nan & Bron, the City & racing brothers[6] &c. It wasn't exciting, & I confess I find Nan Herbert, next whom I sat, a trifle exhausting, with her heaving & palpitating earnestness about not very important things. . . .

I agree about F. McLaren – to the extent that he ought to do *something*, but I don't see him leading a forlorn hope or even conducting a rear-guard action. Poor Mary Herbert was here to lunch: she looks worn with anxiety. As I fancy that Aubrey is with the Irish Guards, I didn't like to tell her that we heard this morning that Major Crichton was killed, & Colonel Morris wounded, both of that regiment.[7] Another of the killed is Colonel Ansell of the 5th Dragoon Guards whom I met at Aldershot 2 months ago – a very clever officer.[8] There is of course a second casualty list much overdue.

We had a Cabinet this morning – a mass of details, but nothing really interesting, except that Winston has sent 4 of his aeroplanes to Antwerp to scuttle the Zeppelin that has been throwing bombs there.

We dine with the Bencks to-night at Stanmore. . . . I have blocked out part of my [Guildhall] speech, and shall try to finish it in my bedroom to-night. I think I shall again go to Lympne for Sunday: it is restful & I love the view. My own love, how I long for you!

[P.S.] Is this too long?

[1] Kitchener saw French, 'whom he clearly considered distraught', Hobhouse noted after K's report to the cabinet.

[2] He had become Minister of War when the Government was reconstituted on a broader basis.

[3] They embarked for St Nazaire, 8–9 Sept., and arrived at the front on the Aisne, 16 Sept.

[4] It never came to 'an investment of Paris'. The German 1st Army were exhausted: 'The men stagger forward', one of their officers wrote on 2 Sept., 'their faces coated with dust, their uniforms in rags; they look like living scarecrows; they march with their eyes closed.' On 1 Sept. Royal Flying Corps reconnaissances, and a map found on a wounded and captured German officer, told Joffre that the German 1st Army had turned south-eastwards away from Paris. The 1st Army commander, von Kluck, thought that he faced a beaten rabble, and that by making this wheel he could drive them away from their bases. In fact he was exposing his flank to formations which were ready, and even eager, to end their retreat and attack.

[5] By 10 Sept. the Austrians had lost 250,000 casualties and 100,000 prisoners, and had retreated 150 miles. The Austro-Hungarian army never recovered from this reverse.

[6] Probably Lord Swaythling and Lionel Montagu.

[7] Asquith's fear was well founded. These casualties occurred on 1 Sept. when the 1st Irish Guards were engaged near Villers-Cotterets; Aubrey Herbert was wounded and captured in the same engagement; but see Letter 147, n. 3.

[8] At Néry on 1 Sept. the 1st Cavalry Brigade were surprised by a German cavalry division, but fought back and inflicted severe losses on it. Lt.-Col. Ansell was killed when leading a charge in this action. The contrast between French's account of his 'shattered force' (Letter 141), and the performance of this brigade just after he had given it, is striking.

144

Fr. 4 Sept 1914

I was not exactly nervous about my speech to-day: I am very rarely that; but having made up my mind as to its general lines, and gone to bed & to sleep on that assumption; when I woke this morning & my letters were brought in I was anxious (as I always am) to feel sure that you thought the same, or were at any rate thinking in the same sense & spirit (I am writing this at the Cabinet & have to be careful) so I was more than disappointed to find no letter! It came, at last – after I got back from the meeting – and was all that I could have wished for, and of course I loved to have the sprig of myrtle, which I shall press & keep. Lucky or not, I should certainly have put it in my buttonhole (or nearer the centre, if it can be discovered & localised, of one's activities). As it is, I shall treasure it for its own sake & yours.

It was very nice of you to say what you do, my own darling, (I dared not write this with Loulou on one side & Kitchener on the other!) about my speech, tho' there is never any occasion for *you* to envy me.

Shall I tell you about it? We i.e. Margot Violet & I, left here in the motor about ¼ to 12. (Lucy Frances & Dinah had preceded us, & Countess Benck. was also of the company) There was a lot of cheering in the rather crowded streets as we drew near the Guildhall, and when we got inside it was quite a wonderful sight. You know the old hall with its monuments & stained windows and fine historic air. It was absolutely crammed with men (practically no women, except our select lot, Clemmie &c, in the Lady Mayoress' little side box) all standing (for there was no room for more than about 150 seats), many having been there for hours, the sun streaming in, & the atmosphere almost like that of hell. I started at once & spoke at *great* length for me (this I think will please you): in plain English for I suppose a little more than 40 minutes. I was rather carefully prepared (lest I should say something foolish on the spur of the moment) and I think I got through all right,[1] tho' I am anxious to know your judgment which I am sure you will give me without fear or favour. The audience was quite enthusiastic. B. Law

followed, & I thought he was quite good: then (tho' not in the programme)
A.J.B. was called for, & also Winston, both of whom were brief & to the
point. We lunched afterwards at the Mansion House & I got back here
before 3 in time for the Cabinet, wh. is just over: rather boring & mostly
about small points. I am going in ¼ of an hour to board the motor & drive
down to Hackwood² to George Curzon's to meet the Queen of the Belgians!³
I shall drive back about midnight: I enjoy the calm & freshness of the night
air. It is much better than a stuffy bedroom in a country house, with all the
horrors of breakfast & an early start. I shall do a morning's work here
to-morrow (Sat) & then drive to Lympne, returning as usual on Sunday
night. I count on getting a letter from you there on Sunday morning & on
Monday morning here.

I am sorry the Assyrian has been 'grousing' to you. I am always saying
'something nice' to him, & he has really no reason to complain of want of
appreciation. He is *very* efficient, but I wish of him (as of others) that he was
rather more self-dependent. The young & semi-young men of the present
day seem to need such a lot of cosseting. (Is that a word that you pass?)

Darling – I *do* wish that I could hand over some of '*my* jobs' to you; but
you take in hand much the most serious of them. *Do* send the photograph: I
will pass a rigorous judgment upon it. Spanish? I doubt it. You are quite
right to embark on the *Dunciad* – if you have an edition with good notes;
but you must skip freely & judiciously. Violet is full of Committees &
organisations & every kind of 'useful' work. I'll tell you soon what I think
you *might* do. (Secret) The Japs rather jib at sending their troops to Europe.
Our aeroplanes have done *excellently*. I *love* you more than I can tell you.
But I *must* stop.

P.S. 'Much' would have more, but never less than *much*!

---

¹ 'The Prime Minister', the *Daily Telegraph* reported, 'delivered the greatest speech of his
career.' The *Observer*, also a Conservative paper, referred to Asquith's 'surpassing oration'.
² See Appendix 3.
³ Curzon had become friendly with the Belgian royalties in the south of France during the
winter of 1905–06. In Aug. 1914 he offered them the use of Hackwood and the three royal
children spent the war years there.

145

Sat 5 Sept 1914

My darling – you will know by this time that your fear that I shouldn't write
yesterday was unfounded. Have I ever missed? I confess I have rarely
written under greater difficulties. We had to go to a boring luncheon at the

Mansion House after the meeting, and did not get here till nearly 3 when there was a Cabinet. As I was bound to leave soon after 5 in order to get to Hackwood in time for dinner, you will realise that I had to make the most of a few little interstices to provide you with your letter. I dare say it was a little incoherent & mixed, owing to the conditions of its composition, but I hope it told you the things you most wanted to know.

The papers I see are crying out (not without reason) for news, of which they have had precious little all this week. I am just going to tell Winston to repeat his feat of last Sunday, and to dish up for them with all his best journalistic condiments the military history of the week. K. is absolutely no use for this kind of thing, and has an undisguised contempt for the 'public' in all its moods & manifestations.

I motored down alone to Hackwood along that road (thro' Egham &c) which you & I know so well, and I thought of those heavenly journeys: when shall we have another? I arrived shortly before dinner – the rest of the company, with our host & the Queen of the Belgians & her suite, being composed of Margot, the Lansdownes, Bonar Law, and Mr & Mrs Walter Rubens! rather an odd lot. The last named lady 'obliged' after dinner – with her husband at the piano, giving us among other morceaux, the most wall-and-ceiling penetrating version of 'Annie Laurie' that I have ever heard.[1]

The Queen is a very small pink flaxen German (from Bavaria),[2] quite without any kind of distinction: she might well have been taken for the Governess. She seems however quite intelligent & talks & understands English very well. She has 4 children with her, ranging I shd. think from 8 to 2,[3] who were ushered into & out of the drawing room before dinner. I sat next her at dinner, and also talked to her afterwards. Notwithstanding her origins, she is of course violently anti-German. She had very little to tell about the war, of wh. she hadn't seen much, but is naturally very keen about the Belgian refugees, some 50,000 of whom wish to find an asylum here.[4] At present we have only found places for about 6000. Indeed one of the most troublesome things that have to be dealt with just now is the influx by every boat of hundreds & thousands of French & Belgians – for the most part quite well to do people – who have run away from home in a panic. She was very grateful for our sympathy here & thanked me for my speech. I didn't have (& didn't want to have) any separate talk with Lansdowne & B Law,[5] Lady Lansdowne talked to me for some time: she is 'nice', but *au fond* quite a cat. The Curzon daughter has none of her mother's looks:[6] she seemed quiet & a trifle gauche. I expect he is rather an overwhelming father.

It was a most beautiful moonlight night & quite warm. I left about 11 and drove home in the open motor – 40 miles in little over $1\frac{1}{2}$ hours; which is not bad, as it included Brentford & other horrors, well known to you & me.

I am glad that Oliver has got to Shorncliffe. I hope with you that Anthony is now on the staff. The Irish Guards evidently had a rough time. . . . There is a priceless picture in to-day's *Daily Sketch* of the Guildhall meeting. . . .

As to your questions which (as always) are much to the point, I don't think there will be serious difficulty in keeping pace with the demand for rifles & small arms ammunition, tho' of course with the new recruits coming in the drain will be very great. All the factories are at work all day & night, & in most of them additional plant has been or is being laid down. Much against our will, we had to send the poor Belges 20 million rounds last week for the defence of Antwerp. It is otherwise with field guns; they take a long time to make, and it will be all we can do not to fall short.[7]

The proportion of deaths to the total casualties continues to be surprisingly small, and that of 'missing' surprisingly large. Some 2 or 3 thousand at least of these are expected in time to return. Among the dead to-day is young Lambton – just your age – & only married as lately as last June.[8]

The Americans (as a State) have not behaved over well to us so far; but President Wilson said to Spring Rice one day this week 'Everything that I love most in the world is at stake'. I hope you liked what I said in my speech about the larger issues.

Violet is busy with her Committees &c. but goes for relaxation to Esher for Sunday. Katharine has got influenza at Mells – so Elizabeth will motor with me to Lympne. I believe Teddy Grenfell & his wife will be there. I shall come back as usual late Sunday night. Your myrtle still smells sweet, but I have locked it up 'for future reference'. What progress (if any) have you made with the *Dunciad*? I began last night the Rhoda you sent me. It is not bad so far, but her hand (no wonder) has not its old cunning. Did I ever tell you how she once said sadly to me that she had seen on the bookstall at Newcastle station a bundle of secondhand novels tied together with a string & labelled 'Rhoda Broughton: Soiled and Cheap'!

I am rather alarmed at your new sources of erudition – 'Gazetteers' &c. I sometime ago abandoned my dictionary-reading, and I am afraid I am getting rather rusty. . . .

I must send you the enclosed despatch of E. Grey's. It shows the kind of almost school-boy simplicity both of mind & speech which is intertwined with great qualities.

I must bring this rather garrulous out-pouring to a close as it is nearly lunch time, & I have still to write my Cabinet letter to the King. I *love* your recent letters more than I can say; they help me to follow all your life and almost to live in it: which is what I love best – my *own* darling.

¹ Margot recorded that during this recital her husband 'removed himself as far as possible from the piano and fingered a Bradshaw. . . . Mr Bonar Law looked like a Scotch grieve who had heard that "the . . . war has held back the bidding for black-faced rams at Lanark" (an item of news . . . that morning in the *Scotsman*).'

² Queen Elisabeth's father, Duke Charles Theodore of Bavaria, practised as an oculist in the Munich hospitals. Her sister (d. 1912) had been married to Prince Rupprecht, who commanded the German 6th Army. She sailed for Antwerp soon after Asquith's visit.

³ She had only three children.

⁴ In all, the Local Government Board dealt with 119,000 Belgian refugees. This figure excludes nearly all the 'better class refugees'. See *Parl. Papers* 1919, CMD 413, xxiv. 482–7.

⁵ Curzon or some of his colleagues may have had a political object in inviting the Prime Minister. If so this was frustrated, for as J. S. Sandars reported to Leo Maxse,' 'Squith ran away immediately after dinner, presumably . . . to avoid a Home Rule discussion with Lansdowne and B. Law.' Maxse MSS, 469 f. 523.

⁶ Curzon's beautiful American wife, Mary Victoria, had died in 1906.

⁷ The difficulties were even greater than Asquith predicted. Practically no one foresaw at this date the enormous expenditure of ammunition which prolonged trench warfare, and barrages by quick-firing artillery, would involve, or the extent to which armament contractors, faced with labour shortages, would fail to meet delivery dates. See also Letters 176, n. 6, and 193, n. 5.

⁸ Geoffrey, a Lt., Coldstream Guards, 2nd son of the Earl of Durham's twin brother: a daughter was born, Mar. 1915.

146

Lympne Castle,
Lympne,
Kent.

Sunday 6 Sept 14

My darling – your dear letter this morning was most welcome. I am glad that you approved of my speech. I should have liked you to be there (as you know for 1000 reasons and one more) to see the audience all standing & packed so tight that most of them could not clap, and not a few were carried out fainting.

You are quite right in what you say about the Irish. They will not flock in until they are sure that their Bill is going to be put on the Statute Book. We shall have to settle this up during the next fortnight. After that I believe they will come 'not single spies but in battalions'. It would have looked better if they had faith enough to do it now, but their history has made them suspicious – not without some reason. You would see that Carson led in a lot of his flock to the recruiting office in Belfast this week. The 100,000 of whom we used to hear will I fancy melt down to 20,000 or 30,000. Far the most serious difficulty in dealing with the huge numbers who are now coming in is to find officers & non-commissioned officers fit to train them. They cannot be manufactured by working over-time, like khaki cloth & rifles.

I wrote you a long letter last night after I got to my bedroom, which you were only to open & read in case of accident. But on second thoughts I will not send it – not now at any rate.[1]

Elizabeth & I had a fine drive down here yesterday afternoon. Guy & Frances are here, and Teddy Grenfell & his wife (who used to be Florrie Henderson – do you know her?) Dinah comes to-day and your brother Oliver this evening. It is a lovely day and the view is as beautiful as ever: some aeroplanes have been flying round the house this morning, but the sea is choppy & one cannot see any ships. It is delightfully quiet: perhaps if I do not feel too lazy I shall have a round of golf this afternoon. I have had no exercise for weeks, but I am quite well, and you will be glad to hear that my eye has resumed its normal colouring. When I have posted this (the Sunday post is very early) I shall return to Sir W Scott's journal & finish it.

Eileen Wellesley came to lunch with us yesterday: I had not seen her for years, and thought her looking well. Her particular job is to sort & readjust second-hand clothes which are given for the benefit of the destitute Belge refugees: she says it is a particularly repulsive occupation. A.J.B. is coming to dinner on Monday – for the first time for ages. Margot & Eliz[th] join Puffin at Hopeman on Tuesday night. On Wed. alas! we have the House again.

Soon after my arrival here Masterton Smith telephoned to me the bad news of the loss of the *Pathfinder*, thro' striking a mine. The worst of it is that the mine was actually in the Firth of Forth – not very far from Archerfield – in a line between the May island & St Aff's Head. No one suspected that there was anything of the sort so near shore. Of course they can be laid with the greatest ease by trawlers, and the only thing to do now seems to be to prohibit *all* trawling British or foreign, within 50 or 60 miles of the coast. This will of course be a great blow to the fishing population, and will also cut down the supply of fish. But you cannot distinguish at sight British from foreign trawlers – they fly all sorts of false flags – and it would take a whole fleet to board & examine them all. The *Pathfinder* was a comparatively small cruiser, with a crew of about 200, of whom so far we don't know that any were saved.

There was absolutely *no* news from French yesterday,[2] nor has he yet sent a despatch describing the fighting at Mons[3] – a fortnight ago. I wrote a pretty stiff letter yesterday to Kitchener on the subject, and he replies this morning that he has sent it on to French, as a 'gentle hint'.

It has become so natural to me now darling to tell you everything, that I let my pen run on without stopping to think whether or not it will interest you. But I know you wish me to do so, dont you? You will see in to-morrow's paper the Peace 'formula' of the Three Allies wh. we have been discussing in the Cabinet.[4] Think of me beloved all the week and every day of the week. I wish I could make you feel how much I love you!

¹ This letter was presumably destroyed.
² On 5 Sept., after Joffre had visited the British HQ at Melun, French promised the complete co-operation of the B.E.F. in the general advance planned for the following day. Between dawn on 24 Aug. and nightfall on 4 Sept. the B.E.F. had retreated nearly 200 miles from Mons, the infantry averaging perhaps 4 hours rest in every 24, the mounted troops less. 'I would not have believed', said one officer, 'that men could be so tired and so hungry and yet live.' Morale was high. 'About 6 p.m. [5 Sept.] the Major came into the lines', according to the account of one artillery battery, 'with a paper in his hand. . . . "We are going to advance," he said. . . . There was a cheer which must have startled the French government in Bordeaux. . . . The drivers rushed at their horses, the gunners rushed to limbers to help hook in. . . . The men were ready to go on for a week.'
³ Writing dispatches, French told Mrs Bennett in 1915, was 'the most uncongenial work I have to do. I simply *loathe* writing – except to you:' French MSS, Imperial War Museum.
⁴ 'The British, French, and Russian governments mutually engage not to conclude peace separately during the present war. . . . When terms of peace come to be discussed no one of the allies will demand terms of peace without the previous agreement of each of the others.'

147

8 Sept 14

Most dear – we had a heavenly hour together yesterday – hadn't we? tho' as I went home I remembered countless things that I had meant to say to you & didn't. These are days when more than ever one feels Marvell's lines –

> 'For ever at my back I hear
> Time's winged chariot, hurrying near;
> And yonder, all before me, lie
> Deserts of vast eternity'.¹

(I dare say it is not quite rightly quoted – but you know it well).

I thought our dinner quite a success – A.J.B. is as good company as anyone can wish for, & Winston when (as last night) his copiousness is under control, is a great social asset. Poor Bluey's deafness, and I fear a distinctly growing intellectual & moral anaemia, prevent him from taking his proper part. I revelled in the sight of you, like a parched & starved mariner who has for weeks been 'ever climbing up the climbing wave', and is then rewarded by the vision, which colours his dreams & hopes, of what he loves best. But perhaps you would rather that I should write about Home Rule?

I have just been having a business talk with the Assyrian, who tells me that you all lunched at Winston's & that Clemmie is driving with you to Blackdown. Did you get any nearer to a practical view of Winston's plan for Saturday? The *Enchantress* is laid up (I hear) and we must try to contrive something better than tramping about dockyards and feeling the pulse of sick or wounded cruisers & destroyers. At any rate you will dine here on Friday – my birthday eve: and I shall try to motor down in the afternoon and bring you up.

I sent you a little pencil note from the Cabinet about the casualties, as soon as I read them.[2] I hope you got it. I am rather anxious about poor Aubrey – for he is reported to be *both* wounded & missing.[3] We are trying to make sure that Mary hears of it quietly, before it is published in the morning papers.

We had a long Cabinet this morning, rather cheered by French's latest telegrams.[4] I have sent him a letter to-day of warm appreciation.[5] I still have a lurking or more than lurking doubt as to the wisdom of taking the offensive so soon. I believe it would have been better to wait another week.[6] I have just been reading a telegram from Bucharest to the effect that the Kaiser had written to the King of Roumania,[7] (whom he is most anxious to enlist on his side) that the German troops in France will have crushed the Franco-British forces in 20 days. He says he will then leave 500,000 German troops in occupation of France, and will 'turn his attention' to Russia!

Qui vivra verra. Meanwhile Kitchener calculates that in 6 months time he will have 50 divisions of trained troops, which means a little more than a million of men. I told him (what Blanche had told Bongie) that the new recruits were badly overcrowded – 1400 in barracks at Blackdown wh. have hitherto accommodated only 800. He didn't deny it but smiled grimly & said the damned fools of doctors were always insisting on ridiculous allowances of cubic spaces. 'They wouldn't allow in this room (the Cabinet room) more than 8 men, while we know it can easily accommodate 16 & more'.[8] He added that there was an ample supply of tents, which in this weather one wd think preferable to barracks.

He (K) lunched with us: also Lady F. Balfour, Mrs Drew, & Masterton Smith. We keep up our best menagerie standard for variety & incongruity – don't we?

Margot has gone to see Con, who must be distressed that John is 'missing': but he is a very handy fellow[9] & I expect (unless wounded) that he will find his way back to the lines. The Guards evidently had a rough time.

My darling I am looking for the photographs wh. haven't yet come. It is a joy (of a tantalising kind) to know that you are so much nearer. Write to me. You know how much I love you – perhaps you are weary of being told.

---

[1] A free version of Marvell, 'To his Coy Mistress'.
[2] Missing.
[3] He was left behind by the Germans retreating after the Marne battle, and found by the advancing French on 12 Sept.
[4] The advance of the B.E.F. on 6, 7, and 8 Sept., made over difficult country against skilful rearguards, has been judged over-cautious. It was a deciding feature in the Battle of the Marne,

since the attack from the Paris sector had forced the German 1st Army away from the 2nd, and the B.E.F. was able to push into the resulting gap.

⁵ French gave the text in the 2nd edn. of his *1914* (p. xix), when replying to Asquith's criticisms.

⁶ The civilian strategist was at fault here. The German High Command had allowed the 1st and 2nd Armies to remain so far forward only because a breakthrough in Lorraine to relieve the pressure on them was daily expected. On 8 Sept., when Moltke realized that the French defence round Verdun and Nancy could not be broken, he sent a staff officer to the right wing with powers to order a general retreat. These were promptly used. If Joffre had 'waited another week' he would have faced armies far better placed to repel his attack.

⁷ King Carol of Romania was a Hohenzollern. He died on 10 Oct. 1914.

⁸ The doctors were, however, right: overcrowding contributed to the spread of cerebro-spinal meningitis, which took a heavy toll of the Kitchener armies in training.

⁹ John Manners had been killed at Landrecies on 1 Sept. Asquith probably refers to his prowess at cricket and other games.

148

9 Sept 14

My darling, I was glad to get your little pencil note. I hope you had a good drive, and that you find the surroundings less depressing than we feared. I have just been looking at a revised casualty list; the only new name at all known to me is Colonel Hogg of the 4th Hussars (wounded) – Frances Horner's nephew, who behaved so well in the Curragh affair. I should rather fear that John Manners & young Cecil[1] may have been too impetuous and been taken prisoners. On the other hand they may be able to straggle back, as so many of the 'missing' have done & are doing; whereas poor Aubrey, who is both wounded & missing, stands a much worse chance. Mary Herbert was here before dinner last night: she is very brave & collected, but one can see that she suffers badly. Young Castlerosse[2] too, who made friends with Elizabeth in Holland and came to tea here a month ago, is in the same category. He had only just joined the Irish Guards.

What are your plans? Have you had time yet to make any? Will you get free before Sunday or not till after? Anyhow you will dine here on Friday night. (I called at Mansfield St and stole the photographs, which I found lying on the table. The one with the aigrette grows on me more than the other, which is too set & solemn. But I love to have them both). I doubt whether Winston's proposal for Saturday would turn out to be repaying. There wd. be lunch on the *Enchantress* & then a lot of dockyard sight-seeing &c, which would be rather hot & exhausting and give one few opportunities for talk. And one wd. have to return to London the same evening. If you are staying, I wd. rather put myself on at Munstead & we cd. have a drive. Tell me exactly what you think. *Entre nous*, the adventurous Winston is just off to Dunkirk to superintend his new flying base: he will be back by lunch time to-morrow. Don't say anything of this, as he doesn't want the colleagues to know. He has shown me a *very private* letter to himself from French, who keenly resented K's visit. 'He came over in F.M.'s uniform to lecture me'! &c &c.[3] He seems in quite good spirits & very pleased with his army. If it were multiplied by 6, he says he cd. get to Berlin in 6 weeks without French help. The big battle so far seems to be going well, but it may last for days, & it is too soon to forecast the issue.

I dined last night with Violet at Bluey's. He had darkly hinted to her that he had one or two dramatic coups in store for us in the way of guests. It was therefore a mild shock to find that we were invited to meet the Islingtons & Pauline Cotton, & the Jack Tennants. Frances Horner came in after dinner. I played a mild game of Bridge & retired early. This morning Beb & Oc came up for the day from their camp at Tidworth, both much bronzed with sun & wind. They are liking their time very well, and say that Cys is wonderfully better for it.

We had the usual Cabinet this morning & discussed among other things the procedure in regard to the Bills. Since I came to the House Redmond & Dillon have been to see me with Ll. George & McKenna. The result is that we must clearly stick to our first proposal – to put the Bill on the Statute book but suspend its operation until 12 months or the close of the war – whichever is later; undertaking in the meantime to introduce and prosecute an Amending Bill. I think a large number of moderate & sensible Unionists will think this a perfectly reasonable course: the *Daily Telegraph* for instance endorses it.[4] The leaders are bound to protest as sharply as they can, but I fancy they will content themselves with a verbal demonstration & not divide. The '6 counties' could not at this stage be managed. I hope you approve my darling.

I have just read French's first despatch, which has at last come in. We have pruned it a bit, but I think you will be moved by it.[5] I have rarely seen the House more enthusiastic than when, this afternoon, Charles Roberts read out the splendid catalogue of Indian gifts & promises.

I am going to dine with the McKennae to-night & with the Bencks to-morrow. Margot & Eliz are gone to Scotland, and Miss Way is about to take a holiday: so V. & I have No 10. to ourselves. Your photographs are a great resource & solace – at odd moments of the day & night. But nothing can make up for not seeing you. Be dear and write me a nice full letter. I love you so much now & always – to the end of what lies before me.

[1] In the woods N. of Villers-Cotterets on 1 Sept. two platoons of the 2nd Grenadiers were surrounded, having never received the order to retire. They fought on until all had been killed or wounded. Manners and George Cecil, officers of these platoons, were both killed.

[2] Viscount Castlerosse, like Aubrey Herbert, having been wounded and captured on 1 Sept., was found by the French 11 days later during their advance. Herbert described his

experience in *Mons, Anzac, and Kut* (posthumously published, 1930), pp. 64–82. See also
G. M. Thomson, *Lord Castlerosse* (1973), pp. 42–9.

[3] 'I do beg of you, my dear friend,' French wrote to Churchill, 'to . . . *stop this interference*
with field operatives.' Churchill sent emollient replies, adding: 'In case any further difficulties
arise . . . you have only to send for me; and subject to the naval situation I could reach you
very quickly.' 'I fear I was a little unreasonable about K. and his visit,' French answered on 10
Sept.; 'but we have been through a hard time and perhaps my temper is not made any better
by it.'

[4] On 2 Sept. (leader, p. 6e); by 15 Sept., however, the *Daily Telegraph* had turned round
(p. 8e). On 13 Oct. the *Observer*, the Conservative Sunday paper, which J. L. Garvin edited,
came out in support of the Government's scheme.

[5] It appeared in the press on 11 Sept.

149

10 Sept 1914

My darling – I was so glad to get your little letter this morning, & I quite
understood why you were not able to write more. Never say 'forgive': I
have nothing ever to *forgive* in what you either do or don't do: I am always
grateful, & if not content, that is only because I am apt to be unreasonably
exigent.

　You must have had a hot & dreary day & I am delighted that you will get
release as soon as Friday. The House is not going to sit to-morrow: so I will
drive down in the afternoon, and bring you back at 5.30 or 6.0 or whenever
you like to start. We can if necessary make a little detour so as to see the
beautiful Surrey country putting on its autumn clothes. You shall certainly
sit next either Birrell or Tyrrell – not I think *both*, because I want to be on
one side of you. As to Saturday, if you think it would be really nice, we will
go to Chatham, perhaps with Violet, & see whatever show Winston has to
exhibit. I gather you will need to be back in London not later than 7 or
thereabouts if you want to go to Penrhos Sat. night. Perhaps when you get
this to-morrow morning you would send me at once a wire to Downing St.
as to Sat. plans, and then I can arrange things. I have some thought of going
to Munstead for Sunday, but I am rather fluid on the subject. If only I cd. go
with you to Penrhos! But that is alas! quite unattainable – for the
present. . . .

　We had the usual mélange at lunch to-day – Lady Aberdeen, Ava Astor,
Edgar Vincent, Masterton Smith. The last named told us about the loss of
the *Oceanic* – a huge liner converted into an 'armed merchant ship'. The
Admiralty got rid of the merchant skipper who had navigated her thousands
of times across the Atlantic, & put her in charge of one of their most
experienced & competent post-Captains who straightway ran her on to a

rock on the Shetland coast & she became a perfect wreck! We shall have to pay I suppose £300 or £400,000 to the White Star Company for their little adventure.[1]

Winston had not yet returned from his secret visit to Calais and Dunkirk, but was expected at 3.30 this afternoon. He is engaged in another little 'scoop' (almost as bad a word as 'stunt') in the Heligoland bight, but Masterton informed me with an air of mystery that, as yet, there were 'no fish in the pool'.

We had a Cabinet this morning (without Winston). K. now appears in the undress uniform of a Field Marshal. He was angry that the W.O. behind his back had, very wisely, agreed to pay 3/– a day to recruits who were sent back home until barrack accommodation & training could be found for them. I was convinced that this was right, & forced him to agree, & have since announced it to the House amid universal applause, & with the result that all the grievance-mongers – and they were many, for some of the recruits have been shockingly provided or unprovided for – held their tongues. We got our vote of 500,000 additional men in about ¾ of an hour. I had to defend the W.O. on the ground of excessive over-pressure. Sir H. Rawlinson, who now looks after recruiting & is one of the best of our younger Generals, came to see me. I thought he seemed business-like & capable.

I have been reading Cramb's *England & Germany*. Did you ever hear him lecture to young ladies? – wh. I believe was his profession. It is a rhetorical prejudiced book, but gives one an interesting picture of Treitschke, who was to me only a name: with Nietzsche he is the real founder of modern Germanism. I had got to the last page[2] (I suppose about 1 a.m.) when I did what I rarely do – fell asleep in my chair and did not wake till the middle of the night. V & I dine with the Bencks. My own darling – do you care to read all this? I *love* you.

[1] The *Oceanic* (built 1899) was 'huge' only by the standards of 1914: net tonnage 17,274. She was one of nine liners taken up by the Admiralty at the start of the war as part of the mobilization programme. The loss, which occurred on 8 Sept., had already been announced in the press when Asquith wrote.

[2] These lectures had been delivered at Queen's College, Harley Street, where J. A. Cramb was a professor, in Feb. and Mar. 1913, a few months before his death. 'If the dire event of a war with Germany . . . should ever occur,' the final passage reads, 'one can imagine the . . . mighty deity of all the Teutonic kindred . . . looking serenely down . . . upon his favourite children, the English and the Germans, locked in a death-struggle.'

150

Sat 12 Sept 14 [i]

My darling – our conversation this morning was necessarily rather *décousu*, the conditions not being satisfactory. But we never had a better talk than on the drive yesterday; it was divine, & I shall always remember it. The vigil dinner too was quite a success. It was worth a million birthday presents to have so much of you on one day. I treasure the little Keats above everything.

Since you left I have had talks with Crewe & Illingworth. Both take a serene view of the domestic situation. They think our plan will commend itself to the man in the street as quite fair & reasonable, and that that potent person will decline in existing circumstances to be dragged into, or to countenance, a factious fight. I expect they are right – & that even without the 'America' argument, at which you rather smiled as in the nature of a make-weight or after-thought[1] – it will be comparatively easy to make a very strong parliamentary case. We shall see: as always happens, you will be 'far away' not 'on the billow' but in cross-country trains. At any rate it will be the last of our black Mondays for some time to come.

I was depressed as I watched you & Violet walking across Horse Guards Parade. It is rather a gloomy kind of birthday (especially after yesterday) – dull sky & wind, no news from French (like you I am anxious about the Vitry appendix),[2] the imminent row next week, and the prospect of a Munstead Sunday (That sounds ungrateful – especially as I am bringing my own fellow guests!) I wish I could have gone to Mells. We are going to lunch with the Winstons: I am afraid you will adhere to the 'silken tent'. There are about 1000 things I want to say to you, now that you are out of sight & hearing. Do you ever feel that? I am giving you short measure beloved to-day, but I will write you a real letter from Munstead to-morrow & send it to Penrhos. Bless you – think of me – and send me your love. All mine.

[1] In his speech on 15 Sept. Asquith referred to the effect of 'an indefinite postponement' of Home Rule 'upon the Irish race in our Dominions and in the great kindred country, the United States'. Support for Home Rule in America was by no means confined to Irish Americans or to friends of Asquith's Government. On 4 Sept. the Washington correspondent of the *Morning Post* told Leo Maxse:

If there is any sense among Englishmen they will settle with Ireland . . . at almost any price, and make relations with the U.S. much easier: (Leo Maxse MSS, 469 f. 521).

For Theodore Roosevelt's view see p. 145, n. 15. For the effect of the Government's Home Rule policy on opinion in Chicago, Feb. 1915, see Letter 317.

[2] The Germans had maintained a salient at Vitry on the River Marne and had fortified the town. They were forced to evacuate it, however, on 11 and 12 Sept.

151

Munstead House,
Godalming.

Midnight Sat 12 Sept '14 [ii] my birthday

My darling, I have been wondering at odd moments all day why (after declaring that you *must* go to-day to Penrhos) you so suddenly & with such resolution switched off to Mells. Tell me.

It was the greatest joy to get the 'sombre' portrait & its beautiful frame. Thank you 1000 times. On fuller acquaintance it grows on me. I have them both here, and they are a solace & stay & happiness. I also brought with me the Keats, which I prize more than I was able to tell you this morning.

Violet & I lunched at the Admiralty with the Winstons and E. Grey. The two latter were in high spirits at the latest news[1] . . . and Winston showed me an *excellent* letter wh. he has written to Austen Ch^m & Hugh Cecil, in reply to violent complaints of theirs of our breach of faith, chicanery &c, about the Bills.[2]

I motored here with Barbara in pouring rain, & we were followed by the Assyrian with V & Bongie. It gave me a certain malevolent satisfaction to realise that you were going down to Mells in Bluey's company. Aggie was most hospitable & *avenante* to all my Comus crew.[3] She is a really efficient person, with a vast wardrobe of dressing gowns & other garments, wh. she has fabricated for the soldiers' wives and dependents. She gave me a delightful birthday present in the shape of 2 old maps, beautifully coloured with little forests & fortresses, of the N.E. of France (just where they are now fighting) dating from 1694 – Louis XIV – and all the names Vitry, Lafère &c &c just the same as now. She had picked them up in a stray shop at Guildford! We played some Bridge, & now I am in my bedroom – and thinking of you. We shall drive after lunch to-morrow (Sunday) to Alder- shot and see the beehive, in wh K's new recruits are humming & buzzing, & beginning to form their combs.

I haven't had much of a birthday – except for the sight of you this morning. I wonder (if I live) where & how the *next* will be spent. Goodnight my blest & beloved – give me your thoughts – and if you can your love.

[1] French had written to both Asquith and Churchill on 10 Sept. 'This very day', he told Churchill, 'we have captured several hundred, cut off a whole lot of transport and got ten or twelve guns; and the ground is strewn with dead and wounded Germans. Something like this happened yesterday and the day before. But that is nothing to what they have lost in front of the Fifth and Sixth French Armies which have been much more strongly opposed. They are indeed fairly on the run.' The advance continued until 13 Sept. when the Germans made their stand north of the R. Aisne.

[2] Chamberlain was complaining that the Government had abandoned Asquith's tentative scheme designed to achieve agreement between the English parties (p. 173: 'the second

possibility'). 'There is . . . no practical difference', Churchill replied, 'between the course we propose and the one you ask for, except this: that your course involves a quarrel with the Irish nation, and ours does not.'

³ Comus, the pagan god in Milton's *Masque*, tempts men and women to drink a magic potion which changes their faces to those of wild beasts. He is accompanied on his first appearance by a 'rout' of these monsters. The entry in the cast list is 'Comus with his crew'.

152

[Munstead House,
Godalming.]

Sunday morning [13 Sept. 1914 (i)]

I read part of a book published at Oxford by a lot of the history lecturers there called 'Why we are at War'.¹ It seems very full & thorough tho' perhaps a little juiceless. I wonder if you would care to have it? I stayed late in bed, but found that others had done likewise, for the breakfast table was still encircled by human figures devouring the Sunday papers. There does not appear to be anything new, except an official statement by the Germans of their casualties, which cannot possibly be near the truth. I am afraid that the number they claim of British prisoners may be nearly accurate. It accounts for far the larger proportion of our 'missing'.

The Tories object to our taking our Suspensory Bill to-morrow on a technicality about want of notice: so we cannot table it till Tuesday. Meanwhile the Sunday papers say that Lansdowne will cut in to-morrow in the Lords with a Bill of his own to 'suspend' the Irish & Welsh Bills i.e. to prevent them being put on the Statute Book this session. The world at large will probably think that there is not much difference between this proposal & ours; but you & I know better; to both Irish & Welsh to have their Bills *law*, however long their operation is postponed, is everything, and the majority of the House of Commons will not be content with less.

Reggie & Pamela join us here after lunch; they are staying with Brother Ernest in a *nid d'amour* which he & his new wife have set up not far from here. It is a gusty day with glints of sunshine: everything begins to look & feel autumnal. Do you remember our sunset on Friday, & Hampton Court in the gloaming, and dimly lighted London, and our long delicious talk? 'Not Heaven itself upon the past has power'.² All my love my own darling.

¹ All the authors were college tutors, except for C. R. L. Fletcher who had given up his tutorship some years earlier. The Secretary to the Delegates of the Clarendon Press is said to have engaged them for the work by cycling round until he had run each to earth.

² Dryden, *Translations from Horace, Ode 29 of Book iii.*

153

Munstead House,
Godalming.
                                        Sunday – midnight 13 Sept 1914 [ii]

My darling . . . I don't know what you may have done in your rather
mysterious Mells Sunday this afternoon, but I doubt whether it was more
interesting than ours. After lunch we set out in 4 motors to Aldershot, and a
more wonderful transformation of the whole place since I spent a Sunday
there with the King and Queen in July[1] it is impossible to imagine.

All the streets & byroads are swarming with K's new army – some in
regulation khaki, but the vast majority loafing about in East end costumes:
such a rabble as has been rarely seen. We (i.e. Violet & I) paid a visit of
ceremony to poor deserted Lady Haig – just about to vacate Government
House in favour of the Hunters; and then we drove to Farnborough, where
are the air factory & the aeroplanes. We found an excellent soldier – Colonel
Trenchard of the Scots Guards, whom you may remember at Netheravon –
in command, and then we saw a most interesting & even thrilling thing – an
aeroplane . . . piloted by de Havilland (the best pilot we have) accompanied
in the front seat by Major Musgrave – on a bomb-throwing expedition. The
bombs – 3 in number – are placed side by side in a little cradle at the front of
the machine, and thence are let loose by wires by the bomb-thrower. It
made a magnificent flight, 4000 or 5000 feet high, and circled up & down in
every direction. We could not see the bombs fall – miles away – but this
morning he dropped two, one 70 feet away from the object, & another only
$4\frac{1}{2}$ inches. They are hellish looking little things (like a Thermos bottle): I
wish you could have seen them. Then we went on to the barbed wire camp at
Blackdown, where the German prisoners & spies are confined – quite near to
Blanche's. We got hold of the Commandant, who took us in, our ladies
being the first women who had ever been admitted. He demurred at first to
taking them in, on the ground that the Germans might be rude &c; but we
insisted that they should come, & we all went unmolested all over the camp.
It was one of the most pathetic things I have ever seen: all the sailors from
the *Mainz*,[2] 40 Uhlans captured near Paris & only brought in yesterday, &
every kind of soldier & reservist – some 2000 in number. They have to sleep
12 in a tent, & cook their food, as we saw them doing, in open air furnaces.
There are among them one or two so-called 'swells' – including Metternich,
a nephew of the late Ambassador,[3] who was collared as a spy in his honeymoon journey in Devonshire. We mingled with them & talked to them as
best we could. Their main complaint was that they were cold at night – only
one blanket, & no pillow. We pointed out that our soldiers had also only one

blanket, but they said they had no underclothes. We are going to send them some woollies – socks, sweaters &c to keep out the cold.[4] 500 more are coming to-morrow. It was a most interesting & moving experience.

[1] The date is wrong: he had spent Sat. 16 and Sun. 17 May at Aldershot, attending a Royal tour of inspection.
[2] Sunk in the Heligoland Bight action, 28 Aug.
[3] Count Paul Wolff-Metternich, German Ambassador in London until May 1912.
[4] The Asquiths disdained popular gestures. It was characteristic of them to make German prisoners their care when the women in every other family were knitting for the British troops.

154

Monday 14 Sept. 1914 [i]

I drove up this morning with Pamela, & it was a blow not to find any letter from you: nor has the second post been more productive. Perhaps the Mells posts are erratic – for I know you would not willingly fail.

We had a longish Cabinet mostly occupied with odds & ends. It is rather interesting to know, as Kitchener told us, that we have by now sent out to French 213,000 men & 57,000 horses. The news from him is still very good. They seem to be really rolling up the Germans. But it does not do to be too confident.[1] I quite expect to hear before long that they have been reinforced & are concentrating, & resuming the offensive. The tide must ebb & flow in this way for some time – probably a long time. We hear to-day of some one who actually saw Aubrey Herbert shot in the lower part of the back. One of our doctors at first attended him, and thought well of the wound; but then they had to retreat & leave him to the Germans. Nothing has since been heard. . . .

You wd. see in the papers the notice of Lansdowne's bill which he is going to introduce in the Lords to-day. It is of course, innocent tho' it looks, a most provocative measure; for it wd. leave the whole work of this Parliament at the mercy of the next House of Commons, wh. must be elected in the autumn of next year, and if it had the minutest Tory majority could by a single vote deal a death blow at Home Rule; Welsh Dis^t, & the rest.[2] The House here to-day was quiet & even lethargic, and I gather that the Tories are very divided & not at all disposed to dance to the piping of the Carsons & the Cecils. V & I are dining to-night with the Assyrian – by way of a change. I wish I were at Penrhos. Darling how did you enjoy your Mells Sunday? I think of you making a rather weary train journey thro' the day. Write to me like the angel you are. I shall have to make a speech to-morrow justifying our position – not a specially difficult task. I should have loved you to be there. Alas! There is none upon earth – Tell me everything. You know that I love you – but not how much.

¹ Compare Wilson's diary, 13 Sept. 'Berthelot (of Joffre's staff) asked me when I thought we should cross into Germany; and I replied that unless we made some serious blunder we ought to be at Elsenborn in four weeks. He thought three weeks.' Although the German armies were given permission from H.Q. on 14 Sept. to fall back farther, this was not used. The Aisne position was very strong and a long period of static warfare now began. As far as the front from Compiègne to Belfort was concerned, for three and a half years the ebb and flow of retreat and advance was never to reach ten miles.

² The Controversial Legislation (Suspension during War) Bill, sponsored by Lansdowne, embodied the 'fourth possibility' discussed on pp. 173–4.

'The Irish breast high for loyalty and recruiting'
(Letters 146, 155, and 239)

ASQUITH was mistaken in supposing at this date that the Irish were still 'breast high for . . . recruiting' (Letter 155). The War Office had done nothing to support Redmond in the pro-British stand which he had made on 3 August (Letter 114). 'Lord Kitchener . . . , I think,' Asquith had told the Commons on 10 August, 'will do everything in his power by consultation with gentlemen in Ireland to arrange for the full equipment and organization of the Irish Volunteers.' Yet the National Volunteers had not been given official recognition. Recruits from Ireland had not been kept together in an Irish Division. This contrasted glaringly with the terms which Carson had announced in Belfast on September 3 (p. 174; Letter 146). The men in the Ulster Division were to 'be allowed by the War Office to have . . . their old officers [i.e. the officers of the Ulster Volunteers] and . . . to have back . . . any of the officers who have had to mobilize'. They were to do their early training in Ulster camps. Carson had obtained these terms despite his refusal to allow co-operation between the Ulster and National Volunteers, and without giving any undertaking to abstain from a provocative defiance of Home Rule during his recruiting.

In his Dublin speech on 25 September Asquith repeated his wish 'to see an Irish brigade, or, better still, an Irish Army corps'. Eventually in mid-October it was made known that the Sixteenth Division, then being formed, was to be an Irish Division. An elderly general from India, bred in the regimental traditions of the regular army, was chosen to command it. Like nearly all his officers, he was a Protestant and an opponent of Home Rule. He refused a commission to Redmond's son (who was to prove his fitness for one by ending the war as a captain in the Irish Guards with a D.S.O. and two mentions in dispatches). By then the chance of effective recruiting in southern Ireland had disappeared.

'I am the last person to deny', Asquith told the Commons in October 1916, that the Irish recruiting had been the scene of 'dreadful mistakes and most regrettable blunders'.[1] It is not hard to find excuses for Asquith and Kitchener. Both were very hard pressed in the opening weeks of the war. Most British army officers regarded Redmond's men as little better than rebels. Even if Kitchener and the War Office staff had been determined to counteract this view, instead of being tinged with it, they might have found themselves thwarted. The National Volunteers were not as well disciplined or trained as their opposite numbers in the north; and Redmond's hold on them was far from complete. Giving them recognition and privileges would have entailed risks.

The risks of neglecting Redmond's demands, by relegating them to the 'storm-in-a-slop-basin' category (Letter 239), were far greater. When Carson and Kitchener treated the National Volunteers as unreliable allies, the prophecy was self-fulfilling. Having taken a pro-British stand, Redmond had to deliver the goods to hold his own against the extremists who wanted to cut the British connection. An inoperative Home Rule measure on the statute-book was not enough. Redmond's humiliation spelled danger for Britain.

[1] *Parl. Deb.* lxxxvi. 632–3.

155

Monday 14 Sept 1914 [ii] Midnight

My darling – no letter from you. I feel sad & impoverished, but I am sure it is not your fault. You wd. never fail me – only some infernal mischance. I look at the 'sombre' face – & feel sure. We have just come back from the silken tent – Goonie, Winston & Clemmie, Bluey (!), Bongie – *plus ça change, plus c'est la même chose.* I have just been stringing together some disjointed notes about what I am to say to-morrow. I don't think it will be very serious – for the Tories at their party meeting to-day resolved to have only a single speech – a snarl from B Law – & those damned Cecils who wanted to roam & raven at large seem to have been snubbed & silenced. It will be a really big thing if before the end of the week we get H.R. on the statute book – after 3 years of ceaseless conflict & worry: the Irish breast high for loyalty & recruiting – & the Tories with nothing better than a grievance wh. they dare not & cannot parade. If this comes off, I might almost begin to intone 'Nunc dimittis'. But unlike the venerable Simeon, I am not yet out of the wood. All the same, we might have a good time in Dublin – perhaps at the end of next week. I often wish I had your wonderful

& unique gift of 'unsurprise'. Do you realise what I mean? I believe you do – but I am not *quite* sure.

If present arrangements hold good, I shall go to Edinburgh Friday morning & after my speech there come back the same night, arriving here Sat. morning – perhaps spending Sunday at the Wharf with Puffin, who then goes back to school. Apart from the excitements of the war, it will I expect be pretty dull here for some time to come. But I don't see how I can get away to any distance. Did I tell you that E. Grey's brother Charles has been wounded & had his arm amputated in some of the fighting in E. Africa near the Victoria Nyanza? the same region in wh. a year ago his other brother George was mauled & killed by a lion. It is getting autumnal here – Violet & I drove before dinner in Richmond Park – that same round wh. you & I know so well. I am tempted sometimes to take refuge in the old formula – *tout casse, tout lasse, tout passe*. I suppose Providence must have endowed me with some hidden spring of vitality, and even *you* have said, more than once, that there are moments when you envy me & my chances. What am I to say at Edinburgh? It is no good hammering away at the old clichés – (if that is an allowable metaphor). I often wish I had something of what I once called the 'supreme effortlessness' of Sir Walter Scott – or (to come to more modern man) the unbaffled confidence of Winston – or (shall I say?) the unperturbed complacency of the Impeccable? Which of all these things do you my darling miss most in me? I wish you would tell me candidly some day. I must go to bed. I hope you are safely back at Penrhos, with the Penguin, & Huck, & the small McKennae, and your wall-scaling pony – whom one & all I envy, & *hate*, because the Gods are so uneven in their apportionment of the best things. Good night – I bless & love you.

156

Tu. 15 Sept 14 [i]

I was delighted to get your pencil letter written on your journey this morning. Poor darling! what a day. So far there is no further news of John Manners, but Aubrey had actually got to Havre last night & was expected at Bruton St to-day. It is a real case of a *revenant*. I suppose his wound must have been less serious than one thought, and evidently the Germans did not capture him. Young Castlerosse too who has been reported dead for some days is alive & on his way home, and Needham who was with John Manners has turned up slightly wounded in the French hospital at Neuilly.[1] I telegraphed to you, as I knew you would be relieved about Aubrey. French's telegram to-day says that he has made no further advance but has held his ground. A lot of fighting, & his casualties were rather heavy. Kitchener thinks that the Germans may now be rolled back to the Meuse – in wh. case we shall have won the first bout. Nothing interesting at the Cabinet this morning. It is just lunch time, & then I go down to the House & make my speech on the little Bill. Judging from the amenities at the Carlton meeting yesterday, we may have a rather lively time, as our men who are spoiling for a fight will certainly join in. But I hope the debate will be very short. I will report to you later.

[1] See Letters 143, n. 7, and 148, n. 2. All three had been left behind during the German retreat and picked up by the advancing French. 'I never knew anything more characteristic of Aubrey', Hugh Godley told Violet, 'than just to turn up, more or less all right, . . . after a very circumstantial, and apparently quite hopeless, story had been generally circulated about him.' Aubrey Herbert's pre-war career had included unusual incidents. During his mountaineering he had climbed in the Balkans; and he was said to have been offered the crown of Albania when that country achieved its independence.

157

Later 15 Sept 1914 [ii]

House of Commons – Treasury Bench – 5.45 p.m. I wish you had been here this afternoon; it has been quite dramatic. I made a quiet rather humdrum speech, pitched purposely in a low key, wh. was well listened to by the Tories on the whole. Then B. Law followed, with his usual indictment of us & me in particular for lying, breaking faith, treachery &c &c. He was so offensive that both Illingworth & McKenna who were sitting by me left the House, lest they should be unable to over come their impulse to throw books, paper knives, and other handy missiles at his head. He didn't really make out much of a case, and watching his people carefully I didn't think they were at all united or enthusiastic. At the end of his speech the whole Tory party walked out of the House, by way of washing their hands of responsibility for our wicked ways. It was not really a very impressive spectacle – a lot of prosaic & for the most part middle-aged gentlemen trying to look like the early French revolutionists in the Tennis Court.[1] Still it was unique in my or I think anybody's experience. Several of the Irish & of our Radicals went & sat on the Opposition benches above the gangway. Redmond made on the whole a judicious speech, & he has been followed by Wm O'Brien, & now by Arthur Henderson on behalf of the Labour party. We shall pass the little Bill now through all its stages at once. Meanwhile the Lords are at work on the corpses of the Home Rule & Welsh Bills. We shall be up on Friday I think.

Since the above I have formally introduced the Bill by bringing it up from the Bar. The whole House rose & cheered wildly: for it was the end of the Home Rule controversy, and a really historic moment.

Edgar Vincent & Winston & Clemmie are dining with Violet & me to-night. I must close this to catch the post. As you may imagine I have only been able to write at intervals of the day. I love you my darling – send me *your* love.

¹ On 20 June 1789 the members of the National Assembly (lately the Third Estate) found the hall in which they had been meeting at Versailles closed against them. They assembled in a neighbouring tennis court and took a solemn oath not to separate until the constitution had been firmly established. The scene was painted by David.

158

Tues. 15 Sept 14 [iii] Midnight

My darling – I feel as if a great weight were off my chest. The Suspensory Bill went thro' all its stages on oiled castors in about 7 minutes. The result is that before the week is over, the Home Rule Bill will be law.¹ No one who has not gone through the whole business for the last 3 years (as I have) can realise fully what that means. But you, who have been my confidante & counsellor, in so many of its stormy & dubious phases of fortune, & who have always given me good advice or sustained & helped me in what I thought best, must share my joy. I owe you more than I can ever forget. Aren't you glad? & don't you feel that you have a share in what history will record as a really great achievement?

The universal opinion of our friends is that B Law never sank so low in his gutter as to-day. He tried to make capital out of the private letter I wrote to him last week.² And not content with that, he stooped to a really infamous depth of degradation, when he quoted a passage from my speech on the war,. & (in effect) compared me to the Kaiser as a liar & cheat.³ The indignation of our people knows no bounds. McKenna left the bench & (as he told me) lay down on his sofa upstairs, lest he shd. succumb to the temptation of going for him – physically & muscularly. Violet & Clemmie were in the Ladies' Gallery, and said they felt quite sick.

We had a small dinner here afterwards – Kitchener, Edgar, Winston & Clemmie, Eddie Marsh, Benckendorff, Bongie. How I miss you! You would have enjoyed it, & we had a really good rubber afterwards.

I *so* agree with what you say about both the Assyrian (who can be *excellent* company) & Cicely Horner. Edgar is a curious study – fine intelligence, undeniable charm, and the simulation of bigness without quite the reality. What is it, do you think, that has prevented him (with all his faculties & his enormous industry) from being a really effective figure?⁴ I must go to bed, & will pursue my ramblings to-morrow. Good night – dearest & best.

¹ For the Suspensory Bill see pp. 173–5. When the Home Rule Bill and the Welsh Church Bill received the Royal Assent on 18 Sept. Asquith was on the way to Edinburgh: Letter 163. The Suspensory Bill became law on the same day.

² Bonar Law's argument (like Austen Chamberlain's, Letter 151, n. 2) was that, having failed to achieve an agreed solution, the Government should have established 'a real moratorium', and kept the Home Rule Bill in the state in which it had been on 30 July. He used Asquith's letter to establish that it was the Government's supporters, and not the Opposition, who had balked at the formula for agreement which Asquith had put forward.

³ He quoted the passage in Asquith's 6 Aug. speech describing the promises which Germany was prepared to give in return for Britain's neutrality, and equated these with the Government's promise not to bring Home Rule into effect until Parliament had discussed an Amending Bill.

⁴ From 1920 to 1926 Lord D'Abernon was the highly effective British Ambassador in Berlin.

159

Wed 16 Sept [i]

Thank you darling for your dear letter this morning. I am glad to think of you back at Penrhos: I have never seen it in the autumn, but hope to do so next week. They want to hurry on the Dublin meeting: it may probably be Friday week 25ᵗʰ. The sooner the better – for I shall then see you again.

I telegraphed to you the sad news wh. came this morning that young Percy Wyndham was killed in action yesterday.¹ It seems only yesterday that they were married, & I am trying to find out where poor little Diana is: she is only 21, if that. I gather from French's telegram this morning that they are not doing more than holding their ground: he estimates his casualties these 2 or 3 days at something like 5000, the loss of officers being exceptionally heavy. He mentions in this connection (& for the first time) the 2ⁿᵈ battalion of the 60ᵗʰ: I trust that Blanche's husband is still safe, but it makes one feel rather anxious.² I will telegraph to you as soon as I get any news – good or bad.

We had a long Cabinet this morning, & decided the much vexed question of 'separation allowances', wh. we have settled I think on a very generous scale – a minimum of 12/6 a week for a childless wife, & a maximum of 22/ for a wife with 4 or more children, with an intermediate sliding scale. Many of them will be better off than they ever were before in their lives. Winston has gone off just now (*furtively*) to Loch Ewe on the West coast of Scotland to confer with Jellicoe. He will be back Saturday morning.

After the Cabinet I went to lunch with St Loe Strachey – Editor of the *Spectator* – to meet about 20 American journalists.³ They are all very sore about the Censorship, and would not admit that matters had much improved under the new M⁣ᶜKenna régime. I used soft words to them, and oddly enough, since then, T.P.O'Connor has brought to my room here (at H. of Commons) an American lady, daughter of O'Reilly who was sentenced to death in old days as a Fenian[4] in Ireland, and herself the proprietor of a lot of American papers.[5] She squeezed out of me with great difficulty a terse & not very juicy message to the 'American people'.

The only business we had in our House was a motion about the Indian troops which I made & wh. was seconded by Bonar Law. He is so loathed and scouted by all our men after his performance yesterday that I was afraid they would howl at him. Fortunately it was a very thin House & so we escaped a scene. The centre of interest, or at any rate of activity, is for the moment transferred to the House of Lords. They have got both the Parliament Act Bills & our Suspensory Bill of yesterday on the stocks to-day. The Archbishop is snivelling about, & trying to get better terms for his Welsh Church, but the blood of our people is up & I think he will whistle in vain. There are all sorts of technicalities wh. have to be provided for (as the Tories are watching like cats and will pounce down upon any slip) in order to get our Bills safely on the Statute book in time for a prorogation on Friday. As ill luck will have it, the Speaker – who has to certify – is laid low with a bad attack of gout somewhere in Norfolk,[6] and I expect I shall have a rather *mauvais quart d'heure* with the poor King.

Still we are now in sight of port – after a long & most tempestuous voyage. Are you glad? . . . .

I think that my Edinburgh meeting for Friday night will hold good. I shall go down on Friday morning & return by the night train: so please write both days to Downing Street. I may spend Sunday at Esher, but I will tell you later. I have just read a telegram from our Ambassador at 'Petrograd', who reports that in Galicia up to Sept 11ᵗʰ the Russians have taken 200,000 Austrian prisoners. I am dining to-night (again by way of change!) with the M⁣ᶜKennae. Just seen Redmond: he thinks Friday 25ᵗʰ wd. do for Dublin. Bless you dearest – this takes all my love.

¹ He was in the 3rd Bn., Coldstream Guards.
² Lt.-Col. E. Pearce-Serocold commanded the 2nd Bn., King's Royal Rifle Corps. Having crossed the Aisne on 13 Sept., this battalion was counter-attacked heavily at Troyon the following day, when it lost more than 300 casualties, including 8 officers among those killed.
³ See Thomas Jones, *Whitehall Diary*, ed. K. Middlemas, ii (1969) 159, 27 Nov. 1928, Evelyn Wrench to T. J.: 'If I were to arrange a little dinner of all the American correspondents in London, similar to those which Strachey used to arrange during the early days of the war, which Asquith used to attend, would the P.M. come?'
⁴ The sentence was commuted to 20 years penal servitude. After 3 years in Western Australia he escaped to the United States, where he became Editor and part proprietor of *The Pilot*, the Irish-American paper in Boston.
⁵ She was an editorial writer for the *Boston Herald*.
⁶ He was at his house at Campsea Ash, Suffolk.

160

Wed 16 Sept 14 [ii] Midnight

My darling – before I go to bed I must have a little talk with you. I suppose you are in bed already – & possibly dreaming – not I hope of another quarrel between us! That has never happened – except in dreamland (not mine but yours) & pray God it never will.

The Lords went havering on over the Welsh Bill – so soon after 6 we adjourned. They have made some amendments wh. I expect will have a short shrift to-morrow.

Why don't you send me something – ideas, phrases, allusions, metaphors – clay or straw – for my next layer of bricks at Edinburgh on Friday?

I feel more sad than for any loss that has yet happened in the war, at the death of young Percy Wyndham. . . . What can one say to her [Diana Wyndham]? Unfortunately there is no child, nor (so far as I know) prospect of one. War is a hellish business at the best – and I am inclined sometimes almost to shiver when I hear Winston say that the last thing he would pray for is Peace.

After I wrote to you, I sketched out a King's speech for the prorogation – of unexampled brevity – not more than a dozen sentences. I wish you were here to show it to – but as you are not I have sent it in. I am afraid we shall have to face a terrific list of casualties these last 3 days. There is a report to-night (only a report) that John Manners also is among the dead.[1] There are worse things. Do you remember Browning's lines in the 'Toccata of Galuppi'?

> 'One by one – some with lives that came to nothing –
> Some with deeds as well undone –
> Death stept tacitly, & took them
> Where men never see the sun'

A 'crowded hour' is better than that. But for those who are left – wives, mothers, friends – there is the gap that cannot be filled, & nothing to be said, except 'behind the veil'.

I have just come back from dining with the McKennae – Herbert Gladstone & Dolly, Crewe, Lady Scott, & a Trade Union lady Miss MacArthur.[2] Little Pamela is a good hostess. Lady Scott – like some other women – complains that she can't find a place in this new world of busy & buzzing organisations – except as 5th or 6th wheel in an already over-wheeled coach. She has had to content herself for the moment with housing two desolate little Belgian orphans. It is sad that General De La Rey, who was one of the best of the Boer Generals in the war, should have been shot by a stupid policeman.[3] Violet, who has been at the Club, has just come in, to tell me she went to Park Lane. She had just a glimpse of Lady Grosvenor – wonderfully composed – and a message from Laura, who was with poor little Diana, to say that she would come & see us in the morning. I can't help being rather anxious for your Blanche. Oswald Balfour (son of Lady Frances) is an officer in his battalion.[4]

I ought to be trying to collect my mind as to what I am to say at Edinburgh. But these troubles & anxieties distract me. Bless you my darling – good night – you are always in my thoughts.

[1] The long uncertainty about John Manners illustrates how difficult it was to compile accurate casualty lists during this first phase of mobile warfare. When he was killed on 1 Sept. every other member of his platoon was either killed or wounded, some of the wounded being taken prisoner. The list showing him as killed in action was published on 19 Sept.

[2] The most prominent woman trade-unionist of her time. She had become famous by helping to secure, through the Trade Boards Act of 1909, a minimum wage for sweated women workers.

[3] He was accidentally shot while the police were rounding up a gang of desperadoes who had been terrorizing the suburbs of Johannesburg. His death had serious political repercussions, in that he was believed by his close friend De Wet to have been killed by order of Botha's Government. This goaded De Wet towards armed revolt.

[4] That is, in the 2nd Bn., K.R.R.C., commanded by Blanche's husband.

161

Thurs. 17 Sept [14 (i)]

. . . A most dear letter from you this morning. I knew you would feel poor Percy's death acutely. So far there are no particulars, and as I have been at the Cabinet most of the morning I haven't yet heard about Diana. You may well ask 'Who will be next'.

I confess I can't quite fathom your sudden & almost violent revulsion of feeling in the case of the unfortunate Bluey. 'Sapless' no doubt, but he has just as much as he had when I first knew him – I suppose about 12 or 13 years ago. There is no question that he belongs to the category of 'life-takers'. Still his brain is a deft smooth-working machine, and I think (tho' a great gossip) that he is really fond of his friends.

The Speaker is still prostrate with the gout in the country, and the two Bills have been sent down to him by a messenger for his certificate without which they cannot pass under the Parliament Act. It is the first case that has happened. Winston disappeared noiselessly last evening. There was no telegram from French this morning: the wires are interrupted, but this may be due to the gale wh. is raging everywhere.

Later. I am now at the House, where I announced the very liberal recasting we have agreed to of the scale for what is called 'separation allowance' for wives & children of fighting soldiers. It seemed to be well received. We then got rid of the Lords Amendments to the Welsh Bill, and I saw two historic documents – the Irish & Welsh Bills with the Speaker's certificate that, although the Lords had not agreed to them, they had satisfied the conditions of the Parliament Act[1] & were ripe for the royal assent. Oddly enough I have had no invitation (as I rather expected) from the King to go & see him, before the Council at 6 p.m. where he gives his assent. I thought he would probably like to blow off a little regal steam; but he is well advised to acquiesce without further protest or demur. So now to all intents & purposes this strange & eventful Session comes to an end: which has cured one (as you wisely say) of ever counting on any 'sequence of circumstances', however likely.

I have been looking at my little pocket diary & I find I was at Alderley on the 1st, the 23rd, & the 30th Jan. Those were golden times, when I think that I can barely count now in Sept on 2 or at outside 3 days at Penrhos. And all through March & later you drove with me here, not less than once a week. (Do you remember all the troubles & incipient crises with the Beagles over the Navy Estimates?) Then came the Curragh business which started when I was dining with you on the Friday evening – March 20th, and after a week of ructions (we sat practically the whole day in the Cabinet on Friday 27th) the Arch Colonel resigned & I went to the War Office (March 30). You were away, but I shall never forget the letter you wrote me, most beloved, the following day. Then there was my journey to Fife – send off at Kings Cross – & re-election. We were no sooner out of that than we had the gun-running (April 25) – our Sunday at Kimpton (May 10) – 3rd reading of H.R. Bill – & then Penrhos for Whitsuntide – a heavenly time with chequered moments. The King's Birthday, our visit to the Flying Corps, Winston's review (which neither you nor I were able to see),[2] the Buckingham Palace Conference (July 21st) – a most divine hour I spent with you at Mansfield St late on July 22nd (I wonder if you have forgotten it?) – your departure on the 24th – the day of the breakdown of the Conference; the Dublin 'crisis' on the following Sunday (26th) which was the first day of the week that opened on the War. Since then I have seen you exactly 7 *times* – most of them hardly to be counted.

There! that is a veracious narrative. And now? At any rate your Indian adventure is off,[3] and when you get to Alderley access may be easier.

We (V & I) dine with the Bencks at Stanmore to-night, & at 10 to-morrow morning we go from Kings X – in company with Raymond, Kath. & Cys – to Edinburgh. We shall be a formidable family party at the meeting to-morrow night. On the whole, I am *very* glad that you are going in preference to Dublin. It is practically fixed for next Friday. I *must* stop now: even *your* patience must be near exhaustion. But this daily interchange of ours is the salt of my life. Darling send me *your* love – you *know* that you have mine.

¹ The Bills were required to have been passed by the Commons in three successive sessions, and to have been sent in each of them to the Lords 'at least one month before the end of the session'. Two years had to elapse between the Commons second reading in the first session, and the date on which it passed the Commons in the third. By the Parliament Act, 1949, the three sessions became two, and the two years one.
² The Royal Flying Corps were in camp at Netheravon at the beginning of July. The Naval Review took place on Mon., 20 July. Asquith had been a guest on the Royal Yacht over the weekend, but had been obliged to leave for London early on the Mon. morning (Letter 100).
³ See Letter 93, n. 4.

162

Thurs 17 Sept 1914 [ii] midnight

. . . All our Bills will be on the Statute Book to-morrow, and I hope you will approve of my little King's speech, which has passed without alteration. I have rather a sad little letter from the King to-night (which I will give you sometime if you want it). He says that in giving his assent he 'feels deeply the gravity of the political outlook, as evidenced by the recent debates in both Houses', and trusts that 'by the end of the war there may be a marked change for the better in the attitude of the different political parties' so far as Ireland is concerned. I have sent him a sympathetic reply, expressing warm appreciation of his patience, & of the correctness of his constitutional conduct. I cannot help feeling satisfaction that all the bluffing & outrageous manoeuvring of the Tories has been frustrated. What a help you have been to me in these anxious months! I cannot tell you how grateful I am to you – Good night darling. . . .

163

Sat 19 Sept '14

. . . We arrived in Edinburgh about 6.30 p.m. and dined at Haldane's brother's. There were no less than 8 Asquiths at the table (Margot & I, R & Kath, Cys, Violet, Puffin, Eliza) also the Lord Provost & General Ewart. It was a very fine meeting – entirely men except on the platform – in a new so-called 'Usher' hall.¹ I spoke about 40 minutes, amid alternations of deep silence & wild enthusiasm. I think I took the right line, but I am anxious to know what you think of it. There were such enormous crowds in the streets that they improvised an overflow meeting in the Synod Hall, and as soon as I sat down I went on there. It was really the better meeting of the two, –

some 3000 or 4000 people – having perhaps a greater air of spontaneity. I had to speak to them impromptu, and the atmosphere was so catching that I went on, I suppose for about ¼ of an hour. They were all at fever heat. After supper we caught the midnight train & got here before 8 a.m. R & K, with Cys & Violet went North to Hopeman.

On the whole it was a moving experience.

After I had slept a little, or rather dreamt over your dear letter in a kind of Kubla Khan mood, I again confronted stern realities in the shape of Kitchener & Winston – the latter just returned from his flying & secret visit to Jellicoe, somewhere in the North of Scotland.[2] Joffre is very anxious that we should make a diversion on the N. coast of France to frighten the Germans as to their lines of communication. (This is *very secret*): so Winston has sent there to reinforce his aeroplanes & armed motor-cars his Marine Brigade (about 3000 men). As he mentioned 'cavalry', I thinking of old jokes about 'horse-marines',[3] began to chaff him as to the composition of his force. And what do you think I discovered? That he had (with K's consent, who is heartily glad to get rid of them) despatched the Oxfordshire Yeomanry! his own corps, with brother Jack (who is a Major in it) &c. I am afraid poor Goonie will be in a state of terrible anxiety, and not without reason. There are about 450 of them, all told, and if they encounter the Germans in any force, I fear we shall see very few of them back again. I hope, however, that like that other little jaunt to Ostend, of wh. I told you some weeks ago, they will follow the example of the 'good old Duke of York', who 'led his men to the top of a hill', and 'led them down again'.[4]

I gather from what W. said that the Admiral & his colleagues (with their 40 Dreadnoughts) are a good deal perturbed by the fear of submarines. (They are all against any attack on Heligoland.) In the Scapa flow where they have been of late, there are small whales, or big porpoises, which in their playful flounderings with all manner of fins & tails, often give the impression of a 'periscope', & have been fired at as such.

French's telegram to-day shows that the two armies on the Aisne (each strongly entrenched) are much as they were, but Joffre appears to be contemplating an extended outflanking movement West of *Noyon*.[5] (This too is secret.)

There is a bad casualty list to-day. The 2ⁿd 60ᵗʰ must be almost denuded by this time of officers, and some other battalions are even in worse case. Percy Wyndham's death is officially confirmed, and amongst the other 'killed' are Rivvy Grenfell (brother of Francis – did you ever dance with him?), Lord A. Hay (Tweeddale's brother) and Guernsey (Aylesford's son). Clare Tennant's admirer Gordon Ives is wounded:[6] also Dermot Browne (slightly) and Eric Drummond's brother, and among the missing are Freeman Thomas (the Willingdons' son) & Lord G. Murray (Tullibardine's brother).[7] There is a great number of other officers killed or wounded – including Grant-Duff[8] a very good soldier who served under me for years in the Committee of Imperial Defence. As you say, one wd. like those one cares for to be sufficiently wounded to bring them home; but the God of War is no respecter of persons.

Hankey has just sent me a letter from Swinton who is now at the front & writes the official battle-descriptions, of wh. the first appeared a couple of days ago: also a C.I.D. man.[9] He ends up from the great battlefield: 'I say nothing of the news except that we are carrying on, but it is a stiff proposition against superiority of men & guns'.

In regard to our own affairs, I see that you have still a superstitious feeling (founded I am bound to confess on past experience) that something might 'happen' between now & next Friday, I pray not. Margot wd. like to come to Dublin, and Elizabeth: Violet will make her way as best she can from Hopeman, & I imagine that completes the family 'tale'.

Don't you think my idea a good one to come to you Thursday, & return to Penrhos Sat. morning for Sunday? I suppose Bongie will be of the party, & I see you also promise the McKennae & the Assyrian. *A la bonne heure*! wh. means (in this connection) that I hope & *intend* to get my share (& if possible more) of one person's companionship.

Eliz. & I are off to Esher, but I return Sunday night, so please write to Downing St. I am turning out all my accumulated & undigested papers about the H.R. Bill – that they may be locked up in a tin box. Must stop now – all blessings & love, my own darling.

[1] In Lothian Road. It was named after the donor, Andrew Usher (d. 1898), and had been opened in Mar. 1914.

[2] Loch Ewe, on the west coast of Scotland.

[3] Kipling used this 'old joke' for his story 'The Horse Marines', first published in Oct. 1910.

[4] This diversion greatly alarmed German HQ. The force, nicknamed the Dunkirk Guerrilla, suffered no losses during the month of its independent operations.

[5] The so-called 'race to the sea' which had now begun was in reality a series of attempted outflanking operations, each side seeking to move round the northern end of the other's line.

[6] He had died of his wounds on 16 Sept.

[7] Both the 'missing' had been killed in the Aisne Battle on 14 Sept. In the case of Freeman Thomas this was confirmed only after a long interval.

[8] On 14 Sept., when commanding a battalion of the Black Watch.

[9] Ernest Swinton, who was in the Royal Engineers, had become Assistant Secretary of the Committee of Imperial Defence in 1913. His writings on warfare (*The Defence of Duffer's Drift*, 1904; *The Green Curve*, 1909) had been very successful; and Kitchener chose him to fill the gap left by the ban on war correspondents at the front. He reported as 'Eyewitness'. Quickly becoming familiar with the conditions under which the B.E.F. was fighting, he realized the need for new means of overcoming machine-gun fire from entrenched troops protected by barbed wire, and was a pioneer in the development of the tank.

164

Esher Place,
Surrey.

Sunday 20 Sept 14

My darling – there was no letter from you this morning, but I dare say you took my hints about Sunday posts & are writing to London. It seems almost unnatural, doesn't it? *not* to hear? But neither of us has any right to complain, and you have shown yourself a perfect angel of goodness, as well as a past mistress of the most difficult form of architecture which has to build with the minimum of clay or straw in the 'daily round'. There is nothing I enjoy more than your narrative of your walks & rides & cooking classes.

I don't think I told you yesterday that the D^{ss} of Sutherland (Millicent) just back from Namur & Maubeuge lunched with us.[1] She saw the 30,000 French who to their shame surrendered at Maubeuge being escorted along the road to Namur as prisoners by the Germans. She also saw a certain amount of the Bud & Angie, whom she left at their job. They are in want of money & it is very difficult to get any to them. She showed us her German passes which are real curiosities, and read from her diary an account of the siege of Namur, with map showing the forts &c. She is a very curious woman; I think on the whole I like her rather than otherwise; but like all her family she has the passion for *réclame*.[2]

Edward Grey came to see me to talk over the military situation. He is in better spirits than he was, and Margot elicited from him at tea time that our Pamela[3] was arriving, to take her usual part in his weekly rest cure. I don't think you know him well do you? Elizth & I drove down here in the gloaming. There is a small & rather Esher-ish party: Muriel Wilson, the Maguires, two Scots Guards officers Morrison Bell & Holbeach, and a Miss Halton from Venice. It is not at all exciting but quite pleasant: no one talks of anything but the war, the casualty lists, the victory of the Russians, & topics of the same kind.[4] The Guards have suffered very heavily in officers in these recent fights: I saw to-day the name of one young fellow who was barely 19; and the men here say (Scots Guards) that we have not yet got the list (a serious one) of their battalion.[5]

Rather a good description of Charlie Beresford's platform oratory, given by one of the Illingworth family who heard him at Bradford a night or two ago, on the war: 'A bumble bee in a foxglove'. Buckmaster seems to have been the orator of the occasion: I don't think you share in Violet's *culte* of *him*?

I have got a slight cold in the head – the result I suppose of 800 miles in the train on Friday – which makes me a little raucous. Probably it has not been improved by 2 rounds of golf (the first I have played for about 6 weeks) in intermittent showers of pelting rain. I shall, I hope, have my vocal chords again in good order by Friday. You would never guess who my partners & antagonists were – in the morning I played one ball & Edgar & Julia Maguire another; and we halved the match. This afternoon I encountered Crewe (who came down from London to lunch) in a single, & beat him heavily. I am rather disturbed by your addiction to tennis and your renunciation of golf. Do try & fit it in. It would be such a resource & delight if we could play together.

I have only glanced at the Sunday papers & have got no telegram from Kitchener or anyone else in London. Ll. George seems to have made a very characteristic speech, with some excellent 'purple patches'.[6] It is a great relief that the House of Commons is no longer sitting: no answers to questions, or the daily attempt to endure fools & bores gladly. I am disposed to make the prorogation as long as possible.[7]

Edgar is in very good form, & has ideas of strategy. Helen's temperament & methods do not change with the years – any more than the bloom on her cheeks.[8] I remember, years ago, saying that on the whole I preferred her when she was floating on the ripples of platitude, to when she was scaling the cliffs of paradox. I don't suppose that her life has been quite a success, tho' she has had, & has, many things that most people envy. The young woman from Venice reminds me of Ibsen's Lady From the Sea. There is something incomplete and yet rather suggestive about her. But not very much.

I am afraid this won't reach you till the 2nd post. Eliz. & I return to London after dinner to-night, & I know I shall hear from you in the morning. I re-read last night Birrell's essays on Newman & M. Arnold: both quite good. I have been rather depressed at odd moments to-day, thinking about the future and what it may have in store – for you, & for me. God be praised that we don't know. I wish you knew *how much* I love you!

---

[1] She had arrived back in England with a doctor and 8 British nurses, having travelled, with American help, via Holland. In Oct. she published, in co-operation with *The Times*, a booklet on her party's experiences (*Six Weeks at the War*); all the profits were given to war charities. She later ran the Hôpital Bellevue, Malo, Dunkirk.

[2] Asquith may have been thinking particularly of her half-sister, the Countess of Warwick, who had been well known when young as the intimate friend of the then Prince of Wales, and had been converted in 1895 to socialism. Lady Warwick's toils in that cause became as conspicuous as her earlier conquests in society.

[3] Margot's sister-in-law, Lady Glenconner.

[4] In the battle near Krasnik the Russians had taken 30,000 Austrians prisoner and captured 400 guns.

[5] The 1st Bn., Scots Guards, had been heavily engaged near Vendresse during the Aisne Battle.

[6] At Queen's Hall to the London Welsh, 19 Sept. It marked Lloyd George's emergence as a

popular war leader. 2½ million copies of this speech had been produced by the first week of Nov.

⁷ In 1940 Lloyd George quoted Maurice Bonham Carter as having said: 'During the first six months of the Great War, Asquith had not a care because he was not bothered with questions in the House.' Thomas Jones, *Diary with Letters* (1954), p. 470. While the statement is of interest it should be treated with reserve.

⁸ Lady D'Abernon had been a famous beauty and was now in her late 40s.

165

Mon 21 Sept 1914

. . . Kitchener was rather in the dumps to-day about the military situation. He thinks the two forces are too close – suffering in fact from lock-jaw, and is rather doubtful whether Joffre has enough men to outflank the German right. Meanwhile (but this is *secret*) the Portuguese offer to supply a large number of *mitrailleuses*, & about 10,000 horses & 3 or 4000 troops. This will make them belligerents on our side, & may *froisser* the Spaniards; but everything helps, & I am all for taking it. We shall also (this again is rather private) get some 30 or more additional battalions from India. The first instalment of the Indian troops (about 12,000) lands at Marseilles on Friday. We hear that the Germans have already compiled a prospective dossier of their nameless outrages. After the bombardment of Rheims Cathedral – the worst thing they have done – I doubt if the world will listen to them. . . .

I am afraid dearest this is a dull matter-of-fact letter: perhaps you really like that sort best?. . . . After Wednesday, we shall give up for the present the daily Cabinet.¹ Reggie has just been to see me to suggest Buckmaster as F. E. Smith's successor at the Press Bureau. F.E. is going to join the Indian troops (with the temporary rank of Major) in order to furnish flamboyant reports of their doings to India, and to counteract the lying German legends of atrocities. I was not altogether surprised that Buckmaster (who is a first rate man in his way) was willing to take it: I gather that the Impeccable, in the irritable stages of moral convalescence, has these last weeks led him the life of a dog.² You can always really test a man by his relative behaviour in times of crisis to his superiors & his subordinates. Your friend R. McK told me [he] had been on a sick bed at Munstead from Sat. till this morning – suffering from an 'inflated liver' (whatever that is); it sounds nasty but is perhaps less noxious than a swelled head. My darling – I *must* stop now; if I went on much longer you would cry halt! I love you – more than ever.

¹ There was still no committee to which day-to-day questions about the conduct of the war could be remitted. The War Council was not constituted until late in Nov.

² Asquith refers to Simon's 'near resignation' on 2–3 Aug.

The Three Cruisers (Letter 166)

LETTER 166 begins with the first serious reverse suffered by the British Navy in the war. In order to protect the cross-Channel traffic, and impede minelayers, a patrol was maintained across the southern part of the North Sea. It had lacked its destroyer screen since 19 September because of bad weather. On that day it had been moved by Admiralty order to the Broad Fourteens nearer the Dutch coast. By daylight on 22 September the weather had improved enough to make submarine action possible; but the cruisers were steaming in this very dangerous area at under ten knots, without zigzagging. The *Aboukir* was torpedoed by a submarine at 6.30 a.m.; she sank quickly, some of her boats being smashed in the explosion. The two other cruisers hurried to the spot and lowered their boats; they thus became standing targets, and they also were torpedoed and sunk. More than 1,400 from the crews, including a number of Osborne cadets, were lost. The resulting criticism of Churchill, alleging that he had overruled the sailors, was particularly unfair.[1] On 17 September he heard the patrol called 'the live bait squadron', and on the following day he moved the First Sea Lord to institute a safer system of patrolling; but this had not yet gone into effect. Hankey lunched at 10 Downing Street on 22 September. He wrote years later of this incident (and of the naval losses in home waters in October and November 1914): 'I do not remember any events in this part of the war which caused such an atmosphere of depression.'

The consternation caused by the sinking of the *Audacious* (Letters 191 and 192) is even more striking, since that entailed no loss of life. All this reflected the importance attached to the British margin of superiority in capital ships and cruisers. The commissioning of the *Dreadnought* in December 1906 had devalued all existing navies. For the next eight years Britain had maintained a lead over Germany in Dreadnoughts; but it was not a large one and there was little possibility in war of adding much to it. Mines and submarines had not lessened the importance of the capital ship: they had merely made her extremely vulnerable. Naval losses reminded people how small and precarious the margin of superiority was. Perhaps the German navy might be able to emerge at last and fight on better than even terms. Sir John French could not lose the war in an afternoon: Jellicoe could.

---

[1] See, for instance, Leo Maxse to J. S. Sandars, 8 Oct. 1914: Maxse had heard from the 'naval expert' of the *Morning Post* that 'the sinking of the three cruisers was directly due to Churchill': Sandars MSS, f. 22.

166

Tu 22 Sept 14

. . . We have just had some very bad news: the worst, I think, since the war began. Three good & powerful cruisers of an old but not obsolete type – the *Cressy* & 2 of her sisters – were sunk this morning in the North Sea.[1] . . .

. . . The navy is not doing very well just now: there are nearly ½ a dozen German cruisers, *Emden, Dresden, Karlsruhe* &c, which are at large on the high seas & in all parts of the world are sinking or capturing British merchantmen.[2] Things came almost to a climax at the Cabinet to-day, when we learnt that the New Zealanders absolutely decline to despatch their expeditionary force – all in transports & ready to sail to-morrow or next day – unless we can provide them with a sufficiently powerful escort to convoy them in safety from Wellington to Adelaide, where they were to join up with the Australian contingent. The Admiralty think there is no real risk, but I am inclined to agree with the New Zealanders, and as there are no available ships at hand of the requisite strength, we have been obliged to tell them to wait for what may be as long as another 6 weeks. This will probably excite a good deal of resentment & indignation in N.Z.[3] Unfortunately, on this day, when of all others he was most needed, Winston is away, on one of his furtive missions, – this time again to Dunkirk:[4] and is not expected back till evening. I think (between you & me) that the Admiralty have not been clever in their outlying strategy.

Kitchener presented himself to-day in what he called frankly a 'white sheet', admitting that the recruits had been & were being badly treated in the way of clothing boots & other necessaries. He says that his orders have not been carried out & is furious with the W.O. We agreed to dismiss the chief director of contracts – one De La Bere: and to set on foot a better & more businesslike system. I thought that this had been done – it was certainly ordered to be done – at least 3 weeks ago; but the officials who are quite good in peace time seem hopelessly incompetent to deal with the problems which war throws up. . . .

---

[1] The *Cressy* had been launched in 1899, the *Aboukir* and the *Hogue* in 1900.

[2] When the war began 2 German cruisers were stationed in the West Indies, 1 in the Indian Ocean, and 5 under Admiral von Spee's command in the Pacific. All of the first 3 were out of action by mid-Nov. 1914. The *Karlsruhe* was sunk by an internal explosion on 4 Nov., the *Emden* driven ashore and destroyed by the Australian light cruiser *Sydney* on 9 Nov., and the *Königsberg* blocked into the Rufiji River in East Africa on 10 Nov. (see Letter 198, n. 8). For the destruction of von Spee's squadron at the Falkland Islands see Letter 202, n. 2. The *Dresden* escaped from that engagement, but was hunted down and destroyed in Mar. 1915 in the Chilean islands of Juan Fernandez. To the end of Jan. 1915 the British merchant navy lost

273,000 tons by enemy action. This represented some two per cent of British merchant tonnage; and a further 1½ per cent was detained in German and Turkish ports. These losses were quickly replaced by new building. Surface raiders accounted for 215,000 of the 273,000 tons; and they sank another 227,000 tons during the rest of the war. Compare with that the six and half million tons which were to be sunk by German U-boats.

³ The troops had embarked at Wellington, and two transports had actually sailed from Auckland, when the order postponing the expedition was received early on 25 Sept. It eventually sailed for Egypt on 16 Oct.

⁴ Churchill wrote later of the 'Dunkirk Guerrilla' and similar episodes:
Looking back . . . I seem to have been too ready to undertake tasks which were hazardous or even forlorn. . . . I believed . . . that the special knowledge which I possessed, and the great and flexible authority which I wielded in this time of improvisation, would enable me to furnish less unsatisfactory solutions . . . than could be furnished . . . by others in less commanding positions.

The World Crisis, 1914 (1923), p. 322.

167

24 Queen Anne's Gate,
S.W.

Mond 28 Sept 1914

. . . In regard to Ireland & the succession to the Aberdeens, they [Montagu and Eric Drummond] were both anti-Wimborne & anti-Dick Cavendish, & strongly in favour of the Gladstones.¹ Tell me what you think about this: you know that your judgment comes first with me. . . .

¹ Of the 'possibles' discussed for the Viceroyalty of Ireland, Viscount Gladstone, W. E. Gladstone's youngest son, was the oldest and by far the most experienced. He had been Home Secretary (1905–9) and the first Governor-General of the Union of South Africa (1910–14). Lord Wimborne and Lord Richard Cavendish had both joined the Liberals in mid-career as a result of the tariff reform controversy.

'The Americans are making themselves disagreeable about the seizure & detention of cargoes' (Letter 168)

On 28 September W. H. Page was instructed by cable to see Grey and express the American Government's grave concern at the system for denying supplies to Germany which had been established by the Order in Council of 20 August. American commercial interests had been rather slow to protest; but when they found contraband control by the British to be a reality they inundated the President and the State Department with their complaints. The day after he had delivered this *démarche* Page was obliged to tell Washington that unwrought copper had been added to the contraband lists.

The 'instruction' to Page had originally been conceived as a formal note of protest; but in the light of discussions between Colonel House and the

British Ambassador, Sir Cecil Spring-Rice, it was decided to adopt the less abrasive alternative. After some weeks of intensive discussions the Americans let Grey know on 23 October that they would no longer press him to curtail contraband control by adopting the Declaration of London in entirety. This cleared the way for tighter contraband lists and for a revision of the British system of search and forfeiture. These changes were made on 29 October, the preamble to the new Order in Council stating that the revision was intended 'to minimize, so far as possible, the interference with innocent neutral trade occasioned by the war'.

This dangerous corner for Britain was turned, not only because of Wilson's respect, and Page's affection, for Grey, but because during October many American commercial men began to realize how profitable war trade might be to them. The Allied countries had taken a large proportion of American exports in peace: when their war effort came into its stride they could absorb nearly all that America could export. British agents agreed to good prices; and the firm which sent its goods through British ports could be reasonably sure that the buyers would receive them, and pay for them, promptly. By the third week of October insurance rates between America and Britain had fallen to ten shillings per £100 of cargo, or three-quarters of that in the case of fast liners.[1] By March 1915 the British controlled 95 per cent of exportable American copper.

The policy of mining in the North Sea to which Asquith had been converted was dictated, not only by the activities of German submarines in the Channel, but by the needs of contraband control. If the Germans continued to lay mines, while the British abstained, it would eventually become safer to take an American ship into Rotterdam than into Liverpool. Churchill was the opponent of minelaying. On 29 September Asquith urged him to 'start mining . . . without stinting, and if necessary on a Napoleonic scale'. The cabinet approved the policy on the following day; and the Admiralty published a description of the mined area on 3 October. The neutrals naturally grumbled; but in the face of the German 'ambush' mining the existence of a British minefield which was marked on all charts did not give great cause for complaint.

[1] These were the commercial rates. Cargoes in British ships were insured under the state scheme at 2 per cent: C. E. Fayle, *Seaborne Trade*, i(1920), 40–44 and 306.

168

Tu 29 Sept 1914

My darling – you will never guess how many times I have read over & over (on a very busy day) your precious letter of this morning. Writing is indeed (as you say) a 'wretched make-shift'. They talk of 'Life's little Ironies', but its cruel & terrible partings (even with radiant memories behind, and rainbow hopes in front) plunge one for the time into black fathomless depths of actual solitude. Here am I in the midst of anxious & distracting affairs (it is now 3.30, and I have been at it without a moment's intermission since 10 this morning), and all the time, when I find a moment to myself, a great wave comes over me, and I feel that the best thing in life, on which all my trust and all my hopes are centred, is removed from me by unbridgeable chasms & untraversable leagues. Darling don't ever wish that I had 'not made you want more'.

Can we ever forget those divine hours on Saturday & Sunday?[1] They are part of us both, beyond the reach of chance or change – an ineffaceable memory – the little sheltered slope with the long grass, and the dogs in attendance, and the delicious alternations of silence & speech; and later on, the twilight on the wooden bench in the garden, with the moon & the evening star & the Great Bear, and – but it is too cruel to recreate what, until the lapse of many weary days & nights, we cannot renew. The price of absence & separation is heavy indeed, but not too heavy if (as I firmly believe) there is even more for us in the future than there has been in the past. . . .

. . . Now I will tell you a great *secret*. French intends – if he can get Joffre's assent, and if Joffre can spare enough men to fill the gap – to 'disengage' as they call it i.e. to unlock his troops from their present position, and to make with his whole force a great outflanking march via Amiens, Arras, Douai, Tournay, to the line across Belgium from Brussels to Cologne. He thinks he could do it in a week or 9 days, and the long march would be good for his troops. It would relieve Antwerp (wh. is going to be sorely pressed) take the Germans in their flank & rear, break up their communications, & if successful put an end to the invasion of France. It is a great scheme (heartily approved by Kitchener) and I hope Joffre won't thro' timidity or over caution put spokes in the wheel. . . .[2]

There was no Cabinet to-day – but we had a long conference here – Grey, Crewe, Runcy, McK (not Wood), Impecc[ble], Haldane, & Rufus. The Americans are making themselves disagreeable about the seizure & detention of cargoes sent in their ships ostensibly to Holland, but for German consumption. We naturally don't want to have a row with them, but we cannot allow the Germans to be provided for. I am reluctantly convinced that the only thing to be done is to sow the Eastern part of the North Sea with mines – right down to between Rotterdam & Flushing. I have been urging this strongly on Winston, & I think he is disposed to take the same view. . . .

Take a solitary walk to-morrow beloved to our dear little hollow, and think of me & of our heavenly hour there. How I try to recall all you said, and every turn of your head, and every look of your face, and the touch of your hand, and –. I hardly dare: the contrast makes things look so drab. I love you more than words can say – with every fibre, & whatever I have that is worth having & giving.

[1] Asquith spoke in Dublin on 25 Sept. and stayed with the Stanleys at Penrhos on the return journey.

[2] French had outlined this plan to Churchill, who visited his H.Q. on 27 Sept. While its soundness has never been doubted, some of Asquith's comments on it reflect French's over-optimism at this stage of the campaign. The cavalry could go by road; but moving the rest of the B.E.F. would monopolize the rail resources of the area and prevent any other large-scale movements. Thus the operation of closing a large gap in the Allied line was not a small one for Joffre. The 2nd Corps entrained on 4, the 3rd on 7, and the 1st on 17 Oct. The weak French force which replaced the B.E.F. was driven off the Aisne heights, and – far more important – Lille was lost, possibly because, with the railways pre-empted, no reserves could be brought to its defence.

169

Wed 30 Sept 1914

. . . Sir Ian Hamilton came to lunch: he commands all the Territorials, and is very pleased with a lot of them. Curiously, in England far the best are the North & South Midlands – Stafford, Warwick, Northampton, Derby, Notts &c. Of the Scotch, he puts the Lovat Scouts first. It is strange that the Scottish officers – lairds & sons of lairds &c – are very inferior to the English professional men from the Midlands, solicitors, doctors, architects & such. He is a sanguine enthusiastic person, with a good deal of *superficial* charm (do you know him?) and much experience of warfare (one of the few survivors of Majuba Hill[1] in 1881) but there is too much feather in his brain.[2] . .

[1] Where he was mentioned in dispatches and had his left arm crippled.

[2] Yet it was by Asquith's insistence that Hamilton was sent, in Mar. 1915, to command the Dardanelles expedition (Violet Asquith's diary).

170

Thurs. 1 Oct 14

. . . The Germans are pounding away with their big guns at Antwerp, and tho' the Belgians are in large numerical superiority[1] they seem to have lost morale & nerve, and are making the most piteous appeals for help. One cannot be surprised, or blame them, for the Germans have been unusually active these last few days in burning their villages & shooting the inhabitants. It is now clear that the German soldiers were equipped each man with a supply of small discs of compressed benzine (not much bigger in diameter than a lead pencil) and that with these wh. flare up into a big explosive flame, first breaking the windows & then throwing in the disc, they destroyed the interior of the houses in places like Louvain & Termonde. Whitehouse M.P. who has just come back from Belgium told me this morning that in Termonde² there is not a stick of furniture left in any of the houses, all having been blown up in this fashion from the inside.³ The fall of Antwerp would be a great moral blow to the Allies, for it would leave the whole of Belgium for the moment at the mercy of the Germans; the Cardinal⁴ telegraphs that he does not think they can hold out for more than another 3 days. Of course it would be idle butchery to send a force like Winston's little Army⁵ there: if anything is to be done it must be by regulars in sufficient numbers. We had a conference here last night & sent over in the night 3 good officers to report, and to urge upon the Belgians to disregard their forts and to entrench themselves. The French telegraph that they are willing to send a division (of 15,000 to 20,000) & to put it under a British general – but they do not say what is the quality of the soldiers, who may be, very likely are, only Territorials. However, we resolved at the Cabinet to-day that, if the French cooperation is satisfactory, we would divert our 7ᵗʰ Division (of the finest troops)⁶ wh. was just going to join Sir J. French, and not throw it into Antwerp but endeavour to raise the siege & capture the German big guns. In the meantime Winston is going in for a big mining operation in the North Sea, which ought to make things easier. All the same I can't help being anxious about Antwerp, & the course of events in the next few days.⁷ If Sir J. French, as he says he hopes, can disengage himself & come round the German right in the direction I told you of, the whole situation wd. be changed enormously for the better.

Darling – I know all this doesn't bore you, but sometimes I am afraid that I may burden you too much with my preoccupations. After all, this is the biggest thing we are ever likely to see, and I shall & *must* take you with me *every day* until it is carried through, or I succumb. . . .

Do you ever 'day-dream'? by which I mean lean back in your chair & close your eyes, & reconstruct the back-ground of memory? Half-forgotten events & people live again, old hopes & fears, critical moments, the seemingly unimportant but the really meaning choices & decisions of one's life. Some day I will tell you, when we are sitting close together, of those which stand out for me: and, among them, of the one which has been to me the most enduringly good. Though you don't really need most beloved to be told. I wonder when I shall see you again: perhaps on Saturday. I feel honestly unworthy of all you have been, and are, & will be to me. *My love!*

¹ This was only a slight exaggeration. The immense Antwerp perimeter held at least 65,000 of the Belgian field army and about 80,000 Belgian garrison troops. For the attacking forces see Letter 172, n. 2.
² Now Dendermonde, 25 miles S.W. of Antwerp.
³ See the article by J. H. Whitehouse in the *Nation*, 3 Oct. 1914, and his book *Belgium in War* (1915).
⁴ Cardinal Mercier, Archbishop of Malines; he had visited England in Sept. 'Cardinal' was altered to 'commander' in *Memories and Reflections* and to 'Minister' in *Churchill: Companion Docs., 1914–1916*.
⁵ Asquith refers to the 'Dunkirk Guerrilla' (Letter 163, n. 4).
⁶ This division had been formed from regular units relieved in their overseas garrisons by the Indian Army.
⁷ If Asquith had been served by a stronger war staff he would have become worried about Antwerp earlier than this. Before the end of Aug., Hankey was agitating for some action to be taken to deprive the enemy of the use of German merchant shipping detained there on the outbreak of war. On 7 Sept. Churchill had suggested using the Schelde to supply Antwerp (despite Dutch objections), and sending Territorials to aid in its defence. After discussion in cabinet the first proposal was vetoed by Grey, the second by Kitchener.

171

Fr. 2 Oct. 14 1 p.m.

. . . The news from Antwerp this morning is far from good & gives me some anxiety. The Germans battered down 2 of the forts, and what is worse got in between them & drove a lot of Belgians out of their entrenchments. Meanwhile the only relieving force that the French offer is a mass of Territorials & the like, who would be no use for hard fighting and are quite unfit to co-operate with a trained division of ours like the 7ᵗʰ. On the other hand to send the 7ᵗʰ alone is to court almost certain disaster. It is a very difficult situation – particularly as our officer reports that it is the morale of the Belgian Commanders rather than of the men wh. shows signs of collapse. He says (early this morning) that 'any definite statement of assistance that could be given to Belgian Government would have immediate & excellent effect'. But it is no good to lure them with false hopes. . . .

172

Sat 3 Oct 14

. . . I found on my return¹ that strange things had been going on here. The Belgian Government, notwithstanding that we were sending them heavy guns, and trying hard to get together troops to raise the siege of Antwerp, resolved yesterday to throw up the sponge & to leave to-day for Ostend, the King with his field army withdrawing in the direction of Ghent. They calculated that after their departure Antwerp might hold out for 5 or 6 days – wh. seems very doubtful. This is a *mad* decision, quite unwarranted by the situation, for the German besieging army is only a scratch force, and one way or another a diversion is certain in the course of a few days.[2] So we at once replied urging them to hold out, & promising Winston's marines to-morrow, with the hope of help from the main army & reinforcements from here. I was of course away, but Grey Kitchener & Winston held a late meeting, and (I fancy with Grey's rather reluctant assent) the intrepid Winston set off at midnight & ought to have reached Antwerp by about 9 this morning. He will go straightway & beard the King & his Ministers, and try to infuse into their backbones the necessary quantity of starch. Meanwhile Sir J. French is making preparations to send assistance by way of Lille. I have had a long talk with K this morning, & we are now both rather anxiously awaiting Winston's report. I don't know how fluent he is in French, but if he was able to do himself justice in a foreign tongue, the Belges will have listened to a discourse the like of which they have never heard before. I cannot but think that he will stiffen them up to the sticking point. Don't say anything of Winston's mission, at any rate at present; it is one of the many unconventional incidents of the war. . . .[3]

At Cardiff yesterday we had all the appropriate humours & accompaniments of a Welsh meeting – 'Land of my Fathers', 'Men of Harlech', Ellis Griffith, William Jones, cheers for Lloyd George, cries of 'Clwch' (if that is the way to spell it) &c &c. You know them well from your experiences at Holyhead & elsewhere: happily we were spared the usual speech or speeches in the vernacular. Poor Lord Plymouth[4] was on the platform and made quite a nice little speech.

K. who generally finds out things sooner or later – as a rule rather later – discoursed to me this morning at great length & with much vehemence on the shortcomings & stupidity of the medical & other arrangements for the wounded at the front. He has dismissed his principal Army Medical Officer for incompetence & disobedience,[5] and declares that everything now is in good train.[6] He says the deaths from tetanus, wh. have been very many, are due to the doctors not treating gunshot wounds at once with antiseptic inoculation. He ordered this to be done weeks ago, but unavailingly. . . .

---

[1] From his recruiting speech in Cardiff.
[2] It was not 'mad'. The Belgians aimed to safeguard their field army at all costs; its retreat westward from Antwerp was already seriously threatened. The Antwerp fortress commander was to be told to resist to the end in each fort (an instruction which he did not obey). About

1 a.m. on 3 Oct. Kitchener received a telegram from the British Ambassador to France now at Bordeaux, relaying news given to the French Government by its attaché in Antwerp. This suggested, quite wrongly, that the force attacking Antwerp had only a limited siege-train. The German commander was short of ammunition; but he disposed of 173 heavy guns, the largest being of 420 mm. calibre. These gave him his main strength. Apart from them he had only 5 inferior divisions.

³ Churchill had been travelling to Dover by special train, intending to visit Dunkirk, when the message about the field army leaving Antwerp was received. He was hauled back to London and joined Grey and Kitchener in conference. About 2 a.m. on 3 Oct. he left Victoria in his special train for the second time. His action was much misrepresented. He was said by one of the Civil Lords of the Admiralty (writing to the King's Secretary, 6 Oct.) to have left 'in spite of the remonstrances' of his two colleagues. For his fluency in French see Letter 293.

⁴ His son Archer Clive had died of wounds: Letter 137, n. 3. He was Lord-Lieutenant of Glamorgan and President of its Territorial Army Association. He had also chaired Lloyd George's meeting on 19 Sept.: Letter 164, n. 6.

⁵ Sir Arthur Sloggett. When removed from the Director-Generalship of Army Medical Services, he was sent to France as Director-General of Medical Services in the B.E.F. Lady D'Abernon, who was nursing there in 1916, found him 'quick, vain, irritable, kindhearted. . . . He has an open mind,' she wrote, and 'a hatred of red tape, and is presumably an able if extravagant administrator': *Red Cross and Berlin Embassy, 1915–1926* (1946), p. 11.

⁶ Kitchener recalled Sir Alfred Keogh, who had been Director-General of Army Medical Services, 1905–10, and had left to become Rector of Imperial College. Keogh served in his old post as Director-General for the rest of the war.

173

Ewelme Down,
Wallingford.

Sunday 4 Oct 1914

. . . We were reinforced last night at dinner by an oddly assorted couple – Viola Parsons & Harry Wilson. The latter, who was attired in a very smart suit of Indian khaki, has been given the command of the 'Middlesex Hussars'¹ – a London yeomanry regiment who are encamped with 2 others near here on the river at Streatley. Like so many others of their kind, they expect to be ordered to the front 'next week'! Harry, who is quite a good soldier, declares that they are 'real good stuff' and that he will soon be ready to take the field with them. Viola's explanations of her whereabouts & doings were rather vague: apparently she had come at Harry's invitation to 'look at the soldiers': and after dinner she disappeared with him in a thickish fog in his motor bound for London, whither Harry asserted he was going to try & get some rifles out of 'old K'. . . .

. . . K in his talk with me yesterday morning said that after carefully looking over the Territorials, while there were some quite good units (such e.g. as the London Scottish who are now at the front with French) he didn't think there was any Division which as a Division is, or for a considerable time will be, really fit for the fighting line. I bucked them up as much as I could in my speech at Cardiff, because if the idea spreads that they are to be sacrificed or pushed aside in favour of K's new recruits, there will, at any rate as soon as the war is over, be an end of the Territorials.

I have a letter from Oc from the 'RND'[2] camp at Betteshanger reporting progress. He seems to be quite happy, and has been attached to a battalion, wh. is called the 'Anson' (I suppose to keep up the fiction that they are all at heart sea dogs) & is commanded by George West![3] . . . . Winston's tolerance is wonderful, when his patriotic spirit is fairly aflame. . . .

[1] Originally (1797) the Uxbridge Yeomanry Cavalry; renamed Middlesex (Duke of Cambridge's Hussars) Yeomanry Cavalry, 1884; fought in Boer War and both world wars.
[2] Royal Naval Division.
[3] Lady Randolph Churchill's second husband, Lt.-Col. George Cornwallis-West: they had been divorced in 1913.

174

Monday 5 Oct '14

. . . Winston succeeded in bucking up the Belges, who gave up their panicky idea of retreating to Ostend, and are now going to hold Antwerp for as long as they can, trusting upon our coming to their final deliverance. Winston had already moved up his Marines from Dunkirk, and they are now in the Antwerp trenches, where we hear to-day they are doing well but have already had 70 casualties. He had also sent for the rest of his Naval Brigade from Betteshanger,[1] and I have a telegram from Oc, sent off from Dover pier on Sunday evening: 'Embarking to-night: love.' I suppose most of the territorials & recruits would envy him, being sent off after 3 days to the front! I am sure he will do well, but it is a hazardous adventure.

We are doing our best for the Belgians, for tho' we are dangerously short of regulars in this country, K. is sending off to-day to their help an Expeditionary Force, consisting of the 7th division[2] (18,000 of our best infantry) and a Cavalry Division (also of the best) running to 4000. These with 8000 Winstons make 30,000 men & 87 good guns. The French force wh. is to co-operate with them – mainly Territorials & 'Fusilier Marines' – will amount to 23,500 men & 40 guns; wh. gives a total of over 53,500 men, & 127 guns: quite a big army. They ought all to be in Belgium by Wednesday or Thursday at the latest, and it is to be hoped that Antwerp can last as long as that. K. has appointed one of the best of our younger generals – Sir Henry Rawlinson – to command the whole.

Then comes in a real bit of tragi-comedy. I found when I arrived here this morning the enclosed telegram from Winston, who, as you will see, proposes to resign his Office, in order to take the command in the field of this great military force! Of course without consulting anybody, I at once telegraphed to him warm appreciation of his mission & his offer, with a *most decided* negative, saying that we could not spare him at the Admiralty &c. I had not meant to read it to the Cabinet, but as everybody, including K, began to ask how soon he was going to return, I was at last obliged to do so, carefully suppressing the last sentence, in wh. he nominates *Runciman* as his successor!

I regret to say that it was received with a Homeric laugh. W. is an ex-Lieutenant of Hussars, and would if his proposal had been accepted, have been in command of 2 distinguished Major Generals, not to mention Brigadiers, Colonels &c: while the Navy was only contributing its little brigades. I send you the original, which I know you won't show to anybody, to add to your collection of *mémoires pour servir*, with K's marginal pencil annotation. Even now, I don't know how or how soon, we shall get him back.[3] . . .

[1] Churchill's telegram to Kitchener (received 9.45 p.m., 3 Oct.) proposed, as part of the relieving force for Antwerp, 'both naval brigades, minus recruits'. 'The proposal', as Hankey records, 'was sanctioned, but by whom is not clear.' A brigade which included Arthur Asquith and his friends when it reached Belgium could hardly be said to have arrived 'minus recruits'. Churchill was criticized later for these arrangements, not least by Asquith: Letter 182.

[2] Regular troops who had been at overseas stations at the outbreak of war.

[3] After the war Venetia sold this telegram to Lord Beaverbrook and it is now in the Beaverbrook MSS. Kitchener's annotation reads: 'I will make him a Lieut. General if you will give him the command.' Churchill referred to his offer to resign and take the command in *The World Crisis, 1914*, adding: 'I have since learned that Lord Kitchener wrote proposing that it should be [accepted], and wished to give me the necessary military rank.' When this was published (1923) he possessed no copy of the telegram. In *Politicians and the War* (1928) Beaverbrook published the full text with Kitchener's note. Churchill commented, when sent the proofs by Beaverbrook: 'It was a sporting offer, and I was very lucky not to be taken at my word:' *Churchill: Companion Docs., 1922–1929*, pp. 970–1. Churchill said to Alexander during the 2nd World War: 'I do envy you; you've done what I've always wanted to do – to command great victorious armies in battle. I thought I got very near it once . . . when I commanded those forces at Antwerp. I thought it was going to be my great opportunity.'

The reply to Churchill's telegram told him that Rawlinson would arrive in Antwerp shortly; he was asked to do his best meanwhile.

Weaponry: 'Almost every "lesson" learned in the Boer War has to be . . . reversed in this' (Letter 175)

IT was no doubt true that the British Army had relied too much on its Boer War experiences, and had learned too little from other recent wars. When Sir Ian Hamilton returned from the Russo-Japanese War convinced of the power of the defence based on well-sited entrenchments, his advice was perhaps better taken abroad than at home.[1] Again, it was not appreciated in Britain how far the Turkish defence of the Chatalja lines at the end of the first Balkan War had demonstrated the difficulty of storming strongly defended trenches. A war of movement against a force of lightly armed but well-horsed marksmen did not provide the best preparation for meeting the German army. The machine-guns, which had so often jammed on the dusty veld, were devastating on the muddy plains of Flanders.

The 'lessons' of the Boer War were, however, only one cause of the B.E.F.'s troubles. All the armies of 1914 had been trained and equipped for mobile warfare. A good deal of 'German superiority' rested on a powerful armaments industry. British heavy armaments firms were essentially naval suppliers. Britain had no firms to match Krupps' and the Austrian Skoda works in producing super-heavy artillery for land warfare. The German high command had concentrated on big guns because their plan of campaign had depended on reducing the forts of Liège and Namur in the minimum time.

Some of the 'German superiority' was mythical. At the start of the war the German infantry deployed no more machine-guns than the British, though they may have made better use of what they had. All the pre-war military staffs had their blind spots, British deficiencies being no worse, on balance, than those of France (p. 194). In 1910, for instance, Foch pronounced an army's use for aeroplanes to be 'zero'.[2]

---

[1] Some of the problems had become apparent in the Boer War itself. In evidence to the Royal Commission on it Hamilton had advocated steel shields on wheels to protect infantry in bullet-swept zones. He recorded his experiences with the Japanese army in *A Staff Officer's Scrap Book*, 2 vols. (1905, 1907). In 1906 the War Office rejected a proposal for a mortar to give the infantry support: E. L. Woodward, *Great Britain and the War of 1914–18* (1967), pp. 40 n. 1, and 44 n. 1.

[2] Tuchman, op. cit., p. 261.

175

Tu 6 Oct 1914

. . . Freddy Guest came here to lunch to-day & told us some interesting things about the campaign. He has been at the front, driving Sir J. French every day in his motor, since the beginning of the war. He says (as others do) that the Germans owe such success as they have had entirely to their heavy howitzers,[1] which outrange all our guns & drop the shell perpendicularly at the end of its flight, like this – ⌐⌐ – instead of ⌒ : with the result that cover is almost useless.[2] Also they enormously outstrip both us & the French in their machine guns. It is curious that our War Office, after carefully considering the German superiority in these respects during the last few years, resolved to make no change. The fact is that almost every 'lesson' learned in the Boer war has to be, not only unlearned, but almost exactly reversed in this. The English & German trenches are so near (only 300 yards) that the soldiers chaff one another – the Germans singing 'Tipperary', & the English calling out 'Waiter' & 'sausage' – & other such pleasantries. . . .

[1] One of Moltke's reasons for confidence in July 1914 was apparently the superiority of German artillery. 'France and Russia have no howitzers', he was reported as saying, 'and cannot therefore fight troops in covered positions': F. Fischer, *War of Illusions* (1975), p. 402.

[2] At extreme range the low-angle gun and the howitzer are both pointed at an angle of 45 degrees from the horizontal. When the range is to be shortened, the angle of the barrel is swivelled in the first towards the horizontal, and in the second towards the vertical.

176

Wed 7 Oct 1914

. . . I am glad that you have Goonie with you – she is both restful & interesting, which is a rare combination in a companion. Give her my love. She has less occasion to be anxious than I have just now: for the Oxfordshire Yeomen are back at or near Dunkirk, while Oc & his naval men at arms are lining the entrenchments of Antwerp & sustaining the full force of the German bombardment. The Court & Ministers have retreated to Ostend, and the Belgian army is completely worn out & demoralised.[1] The trenches are good & strongly protected, and our men could I believe hold them against any assault that the second or third rate German besiegers could deliver for an indefinite time: certainly until relief comes. But when the bombardment of the open town once begins the inhabitants (some 300 or 400,000) are sure to get into a panic & to demand a capitulation. Our force will in no case surrender, but if the worst comes will retire on the road to Bruges & Ghent where they will find Rawlinson's Corps entrenched & waiting for reinforcements. But one fears there may be a lot of casualties, from these hellish shells which every one agrees are the German's really formidable weapon.

Much of this I got from Winston who returned from the front early this morning[2] to find himself the father of a new daughter[3] who arrived with the minimum of fuss & pain in the middle of the night. . . .

. . . K. thinks it not improbable that both in the West & the East the big opposing armies may in some months' time come to something like stalemate; in which event he considers it might not be bad strategy for the Germans to try a descent on our coasts. We[4] came to a pretty unanimous conclusion that whether attempted on a large or on a small scale it would be a disastrous operation – for the Germans. Sir Ian Hamilton who commands the home army gave a very good account of the preparations he has made against anything of the kind. The trains are all ready with steam up.[5] *Strictly* between you & me, much our weakest point is deficiency in guns & ammunition; this will not be put thoroughly right until the beginning of January, tho' everybody concerned is working night & day.[6]. . .

. . . I have had a long call from Winston, who, after dilating in great detail on the actual situation, became suddenly very confidential, and implored me not to take a 'conventional' view of his future. Having, as he says, 'tasted blood' these last few days, he is beginning like a tiger to raven for more, and begs that sooner or later, & the sooner the better, he may be relieved of his present office & put in some kind of military command. I told him that he could not be spared from the Admiralty, but he scoffs at that, alleging that the naval part of the business is practically over, as our superiority will grow greater & greater every month. His mouth waters at the sight & thought of K's new armies. Are these 'glittering commands' to be entrusted to 'dug-out trash', bred on the obsolete tactics of 25 years ago – 'mediocrities, who have led a sheltered life mouldering in military routine' &c &c. For about $\frac{1}{4}$ of an hour he poured forth a ceaseless cataract of invective and appeal, & I much regretted that there was no short-hand writer within hearing – as some of his unpremeditated phrases were quite priceless. He was, however, quite three parts serious, and declared that a political career was nothing to him in comparison with military glory.[7] He has now left to have a talk with Arthur Balfour, but will be back here at dinner. He is a wonderful creature, with a curious dash of schoolboy simplicity (quite unlike Edward Grey's), and what someone said of genius – 'a zigzag streak of lightning in the brain'.[8]. . .

[1] The decision to withdraw most of the Belgian field army had been taken on the evening of 6 Oct. The bombardment of the city and of the inner line of forts began at midnight on the 7th. The British naval brigades were evacuated the following night and withdrew towards Ghent and Ostend. Towards evening on the 9th German patrols entered Antwerp; the garrison surrendered on the 10th. The effort at relief had prolonged the defence by some five days.

[2] He had left the city late on 6 Oct. with Gen. Rawlinson and had crossed from Ostend.

[3] Sarah Churchill.

[4] The Committee of Imperial Defence.

[5] The German high command never seem to have given the possibility of a landing serious consideration; but, as the Admiralty could not guarantee to intercept a raiding force, substantial numbers of troops had to be kept to garrison vulnerable points during most of the war.

[6] Lloyd George had already placed £20 million at the disposal of the Master-General of the Ordnance, in an effort to obtain increased capacity from the established armaments firms, and had virtually freed the Ordnance Department from Treasury control.

[7] In Nov. 1915 a naval commander wrote to Churchill, 'You told me once, on the bridge of the *Enchantress*, during a night watch, that in the event of a war with Germany your greatest regret would be that, owing to your official position, you would be unable to take a fighting part.'

[8] From P. J. Bailey's *Festus*: one of Asquith's favourite quotations, which he applied also to Disraeli and the Kaiser.

177

Thurs. 8 Oct '14

My darling – there is certainly something rather rotten about your posts at Alderley, wh. seem to be very inferior to those at Holyhead. Yesterday your letter arrived in the course of the morning, but to-day up to now (3. p.m.) nothing has come. I know that you never fail to write, but it is rather disquieting to be in doubt as to when one will get what one wants most in the whole day. Of course it is no fault of yours, but it seems strange that, being as you are about 100 miles nearer, you are for practical purposes farther away. This is the grumble of a hungry man – to whom your daily letter brings more nutrition & stimulus than the blood of 1000 Argentine steers, or than all the strychnine in the laboratories of Europe. . . .

The news this morning from Antwerp was distinctly bad. The Germans had been bombarding away all night, and General Paris, who commands Winston's Naval Division, talked of evacuating the trenches, while Gen. Rawlinson who is at Bruges sent a panicky report that the Germans had advanced through Termonde, & were threatening to cut through the line of retirement on Ghent both of the Belgian field army and of our Naval force. The Arch-Colonel on the other hand who has turned up at Antwerp, full of fight & hope, gave a much more optimistic view of the situation.[1]

When the Cabinet met, Kitchener being away inspecting on Salisbury plain, E. Grey (as usual) was most dolorous & despondent. The French have played a poor part as they have diverted the relief force wh. they had promised to send. Winston was furious (and I quite share his anger) at his General, who is in an almost impregnable entrenched position & ought to hold on even by his eye-brows, until either the situation becomes really desperate, or succour is at hand. Rawlinson with his 7th Division (unsupported by the French) is not quite strong enough to keep the road of retirement open. Winston got on the telephone with Gen. Paris & put the fear of God into him, and the reports both as to the effects of the bombardment & as to the German flank movement now seem to have been grossly exaggerated. Kitchener has just been with me, & is coming again in an hour's time to confer with me & Winston. I have still some hope that things may come out right, but both at Antwerp and on the extreme left in France, the next 48 hours are a critical time. Sir J. French ought to-day to be at Abbeville (Secret). If you look on the map, you will see what a wide sweep he has made from Soissons and the banks of the Aisne. . . .

Later. Just had conference with K & Winston. The French having failed us, & the Belgian field army being quite untrustworthy, there is alas! nothing to be done but to order our naval men to evacuate the trenches to-night & Rawlinson will meet them & the remains of the Belgians at Ghent, after which point they are safe. Antwerp is I am afraid now in flames, but if the naval men get safely away, Sir J. French's army will be well reinforced, and ought to be able to make what Winston calls a 'punch' of an effective kind on the German right. Poor Winston is very depressed, as he feels that his mission has been in vain. . . .

[1] Texts of these signals, and of Churchill's rejoinder to commander, Naval Division, are in P.R.O. CAB 37/134/33, pp. 23–4.

178

Friday 9 Oct 1914

My darling – I am glad that your 'daily bread' comes to you with such mechanical regularity – like the manna, which we are told appeared in time for breakfast every morning. Mine (as you know by my grumblings) is a more 'moveable feast'. All yesterday I lived from hour to hour in a condition of growing starvation, and at 1 a.m. went to bed suffering the pangs of unappeased hunger. You may perhaps imagine the joyful reaction when I woke up & found 2 of your most divine letters by my bedside. Thank you from the bottom of my heart most beloved. As you know your daily letter is everything to me, and you have never failed, & I know never will. . . .

Rawlinson telegraphs this morning that 2000 of the Naval Division passed through Selzete (close to the Dutch frontier) this morning, making their way via Bruges to Ostend, & that the remainder were expected to go through before dark this evening. . . . They have paid their toll – which I pray does not include Oc, whom (if one must have preferences)I put first in character & nature among my children.

Edward Grey & Winston dined here last night: it is impossible to imagine a greater contrast. Pamela Glenconner, who sat next to me, kept a watchful eye on E.G.[1] I am afraid she is rather losing her look of distinction. . . .

Dinah Tennant goes off to-morrow with the two poor young widows Diana & Rosabelle,[2] to try & pick up & minister to the wounded. They have with them some motors & a nurse & doctor & the architect Detmar Blow.[3] It is quite right that they should go, but one cannot help being rather distrustful of amateur effort in what is in these days a skilled & scientific business.

I quite understand your sudden wave of devotion & hagiolatry (I believe that is the right word). If one could only shut one's eyes & close one's ears & drug one's intelligence – & believe enough! . . . I so agree with your comparison between Goonie & Clemmie, but it is pathetic to think her [Goonie's] reading of poetry has been confined to 'Endymion'. I shouldn't mind (whatever E. Marsh may say) being cut off from the Georgians – 'the sons of Wat of David & of Thomp'[4] – but with no Shakespeare or Wordsworth one's mind & memory would be an 'unweeded garden'.

I was much interested in your reflections on old letters. I suppose one ought to make a holocaust of them from time to time. 'Milestones' indeed. I don't believe it is possible for one to be always keeping & yet always gaining – unless one were a superman or superwoman, & that is not human. Nothing is really lost, but there are some things that cannot be revived. The perspective changes, as one lives & grows: unless one can frankly adopt Talleyrand's prescription for happiness – 'a bad heart & a good digestion'. Darling I was touched by what you said – that you thought your losses had been made good by my love & companionship. It is surely the most wonderful (I mean our relationship) in the world: I have never known or heard of any at all like it. I am often afraid of tiring you by telling and retelling what it has been & is & will be to me. Winston said last night to Margot in his magniloquent & grandiose way: 'Oh, your husband is the biggest man in Europe'. That of course is kindly nonsense, but you know how sincerely & honestly & *truly* I prefer *your* judgment, & *your* approval, & *your* love, to anything that the whole world can give. Do you know the lines –

> 'Name & fame, to fly sublime
> Thro' the Court, the Camp, the Schools,
> Is to be the ball of time
> Bandied by the hands of fools'?[5] . . .

[1] Margot's brother, Lord Glenconner, died in 1920 and Grey married his widow in 1922.

[2] Diana Wyndham and Rosabelle Bingham whose husbands had been killed.

[3] Blow was a good guide to France; well connected, and had worked on great houses (see Appendix 3); in partnership since 1905 with a French architect.

[4] William Watson, John Davidson, and Francis Thompson. Only the first survived into George V's reign. *Georgian Pòetry, 1911–1912*, edited by Edward Marsh, had established 'the Georgians'. It was to be followed by 4 similar volumes.

[5] Tennyson, 'The Vision of Sin', pt. iv.

179

Sat 10 Oct 14

My darling – I told you there was something hellish in your postal arrangements at Alderley: they pass all understanding. I am *most* sorry that you should have been disappointed on waking of your 'daily bread': I know the sensation only too well from my own experience. It so happens that I remember well posting that particular letter with my own hand at the Athenaeum *before* 6 p.m. (for I looked at the clock). I am glad that you got it before the day was out & that your unworthy (!) suspicions were dispelled. How could you think for a moment that I should fail to write? Have I ever – on the busiest & most crowded of days? . . .

It is a bright autumn day, and Violet & I are thinking of motoring via Skindle's (long 'unvisited': do you remember when I was gruff with you there once upon a time?) to Huntercombe, where we may play a little golf before the twilight with Dick & Moyra Cavendish. Then to the Wharf – but please write here: I shall be back Sunday night or early Monday morning.

The news of our Naval Division is still rather patchy & not wholly good. The bulk of them – including I hope & believe Oc's brigade – got through yesterday to Blankenbergh (just by Ostend), but the last lot of about 2000 finding the railway cut took refuge in Holland. It is better than being killed or captured by the Germans, but I am afraid it involves their being 'interned' by the Dutch for the rest of the war.[1] As they are presumably good

Naval Reserve men, this is a serious loss & I am afraid will be a sore affliction to Winston, who was taking complacency in Spencer Gray's daring & successful raid on the Zeppelins at Düsseldorf[2]. . . . Meanwhile Sir J. French is swinging round & is almost in touch with Rawlinson: it looks as if the next big tussle would be actually on the Belgian frontier.[3] It would be a great thing to drive the Germans out of both Antwerp & Brussels. . . .

. . . Sir J. Simpne has just done Raymond a good turn, by making him junior counsel to the Inland Revenue, which ought to be worth £1000 a year or thereabouts. Haldane paved the way by giving 'silk' to the present holder of the post – Sir R. Finlay's son. A welcome stroke of fortune in these bad times.

I have had poor Aberdeen's reply to my letter this morning: it covers 7 quarto pages. Violet also had an even more poignant appeal from Lady A: 'how can your Father wreak such havoc upon Archie's parents?' &c (*Dont* ever say I told you a word of this)[4]. . . .

Winston has just been in to talk over the situation. We both agree with Hankey (who is a good opinion) that this last week – which has delayed the fall of Antwerp by at least 7 days, and has prevented the Germans from linking up their forces – has not been thrown away, and may with Sir J. French all the time coming round have been even of vital value.[5] Seely sends word that Oc has got through & is all right – also Violet's (& your?) friend Rupert Brooke – one of Winston's variegated gang of officers.

The Arch Colonel himself – characteristically – was the last to leave Antwerp, and came the whole way with the General in a motor.

Winston is anxious about his (i.e. Seely's) future. He says he has a bad name at the front, where he is not liked, partly because of his War Office record, & partly because as W. says 'he is a brave man who bucks'. Comes in to breakfast rubbing his hands: 'I have just shot a German, and by George! my chauffeur ought to have the Victoria Cross.'[6] 'Why?' 'You should have seen the way he piloted & followed me yesterday'.[7] And so on. I don't know what can be done for him: unless some fattish Colonial Governorship were to turn up[8]. . . .

[1] During the Antwerp expedition the Naval Division lost:

	Officers	Other Ranks
Killed	7	50
Wounded	3	135
Interned	37	1,442
Prisoners of War	5	931

[2] Another naval airman, Comdr. Marix, was also involved in this raid.

[3] Asquith probably did not realize that the fall of Antwerp had given the Germans numerical superiority in the northern sector and an enormous preponderance in heavy

artillery. Falkenhayn, who had replaced Moltke as C.-in-C., meant to break through to Dunkirk, Calais, and Boulogne before the B.E.F. could be reinforced with Indian or Territorial divisions.

⁴ Asquith had written to the Lord-Lieutenant of Ireland intimating that, as he would soon have held the post for 9 years, the time had come for his retirement. In her appeal to Violet Lady Aberdeen referred to her son Lord Archie Gordon, who had died in December 1909 after a motoring accident (and to whom Violet had been attached): see p. 1.

⁵ See Letter 176, n. 1. Every day on which Antwerp held out gave more time for the defence of the Channel ports, which would have been in great danger had the troops and guns attacking Antwerp been available for a push to the Channel coast a few days earlier. Some of Churchill's critics, Lloyd George among them, refused to recognize this: *Political Diaries of C. P. Scott* (1970), p. 112, 27 Nov. 1914.

⁶ Seely's chauffeur, Sgt. Anthony, showed courage and resource both during and after the war. French became Lord-Lieutenant of Ireland in May 1918; and a serious attempt was made on his life in Dec. 1919. He was lucky to have Anthony driving him on that occasion.

⁷ In the finished form of this legend Seely's recommendation of his chauffeur-servant for the V.C. stated that the latter had stood 'never less than twenty yards behind me throughout the engagement': John Colville, *Footprints in Time* (1976), p. 82.

⁸ Seely was called home by Kitchener soon after this to command the Canadian Cavalry Brigade. After retaining this command for most of the war he was gassed in 1918, and retired from active service with the rank of major-general, 5 mentions in dispatches, and the reputation of having been 'the luckiest man in the army'.

180

*War Office,
Whitehall,
S.W.
*a relic of departed greatness!

Sunday 11 Oct 14

My darling – I am writing from the Wharf with open windows on one of the most beautiful days even of this wonderful summer & autumn – bright sun, not a breath of wind, and the colours one only gets when autumn 'lays his fiery fingers on the leaves'. I drove here yesterday with Violet, & on the way we played a little golf at Huntercombe with the Dick Cavendishes. He is encamped near here with his Lancaster territorials engaged in the dismal & fruitless task of guarding 50 miles of the G.W. Railway with headquarters at Didcot. They have been at it now for nearly 2 months and their casualties amount to 4 men killed – 2 (I think) run over, & the other 2 shot accidentally by their comrades. Such are the hazards of war. The Cavendishes have taken the little red house next door to this for the time – & all came to dinner last night – Dick & Moyra, her sister Lady Alix, and the daughter Betty – a very nice girl of Elizabeth's age. Cys has been staying with them at Holker, where Margot hoped that he & Betty might be mutually attracted.¹ I am rather afraid that he casts a preferential eye on that hussy, Nancy Cunard, who is staying with us for the Sunday. They are out on the river now, while Margot & the Assyrian (who has motored over from Cambridge) are pacing the narrow garden walk, Puffin out from school hovering around, & Violet reading Winston's official report in to-day's *Times* of the doings & undoings of his Naval Division. You will see it in to-morrow morning's papers, but it does not disclose (what appears to be the fact) that in addition to the 2000 sailors who are 'interned' in Holland, a battalion of Marines has disappeared & is still unaccounted for. The situation during these next 2 or 3 days will be as interesting & critical as any since the war began. Meanwhile the remains of the Naval Div^n set sail for home last night, & I hope that Oc (tho' we haven't yet heard from him) is once more safe in his camp at Betteshanger. I don't think that Oliver is likely to go out for some time, as the 8th Division which is the next in order, will certainly not be fit to go abroad for another 3 weeks.[2] The Indians of course are coming up from Marseilles & Fontainebleau.

I am getting to be more sanguine about next Sunday. Wouldn't it be heavenly if I could come to Alderley Friday night? Would you be *really* glad? I do believe you would. I will write to your Mother.

The photographs wh. were taken with so much fuss & pomp at Dublin have now arrived. They are very depressing, except perhaps one, which I will bring with me & submit for judgment. I was rather touched that Sir Matthew Nathan asked for a photograph to take with him to his new post, upon which he enters to-morrow. It looks like a clean sweep in Ireland – Dougherty gone, the Aberdeens going (God knows precisely when), & Birrell following – tho' don't say anything about it to him – or to others. He is sick & tired of his job (no wonder), and doesn't really care for administrative work. I shall insist on his staying in the Cabinet: the Duchy of Lancaster was made for him & he for it[3] – if one could shuffle Masterman elsewhere. What do you say to sending Jack Pease (!) to Ireland (it doesn't want a clever man just now) & Mast^m to Education? Winston is of course very *intrigué* about Cousin Wimborne & the Lord Lieutenancy. I told him yesterday that tho' I am not personally adverse, Wimborne is in fact not a very popular man. Others are strong for the Dick Cavendishes – for whom there is much to be said. Bron & Nan have, I think, passed out of the running. I suppose it might be some consolation to poor Aberdeen to be made a Marquis – tho' I believe he would prefer a Dukedom! I think I shall probably drive up with the Assyrian after dinner to-night.

I didn't of course expect a letter from you darling to-day, tho' not to have one makes a sad blank. I am thinking of you in your curious entourage, & hoping that this time next Sunday we shall be alone together. Don't presume on your 'ox-strength', but eat & sleep like the beasts that perish. And think of me, who love you all day & every day.

¹ Cyril Asquith wrote to Violet from Holker, 23 Aug.: 'Betty is *very* attractive and quite unspoilt by a quarter of a London season, with tentative speech and diffident eyelashes, dewy, demure, and decorous. . . .' He did not marry either Elizabeth Cavendish or Nancy Cunard.
² It was at the Front by 3 Nov. It consisted, like the 7th Division, of regular units from overseas garrisons which had been replaced by the Indian Army.
³ Birrell remained Irish Secretary until May 1916.

181

Monday 12 Oct 14

. . . Why do you think that Raymond is one of the people who 'ought to have been rich'? I sometimes think the exact reverse. He is rarely endowed but needed a goad – or spark. . . .

I have just . . . had one of the most curious & in some ways nerve-harrowing interviews with Lady Aberdeen. I had of course no difficulty in disposing of her arguments about the terrible ruin that would be wrought to Ireland if her 'great work' (sanatoria &c &c) were now to be interrupted. I told her brutally that if her efforts & organisation were of any real value, they would go on after her disappearance from the scene: '*car il n'y a pas d'homme ni de femme nécessaire*'. Then she came to the pecuniary aspect of the affair, with a most piteous tale, and when I pointed out that the Viceroyalty was from its nature a spending & losing concern, which made a heavier drain every month that it lasted, she replied that owing to the War there would be no Dublin season, and so they would be able this next year to make large savings! This roused me, I confess: 'So you want me to continue you in an office, which in the public interest you ought to give up, in order that out of the retrenchments required by a national calamity, you may fill the gaps in your private purse'! It was most painful, as you do not need to be assured. She wept copiously, poor thing, and you know what a coward I am *au fond*: so in the end I gave them till the beginning of Feb, and he is to write a beautiful letter announcing his wish to retire now that his life-work in Ireland is done, and I am to ask the Sovereign to give him some mark of appreciation. Then *we kissed*, and she left agitated but I think appeased, and I felt for once really exhausted. This is all, I need not say, for your private eye. . . .

182

My darling – thank you for your dear letter this morning. I can imagine that Goonie . . . was troubled what answer to give about Port Royal[1] (I wonder what you would have said: are you well up in Pascal, and Mère Angélique, & the sacred thorn, & the controversy about Grace &c &c – perhaps! most of it now-a-days is of little more importance than the price of coals at Brentford). . . .

Oc came to London yesterday & I had a long talk with him after midnight, in the course of which he gave me a full & vivid account of the expedition to Antwerp & the retirement. Strictly between ourselves, I can't tell you what I feel of the *wicked* folly of it all. The Marines of course are splendid troops & can go anywhere & do anything: but nothing can excuse Winston (who knew all the facts) from sending in the two other Naval Brigades. I was assured that all the recruits were being left behind,[2] and that the main body at any rate consisted of seasoned Naval Reserve men. As a matter of fact only about ¼ were Reservists, and the rest were a callow crowd of the rawest tiros, most of whom had never fired off a rifle, while none of them had ever handled an entrenching tool. Oc's battalion was commanded by George West – an ex (very-ex) Subaltern in the Guards who was incompetent & overbearing & hated impartially by both officers and men. Among its principal officers were R. Brooke (the poet) Oc himself & one Dennis Brown (a pianist), who had respectively served 1 week, 3 days, & 1 day. It was like sending sheep to the shambles.[3] Of course when they got into the trenches they behaved most gallantly[4] – but what could they do? The Belges ran away & had to be forced back at the point of the bayonet into the forts, while the Germans at a safe distance of 5 or 6 miles thundered away with their colossal howitzers. When at last (most unwillingly) our men obeyed the order to retire, they found the bridge across the Schelt & most of the lighters & boats in flames: they just got across on a pontoon, but Oc says that if the wind had blown the other way they cd. never have crossed & would have been left in the burning town. Then for 7 or 8 hours they marched (the one thing sailors can't do) for more than 20 miles over cobbled roads, with a ceaseless stream of Belgian refugees & soldiers blocking the way; and at last, more dead than alive, got into trains at St Gilles, wh. gradually took them to Ostend. If the Germans had had any initiative, they might with a couple of squadrons of cavalry have cut them into mincemeat at any state of their retreat.[5] No doubt it is a wonderful experience to look back upon, but what cruel & terrible risks! Thank God they are all now back in England, except the 1500 who, when dead beat, crossed the Dutch frontier in despair, & are now interned in Holland.

I trust that Winston will learn by experience, and now hand over to the military authorities the little circus which he is still running 'on his own' at Dunkirk – Oxfordshire Yeomen, motor-busses (more or less organised by Geoffrey)[6] armoured cars &c &c. They have really nothing to do with the Admiralty, which ought to confine its activities to the sea & the air.[7]. . .

We had a very rare experience at the Cabinet to-day. We had to settle the rate of pension for the widows of soldiers & sailors killed in the war. There was an elaborate report from a Committee consisting of the Assyrian Baker Macnamara & one or two others, in which they differed a good deal from one another. Finally the question emerged whether a childless widow should get per week (as now) 5/- (Montagu & Baker) or 7/6 (Macnamara) or 6/6 (proposed by Kitchener as a compromise). The argument in favour of not more than 5/- is almost overwhelming, but as the childless widows are estimated to amount to no less than one-third of the whole, & they wd. be left as they are, a 5/- rate would be generally condemned outside as mean & ungenerous. There was a long dreary desultory discussion, and in the end I said I would do what I have done (I think) only twice before in nearly 7 years – take a division in the Cabinet. The voting was very curious: (a) for 7/6 – 1 (b) for 5/– 8 (c) for 6/6 – 9. So 6/6 carried the day by a majority of one! It may amuse you to conjecture how the different people voted, and I will give you on Friday a really valuable prize if you don't make more than 5 mistakes. So send me your guesses. Some of them wanted to vote by ballot, but I said that would be cowardly & we reverted to the good old English plan of open voting.[8] We hope that French will complete his turning movement to-morrow.[9]

What a vast letter! My own darling – you were never more dear to me, and I hunger to see you. All *my love*. Write me a *nice* letter.

---

[1] Port-Royal was the convent which Pascal visited and which his sister eventually joined, at which the 'Jansenist' miracle of the Holy Thorn occurred.

[2] See Letter 174, text and n. 1.

[3] Most of these recruits went to Antwerp without water-bottles, haversacks, or bandoliers, carrying ammunition in their pockets and bayonets in their garters.

[4] According to a private soldier in the Royal Marine Light Infantry Arthur Asquith was 'as daring as anybody'. 'Officers like him', the statement ended, 'make a lot of difference . . . and there isn't one of us that wouldn't go through fire and water for him' (*Evening News*, 26 Oct.). He was to have a distinguished war career, gaining the D.S.O. and 2 bars, and the Croix de Guerre, and rising to be a Brigadier-General before being disabled by a leg wound in which he lost a foot.

[5] The Bavarian brigade which nearly cut off the retreat consisted of Landwehr, i.e. reservists.

[6] Geoffrey Howard.

[7] On 13 Oct. the *Morning Post*, commenting that nothing except a 'properly trained and equipped relieving force' could have saved Antwerp, asked:

On whose authority was this adventure arranged and conducted? . . . Is it not true that the energies of Mr. Winston Churchill have been directed upon this eccentric expedition, and that he has been using the resources of the Admiralty as if he were personally responsible for the naval operations?

8 There were 10 votes for 6/6d according to the list which follows. The cabinet reconsidered the question on 4 Nov. and decided on 7/6.

9 The previous day (12 Oct.) has generally been taken as the start of the 'first battle of Ypres'; it was to last for a month.

183

CABINET – 13 Oct 14 [ii]

7/6	6/6	5/-
WSC	Self	Ll George
	Lulu	Lucas
	Simon	Wood
	Emmott	Runciman
	Pease	McKenna
	Haldane	Grey
	Masterman	Beauchamp
	Kitchener	Hobhouse
	Crewe	
	Samuel	

184

Wed 14 Oct 14

. . . I am writing this in the Cabinet room after lunch, and Bongie is distressing me by one of his most irritating habits: coming in every 2 minutes with one set of papers after another, and a few disjected comments, instead of allowing them to accumulate for at any rate half an hour – at a time. You can't imagine what I suffer (in a small way) from these intermittent & recurrent & most gratuitous incursions, just when I am in the mood to have a real talk with you. It is as though we were in your little room at Alderley, and the servant popped in & out first to poke the fire, & then to draw the blinds, & then to bring in tea, and then again to ask if there were letters for the post! 'These are my crosses, Mr Wesley': do you recognise that quotation?[1] Like you, I have always hated 'having it out' with people, and I believe from that kind of passive cowardice have more than once failed in my duty. I haven't a trace of the missionary spirit of the Tennants, who revel in such situations, not out of cruelty or even complete insensibility, but from a dominating passion to improve people, and (as the Apostle says) 'to tell the truth in love'. I am not at all (as you suggest) *hardened*. And I have only this morning got quite an affectionate letter from Alice Guest, whom I fear (with your complete approval) I shall have to disappoint & perhaps plunge in despair by refusing to make her Wimborne the successor to the Aberdeens.[2]

Edgar Vincent came here to dinner last night, and we played a little mild Bridge while Margot & the rest went to a Music Hall to see & hear Gaby Deslys &c. They found it rather dull, & not enlivened by pictures of the siege of Antwerp, flight of refugees &c. Ettie & Frances Horner were at lunch to-day, also Haldane, & Nan Tennant. Oc is, of course, the hero of all our meals, and these large-hatted ladies hang on his modest lips, while he has reluctantly drawn from him narratives of his experiences in the trenches & on the retreat. Julian Grenfell[3] is with his regiment – the Royals – in the Cavalry Division with Rawlinson:[4] they will get in touch to-day with French, who was fighting all yesterday on the extreme left, and now has his head-quarters at St. Omer. . . . The Russians seem to have had at any rate a check,[5] and French in his latest message appears to fear that the Germans in France may consequently get considerable reinforcements: he wants (between you & me) to be secured, in case of difficulty, by entrenching Calais or Boulogne – a very difficult operation. I should much prefer Dunkirk for a base, but the French make difficulties. We shall see how this works out.

Later I have just had a long call from Stamfordham. I am glad to say that the King now realises that he *must* open Parliament, and the whole question is reduced to one of those infinitesimal problems which perplex and perturb the Court mind – whether he should drive to Westminster in the old ginger-bread coach surrounded by Life Guards & Blues – or such as are left of them – or (as I should think better) ride on his charger with the streets lined with khaki-men. Isn't it marvellous that such things should be regarded as worth 5 minutes discussion?[6] I am going to see him (the King) early to-morrow to settle this & other equally momentous issues – e.g. whether Aberdeen should be given by way of *solatium* a Garter or a Marquisate![7]. . .

Last night – stung by your reference to Port Royal – I began digging about into the life of Pascal: certainly one of the greatest geniuses (he died at 39) of the modern world. Did you ever read the *Provincial Letters*? if not, do.

---

[1] 'A gentleman of large fortune' exclaimed this to John Wesley when a clumsy servant made up his fire and a puff of smoke escaped into the room. Wesley replied: 'Pray, Sir John, are these the heaviest crosses you meet with?' He used the incident to illustrate how the rich were tempted towards 'fretfulness and peevishness': J. Wesley, *Sermons*, viii (1788), 287.

[2] Wimborne was, however, appointed Lord-Lieutenant of Ireland.

³ One of Lady Desborough's sons; died of wounds 26 May 1915.
⁴ The 1st Dragoons (The Royals) formed part of the 3rd Cavalry Division, which had been sent over, with the 7th Division, to relieve Antwerp. This force under Rawlinson, henceforth constituting the 4th Corps, had come under the orders of French on 9 Oct.
⁵ The Germans had won the race to the Vistula, and had, with one exception, thrown back all the Russian forces which had crossed the river.
⁶ The King went in the glass coach, despite the advice of *John Bull* against doing so.
⁷ Aberdeen was already G.C.M.G. (1895), K.T. (1906), and G.C.V.O. (1911). The hope expressed by the *Manchester Guardian* in Dec. 1914 that he would be given one of the vacant Garters was not fulfilled. Eventually he was created Marquess of Aberdeen and Temair, 4 Jan. 1916.

185

In train Tu. 20 Oct 14

. . . It was really a piece of heavenly luck in this ill-starred crisis-riddled year to have had 3 whole days with you. I curse that little toad Mikky who did his best to spoil our Saturday, but after that we were really fortunate.¹ . . . I go back in thought, & often shall, to those delicious hours when we read together & were silent, & read again & talked. You remember what we said about short & long lives? Anything would be better than to *rust*. Better far to leave Ithaca & its rocks & 'twinkling lights' to some Shuttleworth-Telemachus,² and start on a new voyage:

> 'It may be that the deep will draw us down,
> It may be we shall reach the Happy Isles,
> And see the great Achilles who we knew'.³

Modern conditions are not favourable to this kind of adventure; if so, the only attraction may be to shuffle off the coil, and, as I think Macbeth says 'jump the life to come'.⁴ Meantime (whatever that means measured by clock & calendar) one must 'bear fardels', and 'grunt & sweat',⁵ and be patient of the yapping of the little dogs, and cultivate an optimistic view of men & things & the world, and hope –. As I said yesterday – whatever is in store for us, you & me – we have not fallen into the feckless blunder of the 'frustrate ghosts' – the unlit lamp & the ungirt loin.⁶ Thank God for that.

After I left you last night I found a volume of Jowett's Plato in my bedroom & partly perhaps because of our conversation & of our reading of 'To be' the evening before, I read over again (after many years) his introduction to the *Phaedo*, & part of the dialogue itself – one of the most wonderful things ever written – especially the last 3 or 4 pages which describe the last conversations & the death of Socrates. If one cd. die like that one would not pray for the *coup de foudre*.⁷ But the arguments for immortality – wh. is the main theme – are not very convincing. After all that the philosophers have said, when one tries to conceive of a complete divorce between soul & body which yet leaves personality intact, one is driven to fall back upon the authority of instinctive beliefs. . . .

[1] Asquith had been at Alderley. 'Mikky' was Roderick Meiklejohn.

[2] Ulysses is here seen as departing on his Tennysonian voyage and leaving Ithaca to Telemachus, his son and heir. Lord Shuttleworth, an elderly Liberal peer, was nicknamed Telemachus, an allusion presumably to the legendary work which Telemachus's mother, Penelope, had performed with her shuttle.

[3] Tennyson, 'Ulysses': a free rendering.

[4] *Macbeth*, I. vii.

[5] The phrases are from Hamlet's famous soliloquy in III. i.

[6] The theme of Browning's poem 'The Statue and the Bust' is missed opportunity: two lovers plan to elope but procrastinate too long. The lines which Asquith had in mind are:

> And the sin I impute to each frustrate ghost
> Is the unlit lamp and the ungirt loin,
> Though the end in sight was a vice, I say.

The poem might have prompted different reflections, as the title-page to this volume suggests.

[7] This was to become a recurrent theme of Asquith's reflections: see for instance, Letters 357 and 365. Venetia was not the only one with whom he looked forward to his death and discussed the problems of an inactive old age. See diary entries of Lady Scott in *Self-Portrait of an Artist* (1949), pp. 134 (where Asquith gives her a volume of poems, and writes in it: 'Let me not live . . . after my flame lacks oil'), 145 ('. . . a ridiculous world, he said seriously that he often wished he could get out of it'), and 148 ('He said that . . . if he kept his . . . activity, it might be an irritation to want to do things and to be powerless to do them. I said he would probably get suddenly old and gaga; he said he thought that one might perhaps just die'). When Asquith died, in his 76th year, Lady Scott wrote: 'Now that he is actually dead, I feel overcome . . . I can't write to anyone to say I'm sorry . . . I have wanted him to die for ten years': ibid. pp. 259–60.

186

Wed. 21 Oct 14

. . . We had a long Cabinet this morning. Poor Winston is in rather bad luck just now; that infernally elusive craft the *Emden* has mopped up 6 or 7 British merchant ships (including what she most needs – 2 colliers) some-where off the West coast of India south of Bombay, despite the fact that she is being assiduously hunted night & day by the *Yarmouth* & the *Hampshire* and a very quick unpronounceable Japanese cruiser.[1] Also a submarine of the best class – E3 – is reported to have been sunk by the Germans in one of their bags.

We have (but this is secret) succeeded in sending 3 submarines all the way into the Baltic to deal havoc among the German war-ships there. Unluckily they began their proceedings, & advertised their presence, by attacking a *Danish* vessel! It is rather an adventurous démarche in any case, as they have no parent ship with them, and like the man in the hymn are 'far from home': but in case of need they will put into Libau, which is a Russian port.

We had a rather interesting discussion on home defence & the possibility of German invasion, which pre-occupies & alarms the mind of Kitchener. His view is that the Army is doing all it can both at home & abroad, and that some of the big ships ought to be brought into the home ports. Winston made a very good defence of his policy, which is (in a word, or at least a few words) that the function of the Great Fleet[2] is not to prevent the landing of an invading force (which is the business of the torpedo flotillas & submarines) but to strike at & destroy the enemy's covering fleet. All the same it is agreed to be desirable to have a lot of sheltered or protected harbours wh. no submarine can penetrate, & in which some battleships & cruisers can lie in safety.[3] This is being done, & (tho' I have never shared K's fears)[4] in a very short time we ought to be absolutely secure even in the judgment of the most doubting pessimist.

Ll. George, who generally has a point of view of his own, is very down on the Russians for not taking us more into their confidence both as to the actual & potential strength of their armies, & as to their real plan of campaign. He says quite truly that for aught we know the Germans may be holding them back by a mere screen of troops, while they are massing their real attack upon the allies in Belgium & France. It is difficult, but we must try to get them to be less secretive, and to throw more of their designs into the common stock.[5] There is the greatest difference of opinion as to the actual quality & equipment of their troops.

Another urgent matter (upon wh. there threatens to be acute difference of opinion among us) is whether or not we should supply the starving civil population in Belgium with food. E Grey & I are rather *pro*, Ll. George, McKenna, Kitchener & others strenuously *contra*. We shall have to decide this to-morrow. . .

---

[1] H.I.J.M.S. *Chikuma*.

[2] The Grand Fleet, as it was more usually called, which Jellicoe commanded.

[3] In Nov., despite Jellicoe's protests, the 3rd Battle and 3rd Cruiser Squadrons, with 8 destroyers, were brought from the Scapa-Cromarty area to Rosyth. For a period in mid-Nov. tides and moon were favourable to a night landing.

[4] Asquith made this clear in cabinet. 'K. is very apprehensive as to a German attack in force,' Hobhouse noted on 14 Oct.; 'the P.M., as representing the CID, very scornful of its possibility.'

[5] 'Either our attaché is a very incompetent person', Hobhouse noted, 'or else the Russians don't let him send us what he knows.'

187

Thursday midnight 22 Oct 14

My darling – before I go to bed I must send you a word of greeting. We had a heavenly half hour – far too short – this evening – but it has made all the difference in the world to me. I had had a long & tiresome & worrying day, and I am afraid I showed it. But I came away a new man – thanks to your life giving & unfailing power of restarting run-down springs, and re-filling exhausted reservoirs, and regenerating the whole being & life of a man.

Do you realise that you have that power? Where you get it, & why you have it, & how you wield it – I don't know – nor do I care to know.

All I know is that to me, it makes the difference between wearily working against the collar on an up-hill ascent, and feeling that – if the course were open – one might be a Derby thorough-bred, or the best Rolls Royce.

I hate your lunching to-morrow with the Assyrian – not that I should have had any real talk with you here; but to *see* you is so much. Damn!

I had a nice talk with John Morley: he & Birrell are the best of all company. None of these younger men can compare with them. Kakoo was here & says that Lympne is full of wounded & rheumatic Belgians.

I *must* see you Monday – even if you have to go back to Alderley by the evening train. We go Munstead Sat. afternoon. My love! try to love me. I don't need to try to *love you*. Good night.

188

Fr. 23 Oct 1914

My darling – I hope you got my pencil letter this morning. . . . At the front things move slowly, though so far as one can judge not badly; but there are some bad losses: John Cavendish of 1st Life Guards (brother of Dick) killed; also Norman Leslie of Rifle Brigade, Leonie's son & Winston's cousin.[1] A telegram has just come in from French dated this morning. He says that for last 24 hours 'violent infantry attacks' have ceased, but heavy artillery bombardment has proceeded. The battle during the 20th and 21st (Tu & Wed) was one of the most desperate of the war, & he thinks that in it the Germans 'incurred the heaviest losses they have suffered against us in the campaign'.[2]

(Your little pencil note has just been delivered. I gather you are going to stay in London for Monday night: where do you think of dining? I shall come to you very soon after 6. That will be a real joy, & some little compensation for this wasted week-end.)

To go back to the Cabinet: the Turks seem to be seriously meditating an invasion of Egypt, where the fellaheen are rather disappointed that they cannot get money for their cotton crop. We have suggested to Italy that this is a *nouveau fait* which might affect her.

Grey & Haldane were very fussy & jumpy lest the Germans should establish a base at Ostend and keep there a new nest of submarines. Winston (I think with perfectly good reason) derides this, and declares that to-morrow (if necessary) he will shell Ostend into ruins & make it uninhabitable. I wish some people (E.G. for instance) had more sense of proportion and perspective.

We had the French General Deville at lunch (with Harry Cust, Algie West, D. D. Lyttelton[3] – the usual incongruities). After the ladies had gone I had quite a good talk with the General, who is perhaps the greatest living authority on artillery. He is all against our 6 gun batteries, says that 4 guns is the maximum, & that a battery of even 2 well supplied with ammunition is a most effective thing.[4] Old Sir Charles Douglas has cracked up in health, and K. is putting Wolfe Murray (back from S. Africa) in his place as Chief of the General Staff.[5]

'Aunt Blanche' appeared this morning from Manchester[6] – radiantly got up (as your Mother & Sylvia will tell you) tho' she complained to me of their grinding poverty. She came to try & save from the McKenna net an alien called Brun, technically a German because born in Alsace since 1871, but to all intents & purposes a Frenchman. I arranged with McK. for his immediate release. I am going to see the King at 5.30: I don't quite know why. . . .

[1] His mother was Lady Randolph Churchill's sister.

[2] For their attempt on the Channel ports the Germans had assembled the troops released by their victory at Antwerp, with an army collected from all parts of the front commanded by Prince Rupprecht, and another of 4 corps newly arrived in the war zone commanded by Duke Albrecht of Württemberg. This last army consisted largely of troops trained only since the outbreak of war, led by retired or reserve officers ('the men too young and the officers too old'); their losses on 20 and 21 Oct. were very heavy.

[3] Edith, widow of Alfred Lyttelton. 'D.D.' was a nickname.

[4] For Kitchener's rejection of the French type of artillery ammunition see Cassar, *Kitchener*, p. 336.

[5] The new C.I.G.S. could not stand up to Kitchener and was soon known as 'Sheep Murray'.

[6] The Dowager Countess of Airlie, widow of the 5th Earl, a sister of Lord Sheffield, for whom see N. Mitford (ed.), *The Stanleys of Alderley* (1968), p. xiii.

The First Lord of the Admiralty (Letter 189)

THOSE who longed 'for an expert instead of a civilian at the head of the Admiralty' may well have deserved Asquith's laughter. But behind all the allegations that Churchill interfered with the experts lay a problem of great importance. In 1869 and 1872, when imposing economies on the Navy, Gladstone had secured Orders in Council under which the First Lord was responsible to the Sovereign and 'to Parliament for all the business of the Admiralty'; and this position had never been reversed. Churchill had become accustomed in peacetime to initiating orders to the various ships and fleet units; and he continued in this practice in war, though he never gave an instruction of any importance without securing the concurrence of the First Sea Lord. Although this degree of direction by the political head of the Navy was unquestionably lawful, most naval officers regarded it as contravening acceptable practice.

In July 1917 Churchill 'admitted' to Hankey 'that he had been "a bit above himself" at the Admiralty'.[1] His practice entailed both strategic and political dangers. One of Asquith's objects in setting up the War Council (p. 184) was to enable leading ministers to question the service chiefs. But a First Lord who had taken over so much of what others regarded as the First Sea Lord's role did not encourage his political colleagues to question the latter. Balfour wrote in September 1915 that Churchill would not 'have tolerated for a moment the independent examination' of the First Sea Lord by a member of the War Council.[2] Thus it was easy for the Council to gain mistaken impressions about the balance of professional opinion within the Admiralty. Politically it was dangerous for a minister who was often accused of self-aggrandisement to make what his critics thought excessive claims about his own position. Naval successes, in ensuring that sea-borne supplies reached Britain, and were denied to Germany, were invisible. Naval losses were known everywhere; and Churchill had ensured that he would be blamed for them all. In war an unpopular First Lord represented one of the worst liabilities which the Government could incur.

[1] Stephen Roskill, *Hankey* i (1970), 415.
[2] Spender and Asquith ii. 187. See also Hankey, diary, 12 Mar. 1915.

189

Sat 24 Oct 14

. . . We shall motor down to Munstead some time after lunch, & I suppose spend Sunday in an atmosphere more or less permeated (a word wh. K. pronounces as if it were spelt perm*ee*ted) by the McKennae. . . .

After writing to you yesterday I went to Buckingham Palace & had an hour's chat with the King. He told me that my Cabinet letters were his only means of knowledge (except the newspapers & gossip) of what is really going on.[1] I generally write him one every other day or so, with a kind of auctioneer's catalogue of the topics we have discussed. He is a good deal agitated about Louis of Battenberg's[2] position: he & the Queen receive heaps of letters abusing them for their cousins (Albert of Sch. Holst. & the Duke of Coburg) who are actually fighting against us and for 'the damned German spy' whom their relationship keeps at the Admiralty. He told me rather naively that Cousin Albert is 'not really fighting on the side of the Germans': he had only been 'put in charge of a camp of English prisoners' near Berlin! – a nice distinction. . . .

. . . (Most secret). . . The plan I have long been urging is about to come off. That is to say that to-day a certain number of old & specially prepared ships go to within about 30 miles of Heligoland, protected by destroyers & cruisers. From there, as from a spring board, a detachment of sea planes will fly straight for Cuxhaven: spy out all the German preparations there & in the Kiel Canal; make havoc if they can of the Zeppelins & their sheds; and return (if they can) to their ships. As Winston grimly says, a lot of them will never be able to use the second half of their return tickets. But this is far the most romantic & adventurous side of modern war. *Nobody* knows of this – except W & myself. It may or may not come off – but it is worth trying.[3]

Then he unfolded to me his schemes for cheating & baffling the submarine. Some of the ships are to be clad in enveloping & protecting 'shoes', others to be provided around their keels & lower parts with safe-guarding 'saddle-bags'. And beyond all this, he is going to establish by means of a huge net-work of wire & nets a 'hen-coop' – somewhere off the East coast – with a couple of doors, in which from time to time our big ships can refuge & nestle, without any fear of torpedo attack. A little later we hope we may have a still larger 'bird cage' of the same character further North.[4] I like this: it is inventive & resourceful, & shows both originality and dash. I laugh at our idiotic outside critics who long for an expert instead of a civilian at the head of the Admiralty. Nothing truer was ever said than that 'experts are good servants but bad masters'. I am not sure that we are not really suffering from a neglect of this sound maxim at the War Office. The lunatic who edits the *Morning Post* writes me a long private letter this morning, urging the supersession of Winston by Jellicoe![5] . . .

[1] They were also the only record of what the cabinet had decided.
[2] Prince Louis resigned his appointment as First Sea Lord on 28 Oct., recognizing, as he told Churchill, that his usefulness was impaired by his German 'birth and parentage'. He had settled in England, and been naturalized as a British subject, in boyhood. Lord Charles Beresford, M.P., a retired admiral of some influence, had apparently announced in the Carlton Club before the end of Aug. that Prince Louis 'should resign'.

[3] A modified version of this plan was attempted on 24 Nov.; but the weather was so bad that the seaplanes could hardly be used: see Letter 215.

[4] Some of these measures are outlined in Churchill's directive, 2 Nov., given in *The World Crisis, 1914*, pp. 392–5.

[5] Gwynne's criticisms of the Antwerp expedition were not unlike Asquith's (Letter 182). In the *Morning Post* Gwynne called (19 Oct.) for Churchill to be, not replaced, but controlled: 'There is an ample field for Mr Churchill's talents, which are considerable, . . . in securing for the experts of the navy complete command of resources and complete freedom from political or amateur interference.'

190

Munstead House,
Godalming.

Sunday 25 Oct 14

. . . Our party here is . . . 2 M^cK's, 2 M^cL's, Bluey & Belloc. The last named who is very *dévot* has gone to mass – so that for a couple of hours the house is free from the echo of his roarings. He never ceases, & rarely listens, with the result that, tho' he says some good things, and has a marvellous wealth of information, he is not far removed from a bore. He thinks that Verdun, to which he attaches great importance, is now safe.[1] . . .

Sunday   Midnight   Later.

. . . It has been a horribly wet day, & after lunch we went in our motor to Aldershot in the hope of seeing something of K's armies. . . . We went to Deepcut[2] to see once more the prisoners' camp. It amounts now to about 4500 men, of whom nearly $\frac{1}{2}$ are the civilians who have been herded there during the last week under McKenna's orders. They were a rotten looking lot – waiters, hairdressers & the scum of Whitechapel & the East End with a sprinkling of doctors, professors, & educated men. We walked about among them & talked to them; a sad & sorry experience. They are going to be transferred to ships,[3] and their most urgent need is to be sorted & classified. McKenna, who was with us, will see to this. . . .

[1] Hilaire Belloc, the son of a French father and an English mother, had done his military service for 10 months with the French artillery in 1891–2, and had retained an interest in military affairs. Already a famous novelist, poet, and polemicist, he was writing for a wartime weekly journal, *Land and Water*, which reached a circulation at its peak of 100,000.

[2] About 2 miles N.E. of Farnborough. In Letter 198 Asquith refers to the camp as 'Frimley'. The *Frankfurter Zeitung* carried a report on conditions in it, 14 Nov.

[3] This was a tented camp. The prisoners and internees were transferred from it during Nov.

191

Tues. 27 Oct 1914

My darling – you came this morning to see Violet (so I heard) and I never saw you! I was what is called busy, but if you had opened the door (why didn't you?) I should have been more than happy. However, I can't & don't complain for you were an angel yesterday. But I miss so much the least & briefest glimpse of you. I don't think you know how much.

We had no Cabinet this morning, but I had long visits from K, Haldane, Grey & Winston. French's 1ˢᵗ telegram says that 'tremendous losses have been suffered by the Germans all along our front', and that he believes 'they are dispirited & quite incapable to making any strong & sustained attack'. In his second telegram he sends a message from Joffre, who declares 'the enemy to be quite exhausted, & bringing up his last resources', adding that 'a general offensive to-morrow by all our troops will entail an important success'. French says he has captured 1300 prisoners. This sounds well, but Kitchener, who is generally right about the war, is not altogether free from anxiety.[1]

General Murray, who is Sir J. French's chief of staff, is over here for the day. He said a very good thing to K. this morning, K having asked him what he thought of Joffre: 'Joffre is a very good man – capable, phlegmatic, equable: he has only 2 defects: the first is, that he is always 2 days too late, and the second, that he is always 2 divisions too few'. No one cd. ever have said that of Napoleon. He (Murray) has just been to see me. I cross-examined him closely about the whole position. He has left me some excellent maps, showing the relative situation of all the forces. He says (as everybody does) that our infantry & cavalry are immeasurably superior to both French & Germans: the French always give us the difficult thing to do; with the result (as I told you earlier) that our casualties are very heavy.[2] But the losses of the Germans are almost indescribable.

Winston came here before lunch in a rather sombre mood. Strictly between you & me, he has suffered to-day a terrible calamity on the sea,[3] which I *dare* not describe, lest by chance my letter should go wrong: it is known only to him & me, and for a long time will & must be kept secret.[4] He has quite made up his mind that the time has come for a drastic change in his Board; our poor blue-eyed German will have to go, and (as W. says) he will be reinforced by 2 'well-plucked chickens' of 74 & 72.[5] . It will be curious to see how the public receives the changes of personnel when they are announced. I can't help being very fond of him – he is so resourceful & undismayed: two of the qualities I like best. K – with all his drawbacks – has the supreme merit of taking everything calmly, never either exalted or depressed. A great contrast to E. Grey: who is always up & down. He (Grey) wants to get away for a week's rest & change, & Haldane & I are quite ready to take on his job, while he is away: perhaps from next Sunday night. I think it a bad form of medicine: you can be just as worried & perturbed 200 miles away as if you were in Downing St. And what different things perturb different people! Me & Grey for instance!

I lunched at the Assyrian's, with a lot of colleagues Ll George, Crewe M⟨c⟩Kenna &c, and the Governor of the Bank & Rufus.[6] We talked financial shop: at what price & on what terms the War Loan of 250 millions is to be issued. M⟨c⟩K, Rufus, & Bradbury good, and I was glad to find that my old Exchequer cunning had not altogether rusted.

Bluey has just been announced: some infernal War Office mess to mop up, I suppose. . . .

[1] Kitchener's anxiety was justified. The German Commander-in-Chief was at Prince Rupprecht's HQ planning a new offensive as Asquith wrote. This was to be made against Haig's 1st Corps by a newly assembled formation (Army Group Fabeck); it started at 5.30 a.m., 29 Oct.

[2] 'First Ypres' marked the end of the original B.E.F. The 2nd Highland Light Infantry may be taken as typical enough. When they were relieved at the end of the battle, scarcely 30 officers and men were left from the thousand odd who had been mobilized 3 months earlier.

[3] A German minelayer had operated off the N. coast of Ireland in order to disrupt the Liverpool trade route. Jellicoe took the Grand Fleet there for a few days' rest and gunnery practice; and one of the newest Dreadnoughts, the *Audacious*, was sunk by a mine. She went down slowly and the crew were saved; but the crucial margin of superiority of the Grand Fleet was reduced (see p. 252).

[4] It was not known to the German fleet for five weeks; and even then they were not certain that the rumour was true.

[5] For Prince Louis of Battenberg, see Letter 189, n. 2. The 'well-plucked chickens' were Lord Fisher, aged 73, and Sir Arthur Wilson, 72.

[6] Walter Cunliffe and Rufus Isaacs, Lord Reading.

'A royal row . . . about . . . the Welsh Army Corps'
(Letters 192–5 and 200)

MANY of the men who answered Kitchener's recruiting appeal wanted to serve with their friends and peacetime associates. Middle-class volunteers, as L. S. Amery wrote privately on 1 Sept., objected to 'being put down in the barracks next to a couple of lousy and swearing hooligans'. By mid-September 1914 those enlisting provided a panorama of pre-war Britain. Such bodies as the Gentlemen Jockeys, the Glasgow Tramwaymen, and the Football Association were all forming their own units. On 16 September the London Welsh met to form a battalion. When Lloyd George spoke in the Queen's Hall three days later (Letter 164) he put Welsh nationalism behind the recruiting drive in the Principality by suggesting the formation of 'a

Welsh army'. The scheme succeeded, in that Wales soon rose above the average for Britain in its contribution to the Kitchener armies. The original object of a Welsh army corps was not attained; but the 38th Division, which was formed as part of the Kitchener armies, remained a distinctively Welsh formation throughout the war.

The recruiting methods of the War Office were almost as unimaginative in Wales as they had been in Ireland (pp. 236–7). Welsh Nonconformists had been taught from childhood to condemn militarism, and Lloyd George had a hard task in bringing them to the colours. He needed to exploit the rivalry between church and chapel; but the entry for 'religion' on the enlistment forms allowed no mention of some Nonconformist denominations. He had a struggle with Kitchener over the enlistment of Nonconformist chaplains. Finally, in the last week of October an army order was issued that recruits were not to speak Welsh even in their billets.

Lloyd George was too powerful a recruiting sergeant to be denied. He overcame Kitchener's resistance on all these issues. The latter's doubts about a Welsh 'political army' are understandable, however. His belief that 'purely Welsh regiments [were] always wild and insubordinate' (Letter 194) was not the only ground for uneasiness. The commanders nominated by Lloyd George were effective at recruiting, but no good at the front. The first brigade to be formed went to Owen Thomas,[1] who was reported in September 1915 to be too 'lacking in military knowledge and training' to command it in France.[2] He was relegated to command a reserve brigade in Wales, and was removed even from that appointment in June 1916.

The first commanders of the 38th Division and of the 14th Royal Welch Fusiliers, Ivor Philipps and David Davies, were both Liberal M.P.s closely associated with Lloyd George. Philipps was removed from his command early in the Somme battle. Before Thomas and Philipps were given their commands Lloyd George seems to have reached an understanding with them about A.D.C.-ships for his sons. The first appointed William Lloyd George as his A.D.C., and the second Gwilym. These political undertones disappeared from the 38th Division long before the end of 1916; and it achieved a notable fighting record during the later battles on the Western Front.

---

[1] For Thomas's surprise at being appointed to command the brigade see A. J. P. Taylor (ed.), *Frances Stevenson's Diary* (1971), p. 11.

[2] Report p. 8; *Parl. Papers* 1917–18 CD 8435, iv. 334.

192

Wed 28 Oct 1914

. . . The disaster of wh. I wrote to you in veiled language yesterday was the sinking of the *Audacious* – one of the best & newest of the super Dreadnoughts, with a crew of about 1000 and 10 13.5 inch guns, off the North coast of Ireland. They thought at first that it was due to the torpedo of a submarine, but it is now clear that she hit up against a new mine-field, laid by the Germans most unsuspectedly in those waters, which in the course of the day blew up 2 merchant ships.[1] The mines must have been laid by vessels flying neutral flags, and as they were placed directly in the route which the great liners take, going from Liverpool to New York, they were probably not intended for the fleet.[2] All the greater must be their satisfaction at such a valuable & unexpected bag. The *Olympic* came up & took the *Audacious* in tow: she remained afloat for about 8 hours and the whole of her crew except one man were safely landed. But the ship itself sank before reaching the coast. It is far the worst calamity the Navy has so far sustained, as she cost at least 2½ millions. It is cruel luck for Winston.

Poor boy he has just been here pouring out his woes. . . . After a rather heated discussion in the Cabinet this morning, we resolved *not* to make public the loss at this moment. I was *very* reluctant, because I think it bad policy on the whole not to take the public into your confidence in reverses as well as in successes. And I only assented to immediate reticence on the grounds (1) that no lives were lost and (2) that the military & political situation (especially as regards Turkey) is such that to advertise at this moment a great calamity might have very bad results. I am I confess rather uneasy about it, & I hope you think, on balance, that I was right.[3] . . . Of course you will say nothing about the *Audacious*, till it is public property. Winston's real trouble however is about Prince Louis & the succession to his post. He *must* go, & Winston has had a most delicate & painful interview with him – the more so as his nephew Prince Maurice was killed in action yesterday. Louis behaved with great dignity & public spirit, & will resign at once. Then comes in another trouble. W. proposes to appoint Fisher to succeed him & to get Wilson to come in also as Chief of Staff – which I think wd. be very popular. But Stamfordham (who came to see me just before W) declares the King's unconquerable aversion to Fisher (he – the King – was always a Beresfordite[4] in the old quarrels) and suggests nonsense people like Hedworth Meux & Sir Henry Jackson,[5] whom W. will not have at any price. I said that nothing wd. induce me to part with W, whom I eulogised to the skies, and that in consequence the person chosen must be congenial to him. So there is for the moment a complete *impasse*, & it requires all my ingrained & much-tried optimism (wh. sometimes amuses you) to forecast a way of escape. Happily I have some experience in building bridges over gaping chasms: whether I can engineer this situation remains to be seen.

French sends a rather sanguine telegram this morning.[6] . . . (Meanwhile the irrepressible *Emden*, with a faked 4th funnel, wh. made her seem like a British cruiser, has turned up at Penang, & sunk a small Russian war-ship. She is certainly an undefeated sportswoman! 7 ships are hunting her, but she seems to have a charmed life & an unfailing reserve of resource.)[7]

Privately, we had a royal row at the Cabinet to-day between K & Ll. George, about Welsh recruiting & the Welsh Army Corps. They came to very high words, and it looked as if either or both of them wd. resign. The whole thing cd. be settled in 10 minutes by the exercise of a modicum of common-sense & imagination. K. is much the most to blame: he was clumsy & noisy: he has spent so much of his life in an Oriental atmosphere that he cannot acclimatise himself to English conditions.[8] I have told Winston to go & see him, and try to infuse some sense of proportion. . .

---

[1] The minefield was 20 miles from Tory Island, off the Donegal coast. Two 'merchant ships' were lost on 26 Oct., but only one of them from these mines. This was the *Manchester Commerce* (5,000 tons) bound from the Mersey to Montreal. The other, the *Amiral Ganteaume* (4,500 tons) foundered in the Channel while carrying 2,000 refugees from the Pas de Calais to Le Havre. She had not been mined, as was at first thought, and her loss was a portent. She was proved to have been torpedoed without warning by a German submarine. 14 lives were lost from the *Manchester Commerce*, and between 30 and 40 from the *Amiral Ganteaume*.

[2] They had been laid by the *Berlin* (17,000 tons), a Norddeutscher Lloyd liner, armed for commerce raiding and equipped as a minelayer. She tried to return to Germany; but putting in at Trondheim on 16 Nov. with only two days' coal in her bunkers, and asking to make good engine room defects, she was immediately interned by the Norwegian authorities. Asquith's remark that the minefield was intended to catch merchant ships, and not the fleet, was almost certainly right. The *Berlin*'s operations happened to coincide with the removal of the Grand Fleet to the N. coast of Ireland: see Letter 191, n. 3. The belief that the Germans used neutral flags or fishing craft for minelaying was general in Britain; but it does not seem to have been well founded. The Spurn Head and Tyne minefields, which had been laid on the night of 25/26 Aug. 1914, were attributed to German fishing craft, but later found to be the work of a minelayer and of light cruisers equipped for minelaying.

[3] The *Olympic*'s passengers had seen and photographed the sinking *Audacious*. Churchill's appeal to the press had some effect; but there was much use of 'audacious' in the papers, and even an illustration of the disaster entitled 'An Audacious Picture'. One of the photographs taken from the *Olympic* was reproduced on 14 Nov. in the Philadelphia *Public Ledger*. German intelligence services do not seem to have been monitoring the British and American press at this time: see Letters 191 n. 4; 193, n. 3. Asquith later told Margot that the whole cabinet, except for Lloyd George and himself, had favoured withholding the news.

[4] Fisher had been First Sea Lord from Oct. 1904 to Jan. 1910, Lord Charles Beresford Commander-in-Chief of the Channel Fleet from 1907 to 1909. A bitter quarrel between the two had split the navy so badly that an official inquiry was instituted. The resulting report, while generally favourable to Fisher, accelerated the retirement of both disputants.

⁵ Jackson was to become First Sea Lord on Fisher's resignation in May 1915.

⁶ Soon after this was sent, British GHQ had learned from an intercepted wireless message of a German attack timed to start at 5.30 a.m. on 29 Oct.

⁷ The commander of this Russian light cruiser, the *Zemtchug*, had refused to take any precautions despite the harbour-master's advice. He was court-martialled, cashiered, and sentenced to a term of imprisonment. When leaving Penang the *Emden* destroyed a French destroyer. Her 'charmed life' depended chiefly on her captain's skill in recoaling. His captures included two colliers on the Aden–Colombo route: he also coaled on 4 Oct. at Diego Garcia, where the islanders had not heard of the outbreak of war.

⁸ According to Pease's diary Kitchener 'said he would resign. P.M. said that was not practical.'

Sir Edgar Speyer (Letter 193)

SIR Edgar Speyer was a Jewish financier educated in Germany who had taken out British naturalization in 1892 and had been largely responsible for the electrification of London's railways. He was a generous supporter of the Liberals and moved in London society, his wife being well known for her musical interests. In 1906 he was made a baronet, and in 1909, on Asquith's recommendation, a Privy Councillor.

There were Speyer firms in London, New York, and Frankfurt. Sir Edgar Speyer, his brother James, and his German brother-in-law were partners in all three. James Speyer, who ran the New York firm, was openly pro-German: he had the German Ambassador to the U.S.A. to stay in September 1914. This increased the unpopularity which Sir Edgar Speyer would in any case have incurred in wartime Britain. As the Naturalization Committee of 1921 reported:

He was constantly attacked in the newspapers; he was obliged to resign from hospital boards lest subscriptions should be withdrawn. . . . He was told that unless his children ceased to attend certain classes the other children would be withdrawn. He was in danger of personal violence; and he and his house were under police protection. Crowds assembled outside his door and hooted his visitors; and friends offered to take charge of his children to ensure their safety.

In May 1915 Speyer wrote to Asquith offering to resign his baronetcy and membership of the Privy Council. Asquith replied that the offer was declined by the King, and added:

I have known you long and well enough to estimate at their true value these baseless and malignant imputations.

A few days later Speyer and his family left for the United States where they lived for the rest of the war.

Once in America, Speyer was drawn into various anti-British courses. In December 1921 the Naturalization (Revocation) Committee reported:

1. That Sir Edgar Speyer has shown himself by act and speech to be disaffected and disloyal to His Majesty;

2. That Sir Edgar Speyer, during a war in which His Majesty was engaged, unlawfully communicated with subjects of an enemy state and associated with business which was to his knowledge carried on in such manner as to assist the enemy in such war.[1]

Speyer's name was struck off the list of Privy Councillors, and his naturalization, with that of his wife and three daughters, was revoked.

Asquith never showed his disdain for popular hysteria more clearly than in this case. At first glance his loyalty to Speyer seems wholly admirable. That Speyer, driven from Britain by outrageous persecution, should have repaid ingratitude with the same coin, and committed disloyal acts, was, if reprehensible, hardly surprising. The facts, however, were more complex than at first appears. Speyer was not entirely innocent when the persecution began.

Royal Proclamations against trading with the enemy were issued on 5 August and 9 September 1914. They applied to Speyer as much as to anyone. He was a partner in a New York firm which had intimate relations with one in Frankfurt, and a connection with the Deutsche Bank. Speyer disregarded the first proclamation. He reacted to the second by consulting his solicitor about a way by which he might remain a partner in the American firm without contravening the law. The solicitor advised against attempting this and on 5 October Speyer's retirement from that firm was announced. Like James Speyer's hospitality to the German Ambassador this was duly reported in *The Times*. Thus by mid-October 1914 it was public knowledge about Sir Edgar Speyer that his brother was active in Germany's cause, and that he had not hastened to resign his partnership in the firm through which that brother carried on business with Frankfurt.

Asquith was probably right to scout the notion that Speyer was anti-British; he was certainly right to regard the outcry against Speyer as hysterical and base. In all probability Speyer at this point was neither anti-British nor anti-German. He was a cosmopolitan financier who meant to keep his international links intact if he could. It was brave to invite him to 10 Downing Street; but he was not suitable to be a wartime Prime Minister's guest.

[1] Ctee. Rep. p. 16: *Parl. Papers* 1922, CMD 1569, vii. 156.

Fisher: 'Winston won't have anybody else' (Letters 191–4)

CHURCHILL's position had been weakened by the loss of the three cruisers (Letter 166) and by Antwerp; and he knew that, however unfairly, the mining of the *Audacious* would also be laid at his door (Letter 191). He needed an outstanding First Sea Lord to prop up his régime at the Admiralty. Fisher filled this bill. The objections to appointing him were obvious. He had long been a highly divisive figure in the navy. He had reached an age when his nerves and vigour were impaired. There was, however, as Asquith wrote, no obvious alternative: the navy was not well off for senior admirals of high ability. Fisher's many critics mostly accepted the appointment with good grace because, in their eyes, with all his faults he had one supreme merit. They expected him to be better than anyone else at controlling Churchill.[1]

Churchill's thoughts were the reverse of this. He had no intention of giving Fisher the last word. 'I took him,' he told Violet Asquith in May 1915, 'because I knew he was *old* and *weak*, and that I should be able to keep things in my own hands.'[2] Neither prediction was near the mark. Beatty made the right prophecy when he told his wife on 4 December 1914; Churchill and Fisher 'cannot work together; they cannot both run the show'.[3] Fisher was not so much old and weak as old and wild. An unrepentant navalist, he had never reconciled himself to a British army on the French left flank. He had no experience of working with the Naval War Staff, the creation of which he had indeed obstructed. Now that he was in his seventies the strain of megalomania in his personality had become more pronounced. He wanted to have the same authority over the navy as Kitchener had over the army.

By acquiring as First Sea Lord an old and famous sailor who meant to have his own way Churchill was buying immediate relief at the risk of future trouble. Any major disagreement would present him with the alternatives of giving way, or of allowing Fisher to resign. He had no notion of taking the first path: he was too unpopular to take the second; and, grateful though he was to the statesman who had brought him back to the Admiralty, Fisher was not the man to endure impossible situations patiently. The First Lord and the First Sea Lord were tied together; and the second was quite capable of going overboard, pulling the first with him.

[1] See H. A. Gwynne (Editor, *Morning Post*) to Leo Maxse, 2 Nov.: Maxse MSS 469, f. 584.
[2] Violet Asquith's diary, 19 May 1915.
[3] Marder ii. 266.

193

Thurs. 29 Oct 14

. . . The losses in the 7th Division, which . . . was the last to go out, have been terrific – at least 4000 out of about 12000 men & 200 officers – in these last few days, & Rawlinson is back in London to-day, presumably with the object of inducing K. to send out the 8th at once. K. tells me they are much 'too soft' to go at present, having returned most of them from Bermuda & semi-tropical places, & quite unable to stand the fatigue of long marches. He would like to keep them here for another month. But if the Germans go on lavishing lives at their present rate, and projecting wave after wave to the front, we shall have to give French all the men we can without being too fastidious as to their quality.[1] K. says that the Canadians on Salisbury plain are terrible fellows, without the most rudimentary notion of discipline. If a man dislikes his Colonel, he migrates at once without asking anybody's leave to another regiment.[2] . . .

. . . I had a call just before lunch to-day from Geoffrey Robinson of *The Times* who came to protest against the order for secrecy. I convinced him (tho' I have many misgivings myself) that on the whole we were right.[3] Meanwhile Jellicoe has held up the *Olympic* who tried to tow the *Audacious* to land, and the crew of the *Audacious* have replied to messages from anxious relatives, who had heard rumours of the calamity, that they are quite well and 'cruising about'. I doubt whether such a widely known secret can be kept for many more hours. . . .

We had the Bencks & Nathalie to dinner last night – with some others including the Speyers and the Assyrian & Mrs Lyell. I can't describe my disgust at the conduct of Ruby Peto, in withdrawing at a moment's notice all her investments from Speyer, to whom she & her rotten husband owe *everything* in the world, in order to place them in the hands of an *English* man of business. Ingratitude & baseness cd. hardly go further.[4] . . .

K . . . thinks now that the war will end sooner than he used to expect – from dearth of ammunition. They fire off every day at least 7 *times* as much as in any previous war, and if it goes on at this rate no possible new supply can keep pace with the demand.[5] I shall compose his quarrel with Ll. George.

After lunch I went to see the King, on Winston's business. As you will see in your morning papers, the resignation of Prince Louis is a *fait accompli*, and the King agreed to make him a Privy Councillor, to show that there was no lack of confidence in his integrity & loyalty. Poor man, I am afraid he is broken-hearted, but he admits that he had become quite unfit for his work.[6] It was a much more difficult job to persuade the Sovereign to consent to his being succeeded by Jacky Fisher. He gave me an exhaustive & really eloquent catalogue of the old man's crimes & defects, and thought that his appointment would be very badly received by the bulk of the Navy, & that he would be almost certain to get on badly with Winston. On the last point, I have some misgivings of my own, but Winston won't have anybody else, and there is no one among the available Admirals in whom I have sufficient confidence to force him upon him. So I stuck to my guns, and the King (who behaved very nicely) gave a reluctant consent. I hope his apprehensions won't turn out to be well founded.

Since I began this, I have had Grey & Winston with me, and W. read us a private letter he has just got from French, who is extraordinarily confident, & talks of being in Bruges & Ostend in a week's time.[7] (This is very *private*). The Chilian Minister, who has come from Berlin, says they are very depressed there; their two first objectives – Paris & Warsaw – have proved impossible; and if this (of Calais), which is the only remaining one, fails also, tho' they will have to go on fighting, they will have been checkmated. It is all important to hold them steadily back for the next 3 or 4 weeks. . . .

[Among lunch guests were] . . . Stamfordham, & Commodore Back-house, Oc's commanding officer: quite a splendid type of naval man of great stature & clean features & plenty of intelligence. . . . Both Backhouse & Hankey (who was also at lunch) think the week at Antwerp was well spent, & had a real effect on the general campaign.[8] . . .

[1] The 8th Division was with the B.E.F. by 3 Nov.

[2] The indiscipline of the Dominion troops was a constant theme among British commanders, accustomed both to the strict discipline of the regular army and to a more deferential society than existed in the Dominions. The Canadians, who had disembarked at Plymouth in mid-October, were in wet and muddy tented camps. They proved their fighting quality at Ypres during the first German gas attack in Apr. 1915. For some similar comments on the Australians see Letter 279.

[3] See Letter 191, n. 4. In that the German fleet did not know of the sinking of the *Audacious* for five weeks (and were not sure of it even then) the cabinet must be judged right, though those who had hitherto relied on the completeness of British government statements were led to revise their views. The Admiralty fitted up an old ship to look like the *Audacious*.

[4] As examples of reactions to Asquith's championship of the Speyers:
  a. Sir Francis Bertie noted a 'strong feeling' in London in December 1914 'at Speyer continuing to be a guest at Asquith's, and matters which ought not to be divulged being discussed before him': Lady A. Gordon-Lennox (ed.), *Diary of Lord Bertie of Thame, 1914–1918* (2 vols. 1924), i. 80.
  b. 'Sir Edgar Speyer', L. J. Maxse told a meeting in May 1915, 'dined with the Prime Minister during one crisis of the war. . . . The right place for Germans was Germany (cheers).'
  Ruby Peto (née Lindsay) was a relative of the Asquiths' neighbours at Sutton Courtney. Cynthia Asquith included her among the 'beautiful sirens'.

⁵ The 'Shells Committee' appointed by the cabinet on 12 Oct. were doing something to enlarge munitions production by greatly increasing the orders for guns, underwriting the costs of plant expansion, and enormously enlarging the list of firms with which the War Office placed contracts. But it was chaired by Kitchener, who resented, and eventually eliminated, its 'interference' in War Office affairs.

⁶ Prince Louis's health had suffered under the combined strain of the war and of the attacks about his German origins: Letter 189, n. 2.

⁷ 'I am', French told Churchill (25 Oct.), 'on the very best terms with Foch who is doing splendid work and will be at Ostend and probably Bruges within a week.' The Germans held both places until Oct. 1918.

⁸ See Letters 176, n. 1, and 179, n. 5.

194

Fr. 30 Oct 1914[i]

My darling – a delicious letter from you this morning. I am glad that you welcome the increasing body of imports: so do I. This last 3 months you have never failed, and it is rubbish to talk about 'dreariness': I keep every one, and you don't know & couldn't guess how many times each one is read in the course of 24 hours. (By the way – I love the prefix 'My'!)

It is natural that you should think that the King had no say in such matters as have been agog these last 2 days. But by an odd convention all our Sovereigns (I have now had to deal with *three*) believe that in Army & Navy appointments they have a special responsibility & a sort of 'divine right of Kings' prerogative. Anyhow they have to be humoured & brought in. . . . You may like to have & keep among your *sealed* documents in the 'gaudy casket' the enclosed, which came last night.¹ Keep it carefully, for some day I may have to ask the loan of it.

Old Jacky came to see me before the Cabinet this morning – as fresh as paint – & told me he had just had an hour with the King, with whom he had got on like 'a house on fire', and come to an agreement that they should regularly meet once a week! On the other hand the other veteran – Sir A Wilson – won't have his name mentioned or published, tho' he is quite willing to contribute day by day all his brains & knowledge & experience. . . .

I have a lot of 'crosses, Mr Wesley', through the tripartite warfare wh. is constantly being waged between the Assyrian, Bluey, & Masterman over the sandy & juiceless area of 'separation allowances', and 'death & disablement pensions'. We shall have much trouble about this when the House meets with the Labour party & possibly a section of the Tories.²

We heard last evening that my nephew Lachlan Duff – son of the brother-in-law who owns Hopeman, & a Gordon Highlander, was killed in action 2 or 3 days ago. He leaves a young wife with 2 children & a third just coming.[3] . . .

I got hold of Ll. George before the Cabinet & told him to suspend his feud with K, who is not ill-disposed but inclined to be slow & rather clumsy. K. tells me privately that no purely Welsh regiment is to be trusted: they are (he says) always wild & insubordinate & ought to be stiffened by a strong infusion of English or Scotch. Anyhow we had quite a placid Cabinet, tho' the news both from South Africa[4] & Turkey[5] is rather disquieting.

I liked Winston's remark about the duties of women to those who are at the 'apex' of responsibility.[6] But I loved much more your wish that I was in your little room, and that we could have had another of those heavenly hours wh. are the best things in life. I hope & trust that it won't be desecrated into a 'Matron's room' in your new hospital.[7]. . .

We had a quiet homely evening yesterday: Margot & Lucy & Cys & Bongie & the Assyrian, with some good talk & unadventurous Bridge. . . .

. . . One of our usual variety luncheons to-day. . . . Violet & Eliz were there: also the Duke of W,[8] Ruby Peto (for whom as I told you I have no warm feelings, but who was in wonderful looks – her infernal husband is at the front with the 10th Hussars) old Mahaffy[9] intriguing hard to be made Provost of Trinity Dublin, Mary Tennant, Sir Thos. Esmonde (a nice Irish MP – descended from Grattan) Dunn, & some others. I can't think how such ill-assorted elements gravitate to the same place. . . .

Frances Horner sent me the first poetic effort of Perdita[10] (aged I suppose about 3): it is, I think, terse & good:

> 'I don't like London,
> No, not a bit:
> I like the country,
> Better than it'

Don't you think that shows promise?

I must stop now, & write my Cabinet letter for the King. . . . The secret of the *Audacious* is still kept:[11] Buckmaster, who was here at lunch & is a *very* able man, described to me his 'crosses' as head of the Press bureau. My own darling, how I long (it is just twilight) to be with you & see you & read to you & talk to you and – *feel* that you are near. Alas! *All* my love.

[1] The King put on record to Asquith: 'While approving the proposed appointment of Lord Fisher as First Sea Lord, I do so with some reluctance and misgivings.' George V had wanted to record 'his protest'. Asquith had persuaded him to use 'a less severe term'.

[2] For Bonar Law's view see Letter 207, n. 1.

[3] Only son of Margot's long-dead sister, Pauline Gordon-Duff. By the end of the war, four of Margot's nephews had been killed in France and one had died of wounds in the Dardanelles.

Four Tennant cousins were also killed and one died later after being gassed. One of the families lost three sons.

⁴ A formidable Boer trio – Beyers, De Wet, and Maritz – had risen in revolt against Botha's policy of active, pro-British intervention in the war. Asquith did not know that at Rustenberg on 28 Oct. Botha had given Beyers's main force a fatal blow.

⁵ On 30 Oct. the raid by the *Goeben* and *Breslau* on installations in the Black Sea (Letter 122, n. 5) drew a 12-hour ultimatum from the Russian, British, and French ambassadors at Constantinople. It was unanswered and hostilities began next day.

⁶ See pp. 118–19.

⁷ This plan to turn Alderley into a hospital did not come to anything.

⁸ The 2nd Duke of Westminster.

⁹ He was 75 and had expected to be nominated to this Crown appointment at the last vacancy 10 years earlier. He was made Provost in Nov. 1914.

¹⁰ Daughter of Raymond and Katharine Asquith.

¹¹ By the end of Nov. it was 'rumoured' in some Conservative circles 'that one reason the loss of the *Audacious* has been suppressed is because she is suspected to have been the victim of Irish Nationalist foul play': Leo Maxse to J. S. Sandars, 1 Dec.: Sandars MSS, f. 178.

195

Friday 30 Oct 14 [ii] Midnight

. . . As the result, I think, of talks wh. I have had with both, Ll. George & Kitchener this afternoon have fallen on one another's necks, and are now inseparable friends.¹ I am anxious about the health of both Grey & Haldane – the strain seems to be too much for them. Darling – you say nothing about your health, which worries me more. *Dear love.* Good night.

¹ Churchill also played a part in the reconciliation.

196

Sat morning 31 Oct 14 [i]

. . . One can recreate the past from letters better than in any other way, and how different the perspective often is, when, after years, one reads them again, from what it was when they were written. They are real milestones. I have destroyed by far the larger part of those I have received during my life, sometimes not without a malicious complacency at the disservice I am doing to any biographer who may be foolish enough hereafter to take me in hand.¹ I am certain that *you* won't lend him any assistance.²

I have written to you with more confidence & fullness & intimacy (a thousand times) than I ever have to any other human being, and the 'huge & growing pile', which already takes up so much room in your box, covers some of the most soul-stirring events that have happened or are likely to happen in our time. (I stopped for a moment to watch, out of the window, the last batch of new recruits, marching across the Parade to the strains of the Russian National Anthem: K. having at last provided a supply of bands.[3] It is a bright sunny morning, & they stepped out well.) I was going to add, that I believe hardly any one (indeed, no-one) knows so much of its real inner history as you do. Perfect love coupled with *perfect trust* is the best boon that life can give. . . .

. . . The Turk has now under German pressure taken a hand. . . . Few things wd. give me greater pleasure than to see the Turkish Empire finally disappear from Europe, & Constantinople either become Russian (which I think is its proper destiny) or if that is impossible neutralised and made a free port. By the way, there is a characteristically vain & silly article in *The Times* to-day on the Tweedmouth letter of 1908.[4] Do you remember it, & the row which it created? It was just when poor old CB was on his last legs, and I was becoming Prime Minister. The first thing I did was to put 'Cousin Reggie' in Tweedmouth's place at the Admiralty – not a moment too soon, for within a month or six weeks T. was raving mad, & so continued until his death.[5] His was a tragic case, for he was one of the sanest & most high-spirited of mankind. I shall never forget my bewilderment when, in the course of a longish tête-a-tête in the Cabinet room, it gradually dawned upon me that he was off his head. Rosie Ridley[6] & I spent a whole Saturday afternoon in search of a mad doctor who would certify him to be insane, and at last dragged old Barlow from a death bed to do what was necessary. . .

[1] By these means he 'seriously embarrassed the task of his biographers', as one of them observed: Spender and Asquith, i.211.

[2] Some pathos attaches to this remark, as Asquith, when short of money in his last years, asked Venetia to send him passages from the letters which he published in *Memories and Reflections* (see Appendix 1).

[3] Many persuasions were needed before Kitchener would sanction the expenditure for this morale-raising innovation.

[4] The Kaiser wrote to Lord Tweedmouth, the First Lord of the Admiralty, in Feb. 1908 to controvert the view that the German navy was being built 'against Britain'. He had been particularly annoyed at some recent remarks by Lord Esher, and was 'at a loss to tell whether the supervision of the foundations and drains of the Royal Palaces is apt to qualify somebody for the judgement of naval affairs' (Esher was Deputy Constable and Lieutenant-Governor of Windsor Castle). Tweedmouth seems to have replied to the letter; and news about it and about his reply reached the Military Correspondent of *The Times* (through the agency of a lady with whom Tweedmouth was friendly, as was believed in the Admiralty). Though *The Times* raised the constitutional issue, the Government refused to publish these pieces of private correspondence. More than six years later, on 30 Oct. 1914, the *Morning Post* published the text of the letter. This gave *The Times* a chance of pointing out how right and prescient it had been in 1908 to protest at a potential enemy's attempted interference in British naval policy. See C. à Court Repington, *Vestigia* (1919), pp. 284–5.

[5] Tweedmouth was Lord President of the Council during the first months of Asquith's premiership: he died in 1909.

[6] Lady Ridley was married to a nephew of Lord Tweedmouth.

H. H. Asquith, 1914

Venetia Stanley, about 1914

197

The Wharf,
Sutton Courtney,
Berks.

Sat 31 Oct 14 [ii] Midnight

. . . Cust was in good form at dinner & (like Yorick) now & again 'set the table in a roar'.[1] His wife whom I now see about once in 2 years is a strange devitalised figure: she had a certain rather uncanny kind of attraction when I first remember her, and is highly accomplished & even learned in ways.[2] Their union was a hopeless experiment from the first: as you say in your letter to-day, a 'tremendous argument against marriage'. How many we see! . . . .

You would see from the papers to-day what a mess poor Lady Aberdeen has got into from the publication of a silly tho' strictly private letter about the Red Cross.[3] In the sheaf of telegrams which came in to-day, there was an extraordinary story forwarded by our Minister in Norway, describing the arrival there of two men, one English & the other Norwegian, on a secret mission from the German Ambassador in America to the Chancellor in Berlin. Their object is to organise a raid of Irish Americans of the extreme factions who are to make a descent with ships & arms upon Ireland, & there to be joined by the Anti-Redmond Nationalists (Sinn Fein &c) in a pro-German rising. It sounds like a mad enterprise, but the evidence seems to be fairly good, & it will require watching.[4] . . .

[1] *Hamlet*, v. i.
[2] Nina Welby-Gregory is said to have coerced Cust into marrying her by putting it about that she was with child by him. There were no children of the marriage. She was a sculptress and author; her book on 'the journeys and adventures of four noblemen in Europe during the 15th and 16th centuries' had been published in 1909. After Cust's death in 1917 she helped to edit his *Occasional Poems*.
[3] *Sinn Fein* and the *Irish Worker* had published, partly in facsimile, a private letter which Lady Aberdeen was said to have written to the Editor of the *Freeman's Journal*. Part of this read: 'I am afraid there is a bit of a plot amongst the Unionists to capture the Red Cross Society in Ireland, and to run it in such a way from London and through county lieutenants . . . that it will be unacceptable to the Irish Volunteers' people.' When invited to disavow the letter Lady Aberdeen refused to make any comment.
[4] In Nov. 1914 Sir Roger Casement reached Berlin from America via Sweden. At the end of the month reports appeared in the British press that he had visited the German Foreign Office. A letter by him, promising that Germany would recognize Ireland's independence and send her friendly assistance, was later published in Irish 'separatist' papers; but his attempts to recruit an Irish brigade for the German service from Irish prisoners of war met with no success.

198

Monday 2 Nov 1914 [i]

. . . I am so glad that you can speak as you do about your health – to me the *most* important topic – and I hope you don't keep back anything in that connection wh. is the least disquieting. I don't know what I should do if you were to be really disabled, even for a week. Do you think it is bad to be so dependent? Does it disappoint you in whatever judgement you have of me? . . . .

While we were at lunch Bongie got a message from Blanche. I gather that Eric's wound is not at all serious, but I shall know better in an hour or two . . .

I am not such a novelty-hunter as you pretend to think. I shouldn't care the least if I never made a new friend or even acquaintance, and I entirely agree with you that those we have, & have known well, compare most favourably with the occasional finds which are fished up from time to time from the unknown & unexplored.

We went yesterday afternoon to see another camp of German prisoners at Newbury . . . The civilians were much better assorted than at Frimley last week – the men of education & 'culture' not more than 4 or 5 in a tent. But I came across lots of cases which it was simply cruel & criminal to have treated as 'interned'; and I hope that McKenna will effect a large clearance in the course of the next week. I loathe the excesses of the spy-fever. . . .

. . . We had a Cabinet at noon. Kitchener retailed his experiences at Dunkirk, where he was yesterday & met President Poincaré, Millerand, Generals Joffre & Foch & some other French and Belgian officers. He found them in a highly optimistic mood, this was to be the last big battle of the war, the Germans were really defeated both East & West, and so on in the same strain.[1] K. told them that he did not share their roseate views, that for the last week our men with tremendous losses had been bearing the brunt of the fighting, and that it was time for the French to send them stronger & more effective support.[2] In the end Joffre engaged to send up a French Corps d'Armée to back them to-day. They are really difficult to deal with, and it is curious that they shd. be so ultra-sanguine. K. found Joffre rather inelastic, and was more impressed with Foch. I hope his visit will have done good. It was just as well that they should realise our point of view.[3]

I have just (4 p.m) got French's telegram of this morning. He says he is 'not so anxious to-day' as the enemy appears to be much less active.[4] He adds, I am glad to say, that 'to-day a strong offensive is being taken by the French': all our troops 'need rest badly'. (K said the same this morning: he saw a lot of the slightly wounded at Boulogne & was struck by their drawn & pinched faces, like those of men who had had no sleep & were worn out.)

I hear just now that Francis Grenfell is on his way back, wounded again, this time in the thigh.[5] What bad luck! One piece of news, by the way, that K. brought back with him is that the Kaiser is at Courtrai: so it looks as if he were egging on his troops for this desperate attempt.[6]

The news from South Africa is decidedly better to-day.

Winston is very angry about the torpedoing of the *Hermes* in the Straits of Dover. She was ordered to come back in the dark, when she would have been perfectly safe, but waited until daybreak & was caught. The Captain will probably be court-martialled.[7] On the other hand, he is pleased to think that he will at last catch the *Königsberg*: she is up a river in East Africa, & ought to fall an easy prey to the *Chatham*[8] (Clemmie has had a slight relapse, & cannot have us to dinner to-night).

. . . What do you say to the enclosed letter from Redmond? . . .

. . . I read 3 Acts of the 1st Part of *Henry IV* before going to bed at the Wharf, and thought all the time how delicious it would be if we could be reading them together. . . . I just jotted down for your benefit a few of the 'quotations' which I came across in these Acts: I thought they might amuse you. I must stop now, my own loved and *most* precious darling. Think of me and send me your *real* love.

[1] Both French and British staffs tended to be too easily impressed at this time at the rawness of the newly encountered German divisions: see Letter 188, n. 2.

[2] Now that there was no longer a chance of an Allied turning movement in Belgium Joffre was anxious to gather a reserve for an offensive elsewhere. The moment seemed propitious, as the Germans had been in retreat in Poland since 21 Oct. and they might have to withdraw divisions from the Western Front.

[3] It is doubtful whether Kitchener's remarks at Dunkirk 'did good'. The French were convinced that they could win a decisive success if only Kitchener would send across every available man. They were highly suspicious of an ally who talked 'pessimistically' about a long war. They feared that Kitchener might be keeping his new armies at home in case Britain should want to pull out of the war while still relatively strong.

[4] The attacks of Army Group Fabeck continued with great intensity throughout 30 and 31 Oct. The 1st Corps had no chance to disengage and withdraw; nor were they well placed to do so, with Ypres and the River Yser behind them. French thought the half-hour on the afternoon of 31 Oct. before the 2nd Worcesters retook Gheluvelt 'the worst I ever spent'. The attack was maintained on 1 Nov. though not at quite the same intensity.

[5] He had been wounded on 24 Aug., earning one of the first V.C.s of the war, when his squadron of the 9th Lancers saved the guns of a battery of field artillery. On 31 Oct., three weeks after he had rejoined the 9th, he received a serious thigh wound at Messines. He rejoined on 21 Apr. 1915 and was killed at Hooge on 24 May.

[6] When he learned from a wireless message that the Kaiser was to visit the front opposite

the B.E.F. at Hollebecke, French issued an Order of the Day urging his troops 'to give His Majesty a good demonstration of what the "contemptible little army" could do'.

⁷ Commander C. L. Lambe was promoted to Captain in 1916 when he was transferred to the Royal Naval Air Service. He was knighted in 1931, after a three year tour as Air Officer Commanding Coastal Area.

⁸ The *Königsberg's* captain knew how to exploit the intricate channels of the Rufiji River in German East Africa; and he held out until July 1915. Finally, when the collier sent to help her had been sunk, the *Königsberg* was destroyed by indirect fire from two shallow-draught monitors, the fall of shot being observed from the air.

198a

Private

Crown Hotel,
Harrogate.   31 Oct 1914

Dear Mr Asquith,

I understand it is seriously contemplated to make a change in the Lord Lieutenantcy in Ireland.

Some months ago I was of opinion that a complete change in the Government of Ireland (with the exception of Mr Birrell) would have been an advantage, but the circumstances at this moment are quite different.

The appointment of Sir Mathew Nathan has strengthened the Executive & I see nothing to be gained by superseding Lord Aberdeen. His removal at this moment would be most unfortunate. It would most certainly be regarded as a triumph by Irish Unionists & as the direct result of Lady Aberdeen's unfortunate letter. Whatever else may be said it must be admitted that Lord & Lady Aberdeen have been most loyal & faithful friends of Ireland & it would I think be most regretable [sic] if they left Ireland under a cloud. What I would earnestly urge upon you is that the matter should at least be postponed & that no announcement should be made at present. I trust it is not true that Mr Birrell is thinking of going.

Very truly yrs
J. Redmond¹

¹ Asquith replied 'that Ld. A. had already resigned, but that it was not to take effect until the beginning of February, and that no public announcement was at present contemplated'. When Aberdeen left Ireland he received a letter from the King, which he promptly made public, stating that Lady Aberdeen's work 'would be gratefully remembered by the Irish people' (*The Times*, 22 Feb. 1915, 10c).

199

Monday 2 Nov Midnight [ii]

My darling – I have been reading over again (for how many times do you think?) your dear letter of to-day – especially the part of it in which you describe the sorting & organisation of my multitudinous letters. It is not your way to exaggerate or over-state anything, but I thought you *might* have said that you were glad to have them.* Perhaps you thought I should take that for granted; but once & again one likes to be *assured* even of that of which one is sure. Is that too exacting?

After I wrote to you this afternoon, we had our conference in the Cabinet room at 5: a curious conclave. E. Grey & I, Winston, Kitchener, Fisher, & Jellicoe (who appeared out of space, on terra firma for the 1st time for 3 months). It went on for nearly an hour, & was quite interesting: I listened & didn't say much, but watched the different faces; K's, brick-red short-nosed, blue-eyed; Fisher strangely un-English, twisted mouth, round-eyed, suggesting the legend (which is I believe quite untrue) that he had a Cingalese mother:[1] Jellicoe, small, alert robin-eyed, of (it is said) gipsy parentage; Winston, whom most people wd. call ugly, but whose eyes, when he is really interested, have the glow of a genius; and Grey with his well-cut, hawk-like visage, now rather pinched & drawn. I wish you could have seen them: they wd have appealed to your picture-loving sense. Our main topic was the closing of the North Sea to all vessels, except those wh. are willing to make their way along our carefully selected route.[2] But there were lots of other things: and one felt at once the difference made by the substitution of Fisher for poor L.B – *élan*, dash, initiative, a new spirit. That is all to the good.

Winston wouldn't leave Clemmie – so we dined almost *en famille* – M & I, Violet, Eliz. Cys, Raymond & Katharine, & Hugh Godley. Quite good talk – about possible Viceroys of Ireland &c. If only you had been with us. Good night my own darling.

*P.S. (next day) Don't mind this: it is a case of 'much would have more'.[3]

[1] Fisher's father was an army officer, and his mother the daughter of Alfred Lambe of New Bond Street. Born in Ceylon in 1841, he was sometimes termed, from his apparently oriental features, 'the old Malay'. Jellicoe's father was in the service of the Royal Mail Line and became Commodore of its fleet. His mother was the daughter of a surgeon who thrice served as Mayor of Southampton.

[2] The conference seems to have originated in the Admiralty's plans to safeguard the Scapa base, which was by now known to be within range of German submarines (see Letter 215, n. 3, for a slightly later incident). In themselves the Scapa proposals would have involved shipping restrictions over a comparatively small area. By 2 Nov., however, there was a strong case for extending the control over the entire North Sea. The British mines, which were greatly

inferior to the German in design, often drifted, so that they might be encountered some way from their published locations; by Nov. North Sea shipping was safe only in one of the regularly swept channels. Moreover the announcement by the British Government, on 29 Oct., that the contraband lists were to be enlarged by the inclusion of materials such as nickel (pp. 254–5), had been accompanied by a warning of stricter control over ships *en route* to neutral ports. It was essential to show that this double proclamation would be made effective. Churchill's press statement of 2 Nov. accused the Germans of minelaying under the protection of neutral flags (Letter 192, n. 2), and declared 'the whole of the North Sea . . . a military area'. Captains bound for Norway, the Baltic, Denmark, and Holland were told to come up Channel to the Straits of Dover where they would 'be given sailing directions'.

³ Note added in red ink.

200

Tu. 3 Nov 14 [i]

. . . We have got down to 3 Cabinets a week, and to-day is a day off, wh. is a great relief. I had a long visit from K, who is far from happy about what is going on at the front. French is still quite confident, but his losses day by day are so great that he calls urgently for more men. . . .

K. tells me that his scouts report that a naval action is being fought this morning on the East Coast, but I have heard nothing yet from the Admiralty. He (K) is quite easy now about invasion: Winston & Fisher are (*entre nous*) bringing a lot of big battleships, with Jellicoe's consent, down to reinforce Burney's fleet in the Channel.¹ My own opinion of K's capacity increases daily: I think he is a really fine soldier, and he keeps his head & temper, and above all his equability wonderfully, considering how all three are tried. Ll. George, who has just been here about another matter, is now an enthusiastic K-ite: – speaking of their reconciliation, & of the way in wh. K had met him over his little Welshmen, he said: 'he is a big man, & what is more does things in a big way!' One never gets to the end of human nature, does one? it is lucky it is so, for it keeps one's interest vivid & unjaded. . . .

My dreams continue . . . There was another . . . in which (with the concurrence of all my colleagues) I was supplanted by Herbert Samuel – as Prince Hal says 'a Jew, an Ebrew Jew'.² Do you think that is going to be my fate? I wonder. I take refuge in the Beatitude: 'The meek shall inherit the earth' – and no Jew was ever meek! . . .

I have been turning for diversion over the pages of the Natˡ Dictʸ of Biography, and I will (out of my newly acquired lore) give you what Puffin calls a 'Stunner'. Of what book was it that Dʳ Johnson said, that it was the only one that ever took him out of his bed two hours sooner than he intended to rise?³ . . .

I must now go back to my grindstone. When shall I see you next my darling? Happily it cannot be much more than a week. We must then try to arrange for *real* seeing, not subject to the chapter of accidents. Every day & all day, *all* my love.

[1] Battleship support for the Harwich Striking Force was to be provided from Sheerness. The proposed move of the 3rd Battle Squadron to Portland did not take place because of the reinforcements sent to the South Atlantic after the Battle of Coronel. After a short delay the Squadron was moved to Rosyth: Letter 186, n. 3.

[2] Asquith had just been reading *Henry IV, Part 1*, but he sometimes quoted a little carelessly; the words are spoken by Falstaff.

[3] The answer – Burton's *Anatomy of Melancholy* – was given in a later letter.

201

Tues. midnight 3 Nov 14 [ii]

. . . In the days of the Gladstone Government . . . [Rosebery] & I used every morning to take a walk in Hyde Park, occasionally watching the riders in the Row, and seeing one day Lord Spencer & the present Lord Shuttleworth (both colleagues)[1] cantering along, Rosebery emitted a low whistle to attract their attention, apparently in vain. Spencer told us afterwards that Shuttleworth had said to him, with icy disdain: 'Who are those 2 rude boys trying to get us to notice them?' – R & I being at the time Foreign & Home Secretaries. Do you remember the night, years afterwards, when Bluey led us astray thro' the wilds of Lancashire,[2] & we arrived near midnight at Gawthorpe, and were entertained by the same great man & his 2 daughters? What fun we had! I think, if I remember right, that we started the evening in the company of Ottoline at Burnley.[3] How little we any of us foresaw of the future – least of all I, my darling. . . .

[1] The First Lord of the Admiralty, and the Parliamentary Secretary there, in Gladstone's last Government (1892–4). Asquith was fond of this story: see Hobhouse *Diaries*, p. 84.

[2] During the second 1910 election. Baker sat for Accrington. For Lord Shuttleworth's house, Gawthorpe Hall, see Appendix 3.

[3] On 5 Dec. 1910 Asquith spoke to an audience of 8,000 in the Olympia Roller Skating Rink at Burnley. The speech helped to clinch a Liberal gain, the new candidate, Philip Morrell, winning the seat.

Coronel: 'If the Admiral had followed his instructions . . .' (Letter 202)

On the evening of 31 October Rear-Admiral Sir Christopher Cradock engaged von Spee's Pacific squadron (Letter 166, n. 2) off Cape Coronel, Chile. The German force of two armoured, and three light, cruisers was by far the stronger and von Spee was completely victorious. The two British armoured cruisers were sunk, all their crews being lost with Cradock himself. His one light cruiser and an armed merchant cruiser escaped in the darkness.

In Letter 202 Asquith gives a condensed and very inaccurate version of Churchill's views immediately after the battle. Cradock was not instructed to wait 'on the other side of South America with the *Canopus* and *Defence* in overwhelming superiority'.[1] On 14 October the Admiralty approved his proposal for two forces to operate, one on each coast, each to be superior to von Spee's squadron. On 28 October he was sent an Admiralty signal: it denied him the *Defence*, for which he had asked, and stated, 'This will leave sufficient force on each side.' *Canopus* was an 1897 pre-Dreadnought battleship, manned by an untrained crew composed largely of reservists. She could hardly have given Cradock 'superiority'. The fact that von Spee held the initiative had tempted Cradock and the Admiralty into neglecting a basic principle – concentration of force.

Letter 202 suggests that where the navy was concerned Asquith stood close to the uninstructed man in the street. He was extremely sensitive to naval reverses (p. 252) and not notably perceptive about the navy's role and achievements. The British public had expected their naval superiority to be established in battle early in the war; and Churchill had contributed to their illusions by telling a Liverpool audience on 21 September that if the German fleet did not come out to fight 'it would be dug out like rats from a hole'. Mines and submarines were still recent inventions in 1914; it was easy to forget that these new devices exposed capital ships attacking well-defended positions to unacceptable risks.

On this point *The Times* was more patient and forbearing than the Prime Minister. On 25 August it pronounced:

Though unseen and unheard, the Fleet is exerting continual and progressively stringent pressure upon the vitals of the foe.

'We should regard it as disastrous', a *Times* leader commented on 23 November, 'if any public comments led to the conclusion that there is a foolish desire that the navy should "do something".'[2] Bonar Law was equally judicious. On 27 November, after Churchill had reviewed the navy's work, Bonar told the House:

Taking the work of the Admiralty as a whole, we have every reason to rejoice . . . and to feel that, in spite of these accidents,[3] good fortune as well as good management has been on our side.

---

[1] Asquith repeated his erroneous statement in his letter to the King, 4 Nov.
[2] The restriction of 'the second Navy in the world to the mud-banks of the Elbe' was, for the

National Review (Feb. 1915), 'as supreme an example of superior sea-power as the world has witnessed'.
³ Such as the loss of the three cruisers (p. 252).

202

Wed. 4 Nov 14

[Coronel] . . . If the Admiral had followed his instructions he would never have met them with an inferior force, but would have been by now on the other side of S. America with the *Canopus* & *Defence*, in overwhelming superiority. I am afraid the poor man has gone to the bottom: otherwise he richly deserves to be court-martialled. . . .

Moreover the operations outside Yarmouth yesterday, when the German shells nearly reached the shore, & their cruisers¹ sailed away unharmed into the twilight, are far from glorious for the Navy. As I told Winston last night (and he is not in the least to blame) it is time that he bagged something, & broke some crockery.² The shelling of a fort at the Dardanelles seems to have succeeded in blowing up a magazine, but that is *peu de chose*.³ At any rate we are now frankly at war with Turkey. . . .

¹ In fact, 4 German battle-cruisers: this 'bombardment' covered a minelaying operation.
² Churchill and Fisher soon achieved an outstanding success. By detaching 2 battle-cruisers from the Grand Fleet they contrived the annihilation of von Spee's squadron at the Battle of the Falkland Islands on 8 Dec. Only the *Dresden* and one collier escaped (see Letter 166, n. 2). Fisher was the chief architect of this victory: it was he who insisted on meeting von Spee with an overwhelming force, though this meant leaving Jellicoe slightly inferior to his opponents in battle-cruisers for an indefinite time.
³ What Churchill called 'a demonstration by bombardment' had been made against the outer forts at the Dardanelles on 3 Nov., apparently on the principle that 'it is a good thing to give a prompt blow'. It lasted for ten minutes and was conducted from long range (13,000 yards) by ships under way. 'The bombardment', Churchill told the Dardanelles Commissioners, 'did . . . encourage us to think the ships could injure the forts . . . from ranges at which the forts could not reply.' It was generally conceded afterwards to have been a mistake, since it put the Turks and their German advisers on the alert and deprived the British and French of any chance of surprise at the Dardanelles.

203

Thurs. 5 Nov 14 [i]

My darling – your letter this morning gave me greater happiness than anything that has happened to me for a long time. It was such a sweet and characteristic expression and revelation of your *real* self, which I know so well and love so much more than I can tell you, and which (as you say) you often keep under a veil of natural reserve.

Of course, darling, I *do* know the truth of all you say: I never doubt it: it is the joy & stay of my life: it means more than anything in the world to me. It is not doubt, or unfaith, that prompts me now & again to ask you to lift the veil. It is because I know that, if and when you do, I shall be nearer, if only for a moment, to what I treasure most.

It is delicious to read what you say about your 'lit lamp'.[1]You were not made to put up with rush-lights. And whatever may come in the future, you & I will always know that we refused to play the part of the 'frustrate ghosts'; lived a life of our own together, close to the making of history, in a confidence that was never broken; sharing every counsel, fear, hope, disappointment, exultation, day by day; and you giving to me, without stint, from your own rich nature the stimulus & the strength for whatever I did, or tried to do, that was worth doing. My beloved, no one can say that *we* kept our lamps unlit, or allowed them to grow dim & flicker out.

I, too, don't often 'put down', as you say, what I really feel, but there it is, for once. All I ask for and pray for is that it may be so to the end: till some Power, greater than either of us, extinguishes the light: what Milton calls (to change the metaphor) 'the blind Fury with the abhorrèd shears'.[2] Till then, let us make the most of what we are and can be to one another. That I know is the best that earth has to give *me*. . . .

My darling – if I were to die to-night, your name would be graven on my heart, and the thought and vision of you would be my last & dearest memory.

Write fully and dearly to-morrow. *All* my love: your own.

[1] An adaptation of Browning's phrase in 'The Statue and the Bust': see Letter 185, n. 6.
[2] 'Lycidas', l. 75.

204

Thurs. 5 Nov 14 [ii] Midnight

My darling – your letter of this morning has been like an undertone of the most beautiful music throughout the day, & I shall put it under my pillow when I go to bed, in the hope that it will bring me magic & uplifting dreams. I wrote to you about it earlier in the day, and I wish you to know that nothing I said was in the least degree exaggerated or out of proportion. That is what I really & permanently feel, tho', like you, I don't always or perhaps often put it on paper. It has become the dominant underlying keynote of my life. And *its being there* makes everything else easier & smoother & less hard to adjust & reconcile. Whatever may happen to me, I have nothing but blessing & gratitude, and the tribute of a life saved & enriched, for you. . . .

205

Friday 6 Nov 14 [i]

. . . I am having a rather distracting day. We had a longish Cabinet this morning, with bad news from E. Africa, where our Indian troops have had a very unsuccessful brush with the Germans.[1] In S. American waters, the *Glasgow* wh. escaped has now picked up the *Canopus*, & they are making for the Falkland Islands. There seems to be little doubt that the *Good Hope* was sunk. We are sending out some good ships in support, including two of the big battle cruisers.[2] We are also adding largely – perhaps about 40 – to the construction of new submarines,[3] in place of new battleships which would not be available until the war was over. It is one of the many ironies of the present situation to recall the activity of the Beagles a year ago, when we had the series of crises you so well remember over Navy Estimates.[4]

What follows is *very private*. After lunch (another Zoo-like affair) . . . I found on descending to the Cabinet room Winston & Freddy Guest – the latter on a secret mission from Sir J. French. A *most* disagreeable affair. It has been reported to French (apparently by that poisonous mischief-maker Gen Wilson) that when K. was at Dunkirk last Sunday, he asked the French Generals whether they were satisfied with Sir John, & even suggested as a possible successor Ian Hamilton (whom K despises and would gladly kick round the Horse Guards Parade). I don't believe there is a word of truth, or even a shadow of foundation for the story.[5] But it appears to have given great distress to Sir J. F. (who is very sensitive) & led him to think that he had lost or was losing the confidence of the Government. Hence F. Guest's mission, wh. was to me & not to K. These noxious weeds only grow in prepared soil – in this case, apparently an estrangement, or at any rate a coldness, of long standing between French & K. I have written him (F.) what I think you would agree is a 'very nice' letter, & Winston is going to do the same: but we both feel a certain delicacy in doing this behind K's back, French being very anxious that he should not be told. Rather a difficult situation isn't it? from the point of view of casuistry. But it is *all important* that French should be kept in good heart.[6]

Freddy gives an appalling description of the state of the army, so reduced by losses, that a Corps now numbers little more than a division. The 7th Division (which was our best) seems to have been badly led by Rawlinson,[7] and Capper the infantry commander is said to spend much of his time in a bomb proof hut![8] (This is all *for you alone*). The reinforcements are there or thereabouts, but meagrely officered, and it takes a lot of time to get them to the front & mix them with the depleted cadres. So no one gets any rest, & it is no wonder if their nerves are rather out of order. . . .

[1] At Tanga, where a force of about 7,000 had been landed on 3 and 4 Nov. After sustaining about 820 casualties they were re-embarked on 5 Nov. Much equipment was lost.

[2] See Letter 202, n. 2.

[3] Among other orders Churchill and Fisher placed a contract with the Bethlehem Steel Company for 24 submarines, 'to be completed in the . . . incredibly short period of six months'.

[4] The one achievement of Churchill's critics in the Naval Estimates crisis (pp. 35–8) had been to extract a promise that the 1915 estimates would be substantially reduced. 'When the time came,' Churchill wrote, 'I was not pressed to redeem this undertaking.'

[5] The story was substantially true. When complaints about the handling of the B.E.F. were voiced at the conference Kitchener offered to replace French with Hamilton. While Joffre would have welcomed Wilson as the replacement, he did not want to be faced with a new arrival over whom he might have little influence. He therefore deprecated making a change in mid-campaign and expressed confidence in French, being supported in this by the French President. On 5 Nov. Foch told Wilson of Kitchener's offer, and suggested that French should be told. Wilson readily took the story to his chief, who never again felt secure in his position.

[6] 'I cannot believe', Asquith wrote, 'that there is even a shadow of foundation for what has been reported to you. . . . Lord Kitchener . . . never fails in appreciation of, and loyalty to, you. . . . We think the country fortunate to have at the head of the gallant forces a commander who has never been surpassed in the capital qualities of initiative, tenacity, serenity, and resource.' French replied (9 Nov.): 'I cannot find words which adequately express my feeling of profound gratitude and relief on receipt of your letter . . . It has put me quite at rest . . . Few commanders in the field have had the good fortune to serve under such a true, loyal, and sympathetic chief as you.' According to Lord Esher the 'fabulous story' that French might be replaced by Hamilton was quite widely known and 'met with ready credence'.

[7] Rawlinson's 4th Corps consisted of the 7th Division and the 3rd Cavalry Division.

[8] Maj.-Gen. Thompson Capper; K.C.M.G., June 1915; died of wounds, Sept. 1915. A general in 1914 had no wireless to give him voice control while the battle raged. In view of this he was probably as well informed in 'in a bomb proof hut' as anywhere else: John Terraine, *The Smoke and the Fire* (1980), pp. 170–81.

206

Fr. 6 Nov 14 [ii] Midnight

My darling – after I wrote to you this afternoon I had a long & rather tiresome interview with Ll. George, Rufus Isaacs, Assyrian, Bradbury & Governor of the Bank of England as to the precise terms on which the War Loan of 250 millions is to be issued. Rufus is far the greatest expert of the whole lot, but I like the Governor – a regular John Bull of the farmer type, but wonderfully shrewd & level-headed. When the others had gone, I told him (he is called Cunliffe) that the King had agreed to give him a peerage, and that I proposed to announce it at the Guildhall on Monday. He was not the least *émotionné* & simply said – 'Well, I obey orders.' This lasted until about 6.30 & I went for a short respite to the Athenaeum – one of the few places where one is secure from interruption – & read 'The Double Mr. Burton', not at all a bad novel.[1]. . .

. . . Goonie who sat next me at dinner was in very good form, & talked very shrewdly about the advantages and drawbacks of sending the Wimbornes to Ireland. She agrees that he is rather a bounder, & she rather a 'slacker', but she is disposed to plead for it as a reward, or at any rate consolation, for all that they have endured in the way of insult & ridicule from their old Tory friends.[2] *Ça donne à penser.* I wish you would think it over dispassionately & tell me what your judgment is. . . .

[1] E. Phillips Oppenheim, *The Double Life of Mr. A. Burton* (1914).
[2] Like his cousin Churchill, Wimborne (or Ivor Guest, as he then was) had joined the Liberal party when the Conservatives took up tariff reform.

207

Sat. morn. 7 Nov. 14.

. . . The papers I see are full of rather sentimental vapouring over soldiers' pensions, and I have no doubt that our scheme – which is liberal & even lavish – will be abused in all quarters for shabbiness. It is curious that the Labour people should be so indifferent to the effect on female labour & the standard of women's wages, of letting loose some thousands of highly subsidised widows, childless & for the most part quite young, to compete in the market with the rest. It is just one of the cases in which the House of Commons is very likely to lose its head.[1]

Hankey has just been here for a talk: he has the best head of the soldiers & sailors. He was very strong about the necessity of giving French's troops a rest – which can only be done if the French are willing to take their place for a time. The most demoralising & nerve-shaking thing, as all agree, is the big shell that bursts in a trench, & buries numbers of men alive. They cannot be dug out till dark, & are then found unwounded but dead. . . .

[1] This comment does not show great imagination, whereas Bonar Law had seized quickly on the essential point. The elderly M.P.s who were persuading young men to join up and face great dangers at the front were, in Bonar Law's words, 'calling upon other men to make sacrifices which they did not mean to make themselves'. They would have been a little inhuman had they seen the problem of pensions for war widows entirely in terms of disturbance to the labour market. For the Government's proposal see Letter 182, text and n. 8.
Labour's answer to Asquith's point about 'highly subsidized widows' was given by G. N. Barnes during the Commons debate on 18 Nov. 'The principle I want to lay down', he said, 'is . . . that a woman who is left a widow as a result of this war shall be kept out of the labour market altogether.'

208

The Wharf,
Sutton Courtney,
Berks.

Sunday 8 Nov '14

. . . There is no news this morning except the capture of Tsingtau by the Japs, which is all to the good.[1] So far all the *dramatic* successes in the war have been won on land by the Russians & Japs, and on sea by the Germans. The sort of prolonged & bloody pull devil, pull baker, business, which has been & is going on in France & Belgium, does not appeal to people's imaginations. Winston of course would dearly love to break some crockery, as he nearly succeeded in doing at Antwerp. *Between ourselves*, Hankey is rather apprehensive that he may be drawn into some resounding adventure by the joint influence of those two unquenchable old sea-dogs, Fisher & Wilson. . . .

After I went upstairs last night I tried my hand at drafting a King's speech. Do you remember my composing at Alderley the critical paragraph in the speech of last Feb, and not showing it you, & you being a trifle resentful? I would send you this one, if there was anything in it either to interest or to criticise, but as befits the circumstances it is all 'leather & prunella'[2] – & thank Heaven, not much even of that. . . .

[1] Tsingtao had been in German hands since 1897 and the harbour was strongly fortified. The first landing had been made on 2 Sept., 80 miles to the N.; and a combined land and sea attack was mounted on 31 Oct. The besieging force included British troops from Taku and Wei-hai-wei. The siege and assault were judged to be efficient operations: it had taken the Japanese eight months to capture Port Arthur in 1904–5. In his Boxing Day memorandum (Letter 241) Hankey called this 'perhaps the most grievous loss that Germany has suffered since the war began'. See Letter 121, n. 5.

[2] Worth makes the man, and want of it the fellow;
   The rest is all but leather or prunella.
      Pope, *Essay on Man*, Ep. iv. 203–4.

A draft of the speech, pencilled by Asquith, survives in the Bonham Carter MSS.

209

Tu 10 Nov 1914 Midnight

. . . You may think I am becoming vain if I send you these cuttings – one from a Liberal, the other from a Tory paper.[1] But I think they may give you pleasure. What a joy it is to think of next Sunday! When shall I *really* see you again? Glimpses at any rate to-morrow: something perhaps better Thursday – certainly Friday. All my 'tiredness' is gone, now you are here! Bless you best beloved & good night. . . .

---

[1] These cuttings have been lost. The 'Tory paper' mentioned by Asquith was probably the *Morning Post*, which wrote of his Guildhall speech (9 Nov.): 'No finer appeal has ever been made to the British nation. The nation will respond to the call of its leader.' The Liberal paper may have been the *Manchester Guardian*, which remarked of the speech, 'The Premier was impressive, as always.' An 8-line extract from it has been included in the first three editions of the *Oxford Dictionary of Quotations*.

210

[House of Commons]

Thurs 12 Nov 14 5 p.m.

. . . The debate here this afternoon has been decidedly languid & dismal, only relieved by a prolix & rather vicious attack from Walter Long on the War Office, to which Bluey replied in a very thin House with great ability and in excellent style.

. . . I will . . . ask Hankey to-night to bring the elusive and unfaithful 'Boverton' to lunch one day next week.[1] I wonder what impression he will make on you after your long separation. I will close this now, perhaps write later in the evening. Light of life – I love you more than ever.

---

[1] Sir Boverton Redwood, the subject of Asquith's Venetius joke (Letter 81, n. 2), was at this time helping Hankey in the development of oil-based incendiary devices.

211

H of C

Mond 16 Nov 1914 [ii]

My darling – I drove away with rather a heavy heart; I had so counted on your companionship.[1] But it would be the height of ingratitude to fortune not to be thankful for the last 48 hours. Our drive on Sat. I am sure we shall both agree was one to be always remembered; even Canterbury Cathedral had its alleviating moments; and the gloaming as we came back from Rye, & still more our delicious hour before dinner, make Sunday a red-letter day. It is the combination of so many things in which we have joint interests – poetry, figures, names of places, fortunes of persons, the largest issues of policy, fringes and striped dresses, and above & beneath all a real community of thought & purpose in all that matters & counts – it is this (neither more nor less) that is the heart-spring of my life. Take it away, and I say at once with all sincerity 'tired of all these (i.e. the other things) from these would I be gone'.[2]. . .

A rather dreary Cabinet – to which I invited the Assyrian, in the absence of Ll. George, who was kept at Walton Heath by one of those psychological 'chills' which always precede his budgets, when he does not feel altogether certain of his ground. He has a terrible lack of the best sort of courage. . . .

Treasury Bench later: I deferred my éloge of Ld. Roberts[3] till to-morrow, & made a short dry statement about the Vote of Credit. Walter Long followed in a rambling & not particularly vicious speech, and since then the debate has been dull & desultory, and as Sir W. Byles is now on his legs you may judge that we are reaching the dregs.[4]. . . I have now replied on the debate and (6.30) we have got both our votes: £225 millions in money, & 1 million regulars in numbers of men: not a bad performance for $2\frac{1}{2}$ hours is it? . . .

[1] After a weekend during which they had been fellow guests, Venetia had declined, 'out of good nature to Clemmie', to return to London with Asquith.

[2] Tir'd with all these, from these I would be gone.
                    Shakespeare, *Sonnet 66*.

[3] Field Marshal Earl Roberts, V.C., had died on 14 Nov. while visiting the B.E.F.

[4] Aged 75; the radical founder of the *Bradford Observer*.

212

Tues 17 Nov 14 Midnight

My darling – I should not be telling you the truth if I did not say that I was bitterly disappointed this evening. All day I had somehow counted on finding you alone & having a real talk – such as only you & I can have. And there were so many things – apart from what I told you in the last 3 minutes – which I wanted to say to you & ask you about: and they are so fugitive from day to day that if the chance fails, it may never recur. So – though you were as dear as you could be – I went away in a subdued & hungry mood. You are encompassed by such a *zareba*,[1] that one almost despairs of getting anywhere near the inmost shrine. . . .

I *must* see you to-morrow. May I come before dinner? – say at about 6.15? Or shall I find you there once more the centre of a family circle? Things are very difficult – but to me it makes the whole difference to see you – however shortly – *every day*. We have a Cabinet in the morning, & then the House. But I could get away. *Do* try to arrange it – my most blessed & beloved – and send me a lovely message. *All love.* Good night.

[1] A Sudanese word, meaning a stockade of thorn-bushes.

213

H of C

Wed 18 Nov 14

My darling – thank you 1000 times for your sweet little letter. It has been rather a bungle – hasn't it? – through no fault of yours. But *two* days without any real sight of or talk with you brings me very nearly to starvation point. You will & *must* keep an undisturbed hour for me to-morrow. There is *so* much that I have to say to you. And I find that I am very dependent.

So you think of going again to Belcaire for Sunday! If only I could come! But I am booked for Easton Grey. I wonder if you go Friday or Saturday – I hope the latter.

It was dear of you to say what you did about my Roberts speech. Did you recognise the much mangled quotation?[1]

We had a rather dull disconnected Cabinet this morning. The Budget has been so well taken,[2] that I think we shall finish up this part of the Session not later than next Thursday. I wonder what your plans will be after that. I want particularly to have another Alderley Sunday before very long.

I have answered my questions, & am just going back into the House for the debate on the Pensions Committee,[3] which won't last long, and I shall have to 'chew the bitter cud' of thought between 6 & 8. Alas! But the 'inward eye' has its own field of contemplation & delight – thank God. At any rate, I live (at least I hope I shall) till to-morrow evening. We are dining then (Thursday) with the Horners. Are you coming: *do*: I am certain that Frances wd. be delighted, & to me it would make all the difference. Bless you *beloved*.

6.30 I feel *very* solitary

---

[1] Asquith had applied to Roberts what Spenser wrote of Chaucer:
On Fame's eternal beadroll worthy to be filed.
The Faerie Queene, IV, c.ii.xxxii.

[2] 'In its essential principle', *The Times* predicted, 'the Government policy . . . for meeting the cost of the war will . . . be fully endorsed by the country.'

[3] A Select Committee was established to 'consider a scheme' of war pensions and separation allowances.

214

Sat. morning 21 Nov '14.

. . . We never had a more heavenly talk than in the gloaming yesterday. Don't you look back upon it? There are some conditions under wh. it becomes easy to say things wh. under others are difficult or even impossible. It is the great delight & pride of my life that, the more you disclose of your real self, the more worthy I find it of all the love & devotion which I have given & do give to it.

. . . We drove in the cold to the outposts of Jewry at Gunnersbury.[1] The other guests were the Maguires, Edgar Vincent, & Charlie Grant[2] & Lady Sybil.[3] I was very glad to see him (C.G.) & talk with him: he is one of the best brained soldiers we have and as you know has been killed more than once by report. He has been 60 successive days under shell fire: once wounded, but did not go into hospital. Two things struck me very much in his account of things: one, the extraordinary bravery & resource of very small detachments of our men, often commanded by quite inexperienced officers; and the other, the repeated failure of the Germans to push a success. The Prussian Guard the other day had only at the end of the battle to walk over a single thin line of men in the trenches, but they were so demoralised by the terrible losses they had suffered that they turned round & went back. This has happened many times.

. . . I have a very characteristic letter from Raymond, in which he says (not without truth) that 'one good reason for taking such a step is to avoid the necessity for continuing during the rest of one's life to recite the still better reasons wh. prevented one from taking it'. He thinks he will try to get a Commission 'towards the end of this term'.[4] After what you said yesterday, I don't think I shall attempt to dissuade him.

Later. Just got your note, in the midst of a most boring conversation with Charlie Beresford who came to lecture me on the Navy, with all the obvious criticisms about *Cressy Canopus*[5] Antwerp &c, violent attacks on Fisher, Wilson & the old gang ('nothing personal', of course) &c &c. So you are going (as I thought you would) to Belcaire. I feel very jealous of the Assyrian. Perhaps I shall see you Monday? before dinner. Let me know in your letter to-morrow (to Downing St.). I am rather depressed – feeling what is so well said in our Sonnet.[6] Think of me, most beloved.

---

[1] Leopold de Rothschild's house.
[2] Coldstream Guards.
[3] Rosebery's elder daughter.

⁴ Raymond Asquith was commissioned as a 2nd Lt. in the 16th Bn., the London Regiment (the Queen's Westminsters) on 17 Dec. 1914.
⁵ For the loss of the *Cressy* see Letter 166; for the *Canopus* see pp. 307–8 and Letter 202.
⁶ See Letter 211, n. 2.

215

Tu 24 Nov 1914

. . . The whole of the much tried 1ˢᵗ Army Corps is now out of the trenches & is going to have a fortnight's holiday for rest & refit, most of the officers being over here, among them Sir Douglas Haig, whom I mean to see to-morrow. K. thinks there is a real game going on of pull Devil pull Baker between the Kaiser & the General Staff – the former for a further desperate attempt upon Calais, the latter for concentration against the Russian attack.[1] In Egypt, in another week, i.e. by the 30ᵗʰ, we shall have 50,000 troops – including the newly arrived Australians & New Zealanders: quite enough to dispose of any number of Turks. Meanwhile, protectorate (not annexation) will be the order of the day.

Winston is quite pleased with his raid on the Lake of Constance: a hydrogen factory wrecked, 1 Zepp. probably destroyed, and 2 out of the 3 aeroplanes safely back.[2] As we have also bagged a good German submarine – U.18 – charged & rammed by a small armed fishing trawler![3] and Seebrugge was heavily bombarded yesterday by 2 Duncans,[4] the Navy is holding up its head. . . .

[1] Kitchener was right, except that the protagonists were Falkenhayn (for continuing the attack towards Calais) and Hindenburg (for transfer of troops to the Eastern Front). Falkenhayn, who was both War Minister and Commander-in-Chief in the West, had his way during November; and no considerable reinforcements reached Hindenburg until the end of the month. The dispute is analysed in C. R. M. F. Cruttwell, *The Great War* (2nd edn., 1936), pp. 83–5. The reference to 'the Russian attack' is curious, and shows how firmly the theory of 'the Russian steamroller' was held. In fact Hindenburg had launched a great offensive more than a week earlier. After a savage week-long battle the Russians had just saved Lodz and their 2nd Army; but they were to lose the city on 6 Dec.

[2] 3 planes of the Royal Naval Air Force flew from Belfort, dropping 9 bombs on the sheds and factory at Friedrichshafen. The third plane was shot down, the pilot being captured. The sortie was commanded by Noel Pemberton Billing, who sat in the Commons as an Independent, 1916–21.

[3] The U.18 was rammed in Hoxa Sound at one of the entrances to Scapa Flow, and scuttled near the Pentland Skerries.

[4] 'Duncans' were pre-Dreadnought battleships, each carrying 4 12″ guns.

216

. . . Cassel's dinner was of the usual kind – Mrs Greville, Maguires Mrs Astor &c &c. I sat next his daughter-in-law[1] Lady Helen – wife of Violet's ex-admirer; she is rather a tiresome lady with a lot of 'missions', & talked to me of separation allowances with special reference to the problem of un-married wives, and other such topics. I was more interested in Mrs Greville's[2] account of the numerous attempts of Ruggles Brise to get her to marry him (she has about £100,000 a year) before he took up with 'Jessie, Lady Camoys'.[3] Cassel was very complimentary about the success of the loan, which in the circumstances, Stock Exchange shut &c, he regards as miraculous. I fancy the 'over-subscription' did not amount to much, but to be able to get 350 mill. in a week, after borrowing another 90 during the last 3 months, is as good as anyone could wish for. . . . I won 3 guineas at Bridge, which is a large sum for me. Maud Cunard[4] writes to say that she is 'upset' at hearing of Raymond's military ambitions, and demands that I should nip them in the bud 'by perhaps putting him into Parliament at once & making him an Under Secretary at the first opportunity'. Heroic re-medies! She is a wonderfully active woman: only yesterday she sent me 2 boxes of cigars (which made me a little suspicious), and I now find that she has been even more generous to Bongie, with a hint that one Delius (who composes) should have a Knighthood,[5] and that the Treasury should make a grant to the 'Women's Emergency League', which is I believe composed of ex-suffragettes of the Lena Ashwell[6] type. She will be delighted to hear of the Wimborne appointment (if it comes off): for some reason she has been pushing it all she can. 'Maud moves in a mysterious way.'

In the night I was thinking over our talk yesterday about different modes of expression. 'Arry & 'Arriet on Hampstead Heath and Edwin & Angelina[7] in the politer atmosphere of Brixton are probably more articulate, & at any rate more fully intelligible to one another, than Petrarch was to Laura or the Man in the Sonnets to the Dark Lady. As the Apostle says in one of his profounder moods, somewhere in the Corinthians (I see the exact reference is 1 Cor. XIV. 10!) 'there are, it may be, so many different kinds of voices in the world, and none of them is without signification'.[8] But to find the 'voice' which will give the full 'signification' of what one feels most deeply is far from easy. That, as we were saying, is one of the reasons for which poetry was invented. 'He touched a jarring lyre at first, And ever strove to make it true.' That is what I strive to do my darling, and it is my most cherished faith that you have an understanding ear. . . .

¹ Lady Helen was the wife, not of Cassel's son, but of his nephew, Felix.

² Mrs Greville (née McEwan) had inherited a large Scottish brewing fortune, and had been a widow for 6 years. For a lively sketch of her at a later stage see Kenneth Clark, *Another Part of the Wood* (1974), pp. 268–70.

³ Sir Evelyn Ruggles-Brise had been Chairman of the Prison Commission since 1895. He had married the widow of the 4th Lord Camoys on 3 Sept. 1914.

⁴ For whom see Clark op. cit., pp. 216–20.

⁵ Lady Cunard's protégé, Sir Thomas Beecham, was the first English conductor to recognize the importance of Delius's work.

⁶ She was a member of the United Suffragists, a non-militant body, when war broke out. The reference to 'ex-suffragettes' is thus one more example of Asquith's refusal to distinguish, among advocates of women's suffrage, between the violent and the law-abiding. A well-known actress, she was prominent later in the war in organizing concerts for the troops at the front. She gave an account of the Women's Emergency Corps in *Myself a Player* (1936), p. 182. 3 of the 4 founders of the Corps were actresses.

⁷ The conventional names for middle-class lovers in Victorian humorous writing. See W. S. Gilbert's use of these names in *Trial by Jury* (1875).

⁸ Asquith adds 'different' to the verse as it appears in the Authorized Version.

217

The Wharf,
Sutton Courtney,
Berks.

Sat. 28 Nov 1914 [ii] Midnight

. . . MᶜKenna & I had a walk & talk, about persons & particularly about courage (of which, with all his limitations, he is a shining example). I found that we didn't differ much, both marking Ll. George rather low in this respect, & E Grey too *nervy* to be put really high. Are you reading the new Buckle volume of Dizzy's Life?¹ I have not got it yet. He was the only Jew of our time who had real courage – both passive & active – a rare quality in that race. . .

. . . I had the most extraordinary letter to-day from Ldy Aberdeen: I must show it to you on Monday. It is almost incredible. She wants them to stay on till *April*, & then that he shd. be made an *Irish* Duke! with a seat perhaps in the Senate of the Home Rule Parliament. They honestly think that they are the *homme & femme nécessaires*, and that all Ireland (except a few Ulster families) will go into mourning on their departure. I should think there has rarely been a case of such innocent & misguided infatuation. . .

¹ The first 2 volumes of the *Life of Disraeli* published under the auspices of the Beaconsfield Trustees were by W. F. Monypenny. He died in Nov. 1912 as the 2nd appeared; and the biography was completed by G. E. Buckle, who had been Editor of *The Times*, 1884–1912. The 3rd volume to which Asquith refers here covers the years from Peel's fall to the Crimean War. The 6th and last volume appeared in 1920.

'Haldane . . . is violently attacked . . . as a thinly veiled friend of Germany' (Letter 218)

THE newspaper clamour against Haldane was entirely devoid of substance. The army reorganization which he had effected, as Secretary of State for War from 1905 to 1912, had indeed resulted in some reductions in establishment; but its general effect had been to strengthen the army greatly, and to leave Britain in possession, for the first time, of an effective Expeditionary Force.[1] The *Morning Post*, which was attacking him in November over the 'reductions', had in August joined in the press tributes to him as the creator of the B.E.F.[2]

Haldane was bound to attract the Opposition's rancour and to draw their fire. He had succeeded in army reform where the Conservatives had failed; and it had been his boast that his Territorial scheme would put paid to the ideas about conscription with which some Conservatives had toyed before the war.[3] The vulnerability resulting from his admiration for much in German life[4] was increased by his political isolation. The radicals thought of him as a Liberal Imperialist with an unfortunate penchant for agreeing with Balfour. His taste for philosophy did not endear him to the man in the street.

Fixing the label of disloyalty on a prominent member of the Government helped to re-establish the Conservatives as the patriotic party, while leaving the letter of the party truce unbroken. There was no shortage of noble motives for these base attacks. Haldane's 'presence in the Government', L. J. Maxse told J. S. Sandars, 'is an intimation to the world that we are unreliable as an ally, and shall be ready to patch up a peace with Germany at any moment in order to save our "spiritual home"' (for this phrase see Letter 223, n. 3).

Haldane's courage and candour in debate were not always matched by tact. His methods are well illustrated by the remarks which occasioned the *Morning Post* attack mentioned in Letter 218. On 25 November the Lords discussed, on the initiative of some Opposition peers, what Asquith called 'spies and such nonsense' (Letter 218). Lord St Davids asked:

Have the government any information as to the statements that have appeared in the press of neutral countries that the Germans are putting women and children, and men above military age, into concentration camps, or threatening to do so, under the idea that Germans in this country are being maltreated?

Haldane replied:

No doubt some of our subjects who are [the Germans'] prisoners have been lately removed from the great freedom which they enjoyed of roaming about in places like Baden-Baden and other quite agreeable spots, and placed in prisons. That has been done since we took to interning large numbers of aliens here in concentration camps. The Germans are within their rights, and we are within our rights.[5]

Haldane then added a few words about the need for accuracy of statement if exacerbations between belligerents and reprisals were to be avoided, and congratulated Lord St Davids on having spoken more reasonably than on a previous occasion.

The most damaging attacks came, not from the *Morning Post*, but from popular papers. Even these might not have been effective without encouragement from the Conservative leaders. One of the *Daily Express* columnists told Leo Maxse early in February 1915 that he had 'talked at length with Bonar Law, Carson and Long'. He reported them as indicating 'no desire to abandon the campaign against Haldane just as the scent is burning'. Each was, on the contrary, in one way or another 'anxious to be present in Whitehall or St James's Street when the plump body of the Member for Germany swings in the wind between two lamp posts'.[6]

By December 1914 the partisan attacks by Conservative outriders were not confined to Haldane.[7] In view of this, Asquith's continuing detachment about what was happening to his colleague (Letter 234) suggests an excessive sense of security. Maxse's friend on the *Daily Express* regarded 'the downfall of Haldane' as 'life or death' to the Conservative party, and wrote: 'If we do not destroy him there is no reason why the Radical boches should not go on for thirty years.' The *Daily Express* man was exaggerating absurdly, in his usual fashion. But the converse of his proposition would have been uncomfortably near the truth. The failure to defend Haldane did not augur well for the Liberal Government.

[1] See F. Maurice, *Haldane* (1937), i. 377–9. For a contemporary defence of Haldane's reforms see Basil Williams's letter, *Westminster Gazette*, 8 Jan. 1915, 8c. For a recent repetition of the Conservative charges see *The Times*, 9 Nov. 1964, 11e (Earl of Selborne).

[2] Two other Conservative papers, the *Daily Telegraph* (6 Aug., 6f) and the *Pall Mall Gazette* (20 Aug., 5b) were equally complimentary during the first days of the war.

[3] See *The Times*, 30 Nov. 1907, 6c.

[4] Bonar Law had expressed a similar admiration for German literature: *Parl. Deb.* xxxii. 68 (27 Nov. 1911).

[5] *Parl. Deb.*, Lords, xviii. 140, 143.

[6] Stephen Koss, *Haldane* (1969), p. 136.

[7] Northcliffe produced *Scaremongerings* at the end of Nov. 1914 to show how prescient the *Daily Mail* had been about Germany by comparison with prominent Liberals (A. G. Gardiner replied in the *Daily News*, 5 Dec., 6d, e). Leo Maxse produced his *Potsdam Diary* a few weeks later. He included a few embarrassing quotations from Balfour's speeches to show that he 'was not a mere political partisan': Sandars MSS, f. 179.

218

The Wharf,
Sutton Courtney,
Berks.

Sunday morning 29th Nov [14]

. . . I must take this into Oxford to post – otherwise you won't get it before you leave to-morrow. I have just had a late breakfast with Bluey: do you think he will ever experience a flow of real sap along the nerves of his intelligence? The sky is drab & the air full of drizzle & wind: a most uninviting day. There is no news of interest in my pouch except a strong protest from Delcassé against our proposed mission to the Vatican, which he says will lead to a violent demand from the French Catholics for similar action on the part of their Government. This would be condemned by the Chamber, and there would be a regular hurly-burly just when it is most important that they should present a 'united front' &c. There is a good deal of force in this, tho' oddly enough 2 or 3 days ago Cambon expressed strong approval of the mission to Grey, who is I think more wedded to it than I am. Its main object would be to free the Clerical press in Italy & elsewhere from German & Austrian influence. The Pope himself is believed to be friendly to us.[1]

Desperate efforts are being made to find some territorial formula which will bring Bulgaria & Roumania into the fighting line alongside of Servia & Greece. It is not an easy job.[2] Meanwhile E. Grey is taking a Sunday off – he left on Friday, I need not say for Wilsford:[3] and Haldane is in charge for a couple of days of the F.O. Poor old boy! I see he is violently attacked, à propos of spies & such nonsense, by the *Morning Post* as a thinly veiled friend of Germany, who reduced infantry & artillery, and palmed off on us the Territorial sham.

It is a good thing that the fighting Generals – especially French & Haig – are strongly pro-Territorial, and in this last despatch French says some very 'nice' things of them.[4] .

[1] Benedict XV: he had become Pope in Sept. 1914.

[2] It was almost impossible. In the first Balkan War (Oct. 1912–May 1913) the Turks lost most of their European territory to the Balkan countries; in the second (June–Aug. 1913) the Bulgars made an unsuccessful surprise attack on their late allies and were despoiled of their share of the previous winnings. The entry of Turkey into the war freed Britain to seek the help of Greece and Romania, and to promise Turkish territory to Bulgaria. Unfortunately this was a useless promise. Bulgaria's claims on Macedonia, and her need for an Aegean port, entailed gains at the expense, not of Turkey, but of Serbia and Greece. Any move to enlist Greek or Romanian help increased the inducement for Bulgaria to side with Germany.

[3] Pamela Glenconner's house near Amesbury. See Appendix 3.

[4] In his fourth dispatch (London press, 30 Nov.) French wrote that the performance of the

first Territorial Army units to reach the front gave him 'the highest hopes as to the value and help of Territorial troops generally'.

219

Monday 30 Nov 14

. . . I drove up this morning with the Assyrian & Elizth in his car . . . I mean to make him . . . a Privy Councillor on New Year's Day: he has done extraordinarily well. It is a question whether Bluey (who has a lot of good marks) should be similarly honoured.[1] What do you say?

I have told Bongie to put in hand the other thing in which you expressed an interest. . . . There are a lot of things I want to talk to you about to-morrow . . . the re-shifting of persons & places: and some other things that I can't write down. . .

[1] H. T. Baker became a Privy Councillor in June 1915.

220

Fr 4 Dec 1914 Midnight

. . . I sometimes think how much more you wd. think of me, & how much higher you might possibly rate me, if I were not so fond of you. It is rather sad that one shd. suffer in the estimation & judgment that one most prizes, because one loves so much. I am sure it is so. I should probably feel the same if it were the other way about. Providence, or fate, or whatever it is that determines things, won't allow a perfect equipoise. I can only say that I feel no humiliation – nothing but joy and pride – in what you give & allow me. And you must try, with your rare gift of intuition & imagination, to realise my point of view, & not to brush it aside. . . .

. . . Kitchener, who spent the best part of an hour with me this morning, rather deprecates these frequent visits of W. to the front: the Army think that he mingles too much in military matters, & the Navy that he is too much away in what may be critical moments for them. I am so far disposed to agree that I think, after this, I shan't allow him to go again for a long time.[1]

I must now go to bed. If you were to fail me – I know you won't – I should go down – 'deeper than ever plummet sounded'[2]. . . .

[1] Churchill was flattered by French and his staff, probably in the hope that he would act as a counterweight to Kitchener. Thus on 2 Sept. French talked to F. E. Guest, his A.D.C. and one

of Churchill's cousins, about Kitchener's visit to Paris. Guest was left to convey these thoughts *'privately* to whomsoever in the government I may think fit. As you are the only soldier,' he told Churchill, 'I write to you.' By forming the Naval Division Churchill had given the impression that he meant, in Asquith's words, 'to run a war of his own'. The First Lord's absences from the Admiralty had aroused much critical exaggeration. 'If Winston stayed all day and every day at the Admiralty,' Fisher had told Rosebery on 10 Oct., 'things would be better; but every Friday to Tuesday he is at the war.'

² Shakespeare, *The Tempest*, III. iii.

221

Sat morning Dec 5th 14[i]

. . . We have a very curiously assorted party at the Wharf – the last time we shall be there this year. J. M., Harry Cust & Mrs Keppel, with Clemmie thrown in, and possibly Viola on Sunday – looks like rather a strange *mélange*, and not perhaps particularly restful. I thought Cynthia in good looks last night: Beb is by way of joining his comrades in arms to-day, if he succeeds in finding the way.¹ Cys informed us that he had been rebuking one of his squad for unpunctuality, & that he 'gave the fellow Hell'. Raymond will no doubt be equally strict in repressing coarse or profane language in the ranks of Winston's 'New Model'². . . .

. . . One ought not perhaps to be surprised at anything . . . when a cool-headed man like Hankey came to me yesterday & proposed the immediate arrest of the 25,000 or so German & Austrian subjects still at large in London (including thousands of Poles, Slovaks, Slovenes &c &c who hate their rulers worse than poison) for fear that they may perchance be organising a campaign of sabotage! I gave him a rather curt 'No',³ & diverted the conversation in the direction of Greek fire.⁴ You will be interested (& perhaps a little anxious) to learn that he and Venetius are to-day conducting their great experiment on a remote river somewhere in the Essex flats.

I had a momentary panic after you left yesterday as to whether you had got that telegram safe in your little bag. . . .

¹ Asquith's second son, Herbert, was absent-minded (and a poet).

² Asquith makes play with the moral strictness which prevailed in Cromwell's New Model Army. Having decided to take a commission, Raymond no doubt hoped to serve with one of his brothers. In the event he joined Cyril in the Queen's Westminsters, not Arthur in 'Winston's "New Model"' (the Naval Division).

³ The decision to intern Germans of military age had been taken on 20 Oct. For Hankey's retrospective conclusion that security had been threatened far more by 'society gossip' than by the presence of aliens see p. 419.

⁴ Hankey's experiments for incendiary devices to be used against harbours and shipping.

222

The Wharf,
Sutton Courtney,
Berks.

Sat 5 Dec 1914. [ii] Midnight

W[inston] was . . . crossing to-night to see French. . . . His volatile
mind is at present set on Turkey & Bulgaria, & he wants to organise a heroic
adventure against Gallipoli and the Dardanelles: to wh. I am altogether
opposed[1]. . .

[1] For the preliminary bombardment of the outer forts at the Dardanelles see Letter 202. At
the first meeting of the War Council (p. 184) on 25 Nov. Churchill 'suggested that the ideal
method of defending Egypt was by an attack on the Gallipoli Peninsula'. The destruction of
von Spee's squadron meant that the navy could increase its strength in the Mediterranean. At
this stage, however, Churchill thought such an attack 'a very difficult operation requiring a
large [military] force'. The troops needed for it could not be found. The Greeks would not
supply them, for fear of an attack from Bulgaria. Kitchener said that 'time was required for the
organization of the considerable military forces . . . in Egypt'. For the Turkish attempt to
invade Egypt across the Suez Canal see Letter 288.

223

The Wharf,
Sutton Courtney,
Berks.

[Sunday 6 Dec 1914]

Darling – after all I found quite a good thing in Buckle's Dizzy – the
description by D. of Crewe's father Lord Houghton, who figures in *Tancred*
as Mr Vavasour.[1] It is malignant and life-like: I just remember the old
scoundrel when in his declining years he used to read his Poems aloud in the
drawing rooms of country houses[2]. . . .

[John Morley] had been lunching with Haldane & is painfully struck
with his look of age & illness: also with the fervour with which he declared
his dislike of being on bad terms with Germany – his 'spiritual home', as
Prof. Oncken declares that he called it 2 or 3 years ago.[3] It is not that he is
half-hearted about the war, but that he feels as if he was called upon to fight
to the death his own Kith & Kin. . . .

[1] Buckle devoted Ch. 2 of Book III in the *Life* to a description of Disraeli's novel *Tancred*,
which was published in 1847. When *Coningsby* had appeared in 1844 Monckton Milnes (later
Lord Houghton), who had played a minor part in the Young England group, complained that
no portrait of him had been included. By 1847 Disraeli had good reason to portray Milnes's

foibles in the description of Mr Vavasour. In the breakup of the Conservative party which followed Peel's repeal of the Corn Laws, Milnes abandoned Peel, but announced that it was 'impossible' for him to be led by Disraeli. He joined the Whigs and was raised to the peerage in 1863 by Palmerston.

² In 1874 Asquith spent some months in the Earl of Portsmouth's country houses, Hurstbourne (Hampshire) and Eggesford (North Devon), coaching the Earl's eldest son. The readings by Lord Houghton, who was one of the Portsmouths' guests, took place on Sunday evenings, when no games were allowed.

³ Hermann Oncken, who was a history professor at the University of Heidelberg, published an article saying that he had met Haldane in 1913, and that at the end of the evening Haldane had remarked: 'Germany is my spiritual home.' A correspondence had apparently followed, Haldane writing: 'I owe your country a deep personal debt.' This was all reported in *The Times* on 2 Dec.

224

Tues midnight 8 Dec 1914

My darling – I won't go back on our talk this evening, because I think it was quite perfect, & I want to remember it as it was, without addition or subtraction.

Gosse's dinner . . . was quite a success. We had 2 poets – H. Newbolt & L. Abercrombie[1] – Ld. Parmoor (late Cripps), Harold Cox (editor of the Edinburgh Review), Sir W. McCormick (a rather dim Scotch educationalist) & best of all Henry James . . . They were all very nice to me, and (strangely enough) my sub-conscious self was most of the time a million miles away . . . It is a great thing to get now & again a really big perspective. I can see you smile, & say to yourself The poor man! whom mankind thinks sane & strong, has a touch of phantasy, & 'moves about in worlds not realised'! Perhaps! Anyhow – I hug my chains, if chains they are, and bless what you regard as my impotence. . . . It is almost impossible to continue to look *up to*, and very difficult not to be tempted to look *down upon*, a person whose habitual attitude to one's self is that of unqualified devotion.

I fear alas! that I may not see you until Thursday. 'On the bald street breaks the blank day.'[2] I love you.

¹ This was an annual event. Henry Newbolt's verse had been well known since the publication of *Admirals All* in 1897: Lascelles Abercrombie was already admired as a leading poet of the younger generation.

² Tennyson, 'In Memoriam', vii.

225

Fr. aft. 18 Dec '14[1] [i]

. . . I wrote to Winston as we agreed adding what you suggested about the possibility of concerting naval & military action here at home.[2] He has just been to see me, very sore & angry with K, upon whom he poured a kettle-full of opprobrious epithets.[3] Of course he acquiesced in the decision, and will not now go to Dunkirk till to-morrow, if even he goes then. . . .

. . . I am disposed to think & have told Kitchener so, that it mt. be a good thing if Sir J. were to come here for a couple of days, & talk over things & the future with us. What do you say? It is such a joy & help to discuss things with you, & now you are gone! & the damnable 'shades of the prison-house' blot the whole prospect.[4] My darling – *how* could you? . . .

[1] For the period 8–16 Dec. no letters have survived. Asquith was at Alderley for the weekend 12–13 Dec. As Venetia seems to have been in London the rest of the time he presumably met her often during those eight days.

[2] Asquith wrote: 'After talking with Kitchener . . . I am clearly of opinion that you should not . . . attempt to see French. These meetings have in K's opinion already produced profound friction between French and himself, and between French's staff and his staff. . . . Questions of concerted naval and military action can be best discussed and arranged here.'

[3] Churchill wrote to Kitchener about the objections made to the proposed visit: 'It was not necessary to trouble the Prime Minister; and some of the statements you appear to have made to him are not well founded, and should certainly in the first instance have been made to me.'

[4] Wordsworth, 'Ode. Intimations of Immortality', iv. Venetia was due to start as a trainee nurse at the London Hospital on 6 Jan. See p. 351.

226

Friday midnight 18 Dec 1914 [ii]

. . . Pamela declares that Bonar Law's brother & partner[1] in Glasgow has been caught 'trading with the enemy', & is now only allowed out on bail for £5000 – an amusing development.[2] She (P) thinks it very rash of me to go to Walmer, where I may be bombarded! Sometimes I think that an opportune shell might solve many problems: with some of which you are not remotely connected. By the way she cross-examined me rather closely as to what dress you wore last night! I tried my best, but I am, as you know, a fumbler in these matters: I could only give a vague impression of colours & distinction! . . .

[1] Mrs McKenna was inaccurate on Bonar Law's position. He was not then a partner in William Jacks and Co., though he used the firm as his deposit bankers.

[2] In the end John Law was not prosecuted. Two other partners were convicted of trading

with the enemy and received brief terms of imprisonment . See Blake, *The Unknown Prime Minister* (1955), pp. 257–60. See also Letter 307, text and n. 4.

227

Sat mg 19 Dec 14 [i]

. . . I have heard & seen nothing so far this morning of either of my stormy petrels – K & Winston, and I hope I shall make good my escape before either is well on the wing. . . .

. . . As the inevitable visit from K has now taken place I thought you wd. like to hear about it. W. seems to have sent him a pretty abusive letter last night, complaining of his speaking to me &c – a rather childish performance. K declares that he returned a 'soft answer'.[1] Meanwhile for his own amusement, & the enlightenment of posterity, he (K) has been drawing up an imaginary account of how he secretly induced or bullied Jellicoe into taking 300 War Office steamers & stowing them away off the S.W. coast of Ireland. In order to keep French's visit a secret we have arranged that K. shd. meet him at Dover or Folkestone to-morrow morning, motor him to Broome, and after they have confabulated there bring him over to me at Walmer,[2] where if necessary I can put him up for the night, & he can be shipped off back to France next morning. What a pity you are not to be at Walmer!

I now hear that Winston is on his way over here: so I won't finally seal this up. Thank God he is not coming – after all. Just off with V. *All* love.

[1] See Letter 225, n. 3. Kitchener drafted an answer which was not especially soft (*Churchill: Companion Docs., 1914–1916*, pp. 313–14). He showed it to the Prime Minister, who advised him not to send it, and promised to speak to Churchill himself.
[2] See Appendix 3 for Broome and Walmer.

228

Walmer Castle,
Kent.

Sat midnight 19 Dec 14 [ii]

My darling – this is a real nest. If only you were here!. . . . V & I, as expert Cuckoos,[1] have been appraising the possibilities of the place, & pronounce it very good. Charming bedrooms with strange alcoves & recesses, an abundant supply of bathrooms, electric light everywhere, & mezzotints of past Lord Wardens, & charts of the Downs, on all the walls.[2]. . .

¹ Asquith referred to his extended experience of occupying houses lent to him.
² Before Lord Beauchamp was appointed Lord Warden of the Cinque Ports Asquith had declined the honour, when advised what it would cost him to maintain Walmer and its grounds. Beachamp had now lent Asquith the Castle as a weekend retreat.

229

Walmer Castle,
Kent.

Sunday 20 Dec 1914 [i]

. . . *3.30 p.m.* The Great Men¹ have come & gone: it was really most interesting, and all the time I *longed* for you to be here. They arrived – each with his familiar² – from Folkestone about noon, & I turned them into a room to talk together for about ½ an hour, and then joined them.

I found K, with his chart of Russian & German divisions, emphasising the pessimist point of view. French, on the other hand, will have none of it. He is quite convinced that the Germans have lost all their best troops & officers, and is satisfied that even if they were able to polish off the Russians and push them beyond the Vistula to the Bug (which he believes to be impossible), no troops that they could bring from the East to the West could ever get thro' the English & French lines. He says that the troops they now bring to the front are of the worst quality, & are only forced into action by 'battle police' armed with revolvers.³ On the other hand he thinks our Army better than it has ever been, and the French (tho' not so good as Germans) very well led & generalled.

After K had returned he admitted that they (the F) are disappointing & untrustworthy allies – rarely turning up at the time & in the place they promised: even this week his whole aggressive movement was spoiled because the French sent only 1 Army Corps to his support, instead of the 2 which they had engaged to send.⁴ He says further that they have absolutely vetoed our proposal that he shd. go to the extreme left, & co-operate with the Belgians & our fleet. The Belges were most anxious to work directly with us, but the French sent them a special mission to remind them that *they* (the French) were *their* hosts & paymasters, and expected them always to obey their orders. What allies!

I spoke very frankly to Sir J. F. about Winston's visits, & his intervention in military matters. I found that he was substantially of the same opinion, & with all his affection & admiration for W, estimates his judgment as 'highly erratic'. He & I alone went over the whole ground together, with the result that I am somewhat relieved. If the French cd. only be depended upon, we should be able to repose in more or less confidence. The 2 F.M's are an extraordinarily disparate couple, and not born or moulded to work easily together. Physically, F. is only about 2/3 of K in stature; but he has a really attractive face & manner; while K (as Violet has just remarked) has a face whose network of bloodshot veins reminds one of the 'railways in Silesia', and a kind of barking cynical laugh which instinctively puts you off. I like them both, & each has his special uses; but F. is undoubtedly far more *attrayant.* He looks younger than he did, and was really *émotionné* when I told him, in the simplest words, how admirably he had justified all our confidence.

'Sir Edgar'[5] was a strange figure sitting between the two!

By the way, F. confided to Violet that one of the reasons why he must go to London this afternoon, was that he has a lot of alien *teeth* wh., under the stress of the campaign, have come in need of repair!. . .

[1] Kitchener and French. They motored to London together by way of Broome. 'This was the last', French wrote later, 'of all the many days of happy personal intercourse which I spent with my old South African chief. As a soldier and a commander in the field I had always loved and venerated him; in his capacity as a politician and minister my . . . feelings towards him were never the same.' French's visit was supposed to be a secret and Violet Asquith, when referring to it in a letter, took the somewhat inadequate precaution of writing his name in Greek characters. According to Esher it soon became 'like most secrets throughout the war, . . . the talk of the town': *The Tragedy of Lord Kitchener* (1921), p. 76.

[2] Lt.-Col. O. A. G. Fitzgerald was Kitchener's Personal Military Secretary, Lt.-Col. B. J. H. Fitzgerald one of French's A.D.C.s.

[3] The H.Q. staff of the B.E.F. were still greatly over-impressed by the poor quality of some German divisions first encountered at Ypres: see Letter 188, n. 2. They do not appear to have taken sufficiently into account, first, that this did not apply to more than a small proportion of the German troops on the Western Front; secondly, that, on their own side, the Territorial and Kitchener units now forthcoming could hardly be expected to equal the regulars of the original B.E.F.; and, thirdly, that no troops, whether German, French, or British, could retain after months of fighting the *élan* shown in the August battles. It is very doubtful whether the optimism of G.H.Q. was shared by the front-line troops. A captain in the Coldstream Guards told Hobhouse early in Feb. 1915 that 'Sir John French . . . never, not even at the battle of Ypres, came anywhere really near the firing line'. During the earliest weeks of the fighting the men at the front had been more confident than G.H.Q.: now the position was reversed.

On 10 Dec. 1916 Asquith wrote to Hilda Harrisson:

I am writing in the little room where two years ago one Sunday Kitchener and French visited me and had a battle royal which I had to compose: *H.H.A.: Letters to a Friend* (2 vols., 1933–4), i. 13.

[4] For the engagements to which French refers here see his account in *1914*, pp. 320–26.
[5] Asquith adds the inverted commas because Vincent was by now Lord D'Abernon.

n Montagu

Winston Churchill, 1914

rew Bonar Law, arriving for the Blenheim Meeting, July 1912

Penrhos, Anglesey, about 1914

Walmer Castle: the Drawing Room, 1919

230

Walmer Castle,
Kent.

Sunday midnight 20 Dec 1914 [ii]

. . . Like all our returned warriors, [Sir John French] looks younger than when he went out, & in the best of condition. . . .

A *private* thing that was exercising F. was an idea he had got to replace Gen. Murray, who has been the Chief of his Staff since the beginning of the war, by that poisonous tho' clever ruffian Wilson who (as you remember) behaved so badly at the W.O. this spring about Ulster &c. I am glad to say that after a little talk he quite dropped it, and Murray (who is an excellent tho' slightly jumpy man) will go on.[1] F thinks (*Secret*) the German soldier – not individually but collectively – better than the French: but the French Generals better than the German.

I gave him a full account of the French political & financial situation (wh. I thought he ought to know – don't you?) and it opened his eyes to a lot of movements wh. had hitherto been obscure.

Poor young Hardinge – the Viceroy's son – who was not very badly wounded & seemed to be convalescent – died at Folkestone yesterday. It was *tetanus* – the same thing that killed Col. Cook of the 1st Life Guards. K. (who showed some feeling about it) was very strong that these unnecessary deaths are due to failure to inoculate within 24 hours after the wound: & F. agreed.[2]

One incidental thing to-day that wd. have amused you (why, again I ask, why were you not here?) was K. at luncheon, looking round on the Beauchamp Nouveau art pottery & undistinguished furniture, at last fixing his wall eye on Mr Pitt's chair (a delightful Georgian seat on wh. you straddle looking the wrong way to the book behind you[3]) & at once instructing his familiar (Fitz) to send a carpenter & have it copied for Broome!

Edgar thinks this the nicest house in England, & is keen that we shd. retrieve it. The only practical way of doing so is to send Beauchamp as Gov. Genl to India, and reclaim the Wardenship.[4] What do you say to that?

By the way your member E. Griffith came to me yesterday to say that he had resolved to go back to the Bar.[5] So the Under Secyship at the Home Office will be vacant. Whom am I to appoint? Good night my sweetest & best. I will finish this to-morrow. All my love.

[1] Murray, who had been dangerously wounded in the Boer War, was replaced as French's Chief of Staff early in 1915 by Robertson (for whom see Letter 238).
[2] Tetanus inoculations were already having a dramatic effect. During the first two months

of the war over 8 in a thousand of British wounded developed tetanus; by Jan. 1915 this had
fallen to 0.2 per thousand: Official History, *Medical Services, Surgery*, i (1922), 151–3.
  [3] It is still displayed in Walmer Castle.
  [4] This suggestion became one of Asquith's 'long-running' jokes.
  [5] Ellis Griffith sat for Anglesey.

231

Monday 21 Dec 14

St. Thomas's Day (I am sure you didn't know that!)

. . . I thought Winston's letter about the 'Scarborough baby-killers', wh.
I read in the train rather banal; a lot of cheapish rhetoric & an undertone of
angry snarl![1] He appeared here in person soon after I arrived, and told me he
had had an effusive reconciliation with K. It was all a 'quite trumpery
misunderstanding' &c. He is going this afternoon to see French, who has
dug himself in for the moment in his old lair at Lancaster Gate.[2] . . .

Lady Randolph came to lunch: she is tactless tho' not *au fond* ill-natured.
She told us that Olive Guthrie (who must be well on the road to 50) is going
to marry young Stirling, who you may remember divorced his Gaiety wife,
now Lady George Cholmondeley.

I hope you won't exclude Jan 2nd at Walmer from the sphere of possibility, or even probability. There is no difficulty about room. And it would be
so delicious to spend 48 hours together in new & nice surroundings, before
you 'shut the gates of mercy'[3] and entrench yourself in that horrible
East-end. Again I say, how *could* you? I am still not without hope that,
somehow or other, you will be set free by the veto of Providence. . . .

French pressed me *strongly* to go out for 2 or 3 days: he says the troops
wd. like it. Perhaps I shall – if & when you are immured![4] . . . Suppose you
had gone to India! The War is at any rate to be praised for having put a stop
to *that*.

I am writing in the Cabinet Room, at the beginning of twilight, and thro'
the opposite window across the Parade I see the Admiralty flag flying, and
the lights 'beginning to twinkle' from the rooms where Winston and his two
familiars (Eddie and Masterton) are beating out their plans. . . .

I have been looking thro' the Foreign Office telegrams to see if there is
anything of interest to tell you. But I can find nothing worth repeating,
except that there seems to be some solid reason for thinking that Austria
wd. like to make peace on her own account.[5] . . .

¹ The commander of the German High Seas Fleet decided to make a foray while Jellicoe still lacked the 2 battle-cruisers detached to deal with von Spee. Between 8 and 9.15 a.m. on 16 Dec. German battle-cruisers bombarded Scarborough, Hartlepool, and Whitby, killing 133 civilians and wounding 360. As Scarborough and Whitby were undefended towns bombarding them contravened Art. 1 of the 9th Convention on the Rules of War signed at the 1907 Hague Conference. The bombardment covered a minelaying operation off Filey, and was intended to lure part of the British Grand Fleet on to the newly laid mines; the whole German High Seas Fleet was meanwhile to lie in wait in the North Sea. Though both sides took enormous risks there was, in the event, little contact between the fleets. The main German fleet turned for home before dawn; and the battle-cruisers slipped past the British squadrons in deteriorating visibility, and with the help of a misunderstanding between Beatty and Goodenough. Churchill's letter to the Mayor of Scarborough was written for publication in the press. Asquith's opinion of it was echoed among naval officers, one senior admiral thinking it 'un-English' and 'undignified for the head of the Navy': Marder, ii. 149.

² He shared No. 94 with an American, George Gordon Moore: see Letter 239.

³ Gray's *Elegy*:

> Forbad to wade through slaughter to a throne
> And shut the gates of mercy on mankind.

⁴ Asquith did not go to the Front until 30 May 1915.

⁵ While the old Emperor lived Austrian peace overtures were foredoomed. He would make peace only in concert with Germany and provided that Austria-Hungary suffered no serious territorial losses. He died on 21 Nov. 1916.

232

Tu 22 Dec 1914 3 p.m.

. . . The first of these [four new armies] will be ready in March & the others will follow in quick succession. As you see, they will each be about 150,000, or 600,000 in all: which with the first two already in front will make a total of 900,000.

Then after an interval comes the 7th (Ulstermen, Canadians, Naval Division &c): to be followed in due course by the 8th & 9th: a further 450,000. They will be each (when it goes out) fully equipped: the only substantial change being that the Artillery will be reduced from 6 to 4 guns a battery: wh. means for each Army 48 instead of 52 guns [*sic*]. There! you now know everything that is to be known: of course as *Secret* as can be.

We discussed at length the Russian situation in Poland, & (what is really dependent upon it) French's proposed move to the extreme left flank & the coast.

K. presented the most gloomy view of the Russian position (quite rightly) in what I described as a spirit of the 'most sanguine pessimism'. (By the way W. said to me yesterday à propos of French 'What a good thing it is to have an Optimist at the front', to which I rejoined 'Excellent, provided you have also (as we have in K) a Pessimist in the rear'. Don't you think that is true?)

According to K's estimate, if the Russians lost Warsaw (wh. seems not improbable, with their defective supplies)[1] the Germans might bring back 40 Divisions (i.e. about 800,000 men) to reinforce the attack on the West. I believe (& so I think in his heart does K) that this is an almost ridiculous over-estimate: and of course we did not disclose to our colleagues what French told us on Sunday of the inferior fighting quality of the newer German troops. On the other hand, we & the French have now 20 rounds a gun compared with the Russian $3\frac{1}{2}$,[2] & no one knows what is the corresponding figure for the Germans.

We agreed that, with all these facts & estimates on the table, Joffre & French shd. have an immediate conference as to the best strategy for us in the West during these next 2 or 3 weeks, while the Polish situation is still undecided, and that there ought to be a joint consultation of the 3 Allies as to the best way in which they can concert together for increasing the supplies of necessary ammunition during the next 3 months. There is no doubt that the French have the best available means of production. . . .

. . . The following 'aphorism' occurred to me in the watches of the night: 'In almost every form of human pursuit, the *quest* is more enjoyable than the *quarry*.'[3] It is certainly true (as I have often had occasion to see) in the case of wealth, power, fame. . . .

[1] Warsaw did not fall until 4 Aug. 1915.

[2] At the height of the November campaign the Russian armies are said to have used 45,000 shells a day, when the country's monthly production was only 35,000. The guns of a Russian infantry division had been reduced from 48 to 36. See also Letter 241, n. 6.

[3] Asquith evidently became fond of this *mot*: Margot quoted it in her novel, *Octavia* (1928), p. 83.

233

Wed 23 Dec 1914

. . . One of the Americans – a journalist called Slidell – was fresh from Cracow, & has seen a lot of the fighting in Poland. He says the Hungarians are the worst fighters in Europe, & the Austrians not much better: he is quite convinced that the Germans & Austrians will be killed by the winter. The ground is already so hard that no trenches can be dug,[1] and there is an incessant & pitiless wind wh. blows the snow in sheets; when a man drops wounded he is as good as dead: he is at once half buried in snow, there are no ambulances or doctors, and in the course of a few hours the poor devil, or what remains of him, is devoured by wolves. Nice sort of conditions, aren't they? He is quite convinced that the Russians must more than hold their own. . . .

. . . Maud Cunard brought me a beautiful old copy of Catullus, Tibullus &c, with a small Homer from Nancy. I wonder if this is a thank offering for the Wimborne coup,[2] or a propitiatory gift in the interest of Delius. What do you think? (I hear her nasal accents at this moment in the next room, exhorting or threatening or wheedling poor Bongie. She is quite undefeatable.)

By the way Birrell tells me that the new Lord Lieutenant came to see him in a very sanguine frame of mind. B. warned him that he was not the least likely to see Dillon & Redmond & Devlin with their 'feet under his mahogany' at the Viceregal Lodge, and 'quaffing his mellow wines'. It will take a long time, and a large expenditure of both cash & charm, to overcome inveterate Irish habits. . . .

[1] The Russians had entrenched themselves behind barbed wire in the defences of Warsaw. Ludendorff found that the German armies in the East had the greatest dislike for trench warfare.
[2] The decision to appoint Lord Wimborne as Lord-Lieutenant of Ireland had been made, though it was not announced until 4 Jan., and did not come into effect until 17 Feb. 1915.

234

Thur. 24 Dec '14

My darling – I am certainly not going to be 'put off' (as you call it) by your letters. Why should I? They tell me exactly what I want to know of your life day by day. It may be that I should like sometimes to know a little more of what goes on within, but I think you agreed not long since that in these matters I am not 'exacting'. So I don't ask many questions, or (except perhaps now & then) make appeals. You know (too well) what I feel.

You will be amused at the result of Maud Cunard's mission to buy me a Xmas present, for wh. she had apparently received *carte blanche* from Alice Wimborne. She asked me at lunch whether I would like a 'nice' Petronius or Apuleius, and she evidently went off post haste to Quaritch (the most expensive bookseller in the world). For by tea time there appeared a wonderful copy – in a beautiful old red French binding – of Apuleius' *Golden Ass*, printed at Vicenza in 1488! and once, as the book plate shows, in the Sunderland library at Blenheim. The title page is missing (otherwise it would be priceless) but it is in beautiful condition, and must be one of the earliest specimens of Italian printing. And inside (to keep up appearances) a little slip 'with very best wishes & love from A.W.'. . . .

. . . I was rather disappointed to-day by receiving Ld. E. Talbot's[1] refusal of my offer of Privy Councillorship. It destroys the symmetry of the list wh. wd. have included him (Tory) Illingworth (Lib) Henderson (Lab), with the weighty figure of the Assyrian to tip the balance. We can't think of anybody else whose name wd. produce the same effect. Can you? There is still plenty of time.

Why should Beauchamp's High Churchism unfit him for Viceroy of India? Ripon was a full blown Papist who took with him a father Confessor, and the whole bag of tricks. Do you think an 'Ebrew Jew' better qualified religiously than an Anglo-Catholic?[2]. . .

Thank you for your suggestions as to the succession to E. Griffith. I talked to McKenna (who dined here last night without Pamela, kept at home by headache) and he at once plumped for Harry Verney.[3] I notice that he i.e. H.V. is rapidly becoming what (in a rather higher sphere) the Impeccable used to be – the *homme nécessaire*. For the other day when we were discussing the possibility of a vacancy in the Chief Whip-ship, his was the first & almost the only name suggested. How do you account for this?

I am *so* glad the neuralgia has gone.

. . . W. has now got down in the South & within hailing distance an Admiral after his own heart – Lewis Bayly, who has taken the place of Burney sent North to join Jellicoe. Both are quite good officers, but, as W. expresses it, Burney belongs to the 'No' & Bayly to the 'Yes' school.[4] So W. is now meditating fearsome plans of a highly aggressive kind to replace the present policy of masterly inactivity. The two old sea-dogs at the Admiralty are both of the forward school, and I expect the whole Navy is a little dispirited & chafing under the sense of ill-luck and impatience at purely negative results.[5]

Haldane has just been over to consult me: he is in charge of the Foreign Office while Grey is away for his first holiday: what a thrill of horror would go through our yellow press if this were known![6]. . .

. . . Haldane who looks after the sentences of Court Martials, in relief of K, tells me (this is of course *very private*) that there have been quite a number of cases lately of privates being tried & sentenced for mutilating their left hands, so as to make them incapable of handling a rifle. I knew this had happened with the Indians; that it shd have spread to our men shows what a shattering thing the trenches must be. . . .

---

[1] Conservative Chief Whip.

[2] The Marquess of Ripon was Viceroy of India, 1880–84. He had become a Roman Catholic in 1871. The Jewish candidate under discussion was probably Edwin Montagu, for whose Viceroyalty ambitions see Letters 260, 274, and 337.

[3] Verney, who was 33, had become Parliamentary Secretary to the Board of Agriculture on the outbreak of war. He stayed in that post.

[4] It proved an unfortunate appointment. Vice-Adm. Bayly refused the destroyer escort

which he was offered when exercising his squadron near Portland; and at 2.30 a.m. on 1 Jan. the *Formidable* was torpedoed by a submarine off Start Point. The squadron had been steaming at 10 knots on a straight course in moonlight, and near the Start Light. 35 officers and 512 men were lost with this pre-Dreadnought battleship. Bayly was removed from command; but no other action was taken in his case, because, in Churchill's words, 'to terrorize Admirals for losing ships is to make sure of losing wars'.

⁵ For the importance of these 'negative results' see p. 308.

⁶ On 3 Dec. a correspondent to the *Daily Express* had protested against Haldane's presence in the Foreign Office. In a statement on 30 Dec. about the American Note on the Blockade the Press Bureau revealed that Haldane was again in charge there.

235

Easton Grey,
Malmesbury.

Xmas Day 1914

. . . I have just seen a letter from poor little Diana Wyndham to Lucy from Boulogne: she says – 'last Xmas seems like some wonderful dream, but thank God I dreamt it, & that it was true' . . .

I received this morning a very *secret* telegram from Spring Rice at Washington: he is convinced that both the German & Austrian Ambassadors there are working for peace. The only person they communicate with is the President. I gather that he thinks that the Germans would gladly agree to evacuate Belgium & give full compensation,[1] and securities against future attack. This of course wd. not be enough either for France or for Russia – nor for us[2] – but it is significant as showing how the wind is blowing. Don't say anything. Springy adds that 'meanwhile there is not the least diminution in the Anti-English ferocity of the German agents here'. . . .

As your last letter was written on Tuesday, I feel rather at sea. There are so many questions, that one poses to one's self, but does not ask; so many 'hopes that are too much like despair'; so many dreams that one knows to be 'insubstantial pageants'; so many things that are left unsaid, for fear that they might be spoilt in the saying.

Do you know Pascal's 'I know that, whatever happens, I shall die alone'. In a sense we all live *alone* too. How much of your real & inner life there is that you share with nobody. I share most of mine with you – more than I ever have with anybody – and there is nothing I would not share. . . .

[1] The German scheme was to buy the Belgian Congo at three or four times its value.

[2] 'It was the old problem which had been presented a hundred years before by revolutionary France and which was to be presented later by communist Russia. What is the good of making treaties with a country which, because of its political philosophy, regards itself as free to break them?': A. J. P. Taylor, *The Struggle for Mastery in Europe* (1954), pp. 535–6.

236

Easton Grey,
Malmesbury.

Sat 26 Dec. 1914

. . . As for Italy, the Russian attaché there says that she cannot take an 'active part' in the war before beginning of *March*, when all her artillery will be refurbished & in apple pie order, with 2,400 shells per gun (rather a contrast to what we heard of the Russian supply!).

You will see that they have begun dropping bombs on the coast of Kent. We ought to make quite a good target at Walmer.

One of the false reputations of the war threatens to fall to the luck of Admiral Sturdee. He had to be hustled away with his ship from Devonport, & if he had loitered there, as he wished, he wd. have been from 12 to 24 hours too late to encounter the Germans at the Falklands.[1] He certainly ought to have chased & caught the *Dresden*, wh. is now at large, no one knows exactly where.[2] And he seems, from to-day's papers, to have made a singularly foolish speech when he was fêted for his great achievements at Monte Video, extolling the unappreciated prescience of Lord Roberts, and deploring the folly of English merchants who for 'economic reasons' used to take Germans in to their employ. The authorities should (in Prior's phrase) 'clap a padlock'[3] on the tongues of all fighting men – whether Generals or Admirals.[4]

Death having opportunely removed Sir John Barker of Kensington – Lloyd George & Illingworth's candidate – I am going to make Ld. Hampden Lord Lieutenant of Herts.

Aren't you amused at the electoral experiences of poor Masterman? He goes literally from pillar to post, and despite all that Lloyd George can do in the way both of cajolery & menace, the Welsh won't look at him.[5] I doubt his ever finding a seat in this Parlt. I like the question put to him by one of the little MᶜKennae: 'Have you yet found any of those seats you lost?'

We have been talking just now of curious cases of sudden madness. . . . The Assyrian declares he has a constituent whose wife went mad after hearing Crewe speak for an hour & a half on the land question in the Corn Exchange at Royston! . . .

[1] For the British victory at the Falkland Islands see Letter 202, n. 2. If Sturdee 'had been allowed to pack all the shirts he wanted to take', Masterton Smith wrote to Fisher in Oct. 1919, he 'would have been looking for von Spee still': A. J. Marder (ed.), *Fear God and Dread Nought*, iii (1959), 598. The worst 'loitering' at Devonport had been performed not by Sturdee, however, but by the Admiral Superintendent there. He reported that the *Invincible* could not sail until 13 Nov. and was told by Fisher that she and the *Inflexible* must sail two days before that. They did so, the *Invincible* with a number of skilled workmen aboard.

[2] An Admiralty message told Sturdee on 13 Dec. that the *Dresden* was at Punta Arenas in the Straits of Magellan; but she escaped from there before Sturdee's cruisers arrived. Fisher's statements about Sturdee's 'criminal ineptitude' in allowing the *Dresden* to escape should be heavily discounted: Marder, ii.125–6.

[3] Be to her virtues very kind;
   Be to her faults a little blind;
   Let all her ways be unconfin'd;
   And clap your padlock – on her mind.

   Matthew Prior, 'An English Padlock'.

[4] Asquith's annoyance at the speech made him unfair for once. Fisher now set the tone for Admiralty gossip and he had never been concerned to do his opponents justice. Sturdee, who had been a 'Beresfordite', was anathema to Fisher; he was commanding at the Falklands because he could not be retained as Chief of the Admiralty War Staff once Fisher was in office. He was pompous and unpopular with his fellow admirals; they seem to have blamed him as Chief of Staff for more mistakes than he actually made: Marder, ii. 92–3, 128–9.

[5] A vacancy had occurred at Swansea, where the leading Liberals in the constituency were prepared to support Masterman; but a local candidate with nationalist backing threatened to stand as an unofficial Liberal if this outsider were given the party nomination. The situation was far more complex than Asquith made out. In view of the party truce he could not give Masterman official encouragement to accept a candidature which might bring on a contest; but Lloyd George, who had prepared the ground as best he could, thought that if Masterman accepted boldly his local opponent would withdraw. In the event Masterman declined the formal invitation from Swansea on 7 Jan. and remained out of the House until the 1923 election. It is clear from this paragraph (and from other evidence) that, despite Masterman's great abilities, Asquith had no special wish to keep him. He found Masterman, as he had told Venetia on 5 Nov., 'quite clever but strangely unattractive'. Masterman's unfortunate manner had alienated a number of his colleagues.

237

Easton Grey,
Malmesbury

Sunday 27 Dec 1914

. . . Francis Horner wrote me a description of Katharine's children's party: she deplores that Diana Churchill increasingly takes after her father's looks & not her mother's.[1] By the way I must be rather in Winston's good books just now: he sent me quite an effusive Xmas telegram. . . .

According to the latest conjectures from the various capitals, the probable dates of the 'coming-in' of the halting & wavering Powers are: Roumania, end of Jan: Italy, March; Bulgaria, not before March, if ever; Greece, as soon as she sees a prospect of making a good thing out of it.[2] Of course Roumania & Italy are all important; their intervention would put an end to Austria, and in that case the Bulgarians would almost certainly come in & round on the Turks. All these little Powers hate one another cordially, but when the carcase is ready to be cut up each wants as big & juicy a slice as it can get. . . .

[1] Diana's father had not deplored this resemblance when it originally appeared. The following dialogue on the front bench was recorded in 1909: *Lloyd George* 'Is she a pretty child?' *Winston* 'The prettiest . . . ever seen.' *Lloyd George* 'Like her mother, I suppose?' *Winston* 'No, she is exactly like me.': Lucy Masterman, *C. F. G. Masterman* (1939), p. 144.

[2] Italy, Romania, and Greece eventually sided with Britain, France, and Russia: they declared war in May 1915, Aug. 1916, and June 1917 respectively. Bulgaria sided with Germany and Austria-Hungary and declared war in Oct. 1915.

238

Monday 28 Dec 1914

. . . The Assyrian was in his best form: had long confidential talks with Margot & V: took part in general conversation: & was at any rate moderately sanguine about himself. . . .

Another serious thing – about which K. has just been to talk to me – is the position of our troops in France. As you know, we have been urging the French to let them go to the extreme Left, & take the offensive along the coast. Cambon is now over there & has been pressing our view on Millerand. The reply is (Secret) that Joffre has 'no objection in principle', but feels that 'some time ago he did not receive the support he expected from British troops in carrying out an enveloping movement' (just the complaint we are always making against him), and he attributes it to 'want of energy on the part of the Chief of the Staff – Sir A. *Murray*'. This both K & I believe to be another proof of the constant intriguing of that serpent Wilson, who is just under Murray & wants to supplant him. We are quite determined that he shall not succeed; & K. has suggested with my entire approval, that Murray (if displaced) shall be succeeded by Sir W. Robertson – the man who rose from the ranks, & throughout the campaign has been the most efficient of Quartermasters-General. I will tell you how this progresses. Of course, for *you* alone.

Delcassé, the French Foreign Minister, is very keen to bring a Japanese army on to the European theatre. The Japs have hitherto absolutely declined, & as they have had a Ministerial defeat,[1] and a dissolution, with the prospect of a General Election in March, it doesn't seem a very practical proposal. I am rather against it on its merits: I would much rather the war lasted a few months longer than that the decisive blow was administered by the Yellows. . . .

[1] The Japanese Government had been defeated on a proposal to increase the army. The agitation in France for Japanese help in Europe reflected some French scepticism about the effectiveness of the Kitchener armies. See also Letter 243.

239

Walmer Castle, Kent.

Tu 29 Dec '14 [i]

. . .Poor Birrell . . . is clamouring (at Redmond's instigation) for a 'Badge' for the new Irish Division, on the plea that the Welsh & Ulster Divisions already have one. They had gone so far as to invent a shield surmounted by a gold crown, & with the Arms of the 3 provinces (I suppose excluding Ulster). K, it appears, won't hear of it, and thinks that a 'shamrock on a shoulder strap' meets the needs of the situation. . . . Redmond is in a fine frenzy, threatens to publish the correspondence &c. As Birrell characteristically comments: 'Harness is irksome to the Wild Ass, and after so much *Loyalty* a little free speech will not be amiss to an Irish orator'! I suppose that as usual I shall have to try to compose the controversy – a storm in a slop-basin, if ever there was one.[1]. . .

Geo Moore (that quaint Yankee familiar of Sir J French)[2] has sent me a box of very large cigars, and Violet a huge 8 guinea (price marked) book of 'Remarkable Women' with illustrations, which she is engaged in 'melting' at Humphries' shop (whence it came) into Hardys & Hy. James's &c.[3] I have advised her to buy Dent's Everyman's Library – about 150 volumes at 1/ or so each, and embracing almost every known book. Canadian Dunn's present to me is a rather nice old leather letter case, wh. contains all the various coloured 'books' – White, Yellow, Green, Purple &c – wh. have been published by the various nations about the War![4] What do you think of that? . . .

[1] See pp. 236–7.
[2] George Gordon Moore, a rich American lawyer and engineer. His services in helping to solve engineering problems on the Western Front were described by French in *1914*, pp. 353–5. Lady Diana Cooper gives a vivid picture of Moore in *The Rainbow Comes and Goes* (1958). See also Letters 231, n. 2; and 323, n. 1.
[3] 'Humphries' shop' is Hatchards in Piccadilly, where A. L. Humphreys worked from 1881 to 1924.
[4] These were collections of diplomatic documents produced to justify the course taken by each nation during the crisis leading to the war. On the Entente side, the British produced a White Paper which was much reprinted and translated, more than a million copies being issued. The Yellow Book was French, Russia's colour being orange, Belgium's grey, and Serbia's blue.

240

Walmer Castle,
Kent.

Tues midnight 29 Dec 1914 [ii]

. . . We (i.e. V, Oc, & I) motored over to Deal, & played about 12 holes on most perfect links. . . . As we were approaching in the gloaming the 18th hole, a native appeared, & appealed to me to come & say a word to about 20 wounded soldiers who had been brought over in a char à banc from Folkestone to tea. So Violet & I went in to his bungalow & greeted the warriors who were in charge of a most tiresome member of your new profession: a very full blown Nurse, who informed me in bridling accents that she was 'Sister Harold' – or some such name. I shudder to think of you cheek by jowl with such women. If I had a real genuine belief in the efficacy of prayer, I should even now put up a petition that you might be plucked from the burning. . . .

'A diversion on a great and effective scale'
(Letter 241)

THE memoranda from Churchill and Hankey (Letter 241), together with one from Lloyd George and a second from Churchill which Asquith received on 1 January (Letter 245), began a controversy which lasted throughout the rest of the war. Though often known as 'Easterners v. Westerners' it is perhaps better described as 'peripheral strategy v. Continental'. On the Western Front three inventions of the 1890s – the high explosive trinitrotoluene; smokeless artillery propellants such as cordite; and the recoiling-barrel machine-gun with a lock of the Maxim-Nordenfeldt type[1] – gave decisive advantages to the defence once the first encounter battles were over. The trench systems stretched from the Swiss frontier to the North Sea, so that they could not be outflanked by a land attack. The artillery preparation for an attack deprived the attackers of surprise, and told the defending commander where his reserves would be needed; yet it did not knock out more than a proportion of the wire entanglements and machine-guns against which the bravest infantry were almost powerless. The more thorough the barrage, the more the attackers' front was turned into a chaotic quagmire which would prevent them from exploiting any local success.

Hankey's 'armed rollers' (Letter 241) would in the end help to redress the balance. Hankey was indeed only one of those who were working towards the tank by the end of 1914. All the elements of that solution were already in use – bullet-proof armour, caterpillar tracks, and the internal combustion engine. But combining these elements into an effective war weapon posed formidable problems of design and production, not to mention the retraining of the troops and the re-education of their commanders. Meanwhile the Western Front left Kitchener in complete perplexity. 'I don't know what is to be done,' he told Grey; 'this isn't *war*.'[2]

The attractions of a peripheral strategy based on sea power thus became very great. They were overwhelming for Hankey, Lloyd George, and Churchill. The first, as a navalist (p. 145, n. 7), had never wanted to send British troops to the Western Front. The second did not expect Kitchener's new armies to go to the slaughter in Flanders without protest. The third burned to use the navy in an offensive operation. All three were exceptionally able and persuasive. They made the optimism of the Western Front generals look absurd; but there were more drawbacks to their own plans than appeared at first sight.

[1] For the importance of artillery, as against machine-gun, fire see John Terraine, *The Smoke and the Fire* (1980), pp. 130–42.
[2] Grey, *Twenty-Five Years*, ii. 69.

241

Wed. 30 Dec. [14] [i] in train to London.

There was no letter from you by the early post this morning, but I hope I may perhaps find one on my return this evening.

I am in the train on my way to attend the Cabinet, wh. is at 3 this aft. It is a fine bright day – this South Coast certainly has its full share of sun.

Very Secret

I have 2 very interesting memoranda to-day on the War – one from Winston, the other from Hankey – written quite independently, but coming by different roads to very similar conclusions. Both think that the existing deadlock in West & East is likely to continue, and W. points out that the flanking movement we urged on the French a month ago is much more difficult now that the Germans have fortified line by line almost the whole of Belgium. The losses involved in the trench-jumping operations now going on on both sides are enormous & out of all proportion to the ground gained. When our new armies are ready, as they will soon begin to be, it seems folly to send them to Flanders where they are not wanted, & where (in W's phrase) they will 'chew barbed wire', or be wasted in futile frontal attacks.

Hankey suggests the development of a lot of new mechanical devices, such as armed rollers to crush down barbed wire, bullet-proof shields & armour, smoke-balls, rockets with grapnel, petrol-throwing catapults &c. It will be strange if we are driven back to these Mediaeval practices.[1]

But apart from this, both he & W. are for finding a new objective & a new theatre for our new armies. H. wd. like them to go to Turkey & in conjunction with the Balkan States clear the Turk out of Europe. Germany, & what is left of Austria wd. be almost bound to take a hand.

W., on the other hand, wants (primarily of course by means of his Navy) to 'close the Elbe & dominate the Baltic'. He wd. first seize a German island – Borkum for choice – then invade Schleswig Holstein, obtain naval command of the Baltic, & thus enable Russia to land her troops within 90 miles of Berlin.

This plan (apart from other difficulties) implies either the accession of Denmark to the Allies, or the violation of her neutrality.

There is here a good deal of food for thought. I am profoundly dissatisfied with the immediate prospect – an enormous waste of life & money day after day with no appreciable progress. And it is quite true that the whole country between Ypres & the German frontier is being transformed into a succession of lines of fortified entrenchments. The nearest parallel is what Wellington did at Torres Vedras. I don't see the way to a decisive change before March, but I am sure that we ought to begin at once to devise, in concert with the French & the Russians, a diversion on a great & effective scale.

Later – I have got to Downing St. & found a letter from poor Beauchamp who is too bruised and shaken to attend the Cabinet.[2]

We shall have to consider what reply to make to this American note, wh. is a nuisance, tho' long expected.[3] Their merchants & shipowners have behaved & are behaving as fraudulently as they can, knowing perfectly well that most of the copper &c wh. is shipped often under false papers for Holland & Denmark is really destined for Germany.[4] But they have some technical points in their favour,[5] and the President whose position becomes daily more precarious, dare not offend the powerful money interests. What a country!

Perhaps I may be able to squeeze in a line or two while the Cabinet is sitting.

Cabinet

Russian supplies – we must have a really well-informed & responsible agent of the Russian Govt here. It would seem that they have been (what is vulgarly called) pulling our leg over the whole business. They can (it now appears) turn out in Russia a 1,000,000 shells a month.[6]

E. Grey is back after a week's holiday & looks very well.

[1] Writing for his scholarly Prime Minister, Hankey prefaced his passage on new weapons with a reference to ancient and medieval siege devices.

[2] He had been in a car accident.

[3] The American Note of 26 Dec. complained that 'cargoes passing between neutral ports in the peaceful pursuit of lawful commerce' had been 'detained sometimes for weeks by the British Authorities'. 'Neither government helps me,' Page had written to House a fortnight earlier; 'our government merely sends the shipper's *ex parte* statement. This government uses the Navy's excuse.'

[4] Some consignments of copper to Rotterdam were seized early in Oct. After much American complaining they were proved to have been destined for Krupps'. The British Government paid for them, though they might lawfully have been condemned as contraband without compensation.

[5] The British Government was not complying with precedents, which, in their view, had been made inapplicable by technical developments or by their needs in a struggle for survival. During earlier wars it had been possible to stop neutral ships and search them at sea. The coming of the submarine had made this procedure too dangerous; the suspected neutral had now to undergo the delay of being escorted to one of the British anchorages used for contraband control. In the Boer War Lord Salisbury had laid down that foodstuffs could be considered as contraband only if they were shown to be destined for the enemy's forces. The American Government faced equally embarrassing pronouncements from the past, since their predecessors had maintained the strictest blockade doctrines in order to defeat the Southern States during the Civil War.

[6] This was almost certainly a large overestimate. (Russian monthly production was said later to have reached 550,000 shells per month by Apr. 1915: Sir A. Knox, *With the Russian Armies* (1921), i. 273.) Kitchener had been questioning the Russian Military Attaché in London, but found him 'kept entirely in the dark by his government'. The Russians were suspected of exaggerating their plight in order to hasten a loan of £40m. from Britain for which they were negotiating.

242

Walmer Castle,
Kent.

Wed 30 Dec '14 [ii] Midnight

. . . This year (1914) has been in the fullest sense what the Ancients used to call 'annus mirabilis'. I am not as a rule very sensitive about anniversaries: the 'daily round' is more important to me. But this particular one is an exception. From the world-wide point of view it is impossible to exaggerate the difference wh. it has made in values & the things that matter. I won't enlarge on this. Nor do I think much of the effect wh. its unforeseen unrolling of events has had on my own personal position. . . . But to you & me (I recall the Xmas play at Alderley exactly a year ago, & our New Year's eve, with Commerce, punch &c) it has been a succession of marvellous experiences. Looking back, I can hardly remember a day out of the 365 when I have not either written to you, or seen you, or often done both. And there have been very few when you have not either seen or written to me. We have interchanged everything – the greatest & the smallest; never has there been between man & woman fuller & franker confidence: & whatever may be the case with you, rarely, if ever, has a man gained or owed so much.

I thank you, my darling, from the bottom of my heart, from the very source of my being, for what you have been to me. Without you I must often have failed, & more than once gone down. You have sustained & enriched every day of my life.

That is my New Year's greeting. Do you welcome it? or do you wish it had been otherwise?

Perhaps you don't always realise that I am as fully conscious as you can be of the great apparent difference & disproportion: you in the full tide of your glorious youth: I – according to the Calendar – on the threshold at any rate of the later stages of life. Whatever comes or goes, I am & must be the debtor: hugely overdrawn, often ashamed of what I owe; but – I can't say more to-night.

243

[Walmer Castle]
                                             Thurs. 31 Dec. 1914.

I stopped last night, as you will see, in the middle of a sentence. I won't complete it this morning: you can do so out of your own imagination if you are so minded, darling. I wish I were with you rearranging your books. I can't imagine a more delicious way of spending the last twilight of the year. I shall gradually make a *very select* collection of missing pieces, with which you will have to fill in the flyleaves of my precious book.

'Sir Edgar' & Raymond & Kath. are here, and I think the Assyrian & Eliz. will join us some time to-day. I am glad to say that Margot thoroughly likes the place. Its only defect is that as almost all the rooms – both bed & sitting – are in one corridor, there is such a clatter of housemaids raking out grates &c &c in the early morning as to give one (before one wants it) what Milton calls a 'sober certainty of waking bliss'. This can no doubt be mitigated by better management. It is unluckily pouring with rain to-day, with now & then a lucid interval: nevertheless they have gone off golfing, and I imagine you are once more – for the last time? – in the hunting field, dodging the overflows of the Dane & the Weaver[1]. I am glad Anthony has got such a good leave: give him my love & New Year's wishes.

(I ought to have sent thanks before for a magnificent sirloin from the Prize Beast!)

I am anxious to hear *exactly* what are your plans for next week. We are asking the Bud to stay here for a few days to recuperate: as usual, she seems to have had marvellous experiences,[2] in & out of prison, on her adventurous journey home. K. has seen her & thinks her not looking well.

I have just been showing her (K) the Duke of Wellington's room & our other sights. Her cry of 'Perish India!' is loud & insistent.[3]

I got a lot of figures this morning of which two I think will interest you. One is Winston's estimate of the men (including wounded, prisoners, & refugees) horses, & stores wh. he has transported across the seas since the war began with (as he complacently notes) 'no fatal accident nor any loss due to the enemy'. The total is *men* 809,000: horses 203,000: stores 250,000 tons. This is of course a record – especially when you come to think that large numbers have been brought from the ends of the earth across various oceans in wh. the German cruisers were still at large. The other figure comes from Sir F. Bertie. I think I told you that Kitchener estimated the number of effective French troops at not more than 1,250,000 with the same number in reserve to make good losses & wastage. Delcassé declares that they have 1,400,000 at the front, and not less than 1,800,000 in reserve. This is good, *if* it is true.

I hope this afternoon & or to-morrow to write my mem^m on the present position & future conduct of the war. If you care, I will send it to you.

Delcassé, by the way, is extremely anxious to bring the Japs into the European theatre. He thinks that the addition to the Allies of 400,000 of their troops would at once turn the scale & practically finish the War. The Japanese Gov^t (as we know) is *very* adverse to any such plan, & says that public opinion there would not stand it. Nor is it easy to see what inducement in the way of material gain cd. be offered them: except the certainty of retaining Kiao-Chow.

I confess I am not very much enamoured of the idea that the war shd. be decided by the importation of these Yellow men: but Winston derides any such scruples as born of perverted sentiment: and remarks (with some truth) that the great thing is to *win*.

What do you feel about it? I am pretty certain that no amount of pressure on the Japs will prove effective.

We have lost 5000 men (not more – but that is quite enough) in this desultory trench fighting of the last fortnight.

I told you *very secretly* about Sir A. Murray: the French are very keen to get rid of him as Chief of our staff: they don't seem to have any very specific charge against him except that he speaks poor French & is not *sympathique*. Both K & I think that Robertson is the right man to succeed him. Winston is for Haig, but it would be almost impossible to replace him where he is.[4] This is *most private*.

Darling I could go on talking to you for a long time, but I must get this off by the 2 p.m post, which will give it a chance of reaching you to-morrow morning.

Send me a *nice* New Year's Message, which I can remember and treasure.

Where and what shall we be this time next year? My last word to you *this* year, my own darling, is one of untellable gratitude & unalterable love. *Bless you.*

¹ A Cheshire river and its tributary. The Weaver is joined by the Dane at Northwich and flows into the Mersey at Frodsham.

² While serving as a nurse in Belgium Nellie Hozier had been imprisoned by the Germans, but quickly released.

³ For this joke see Letter 230, text and n. 4. If Beauchamp went to India as Viceroy Asquith could become Lord Warden of the Cinque Ports and so acquire the right to occupy Walmer.

⁴ 'You ought to take the best man in the army,' Churchill told French on 28 Dec.; 'Haig is without equal; and this is not a time when his personal feelings should count a scrap. You must be freed from minor worries. There is no comfort like really high ability working for one.' Robertson was appointed Chief of Staff, B.E.F., however, in Mar. 1915.

PART 3

The London Hospital and the Dardanelles

ASQUITH did not abate his demands on Venetia to make them fit better with the life of a trainee nurse. He claimed the lion's share of her few leisure hours. He asked for a letter 'every day – one line, at any rate, and as many more as you can' (Letter 247).[1] He fussed if his letters or hers were not delivered promptly: he begged as insistently as ever for her advice and support. When on 4 March she warned him to moderate his demands she succeeded only in making him pitiably distressed (Letters 330–32 and 334).

The prospect of a long war, and Venetia's entry into war service, not only subjected the friendship to strain but endangered its whole basis. 'When one looks back at . . . last spring and summer,' Asquith told her in March 1915 (Letter 354), 'it would . . . seem as if we had passed into another world.' He did not appreciate that in this new world of wartime she might reassess her attitude to Edwin. She already knew several war widows. Marriage to someone who was not expected to rush into the forces had grown more attractive. Social bonds were being loosened: it no longer seemed impossible for a Stanley to embrace the Jewish faith.

Edwin showed more perception than his chief. He put his house and car at Venetia's disposal and 24 Queen Anne's Gate soon became the rendezvous for her and her younger friends which 10 Downing Street could never be. 'You have been an angel friend to me,' he wrote to her on 1 February (Letter III, p. 412); 'why not a wife? . . . Have you ever thought again of that?'[2] This time he was not repulsed. A weekend at Alderley early in March encouraged him to persevere (Letter IV, p. 466). The letters which he and Venetia exchanged chart the ups and downs of the courtship which followed. During another Alderley weekend, soon after she had finished her training in April, they moved a stage nearer to an engagement. By the end of that month he had received her definite acceptance and had discussed her conversion to Judaism with her and with his eldest brother. 'We won't increase our difficulties by poverty,' he wrote to her on 30 April (Letter

XXXI, p. 576); 'just dismiss the matter by saying to me "I will go through with it".' One great obstacle to their marriage had been faced.

There was another difficulty which they had not tackled, however. How could Venetia disengage herself from Asquith? The fondness which she and Edwin both had for the Prime Minister stopped them from solving the problem ruthlessly; and they discovered in painful episodes that no gentle solution was possible. At first Edwin 'dreamed of a gradual ending' of the attachment (Letter XIV, p. 530); but it soon became clear that Asquith was too greatly obsessed by Venetia, and too dependent on her, for this to be feasible. She managed to keep both men 'fairly happy' (Letter XXIII, p. 551) while completing her hospital training. The strain told on her, however. During the weekend which all three spent together at Walmer just before her course ended she retired to bed ill, to the frustration of both her admirers (Letters XV–XVI, pp. 536–7; and Letter 394).[3]

The move towards an engagement made at Alderley a week later had to be followed by some kind of warning to Asquith; and on Sunday 18 April Venetia wrote to prepare him for the possibility that she might soon marry. Much shaken, he begged her to let him know 'the worst – without disguise or delay' (Letter 405). From that point his fears of losing her recurred with mounting intensity; and his depression was soon deepened by the news that she was going to France to nurse (Letter 410). But she dared not risk his disapproval of the step she was taking until the arrangements were well in train, and he did not come near to the truth. After each episode in which her distraction showed she made amends and gave him a measure of reassurance (Letters 415–18).

The news about the engagement might have been broken bluntly if a good day could have been found for doing this; but in a wartime Prime Minister's life, as Venetia remarked, there were no such days (Letter XXIII, p. 551). Again, if Asquith had been able to look on Venetia and her prospects with a cooler eye he might have guessed what was happening. He knew that Edwin was to be at Alderley on 17–18 April and he resented that the invitation had not come to himself (Letter 392); but he did not connect this fact with the letter which he received from Venetia immediately after that weekend. None of the Asquiths in 10 Downing Street thought that Edwin might be the man. Margot saw Edwin, not as a suitor, but as an adviser who might persuade Venetia to marry (Letter XXI, p. 547). She told him to exercise these persuasions on both Venetia and Violet.

Events dictated the solution. Venetia was due to report for duty in a war hospital at Wimereux, near Boulogne, on Monday 10 May; and she no doubt intended the news to reach Asquith from there. However, while spending the preceding weekend with the Churchills at Hoe Farm* in

* See Appendix 3.

Surrey, she ran a temperature and had to retire to bed in Mansfield Street. The illness, to which the strains in her personal life had no doubt contributed, was not serious; but it imposed a decision. She could not deceive the Prime Minister any longer: he must not be allowed to remain in ignorance and visit her. The circle of those in the know ranged from Lord Swaythling to Maurice Bonham Carter (Letters XXX and XXXII pp. 575 and 578). There was by now a risk that the news might be unwittingly revealed to Asquith by someone's chance remark. Taking the initiative entirely on her own,[4] she wrote on 11 May from her sick-bed that she was to be married to Edwin.

*   *   *

During April and early May Asquith was beset by public troubles. His war leadership, lately so much admired, came under increasing criticism.[5] The qualities of dignity and good judgement which had won him acclaim when the war began were not thought sufficient for directing the war effort. A display of dynamic energy had become the order of the day; and it was not in him to supply this.[6] Throughout the period when he was in dread of losing Venetia he was thus faced also with acute governmental difficulties. His friendship with her seems up to this point to have enhanced his efficiency. Now he had to envisage the withdrawal of the prop on which he had come to depend. Did his private worries impair his public performance? Did the personal preoccupations to which the Letters bear witness make him less efficient during these critical weeks? There was a notion in governmental circles that something must have lessened his capacity to grapple with problems. Arthur Salter, who was then serving in Whitehall, later recorded:

Before the war had been going six months Asquith appears to have had an illness which, though its critical period was soon past, left some consequences. The capacity for immediate and vigorous action, the constant and unrelaxing concentration on the new issues presented by the war as it developed, were no longer quite what they had been.[7]

Asquith suffered no such illness; but his personal worries may have given some of those close to the Government an impression of impaired performance for which a bout of ill health seemed the only explanation.

Though the Prime Minister's private anxieties may have produced some such effect, it would be absurd to regard them as the chief cause of the Government's weakness. Much of the criticism to which Asquith and his colleagues were subjected in the spring of 1915 was unreasonable. Their performance was much as it had been three months earlier. They came under attack because they were being judged more harshly; it was the public mood which had changed. H. G. Wells wrote of this phase in *Mr. Britling Sees It Through*:

The war which had begun so dramatically missed its climax . . . it had ceased to be either a tragedy or a triumph . . . It had become a wearisome thrusting against a pressure of evils. . . .

Under that strain the dignity of England broke . . . The British spirit . . . wasted its energies in a deepening and spreading net of internal squabbles and accusations.[8]

Eight months of war had brought several intractable issues to the surface. Some of the failures laid to Asquith's charge originated, not in mistakes, but in limitations which would have hampered any Government. The difficulties of organizing manpower without some form of military conscription were becoming clear; yet for the Liberals introducing conscription would have been a political impossibility in April 1915. Kitchener had been the right choice as War Secretary; yet the presence in that post of this all-powerful cheese-parer impeded a solution of the munitions problem.

Other reverses sprang from mistakes made months before Asquith's private worries began. It had been a mistake to plan the Dardanelles attack in January as a wholly naval effort. Once the War Council had succumbed to that temptation, the damage could not be repaired. Any later mistakes and omissions over the Dardanelles with which Asquith can be charged must be judged of secondary importance. To procure the troops for a combined operation while the defences were still weak would have been difficult. To procure the army needed to overcome vastly stronger defences, once the navy had failed, was virtually impossible. That would have entailed a veto on all major British attacks in the West, despite every plea from Joffre and French. It might have meant risking a German breakthrough to the Channel.

Moreover, what seemed negligent may not have been so. The Dardanelles Commission censured Asquith's failure to convene the War Council between 19 March and 14 May, remarking reasonably enough that during this interval the naval attack was abandoned and full-scale military landings substituted.[9] By the last week of March, however, the decisions lay, not with the War Council, but with the commanders on the spot. The most likely effect of summoning the War Council would have been Fisher's resignation; and, as Asquith knew, Churchill's unpopularity was such that the Government could scarcely survive the departure of the First Sea Lord.[10]

The Prime Minister's role at this stage of the war was immensely difficult and, despite all his talents, Asquith did not have the best temperament for it. Even the ideal wartime Prime Minister would have had political troubles in April and May 1915. Asquith, who was not that ideal figure, would have had serious ones even if there had been no personal worries to distract him. It was precisely this vulnerability which made his private apprehensions and distractions so dangerous to him at this time. His fears for his friendship with Venetia came just when he needed to bring every ounce of energy to bear on the problems of his office. Some of the Letters which follow suggest that at certain points in March, April, and early May 1915, these fears may have done something to impair his concentration and vigour. Certainly his Newcastle speech on 20 April showed uncharacteristic ill-judgement. But the effect of Venetia and her plans should not be exaggerated. By the time Asquith went to Newcastle Venetia's future was only one of the anxieties pressing on him.

Notes to the Introduction to Part 3

1. The monthly totals of Asquith's letters to Venetia rose from 27 in Nov. and Dec. 1914, to 45 in Jan. 1915, 48 in Feb., and 58 in March.
2. It is impossible to estimate when the attachment between them moved into this new phase. In Apr. 1915 Edwin referred to the year which they had already 'wasted' (Letter XXVII, p. 562). Practically no correspondence between them survives for 1914.
3. The illness does not seem to have been 'diplomatic'. The strain of personal difficulties would have told with doubled effect at the end of a strenuous nursing course.
4. As is established from a passage, not selected, in Edwin to Venetia, 17 June 1915.
5. In Apr. 1915 L. S. Amery, who was serving in the Mediterranean, could hardly believe that the Government had become as discredited as *The Times* made out: to Milner, 27 Apr.; Bodleian Library, MSS Milner, dep. 350, f. 102.
6. See, for instance, Balfour's remark to Lady Rayleigh, 24 Mar. 1915: 'It is not in Asquith's nature to speed up things'; Max Egremont, *Balfour* (1980), p. 268; and Tom Bridges, *Alarms and Excursions* (1938), p. 134: 'One had to admire . . . Asquith's great qualities . . . though he was not tuned up to the war tempo.'
7. *Slave of the Lamp* (1967), p. 29. Lord Salter recalls Asquith as 'the world's then greatest statesman'.
8. pp. 282–3. *Mr Britling* was published in Sept. 1916.
9. *Parl. Papers*, First Report, 1917–18 CD 8490, x. 463. See also Second Report, 1919 CMD 371, xiii. 729. For Asquith's comments see *Parl. Deb.*, xci. 1765–6 (20 Mar. 1917). In the First Report the Commissioners went so far as to say that, in the absence of a summons from the Prime Minister, 'the other members of the War Council should have pressed for . . a meeting'. The evidence on which the Report had been based was not published.
10. The crucial point was the extent to which Churchill had lost the confidence of the Liberals: Beaverbrook, *Politicians and the War* (1928), i. 125. Asquith was reticent about this in writing to Venetia, because she was fond of Winston and a cousin of Clementine Churchill. It emerges more clearly in Margot's diary.

244

Walmer Castle,
Kent.

New Year's Day 1915 [i]

My darling – it is just after mid-night & the bells have only just ceased ringing. Your dear Xmas present is on my knees, & I am writing with it as a support.[1]

I don't the least know, nor can I guess, what this year is going to bring. But my first thoughts & my first words are for you.

I wrote to you last night and this morning about 1914 – a year of many agitations & anxieties – which through you, has been transformed for me.

Will you be the same in 1915?

My loyalty & love will never grow paler or fainter . . .

> Thy love is better than high birth to me
> Richer than wealth, prouder than garments' cost. . . .
> Wretched in this alone, that thou mayst take
> All this away, and me most wretched make.[2]. . .

Bear with me, believe in me, & if you can love me. Yours through life – always – everywhere.

[1] Venetia had given him a 'Treasury of Sonnets', handwritten by herself: see Letter 391.
[2] Shakespeare, *Sonnet 91.*

245

Walmer Castle,
Kent.

Friday *midnight* 1 Jan 1915 [ii]

My darling – after two days of complete starvation (through no fault of yours) I got at last just before dinner to-night your most dear letter of Wed (30th). You say that when you wrote – evidently tea-time Wed – you hadn't yet got either my Monday or Tues. letter. I wrote Monday – in the midst of travelling – and gave it to one of our trusty messengers to be posted before I left for here by 5 p.m. train. I can't understand why you didnt receive it at any rate by late post on Wed. Then I wrote & posted from here by 2 p.m. on Tuesday; again on Wed. (when I was in London) before returning here: & of course from here yesterday & to-day. This sounds boring, but I wanted you to know that there is *no single day* on wh. I have not written, and (if you have now got them) as you (poor sweet!) may think more than copiously. . . .

I suppose this won't get to you till Sunday at earliest. I shall come up to London Monday morning: let me know by wire to Downing St when you arrive that day. I will come & see you at Mansfield St. between 6 & 7: and I will arrange that we shall dine together that evening – either at Downing St, or possibly at the Assyrian's. Don't bother about this: I will see that it is all right.

As a matter of fact, I could have spotted in one guess his present to you: for last night Kath. came down to dinner in a wonderful *confection* – designed I imagine by the same hand, – at any rate proceeding from the same source. Do wear yours on Monday evening: & we can compare notes & criticisms.[1] . . .

No – I shan't reproach you this time with your pleasure-hunting habits. I almost begin to wish that I had spurred you on: it seems so sombre & bleak – what you are now going to face. My only consolation is that you will be *near*: and that in your little spaces of liberty we can drive together, at any rate as far as Richmond or Barnet.

We have had a nasty disaster to-day: the *Formidable* (a sister of the *Bulwark* wh. was blown up by accident) has been torpedoed somewhere in the Channel by a German submarine.[2] I am sorry for Winston, who seems just now to be dogged by ill-luck.

The Assyrian got a lot of telegrams of congratulations to-day on his P.C.[3] We have been chaffing him at dinner (after drinking his health) on the sources from wh. they came. So far as we cd. extract disclosures from him, the only feminine senders were Fr. Horner & the ever faithful Pamela McKenna!

Unhappily we have had vile weather for New Year Day – pouring rain & gusty winds. Raymond took to his bed with a chill & temperature, but is up this evening & apparently all right. Margot Eliz & I & the Assyrian made a pilgrimage to Canterbury & lunched at the Palace with the Archbishop & his wife. They took us all over the Cathedral, Thomas à Becket's shrine, Black Prince's tomb, &c – quite interesting.

I got a really amusing letter from Paris – from Sir F. Bertie to E. Grey – with an account of a conversation between B & Clemenceau, who is rather violently anti-Poincaré. One thing that will interest you in it is that Gen. Joffre 'rests' every day from 1.30 to 3 p.m, & resented very much that when the President came to the front, on one of his popularity-hunting missions, he demanded that Joffre shd. accompany him to see the troops during this sacred siesta: wh. J. flatly refused to do!

I have also received to-day two long mem^a – one from Winston, the other from Lloyd George (quite good, the latter) as to the public conduct of the war. They are both keen on a new objective & theatre, as soon as our new

troops are ready: W, of course, for Borkum & the Baltic: Ll. G. for Salonica
to join in with the Serbians, & for Syria! I will bring them to you on
Monday, & we can talk it all over. I am summoning our little 'War Council'
for Thursday & Friday to review the whole situation, & as there is a Cabinet
on Wed, I expect I shall be practically in London most of the week. I love the
prospect – for I shall be in close touch with my dearest & wisest counsellor.

I must go to bed – with your dear letter under my pillow. Good night –
most dear – never more dear, or so dear, as on this first night of a New Year.

[1] See Letter I, below, and n. 1.

[2] Off Start Point, east of Salcombe, south Devon: see Letter 249. Over 500 officers and men
were lost. The *Bulwark* had been destroyed by an internal explosion on 26 Nov. 1914.

[3] Montagu's Privy Councillorship had been one of the New Year Honours.

246

Walmer Castle,
Kent.

Sunday 3 Jan 1915

. . . Poor Illingworth died this morning. I had a letter from her [Mrs
Illingworth] only yesterday thanking me for his P.C., and saying that a fall
of temperature had made them begin to hope for better things. He is a great
loss to me: if I told him to go to the top of St Paul's & throw himself down,
he wd have done it without a moment's hesitation. I used to see him every
morning to talk over every kind of delicate thing, and tho' he had none of
the Master's subtlety, he had great Yorkshire shrewdness, & was as straight
and loyal as any man living.[1] . . .

[1] He had succeeded the Master of Elibank as Government Chief Whip in Aug. 1912. His
death (which was said to have resulted from eating an infected oyster) turned out to be quite as
serious a blow as Asquith predicted.

I

E.S.M. to B.V.S.

Walmer Castle
Kent

3 January 1915

My dearest Venetia,

Thankyou a hundred times for your delightful letter and many many
times for your most attractive Chinese poem. . .

I am not satisfied by any means with your dress or Katharine's.[1] I think I
know what is wrong with both but I realise I am too ignorant of the

techniques and terminology of dressmaking to do any good in the way of translating my ideas. So you have my first and last arguments in that direction.

As regards 'the great honour H.M. has done me' (to quote a thousand letters) the one thing certain about it is that it produced a letter from the Prime which was the best thing I have ever had.[2] This is far more than even an 'honour', even one which has in its turn been the reward of merit and the consolation of failure, the personal recognition of services and the aftermath of high hopes, can possibly be. But the letter itself is a glorious possession and makes up for heaps of things in the past and will help with many things in the future.

Well best of friends, *au revoir*. I am at your service from tomorrow onwards. Telephone tomorrow afternoon your commands.

Yrs with much love
Ed S Montagu

[1] See Letter 245. Presumably Edwin had given dresses to both Katharine and Venetia.
[2] In this letter Asquith praised Edwin's work at the India Office and the Treasury and also his 'strenuous and inestimable service since the outbreak of the war'. The letter ended: 'It is, I need not add, the greatest of pleasures to me to be able to offer a public mark of distinction to a friend whose loyalty and affection have never failed me.'

247

The Athenaeum

Tu 5 Jan 1915 [i]

. . . About the Zeppelins, . . . old Jacky Fisher seriously proposed, by way of reprisals, to shoot all the German prisoners here, and when Winston refused to embrace this statesmanlike suggestion (wh. wd. have led, in turn, to the massacre of all our poor men in Germany) sent in a formal written resignation of his office. I imagine that by this time he has reconsidered it.[1] . . .

I will send or bring you all the interesting papers after we have had our War Council on Thursday. . . .

Write to me darling every day – one line, at any rate, & as many more as you can. I long to hear every detail of your new life.[2] I think of you every hour, and your love is the *best* thing in my life.

[1] Churchill told Fisher; 'I sympathize with your feelings of exasperation at our powerlessness to resist certain forms of attack: and I presume I may take your letter simply as an expression of those feelings.' Fisher withdrew his resignation.
[2] As a trainee nurse at the London Hospital.

248

Tu 5 Jan 1915 [ii] Midnight (or after)

My darling – I sent you a little note before dinner from the Athenaeum, whither I repaired after my solitary drive back from Whitechapel. I was at the same time depressed from losing you, and elated by what you had said & been. I can't even yet realise the new conditions of your life. But I am quite determined that this shall not impair our daily love & confidence. . . .

. . . I think it would not be a bad thing if Violet & Rupert Brooke came together.[1] What do you say?

I dined at the Admiralty. Clemmie was the only Doe – there was no Assyrian (I thought you said he was coming?) & the other men were Winston, Freddie Guest, the nice little Scotch laird Sir A. Sinclair,[2] & F. E. Smith (who is now a Major & back for two days from the War).

We had a rather good talk (how I wished you had been there!) about the re-arrangements wh. will have to be made when peace comes. F.E. who has been mostly with the Indian troops – they have lost about $\frac{1}{2}$ their numbers – is keen for sending them with a stiffening of regulars & territorials to Smyrna – to make their way sooner or later to Constantinople. They can't stand the cold & the wet, & he says the Gurkas were almost the worst.[3]

We have now a lot of alternative objectives: (1) Schleswig (Winston) (2) Salonika or Dalmatia (Ll. George – curiously enough, French in his letter to me suggests that we might send a diversion to help the Montenegrins) (3) Gallipoli & Constantinople (Kitchener) (4) Smyrna & Ephesus (F.E. & others – I rather like this). . . .

We had rather amazing Bridge – Sir A.S. & I against Clemmie & F.E. The last named is a foolish & adventurous maker – a regular gambler: & my modest partner & I made (unfortunately at low stakes) many points. . . .

I think I shall write to you shorter letters, but more of them (Poor sweetest! does this make you tremble?) It is such a blessing to be free from the vagaries of the country posts! . . .

You must tell me everything. But if you are hustled or tired, just write two or three lines. *Never less.* That will make & keep me happy . . .

---

[1] Brooke's personal life was already somewhat cluttered. Though 'Ka' Cox and Noel Olivier belonged in a sense to his past, thoughts of them still disturbed him. His romantic friendship with Cathleen Nesbitt was in full vigour and he had recently become attracted to Lady Eileen Wellesley. For his feelings towards Violet Asquith in Mar. 1915 see Letter 407, n. 3.

² In Oct. 1913 Asquith described him to Venetia: 'Owns 100,000 acres or thereabouts, is in the 2nd Life Guards, and when in London flies every morning before breakfast. . . . He has good looks and manners, a slight but attractive stammer, and wears a kilt of a sober but striking pattern.' Sinclair led the Parliamentary Liberal Party, 1935–45, and was Secretary of State for Air, 1940–45.

³ The Indian Corps of some 24,000 men reached the Western Front in Oct. 1914 and saw action in the First Battle of Ypres. It was to have further heavy losses at Neuve Chapelle (Mar. 1915) and at Loos (Sept. 1915). It was then withdrawn from the Front and disbanded, having suffered 10,000 fatal casualties. Indian troops served with far greater success on the other fronts.

249

Wed. aft. 6 Jan 1915 [i]

My darling – I wrote you a little letter from the Athenaeum yest. evening, wh. I hope you got by early post this morning, and another at midnight, wh. ought to have reached you by now. Tell me when they arrived: so that I may be able to gauge your posts. . . .

I have been wondering at odd moments all thro' a rather busy day what you were doing, and trying to picture you in your new costume & your still stranger milieu. Tell me the truth (I know you will) about how you like it & how you feel.

First I will report about personal things. Lucy was here (for her doctor) last night, and when I went to see her just before the Cabinet this morning I found her in the company of Laura Lovat & Diana Wyndham: both in very good looks. I hadn't seen Diana since her sorrow: she was very nice & simple & sensible. All the Dunkirk team are apparently over here, taking a short holiday.¹

After an early lunch Bongie & I went to the Illingworth Memorial Service at a Presbyterian Church near the Marble Arch, wh. was quite crowded. It was a simple Non-conformist service, with hymns like 'O God of Bethel' & 'Abide with me', and extempore prayers; and an address by the veteran Dʳ Clifford,² wh. was good in style & taste, & not too long. I was in the front & couldn't see much of the congregation, wh. was full of politicians London & provincial. I noticed Ld. E. Talbot, & T. P. O'Connor: also all our H. of Commons colleagues. I recalled my close daily intimacy with poor Illingworth in all the crowded & recurring crises of the last 2 years: no one ever had a more devoted and whole hearted friend & chief of staff: I felt very sad.³ . . .

Now to other things.

Winston came in this morning & told me 2 new & not very agreeable Naval stories. The first was that on the luckless day of the Scarborough bombardment, part of the German fleet was picked up by Goodenough & his light cruisers. He saw some of them in the mist & at once opened fire on them with two of his ships: if he had gone on, the rest of the two fleets wd. have been attracted by the noise & come up, and there might have been a general engagement in wh. we were bound to score. Unfortunately Beatty with his battle cruisers – not hearing or knowing of the firing – signalled to G's two unengaged cruisers to sheer off: the message was by some fool's mistake miscarried to G; who thereupon (as he supposed in obedience to orders) ceased firing & drew away.[4] I don't think in the circumstances he was to blame; but Fisher & I fancy Winston think otherwise. Anyhow it was a piece of real bad luck. W's other story was about the *Formidable* & shows that the Admiral – Bayly – was seriously at fault. It was a horrible night & he ought to have taken his squadron of 8 battleships into Portland, where they wd have been quite secure. Instead of that he moved them in a close column towards Torbay, and when they were in the full glare of the Start lighthouse (one of the most powerful) & steaming at only 10 knots, the German submarine found the last ship in the line – the *Formidable* – an excellent target, and drove 2 torpedoes home. Wasn't it tragic?[5]

At the Cabinet K read us French's long mem^m proposing a move on Ostend & Zeebrucke [*sic*], for the success of wh. he computes that he needs 50 battalions from home, & a quite impossible supply of artillery & ammunition. He also proposes to break up K's new Armies, & use them, battalion by battalion, for strengthening & enlarging his force. This, of course, is repugnant in the highest degree to K – also to Haldane – & tho' it has some arguable merits, can, I am sure, never be assented to. K. was also a little irritated that F. had sent his mem^m to me, and that the one wh. reached him purported to be only a copy of mine. There is alas! constant friction between them, wh. is part of the price one has to pay for having a military instead of a civilian Sec^y of State.

Winston is sure that F. & his staff believe that when the pear is ripe, & the new armies are ready to take the field, – say about the beginning of April – K means to supersede F, & himself take the command & finish the war.[6]

I don't as yet see any sufficient reason for such a suspicion: but the fact that it exists constitutes another serious difficulty. . . .

[1] For Percy Wyndham's death in action see Letters 159–61: the nursing team with which Diana Wyndham had gone abroad is described in Letter 178.

[2] The famous Baptist preacher, then aged 78. 'One could not help feeling, seeing the P.M. sitting in the front pew,' Christopher Addison wrote, 'how infinitely better he would have done it.'

[3] According to the *Baptist Times*, 'At the "Dead March" . . . the Prime Minister remained standing for a moment, and then, as if he could bear it no more, sank on his knees and buried his face in his hands.' Lloyd George noticed that Asquith 'sang vigorously all the words of all

the hymns but . . . there was not a note in tune the whole time. He sang in a dull, continuous, deep monotone. He was, however, doing his best and enjoyed his own singing': C. Addison, *Four and a Half Years* (1934), i.56.

⁴ Jellicoe noted after the war: 'Beatty very severe on Goodenough, but forgets that it was his own badly worded signal to the cruisers that led to the Germans being lost': Marder, ii.145, n. 18. Fisher, as usual, urged that heads should roll: Churchill prevented this.

⁵ See Letter 234, n. 4. Bayly was told by the Admiralty that his handling of his squadron 'was marked by a want of prudence and good seamanship in the avoidance of unnecessary risks inexplicable in an officer holding high and responsible command'. He was transferred to the Presidency of the Royal Naval College, Greenwich.

⁶ From the time of his interview with French in Paris (Letters 141–3) Kitchener had toyed openly with the possibility of putting his authority to direct war strategy beyond question by becoming Supreme Commander of the British Armies as well as Secretary of State. This had naturally given rise to the idea that he planned to take over from French in the field whenever victory should be in sight. According to Esher, Kitchener conveyed to French in May 1915 that he had never 'entertained the idea of taking over the command of armies in the field; . . . he never would suggest such a course to the government; and, if it were suggested to him, he would meet it with a strong remonstrance'

250

Wed 6 Jan 15 [ii] Midnight (or after)

My darling – I got back from the Assyrian's feast just before 12 & found your heavenly letter awaiting me. It is just what I wanted, and I hope you won't become less 'verbatim' day by day. I love & long to know everything that you do & experience hour by hour. I was glad to find (from the postmark) that posted at 6 p.m. it got here the same evening. Very different from Alderley & Walmer. I shd. like to know when my first letter to-day (posted about 10.30 in the morning) got in to your hands: also whether you received the same evening my second – posted in a pillar box soon after 5.

I am *so* glad you like the Shelley. I look forward to sending you a really nice book from time to time.

'Charrington'¹ sounds very grim, – cleaning up, sweeping, 'turning' patients &c. It is too horrible! I hope your dear hands won't suffer. Do tell me every detail.

I shall look out for a telegram to-morrow. Either that aft. or Friday is the same to me: I shall be there. I'm afraid your food is disgusting: you must let me know if I can bring anything.

After I wrote to you this afternoon (you must realise that I'm quite close here) I went to the Athenaeum – the only place where I am free – and read a not bad Russian Nihilist novel by Leroux (the man who wrote the *Chambre Jaune*).² I came back here in time to dress for dinner & went to the silken tent, where I found quite a characteristic party – R & Kath – Goonie – & the two sisters Hennessy,³ *plus* Edward Horner, who I need not say arrived about 20 minutes after we had sat down at table. I found Mᵐᵉ de Janzy (if that is her name) pretty tiresome, but had a good talk with Kath – who was on my other side. She is rather disposed to think that something may come of Violet & Rupert Brooke, whom she favours. What do you think of that? We played 2 rubbers – Raymond & Goonie against Edward & me – Edward very reckless – but not much result in money one way or the other. Goonie will come with Clemmie to Walmer on Friday.

Margot wires that after playing a few holes of golf this morning she has taken to her bed, & thinks she has influenza, but she doesn't seem to be really bad. . . .

[1] This ward was named after a family of distinguished benefactors of the London Hospital. It formed part of a wing opened in 1876.

[2] *The Secret of the Night* by Gaston Leroux, which had appeared in an English translation in 1914.

[3] One sister, Olive, was the widow of the Comte de Janzi, the other, Eleanor (Norah), married Paul Methuen, the painter, in July 1915. He succeeded his father as Lord Methuen in 1932.

251

Thurs 7 Jan 1915 3 p.m.

My darling – I got Nurse Downing's telegram before breakfast this morning (is that going to be your *nom de guerre?* I think it is a very good one, & you might register it as a telegraphic address). I was not really disappointed, because I never hoped for to-day, but to-morrow (Fri) I trust it may be different. Do wire *early* to say where & when I am to bring the motor. I have read your letter I don't know how many times, & tried to realise your conditions. They fill me with *loathing*. That you should be turned out at 7 a.m. to sweep rooms & empty slops & do sluts' work is a thought wh. I can hardly endure. I might just as well be employed to run errands, & call taxis, & calculate percentages for Lord Swaythling. It would be about the same disproportion.

I notice that you are in a medical & not a surgical ward. Tho' blood & wounds are not nice things, I shd fancy they are more endurable to contemplate & to minister to, than typhoid & pneumonia. I have been trying (in the intervals of business) to calculate the number of hours a day in which you are actually standing up: it appals me. As Ben Jonson says: 'Is there a Heaven & Gods?'[1]

If we can get 2 good hours to-morrow aft. I will take you into fresh & wholesome air, & we can talk.

I wonder whether you have yet received the letter I wrote at midnight, and wh. was posted soon after 10 this morning? We had between noon & 2 p.m. a sitting of our War Council – quite a good body. Self & A.J.B. – K –

Winston, with his two septuagenarian Sea Dogs Fisher & Wilson, E. Grey, Haldane, Crewe, Hankey. We agreed that we cd. not back up Sir J. French in his projected Ostend-Zeebrugge operation, for wh. he requires 55 [*sic*] more battalions & an impossible amount of Artillery. W. pressed his scheme for acquiring a base at Borkum (wh. we have agreed always to speak of & if possible think of as Silt)[2] – a big business, as it is heavily fortified, and the necessary preparations will take till near the end of March. We gave him authority for this. By May or June there ought to be over 1,000,000 men either at the front, or available to go there; a Special Reserve here (for making good wastage in the over-sea force) of nearly 400,000: and a Home Defence Army of about 500,000 (This of course is *most private*). But I think it makes a good record: and one cannot help smiling, when men like Lansdowne[3] & St John & Curzon, who led us into the Boer war with *no* preparation at all, cavil & carp & criticise.[4]

There remain for discussion the larger questions of theatres & objectives, in regard to the choice of which one must always keep in view the chances of bringing in Italy, Roumania, & such minor but not negligible quantities as Greece & Bulgaria. We shall have another meeting to-morrow (Fri) morning to canvass this ground. And then after lunch I hope to be with you, best beloved. Thereafter to Walmer, where we shall have Clemmie & perhaps Goonie & the McKennae.

I stop now, for I want you to get this before you go to bed. Most dear – never more dear – I love you with heart & soul.

[1] *Catiline*, III.2: Cicero's opening speech.
[2] Borkum is in the East Frisian group, Sylt in the North Frisians.
[3] After the initial reverses of the Boer War there had been calls in the press for the impeachment of Lansdowne, who was then Secretary of State for War.
[4] Curzon's speech in the Lords, 6 Jan., had included some criticisms of the Government; and Lord Midleton (St John Brodrick) had made a similar, though much shorter, intervention in the same debate. Both sides emerged with a grievance. For Kitchener's indignation see Letter 256. Curzon wrote to Bonar Law: 'If we ask perfectly legitimate questions in the . . . Lords we are treated as though we were naughty children.'

252

Friday 8 Jan 1915 – in train

. . . As you said, we (you & I) are very different. There is no older or shallower fallacy than that like loves like. Here I am speeding along in a railway carriage *à trois* – my companions being two very attractive members of your sex – each by the way extremely well dressed – Clemmie fast asleep in one corner, & Goonie trying hard to read Carlyle's *Life of Schiller* in the other. And I all the time am thinking of 'the absent face that fixed me'.

You may say that that is not unnatural, considering everything. But at moments one is tempted to analyse & to seek explanations, if not to discover causes. So I have been thinking about it all – but as yet am not much wiser. Your magnificent equanimity & balance – not as you say looking for things or expecting them, but taking them as & when they come 'unsurprised', is a constant interest & delight to me. . . .

253

Walmer Castle,
Kent.

Sat 9 Jan 1915

. . . I often feel that it is difficult to keep anything like an equipoise between you and me. I *feel* more, and in some way you *understand* more: I sometimes wish that the balance could be redressed.

We are really a huge party here – more than the house, wh. looks big but has few rooms, can comfortably hold. . . .

It was a beautiful sunny morning to-day, and we all went after breakfast to golf on the Deal links wh. are of the highest class – only 12 holes at present, as 6 have been commandeered for shooting &c. by the military. We produced 9 or 10 golfers. I went out with Margot & Puffin, who played quite beautifully, driving a really long ball. I was fairly pleased with my own play. I *do* trust you will, when Providence permits, take to a little golf again: we had some quite good rounds just a year ago now at Delamere:[1] do you remember?

I received this morning 4 quarto pages from the Assyrian – *not* type-written. . . .

A little later. I have now tracked, with dubious & sometimes stumbling steps, thro' the thickets & boscage. It is a characteristic letter, & therefore in criticism shrewd, and in feeling (so far as I am concerned) more than nice. He trembles at the idea of Birrell being replaced – at present at any rate – by Jack Pease, of whom he says, quite truly, that he is a good example of the success of character 'unaided by any intellectual or interesting qualities' – and, therefore & thereby, unequal to cope with what may be or become a difficult Parliamentary situation. Further objections are 'Mrs. Pease in Dublin',[2] & the 'almost certain suicide of Simon' (!) as well as the manifold dangers of putting Masterman, an Anglo-Catholic, into the Education Office.[3] For that post – if it is to be vacated – he favours McNamara. For Chief Whip he is all for Whitley, but adds that (failing him) he was 'horrified to hear' the Ch. of the Ex^r say 'that it wd. be supposed not to be worth my while to go there'. And then, after a modest disclaimer of the 'qualities: physical & personal', which make a good whip, and the check to his main ambitions wh. would be involved, he adds that 'anything is worth my while that you think is useful to you'. Very simple & dignified & touching, don't you think? Of course, I would as soon cut off my right hand as ask him to make any such sacrifice.

But these things rather sweeten politics. I shall write him an appreciative letter. . . .

I have been thinking, at odd moments, of what Sylvia said to me on Monday night of my being both a good & a bad influence upon you. I can see now that I ought to have replied: 'You make a great mistake about the whole situation. The truth is that I have *less* influence upon Venetia than she has upon me. She is one of the least influenceable people in the world. I can say so, because no one knows her better, or has tried harder to understand her mind & character & temperament. The real truth can be best made clear by an illustration from mountaineering. There are various ways of getting, or trying to get, to the summit of apparently inaccessible Alpine peaks. Sometimes you can wind your way up a snow-field, which leads you, after much drudgery & patience, to the top. Others, again, can only be reached by the laborious & often tedious process of cutting steps in the ice. But there is a third class – the rarest, most difficult, most stimulating – wh. cannot be ascended except by *rock-climbing*. Now & again, there is a narrow cranny (perhaps with a hardy Alpine flower in bloom): often, what seems a practicable face is found to be covered with a surface of ice; and the whole way from start to finish (if you ever get there) you are lucky if you can secure sufficient hold for hand or foot, while a false step means not only failure but destruction. Of the last class there is no more conspicuous example than Mount Venetia'!

There, my own sweet darling, you see what I *sometimes* feel. But I mean to persevere, and wd far rather fall into the abyss than cease to climb. I won't ask you what you think of my chances.

I think I ought to close this now. I hope you will get a short respite to-morrow & see some of your friends. Monday & Tuesday I fear, from what you said, you will be shut in. But might not *Wed* be possible, if I came not much later than 2, & picked you up & we tried 'fresh woods' in the direction of Epping Forest? I *must* see you at least *twice* in every week: otherwise I shall starve. It was, in a way, much easier when you were 200 miles, more or less, away: now you are 'so near & yet so far'. I am going to read over again your Xmas present before I go to bed to-night. I wonder if you know *at all* how much I love you?

¹ Delamere golf-course is about 6 miles W. of Northwich, Cheshire. For Asquith's stay at Alderley, New Year 1914, see Letter 23.
² Ethel, daughter of the late Lt.-Gen. Sir Henry Havelock-Allan, Bt., V.C., and grand-daughter of the defender of Lucknow in the Indian Mutiny. From a remark in Asquith's Letter of 28 Sept. 1914 to Venetia (not selected) it would seem that he had no great opinion of Mrs. Pease's tact.
³ The Balfour Education Act of 1902 had greatly increased tension between the Church of England and the Nonconformist denominations; and this was still by far the most sensitive issue in educational policy in 1915.

254

Walmer Castle,
Kent.

Sunday 10 Jan 1915

. . . Winston . . . has been colloguing with K (for the moment they are on the most sugary terms) and . . . they both agree to advise French to take Haig in place of Murray. Technically it is right that the best man next to the C. in Chief shd be Chief of Staff, as K. was to Roberts in S. Africa. But I am not sure that Haig is not irreplaceable as first fighting Commander. On the other hand, Robertson is no doubt extremely useful where he is.¹. . .

. . . Whitley . . . asks for time to consider the offer of the Whipship, but hints that there seem to be 'insuperable obstacles' in the way of his acceptance. If he remains in this frame of mind I must have him up to London & try to talk him over; for, the more I consider the problem, the less hope have I of finding any other suitable man.². . .

No one who has had anything like my experience in judging mankind can doubt (at moments) that there is an element of imagination and even illusion (what you call 'prejudice') in one's conception of the person one loves. But *reality* is always in fact only a relative term. . . . At any rate if I am in chains, I cling tightly to them. The *you* that I see & know & love is, to me, the *Real you*; and . . . I am pretty certain that I am neither mad nor doting. . . .

. . . I believe you are accurate in saying that you rarely, if ever, do or abstain from doing things from a *conscious* reference to a supposed standard of right & wrong. You don't like Wordsworth (alas!) – so I hardly like to quote the lines from the Ode to Duty:

> Glad hearts, without reproach or blot,
> Who do thy work, & know it not³ . . .

¹ Robertson was appointed Chief of Staff in Mar. 1915. See Letter 243, n. 4.

² Whitley had been Deputy Speaker since 1911 and was ten years younger than the Speaker. He wanted the Speakership and virtually held the reversion to it as long as he stayed where he was.

³ This had long been one of Asquith's favourite quotations. Writing just after his first wife's death he had applied it to her. See also Letter 287.

255

Walmer Castle,
Kent.

Monday 11 Jan 1915

My darling (I like to have the prefix now & again, when the spirit moves you). . . . You don't say anything about how you are in body or health – what for instance about the hands, & the ankles, wh. were beginning to be a source of anxiety at the time of our last drive? Figs to eat, at intervals, are better than nothing.

I am sorry if my well-meant & apparently successful efforts to get my letter to you on Sunday caused undue agitation. . . .

I thank God . . . that this is going to be only an episode in your life: otherwise I also shd. become a student of what you call 'toxiology', with a view to discovering the speediest & most painless exit from the disappointments of life.

About plans: I see you say Wed. aft. is impossible, & it is not unlikely that our War Council will go on sitting that day after lunch. I shall count on having you on *Friday* at lunch at Downing St, & to drive afterwards. But if I were free, couldn't I come & see you sometime, & if so when, on *Thurs morning*, when I gather you will be off for a time? Do try to manage this – my own love: I *pine* to see you.

I must now tell you what I have been doing since I wrote yesterday (I hope you got my letter by the first post). . . . On Sunday . . . General Murray . . . sat in my little room here with W & me for over an hour, & talked over the whole situation & prospects at the front. He is a very attractive type of soldier, good looking & soft-voiced, highly cultivated, and (as we both thought) extremely intelligent. For some reason that I don't understand, there has been a set made against him, partly by the French, but more I fancy thro' the intriguings & manoeuvres of that serpent Wilson, who wd. much like to supplant him. I shall speak to French again on the subject when he comes here this week. The real (immediate) difficulty of the position is this: Joffre wants French to re-occupy (thereby setting free French troops) what is called the 'Ypres salient', and Sir John is under some kind of promise to him to do so when called upon. But he (Sir J.) cannot do this, and *also* undertake the flanking coast operation, – with the objective of Ostend & Zeebrugge, unless he is given at least 50 battalions more troops. If Joffre released him from his promise, he would be quite ready to go in without reinforcements for the other job (wh, of course, he greatly prefers, as he wd. have the co-operation of the Navy) provided he can be equipped with 3 or 4 weeks supply of ammunition for his heavy guns. Howitzers with high explosive shells[1] are the only form of artillery that is of much use for knocking to pieces trenches & the variety of improvised fortifications wh. the Germans are so skilful in constructing (Murray told us that an English chemist Robert Mond – brother of Sir Alfred of that ilk – has a plan, wh. Murray thinks quite promising, for undermining, & causing the collapse of great works like those of La Bassée by *waterpower*. It is used apparently a good deal in American mines for big blasting operations. All the ingenious & inventive brains are now at work trying to devise some new mechanical check-mate for the latest developments of the art of defensive war). . . .

. . . One or two other things Murray said will interest you. (1) He does not believe in the possibility of a successful German offensive in Flanders or France, even if we send no more troops. (2) He hinted (this is *Most Secret*) that the points at wh. the French hope sooner or later to break through are at Arras & East of Rheims.[2] (3) He calculates the life of a battalion , in such a war as this, as not longer than 6 months. His own old regiment, wh. arrived in France early in Aug. 1000 strong, is now reduced to 100, i.e. all the other 900 places have already been filled up, to make good losses by death, wounds, illness, prisoners &c. So that by Feb. French's Army – so far at any rate as Infantry are concerned – will be an entirely *new one*: hardly a man in it of those who crossed in Aug. last. Doesn't that strike you as remarkable?[3] . . .

---

[1] As opposed to low-angle field artillery (such as the British 18-pounder) firing shrapnel.

[2] The French attacked 'east of Rheims' on 16 Feb. Between then and 30 Mar. their 4th Army suffered 240,000 casualties without gaining the dominating ground on which the German defensive positions were based. This attack was to be matched by one north of Arras against Vimy Ridge, the combined effect being to threaten the vast German salient, centred on Noyon, which was pointed towards Paris. The British offensive at Neuve Chapelle (Letter 355, text and n. 2) was planned to coincide with Foch's assault on Vimy. The latter became delayed, however, first by the failure of the French operations in the south, and then by the German gas attack near Ypres. When it was eventually delivered on 9 May the French achieved an initial success; but, in a pattern often to be repeated, this could not be exploited and the month-long battle cost them about 400,000 men.

[3] See the account of the First Battle of Ypres in A. Farrar-Hockley, *Death of an Army* (1967).

256

. . . (I was interrupted by a visit from K, who came I think principally to ventilate his indignation over Curzon's speech[1] in the Lords the other day. He says he has now here & in France about 1¾ million men under arms: an absolutely unexampled feat, when you consider that we have only been 5 months at war, & have lost approximately on net balance some 80,000 men). . . .

. . . Goonie was in her most characteristic form. . . . She had been very much bullied at her own old home at Xmas about politics: they were perpetually telling her that Haldane had reduced the artillery: ('do give me the figures, darling, put them down on paper, so that I shall have my reply ready'): and her Mother 'a very stupid woman' had even referred in a gibing way to Marconi![2]

Another rather curious figure in our party was Beb, clad in khaki, & growing an orange-coloured moustache, against wh. all but Cynthia protested (I heard Puffin, who had been among the adverse critics, say to her in a low & sympathetic tone 'I hope I didn't hurt your feelings, Cynthia'). He is more slow in speech & undecided in action than I ever remember him, and the girls say that when I asked him at breakfast if he was going to golf, he looked musingly out of the window (it was a lovely morning) and after a long interval replied: 'My plans have not yet crystallised'. He is full of rather argumentative fads about spies, conscription &c, and, as Cys says, his 'bonnet is a regular bee-hive'. Cynthia was in good looks and very happy & nice. . . .

I think this may amuse you: it is one of the watchwords of the Russian Revolutionaries in the early days of Nihilism – about 1881: 'We are breakfasting on the Jews: we shall dine on the landlords, and sup on the priests.'

We had a Cabinet this afternoon wh. lasted nearly 2 hours, but was not particularly interesting. I brought up the question of the rise in the price of bread, meat, coal &c, wh. is becoming serious, & is due partly to the high freights of ships, & partly to the shortage of dock labour in consequence of the large number of recruits.

The Admiralty have taken up about 1000 or 1100 merchant ships for transport of troops &c – many of wh. they no longer for the moment require; and there are a lot of prize vessels wh. have been captured and wh. ought to be sold more quickly & set free. The increase of labour is more difficult: K. characteristically suggested that women shd. be employed, and when it was pointed out that they are not suited or accustomed to loading or unloading cargoes he replied that they were so employed at Zanzibar! There is no doubt that women might take the place of a lot of clerks, shopmen, & even bus & tram conductors: perhaps you can suggest other trades. . . .

[1] When C.-in-C., India, in 1905, Kitchener had been at odds with Curzon, then Viceroy; and the dispute had led to Curzon's resignation.
[2] Her 'old home' was Wytham Abbey, Oxford. For Haldane and the artillery see p. 323, n. 1; for Marconi, Letter 7, n. 3. 'Goonie' was the Earl of Abingdon's elder daughter by his second marriage. Her half-sister Mary was married to Lord Edmund Talbot, the Conservative Chief Whip.

257

Tues 12 Jan 15 [ii] after midnight

. . . I can't help hating the thought of you ministering, with your dear hands, to these outcast & unmeriting invalids. I *mind* it *more* than I can say. . . .

I weave many visions as to possible futures, but they die down in the hard, cold, clear light of common day. As we drove up this morning in the motor (it is about 80 miles), we had two or three very narrow shaves of collision & disaster. And after each, I said to myself – suppose it had gone wrong, & I had (as Browning says) 'ended my cares'[1] what would have been the consequence?

Lots of stuff in the Press – a 'nine days' wonder in the country: violent speculation as to who was to succeed me – E. Grey, Ll. George, Crewe &c; many obituary notices; and after a week or 10 days (at the outside) the world going on as tho' nothing had happened. Very much what I said to you at Penrhos at Whitsuntide: a few ripples, even, if you like, a bit of a splash in the pool – but little or nothing more.

Of the men with whom I have been most closely associated, I think that those who wd. (for a time) feel it most are, oddly enough Haldane, McKenna & the Assyrian: a strange trinity; of my own family Violet, Oc & perhaps Puffin: and among women I am inclined to think Viola (tho' I am not at all sure about this).[2]

And you – my most dearly beloved, to whom every day & night, I give my best thoughts, my most intimate confidence, my unceasing devotion, my fears & hopes, my strength & weakness, my past my present my future – *you*! what would it mean to you?

I don't know – I can't think. All I know is that I am (whatever you may ever be) always – everywhere – wholly yours.

[P.S.] A stupid letter![3]

[P.P.S.] Wed. morning 13th
Alas! no letter this morning, very hungry![4]

[1] What, you want, do you, to come unawares,
   Sweeping the church up for first morning-prayers,
And find a poor devil has ended his cares
   At the foot of your rotten-runged rat-riddled stairs?
      'Master Hugues of Saxe-Gotha', xxix.
[2] Viola Parsons (née Tree) was to write: 'Mr Asquith, though professedly unmusical, followed my movements with interest. I, in my turn, naturally worshipped him; and he became a tremendous hero and great friend': *Castles in the Air* (1926), p. 140.
[3] Added at top of first page.
[4] Red ink note.

The Dardanelles I: the Naval Attack

THE attack on the Dardanelles was by far the most promising of the possible operations which the War Council reviewed; but it should have been planned as a combined military and naval operation from the start.[1] In the paper which Asquith received from Hankey on 30 December (Letter 241), and in the War Council on 8 January (Letter 251, para. 5), it was advocated and discussed on the assumption that it would be planned in this way. It was Churchill who suggested a solely naval attack at the War Council on 13 January (Letter 258),[2] and who persuaded the Council to decide for that on 28 January, despite Fisher's obvious misgivings (Letter 281).[3]

The idea of a wholly naval attack was fatally attractive. The naval force could be collected quickly, in that the elimination of the German commerce raiders had made a surplus of pre-Dreadnought battleships immediately available. By contrast, an army for the Dardanelles would mean wrangles with Sir John French and with Joffre and Millerand (Letters 272 and 274); and it might entail serious delays. Yet the arguments for leaving the job entirely to the navy proved insubstantial and unrealistic. The initial reason for moving at once despite the risks disappeared before the War Council had even met. The Russian high command asked (1 January), via the British Ambassador, for action against Turkey to relieve the pressure on their army in the Caucasus. The request had hardly been digested before news came of a shattering Turkish defeat on the Caucasus Front.[4] A far more important reason for speed was that enemy submarines were expected at the Dardanelles; but, in the event, they did not arrive until May 1915 (p. 598).

The notion that all the resources were available for an immediate naval attack was mistaken. The most essential component of all was lacking, namely an efficient minesweeping force capable of operating against a strong current, in a narrow channel dominated by shore batteries. The second argument, that a wholly naval attack could be discontinued without loss of prestige if no initial success should be achieved, proved equally delusive. The naval bombardment which began on 19 February was promptly publicized in an attempt to affect the wavering neutrals (Letters 316 and 326). Within five days it was accepted that withdrawal was impossible. 'The effect of a defeat in the Orient', Kitchener pronounced on 24 February, 'would be very serious.'[5]

The idea of a wholly naval operation had faded before the bombardment even began. The abandonment of the plans for a land attack on Zeebrugge (Letter 255), and the failure of the Turkish attempt on the Suez Canal (Letter 288), made some troops available; and the evidence that the navy could not complete the job without military support became too strong to disregard. Hankey was close enough to the Admiralty to know that Churchill was almost the only person there who had ever believed in a solely naval effort; he suspected indeed that Churchill had planned the operation in this way in order to recoup the prestige which he had lost at Antwerp.[6] On 13 February Asquith and Hankey were in agreement that troops should be sent (Letter 303); and three days later it was decided at an informal meeting of the War Council that the 29th Division, the sole regular division remaining in Britain, should be despatched to Lemnos, and a force prepared in Egypt 'to be available . . . to support the naval attack on the Dardanelles'.[7]

Thus the Dardanelles expedition became, too grudgingly and too late, a combined operation of a sort. But the mistake of not planning it as one from the start could not be made good. Though the difficulty of collecting an adequate army for it was very real, this might have proved surmountable if faced at the beginning. Quite a small military force sent promptly would have been worth more than the large one which landed on the tip of the Gallipoli Peninsula in April. Here, as always, the chief responsibility for a mistaken decision lay with the Prime Minister. He knew more than his colleagues on the War Council about Fisher's forebodings. If anyone could have restrained Churchill it was the premier. But Asquith was not the only member of the Council to disregard warnings which should have been heeded. On 19 March Hankey recorded laconically in his diary:

On the first day proposal was made I warned P.M., Lord K, Chief of Staff, L. George and Balfour that Fleet could not effect passage without troops and that all naval officers thought so.[8]

[1] Some of the expectations entertained about it were unrealistic, however. Even if completely successful it probably would not have united all the Balkan countries against the Central Powers.

[2] Asquith's minute recorded that the Admiralty 'should . . . prepare for a naval expedition in Feb. to bombard and take the Gallipoli Peninsula, with Constantinople as its objective'.

³ Fisher had explained these misgivings in a memorandum intended for the War Council, but not circulated to it, 25 Jan., and in a letter to the Prime Minister, 28 Jan.; *Churchill: Companion Docs., 1914–1916*, pp. 451–4, 461–2. Asquith later implied that the entire basis of Fisher's objections was an 'avowed preference for a wholly different objective': *Parl. Deb.*, xci. 1762. In fact, however, Fisher had based his case against an exclusively naval operation in the Dardanelles on the need to maintain a clear superiority to the German Navy in the North Sea. He argued that, even when the ships were expendable, the trained crews were not.

⁴ The London evening papers announced the Russian victory at Sarykamysh on 5 Jan., though its full extent did not become known until the following day.

⁵ *Churchill:Companion Docs., 1914–1916*, p. 559.

⁶ Diary, 19 Mar. 1915.

⁷ See Letters 318 and 322 for the delay in despatching this division.

⁸ See also Hankey's diary, 12 Mar. For the difficulty experienced by the War Council in eliciting the views of the naval and military staffs see Spender and Asquith, ii. 187. Despite these views Hankey defended the War Council decision with his usual ability when questioned by the Dardanelles Commission: G. H. Cassar, *Kitchener* (1977), p. 285.

258

Wed 13 Jan 1915 [i] 3.30 p.m.

My darling – I have just received your most welcome letter, and quite understand why it couldn't have come sooner. I hope I didn't cause further 'agitation' by sending my second letter by messenger this morning. I knew you were going out for the afternoon, & wanted you to get it before you started. I feel rather jealous of the Assyrian & the Bud, who have seen more of you than I have. But I want to mend my luck. So I have wired to you to say that if (as I suppose) you breakfast with Cynthia at Sussex Place, I will come & pick you up about 10.30 so that I could get you back to your place by 11.30, & myself keep a revised appointment with the King at Buckingham Palace by noon. Then you might come here to *dinner* in the evening. (This last I see is wrong: you say your free day is *Tuesday* i.e. next week. Of course I shall keep it free: tell me your hours.) & on Friday you will be here to lunch, & we shall have a *real* drive afterwards. *Friday* is all right. What do you say to this plan of campaign?

We are now (4 p.m) in the midst of our War Council, wh. began at 12, adjourned at 2, & is now sitting again. Sir J. French is here & sits next me. A most interesting discussion, but so confidential and secret that I won't put anything down on paper, but I will talk fully to you to-morrow (if we meet then) or if not in the course of our drive on Friday.

Later. The Council is now over, having arrived harmoniously at 4 conclusions suggested by me, wh. will keep both Navy & Army busy till March. I am keen to tell you all about it, & see if it meets with your approval.

I hope you had a good time off to-day with Kath & the Bud: it wd. be nice if the last named cd. join you in your dismal pilgrimage: as the Assyrian said, sadly & sententiously, at lunch here to-day to Violet (I overheard with the sharpness of ear one has when some one we care for is mentioned): 'She was not meant to be a Nurse'! . . .

We talked about good manners, wh. are not very common in these days: the Assyrian, tho' not perhaps a perfect exponent or practitioner of the art, is critical of others. Viola said that 'for an Asquith' Oc was good. She will hear more of this.

I wished more than once that, like Huck on a famous occasion, you had lain *perdue* (not that he was the least *perdu*) during the War Council to-day. It wd. have amused & interested you intensely – not only for the subjects discussed, but for the curious lights it threw on human nature & character. I maintained an almost unbroken silence until the end, when I intervened with my conclusions but, except for one or two furtive glances at your letter, (wh. only arrived at 3) I kept a careful watch on the rest. French sat next to me on one side & A.J.B. on the other; next to French K, then old Jacky Fisher, Winston & Sir A Wilson (the Naval Trinity); and beyond them Crewe, Grey, & Ll. George. You won't often see a stranger collection of men at one table. Of the lay disputants the best were A.J.B. & Ll. George. French & K were polite & almost mealy-mouthed to one another. Happily the great question upon wh. they are nearly at daggers-drawn (how the new 'K' armies are to be organised – as separate entities, or intermingled with the old units) tho' broached, was tacitly postponed to a later & more convenient date.[1] Winston (if such a phrase is possible) showed a good deal of rugged fluency.

5.20 p.m. Darling I have just got your sweet little note written this morning & finished in the motor. I am rather sorry you have made an appointment with Violet in the morning, as it will, I fear, prevent me from driving you back to your loathsome prison-house. Anyhow I shall see you here at 10.30, unless you wire that I am to come for you.

You are perfectly right to chuck the wretched physiology handbook into the waste-paper basket: never bother about it again.

I resent more than I can say that you shd. spend your days doing what almost any charwoman cd. do. I have *never* in my life known a case of more shocking & wanton waste. I can't even now (after much reflection) quite make out the time-table of your days: is it that, on alternate days, you get 9 to 12 in morning, or 1.30 to 5 in afternoon? & on Sundays rather less? It is hideous to think of – but none the less important to know.

I am going this evening after an early dinner to see *Raffles*[2] with Puffin. To-morrow we have a dimmish lot of people to dinner, and I have a rather busy day. As I fancy it is one of your days 'in', I suppose the only time you can write is in the morning (and you won't be able to do that):- so that you will have to wait until after post-time. You have been such an *angel* in writing that I cannot thank you enough. I hope my pencil letter of last night didn't bore you. It came from the heart. I wish I cd. tell you how I *love* you.

¹ The commanders in France wanted the new armies to be incorporated, in the words of the War Council Minute, 'in units not larger than a brigade with the regular force'. Kitchener pointed out that 'the *esprit de corps* and the spirit of emulation of the new armies would be lost by the adoption of Sir John French's proposals'. The question was agreed to turn on the prospects of a breakthrough in France. French's scheme would be the better if, but only if, the war could be won in 1915.

² A revival at Wyndham's Theatre with Gerald du Maurier once again in the name part. Raffles, the 'amateur cracksman', was the creation of the novelist, E. W. Hornung. He had adapted his story for the theatre with the help of E. W. Presbrey.

259

Wed. midnight 13 Jan 15 [ii] – really Thurs. morning.

My darling – I am a little disappointed about to-day (I mean Thursday) – tho' it is not the least your fault. But when I got your first letter, wh. only came at 3 p.m., – I at once postponed my interview with the King until noon, that we might have the hour 10.30 to 11.30 together. But you had already made your appointment with Violet, & I can see that that was difficult to change. So I suppose I shall have only the briefest of glimpses of you in the morning. . . .

I wanted so much at the earliest opportunity, and while the impressions were still fresh, to talk to you, & get your opinions about to-day's War Council. But I know you will send me a nice letter when you get back to your prison (which I shall sorely need): and on Friday we can have a real talk. . . .

. . . Wimborne . . . is quite inflated about his new Irish career. He is all for comprehension & inclusion – with a view to beating down the Unionist social boycott. He produced a list of his proposed *entourage* – his first name for the principal place (private Sec^y) being Lord Drogheda!¹ I vetoed this at once, much to his surprise & obvious chagrin, & told him to go to Bongie & obtain from him the name of some competent & colourless Civil Servant.

The result of the War Council pleased me: they all parted on the best of terms (including French & K) & with a real, if not ambitious, programme for both Army & Navy. . . .

. . . I recall a little rhyme, wh. I wrote down in the Cabinet & wh. pleased J. Morley, when Ll. George was evolving his Budget of 1909:

George moves in a mysterious way,
His little sums to make;
Loose logic, lax arithmetic
Contribute to the fake. . . .

[1] The Earl of Drogheda had been elected, only a year earlier, to an Irish Representative Peerage by Conservative votes: see Letters 263 and 264.

260

Thurs 14 Jan 1915

My darling – I am really distressed at your thinness: I couldn't have imagined that one week on the treadmill could have taken so much out of you. . . . When the conditions are such that I can do so without giving you away, I shall let that well-advertised figure-head, Lord Knutsford,[1] know in the plainest English what I think of his system. . . .

I had the best part of an hour with the King: he is a strong Kitchenerite, and a little disposed to underrate French.[2] He is very bitter about the German treatment of our prisoners wh. seems to be extremely bad, according to the account given by Capt. Vandeleur, who lately escaped from Crefeld. French had been to see him & was as optimistic as ever. I told him that my view is that neither the French nor the Germans can add anything really substantial to their present forces: that the most they can do is to replace wastage; and that by the end of the summer this process will be coming to an end & they will continue to diminish. The exact reverse is the case with ourselves & Russia (subject to the question of ammunition), and if you add the chance or more than chance of Italy & Roumania coming in, the odds *in the long run* are largely on our side. Do you agree to this forecast?

I had a dullish Committee meeting, and then lunch, where the only new figure was a Croat (sent by Benckendorff) who explained to me at great length – with the aid of maps – the ambitions & hopes of the Croats & Slovenes. The liquidation of Austria-Hungary will be one of the most tangled businesses that has ever fallen to the lot of man.

Since lunch I have had a long interview with Whitley, who firmly declines to become Chief Whip, mainly on grounds of health &c.[3] I asked him to suggest alternatives, and out of a fairly long list wh. he produced (including of course the inevitable Verney)[4] the only name wh. struck me as at all possible was that of Francis Acland, who is now Foreign Under Secretary. Do you know him? He has a foolish Suffragette wife,[5] but is himself a capable, tho' I think a rather angular, man.

Then came in Crewe, wanting to know what answer to send to a message from Hardinge, who rather hinted (in consequence of the War) at a temporary extension of his term of office: it expires in November.[6] We both thought that there was no case for this, & began to canvass the names of possible successors. None of the present Governors (Carmichael &c) will do, and we turned our attention to our colleagues. I ruled out the Islingtons, and then threw a fly about the Assyrian, but it did not lure Crewe at all: he thought it quite an impossible idea, wh. wd. arouse the resentment of the whole Indian Civil Service, be badly received by the leading Native Princes, and be regarded here at home as in the nature of a party job. At the same time he was full of appreciation of our friend's qualifications & merits – in the abstract. Emmott we mentioned & dismissed. But what of Beauchamp or Bron? He was disposed to think that either would be quite good, with a slight leaning in favour of Bron. (Of course we assumed that K.[7] was now out of the question). No choice or announcement need be made till the early summer, and much may happen before then. All this is very *private*. . . .

I had a letter just now from Sylvia of all people, about a silly story, told to her by Blanche Lloyd, that I had said at lunch here on Wed Aug 5th in the presence of Lord Roberts, (the day after the declaration of war) that we did not intend to send out an Expeditionary force. As Roberts did not lunch here until nearly 2 months afterwards, the thing was an obvious lie, and she (B.L) now corrects it by saying Lord R 'had the information from a man who was lunching' with me. The thing is of course an invention, but it shows how malevolent old Roberts was. I could do him a pretty good turn in the way of revenge (if I cared) by relating what is true: that at the War Council that same day, he strongly deprecated the sending of Indian troops to Europe to the horror of K. and all the other Generals who were present. He afterwards wrote me a letter of recantation: but that was his advice at the time.[8] If the Indians knew, they would have given him a very different reception when he went out to see & praise them. . . .

[1] Knutsford had become interested in social reform through the influence of one of his masters at Wellington College, and had been drawn to London's East End by inheriting some East and West India Dock shares from an uncle. As Chairman of the Governors since 1896 he had raised large sums for the London Hospital.

[2] 'French may be a good soldier,' the King wrote to the Duke of Connaught on 23 May 1915; 'but I don't think he is particularly clever and he has an awful temper.'

[3] See Letter 254, n. 2.

[4] See Letter 234, n. 3.

[5] A good example of Asquith's prejudiced views on women's suffrage. Eleanor Acland had been involved with the non-violent Liberal Women's Suffrage Union: she was a suffragist, not a suffragette. She and her husband had, however, tried to mediate between the suffragette leaders and the Government; it may have been this which had aroused Asquith's annoyance.

[6] In Mar. Asquith became so disturbed by Hardinge's telegrams that he wondered whether the change ought to be made sooner than Nov. The Viceroy, worried by internal unrest, had

almost refused to send troops to Mesopotamia: Asquith to Montagu, 7 Mar. 1915, Montagu MSS.

⁷ Kitchener had been a strong contender for the Viceroyalty in 1910; but Morley, then Secretary of State, had foreseen ill results from sending a famous soldier as Viceroy, with all the fears of paternalism and repression which this might evoke, immediately after the passage of the India Councils Act, 1909.

⁸ See Letter 134, n. 5.

261

15 Jan 15 [i] in train

My darling – this has been an afternoon of narrow shaves, & almost the narrowest was that by wh. I caught this train at exactly ½ a minute after 5: they kept it so long for me. We had terrible blocks in Whitechapel & Aldgate, but Horwood was on his mettle, & sprinted along the Embankment & thro' the Mall in defiance of every law at more than the pace of a Derby winner. . . .

Despite the 'regrettable incident' of the knocking down of the errand boy, & the time wasted in our futile & irritating quest of a doctor, I think we have rarely had a more heavenly drive. Apart from a slight suggestion of weariness in the corner of your eyes, I have never known you in better looks, but *please* darling don't get any thinner. Do weigh yourself from time to time. I can hardly bear to think of you now, in your disguising uniform, ministering to those undeserving aliens. And 'to-morrow & to-morrow creeping, in its petty' & squalid pace, from day to day, for more than another 2 months! . . .

I don't believe I had time to tell you of my talk this morning with Lloyd George and the 2 Buxtons, who were both shot (one in the lungs) by a young Turk at Bucharest some weeks ago,¹ and have employed their time of convalescence in going round the Balkan States, & interviewing the leading so-called 'statesmen' of that devil's kitchen. They are strong pro-Bulgars, and are quite sure that if we offered (1) Bulgaria, the slice of Macedonia Irredenta which (Monastir, &c) the Serbs stole from her 2 years ago² (2) Servia, Bosnia & a good bit of the coast of Dalmatia (3) Roumania, Transylvania & one or two oddments & (4) Greece, Southern Albania, Rhodes & the other islands, & perhaps Smyrna & a strip of the shore of Asia Minor in that region – we could bring the whole lot in to fight on our side. They all hate one another & are as jealous as cats – particularly the Serbians & Bulgarians; but in the case of the 2 latter we cd. save them from the repulsive necessity of fighting side by side, by putting them back to back – the Serbs

going for Austria & the Bulgars for Turkey. This (with our Gallipoli enterprise, of wh. of course I did not tell them) might conceivably make a huge &
even decisive diversion. It wd certainly compel Italy to come in.

On the whole (tho' the difficulties are prodigious) I am attracted by the
plan. How does it strike you? . . .

Suppose we had come to grief this afternoon, & what remained of us had
been picked up by the Countess Benck! . . .

[1] Charles and Noel Buxton had gone to Bucharest, with the blessing of Churchill and Lloyd
George, but with little encouragement from Grey, nominally to attend the funeral of King
Carol of Roumania, but in fact hoping to enlist a Balkan confederation on the side of the Allies.

[2] The Buxtons and those who thought with them argued that King Carol's death removed
the leading friend of Germany and Austria from Roumania, while the Bulgars had been
friendly to Britain since Gladstone's time. None of this reduced the difficulty that the Serbs
had gained 'the slice of Macedonia' by repelling an unprovoked Bulgarian attack in June 1913.
They were unwilling to give up this territory whatever compensations they were offered
elsewhere. They were fighting with the Allies; and their lands could not be rearranged
without their consent. See also Letter 218, n. 2.

262

Walmer Castle,
Kent.

Friday midnight 15 Jan 1915 [ii]

. . . We have had a nice quiet yet not uninteresting evening *à quatre* –
Violet & I, Bongie & Cys. It is so peaceful to be remote from the world we
live in every day & all day. I can't imagine anything more heavenly than
having you here for 3 or 4 days under these conditions. We cd. settle so
many outstanding things, and talk, without strain or pressure, about things
that don't need to be settled. I always feel that when we meet in London –
delicious & free as our intercourse is – we have a sense of 'Time's winged
chariot hurrying near': the delight of a place like this is that you feel that his
chariot (or motor) is stabled in the garage, and that you are no longer under
the harassing compulsion either of time or space. . . .

263

Walmer Castle,
Kent.

Sat 16 Jan 1915

. . . Your veto on Neil for Chief Whip is heartily endorsed by both Violet
and Bongie. I wonder why Ll. G. is so enamoured of the idea?[1] I am

beginning to think that, *faute de mieux*, it will be the line of least resistance to promote Gulland. Not good;[2] and to me very drab & wearisome: but can you suggest anything better?

Birrell writes putting in a rather half-hearted plea for Drogheda. I have told him it is impossible for the W's to start with a man in their principal & most confidential place who only last year was elected by the Unionists as a Representative Peer. Of course, a more serious difficulty is the Lady, who wd. be the power behind the (Vice) Throne.[3] The Wimbornes show just the same persistence & importunity about this as they did in urging & engineering their own claims. As I said to Birrell, if this kind of thing goes on, we may before very long be regretting the golden days of Lord & Lady 'Tara': do you see that this is the ridiculous title wh. Aberdeen proposes to add to his own when he becomes a Marquis?[4]

I have told Birrell he *must* come to dinner on Tuesday. I believe you wd. like to have him as much as anybody? And I have suggested to Margot that she shd. ask the Bencks.

I gather from to-day's telegrams that Italy is now hard at work pulling the strings among the Balkan States. One can't afford to be too particular or fastidious in the present condition of the world, but I have enough of the old Adam in me to wish that both Italy & the U.S.A. may come badly out of the whole of this business.[5]. . .

. . . Whatever comes or goes in the near future, sinking or swimming, success or failure or stalemate, rising or falling stars, sunset or sunrise: I shall always think, & feel, that no man has ever, in trying times & circumstances, been so fortunate or so blessed. And that means – *You*. Bless you beloved – think & dwell on it all, and *try* to love me.

[1] Neil Primrose, unlike his father, Lord Rosebery, was identified with the more radical elements in the Liberal party. Lloyd George was well aware that he had endangered his radical links by participating in a war Government. His backing for Primrose probably represented an attempt to repair them.

[2] Gulland was not a success in the post; but he inherited an inadequate Whips' Office.

[3] Wimborne seems to have been attracted by Lady Drogheda. Cynthia Asquith, who had stayed at Viceregal Lodge, noted: 'She is a "dainty dish" – she and His Ex [Wimborne] *are* a couple – . . . . However, . . . she seemed very kindly and I quite liked her.'

[4] The double title 'Aberdeen and Tara' was devised by the retiring Lord-Lieutenant as a sign of his devotion to Ireland. The appropriation of this historic Irish name by a Scotsman was not appreciated, however. On 19 Jan. the *Daily Mail* suggested 'Aberdeen and Britannia' or 'Aberdeen and Sinai' as alternatives, while Margot Asquith remarked that, as a Scot, she would have resented 'and Bannockburn' being added to an English title.

[5] A striking illustration of the way in which the contraband question had affected Asquith's views on American policy. By 'the whole of this business' he seems to refer simply to the war and its outcome.

264

Walmer Castle,
Kent.

Sunday 17 Jan 1915 [i]

My darling – your delicious long letter arrived this morning & has made me happy. . . .

All our guests except the Winstons arrived in time for dinner yesterday – including Eddie Marsh & Davies. We had some excellent talk at dinner, to wh. I am bound to say the Assyrian contributed little or nothing. Dear old Henry James was in his best form,[1] muttering in his staccato way his phrases & epigrams, and (after his fashion) as often as not leaving the building half-finished with the scaffolding still around it. . . .

. . . We had some rather good 'stunts', as you & some others call them: Eddie did his Housman Greek tragedy most excellently, and my young man Davies 'obliged' with a very skilful imitation of George Alexander at his best, and worst,[2] Viola & Alan played the part of appreciative spectators. After I went to my bedroom I took out my secret book, & read & re-read some of the Sonnets that we like best.

It is a most beautiful morning – brilliant sun with a coldish wind. Most of them have gone golfing: I may go after lunch, but I prefer talking to you, and I have besides some odds & ends of work that I ought to clear up.

I am glad you told me exactly what you thought about Neil Primrose. I believe – indeed I am sure – that you are right. The Assyrian is almost past holding when the idea is broached. He is sure that all the existing Whips wd. at once resign. With the passion for begging & pushing wh. characterises the Guest family, Freddie took the opportunity of urging *his* claims to the post upon our friend, with a view of course to their being transmitted to the right quarter. He F.G has no doubt that it would be the best and most popular appointment! the only thing that gives him any pause is the question whether he is not rendering for the moment more valuable service in acting as runner & go-between from French to Winston & vice versa.[3] I told you how Ivor had been again at Birrell over the Drogheda business: this morning Violet has 4 sides from Alice pressing (in the most sugared terms) the same point. You doubt my capacity for inflicting snubs (is it moral cowardice, or some intellectual deficiency?): but I have told Violet to return the short answer that the matter is settled and cannot be reopened – oddly enough almost the same language one latterly had to use to the moribund Aberdeens.

To go back to the Whipship, about wh. I talked a little to the Assyrian – he suggested Maclean, quite an impossible person – I am not sure that I shall

not have to fall back upon Gulland (for the House) and Benn (for organisation & the country). It would not be a brilliant solution, but it wd. offend
nobody, and each of them has the merit of knowing very well his particular
side of the job. It wd. be difficult to justify the putting of Geoffrey over
Gulland.[4] I should be the chief sufferer; a daily interview & intimate
converse with Gulland has no attraction and I doubt whether I could rely
upon him (as I always could upon Illingworth) to 'stick up' to me when his
judgment differed from mine. He didn't mind the least being overruled, but
he always spoke his mind.

Tell me darling what you think of this.

Your quotation about the witches' caldron is very much to the point.
There are a good many other explosive ingredients besides 'Turk & Tartar':
tho' curiously enough 'liver of blaspheming Jew'[5] is not one of them. There
are very few Semites in these countries, except in Roumania, where they are
given the devil's own time. You don't say what you think of the partition on
Buxton lines: it is all at the expense of Austria & Turkey,[6] except the Greek
islands wh. Italy holds in pawn, & will not let go without getting in
exchange a good substantial pound of flesh for herself. I regard it as of the
first importance that, one way or the other, they shd. all be brought in . . .

I have been writing a letter of congratulation to my niece Dinah; she is to
be married next month, and I hope she is not going to be another victim to
the hazards of war.[7] She has always been my favourite in that family, and I
told her that it was not at all a 'niecely' thing to go & get engaged to a man
whom I had never seen. Telegraph in the morning if any name occurs to you
of some one you specially want at dinner on Tuesday. . . .

[1] James, then aged 71, lived in the Lamb House, Rye. He became a British subject in July
1915 and was awarded the Order of Merit, on Asquith's recommendation, in the New Year
Honours of 1916. He commented on his Walmer weekend: 'The sentiment the place makes
one entertain . . . for old England is of the most acutely sympathetic; and the good, kind,
friendly, easy Asquith, with the curtain of public affairs let thickly down behind him and the
footlights entirely turned off in front, doesn't do anything to make it less worth having.' See
Leon Edel, *The Master* (1972), pp. 528–30.

[2] David Davies, who was a friend of Cyril Asquith and a fellow Wykehamist, had joined the
civil service in 1913 and had become one of Asquith's Secretaries. He later married Margaret
Kennedy, the authoress. Sir George Alexander was a well-known actor who had managed the
St James's Theatre since 1891.

[3] The *Manchester Despatch* had pointed out, 4 Jan., that Guest had 'a good social position
and a house in Park Lane'.

[4] John Gulland had been a Junior Lord of the Treasury and Scottish Whip since 1909.
Geoffrey Howard had joined the Whips' Office in 1911.

[5] Venetia had quoted from the witches' invocation in *Macbeth*, IV. i.

[6] But see Letter 261, n. 2.

[7] Sir Iain Colquhoun, 7th Bt., Dinah's fiancé, survived the war, though wounded. He was
court-martialled in Jan. 1916 for allowing his men to fraternize with the enemy on Christmas
Day, and was defended by Raymond Asquith, by then a fellow Guards officer. Raymond

thought Colquhoun 'a perfect man of his type – insolent, languid, fearless, and (in khaki at any rate) of a virile elegance which is most engaging. I give him absolutely top marks for deportment, especially in the dock where few look their best.' Colquhoun was awarded the D.S.O. later in the same year.

265

Walmer Castle,
Kent.

Sunday midnight 17 Jan 1915 [ii]

My darling – I hope you got my rather long & disconnected letter of to-day by the first post on Monday. It took you a great deal of badly or non-expressed love: love wh. *cannot* be expressed. Winston arrived at last – just before 8 p.m – having dropped Clemmie at Gravesend with a headache – & having had a lot of minor adventures with a bad chauffeur in the dark. He was in good form & contributed to our amusement. After dinner we played Bridge – Winston & Violet against the Assyrian & me. We won pretty easily, & as W. insisted on playing 2^d with £1 on the rubber he lost about £4 to Mr Wu.

In the course of dinner talk they extorted from the Assyrian the avowal that he had been writing a letter to you. I wonder what it was like: did he give us all away? I sent all the other men away after dinner to have a talk with W. He is quite determined – and I think rightly – whatever the Army may do – to bombard & if possible destroy Zeebrugge, wh. becomes more menacing & dangerous day by day.

I talked again over the question of Chief Whip with Assyrian & Bongie before dinner. On the whole, they were disposed to acquiesce in my tame and (as you say) 'uninspiring' conclusion to put it in Commission between Gulland & Benn. For Home Under Secy they were rather divided between Cecil Harmsworth & Beck: of the two I decidedly prefer the former. Neil's stock is quite at a discount.

The whole lot of guests will have disappeared by 10.30 to-morrow (Monday) morning: and I am looking forward to a peaceful & almost solitary day: which is (since you are an impossible companion just now) the very thing that I most desire. I begin to covet this place from that point of view. Good night dearly beloved: I hope I may dream of you.

266

Walmer Castle,
Kent.

Monday 18 Jan 15 [i]

. . . Henry James declared he had never enjoyed 2 days so much in his life. He was well worth his salt. . . . H.J. watched [Winston] with much curiosity & not a little bewilderment. We . . . asked him this morning after Winston had gone what he thought of him. He answered in his pauseful oracular way: 'I never had the lively interest of seeing so much of this remarkable young man before.' Then after some compliments to W, and comparing him favourably with his father, he added: 'I confess I am often struck at the limitations with which men of power pay the price for their domination over mankind.'[1]. . .

. . . Young Geo. Trevelyan who is on a Balkan pilgrimage & at present in Servia . . . is very much afraid that the Serbs will be overwhelmed by the new attack wh Austria is preparing unless some one comes at once to their assistance; Roumania for preference, next Greece. Another indication of the importance of getting the caldron to brew the right mixture without any further delay.

Winston tells me that they have recalled Lewis Bayly from the command of the Channel Fleet as a consequence of his loss of the *Formidable*, & have put Admiral Bethell in his place. It is rather disquieting, for Bayly was supposed to be almost the pick of our younger Admirals, & Bethell, whom I used to see on the C.I.D, is to my thinking no flier. We really seem to have better reserves in the way of Commanders in the Army than in the Navy. . . .

[1] According to Violet Asquith, this insight into the limitations of men of power struck James as 'very encouraging: it – er, er – *bucks one up*': to Rupert Brooke, 1 Feb. 1915.

267

Wed 20 Jan 1915. [i]

. . . I long more than words to see you again: *twice* a week is a meagre & *irreducible* minimum, and I don't count yesterday (good as it was) as equal to more than once. Don't laugh, but you looked *beautiful* at dinner: everyone comments on your looks! That ought to be some slight consolation for your privations & drudgery. . . .

268

My darling – I regretfully acknowledge that (not perhaps for the first time, but it doesn't very often happen) I have made a thorough muddle of my arrangements for to-day. I have already explained . . . the mistake about the hour of the Cabinet. There was a further obstacle to our plans (of wh. Drummond ought to have reminded me) in the shape of a luncheon given by St. Loe Strachey of the *Spectator* to me to meet the American journalists in London. This only began at 2, and I tremble to think how I shd. have managed to be outside your front door at 3.5 or thereabouts. The journalists numbered from 15 to 20 and were much of the usual type. The one who sat next me had just been spending a month in Berlin, and gave me an interesting account of a long interview of 3 hours he had had with the Chancellor Bethmann-Hollweg, whom he found rather piano about the war, & who he thinks is likely to be made a scapegoat. Of course, all the German officers, both civil & Military, were more than polite to the American. The one thing they most want is to capture American sympathy. Otherwise the journalists were not interesting, but I suppose the function was worth while from the point of view of international lubrication![1]. . .

. . . I had a long talk with Ll. George who, failing Neil, was inclined to agree that the Gulland–Benn arrangement was the best – tho it is not an ex*h*ilarating one (observe the 'h'!). . . .

[Cabinet] . . . We had a long talk about the Balkans & Greece & how to bring them in. Grey is anxious to be able to dangle before the Greeks Cyprus as a lure. It is not worth much to us, indeed nothing – tho' Kitchener is very loth to part with it, because it is on the high road, via Alexandrett, to Mesopotamia, where we now straddle across the Tigris & Euphrates. Grey thinks it wd. have a good moral effect to show that we were really prepared to part with something we have instead of merely carving out & distributing other people's possessions.

We appointed a Committee on the rise in Food prices, over which they want me to preside, and I shall do so, tho' I rather shrink from adding to one's detailed work. In less than a fortnight the House will be sitting again, wh. is not altogether an alluring prospect.

Hankey came to me to-day to say – *very privately* – that Fisher, who is an old friend of his, had come to him in a very unhappy frame of mind. He likes Winston personally, but complains that on purely technical naval matters he is frequently over-ruled ('he out-argues me'!) and he is not by any means at ease about either the present disposition of the fleets, or their future movements. Of course he didn't want Winston, or indeed anybody to know this, but Hankey told him he shd. pass it on to me. Tho' I think the old man is rather unbalanced, I fear there is some truth in what he says; and I am revolving in my mind whether I can do anything, & if anything what? What do you say?

We had a long & very dusty discussion on the latest phases of the Marconi contract (wh. you might think was by this time in its grave) carried on mainly by the Impeccable, H. Samuel, Hobhouse & McKenna, with occasional irruptions by Winston, and once or twice a lurid flash from K. It has become (from being a scandal[2]) a purely technical matter about strategic & commercial 'points', and we all got so tired of it after a time that I brought it to an abrupt conclusion. When you come into your office (S. of S. for India, isn't it?) I wonder how you will face the tedium of some of these debates. It will be as bad as 'washing 18 patients', which I note with regret you now prefer to playing a full round of golf. . . .

[1] See Letter 159. Strachey held these gatherings regularly, ministers being invited as they were available.

[2] See Letter 7. The cost of the wireless chain had been seriously underestimated. The case reappeared in the courts in 1918 when the Marconi Company sued the Government for breach of contract and secured a settlement. The statements made on their behalf were then challenged openly by Hobhouse, Postmaster-General from Feb. 1914 to May 1915, who was successful in the consequent libel action, being awarded damages and costs.

269

Wed 20 Jan 15 [iii] midnight

. . . A riddle in the papers to-day . . . may amuse you: 'Why is Mr A. such a good host?' 'Because he can always find snug places for his Tennants & Guests.' Do you think this is what the old writers used to call 'a shrewd hit'? . . .

270

Thursday 21 Jan 1915 [ii]

. . . The main point is to do something really effective for Servia, which is threatened by an overwhelming inrush from the Austrians reinforced by some 80,000 Germans. If she is allowed to go down, things will look very black for us, and the prestige of the Allies with the wavering & hesitating States will be seriously, if not mortally, impaired. I have urged Grey to put the strongest possible pressure upon Roumania & Greece to come in without delay, & to promise that if they will form a real Balkan *bloc* we will send troops of our own to join them & save the situation. I am sure that this is right, and that all our 'side shows' – Zeebrugge, Alexandretta, even Gallipoli – ought to be postponed to this.

You may ask – Where are we to get the troops? They must come either from those wh. we already have in France, or from those wh. we were going to send there. There was a report in to-day that General de Castelnau,[1] who is one of the best of the French Generals, is strongly of opinion that things there have reached a condition of stale-mate – that neither side can do more than push a little here & retreat a little there: if so, it seems a criminal waste, at such a critical moment, to pour in new & good troops into that theatre.

There are two fatal things in war – one is to push blindly against a stone wall, the other is to scatter & divide your forces in a number of separate & disconnected operations. We are in great danger of committing both blunders: to neither of which it seems to me is Winston properly alive. Happily K. has a good judgment in these matters – never impulsive, sometimes inclined to be over cautious, but with a wide general outlook wh. is of the highest value. . . .

I sent for Gulland this morning & told him he was to be Chief Whip, with Benn in control of the organisation &c. He wasn't at all elated, having a due sense of the difficulties & dangers of the position, & of his own modest equipment for grappling with them. He is quite a good fellow with a strong strain of native shrewdness, but of course lacking in personality & authority. He may do quite well so long as the 'truce' lasts: at all events I am sure (with you) that Neil wd. have been a grievous mistake. . . .

I have just read a rather amusing letter from Bertie to Grey.
. . . There is a Socialist group in the French Cabinet, & of course a much stronger one outside, wh. is giving trouble. They procured the decoration of some Generals of their kidney, whom Joffre had dismissed for incompetence, and are now intriguing agst Millerand the War Minister,[2] & agst Joffre himself, for whom they want to substitute their own friend Gallieni,[3] the Military Governor of Paris. This if successful would probably create an uprising in the Army, wh. is apparently strongly pro-Joffre. . . .

[1] De Castelnau had been Joffre's chief staff officer before the war. He was an ardent Catholic of aristocratic connections, so that his advancement had never been popular with most French politicians. The report was correct: de Castelnau had told Seely on 1 Jan. that the new armies should be sent to the Eastern Mediterranean: Seely, *Adventure* (1930), p. 215.
[2] Millerand had a socialist past and was regarded on the left as a renegade.
[3] Joffre was not displaced. Gallieni succeeded Millerand as War Minister in Oct. 1915.

271

Friday 22 Jan 1915 [i] 4 p.m.

My darling – I am really depressed to-day. The snow and fog are bad enough, but what weighs much more upon my spirits is that I have not seen your handwriting (I don't count this morning's telegram) since Wed. evening. It is a long time since I have been for so many hours without anything that comes direct from your hand. It is perhaps a mistake (from an abstract point of view) to be so dependent: but the 'infirmity is such' as you will both understand and forgive. It conveys no reproach: you are always considerate, & I know the difficulties; but starvation is (I expect) always an uncomfortable process, and I am at present in the *gnawing* stages. . . .

. . . First I had Grey & Ll. George & Hankey here, to talk over the Servian business, which pre-occupies me a good deal. If we are to send a Corps (50,000 or 60,000 men) to help at the critical time & place, Hankey calculates that it will take at least 6 weeks from to-day to get it there. Plans have to be worked out at the W.O, the actual transport by sea takes at the least a fortnight, stores have to be accumulated, & a large margin allowed for unforeseen delays & accidents. War is a tiresomely slow business. . . .

In view of the urgency of this, it looks as if Sir J. French's proposed operation would at any rate have to be postponed. . . .

After that, I presided for nearly 2 hours over a Committee on Food Prices: quite a business-like body, Crewe, Runciman, Bron, the Assyrian, with Hopwood[1] & Bluey. As there was no rhetorician present, we went over practically the whole ground, and came to a few modest & sensible conclusions. There is no doubt that we are at last beginning to feel the pinch of war, mainly because all the German ships wh. used to carry food are captured or interned, and the Admiralty has commandeered for transport &c over 1000 of our own. Further, the Australian crop has failed, & the Russian (wh. is a very good one) is shut up, until we can get hold of Constantinople & open the Black Sea.

Winston arrived about 1.30 and groused a little about my demand that Jellicoe shd. come up next week to the War Council.[2] He is all for having French at these gatherings, but doesn't like his own man to be summoned & cross-examined.

He stayed to luncheon, where we had Sir D. Henderson[3] who goes back to the front to-morrow morning. He is in my judgment a long way the best instructed & most level headed of our Generals: in fact (if Robertson is unavailable) he clearly ought to succeed Murray as Chief of the Staff. W & I discussed with him the whole position at the front: he does not favour the forward move at present. He thinks the new men who come out excellent material: the difficulty (of course) is to get really good officers. . . .

[1] Additional Civil Lord, Admiralty.

[2] Churchill also wrote Asquith a long letter pointing out that there was 'no similarity between the position and functions of a naval Commander-in-Chief and [those] of a modern General in the field'. In the army it was the brigade, divisional, and corps commanders who coped with emergencies, whereas Jellicoe might have to take the Grand Fleet to sea at any time. Perhaps Churchill did not want Jellicoe telling the War Council that the Dardanelles operation might weaken the Grand Fleet dangerously. He had his way: Jellicoe was not ordered to attend.

[3] He commanded the Royal Flying Corps with the B.E.F. For a peacetime reference to him see Letter 103.

272

Friday 22 Jan 1915 [ii] midnight

[Dinner at Kitchener's] Millerand, the French War Minister, was of course the principal guest. . . . I sat next him . . . & had quite an interesting conversation. He can't speak a word of English, but was apparently able to follow my French. He was all against the proposed démarche of Sir J.F., and says that Joffre is anxious that we should pour all our troops during the next month into his theatre, in order that he may be able to organise & carry out a really effective *coup*.[1] Of course I put to him strongly the Balkan situation, and the irreparable disaster wh. wd. be involved in the crushing of Servia. He professed to be quite alive to this, but not 'dans ce moment' &c. Ll. George (with the aid of an interpreter) & E. Grey after dinner pressed our point. I don't know what the actual upshot will be, but I am sure that it is all to the good that we shd. often have these personal interchanges. They obviate friction, and grease the sometimes rather creaking wheels of the Entente. Millerand is an eminent advocate by profession – leader of the Paris bar: a rather thick set man with white hair and a black moustache: he talks well with the inimitable French *netteté*,[2] and is not at all rhetorical or phrase-making, or epigrammatic. On the whole he left on me quite a good impression of solidity and good sense.

[1] Millerand thought it his overriding duty to support and defend Joffre's schemes.

[2] Millerand's clarity and precision of speech were famous. After the war, when he was an elderly Senator, he would not allow his speeches to be corrected for the parliamentary record: he assumed that no revision would be needed.

273

Sat 23 Jan 1915

My darling – I confess I was *very* depressed when I looked this morning at my letters by the bed-side, & saw no sign of your hand-writing. Thursday & Friday both blank days (except for a little jejune telegram), and Sat. to be the same! You must admit that it was trying, and I began to cherish the fear (at which I hinted before) that I was *overloading* you. However your telegram wh. arrived about noon reassured me – especially its last word, wh. was *more* than welcome. And now I am in the train & looking eagerly forward to your letter of last night.

Darling – you musn't think me over-nervous or exacting: you know I am not. Perhaps a little greedy – but that is because you have been so good. . . .

I had a letter this morning from Aberdeen enclosing one wh. he has written to the King on the subject of the 'Tara' title. I sent it on to Birrell with the comment that both letters shewed unmistakable signs of incipient mental derangement. He still clings to the idea that the bulk of the Irish desire nothing so much as that his name shd be imperishably associated with that of their mythical capital. 'Ishbel Tara' would be a quaint signature wouldn't it: it reminds one of the Vedas, or the Assyrian monuments. Drummond has conceived a happy solution of this ridiculous tin-pot problem: wh. is that 'Garter' Gatty[1] shd. discover in the Heralds' College reasons for doubting whether an actual 'Tara' peerage of about 100 years ago has really become extinct.[2] If a plausible case can be made in that sense, it blocks the way, & our poor friends must have another try. . . .

. . . I will add something when I get to Walmer, & in order to insure your receiving this on Sunday morning, I will put it into a 'P.M.' envelope – so that it may wear the livery of a state despatch. Please write & post tomorrow to *Walmer*: I shall get it (I think) by noon: at any rate before dinner on Monday.

I learnt by heart last night before getting into bed (from the secret book) 'Like as the waves make towards the pebbled shore',[3] and am now I think word-perfect. I will just try & see. . . .

[1] Sir Alfred Scott-Gatty had been Garter King-of-Arms since 1904.

[2] The question was probably whether on the death of the 3rd Viscount Taragh in 1674 the viscounty had become extinct or dormant. On the death of Lord Tara of Bellinter in 1821 that barony had become extinct. Lord Brabazon, who was raised to the peerage in 1942, had a good claim to be Brabazon of Tara: his family came from Tara House, County Meath. Aberdeen eventually took Temair as his second title when raised to a marquessate.

[3] Shakespeare, *Sonnet* 60.

274

Walmer Castle,
Kent.

Sunday 24 Jan 1915

My darling –
   . . . Your *two* letters of Fr. & Sat. arrived side by side by the morning post. They have been already read many times, and have made me a different creature. . . .

   . . . I hope your throat is quite well again: I expect you caught cold wandering about in tubes & buses on those two dismal wintry mornings. You give a lurid picture of your pneumoniac: I trust that he finally passed away when you were not there.
   You don't say anything about politics or the other things of wh. I wrote. We are really at a very critical stage, & it is quite possible as a result of Millerand's mission that we may have a bit of a row with the French. When you remember that we have sent them 3 times the number of men they ever reckoned on (350,000 instead of at the outside 120,000) their demand that we should go on pouring into their theatre every available Division, is more than a trifle greedy – particularly as they continue to assure us that the Germans can *never* break through the present lines. I have just been having a talk with Ll. George, who goes back to London after lunch. His conversation (thro' the interpreter) with Millerand seems to have been of a rather stormy kind. Ll.G. is of course a violent pro-Serb, and disposed to be more down on the French than I am. Meanwhile the War Office are getting out their plans, and by the time we have our War Council on Thursday morning, matters ought to be ripe for a decision.
   Gulland's appointment as Whip will be announced to-morrow morning. He reports to-day that at Norwich, where there is a vacancy owing to the sitting member Low becoming a Judge, the local people won't hear of Masterman & have already got as a candidate one Young,[1] who is a naval lieutenant in Jellicoe's fleet. Shipley – Illingworth's old seat – also refuses to look at Masterman. He has now been nearly a year out of the House, and there is no prospect of his getting back again. This is intolerable in the case of a Cabinet Minister who is responsible for important administration like the Insurance Act. So I have come to the conclusion that he must go, and as I wd. rather the suggestion came from him than from me, I have told Gulland to contrive that some tactful hint in that sense shd. be dropped to him.[2] If this comes off – what follows is *strictly* between you & me – I should promote the Assyrian to the Cabinet, giving him the Duchy[3] and charge of Insurance, wh. I think he would do quite well, tho' Ll. G (who likes him)

seems to think he might fail in quickness of decision. Our friend had confided to him his Indian ambitions.[4] Ll. G. says he was never so staggered in his life. I am sure he would be wise not to nurse that dream, and I shall take some opportunity of telling him so. . . .

Our rather strangely mingled party is going on quite well. Lady Tree & Anne Islington did some good 'stunts' (*locutio non approbanda*)[5] after dinner last night and Ll.G. was also in good form. . . .

. . . I have an amusing letter from Birrell this morning on the subject of 'Aberdeen-Tara'. He says the Nationalists were at first adverse & even inclined to be angry, but are 'too good fellows' to join the Unionist 'mob of vulgarians' in deriding their 'old & loved tho' *not* respected friend'. As he is now the 'stricken deer, wounded by the archers', they will at all events hold their tongues. It is a squalid little comedy. . . .

[1] Edward Hilton Young. He was to marry Asquith's friend, Lady Scott, the explorer's widow, and to end his political career as a Conservative minister.
[2] For Masterman's earlier electoral misfortunes see Letters 38, 70, and 236.
[3] The Chancellorship of the Duchy of Lancaster.
[4] His wish to be Viceroy.
[5] 'An expression not to be encouraged': c.f. Letter 72.

275

Walmer Castle,
Kent.

Monday 25 Jan 1915

. . . You know how I value your judgment: I put it *quite first* among women, and there are only 2 or 3 men to my mind in the same class. And you have now shared my inmost confidence so long & with such unsurpassable loyalty that I can speak to you really *more freely* about the most important things than I can to any other human being. It is a wonderful & I believe a unique relationship. Of course now that you are so hustled for time you can't write much about these things, tho' I hope you will give your view whenever you can. But it is a real necessity to me to see you, especially just now when lots of things are trembling in the balance. Do you understand, sweetest and also wisest? Don't pretend either to yourself or to me that I am *ébloui* & off my balance, & all that. I am not. I was never saner in my life, and I say with the Apostle (in quite a different sense) 'I know in *whom* I have believed'. For 13 months now you have never failed me, & I know you never will. . . .

. . . Lady Tree, who has just left us, is really cleverer than any of her children: she has a good tho' often disguised sense of humour. She said to me at the end of our drive yesterday with much apparent naiveté: 'Do you take an interest in the War?'[1]

While we were at dinner last night a messenger arrived from the Admiralty with a letter to me from Winston, giving a narrative of the naval battle in the North Sea. The *Lion* – Beatty's flagship – was a good deal damaged tho' not disabled: her speed was reduced to 12 knots from (I suppose) 26: and Beatty transferred his flag to the *Princess Royal*. None of this appears in the official account published to-day – from wh. one wd. gather that none of our ships had been touched. Don't you think this kind of secrecy quite puerile? It is not the least likely to deceive the Germans, who no doubt know perfectly well that they hit and injured the *Lion*, and when the truth comes out people here will say with justice that they have been treated with lack of candour. I am all for telling the worst at once, aren't you? All the same, it was the best thing – at least the most successful – the Navy have done so far.[2] . . .

I had a letter from Crewe this morning: he is very anxious that something shd. be done for Neil who needs to be 'steadied by responsibility': an Under Secyship for instance. He also discusses who shd. succeed Wimborne as Lord in Waiting – remarking justly that 'our cellar, so to speak, is not very full'. He suggests for consideration Nunburnholme, Cranbrook (a recent recruit to the party) Rankesborough & Glenconner. Have you any views? It carries with it some small political opportunities in the H. of Lords.[3] . . .

. . . I think I will send you a volume I have just read of short stories by Tchekoff, the Russian. They have all the sombre squalor, interfused with a strange idealising atmosphere, wh. one expects to find in the post-Tolstoi writers. To my thinking, none of them approaches Dostoieffski, but I fancy you may find this man worth sampling. . . .

[1] The question was more dangerous to Asquith than he realized. He was not always seen as a dynamic war leader by his acquaintances.

[2] In the Dogger Bank action (24 Jan.) Beatty's battle-cruisers had the better of Hipper's. The *Blücher* was sunk and the *Seydlitz* badly damaged, well over 1,000 German seamen being killed or taken prisoner. On the British side, while the damage to the *Lion* took four months to repair, the casualties were less than 50. Considering, however, that the initial orders to Hipper had been intercepted and decoded at the Admiralty the British victory should have been more decisive. To Jellicoe's mind the Admiralty were at fault in not giving the main fleet a chance to intervene. In the battle itself the ever present fear of submarines led Beatty into a tactical error. For Churchill's letter see *The World Crisis, 1915* (1923), pp. 142–3. The *Lion*'s speed soon fell to 8 knots; then her engines failed and she was taken in tow by the *Indomitable*.

[3] Ranksborough (a retired military officer raised to the peerage in July 1914) was appointed. He was thought by the King to be more readily available when needed than the others on the list. The Lords-in-Waiting had been thinned by war service. Asquith misspells the name.

276

Tues. 26 Jan 1915 [i] (after lunch)

My darling – we motored back here this morning – Violet Bluey & I – in lovely weather: lots of sun and a mild air, and got here before 2. We found at luncheon Sr Edgar (as usual) & Francis Grenfell – the V.C. – a charming specimen of the best type of simple minded & yet most capable Cavalry officer.[1] . . .

Last night, after I got to my bedroom I wrote you a letter, a real love letter; but this morning casting a fastidious eye over it, (tho' it contained no word that was not literally true) I thought there were one or two things in it wh. you mightn't perhaps altogether like: so I tore it up, & put it in the grate. With a good deal of reluctance, I must admit: it covered 2 sheets, and attained in one passage (I know you will laugh) to what I thought a fairly high level of eloquence (!!). I rather regret now that I didn't risk sending it. . . .

You & I have different ways of saying things: even the same thing. Happily. Do you remember telling me some weeks ago that you were shy at self-expression? So am I – tho' perhaps looking back on a year's correspondence you mightn't think so! But I am really by nature as prone as you are to reserve & under-statement, about the things wh. are near the centre of one's being, & which really matter. I have spoken & written of them more freely to you than to anyone I have ever known: but yet I always know that what I feel in every fibre, every day & all day, remains not only unexpressed but (so far as speech goes) nebulous & undefined: 'airs & floating echoes'. You have an intuition of your own, however, wh. enables you to interpret & realise.

Whatever happens, I want you to know, once & for all, (if this were my last testament) that I bless you as the pole-star of my life.

Don't trouble to answer all this, except to say the one word 'I understand'. . . .

. . . I am dining with Winston to meet the Arch Colonel. I note your vigorous protest agst. his Brigade: so far as I know it is only composed of Yeomanry, and it may be a long time before it is called upon for active work.[2] But I will inquire about this. I agree entirely with your criticism, if he were going to be put in charge of regulars or fighting units at the front. . . .

[1] For the episode which won him the V.C., 24 Aug. 1914, see Letter 198, n. 5. His diary entry on it bears out Asquith's description of him:

It is on occasions like this that good discipline tells. The men were so wonderful and so steady that words fail me to say what I think of them, and how much is due to my Colonel for the high standard to which he had raised this magnificent regiment. . . . My fingers were nastily gashed; . . . a bit of shrapnel had taken a piece out of my thigh; I had a bullet through my boot and another through my sleeve; and had been knocked down by a shell; my horse had also been shot, so no one can say I had an idle day.

John Buchan, *Francis and Riversdale Grenfell* (1920), pp. 197–8.

[2] Seely had been given the command of the Canadian Cavalry and Auxiliary Forces, which he was to retain for most of the war. Despite Asquith's prediction, he and his brigade were soon in action at Festubert. Venetia's protests were widely echoed by officers at the Front; but Seely did well in France. See Letter 179, n. 8.

277

Tues 26 Jan 15 [ii] 7 p.m.

. . . Freddie Guest duly appeared, & brought me some rather interesting messages from Sir J French, wh. are *very private*. First, as to personnel: the Doctor there opportunely reports Sir A. Murray to be so seriously run down & bad in one lung that he must go home for at any rate a month or two. French wd. like him to come out again when he has recovered, & command the third army:[1] he knows every inch of the ground, & tho' he has not been a complete success as Chief of Staff, Sir J. has a very high opinion of his general ability, and (I think) a considerable dread lest Hunter should be sent out. K & I telegraphed yesterday evening that we approved of Robertson as his successor, & he has assumed his new functions to-day. Wilson (I rejoice to say) is put out of the reach of mischief making by being appointed chief officer of *liaison* at the French Headquarters. Robertson has replaced him as Sub-Chief of Staff by one Perceval, a gunnery general of whom I know very little. He has also booted out a lot of the minor men. I feel sure that these are good changes.

Next (this is also *very secret*) an agreement has been come to between Joffre & French for such a rearrangement of troops as will give us the whole of the extreme left flank, and put us in direct touch – without any intervening French – with the Belgians & the sea. This ought to be completed by the first or second week in March. It is also to the good. Meanwhile, I dare say from what F.G. says, & from other reports, that the sedentary expectant life they are all leading just now is bad for the condition & morale of the army. . . . Sir J.F. himself appears to be rather *désoeuvré*.

The Staff's present estimate of numbers (highly conjectural, I imagine) is in fighting line French 1½ million: Germans (taking both theatres) 2½ millions: and each with sufficient reserves of new troops under training to keep up these totals for perhaps another 6 months, but very little longer. If this is anywhere near the truth, it shows (as I said to you some time ago) what a growing advantage we & the Russians ought to have over all the other combatants.

The Balkan situation is still very cloudy, Greece looking for the moment the most promising of the lot. The Roumanians are becoming alarmed at the concentration in Transylvania of Austrian & German troops: a lot of the Germans who we thought were destined for Servia, have apparently been diverted into this quarter. . . .

¹ Kitchener kept Murray in London, making him Deputy C.I.G.S., with special responsibility for the training of the Kitchener armies.

278

Tues. 26 Jan 1915 [iii] Midnight

. . . To-night, at the Wimbornes, I sat next to Goonie, and she told me of your talk with her yesterday afternoon. She *loves* you so much, & I *love* her for doing so. She told me of the things that you have naturally never mentioned to me – the squalor & the horrors & the filth of ministering to these diseased wastrels. Old Jews & Gentiles also, whom your hands ought never to have touched. I had vaguely imagined it all, & it repelled me more than I can say: but as she *effleuré'*d it in her dim & rather dainty way, it became more real to me, and my aversion increased, & almost grew to indignation & revolt. I can't tell you what I feel about it. Thank God, it cannot last long. I have never known such a profanation! & yet I can't say, or think, you were wrong to undertake it. The worst of it is that I am sure, the more you see of it, the more it inspires in you, not of compassion, but of revulsion. I *so* understand it. What a crooked world! . . .

. . . Poor MᶜK – who gets lots of kicks¹ & rarely a halfpenny-worth of praise – was pleased, when I said that there were 2 *men* (& those, tho' I didn't say it – the most unpopular) to whom, in this war, we owed the most – Haldane, who made our Army, & he (MᶜK) who made our Navy. Winston's 1ˢᵗ ship² (*Queen Elizabeth*) is just about to make her début: and Kitchener's Armies are still only in the stage of parturition . . .

. . .Ll. George came to see me before dinner. He has, by his curious tactlessness, provoked something like a mutiny in the Treasury. The Masterman affair is on the point of settlement: he will I think resign, & with Grey's help we can find him out of Secret Service a salary to go on supervising American & other press work. L.G. is dead agst McNamara joining the beagle kennel,[3] & thinks we may soothe any ruffled ambitions he may have by insisting that he is *homme nécessaire* at the Adm^ty, & could not be spared from there during the war. I told him that I thought it wd. be bad for the Assyrian to be at all *désoeuvré* – the Duchy being in itself a sinecure post: he assures me that Insurance seriously taken, is quite enough to absorb the whole of a man's working hours. Like you, he (L.G) is very anxious to bring in Neil. I think in the small general shuffle it might be managed. . . .

[1] As Home Secretary McKenna was responsible for dealing with enemy aliens, about whom various 'spy scares' were raging. The Government's handling of this issue was popularly thought too 'soft'. See next Letter.
[2] Churchill had succeeded McKenna as First Lord of the Admiralty in Oct. 1911.
[3] Asquith's expression for the junior members of the cabinet: see Letter 27, n. 3.

279

COMMITTEE OF IMPERIAL DEFENCE

2 Whitehall Gardens,
·London, S.W.

Wed 27 Jan 1915 [i]

. . . [Cabinet] Winston produced Beatty's preliminary report on the Naval battle; as you wd. see, the damage to the *Lion* is rather tardily admitted in the official communiqué in to-day's papers; she was very unlucky in getting the only shot wh. went home right in her *lung*[1] (this is the kind of metaphor wh. I am sure appeals to you in your present environment. I don't know whether you are still writing notes only about valves & ventricles). Your account of your lectures reminds me of what is going on in the Queen's Westminster: there every Monday evening Raymond & Cys (both Ireland scholars) go with their note-books & listen (or otherwise) to a discourse from a fiery & illiterate Major on the rudiments of tactics & drill. (Yours & theirs are similar cases of *Waste*.) Beatty is satisfied that he did immense damage to at least 3 of the German battle cruisers – the *Derfflinger*, the *Seydlitz* & the *Moltke*. He also thinks that he killed & wounded a great lot of German sailors & marines.[2] On the whole it is the best naval achievement of the war.

K. showed me an interesting private letter wh. he had got from Maxwell, the G.O.C. in Egypt. The Australians there have given a lot of trouble from their want of discipline & their strange habits: at Xmas they made a raid from Mena & painted Cairo red. But they are improving & he says they are splendid raw material.[3]. .

There was a rumour yesterday of an intended Zeppelin raid last night to celebrate the Kaiser's birthday, which is to-day. So the whole of the East of England was plunged in darkness & all the Territorials &c were on the qui vive. Somewhere in Norfolk a vigilant officer discovered suspicious signalling lights going on from the top of a Church tower. He assembled his men who felt their way in the darkness with fixed bayonets to the Churchyard, & were just about to fire, when they discovered that the suspected spies on the steeple were their own comrades from another company, who had seized the opportunity to do a little signalling practice. McKenna gave us an equally amusing commentary on the ridiculous spy fever. The motor car with flashing lights wh., as I dare say you saw, was supposed to have guided the Zeppelins, when they came to Yarmouth & Kings Lynn last week, turns out to have belonged to the Rev. Somebody Grant, Domestic Chaplain to the King, who was on his way to his Rectory at Sandringham. They are going to have another experiment in darkening the coast to-night. The Expected rarely comes off – does it? . . .

Gulland has seen little Benn, who absolutely declines to take on the organising job. He is eaten up with martial ardours, & determined to risk everything at the front. It is a great bore, for he was far the best man for the post. I shall now offer it to Geoffrey, who I fancy feels that he has done his duty by the war, and who will be quite good if he will bestir himself & be ready to 'live laborious days'.[4] . . .

I have been presiding this afternoon – as the earlier sheets of my letter show – at the Committee of Defence. It was what is called a full meeting:[5] A.J.B. was there, and the Canadian Perley, & Lords Nicholson & Esher, as well as the usual lot. They had a long discussion in wh. I took very little part on the 'limits of Enlistment': the object being to devise some way in wh. the necessary industries of the country can be carried on by men of non-military age, or disqualified for health &c, & by women. There was much cry & little wool, and in the end I formulated 2 or 3 rather platitudinous propositions, to wh. they all agreed. In the intervals, I began this letter to you. . . .

[1] The *Lion* was hit by an 11" shell from the *Seydlitz* which knocked out two of her dynamos, and by two 12" shells simultaneously from the *Derfflinger*, one of which drove in the waterline armour and so flooded the port feed-tank. This last hit was the serious one: the port engine had to be stopped half an hour later.

[2] For the German casualties see Letter 275, n. 2. One of the two hits on the *Seydlitz* penetrated the 9" armour and almost knocked out the ship. The only hit on the *Derfflinger* did not do great damage, though it started a fire which could be seen from the British squadron. The *Moltke* was undamaged. By a misunderstanding the *Tiger* failed to fire at her; she was thus left unmolested to fire at the *Lion*. When the *Blücher* was sunk 250 were picked up and taken prisoner out of a crew of nearly 1,200.

[3] Asquith's remarks here resemble those in Letter 193 on the Canadians and show the

impact made by the Australian troops on statesmen and commanders used to strict discipline and deference. Admiration for the splendid physique of the Australians was almost always combined with shocked comments at some aspect of their conduct. On Good Friday, a few weeks after this letter was written, the 'Anzacs' wreaked their vengeance on a Cairo brothel, and started a serious riot in which the military police opened fire and killed a man: P. Liddle, *Men of Gallipoli* (1976), pp. 82–3. When in Cairo in June 1915 Violet Asquith noted of the 'Anzacs':

Their spirits and *élan* . . . are . . . attractive and their . . . appearance is quite magnificent. . . . They are unanimously loathed for their wealth, insolence, crudity, and lack of any sort of discipline, manners, or consideration. . . . At Gallipoli on the other hand they fight with extraordinary dash and courage.

[4] Wedgwood Benn had a varied and most distinguished war career, being awarded the D.S.O., the D.F.C., the Croix de Guerre, and the Italian war cross and bronze medal for valour, and becoming a Chevalier of the Legion of Honour. (Venetia, meeting him in September 1913, had described him to Edwin as 'a strange, keen, alert little creature'.) Geoffrey Howard returned to his parliamentary and party duties in Feb. 1915, having qualified for a mention in despatches.

[5] The first meeting of the full Committee of Imperial Defence since the start of the war.

280

Wed. 27 Jan 1915 [ii] Midnight

' . . . Margot has just come back accompanied by the Assyrian from Bluey's dinner party. . . . We had some talk, & after she went to bed, I sat for a time with the Assyrian, discussing Whips &c, & then unfolded my plan about himself, Bluey &c. He conscientiously put forward the claims of Macnamara, Fr. Acland &c, and even raised a ridiculous scheme under wh. Ll. George was to become Ch^r of the Duchy, McKenna Ch^r of Ex^r, Simon Home Sec^y &c &c.[1] He is *really* sorry to leave the Treasury, especially at this time when it is full of interesting war problems, for wh. the little ripples of the Insurance backwater are a poor substitute. But I reminded him of Mr Gladstone's sound dictum: 'no man shd. ever refuse Cabinet office for the first time; it is the great chance of his life; and it matters nothing what particular place for the moment he holds'. He is of course fully alive to this, & didn't really hesitate. He was very *émotionné* & began to say all sorts of nice things about my friendship for him &c &c – wh. I cut short. I *love* gratitude, but am (as you know) naturally rather unresponsive, & always afraid of forcing the note. It is one of the few *real* pleasures one has to feel that one can open the door, wh. so many vainly covet to pass through, without any misgivings as to capacity & merit, to a really devoted friend. I am sure he has gone back to his tent – for once in his life – a genuinely happy man.

You, I know, will be glad too. Sometimes – in my worst moods – I am jealous of everybody who likes you & whom you like. But that does not last.

If only I could even make you know where I put you – what you have become to me – how I love the thought of you – what the loss of you wd. mean to me of desolation & despair! Good night *best beloved*.

¹ An interesting anticipation of what was to happen in May 1915, when the coalition was formed. McKenna then took over the Exchequer, and Simon the Home Office, Lloyd George going to the newly created Ministry of Munitions.

'A British annexation of Palestine' (Letter 281)

WAR with Turkey stimulated speculation in Britain about the future of the Ottoman lands. On 4 November 1914 an open letter in the *Daily Chronicle* from H. G. Wells asked: 'What is to prevent the Jews having Palestine and restoring a real Judaea?' Unwittingly Asquith gave these ideas added force when he predicted at the Guildhall on 9 November that the war 'had rung the death-knell of Ottoman dominion, not only in Europe, but in Asia'. Chaim Weizmann, the Zionist leader, now revealed his great diplomatic talents. With the help of C. P. Scott, Editor of the *Manchester Guardian*, he managed to meet Lloyd George and Herbert Samuel. He had met and impressed Balfour as early as 1906.

Although Samuel had lost his faith in Judaism while an undergraduate at Balliol, he had kept his synagogue membership. He was thus the first member of the Jewish community to sit in a British cabinet. He described in his *Memoirs* what his attitude had been in November 1914:

It was incumbent upon me at least to learn what the Zionist movement was and what it was doing . . . The more I read the more I was impressed by the spiritual influences that evidently animated the movement; by the sacrifices that were being made, and the results already achieved. . . . The importance of the question to the strategic interests of Great Britain stood out clearly. If Palestine . . . were to be separated from Turkey, for it to fall under the control of any of the great continental powers would be a danger.

Samuel proposed (Letter 281), not an autonomous Jewish state, but a British protectorate with encouragement for Jewish settlement.¹ In March 1915 a revised version of his memorandum was circulated to the cabinet (Letter 347). This elicited an anti-Zionist counter-memorandum (which was not circulated)² from his cousin, Edwin Montagu (Letter 354). In the same month the India Office began to show concern for Moslem claims; and Crewe circulated a paper by a distinguished Anglo-Indian which foreshadowed the inclusion of Palestine in an 'Arab kingdom'.³ When sounded in November 1914 Crewe had been sympathetic to Zionism; and he probably did not realize that the Anglo-Indian's paper concerned an obstacle to Zionist plans more substantial than Montagu's objections.

Asquith's astonishment on receiving the Samuel memorandum may be thought to illustrate his unimaginative cast of mind and his tendency to disregard newer currents of thought. But it is less surprising than appears at first sight. Very few of the well-established Jews in his circle were identified with Zionism, though his friend Mrs James de Rothschild had begun to plead its cause among her husband's family and connections. Many leading British Jews still aimed to show that Britain was their only home and the centre of their allegiance. They knew that Zionism had some odd allies among the anti-Semitic right wing fringe of British politics.[4] In March 1915 Montagu may even have reflected the views of British Jewry as well as Samuel did. The various memoranda of that month prefaced, not a quick victory over Turkey and a clear-cut decision, but many years of struggle. As the war dragged on Zionism became stronger; so did Arab aspirations.

[1] I. Friedman, *The Question of Palestine, 1914–1918* (1973), ch. 1.
[2] As Violet Asquith noted in her diary.
[3] P.R.O. CAB 37/126/8. See also *Churchill: Companion Docs., 1914–1916*, pp. 713–16, for the War Council discussion, 19 Mar. 1915, about the preservation, on the disintegration of Turkey-in-Asia, 'of a Moslem political entity'.
[4] See C. Holmes, *Anti-Semitism in British Society* (1979), pp. 119–20.

The First German Submarine Campaign (Letter 281)

PRE-WAR Admiralty discussions about probable German submarine activity had been almost entirely concerned with the effect on battle fleets. Except for Fisher, who was then in retirement, no one in Admiralty circles had believed that Germany would allow submarines to attack merchant shipping in defiance of the usages of war and the interests of the neutral nations. As Simon told the cabinet (Letter 281), submarine commanders could not operate against commerce within those usages. Unless they were to take enormous risks they could not ensure that their sinkings were confined to enemy, as opposed to neutral, ships and cargoes. If a torpedo were used, instead of gunfire, they could not ensure that the merchantman's crew and passengers would even have a chance to take to their lifeboats.

During December 1914 there was much pressure in German naval circles for a submarine campaign. The surface raiders had failed to disrupt Britain's war supplies and commerce; von Spee's squadron had been destroyed (Letter 202, n. 2): Britain still held the Channel ports and sent her troops to France without hindrance; and her contraband control (pp. 254–5) had begun to bite. On 22 December the *New York Sun* published an interview in which Tirpitz, the German Minister of Marine, hinted that Britain would be starved into submission by submarine attacks against her shipping. On 21

January 1915 a small British steamer, bound from Leith to Rotterdam, was sunk by a U-boat. The submarine campaign was approved by the German Chancellor on 1 February, and by the Emperor three days later. A proclamation was issued instituting a 'blockade' of the British coasts:[1] the seas round them were designated a war zone and the neutrals were warned that from 18 February any of their ships entering this zone would risk being sunk without the usual preliminaries of visit and search.

Countering the U-boats proved very difficult and later in the war they posed an enormous threat to Britain. But in February 1915 the German navy had nowhere near enough of them for an effective campaign. Only twenty-two were available and these had to work in three relays. Cross-channel traffic was not significantly interrupted; and on 10 April, after the U32 had been caught in the Straits of Dover in a net barrage, the U-boats were told to make the journey to the western approaches round the north of Scotland, and not via the English Channel. The campaign was suspended in September 1915 in response to American protests. Four months before that the sinking of the *Lusitania* had pushed the American people towards intervention against Germany (Letter 423, n. 2). From 7 May 1915 complaints about British contraband control were submerged in indignation against the U-boat pirates. 'On two supreme occasions', wrote Churchill in *The World Crisis*,

the German Imperial Government, quenching compunction, outfacing conscience, deliberately, with calculation, with sinister resolve, severed the underlying bonds which sustained the civilization of the world and united even in their quarrels the human family. The invasion of Belgium and the unlimited U-boat war were both resorted to on expert dictation as the only means of victory. They proved the direct cause of ruin.[2]

[1] See C. Ernest Fayle, *Seaborne Trade*, ii (1923), pp. 8–9.
[2] *1915* volume (1923), p. 335.

281

Thurs 28 Jan 1915

. . . Masterman came to see me this morning & we had a rather disagreeable interview. I can see that he labours under a sense of grievance because the Whips have not been able to fulfil their promise of finding him a 'safe seat'. And it is difficult without inflicting unnecessary pain to make him realise that, altho' several 'safe seats' have been & are at this moment vacant, the local people will not look at him. He is particularly angry with Ll. George (his oldest & closest friend) for the Swansea fiasco.[1] In the end, I was obliged to make it clear to him that, much as I compassionate his almost incredible ill-luck, he must go. His wife is ill & he has not yet broken it to her: so I said there was no hurry and any public announcement could be put off until next week.

Then there is real trouble about Macnamara. When he was passed over for the Assyrian, he was assured that his 'political future' would not be prejudiced. He is a popular man in the party, having been for many years a keen wire-puller & favourite platform orator. In the latter rôle he divided the honours with Ure, who has now got into a snug & stormless port at the head of the Scotch Bench.[2] Winston thinks he will be mortally stricken if Montagu – much his junior – is now preferred to him for the Cabinet. Ll. G, & I pointed out that, not only would he be of no real use in the Cabinet, but that it would look bad for him to leave his post at the Admiralty in the middle of the War. I must see him (he is really *au fond* a good fellow) and try to smooth things out: tho' I don't look forward with pleasure to the interview. The Assyrian I believe wd. really prefer to remain for a time where he is, in the midst of interesting & even exciting work, than be shunted into the sheltered backwater of Insurance (what a metaphor!) – particularly as his promotion just now is sure to be represented as another illustration of the favoured treatment given to the 'coterie' of private Secretaries and personal friends as compared with the stalwart hewers of wood & drawers of water in the party. As often happens, an act friendly in intention may turn out to be unfriendly in effect. As you know well, I would myself for every reason like far better to bring into the Kennels 'a hound bred out of the Spartan kind' (tho' I am not sure that that is a happy description of his pedigree) than another baying beagle of the mongrel type.

Another personal matter which rather worries me is the growing friction between Winston & Fisher. They came to see me this morning before the War Council, and gave tongue to their mutual grievances. I tried to compose their differences by a compromise, under which Winston was to give up for the present his bombardment of Zeebrugge, Fisher withdrawing his opposition to the operation against the Dardanelles. When at the Council we came to discuss the latter – wh. is warmly supported by Kitchener & Grey, & enthusiastically by A.J.B, old 'Jacky' maintained an obstinate and ominous silence. He is always threatening to resign & writes an almost daily letter to Winston, expressing his desire to return to the cultivation of his 'roses at Richmond'. K. has now taken up the rôle of conciliator – for wh. you might think that he was not naturally cut out![3] . . .

[Cabinet] . . . Winston is very strong for retaliating on the Germans by 'methods of barbarism':[4] he is very much irritated by the attacks of their submarines on our merchant ships. (I am not myself much moved by this development; the ships sunk have been very small; and any decent paced merchantman can show his heels to the quickest submarine.) The Impeccable made 2 good points against this use of the submarine – (1) that a man of war is always supposed to *capture* (not sink) a prize, & take her to a port (2) that if this can't be done, the man of war, before sinking her, takes her crew on board. A submarine can do neither, being too weak to tow or shadow a prize, & too small to accommodate her crew. So she is, in international law, a pirate.

Maud Cunard came to lunch & brought with her Nancy & a journalist called Williams who seems to be one of the editors of the *Daily Mail*: a harmless looking young man. Maud, having as she fancies filled up Ireland, is now busy in selecting a Viceroy for India. She has apparently been retained by the Islingtons to plead their cause, wh. she did with much fervour. What folly! They wd. never do.[5] . . .

I have just received from H. Samuel a Cabinet memorandum, headed 'the future of Palestine'. It begins by saying that 'already there is a stirring among the *twelve million* Jews scattered through the world'. (Did you know there were so many? I am sure I didn't!) He goes on to argue at considerable length & with much vehemence in favour of a British annexation of Palestine – a 'country the size of Wales, much of it barren mountain & part of it waterless'. He thinks we might plant in this not very promising territory about 3 or 4 million European Jews, and that this would have a good effect upon those (including I suppose himself) who were left behind. 'The character of the individual Jew, wherever he might be, would be ennobled. The sordid associations wh. have attached to the Jewish name would be sloughed off' &c &c. 'The Jewish brain is a physiological product not to be despised . . . If a body be again given in wh. its soul can lodge, it may again enrich the world' – & so on. It reads almost like a new edition of *Tancred* brought up to date. I confess I am not attracted by this proposed addition to our responsibilities. But it is a curious illustration of Dizzy's favourite maxim that 'race is everything'[6] to find this almost lyrical outburst proceeding from the well-ordered and methodical brain of H.S. . . .

[War Council] . . . Happily the weather is so bad & the snows so deep in Servia that there doesn't seem to be any near prospect of anything like a serious invasion. . . .

[1] See Letter 236, n. 5. Masterman did not know the full facts; his anger against Lloyd George was not wholly justified.

[2] Alexander Ure had been appointed Lord President of the Court of Session in Oct. 1913 and created Lord Strathclyde, 1914.

[3] The War Council Minutes show that Fisher was not silent at the start of the discussion. When Churchill had presented the Dardanelles plan:

Lord Fisher said that he had understood that this question would not be raised today. The Prime Minister was well aware of his own views in regard to it.

The Prime Minister said that, in view of the steps which had already been taken, the question could not well be left in abeyance.

Fisher then started to leave the room; but Kitchener pursued him and persuaded him to return to the table. It is not clear whether Asquith's reference is to Kitchener's prompt action in the meeting, or to some further attempt at conciliation which he may have made after it. Asquith, like Haldane and Balfour, told the Dardanelles Commission in 1916 that he had no recollection of Fisher's move from the table.

⁴ Campbell-Bannerman had made this phrase famous in the Boer War by applying it to the British policy of holding the enemy population in 'concentration camps'.

⁵ See Letter 260. Islington had been Governor of New Zealand and Chairman of the Royal Commission on the Indian Public Services. Asquith and his colleagues were not the only people to think that the Islingtons 'would never do'. Hearing the rumour that they were being considered, the Governor-General of Australia, Munro-Ferguson, commented: 'It is hard to imagine anything worse' (Rosebery MSS, Nat. Lib. of Scotland, 10020, f. 101). Munro-Ferguson differed from Asquith in thinking the same of the Beauchamps.

⁶ Sidonia's remark, 'All is race', is quoted from *Tancred* in Buckle's third volume on Disraeli which Asquith had just been reading: Letter 217, text and n. 1. Samuel's memorandum was in line with ideas once entertained by Disraeli, who told Stanley in 1851 that Palestine

had ample natural capabilities . . . . : the ownership of the soil might be bought from Turkey: . . . the Rothschilds and leading Hebrew capitalists would all help: . . . the Turkish government would do anything for money. All that was necessary was to establish colonies, with rights over the soil, and security from ill treatment. The question of nationality might wait until these had taken hold.

John Vincent (ed.), *Disraeli, Derby, and the Conservative Party* (1978), pp. 32–3. Disraeli's emphasis on race may have owed something to the fact that he was not a Jew by religion. For an interesting account of the effect on him of his early travels in the Holy Land see R. Blake, *Disraeli's Grand Tour* (1982), ch. 6. His advocacy of a Jewish return to Palestine was by no means unique. Several Jewish publicists of his time, such as Salvador, Moses Hess, and the rabbi Hirsch Kalischer, championed the same cause. Nor was its popularity confined to Jews: some nineteenth-century romantics made similar suggestions. For a Victorian Evangelical such as the 7th Earl of Shaftesbury the restoration of the Jews to the Holy Land, and their conversion to Christianity, were the prelude to the Second Coming: G. B. A. M. Finlayson, *Shaftesbury* (1981), pp. 112–14.

282

Friday 29 Jan 1915 [i]

My darling – what a horrible day! Bright outside, delightful for a drive, everything pointing that way. But your telegram this morning was a death-knell, and I felt as if the whole week had led up to an anti-climax. I had rather counted, since you were so near, upon seeing you at least *twice* a week, & this week it has worked out at not even *once*. I feel very sore & rebellious: but it is not against you, my sweet: it is against the mechanism of life, & the absurdly unforeseeing arrangements of your damnable Hospital. I hope I may have a line – even one – from you at Walmer to-morrow morning. At any rate you will write Sat. *& Sunday*: I don't mean to come back till Tues. morning – for I know I should not see you – and the only rest one gets in these days is being beyond the reach of bores & fools.

. . . M^cN.[1] behaved extraordinarily well. Nothing wd. induce him to forsake his quarter deck at the Admiralty during the war! Perish the thought! According to Ll. George, his eye flashed & his bosom swelled with patriotic pride & self-devotion. He volunteered to go & see the Assyrian & assure him of his good will – wh. he did. So far, so well. I am not sure that as regards the Assyrian himself, the thing went quite so well. 'Man never is, but always to be, blessed'[2] is a line wh. might well have been written of him. I don't know that he quite goes so far as to envy 'the Doctor'[3] his *beau geste;* but he begins to cast wistful glances upon the closing doors of the Treasury, & to look upon Insurance as rather a boring job, and to doubt whether it is such a great thing after all to be in the Cabinet. At least that is my diagnosis. As I have often said to you, one never gets to the end of human nature.

Masterman, in a penitent mood, sent me quite a nice letter this morning, and I wrote a very appreciative one to McNamara.

The 'Doctor's' devotion to his naval duties makes it impossible to remove Bluey from the War Office, where he is, or ought to be, immersed in equally absorbing responsibilities. So I must send Acland to the Treasury, and (as you suggested) put Neil at the Foreign Office, where I must say he is devilish lucky to find himself. Geoffrey appeared here at lunch to-day in khaki; he is quite willing (perhaps more than willing) to become Second Whip & undertake the organising business. So now our changes are practically complete. . . .

. . . [We had] at lunch the American Ambassador & his daughter, Crewe, & Lady Meux. The Ambassador is a sound & really strenuous friend to us in the war, and it is well to see him from time to time.[4]. . .

---

[1] T. J. Macnamara: see Letter 281.
[2] Pope, *Essay on Man,* Ep. i.96.
[3] Macnamara was an Honorary L.L. D. of St Andrews.
[4] For the help given by Page see p. 170.

283

Walmer Castle,
Kent.

Friday 29 Jan 1915 [ii] ¼ to 8 p.m.

. . . I can't tell you how much I have missed you to-day. It is like having a whole week wasted – the loss of a slice of one's life. The worst of it is that on

Tues. the House begins to sit, wh. always complicates things. Don't you think it might be possible to secure in advance by some sort of arrangement a certainty of next Friday? Or are you what Tennyson calls (for this purpose) the 'ball of time bandied by the hands of fools'?[1]. . .

. . . There is now quite a dead-set against the virtuous Runcie (the 'alabaster statesman' as somebody once called him) because his father owns tramp steamers, & is supposed to be battening on high freights,[2] at the expense of the poor consumer of bread. This is one of the topics with wh. our Committee of this morning deals. . . .

[1] Another old favourite: see Letter 178. Tennyson 'The Vision of Sin'.

[2] The rise in grain freights between Jan. 1914, when they were depressed, and Jan. 1915 was very sharp. With the war creating a shortage of shipping they had more than doubled from New York; from Karachi they were $2\frac{1}{2}$ times higher, and from the River Plate 6 times higher. High freights were only one cause of high bread prices; but they were by far the most visible cause. The Runciman firm paid dividends of 25 per cent for 1913, $12\frac{1}{2}$ per cent for 1914, and 25 per cent for 1915: Runciman to W. M. Crook, 12 July 1917: Bodleian Library, MSS Crook, Eng. hist. d. 393, f. 41.

284

Walmer Castle,
Kent.

Sat aft 30 Jan 1915

. . . Do you know that Helen Vincent has followed in your steps & taken to nursing? She entered Guy's this week: I wonder how she is bearing the yoke of discipline & what the other nurses think of her.[1] The war certainly diverts people's lives into strange & unexpected courses: witness the case of Maxime Elliott,[2] who runs a barge on the river Yser, on some unnamed mission of philanthropy, and has now been joined by Lady Sarah Wilson & Lady Drogheda! The 'Three men in a boat' are quite eclipsed by these three women in a barge. What a Trinity! I am told that Diana Manners feels tempted to throw up nursing & her projected hospital to join the gentle bargees. . . .

. . . [On 28 January] we had a second meeting of the War Council before dinner, and despatched Winston to go & see Sir J. French – in order that both he & Joffre may realise the importance we all attach to being able to send at any rate 2 Divisions to help the Servians, instead of continuing to pour every available man into the North of France. I don't know whether Winston has yet returned, or how he fared with his mission. I suppose I shall hear to-morrow. Curiously enough it was K. who suggested that he should go & pressed it hard.

Winston & Fisher have for the time at any rate patched up their differences, tho' F. is still a little uneasy about the Dardanelles. . . .

. . . I couldn't get hold of Fr. Acland yesterday, as he was not in London. I have very little doubt that he will agree to be promoted: most people do, when it comes to the point. With Neil at the Foreign Office, Cecil Harmsworth at the Home Office, & Beck & Rea as Whips, we shall have a fair infusion of new blood,[3] but the reservoir of available men of any quality is running dangerously low: Were you reassured by what I told you about Seely & his 'brigade'? . . .

Violet told me of an extraordinary conversation she had with McKenna at the Wimbornes' dinner. He dilated at great length & with the utmost vehemence on the untrustworthiness & chicanery of the Master, whom he accused of more crimes than even Leo Maxse has ever laid to his charge.[4] The reason appears to be that he suspects the Master of having 'intrigued' him (M^cK) out of the Admiralty, because M^cK was about to take legal proceedings of some kind against Lord Cowdray.[5] Can you imagine anything more absurd? As a matter of fact the transfer of offices between M^cK & Winston was entirely my doing, & the Master had no voice in it.[6]

I had a curious & rather unpleasant sensation when I was playing golf this morning. I began to feel quite dizzy & nearly tumbled down. No one noticed it & I said nothing, & it passed completely away. I can't account for it, as I am perfectly well, & have been guilty of no excesses either of work or debauchery! . . .

You will have completed your first month on Wednesday. Do you now go on to surgery? I should think it might be more interesting or at any rate less squalid, and I am sure you will turn your back on Charrington[7] without a single 'longing lingering glance behind'. Do you still think that you will be able to last out the whole three months? Goonie proposes to be quite certain that on one of your afternoons 'out' you will simply refuse to return! . . .

[1] Lady D'Abernon became an assistant anaesthetist, and gave an account of her war hospital experiences in France and Italy in *Red Cross and Berlin Embassy, 1915–26* (1946).

[2] An American actress. She had arrived a few weeks earlier to help in a canteen at Boulogne accompanied by a butler and a maid: Lady Angela Forbes, *Memories and Base Details* (1922), p. 185. It was said, however, that in 15 months some 350,000 people were fed and clothed from her barge.

[3] The oldest of the four, Harmsworth, was 45; the youngest, Primrose, 32.

[4] Maxse, the eccentric Conservative who edited the *National Review*, had been active in pursuing the ministers involved in the Marconi scandal, of whom the Master of Elibank (by now Lord Murray of Elibank) was one (Letters 7, n. 3, and 37, n. 4).

[5] The Admiralty were concerned with the extensions to Dover Harbour which were being undertaken by Lord Cowdray's contracting firm. Cowdray was a rich and prominent Liberal,

so that his fortunes during 1911 may well have been of interest to the Master of Elibank, then Liberal Chief Whip.

⁶ The Admiralty had shown up badly in the Committee of Imperial Defence meeting held on 23 Aug. 1911 to discuss Britain's strategy in a European war. The meeting seems finally to have convinced Asquith that a new First Lord was a necessity if there were to be effective war plans.

⁷ See Letter 250, n. 1.

II
B.V.S. to E.S.M.

31 January 1915

You were right as far as dates go. I looked through my letters & see that the first time it was mentioned was on Sunday 24th from Walmer.¹ Still I dont think that proves that it was entirely a plot of Lloyd George's. I know the P.M. has wanted to have you in for sometime. He's *very* fond of you. He says in one letter 'It is one of the few real pleasures one has to feel one can open the door, without any misgiving as to capacity or merit, to a really great friend.'² I also find I did the old boy an injustice, he never said he'd seen Macnamara. . . . I am certain you wont stick in the Duchy for long, & as I am very ambitious for you (!) I welcome this step very greatly.

But you mustnt let the P.M. push Addison in.³ It would be too great an anti-climax. . . .

. . . Next time I have my day off I'm determined, if you can, to dine with you, get a 'late pass' & try & win or lose a little money. Will you arrange that?

Yours ever
Venetia

¹ I.e. E.S.M.'s promotion to the Cabinet: Letter 274.
² Letter 280.
³ Dr Christopher Addison (Parliamentary Secretary, Board of Education) was not moved. The post vacated by Montagu went to Acland: Letters 282 and 284.

285

Walmer Castle,
Kent.

Monday 1 Feb 1915

My darling – your Sunday letter arrived here at noon to-day & was a great joy to me. I rather envied your Sat afternoon: if I had known that you wd be free for so long I shd. have been tempted to postpone coming here. You might perhaps have sent me *one* line from the 'silken tents', but I suppose it didn't occur to you, or you were too pressed for time. At any rate we will have a good time together to-morrow. . . .

I believe Goonie was not far from the truth: you seem to have been strongly tempted to cut adrift from your new slavery on Saturday. . . .

Our party dispersed this morning. You would have been amused to have seen at midnight Sir Edgar, Bongie, & Elizabeth all doing in competition the Swedish exercises. Col Bridges is regarded by the united feminine judgment here as *le plus beau des beaux Sabreurs*. He is certainly a very intelligent soldier, really absorbed in his profession, but to my thinking with a streak – very slight but just perceptible – of the bounder.[1]. . .

[1] (George) Tom (Molesworth) Bridges was then head of the British Military Mission at the H.Q. of the Belgian army.

III

E.S.M. to B.V.S.

1 February 1915

. . . God bless you Venetia. You have been an angel friend to me, why not a wife? I cant guess! Have you ever thought again of that?[1]

Yrs

Ed. Montagu

[1] Edwin was answering Letter II, p. 411. For his proposal to Venetia in 1912 see p. 5.

286

Wed 3 Feb 1915 [i] 5 p.m.

. . . I hope you will like my little tribute to poor Illingworth.[1] Bonar Law was quite good on the subject: he does these ceremonial things much better than A.J.B. We had a very footling debate on small points, in wh. Hogge, King, & others of the asinine type on our side took the main part. I got rather impatient after a couple of hours & flung a little shrapnel among them towards the end to the manifest pleasure of the large majority on both sides.[2]

We had a heavenly hour together yesterday: you were very sweet to me, though once or twice a trifle elusive. But I never loved you more. . . .

Meantime in the interludes of the Cabinet & the House I have jotted down the enclosed outline 'Portrait of a Lady.'. . . . Substantially doesn't it reproduce something at any rate of what you appear to *you?* . . .

¹ This was one of the most admired of Asquith's parliamentary obituaries. Henry Lucy wrote in his (unsigned) *Observer* column:

In the simple, eloquent tribute spoken in broken voice the House discovered full-blooded humanity where it had formerly recognized only intellectual austerity.

Lucy added that the speech had raised Asquith 'to the pinnacle of one of the most popular Prime Ministers of modern times'.

² Asquith's motion concerned the business of the House in wartime. On such subjects as the appointment of a special envoy to the Pope, James Hogge suggested, 'the cabinet have suppressed the free expression of opinion in the public press. . . , just as today they are trying to shut the mouths of Private Members in this House'. Joseph King was concerned with the fate of the Plural Voting Bill, and of such Private Members' measures as the Plumage Bill. 'To listen to some of the criticism', the Prime Minister remarked, 'one would not realize that a great war was being waged, and that six millions . . . of men in arms are fighting one another to the death.'

287

[Encl. 3 Feb. 1915 [i]]

Portrait of a Lady
(Mainly by *herself*) [Part 1]

Tho' she had not by any means an exalted opinion of herself – indeed was singularly free from vanity except in one or two *small* things – she had no ambition to become better than, or different from, what she was. Both by conviction and by temperament, she was sceptical of what is called self-improvement. And unlike some people who are content with themselves, but consumed with missionary zeal, she never made any effort to correct the shortcomings, whether of character or of manners, of her associates or friends. She preferred, not out of laziness or lethargy, still less from want of perception, to take them as they stood and to leave them as she found them. By nature she was not passionate, and for that and other reasons she was free from some of the temptations to which more susceptible and impressionable characters are exposed. When she was for a moment in doubt whether to do or abstain from doing anything, her decision was not as a rule determined by considerations of right or wrong: she was guided rather by what seemed to her at the time being the easier and more convenient, even the more amusing or the more adventurous course. She was not the least selfish or egotistic: on the contrary she was, without effort or self-suppression, kindly, considerate and generous and abounding in *joie de vivre*.

This may almost sound as if she belonged to the class of simple souls, described in Wordsworth's 'Ode to Duty' as

> Glad hearts without reproach or blot
> Who do thy work and know it not.

But that would be an altogether mistaken conception of her. She was by no means 'simple', but (for a woman) exceptionally *balanced* and as a critic once said 'unsurprised', never more conspicuously so than in one episode in her life, when she won, without seeking it for a moment, the passionate love and the unbroken confidence of a man much older than herself.[1]

---

[1] For Parts 2 and 3 of the 'Portrait' see Letters 309 and 356. Henry James's novel, from which Asquith borrowed the title, had been published in 1881.

288

Wed 3 Feb 15 [ii] Midnight

My darling – I shall be curious to know whether the letter I posted to you from the House at 6 reached you before bedtime. I hear from Margot & Violet that after all you were in the gallery, tho' you came too late for my speech. I suppose notwithstanding my wire, you could not have come sooner. Why didn't you send me a little pencil line from above by the messenger? And what about Friday? . . .

I suppose you have had your lecture this evening & produced your notes about valves & the other kindred topics upon wh. you are squandering your time & intelligence. I cant tell you how I loathe the whole business, & when I pay my visit – some Wed. morning isn't it? – after due notice to the bounding Knutsford I hope I shall have grace to be as outwardly sniffy & supercilious as I am inwardly wrathful & sour. I know you don't think that I am capable of such a heroic pose. *Nous verrons*!

I got back from the House about 7 & in the half hour before dressing read a little about Shakespeare's sonnets. Do you know how they differ metrically from Petrarch the original Sonneteer, and from most if not all of his other successors? It is that he always rhymes the 1st & 3rd line of each *quatrain* & the 2nd & 4th, while they for the most part rhyme the 1st & 4th & the 2nd & 3rd – at any rate in the first of the 3 quatrains. Keats, however, perhaps the best of them, often shifts about, as for instance in 'When I have fears that I may cease to be' – wh. is so magnificent in its way that you must some day write it on one of my precious vacant sheets.

. . . The Turks have been trying to throw a bridge across the Suez Canal & in that ingenuous fashion to find a way into Egypt. The poor things & their would-be bridge were blown into smithereens, and they have retired into the desert.[1]. . .

¹ A Turkish force of about 20,000 crossed Sinai under Djemal, the Minister of Marine. Their assault across the Canal was poorly executed, very few of the pontoons or bridges (brought from Germany) being used. Maxwell, the commander in Egypt, wired Kitchener, 7 Feb. 'Numbers of Anatolian Turks . . . deserting. All say . . . few wish to fight English or invade Egypt.' This Canal episode reinforced the low opinion which Asquith and others held of the Turkish army. Yet an abortive attack on Egypt provided no evidence that the Turks would fight badly in a defensive battle nearer home.

289

H of C

Thurs. 4 Feb 15 3.30

My darling – it was the greatest delight to get your dear letter, written under such adverse conditions: it came to me in the middle of the morning when I was presiding over a particularly dismal Committee about Food Prices, and at frequent intervals I refreshed myself by a furtive glance: the nicest of all forms of dram-drinking.

It was very unlucky yesterday that you were just too late. You were right in your conjecture as to the *subject* upon wh. I was scribbling; tho' not as to the exact form. I don't think I should make my maiden effort as a Sonneteer with Jack Pease on one side, & John The Impeccable on the other! One must court the Muses, if not in solitude, at least in more inspiring & stimulating company.

I am glad that you were able to commend the 'Portrait', without your usual qualifying epithet. . . .

A little later. We have got thro' an enormous list of questions & the House has now settled down to 'Supplementary Estimates.'. . .

I did not know until your letter to-day that you liked Winston *quite* so much as all that, tho' I don't at all suppose that you are making an overdraft on what the Painter calls your very moderate reservoir of Vanity in think-ing that he likes you. But I quite agree with what you say as to the difficulty of having a 'nice' talk with him. He never gets fairly alongside the person he is talking to, because he is always so much more interested in himself and his own preoccupations & his own topics than in anything his neighbour has to contribute, that his conversation (unless he is made to succumb either to superior authority or to well-directed chaff) is apt to degenerate into a monologue. It is the same to a certain extent in the Cabinet.[1] And to do him justice I don't think it makes any difference to him whether his interlocutor is the dreariest dry as dust (like our friend Telemachus Shuttleworth)[2] or the most charming of women.

¹ Haldane once likened an argument with Churchill in cabinet to 'arguing with a brass band': N. A. Rose (ed.), *Diaries of Blanche Dugdale* (1973), p. 39.
² Asquith and Venetia had visited Lord Shuttleworth during the second election campaign of 1910: see Letter 201.

290

Walmer Castle,
Kent.   Sat 6 Feb 15

. . . We talked (you & I) no politics yesterday, except personal things, such as Winston for India.¹ He (W) has sent me to-day his proposed counter-blast to the truly absurd German 'blockade' of our seas & coasts. In effect it comes to this – that we shall seize and detain all ships containing cargo of a useful kind (particularly food) going to Germany, or presumed – wherever ostensibly going – to have a German destination. I am rather disposed to confine it in the first instance to food. We shall get into the devil's own row with America if we seize all the cotton shipped from the Southern States directly or indirectly to Germany.² I shall see what Haldane thinks about it.

Poor Birrell writes rather wistfully about the Assyrian's promotion to the Duchy: the office on wh. he had set his affections in the event of his hoped for release from Ireland coming off at an early date. Redmond, whom I saw this week, is most anxious that B. shd stay on for some time, well as Nathan is doing. He R. does not drop many tears over the Aberdeens, and thinks the 'Tara' business the extreme height of folly. Poor Mrs Birrell, who is *in extremis* & always wandering in mind, nevertheless continues to maintain (as her husband says rather ruefully) an 'astonishing heart & pulse'. It is not to be wished for anyone's sake that she should struggle on. . . .

¹ See Letter 295, n. 5.
² See Letter 326, n. 3.

291

TO

B.V.S.

6 Feb. 1915

I thought of wasted Toil, of Hope betray'd,
Wreck'd Argosies freighted with golden Dreams,
Faith's sun gone down in fitful fading gleams,

And puissant Purpose blighted and decay'd.
I thought of Triumphs bitterer than defeat,
Of Wreaths that crush and pierce the victor's brow,
Repute that Honesty would disavow,
Fame's mocking foil, and Power's grim deceit.
These had I seen and known – still left in doubt
Whether to pray high Heaven for Life or Death:
When, from the unforeseen, Thy healing Breath,
Thy steadying Hand, put my sick fears to rout:
Come what come may – I stand aloof, above,
Strong in Thy strength: I live because I love.

292

Walmer Castle,
Kent.

Sunday 7 Feb 1915

My darling – I cannot thank you enough for this morning's letter: one of
the most delicious I have ever had from you. It delights me to think that I am
able to give 'point' to your life. You do indeed give me what I 'value &
want'. Looking back I find it difficult to realise how I fared without it. It
seems now so natural, and when you talk as if absence in Servia, or in the
uttermost parts of the earth, could change what I feel, I know that you don't
in your heart believe that it ever could. Sometimes a horrible imagination
seizes me that you may be taken from me – in one way or another; with you
would vanish all the colour and 'point' of my life; and tho' I might struggle
on for a time from habit, or a vague sense of duty, or the instinct to finish off
a half-done job – that would be all. You won't suppose that this is said by
way of half-reproach. It isn't at all. These last two years the love of you &
trust in you, and your never failing return, have made life worth living. You
know better than anyone what I may call my larger worries. I don't often
speak even to you of my smaller ones, wh. are occasionally depressing. I
believe I am endowed with rather more than an average stock of patience,
but sometimes (this morning, for instance) it is tried almost to bursting
point, and, like the Psalmist, I have to put a guard on my lips that I 'sin not
with my tongue' . . .

. . . I have talked a lot of shop with Haldane about Serbia, Bulgaria &c.
K's idea of the most effective stroke that cd. be put in for Serbia is that an
Entente force – say 1 Russian Corps 1 French Div^n & 1 English Div^n should
promptly appear on the scene. The Bulgarians will never fight against the
Russians, and the Roumanians, who are for the moment in a funk & very

much 'off colour' could hardly fail to be drawn in. There is a good deal to be said for this. No real fighting can begin in Serbia until well on in March when the spring has set in. My darling I do hope that your 'wandering footsteps' won't take you so far afield! . . .

. . . I have a letter from K to-day proposing to form a battalion of *Welsh* Guards.[1] He remarks characteristically that he hears 'the Welsh wives declare they never knew their husbands were worth as much as 12/6 a week' (the minimum separation allowance) 'and are driving them into the Army neck & crop'.[2] . . .

---

[1] The suggestion seems to have originated with the King.
[2] Kitchener also reported: 'Lloyd George's division in Wales has formed well': see p. 289.

293

H of C

Monday 8 Feb '15 3.30 p.m.

. . . I heard Jack Tennant introduce his Estimates: the House was three parts empty, and of course he had to be reticent about everything that matters, but he got on very well & I think distinctly improved his position. I have left him & the vigilant Bluey as watchdogs on the Bench while Walter Long is declaiming, after his fashion, a series of shambling perorations. There is no life in the debate wh. looks as if it would very soon peter out. I have had my interview with M. Bark,[1] quite a good type of Russian of German rather than Mongolian features, who intermingles English & French in his conversation. He is (as he said) *très* optimistic, and says that the *haine* against Germans & everything German is growing every day in Russia in an almost incredible fashion: they are quite determined to fight the thing out now once for all *jusqu'au bout*, &c. Ll. George, by the way, has managed to extract from both Russians & French 7 millions each in gold to be sent here to help to finance our joint operations. He found the French far more close-fisted & *difficile* than the Russians.

I had rather an interesting luncheon at Edward Grey's: Delcassé, Cambon, Kitchener & Winston. Winston was very eloquent in the worst French you or anyone has ever heard: *s'ils savent que nous sommes gens qu'ils peuvent conter sur* ('count on') was one of his flowers of speech.[2] We were all agreed that (1) the Serbian case is urgent (2) we must promise to send them 2 divisions – 1 English 1 French – as soon as may be to Salonica, & *force in* the Greeks & Roumanians (3) we must try our damnedest to get the Russians to join if possible with a corps, not of their good troops, but drawn from the vast reservoir they can't at present get to the front or use against

Germany & Austria. Ll. George thinks he has got Sir J. French's assent to this; but I have told K to send for him & he is coming over to-night in one of Winston's Destroyers. All this, of course, for *you alone.*

5.40 Your dear letter of Sunday has just come, and has moved me more than a little. . . .

---

[1] Russian Finance Minister; later adviser to the Bank of England on Central European Affairs: knighted, 1929. 'An odd name,' Asquith remarked in another letter to Venetia; 'where, by the way, is poor bereaved Huck [Venetia's dog] all this time?'
[2] Writing of his meeting with General Gamelin in Paris on 16 May 1940, Churchill described himself as 'breaking into French which I used indifferently (in every sense)': *Their Finest Hour* (1949), p. 42.

294

Tues. 9 Feb 15 [i] noon

My darling – your dear little pencil note greeted me on my return home after dinner last night. I am more glad than I can tell you that you like the Sonnet; it halts here & there, but it came (as you know) straight from my heart. 'Come what come may' – I suppose that is what you may think rather banal? & so indeed it is – *very*. . . .

The dinner at Cambon's last night reached the very nadir of dullness, and I am thankful – as the Countess Benck, whom I sat next, said to me – that I am not going to a similar one wh. she, poor thing, has for her sins to give to-night. . . .

Security: 'This . . . is supposed to be a secret' (Letter 295)

SECURITY was extremely lax in the first year of the war. Those in London society were accustomed to gossiping freely and continued to do so (see, for instance, Letter 229, n. 1). Some senior serving officers were almost as indiscreet as the civilians.[1] The American Ambassador was convinced that through the social contacts of his staff he had 'the best secret service that could be got by any neutral'.[2] Great public attention was paid to the danger of allowing enemy aliens to remain at large; but Hankey looking back recalled that the internment measures left untouched the most dangerous of all sources of information to the enemy, 'namely, society gossip'.[3]

One of the worst features of this laxity was the way in which it reinforced

Kitchener's secretiveness. He would tell his cabinet colleagues everything, he said, 'if they would only all divorce their wives'.[4] Not all of the information which was tossed around reached the enemy. The Germans did not start the war with any monitoring service; and their high command and admiralty, so far from picking up all the gossip of London's clubs and drawing rooms, sometimes missed items in the American press (see Letter 121, n. 2, for arrival of B.E.F. in France; Letter 192, n. 3, for sinking of the *Audacious*).

There seems to be no evidence that any of the information which Asquith sent Venetia found its way into the wrong hands.[5] A few secrets were kept even in April at Gallipoli when the military arrangements posed almost insoluble security problems. The defenders knew when to expect the landings, but not exactly where they would be made.

[1] For instance, it was easy to infer from the house-hunting activities of Lady Beatty around Edinburgh early in the war that Beatty's battle-cruisers must be coming south to Rosyth: C. Beatty, *Our Admiral* (1980), pp. 76–8.

[2] B. J. Hendrick, *Walter H. Page* (1923), ii. 416.

[3] *Supreme Command*, i. 220. See also Hankey's diary, 27 Apr. 1915 ('Some of these women . . . know too much'), and S. Roskill, *Hankey* i (1970), 422. Some public men did not set the women a good example. Churchill revealed to Violet Asquith that the Naval Division were bound for the Dardanelles and allowed her to 'tell Oc and Rupert . . . but *no one* else': *Winston Churchill as I Knew Him* (1965), p. 361. Mallet's indiscretion in her presence is mentioned in Letter 295.

[4] *Supreme Command*, i. 221.

[5] Asquith complimented Lady Scott on her discretion (as she remarked in her diary, 28 Dec. 1915: Kennet MSS). 'It was the excitement of discretion that was so thrilling,' she noted in 1928; 'it was an acrobatic stunt, to know so much during the war, and not only not to tell, but not to let anyone know I knew': *Self-Portrait of an Artist*, p. 260.

'Winston . . . is always hankering after coalitions' (Letter 295)

CHURCHILL had a Tory past, and had earned much Conservative praise for the naval precautions at the end of July 1914 and for his part in bringing Britain into the war; he was very friendly with F. E. Smith and admired Balfour. It was known to a number of Liberals that, when the Government had almost broken up over the war crisis, Churchill had been in touch with his Conservative friends. During the first days of the war a rumour that he was working for a coalition reached the press. In Liberal eyes his advocacy of conscription gave still stronger evidence of his Conservative inclinations. He was told by a Liberal Whip in May 1915 that his 'rumoured leanings towards a coalition' had been the talk of the clubs for months.[1]

These Liberal suspicions were well founded. Commenting on the presence of Bonar Law and Lansdowne at the War Council meeting about the future of Constantinople (Letter 341), Churchill wrote in *The World Crisis, 1915*:

I had long wanted to see a national coalition formed. I viewed with great disquiet the spectacle of this powerful Conservative party brooding morosely outside, with excellent information from the services and complete detachment from all responsibility. . . . We needed their aid. The Empire needed their aid. . . . I had frequently talked to Mr. Asquith in this sense.

A statesman who seemed none too securely anchored to his party was not well placed to persuade his Liberal colleagues of the virtues of a broad-based government in wartime. Churchill's advocacy of coalition at this period illustrates both the strength of his patriotism and his insensitivity to political atmosphere. By it he lost Liberal sympathies without gaining Conservative support.[2] By his wartime conduct as First Lord he had made Bonar Law think his mind 'entirely unbalanced'.[3] He probably realized how far the war had weakened the Liberals better than Asquith did. But there was no movement towards coalition in February 1915. When the move was made three months later Churchill was excluded by Conservative command.

[1] By Cecil Beck, 26 May: *Churchill, Companion Docs., 1914–1916*, p. 955.
[2] The Conservatives were no longer greatly influenced by Balfour; and most of them distrusted F. E. Smith.
[3] Robert Blake, *The Unknown Prime Minister* (1955), p. 234. Bonar Law wrote on 14 Oct. 1914 (Bonar Law MSS, House of Lords, 37.4.21).

295

Tues 9 Feb 1915 [ii] 3 p.m.

. . . I am carrying about with me in my pocket the most delicious letters you have ever sent me. Nothing for years has given me such intense pleasure as your assurance that you don't want me *ever* to stop loving you & wanting you. That could never happen.

I have just come back from a huge official luncheon given by the Ch^r of the Ex^r in honour of M. Bark the Russian. There was the whole Paris team – Assyrian, Governor of Bank &c – with Grey, Crewe, Winston, and some 'meaner beauties' thrown in. It made me think of old Cornewall Lewis's[1] grim but illuminating dictum: 'Life would be very tolerable but for its pleasures.' I am now back at the House with no questions to answer, and a dull sitting in prospect. At 5 we have a War Council at No 10, wh. Sir J. French has come over to attend. The main question of course will be how soon & in what form we are to come to the aid of Serbia, & whether & how far the French & Russians will join in. French will no doubt kick even at a single Division being abstracted from his forces, but he must be made to acquiesce in this. The two danger points at this moment are Serbia, & Mesopotamia, where we have a rather weak Indian force at the confluence of the Tigris & Euphrates, threatened by what is reported to be a heavy Turkish advance.[2] Our men must be reinforced promptly from India & possibly from Egypt, whence the Turks have for the moment retreated baffled & broken.

I can't help feeling that the whole situation in the Near East may be virtually transformed, if the bombardment of the Dardanelles by our ships next week (*Secret*) goes well. It is a great experiment.

Lloyd George & Montagu have come back from Paris, where they saw all the people who count, much impressed by the weakness & timidity of the present French Ministry. It is a kind of coalition Government of 'all the talents';[3] its members hating and distrusting one another; afraid of the Chamber; afraid of the Press; afraid (from the President of the Republic downwards) of their own shadows. It is (except perhaps the poor fugitive exiled Belges) by far the most unstable Government among all the belligerent powers on both sides. Isn't it extraordinary that a country so rich in resources, human & others, as France, should not have been able at a supreme moment in her history to throw up into the highest places what the French themselves call *hommes de gouvernement?* Throughout these financial negotiations, as I told you yesterday, the Russians have shown far more backbone; and I am not sure that it is not going to be the same in the sphere of diplomacy. (There, my beloved, I have got for a few moments at any rate far away from my favourite theme – wh. I hope doesn't yet bore you – of *analysis*, of You, & of our relations to one another). . . .

I am afraid I can't escape going this Sunday to Easton Grey, where Lucy is entertaining my 3 Lister nieces; it sounds churlish to say 'afraid', but I so much prefer the sea air & freedom of Walmer. If I find I have to do this, I shan't leave till Saturday: so we shan't be haunted & fettered in our drive by fear of losing the train.

I hate beyond words only seeing you *once* in the week. Judging by present appearances I don't think the House can sit longer than the end of the first week in March, wh. would give one a good deal of greater freedom. That would be much better, wouldn't it?

I begin to feel rather anxious as to your future plans, when you escape from your prison house. Please, my own darling, don't *commit* yourself without consulting me first. . . .

To whom shall I give Londonderry's K.G?[4] I have thought a good deal of what you said about Winston & India. He has never hinted at anything of the kind, & of course it couldn't come off unless Hardinge's term was extended to well over the finish of the War.[5] I gather that you are rather in favour of it. It would, of course, for the time close down his political chances here, and no one ever comes back from India into English politics without a considerable handicap. On the other hand, it is not easy to see what W's career is going to be here: he is to some extent blanketed by E. Grey & Ll. George, & has no personal following: he is always hankering after coalitions and odd re-groupings, mainly designed (as one thinks) to bring in F. E. Smith & perhaps the Duke of Marlborough. I think his future one of the most puzzling personal enigmas in politics – don't you? . . .

. . . The only exciting thing in prospect (after seeing you on Friday) is what will happen in the Dardanelles next week. This as I said is supposed to be a secret, and indeed I believe it isn't known to some members of the Cabinet, tho' Violet heard Louis Mallet[6] talking about it most indiscreetly at dinner one night. If it is successful, it will smash up the Turks, and, incidentally, let through all the Russian wheat wh. is now locked up & so lower the price of bread. But it is full of uncertainties – naturally I shall tell you *everything*. . . .

[1] Sir George Cornewall Lewis (1806–63), a leading minister in Palmerston's Governments: Chancellor of the Exchequer, 1855–8; Home Secretary, 1859–61; Secretary of State for War, 1861–3.

[2] This force had been sent to protect the oil pipeline on which the Navy depended, and which ended in the Shatt-al-Arab about 30 miles from the Persian Gulf. Unfortunately the Indian Viceroy, Lord Hardinge, who had just visited it, was less worried about its prospects than the Prime Minister, despite the admitted impossibility of sending substantial reinforcements from India. It came to grief at Kut in Apr. 1916 less from the strength of the opposing Turkish forces than from the rashness with which its commanders had pushed far inland.

[3] On 28 Aug. 1914 Viviani's Government had been converted into one of 'sacred union'.

[4] The Marquess of Londonderry had died on the previous day. Kitchener became a Knight of the Garter in June 1915. By then he had been attacked in the Northcliffe press and the King was anxious to show confidence in him.

[5] Churchill had expressed an interest when the Viceroyalty was vacant in 1910. According to Margot Asquith he had told her in Jan. 1915: 'I would not be out of this glorious delicious war for anything the world could give me.'

[6] Ambassador at Constantinople until the declaration of war against Turkey. He was not re-employed and retired in 1920.

296

Tuesday 9 Feb [iii] midnight

My most beloved – I got your little pencil letter written in the motor about 7, & it gave me the greatest delight. There is something so irregular & incalculable in your hours of freedom & servitude that it baffles all one's plans. For instance, if I had known that you had been free this afternoon, I could at any rate have had half or even three quarters in your company. And what a difference that would have been! – to me at any rate, & I hope to you.

We had a longish War Council, which lasted from 5 to 7. French was there, as always optimistic, quite convinced that the Germans couldn't ever break through in France or Flanders, certain that the Russians were doing well in the Eastern theatre, and altogether sceptical as to a German-Austrian attack on Serbia. He told us, among other things, that Joffre was equipping himself with a full apparatus for bridging the Rhine!

With some difficulty, we brought him to the point of agreeing to send *one* division to Salonica, if he got a good Territorial Division in exchange.

The result is – that we try the Dardanelles bombardment next week, & with the French, & we hope & believe the Russians, make the Serbian démarche by or about the beginning of March. This is all for *yourself alone*. . . .

297

Wed 10 Feb 1915 [i] ¼ to 4

. . . Like you, I earnestly trust that nothing will interfere with Friday: but if by chance you were kept in, I shall be here Saturday, and we could talk at Mansfield St. or drive, that afternoon, before I have to leave for Easton Grey. I am hideously jealous that other people shd. get chances that are denied to me. Is it a pity, or a gain, to be so dependent? I have no doubt about the answer myself. . . .

. . . I have just come back from Dinah's wedding at the Guards Chapel – rather a gaunt ceremony, all the young men in khaki, and only a single bridesmaid, Kakoo, who looked lovely. Dinah, unlike most brides, was in her best looks, but I can't pretend to be enthusiastic about the choice she has made.[1] I have always had a specially tender place for her in my heart among my nieces, and christened her 'wunderschöne' at least 10 years ago. I loathe the Wedding Service, wh. is a reproach to Cranmer & all the experts in what you call 'Tudor prose'. And quite apart from the rite itself, I always feel as if I were present at a sacrifice like that of Iphigenia in Aulis. It means in many ways so much more to the woman than it does to the man: the end of freedom, the opening of a new book, which in perhaps one case in a score,[2] begins a real & living partnership, and in the rest exhibits all the many shaded gradations between serfdom, colourless acquiescence and habit, a more or less workable *modus vivendi*, and hunger & mutiny. Perhaps a too summary & cynical judgment upon the most venerable & apparently impregnable of human institutions! On the whole, I confess that I prefer a funeral. . . .

6.15 . . . I have been sitting all the last 2 hours on our Committee on 'Food Prices' – its last meeting, as we have the debate to-morrow, when I must let loose such information as I have acquired. Runciman has been our most useful member, altho' Crewe Bron & the Assyrian have all contributed something, and we have a clever young Cambridge don called Keynes[2] as Secretary, upon whom I rely for my brief to-morrow.

Do you really want me to write another Sonnet?. . . . There are moments when I can't help feeling that you may *possibly* say to yourself 'I have heard all this before.'. . . One of the penalties of being *so* much loved is to be told it again & again. . . .

[1] See, however, Raymond Asquith's regard for Sir Iain Colquhoun: Letter 264, n. 7.
[2] Asquith first wrote 'a hundred'.
[3] J. M. Keynes had joined the Treasury in Jan. 'for the duration'. Even as an outsider, in the opening days of the war, he seems to have had some influence on financial policy through a Treasury friend, Basil Blackett.

298

Wed 10 Feb 1915 [ii] 8 p.m.

We had a Cabinet this morning – the first that the Assyrian has attended – but tho' fairly long it was not particularly interesting. The main point was to re-draft in the best form Winston's counterblast to the German threat of blockade & ship-sinking. We intend by way of retaliation to seize & keep every ship & cargo, wherever found, which is German in origin, ownership, or destination, by whatever disguises its real character may be concealed. In the course of the discussion Runciman produced a paragraph of his own on wh. he had evidently bestowed much pains & thought, branding the German methods as 'inhum*ane*'. I denied that there was any such word in the English language, and it was struck out. Runcie was perhaps a little mortified; at any rate he has since been diligently at work in the Dictionaries; and this afternoon he produced me a passage from Butler (the 'Hudibras' man) in wh. (under the stress of metre) 'inhuman*e*' is made to rhyme with 'vein'. He admitted that he could find no other instance except in Longfellow & the inferior American writers. Does this amuse you at all?

We agreed to join with France & Russia in lending the Belgians 20 millions. They are in a very bad way, and there is a serious risk, if we do not back them up by every means in our power, of their going over lock stock and barrel to the Germans. A pretty end to our 'scrap of paper'[1] – wouldn't it be? They are certainly the most disenchanting of protégés.

A destination & use has at last been found for Winston's squadron of armoured motors, which has been lying practically derelict at Wormwood Scrubs for the last 2 or 3 months. They are to be sent out to take part in the War in German *South West Africa*, with Josiah Wedgwood as first & Francis McLaren as second in command! I doubt whether there [are] any roads in the country, but I suppose they may be able to trek across the veld & the scrub.[2] . . .

A secret telegram came this morning, wh. has only been seen by Winston Grey K & me, from the Admiral (Carden) that the business out there, wh. was to have been begun next Monday, has had to be postponed for a few days, as the requisite mine-sweepers could not be got together sooner. I hope it won't be delayed any longer,[3] as it is all important as a preliminary to our démarche in the Balkans. So far it has been on the whole a well kept secret. . . .

I always want you to know everything. . . .

[1] The phrase came in the final dispatch from the Ambassador to Berlin. He represented the German Chancellor as using it to denote the 1839 treaty guaranteeing Belgian neutrality. The dispatch was published on 28 Aug. 1914. *A Scrap of Paper* was the English title of a play by Sardou, which had been well known since its first performance in 1860. It is not clear whether Bethmann-Hollweg used exactly these words, or indeed whether he spoke to the Ambassador on that occasion in English, German, or French. See C. H. D. Howard (ed.), *Diary of Edward Goschen, 1900–1914*, (1980), Appendix B.
[2] Botha declined the offer and the unit went to the Dardanelles, where the machine-guns were useful though the vehicles were not.
[3] The Dardanelles bombardment was deferred only from 15 to 19 Feb.

299

Thurs 11 Feb 1915 [i] 11 a.m.

. . . Roughly speaking the figures of our casualties up to about a week ago (104,000) work out as follows: killed 16,000: prisoners 20,000: incapacitated by wounds 27,000: wounded & recovered & returned to duty 41,000. Dont you think the numbers rather striking (1) small (comparative) proportion of killed (2) large number of prisoners (3) high percentage – no less than 60 out of 100 – of the wounded who have gone back. . . ?

Later . . . Nothing from you yet! I hope for a scrap of paper during the afternoon. And what about to-morrow? You see where my thoughts &

hopes are centred: always the same – does it seem strange to you, or quite natural? Somehow I can't imagine it being different, unless & until some *coup de théâtre* blows me into the inane. 'But that to die, I leave – ' O, my darling – . . . .

300

Thurs 11 Feb 15 [ii] 7. p.m.

My darling – I sent off my letter unfinished so that you might get it this evening. I have been reading yours over again – a very delicious one. . . .

. . . I so far agree with what you say that I wd. rather see you go even to the Balkans than to these overstaffed annexes of London Society in Boulogne & Wimereux[1] & the rest. Not that I should feel at all comfortable or anything but deeply anxious if you were to go to the Near East. Typhus (which we don't any longer know)[2] is raging there & killing off the troops by hundreds & thousands, and all the conditions are primitive & even savage. I can't think that you would be right to run such risks – let alone my own selfish reluctance even to *dream* of you for so long so far away. Darling, it would afflict me night & day more than I can tell . . .

I am writing on the Treasury Bench in a House which holds I suppose at this moment not more than 50 members. Poor devils – they are not here to listen to one another: each of them wants to speak & to be reported in his local newspaper. Politics is a wonderful profession: the more one sees of it, the less one understands of the 'vaulting ambition' of the average M.P. B. Law made rather a good speech, but it is a dismal debate.[3] I shall go home to dinner. . . .

---

[1] It was however to Wimereux that Venetia went in May 1915.
[2] The 'gaol fever' of the Middle Ages: it is spread by lice.
[3] Pease thought Asquith's speech 'a masterly exposition'. Bonar Law's main points were that the Government should have bought wheat when they knew that war was imminent, and again when they expected a war with Turkey which would close the exit from the Black Sea; that the Admiralty was hoarding more shipping than they needed; and that shippers could not be allowed indefinitely to make excess profits from the war.

301

The Athenaeum,
Pall Mall, S.W.

Friday 12 Feb. 1915 7 p.m.

. . . My darling, I was so oppressed to-day by the terror of *losing* you that I am afraid I was rather a gloomy companion.[1] I will try to banish such chilling imaginations. All this week you have been divinely good to me, and I love you more than ever – more than life!

[1] This probably refers to the prospect of Venetia serving overseas rather than to the possibility of her marrying.

302

Sat 13 Feb '15 [i] 11 a.m.

. . . After I got home, I took up my pencil to see if I could make any way with the Second Sonnet. . . . I find I have discovered for myself a new & fascinating pastime.

I have just been going through Sir John French's very belated despatch; it professes to give a narrative of what has happened since the middle of November, and is really a most curious lop-sided document. He gives a number of isolated incidents – especially about the Indian troops – in great detail, and then suddenly jumps from the 23rd Dec. to the 25th Jan – a whole month, without a single word either of story or of comment. All the same it is quite well written with interesting passages.[1] K's comments (he is the only person who has yet seen it) are caustic and terse. . . .

[1] The dispatch was published on 17 Feb.

303

Sat. 13 Feb 1915 [ii]

. . . I meant to tell you yesterday of a curious thing about which the Impeccable consulted me. You know that at one time King Ed VII, when Prince of Wales, was violently enamoured of Lady Warwick (Brooke, as she then was). It went on for a considerable time, and he wrote her a lot of letters, of which she claims to be in possession of over 30. Some of them have been subjected to the scrutiny of our Sinless friend, & he pronounces them to be 'very bad' – particularly in some of the references to Queen

Violet Bonham Carter, November 1915

Lady Gwendeline Churchill
('Goonie'): a portrait sketch by
Lavery

Hoe Farm, Hascombe, Surrey,
rented by the Churchills in 1915

Alexandra. Lady Warwick, being very hard up, wants to make money out of this precious correspondence, and hints to would-be purchasers that, if they will put down a good price with an undertaking to destroy, they will acquire 'merit' in the eyes of the Court, & may look forward to marks of honour &c. There is naturally a good deal of perturbation in the highest quarters, and the King's Trustees have in the secrecy of Judge's Chambers obtained an injunction to prohibit her for the time from parting with or showing the letters. There is now proof that she has been disobeying the injunction, & is again hawking some of them. So the Impeccable proposes to go to a Judge & ask him to 'commit' her – in vulgar language to send her to prison till she amends her ways. The risk is that she might appeal to a higher Court, in wh. case the whole thing would become public. But both he & I were of opinion that the risk must be run: it is a golden rule never to parley or traffic with blackmailers.[1] The poor King was lucky when he transferred his affections & his confidences to the safe keeping of Mrs K.[2] . . .

Saturday is a good day for cleaning up miscellaneous arrears, of wh. I am glad to say I have very few – a great tribute to the efficiency of the Private Secretaries. The latest comer, Cys's friend Davies, is very capable. . . .

I have just been having a talk with Hankey, whose views are always worth hearing. He thinks very strongly that the naval operations of which you know should be supported by landing a fairly strong military force. I have been for some time coming to the same opinion, and I think we ought to be able without denuding French to scrape together from Egypt, Malta & elsewhere a sufficiently large contingent. If only these heart-breaking Balkan States could be bribed or goaded into action, the trick wd. be done with the greatest of ease & with incalculable consequences. It is of much importance that in the course of the next month we should carry through a *decisive* operation somewhere, and this one would do admirably for the purpose.

We both agreed that the Admiralty have rather got the 'submarine peril' on the brain. I asked H. how many submarines, capable of effective use, he thinks the Germans now have. He can't make them more than 30. It is ridiculous to think – even if they cd. employ them all here – that, unsupported as they will be by a single cruiser, they can do any real havoc to our merchant ships. No ship of any size or speed ought to surrender to them; as a rule the ship can outpace them, & nothing is more difficult than to aim a torpedo with any accuracy at a running target.[3]

My main anxiety just now is about Serbia. Apart from the typhus & the small pox, they are very badly off both for food & clothing. We are sending them 50,000 great coats, & from Egypt 5000 tons of flour. I have just been reading a letter from George Trevelyan – the clever one – who is there to F.

Acland. He says that, tho' stout & stiff, the Serbs are a very mercurial & impressionable people, and is very strong on the moral effect which the appearance of even a small contingent of British troops wd. produce. As you know we have decided on this in principle, but the wheels of diplomacy move with damnable slowness, and even the Greeks (not to speak of Bulgarians & Roumanians) require to be *menagés* in every kind of way. What a true saying was Lord Carnarvon's as far back as 1878 – 'the crux of the Eastern problem is that the Turks are half-dead and the Christians are only half-alive'. In the 40 years, or so, that have since passed, the Turks have become at least three quarters dead, & the Christians, though much more than half alive in force & fighting power, are more distrustful of one another, & more quarrelsome among themselves, than they have ever been before. . . .

[1] At the end of July 1914 Stamfordham, the King's Secretary, and two colleagues had obtained an interlocutory injunction restraining the Countess of Warwick from infringing copyright by publishing anything from the letters. On 5 July 1915 they obtained a second injunction that 'all further proceedings in this action be stayed until further order': the letters were to be destroyed and 'all affidavits filed in this action . . . to be taken off the file of the court and returned to the present solicitors of the parties who filed them'. Lady Warwick did not obtain money from the letters either for her creditors or for herself and the matter did not 'become public': T. Lang, *My Darling Daisy* (1966), p. 185.

[2] Mrs Keppel's 'wonderful discretion' was the subject of a private note by the Permanent Under-Secretary at the Foreign Office recorded when King Edward died. Hardinge wrote: I would like to pay tribute to the excellent influence which she always exercised upon the King. She never utilized her knowledge to her own advantage, or to that of her friends; and I never heard her repeat an unkind word to anybody. There were one or two occasions when the King was in disagreement with the Foreign Office, and I was able, through her, to advise the King with a view to the policy of the government being accepted. She was very loyal to the King and patriotic at the same time.

[3] In the short run Asquith was right. Between 18 Feb. and 30 Apr. German submarines sank 39 ships, or 105,000 tons of shipping. This was about two-thirds of the tonnage sunk by cruisers and armed merchantmen in Sept. and Oct. 1914. In the same period 40 ships were attacked but escaped: in nine cases the torpedo missed; in the others the merchantman 'outpaced' the submarine. As the figures suggest, there was little risk to the larger and faster ships.

304

Easton Grey,
Malmesbury.

Sunday 14 Feb 1915 [i]

. . . Clare Tennant is here, in good looks, and a Captain Harrisson & his wife. He is a small-sized gunner who has been all through the war without getting a scratch, & is home on short leave. He used to know Oliver.[1] . . .

[1] Clare was Lord Glenconner's eldest daughter and thus one of Margot's many nieces. Harrisson was killed in action in 1917; his widow became the closest friend of Asquith's old age. Venetia's brother Oliver survived the war, though twice wounded.

305

Easton Grey,
Malmesbury.

Sunday aft 14 Feb 1915 [ii]

. . . It is 3 years (do you remember?) since you became the pole-star. My allegiance has never wavered – and never will.[1]. . .

[1] Asquith refers to the Sunday morning when he was with Venetia in the dining-room of Hurstly and 'the scales dropped' from his eyes: see p. 2 and Letter 385. The date was almost certainly 25 Feb. 1912.

306

Monday 15 Feb '15 1 p.m. [i]

. . . I quite understand your decision about Tuesday's dinner. I shall be with you at 6.15 and we will have one of our most heavenly talks, wh. will console me for not seeing you (perhaps in the white dress?) on the other side of the table.

What you say about not 'losing' you gives me relief & happiness. . . .

307

Monday 15 Feb '15 [iii] 7 p.m.

My darling – I sent you off a rather skimpy letter composed under difficulties on the Treasury Bench: so that you might get it this evening. As we are to see one another at 6.15 to-morrow, I suppose most people would say that I might keep anything more till then, and give you a free morning. But I don't believe that you would say so, and I like to write to you about things when they are still quite fresh.

I have a nice little note from the Assyrian (the *guest-thief*) who says that, of all the things I have done for him, he values most the 'introduction' this afternoon.[1] It was a cheap way of earning so much gratitude, & I am glad I did it.

Cambon brought here (H of C) at 5.30 M. *Sembat* the French Socialist Minister, who came over to attend a Sunday reunion yesterday of extreme men, Keir Hardie, R. Macdonald, & Belges French & Russes of the same kidney. He says that Keir H. & Ramsay M. are feeling their isolation from the main body of Socialists, who are pro-war & anti-German. He is rather a remarkable looking man, I should think what they call 'sprung from the ranks', & talks, unlike most French speakers, very slowly with long pauses. He is said to be the most powerful man of his class in France. He is all for carrying on the war to the extreme end, without giving way to what he seems to have called at the Socialist meeting yesterday 'une paix boiteuse':[2] rather a good phrase don't you think? I liked him better than the others I have seen: Millerand, Augagneur, Delcassé &c. . . .

I must see Gulland now. . . .

After dinner. I dined at Grillions, & sat next Mr Justice Darling, who is *au fond* a bore & a bounder,[3] & opposite Mr Bonar Law! Stamfordham was on my other side, & I tried to impress on him the importance of the King having a really good *civilian* among his Secretaries, instead of always drawing them from more or less (mostly less) instructed soldiers. He was quite disposed to agree.

I think I told you some time ago that the firm in Glasgow to which B. Law used to belong – dealers in pig iron – are accused of 'trading with the enemy', by supplying since the war began iron & steel to Krupps'.[4] Two of the partners were arrested some time ago, & now the rest (including B. Law's brother) have suffered the same fate. It will be one of the ironies of fortune (after what we innocently suffered over Marconi) if B.L. (equally innocent) were to encounter a like injustice. . . .

[1] Montagu's promotion to be Chancellor of the Duchy had entailed vacating his seat; after being re-elected for the Chesterton Division of Cambridgeshire he had been introduced to the House by the Prime Minister and the Chief Whip.

[2] According to Sembat the meeting resolved unanimously to pursue the fight against German imperialism 'until it had been utterly destroyed' (*The Times*, 16 Feb., 5d).

[3] Darling was famous for his witty remarks on the bench which sometimes cost him the respect of the jury.

[4] When war broke out a ship chartered by this Glasgow firm, William Jacks and Co., was *en route* from Nova Scotia to Rotterdam with a cargo of iron ore for various German firms including Krupps'. William Jacks and Co. tried but failed to divert it to a British port. It docked at Rotterdam and began to discharge its cargo on 11 Aug., six days after the first proclamation against trading with the enemy; and William Jacks and Co. authorized the delivery of 7,500 tons of iron ore to Krupps' and two other German firms in return for a financial settlement. In the end no proceedings were taken against Bonar Law's brother, John; but two of the other partners who had been responsible for the transaction were convicted and sentenced to brief terms of imprisonment. See also Letter 226, n. 1.

Bonar Law was much distressed by the prosecution.

308

Wed 17 Feb 1915 [i] noon

. . . I have been spending a quiet morning among telegrams and despatches, varied by visits from Gulland & Runciman & now in a few moments from Ll. George. In the intervals I have jotted down and now send another instalment of the 'Portrait of a Lady' – some traits in which you will recognise as borrowed from or suggested by yesterday's talk. . . .

. . . I finished the Sonnet after a fashion last night, but what I added won't stand the garish light of day, & has been already committed to the flames.

I have just had Ll. G. here for ½ an hour, talking at large on the situation. Our Serbian démarche is off for the moment, as the Greeks shy at it (we *fear*, under French instigation). So one's eyes are now fixed on the Dardanelles. . . .

309

[Encl. 17 Feb. 1915 [i]]

Portrait of a Lady
(Continued by Herself) [Part 2]

From the point of view of technical 'religion' she offered little encouragement to preachers and evangelists. She had no 'sense of sin'; no penitential moods; no waves of remorse; no mystic reveries; no excursions (after the fashion of St Paul) into the Third Heaven, and hearing of 'unspeakable words that it is not lawful for a man (or a woman) to utter'. She was no subject for William James.[1] The wings of her imagination – and it had wings as well as feet – when it left the ground took quite a different flight. Poetry and music fed & sustained it.

She was not, as might seem from some phrases in what goes before, at all self-complacent. She was genuinely sorry if, to please herself, she had disobliged or put off a friend. In argument she was always ready (if convinced) to confess herself in the wrong. She hated quarrels, and would sacrifice a strong position for the sake of 'making it up'. She had no rancours against people who had offended or wounded or slandered her; she was, if anything, forgiving to a fault.

If asked whether she had *any* guiding principle she would, in some moods, declare that it was to get 'the maximum fun' out of life. In other moods, perhaps more often, she was inclined to doubt whether (in the words of a friend) the 'quarry was worth the quest'.[2] She was preserved from cynicism, and from living at hap-hazard by the native energy of a healthy temperament, and by a capacity for *real* devotion where she really cared.

[1] The psychologist and philosopher, best known for his book *Varieties of Religious Experience*: died, 1910. Elder brother of Henry James, the novelist.
[2] For this Asquithian epigram see Letter 232.

310

Wed 17 Feb. 1915 [ii] *4.30*

My darling – I am writing from the House in continuation of the little letter I sent you this morning. . . .

. . . The war just at present, tho' not fertile in incidents of a dramatic kind, is very costly: K. told me yesterday (I forget if I told you) that in the last *10 days* Sir J. French's force has lost 100 officers and about 2600 men. And very little that is ostensible to show for it. Meanwhile the Russians seem to be doing badly: happily they have wonderful powers of recuperation, and those wretched little Balkan States (all except your protégés the Serbs) are bickering and cowering & holding their hands after the Italian pattern. It is a sorry spectacle, & makes me sad.

The Dardanelles affair will begin – we hope – on Friday morning. It is an absolutely novel experiment, & I am curious & rather anxious to see how it develops. . . .

I had rather an interesting lunch at Edward Grey's – the only other 2 guests being Page the American Ambassador, and Colonel Howse [*sic*][1] who is the President's most intimate friend, & goes in America by the name of Warwick, the King Maker. He is quite sympathetic to us & wants us to win, but he keeps up relations with the German Government, & is by way of being on his road to Berlin. His main object is of course to obtain for Pres. Wilson the kudos of having brought about peace. I told him I thought it a bad psychological moment: there are 2 strong parties in Berlin: the war at any price lot, headed by Hindenburg, the popular hero, & the Crown Prince; and the peace lot, led by the big business men, mainly German Jews like Ballin & Stinnes. The right time, if it ever comes, for the Americans to try & help the latter is when the German star is for the moment on the wane, & not when (as now) they are all full of hope & confidence that they are going to smash the Russians & take Warsaw.

He (Howse, wh. means I suppose Wilson) has a lot of rather chimerical ideals: one is that of a Union of all nations, including the United States, to fight against any one of them that breaks the peace, and in the meantime the compulsory closing of all the great armament producing works, such as Krupps, Armstrongs, Vickers &c.[2] I doubt whether, even if the war goes as well as possible, we shall be as near the millennium as that! What do you think about all this? . . .

[1] Edward M. House had declined to take office under Woodrow Wilson, though offered his choice of cabinet posts. He was in Britain from 6 June to 21 July 1914, when he met Asquith, and from 6 Feb. to 11 Mar. 1915. British statesmen, who had been wary of House before the war (p. 93, n. 1), were naturally still more distrustful when he flitted from one warring alliance to the other. For Asquith's view of House in Feb. 1916 see Lady Scott, *Self-Portrait of an Artist* (1949), pp. 135–6.

[2] In Aug. 1914 Wilson had expounded his ideas to his brother-in-law, Stockton Axson, along the following lines:

1.   No nation shall ever again be permitted to acquire an inch of land by conquest.
2.   There must be a recognition of the reality of equal rights between small nations and great.
3.   Munitions of war must hereafter be manufactured entirely by the nations and not by private enterprise.
4.   There must be an association of the nations, all bound together for the protection of the integrity of each, so that any one nation breaking from this bond will bring upon herself war; that is to say punishment automatically.

311

To
B.V.S.

17 Feb. 1915

The Hand that saved and healed me, did I praise?
My Love importunate goes out to Thee:
Pulse of my Being, pivot of my days,
My life-ship's Compass on the uncharted Sea:
The haunting Magic of thy lucent Eyes,
The sweet enigma of thy pencill'd Brow,
Brooding in thought, or lit with gay surmise,
A baffling counterchange of ebb and flow:
How shall I liken Thee, my Love, my Fate?
A Tower with bells that chime or toll at will:
A sky now lowering, now irradiate:
A rippling Pool, anon serene and still:
 Thy contrarieties endear the more
 The deep unchanging Self, that I adore.

312

Thurs. 18 Feb 1915 [i] 11.15 a.m.

. . . We dined last night with the Walter Burns's,[1] and I played Bridge in a rather Judaeo-American atmosphere – Sir E. Cassel, Mrs Sassoon &c. I sat at dinner next Mrs Keppel: she has just come back from a fortnight's stay in Paris,[2] where she met among other people an American yachtsman called Iselin, who is an intimate friend of the Kaiser's and had just come from Berlin. He had seen a lot of German officers &c returned from the front, and says that they think very highly of Joffre & rather poorly of Sir J. French, and that they all consider the British troops far the best fighters.

I am rather vexed with Winston who has been tactless enough to offer Sir John F[rench] (behind K's back & without his knowledge) a brigade of his Naval Division, and 2 squadrons of his famous Armoured Cars which are being hawked about from pillar to post. K. came to me & complained very strongly both of the folly of the offer itself & of its being made without any previous consultation with him.

French was evidently very puzzled what to do with these unwelcome gifts – the Naval battalions being still raw & ragged, and the only use he would suggest for the cars being to remove from them their Maxim guns for the use of his troops. The whole thing is a bad *bêtise*.[3] . . .

Kitchener takes rather a gloomy view of the Russian situation. The Germans have undoubtedly given them a bad knock & taken a large number of prisoners: happily the weather there is still very wet, and the country being sodden as well as naturally swampy & wooded, the German pursuit will be hampered, & the Russians may be able to get back into cover. They tell us they have 900,000 men in reserve at this moment, ready to fight, and clothed & equipped – except that they have *no rifles*. You remember a similar tale of woe about 2 months ago. One never knows what to believe of what they say, or what to expect they are capable of doing.[4]

We are at the moment confronted with all sorts of difficulties – not 'single spies but in battalions' – in all parts of the world – Persian Gulf, South Africa,[5] not to mention Serbia and the Dardanelles. The French & the Russians are both rather *mauvais coucheurs* (of the two I think, between you & me, that the Russians are the straighter), and you know what I think of the Balkan lot.

Then we have got to make effective reprisals against the German 'blockade', & this brings us into all sorts of possible troubles with the neutrals & especially America. Winston M[c]Kenna, Ll George &c are full of blood and thunder, but they haven't half thought out the thing & its consequences:

and so I determined to have a second Cabinet this afternoon, and a War Council to-morrow morning.

So you see, my most sweet & dearly beloved, that *all* my time is not taken up in drawing Portraits and building up Sonnets: tho' they are by far my most attractive occupation, and I can honestly say that not an hour passes without thought of *you* – the 'beauty coming & the beauty gone'. . . .

I am sorry that your dinner at the Assyrian's didn't give you much pleasure: your cold was too bad. Violet thinks that Ll.G. was not *at all* attracted by Diana! She or Eliz[th] had a letter this morning from Fraü at Munich, which shows how the Germans keep up their information, for she refers to our friend, and expresses a doubting hope (well founded as to doubt) whether 'die arme Tante' will be with his 'neuen Post (I forget the gender) zufrieden.'[6]

[1] Burns, whose family came from New York, was Lewis Harcourt's brother-in-law.

[2] Mrs Keppel was concerned with a nursing unit which had been moved from Paris to Boulogne.

[3] Churchill was angry that Kitchener, instead of speaking to him, had gone to the Prime Minister. To Asquith he wrote: 'I wish you had heard what I had to say before assuming that I was in the wrong.'

[4] All the enquiries of the British attaché at St Petersburg were met with evasion or lies. At the beginning of 1915 the Russians had 6,250,000 men nominally with the colours, of whom at least a third had no rifles. Commanders were threatened with court-martial if they used more than three shells per gun per day.

[5] For the Gulf see Letter 295. The reference to South Africa is puzzling. The main body of the rebels had surrendered on 2 and 3 Feb.; and Botha was almost ready to attack the Germans in South West Africa. Asquith no doubt appreciated that an offensive in that hot, waterless region presented many difficulties. Botha was a fine commander, however. The Germans finally surrendered on 9 July 1915. Botha, who deployed up to 40,000 men in the campaign, had suffered only 269 fatal casualties.

[6] Fraü may have realized that Montagu's promotion to the cabinet had taken him out of the mainstream of the war effort (Letter 280). More certainly she knew that he was never easily contented.

313

Thurs. 18 Feb 1915 [ii] 7.30 p.m.

My darling – I sent off my letter from the House before going to the King, with whom I talked for about ½ an hour about Russia, our prisoners in Germany, & such things: nothing of any interest or importance.

Then I came here to the Cabinet which has only just broken up having spent the best part of 2 hours in settling the terms of our Declaration about Reprisals – a most wearisome task, when you have some 10 or a dozen men starting off at tangents every other minute, with suggestions as to the remodelling of this phrase or that. We got it through the mill at last, and like most documents of composite origin it is far from being a model of English undefiled.

The result is that for once I feel rather exhausted, and I would give more than I could say to come to you for half an hour: the 'healing breath' & 'steadying hand' would be worth all the world to me. The last Sonnet is full – perhaps too full – of metaphors, and you may think that it represents you as more double-sided or double-mooded than you really are. All the same I hope you will like it. . . .

The Dardanelles II: de Robeck and Hamilton Decide

THE naval bombardment of the Dardanelles forts began on 19 February, a detailed account being given to the press the following day (see p. 374). On 2 March the Admiral estimated that he needed fourteen days of fine weather to force his way into the Sea of Marmara. Then difficulties accumulated. The minesweepers had civilian crews and little protection against gunfire. In the Dardanelles current they had to do all their sweeping downstream. Their sweep-wires, not being serrated, did not always cut the mine moorings. They were harassed by mobile field guns and howitzers and were quickly picked up by searchlights at night. Battering the enemy's forts by naval gunfire did not knock out his mobile artillery;[1] and the weather often prevented the seaplanes, on which the fleet relied for spottings, from flying at all. Ten rows of mines in a narrow channel, well covered by gunfire, were a formidable obstacle (Letter 355).

Meanwhile the collection of a sizeable army for the Dardanelles became subject to set-backs and delays. On 3 March an offer by the Greek Government of three divisions or more was vetoed by Russia (Letters 328 and 335); the Tsar and his ministers would not allow the Greek army anywhere near Constantinople. Kitchener became afraid that Russian defeats would release German divisions for use against the British Front in the West. He therefore went back for three weeks on his agreement to allow the 29th Division to leave for the Dardanelles (Letters 318 and 322). None of its transports sailed until 16 March.

On 18 March de Robeck, who had succeeded Carden in the naval command, made a full-scale, daylight attack on the forts at the Narrows. Two of his British battleships, and one French, were mined and lost and he suffered some damage from gunfire. The minesweepers again proved ineffective. The Narrows forts were, however, substantially damaged. On the following day the War Council heard Churchill's report on the action and authorized him 'to inform the Admiral that he could continue the operations against the Dardanelles if he thought fit'.[2] Asquith did not refer to this meeting in his two letters to Venetia of 19 March, both of which reflect his agitation at what she had just told him about her future (Letters 357 and 358). The War Council was not convened again until 14 May, except for one short informal meeting on 6 April.

General Sir Ian Hamilton arrived to command the Dardanelles army in time to see the naval attack of 18 March. Kitchener's instructions to him were not to attack until the navy had made its full-scale attempt on the defences at the Narrows, and until his force was complete. He reckoned the earliest date for a military landing to be 14 April. De Robeck and Hamilton now had to decide, amid appalling difficulties, the question which the War Council should have decided after proper staff appreciations in January: how could naval and military efforts at the Dardanelles best be co-ordinated? On 22 March they decided that the navy should not make a further major effort until the army was ready to land.

Although this was not recognized at the time, even by the commanders themselves, de Robeck and Hamilton had put an end to the navy's effort to force the Dardanelles and had handed the whole operation over to the army. Two sets of casualty figures may suggest how much hinged on their decision. When the two British battleships were sunk on 18 March most of the crews were saved: the British navy lost only fifty men killed that day.[3] Between the landings on 25 April and 8 May the forces under Hamilton's command suffered more than 20,000 casualties. Even the limited efforts which de Robeck undertook to make in advance of the landings turned out to be impossible. His improved minesweeping force was not ready until 4 April; and by that time the navy's overriding preoccupation was how to put the army ashore. Asquith, advised by Churchill, disapproved of the navy breaking off its attack (Letters 363 and 366); but he could hardly have ordered de Robeck to renew it on 4 April in full force. If he had done so the result would have been Fisher's resignation and a major governmental crisis (see p. 294).

A renewed naval attack on the Narrows might well have failed; but it would have had a better chance of success than the army landings. By the evening of 18 March the German and Turkish gunners were short of ammunition. Their five 14" guns had less than sixty rounds each: their eleven 9.4" the same or a little more. The howitzers and mobile batteries had fired off half their shells. The Turks were so short of mines that they were using a number which the Russians had floated down at them. Nothing could be done about these shortages. By contrast de Robeck's strength was increasing. He was being sent replacements for the three obsolescent bat-tleships lost. These three had struck a line of mines laid on the night of

8 March beyond the main minefield. De Robeck and his officers were unlikely to be caught again like that. Their aerial spotting system, like the all-important minesweeping force, was being improved.

Unlike de Robeck, Hamilton could not know the size of his problems. Everyone saw the difficulty of landing on a defended shore; but it was all too easy to suppose, as Asquith did (Letter 423), that once the landings had been successfully made the Peninsula must be captured. In the event the attackers never reached positions from which they could have dominated[1] the Narrows and helped the navy. The Gallipoli battles differed from those of the Western Front; but the balance of advantage was the same in both. Under German leadership the Turkish army soon belied the performance on the Suez Canal at which Asquith had sneered (Letter 288). Both sides at Gallipoli commanded immense courage and skill and roughly equal resources. In 1915 where that was so the odds were on the defence.

[1] After the German successes at Liège and Namur it was easy to overestimate the effect of bombardment on fortifications, and to forget how different naval gunfire was from that of land-based howitzers. See Letter 315, n. 1.
[2] The Council was told that the Turks were believed to be 'short of ammunition and mines'.
[3] The French navy had suffered more heavily, 640 being lost when the *Bouvet* was sunk.

314

In train

Friday 19 Feb 15

My own darling – we never quite hit this off. I was 10 minutes too soon for the train, & cursed my ill-luck, as I calculated that I might easily have had $2\frac{1}{2}$ *minutes* more of you without any risk. But I hope you will bear in mind possibilities next week, when you have a fullish afternoon off, of my driving you back. The solitary return journey would be cheaply purchased at that price.

We have never had a more heavenly drive than to-day's – don't you agree? You said some dear & delicious things that I shan't forget, & we were all through in complete understanding. What a joy that is! There is no one *except you* with whom I ever get it. . . . Never was a man so fortunate as I: to have found, before this cosmic hurly burly began, the one perfect companion, whom I can love not only with a whole heart, but with the feeling, wh. never falters for a moment, that she is worthy & more than worthy of all my love & devotion: and to have discovered, when the critical time began, and as it has developed, day by day & month by month, an ever growing wealth of insight, & the best wisdom, and the most unshaken trust, which I know will go on unfailingly to the very end – it is the best thing that life has given, or could ever give. . . . A year ago I shouldn't have thought it possible, but as we said today there are things more incredible than miracles.

I hope you won't think from anything I said that I resent or complain of 'under-expression' on your part. You are truth itself, and if I could doubt you I should welcome death.

Darling – it was more sweet than I can tell you to be assured that what I pour in upon you – '3 letters in the day' – is welcome & does *something* to enrich your life. I shall go on – always – till you tell me – if you ever do – that you have had enough. . . . I am tempted after what you said to start a new Sonnet! . . .

315

Walmer Castle,
Kent.

Sat 20 Feb 1915

. . . I hoped to have heard this morning from Winston some news as to how the bombardment had begun & was going on. So far nothing has come. The forts at the entrance of the straits are I fancy the toughest & best armed.[1] If all goes as well as possible the operation of reducing the forts up to Gallipoli[2] will take the best part of a fortnight. . . .

It is curious that we shd have passed yesterday that rather squalid little house in Liverpool Road[3] in which I spent the best part of two years of my youth. I remember vividly the guilty sense of adventure with which I slipped out early one evening to pay my first visit to the Theatre, and the care wh. I took to cover my tracks on my return. We had been brought up to regard the theatre as one of the devil's most damnable haunts; I am sure my Mother had never entered one in her life, and her scruples were fully shared by the old Puritan couple – a Dispensary Doctor & his wife – with whom I lodged. I must have been quite 16 when I took the plunge: the play was a now forgotten one of Robertson's called *Dreams*, and the heroine's part was taken by Miss Madge Robertson – now Mrs Kendal – whom I regarded with true moon-calf devotion.[4] *Ce n'est que le premier pas qui coûte*, and after a time I became an habitual play-goer, i.e. by careful economy I saved up in the course of a fortnight the 2/– needed for a seat in the pit, and in order to secure a place in the front row I have often stood outside the door for one or even two hours. . . .

. . . One may be as sceptical about so-called Science as about so-called Religion. Huxley[5] & his school used to be just as dogmatic about Evolution (with all its gaps & fallacies) as any of the Popes & Councils & Inquisitors were about the Nicene Creed. The old proverb says that the Cowl does not make the Monk: the converse is equally true – that you may have the spirit & temper of the Monk without bearing the Cowl; and tho' Darwin himself was a modest & humble man, his disciples – until they were split up by hopeless quarrels among themselves – almost surpassed the theologians in their arrogance. Enough of this; it is rather a favourite theme of mine: and I am afraid I have inflicted it on you more than once . . .

[1] Asquith, like everyone else, was thinking of the guns in the forts; but the mobile batteries some miles from the entrance formed the core of the problem. It was extremely difficult to locate them from the water and knock them out with naval gunfire; and while they remained in action the minesweepers could not deal with the minefields.

[2] Gallipoli town is on the north shore of the Dardanelles near to the Sea of Marmara.

[3] In Islington. Asquith was then at the City of London School.

[4] See Letters 317 and 340.

[5] Thomas Henry Huxley would, when lecturing, take out his watch and invite God to prove his (God's) existence by striking him (Huxley) dead within the next minute.

316

Walmer Castle,
Kent.

Sunday 21 Feb 1915

My darling – it was sweet of you to find time to send me your little note yesterday. I am very glad you liked my *love* letter (for such it was) from the train. . . .

I like our American guests very much – particularly the daughter who is quite a nice girl, violently pro-English, and free from most of the irritating foibles & mannerisms of her countrywomen.[1] The rest of the company is rather vieux jeu – Bongie Bogie[2] Bluey & Co – safe but unexciting. . . .

Winston wires that the Dardanelles operations had been delayed by weather: they began very well.[3] Happily our ships have a good & sheltered anchorage close by in Mudros Bay in Lemnos[4] – one of the best harbours in the world. The news from Russia is better; they claim to have extricated the Army wh. the Germans had beaten & wh. was in retreat, and declare that the German account of their losses is grossly exaggerated, and that they are now quite safe. *Nous verrons*: hitherto they have always got well out of their scrapes, but their casualties in men & rifles must be very heavy, and one cannot feel sure that there are enough rifles in reserve to arm the men who are to fill the vacant places. . . .

[1] Katharine Page, the Ambassador's only daughter.
[2] Henry Harris, then in his early 40s, was always known as 'Bogie' or 'Bogey'. In 1916 Cynthia Asquith called him 'somewhat of a mystery . . . No one knows his income, occupation, or love affairs.' He had long been in society, and had lost much of his inheritance playing baccarat with 'the Prince of Wales's set' before the turn of the century. Lord Clark remarks of him: 'In a society composed of bursting egos anyone who is recessive without being dull is always welcome': *Another Part of the Wood* (1974), pp. 179–81.
[3] An optimistic view. The firing from ships under way had not been very accurate. To knock out the Turkish guns it would clearly be necessary to go closer inshore.
[4] It became the main base for the Dardanelles expedition.

317

Monday 22 Feb 15 [i] 4 p.m.

My own darling – Violet & I motored up from Walmer, and on my arrival I found your dear letter, one of the most delicious that I have ever had from you. You say that you are so convinced that I realise what you feel about our relation to one another in all ways that you are inclined to let me 'take it for granted'. Like you I am naturally not prone to take for granted what anyone else feels for me. I try to do so in your case, for you have shown a constancy & a devotion, and a power of insight & understanding, and I think I may say *love*, which I have never experienced from any other human being. 'The flesh is weak', and, now & again at any rate, one likes to have one's unshakeable & undying faith confirmed by outward sign & expression. If that is a weakness, I confess to it; but don't ever think for a moment, my sweetest & dearest, that the faith is not *always* there.

I am glad that you saw Oliver & had your little jaunt with him – even in your hated uniform. I *must* have a glimpse of you in it, sooner or later. Your poor dear knuckles! Do take care of them: they haunt me. It is very strange & quaint to see you gradually succumbing to the 'bouquet' of your foul environment – hymn-singing included! . . .

. . . I have pretty well got rid of the Puritanism in wh. I was bred. It had its uses, but it tends to make people intolerant & censorious. And I suppose in me it never quite subdued or expelled the Old Adam. I believe that Mrs Kendal (I was only 16) was the first woman that I at all idealised: she was not really beautiful, but had a most alluring voice, and to a callow novice in the pit seemed almost more than human. But of course she was as remote as a star from one's daily life. The first *real* one – in your sense – was Helen who afterwards became my wife. I showed the same constancy wh. has since been practised by my sons, and waited from about 18 to 25 (hardly ever seeing her in the interval).[1] . . .

. . . I gather from French's messages that in all this dim & obscure trench fighting during the last 10 days our casualties have been very heavy. Among them, as perhaps you have seen, was W. Tyrrell's son, who only joined the Guards last September.[2] He (W.T.) was already laid aside by influenza & nervous complications, and they say now that he will not be fit for work for many months.

This is very sad, and it threatens to affect me personally, for E. Grey has just been here, bemoaning his own bereavement of his right hand man, and asking me to give him back Eric Drummond. In the circumstances I can't refuse, if E.D. is willing to go, but it will be a terrible mutilation of my staff. He is in some ways far the best Private Secretary I have ever had: careful, capable, admirable in dealing with bores & dry as dust officials, always in good spirits, never in a bad temper. When I took over the War Office, & used to have about 100 questions a day about that wretched Curragh incident & its sequels, he was quite invaluable & never let me in for a single mistake. And since the war began his Foreign Office training & knowledge have been worth anything to me. I don't know how or where to replace him, but I fear I must let him go. Grey is really in a bad way & very sorry for himself. First & foremost, he is very anxious about his own eyes, which are getting worse, and some foolish oculist has told him that he ought to go away *for a year* if he is to keep his sight. Of course he says he will stay till the war is over, but he does his daily job like a man under sentence of death, or – what is really worse, of blindness. Then the Under Secretary Sir A Nicolson,[3] who has been a good man, is quite unequal to the wear & tear of the war, and all the capable people in the office are switched off to specialised work. (Grey is very pleased (by the way) with Neil, who he says is shaping excellently.) I strongly urged him to bring in Sir M. de Bunsen as Nicolson's under-study.[4] He is out of work, & did very well in Vienna up to the outbreak of war. We have rather an interesting American at lunch to-day – one McCormick, editor of the *Chicago Tribune*[5] wh. has the largest circulation in the States. The American Germans are very strong in that part of the country, and he says our case has been badly presented. Oddly enough he adds that the Irish, who are stronger still, are almost to a man on our side – a clear result of Home Rule.[6] . . .

[1] When widowed, Asquith's mother settled at St Leonard's on the Sussex coast. Her two sons became friendly with a family there who were regularly visited by cousins from Manchester. One of these cousins was Helen Melland with whom Asquith fell in love.

[2] The war was to take Tyrrell's elder son too in 1918. For the 'obscure trench fighting' see Letter 325, n. 3.

[3] Sir Arthur Nicolson was 65 and in failing health. He retired in June 1916 as soon as Hardinge had returned from India and was available to replace him.

[4] Sir Maurice de Bunsen worked in the Foreign Office until 1918.

[5] Describing this visit Joseph McCormick wrote:

Mr. Asquith reminds me very much of the Lincoln of war times . . . my grandfather described – the patient, comprehending politician, who bore on the force of his personality the strains of jealousies, hatreds, and distrusts which threatened to wreck the machinery of his government.

With the Russian Army (1915), p. 2.

⁶ See Letter 150, n. 1.

318

H of C

Tues 23 Feb 1915 3.30

My darling – your letter of this morning reached me just as I was starting for the House & gave me infinite pleasure. I envy the Assyrian the innumerable little opportunities he seems to find or make for seeing you. I wish I cd. do the same. I hope he takes too gloomy a view of his symptoms: it sounds rather a brutal thing to say, but the less one broods over one's inside & one's outside symptoms, the better one's hopes of health. Moral & physical introspection are dangerous habits. Bluey is a victim to them both. . . .

. . . The gale has at last abated in the region of the Dardanelles, and the ships were going to resume this morning their pounding of the forts. Winston is sending off his Naval Division on Saturday to be at hand when the military part of the operations becomes ripe. . . .

. . . We had a very boring Committee of the C.I.D, which A.J.B. attended, to settle a lot of purely academic questions as to where refugees shd. be dumped, & cattle driven, & lunatics & school girls and prisoners disposed of, in the event of an invasion or raid.[1] That problem, in all its aspects, has faded into the impalpable.

A much more serious thing is coming on at 6, when we have another War Council. We are all agreed (except K.) that the naval adventure in the Dardanelles shd. be backed up by a strong military force. I say 'except K', but he quite agrees in principle. Only he is very sticky about sending out there the 29th Division, which is the best one we have left at home.[2] He is rather perturbed by the strategic situation both in the East & West, and wants to have something in hand, in case the Germans are so far successful against Russia for the moment, as to be able to despatch Westwards a huge army – perhaps of a million – to try & force through Joffre & French's lines.

One must take a lot of risks in war, & I am strongly of opinion that the chance of forcing the Dardanelles, & occupying Constantinople, & cutting Turkey in half, and arousing on our side the whole Balkan peninsula, presents such a unique opportunity that we ought to hazard a lot elsewhere rather than forgo it. If he [Kitchener] can be convinced, well & good; but to discard his advice & overrule his judgment on a military question is to take a great responsibility. So I am rather anxious. . . .

Rather a wave of depression has come over me: through no fault of yours, my light & hope. 'Not Heaven itself upon the Past has power',[3] but the future in all its aspects, public and private, is wrapp'd in what Carlyle wd. call a 'fuliginous cloud'. I call'd you with truth & without any flattery 'my compass'. But you are *so far* away – not with me or near me 'every passing hour'. And you have your own ship to steer. So there are moments when I see no discernible goal, and begin to think that the happiest thing would be to become the sudden prey of one of Fate's lurking submarines. One would at any rate carry down with one to the bottom a golden freight of memories, and escape the living hell of frustrated hopes & unattainable desires. Don't think, my sweetest, that I am morbid. It is all quite sane & true.

I remember a thing I wrote down one night at Littlestone years ago when you & Archie & Violet & I were staying in one of those gaunt lodging houses . . .: it is somewhere in Cicero: 'Vetat Pythagoras hominem injussu imperatoris, id est Dei, a statione discedere' – which being freely translated means – that according to Pythagoras, man, being a sentinel, ought not without the order of his Commander to leave his post.

'Thy healing Breath, thy steadying Hand' are everything.

Most dear and precious – your love *is* my life.

———

Don't let my depression (which will pass) infect you my own beloved.

[1] The last Committee of Imperial Defence meeting of Asquith's premiership. The next was held in June 1920, the Committee having been superseded during the War by Asquith's War Council, and eventually by Lloyd George's War Cabinet.

[2] A division of regular units from overseas garrisons, where they had been relieved by Territorials.

[3] Dryden, *Translations from Horace, Ode 29 of Book iii.*

319

Wed 24 Feb 1915 [i]

My own darling – I have just got back to the House, and my solitary drive seemed shorter than it has ever done before. I can't give you any idea of the good it has done me to be with you for that too short hour. I was *really* very depressed, not so much with the worries & anxieties which come with almost unfailing regularity, and form part of the daily tale until 'the belles ringeth to evensong'.[1] It came from other and deeper things which you know & understand, and which there is no need to describe.

But you have cleared away the cloud, and the 'wave' has for the time at any rate spent its force. It sounds rather as if I were trying to make you responsible for the darkness, as well as for its dissipation. But you know me better. I had a million times rather feel like I did last night, & to-day until I saw you, than lose what has become & will remain the mainspring of all my strength & happiness. I bless you, as I love you: you are *everything* in my life. . . .

[1] Stephen Hawes, *Passetyme of Pleasure*, cap. 42.

320

Wed. 24 Feb 15 [ii] Midnight

. . . I think I shall take to reading Montaigne (1533–1592) – whom I know only at second-hand – in Florio's translation – good *Tudor* Prose. . . .

The Impeccable has sent me some passages from Thucydides which are strangely modern: Plataea taking the place of Belgium, & Sparta that of Germany.[1] He also transmits a report of a really admirable speech wh. he made at Edinburgh in Dec 1913, in proposing as a toast the 'Immortal Memory of Sir Walter Scott'. . . .

Crewe at the same time sends me 8 lines from the Third Book of Lucretius, which (as he says truly) have a real application to Germany & the Food problem.[2] . .

So you see I have still some cultured colleagues. . . .

[1] The passages must have been carefully selected. Plataea, far from being a neutral state like Belgium, was allied to Athens before the start of the Peloponnesian War; and Thucydides makes clear, in Book II, that the attack on Plataea was by the Thebans (who had been invited by dissident Plataeans), and not by Sparta, so that the parallel between Plataea and Belgium is hardly complete.

[2] Simon, like Asquith, had taken a First in Greats at Oxford. Crewe, a graduate of Trinity, Cambridge, was both a sound classicist and a poet. His best-known verses, 'A Harrow Grave in Flanders', were written in 1915.

321

Thurs. 25 Feb 1915 [ii]

My darling, it would amuse you if (like Huck once upon a time) you were lurking unseen under the table, or behind a curtain, at this moment in this, the Cabinet room. A most animated wrangle is in progress as to the conditions of price, qualities &c under which the Indian Government are to be allowed to export the surplus of their wheat crop.

The parties to the dialogue are only 5: Crewe, McKenna, the Assyrian, Bron & Runciman. I am a more or less detached spectator, occasionally throwing in a question wh. sets them all by the ears. The 4 others have combined their forces against McKenna, who maintains his front with characteristic tenacity and self-confidence. All the same the decision will have to go against him. . . . He now accepts defeat, and comparative peace has been restored. They are all sensible men of real business capacity, and the discussion contrasts favourably with the turbid torrent of diffuse & shambling unreason (I am afraid I am getting rhetorical!) which was poured forth on the subject of strikes, & compulsory labour, & martial law, by Winston & Lloyd George at the Cabinet yesterday.[1]

1.30. It is over now, & I have just settled the answers to my questions for the first time for years without the help of Eric Drummond, who has started on his new duties to-day. He resolutely declines to go to Grey for more than a month, after wh. I am glad to say he will come back to me, and in the meantime we can scramble on short-handed quite happily. . . .

I am much happier than I was on Tuesday night & when I came to you yesterday. . . .

. . . When I think of what I was 3 or even 2 years ago, and what I am now – of the incredible revolution in my inner life – of the way in which you have helped me over unspanned gulfs, of the inexhaustible wealth of delight which I enjoy in the sight of your face, the touch of your hand, the sound of your voice, your smile, your silence, the thought & the hope of you in absence, the infinitely greater charm of the actual reality over even the most sanguine and golden-misted dream: then I know that I would not 'change my state' – I won't say with Kings, the creatures & puppets of a day – but with 'Angels & Archangels and the whole Company of Heaven'.

Does it give you any happiness to know *how much* you have done & *what* you are? *Your own.*

---

[1] The cabinet was highly dependent, however, on Lloyd George's powers of persuasion with the trade unions: see p. 461.

322

26 Feb 1915 [i]

. . . Margot & Violet have both been away at Poole seeing the last of Oc, before he starts to-morrow for 'Aleppo',[1] or more literally Lemnos at the mouth of the Dardanelles. Their lot includes Patrick Shaw-Stewart, Rupert Brooke & Charles Lister: how lucky they are to escape Flanders & the trenches and be sent to the 'gorgeous East'. . . .[2]

. . . Our War Council lasted nearly 2½ hours. Winston was in some ways at his worst – having quite a presentable case. He was noisy, rhetorical, tactless, & temperless – or -full. K., I think on the whole rightly, insisted on keeping his 29th Division at home, free to go either to the Dardanelles or to France, until we know (as we must in the course of the next week) where the necessity is greatest. The Russians are for the moment retiring & out-manoeuvred: tho' one knows that they have a curious knack of making a good recovery. And the difference between sending to the Dardanelles at once 60,000 troops (which we can certainly do) & say 90,000 cannot, I think, for the moment at any rate be decisive. Ll. George is (between us) really anxious to go out as a kind of Extra-Ambassador & Emissary, to visit Russia & all the Balkan States, & try to bring them into line. Grey is dead opposed to anything of the kind. We accepted K's view as right for the immediate situation to Winston's immense & unconcealed dudgeon. . . .

The Assyrian, who has been lunching with me, says he is engaged to join you . . . to-morrow. I envy his chances. . . .

[1] The presence of the *Tiger* at the Dogger Bank action had led Asquith to ask (26 Jan.): 'In what play of Shakespeare do you find mention of a ship called the "Tiger"?' He gave Venetia the answer the following day:

Her husband's to Aleppo gone, master o' th' Tiger.
Macbeth, 1. iii.

[2] Wordsworth, 'On the Extinction of the Venetian Republic'. Violet Asquith wrote to Rupert Brooke, 28 Feb.:

Then one morning the gliding into strange, bright seas, strewn with shining islands, – the first sound of our ships' guns, the landing on a tongue of foreign soil, and you leading your whiskered stoker children against the *Paynims*. The luck of there being such an adventure left in the world and you there to have it.

This exaltation was not confined to those left behind in London. John Masefield, who served on a hospital ship at the Dardanelles, wrote of the assault troops as they left Mudros Harbour on 23 Apr.:

All that they felt was a gladness of exultation that their young courage was to be used. . . . They cheered and cheered till the harbour rang with cheering. . . . This tumult of cheering lasted a long time; no one who heard it will ever forget it, or think of it unshaken.

Gallipoli (1916), pp. 34–5.

Of the four named, Arthur Asquith was the only one who survived the war. He was wounded at the Dardanelles, but not severely (Letter 419): he rose to be a Brigadier-General and was then wounded for the fourth time and disabled, losing a leg below the knee. Shaw-Stewart was killed at Welsh Ridge, on the Western Front, in Dec. 1917. Brooke died of septicaemia on a French hospital ship on 23 Apr. 1915 (Letter 407). Lister was twice wounded at the Dardanelles and twice returned to the battle; in Aug. 1915 he was wounded again, this time fatally.

323

In train

Fr. 26 Feb 1915 [ii]

My darling. I am afraid this is going to be very illegible, but last time you found you were able to read it. It was a real disappointment that I could not make my visitation this afternoon. But things were very adverse, & I should have been late in arriving & probably have missed my train, & only seen you in the most tantalising & unsatisfying way. I wired to Knutsford that I hope for better luck next week.

The Naval Division starts on Sunday night from Avonmouth. Margot saw them reviewed yesterday first by Winston & then by the King: Oc's battalion, called the 'Hood', seems to be admittedly the best. At the eleventh hour it seems to have been discovered that they were without either doctor or drugs, & Clemmie showed a good deal of resource, with the result that they will pick up some necessary 'details' at Malta, but it doesn't look as if the organisation was well thought out. Rupert Brooke is quite convinced that he will not return alive.

We are a snug little party in this carriage – Edgar enveloped in furs, the Assyrian coated in Astrakan, Bongie looking as if he were cut out of leather, & I – (as usual) thinking of & writing to you! . . .

You will find a moment won't you? to write to me to-morrow, & next day one of your most heavenly Sunday letters.

I have got to make a speech in the House on Monday on the new vote of Credit, when I must make an effort to survey the situation. Is there any chance of you being there? Winston was rather trying to-day & I felt constrained to talk to him afterwards a little for his soul's good: a task wh. as you know I do not relish, & in which I fear I do not excel.

You know the mysterious 'George Moore' the American – French's *âme damnée*? A curious secret telegram came to-day from Spring Rice at Washington, who says that Moore's wife lives at the Hotel Ritz at New York, wh. is the head quarters of the German Americans, & is suspected of getting, thro' her husband, all kinds of spying information. He suggests that the husband's correspondence shd be opened & examined here. I have always heard that he was on very distant terms with his wife, who is never seen over here, & I imagine that the whole thing is a mare's nest.[1] But I have put it in the trusty hands of McKenna.

There is a lot of snow still lying about in the country. Do you remember a delicious drive we had thro' Kent that day that we went together to Belcaire?[2] I get very tired of seeing people who pop in at all hours, & bother me about things small & great: that is one reason why it is such a good plan to get away from London on Fridays. But to-day I feel starved for want of my Friday drive. I wonder how many of them we have had together? How are your dear hands? I shall try to-night or to-morrow to add to the Portrait – if only the hand could draw what the eye sees – the 'inward' as well as the outward eye.

Of my varied assortment of metaphors, I am not sure that I don't like the tower with bells the best. Do you agree? My own most dear, I am now going to close my eyes & think of you.

Later. We have got to Walmer – a beautiful full-moon night. It is very peaceful here, and I would give anything for you to come. It seems unnatural that you should never have seen this place: the only 'nest' of mine in which you have never folded your wings. My precious darling, I must stop now for the post. You are always with me, nearer and dearer every day. Your *own*.

[1] The Ritz Carlton. McKenna became so anxious about the spy network in this hotel that in Mar. 1915 he arranged with the Postmaster-General for the Dutch mail-bags to New York to be unsealed, and for the letters addressed to the Ritz Carlton to be opened: Hobhouse, *Diaries*, pp. 226–7. The 'spy mania' was now at its height and a friendship between the Commander-in-Chief and a member of a neutral state aroused suspicions and rumours. In Mar. 1916 Moore won a libel action against the *Manchester Evening Chronicle*. He vindicated his devotion to the Allied cause triumphantly, French testifying on his behalf. See also Letter 239, n. 2.

[2] See Appendix 3 and Letter 372, text and n. 3.

324

Secret
Walmer

Friday midnight 26 Feb 15 [iii]

My darling – We had quite a good talk at dinner, & then Bridge in wh. I fared disastrously: I hope mainly from lack of cards.

Afterwards I talked with the Assyrian, & gathered from him his impression after about 4 meetings of the Cabinet. I was glad to find – because I think him quite an astute judge of men (I am not sure I should say the same of women) – that he had already got a sane & sound view of what is vulgarly called the hang of things.

I will give you what I think (if it were an examination, & you had to classify the candidates – like a Tripos at Cambridge) is the order in which I should put them: I leave out myself & him (the A) as a new comer – & our dear Birrell, who is in a class by himself.

1. Crewe
2. Grey
3. McKenna
4. (bracketed) ⎰ Ll. George
             ⎱ Winston
             ⎱ Kitchener (he ought perhaps to be
                          put in a separate class)
7. Harcourt
   Simon (again a bracket)
9. Haldane ⎱ bracketed
   Runciman ⎰
11. Samuel
12. Pease
    Beauchamp
    Emmot
    Lucas
    Wood

This is most secret – *tell me what you think*. Most darling of darlings.

Your own.

325

Walmer Castle,
Kent.

Sat. noon 27 Feb 1915

. . . On looking over my class list in the cold light of a very wet & windy morning, I think it stands the test of reconsideration, and is fairly accurate in the main. Our two rhetoricians (Ll.G. & W.) as it happens have both good brains of different types: but they can only think writing: only the salt of the earth can think *inside*, and the bulk of mankind (including a still larger proportion of women) cannot think at all! There is a pretty sweeping judgment for you, but I am sure you agree. You are the only woman I have known who can *think* in the real sense, and I don't know in the least how you acquired the faculty. It isn't as if (as Dr Johnson says) you had 'taken infinite pains with yourself'. As you have already pointed out in one of your contributions to the 'Portrait', you are without the passion for self-improvement which consumes (and often deludes) some excellent people. So I suppose it was born in, & with, you: which is another way of confessing one's ignorance. . . .

I hope to-morrow to receive from the Treasury some material for my speech on the Vote of Credit. I shall be grateful for any suggestions that occur to you: one can switch on to any topic that has anything to do with the War. I think I shall have to say something about piracy & reprisals & the Dardanelles: the question is exactly what? You are much too modest & unforthcoming when I mutter these appeals to you, my wisest and sweetest.

I went for a moment into the tea room & found it occupied by Pamela & her Reggie – the former inclined to *bouder* because the latter had absorbed himself in *Land & Water*.[1] I reminded them mordantly of Dizzy's famous antithesis in one of his attacks on Peel between 'the hours of courtship & the years of possession'.[2] On the whole I think they have kept up attachment & its outward forms better than most married couples – don't you? . . .

. . . I don't think that our men have been doing wonderfully well at the front the last 10 days, and the casualties have been quite out of proportion to any ground gained.[3] On the other hand the sweeping of the minefields in the Dardanelles seems to be going on well: but they have not yet come to the really difficult part – Chanak and what are called the 'narrows' – where are the strongest forts and the heaviest guns[4]. . .

[1] A wartime weekly journal which had reached a circulation of around 100,000. See Letter 190, n. 1.

[2] 17 Mar. 1845. Disraeli was contrasting the way in which Peel had courted the landed interest while in opposition with his ill treatment of it when in office. The peroration of his speech is given in Monypenny, *Disraeli*, ii. ch. 11.

[3] On 5 Feb. French drew attention to the 'importance of constant activity and of offensive methods' during the stalemate in the west. He wanted 'local attacks . . . with a view to gaining ground and taking full advantage of any tactical or numerical inferiority on the part of the enemy. Such enterprises . . . relieve monotony and improve the morale of our own troops while they have a corresponding detrimental effect on the morale of the enemy's troops.' This set the pattern for the 'trench raids' which the British used on a scale not matched in the French or German armies. It was never clear how far morale was improved by a policy which entailed accepting increased casualties.

[4] See p. 438 and Letter 315, n. 1.

326

Walmer Castle,
Kent.

Sunday 28 Feb 1915

. . . I have got this morning the Admiral's full report of the Dardanelles bombardment. The only ship hit during the operations was the *Agamemnon* which had 3 men killed & 5 wounded, and some slight damage to herself wh. can easily be patched up. All the ships seem to have fired well, especially the *Queen Elizabeth* with her long range 15 in. guns: the first time any such gun has been used.[1]

The French are prepared to send off on Tuesday a Division of about 18,000 men to join our landing force out there. . . .

Later I see from the Sunday papers that the Admiralty have published a pretty full account of what has been done in the Dardanelles. It makes excellent reading after the daily bulletin from the trenches.[2]

I have been trying to collect some ideas for my speech, and have now framed a sort of skeleton: (1) finance (2) general & very brief summary of military situation with *éloges* of Allies, Belges &c. (3) Dardanelles, in more detail (4) the 'Blockade' & our reprisals, at some length[3] (5) appeal: more men, no strikes, better organisation of work, higher wages to meet prices &c – patience & resolution. That looks rather banal, but as your knowledge of anatomy teaches you, an unpromising looking skeleton can be made into a living thing if you can clothe it with a proper vestment of flesh, & give it 'auricles & ventricles', and make due provision for oxygenating its blood. All which in this case remains to be done!

. . . They are now having tea & starting Bridge: so I have retired to my fastness. I think I must not begin another sheet, as I ought to give a little time & thought to my speech, wh. bristles with topics on wh. it is perilously easy to say too much or too little – especially too much. In particular, one has always to keep both the infernal Yankee and the slippery Balkan Christian in mind. So my sweetest I will stop now. I hunger to hear of & from you. Don't forget me, love of *my life*.

---

[1] The bombardment begun on 19 Feb. was resumed six days later after a spell of bad weather. On 26 Feb. demolition parties landed and completed the destruction of the guns in the outer forts. At this date the Turkish infantry force at the Dardanelles was not large.

[2] This suggests strongly that, while Asquith had not suggested publicizing the bombardment, he scarcely realized the effects of doing so. For these see p. 374. The publicity aroused 'some murmurings' against Churchill: Violet Bonham Carter, *Winston Churchill as I Knew Him* (1965), p. 359. For Hankey's view that the operation was being run 'like an American cinema show' see Robert Blake (ed.), *Private Papers of Douglas Haig* (1952), p. 90.

³ See p. 404. The German proclamation of 4 Feb., marking the start of the U-boat campaign, declared the waters round Great Britain and Ireland to be a 'war zone': all merchant ships found in them would be sunk 'without it always being possible to avoid danger to the crews and passengers'. As Asquith indicates by his inverted commas, this was not a blockade in the sense in which that term had been previously used. The British 'reprisal' was to stop all German trade, and not merely the import of contraband goods. As this ran counter to the Declaration of Paris, 1856, the British Government relied on a belligerent's right of reprisal in reply to a contravention of international law: M. C. Siney, *The Allied Blockade of Germany, 1914–1916* (1957), p. 67.

327

Monday 1 March 1915 [i] 5.40 p.m.

My darling – It was such a relief to get your dear letter of yesterday just as I came down to the House. I was beginning to think that I was quite forgotten. But I know you were very hard pressed on Saturday. . . .

It is very sad about your chilblains, & I am anxious to hear the Dʳ's verdict. I am afraid it will disappoint you if you have to suspend your vocation, & I shan't profit by it if you retire to Alderley. I hope in any case it is all right about to-morrow (Tuesday): unless I hear to the contrary I shall come to you at Mansfield St at 6.15. Afterwards we dine with the Assyrian. There are such heaps of arrears to make good on all sorts of topics with you that I shall not know where to begin. . . .

328

Monday 1 March 15 [ii] 11 p.m.

My own darling – I hoped after getting your letter that there might have been a possibility of seeing you at or after the House. I was particularly anxious to hear about your hands – and your plans! I shall probably – I hope – hear from you in the morning. Meanwhile I assume that I shall see you at M. St.¹ to-morrow 6.15.

I wish – more than I can say – that you had been at the House this afternoon. Not that I think that I made a particularly good speech:² but whenever I make a special effort of this kind, I want you to be there, & to tell me afterwards, as I know you will, what is your judgment upon it. I have become so habituated to living under your vision, whether actually present or absent, that I hate your getting things second-hand.

I dined at Grillions – the usual lot, Haldane, Abp of York, Lord St Aldwyn &c &c. But happily, coming in late, I found myself next John Fortescue, who knows more about military & naval history than anyone in this country, and has in addition a nice acidulated humour, like the apples of Devonshire, from which county he comes.[3]

Winston is breast-high about the Dardanelles – particularly as to-night we have a telegram from Venizelos announcing that the Greeks are prepared to send 3 divisions of troops to Gallipoli. It is really *far* the most interesting moment up to now in the War, & I long to talk it all over with you, my dearest and wisest. Don't fail me to-morrow. I live till I see you. *Your own.*

Nearly midnight – so I must send this.

[1] The Stanleys' house in Mansfield Street.

[2] The *Daily Mail* called the speech 'stirring and splendid'. To *The Times* it was 'one of those speeches which themselves are history'. It corresponded closely to the outline in Letter 326.

[3] He was a younger brother of Earl Fortescue, and thus belonged to a well-known Devon family.

329

Thursday 4 March 1915 [i] 1 a.m.

For it is now Thursday! My own most dearly & entirely beloved, I had the most heavenly time with you before dinner (you were never more dear), and it was an unspeakable joy to see you at & after dinner, more beautiful than I have ever seen you, and full, as you always are, of wise counsel & infectious courage. No greater blessing ever befell any man than has befallen me, in knowing & loving you: And whatever happens, nothing can ever take that away from me.

Of course, it follows that you can (if you were so inclined) give me more pain than anyone else in the world. I have quite forgotten the little transient stab of last night, which you so quickly & so sweetly healed. I know well that you are far too kind by nature (even leaving out any special feeling you may have for me) ever voluntarily to inflict a wound. . . .

All that I do & try to do, I do with the hope of earning your praise. There is nothing else in the world that I would put in comparison with it. Your *own – in life, & till death.*

330

Thurs. 4 March 1915 [ii]

My darling – I am so unhappy.

It is no use saying anything – but I am.

I think of Landor's lines – 'I warmed both hands before the fire of life; It sinks – & I am ready to depart'.[1]

Your own.

[1] It is not clear exactly what Venetia had done to distress Asquith. His remarks in Letter 332 imply that she had warned him not to claim all her free time. She may possibly have hinted that she might soon be married; but it seems more likely that she did not do this until 18 April: see Letter 399. For his disappointment at not being invited to Alderley for the weekend see Letter 332.

It may not be altogether a coincidence that the very different, but equally intense, romance in the life of Asquith's leading colleague came under strain at just this time, when Frances Stevenson's parents made great efforts to separate her from Lloyd George. A few weeks earlier Sir John French and Mrs Winifred Bennett had found themselves to be 'two ship-wrecked souls' made for each other: Richard Holmes, *The Little Field-Marshal* (1981), p. 278. The burdens of wartime leadership made an escape into a romantic attachment more than usually tempting; and such attachments seldom went smoothly in wartime conditions.

331

Thurs. 4 March 1915 [iii] Midnight

My own darling – thank you with all my heart for your little note, which I got at dinner at the McKennas. It made me less unhappy. But I am.

If you are free, I will call for you in the motor at *5 to 3* to-morrow (Friday) and we will have a drive.

Your devoted – always –

332

In train

Fr 5 March 1915 [i]

My own darling – I had a very healing hour & a half with you and feel far happier than 24 hours ago I thought wd. ever be possible. I didn't really exaggerate in what I said to you: the *coup foudroyant* (in the literal sense) would have been welcome all yest. aft. & night. It may not be wise to be so dependent: to have put everything that one has or hopes for into one investment: to stand or fall entirely by one person: but it is too late now to make these calculations, & to attempt to draw up a balance sheet. *J'y suis – j'y reste.* I can never make out tho' I often speculate, exactly how much it means to you: naturally not nearly so much as it does to me: but still I have (except in bad moments) an unshaken faith that it is a real & vital part of your life, and that if anything were to crush or annihilate it, you would feel a certain mutilation, or, if that is too strong a word, a sense of permanent loss. And that is something – a great deal – indeed everything to me.

I hope you won't think, when you reflect on my confessions of to-day, that I was suffering yesterday from a spasm of epilepsy – the first symptom of morbid degeneration, & perhaps ultimate paralysis. It really wasn't that. My case may not bear cold analysis; but I felt as much as, & far more than, I expressed.

I am reassured by the sweet & true things that you said to me to-day. Believe me, most precious, that I don't want to impoverish your interests, or restrict your friendships, or in any direction to fetter your freedom. I don't wish to change you in any way, or to exclude, thro' jealousy or censoriousness, any element personal or external that contributes to the fullness & many-sidedness of your life. But I *do* treasure above everything I have ever had, or have, or hope to have, my own share in you, & that I *couldn't bear* to partition or divide. There is rarely, if ever, complete equality in the relation of two human beings – certainly there is not in ours. In that I acquiesce: it is the decree of the gods. But I should love you always to know & feel that to me you are *everything*.

It has been in some ways a disappointing week, although I have not often had more of the things – praise, flattery &c[1] – wh. no one but a fool or a coxcomb can affect to despise. What is much better, I have had 2 or 3 glorious hours with you, and to-day you were more sweet and angelic than words can say: so I will poke up the 'sinking fire'. All the same, how I long to be in the train for Alderley!

Violet & I are going down together: no one else to-night wh. is quite a peaceful prospect. She tells me that Parky was very strong in the opinion that, until your circulation is better, you ought not to go back to the Hospital. You are the best judge, but perhaps it might be wise to give yourself a few more days of rest & clean & comfortable conditions: wh. is very disinterested of me.

Still more disinterested is my promise to do what I can to promote the voyage of the Hospital Yacht. . . .

---

[1] On 3 Mar. Asquith followed up his success of the previous day with a 'brief but eloquent speech' (*Daily Mail*) on the Universities Emergency Powers Bill. The *Daily Sketch* commented (4 Mar.), on his 'noble . . . unforgettable appeal':

that Mr. Asquith can so well call upon us for . . . 'patience and tenacity' . . . is no doubt because, in himself, he exhibits those qualities admirably. All of us are determined not to fail him and his fellow-workers, any more than in these few memorable months to come there is likelihood of their failing us.

Neither of these papers had been notably favourable to the Liberal party before the war.

333

Walmer

Friday 5 March 1915 [ii] Midnight

My most beloved – I wrote you a little letter in the train wh. I hope you will get by tea-time to-morrow (Sat.). I don't suppose it was at all adequate, but it will at any rate have conveyed to you that, after our divine drive to-day, I am no longer in a suicidal mood. I wish more than ever that I had had the courage to press upon you to come here for Sunday. I am afraid you wd. have said *No*, but it was quite worth trying (as I think was the other alternative, in regard to wh. I blame myself quite as much as you). But seriously it wd. have been delicious this evening if you cd. have made a third with Violet & me. We had dinner together and a really good talk, in the course of wh. we passed most of our friends in review, not to speak of politics & other things. We (she and I) are as you know always the best of friends, and never *froisser* one another. It wd. have been *divine* if you cd. have been with us. After a prolonged talk 'over the walnuts & the wine' we solemnly adjourned to a Bridge table, & for 1½ hours played double dummy. Skip-about wd. have been more amusing, but we had lcts of 'fun'. In the intervals, she recalled her old visits to Alderley (long before I was admitted there) & contrasted what it was with what you have made it. You are not only a life giver but a life maker. We are absolutely alone in this ambitious looking Castle; and (if only you cd. have joined us) we should have had the best of Saturdays & Sundays. It won't be nearly so 'nice' when to-morrow's Comus crew arrives – Ld. Reading, Sir C. Mathews, possibly Bogie, – not to speak of Clemmie & Goonie, whom (as you know) in their special ways I love. But it is an infinite relief to be so far away from London & the unending succession of interviews with colleagues, Americans, Frenchmen, Belges, & miscellaneous bores. But I would give all the peace & comparative tranquillity a hundred times over, for a walk with you to the little wooden house which overlooks the mere & the Church, and wh. is associated with some of my dearest & most blessed memories.[1] And your dear room, & the gaily coloured box,[2] into which you will have to drop (poor sweet) such a mass of new stuff. Four letters in one day! it is almost incredible: but I warn you it may happen again. Violet is most loyal & true to you, and some of the things she said about you gave me a real thrill of pleasure. . . .

[1] Venetia was at Alderley. See Letter IV (p. 466).
[2] The box in which Asquith's letters were kept was painted green and white.

334

Walmer Castle,
Kent.

Sat morning 6 March 15. [i]

My darling – I had quite a good sleep last night, unlike the night before,
when I woke very early and had a hellish time. . . .

. . . I have rather a heavy post of telegrams &c this morning. . . .

As E. Grey says, the moment the military & naval[1] situation improves
the diplomatic sky begins to darken. Russia, despite all our representations
& remonstrances, declines absolutely to allow Greece to take any part in the
Dardanelles business, or the subsequent advance on Constantinople; and
the French appear inclined to agree with her. On the other hand the Greeks
are burning to be part of the force which enters Constantinople, and yet
wish to avoid committing themselves to fighting against anybody but the
Turks & possibly the Bulgarians. They won't raise a finger for Serbia, and
even want all the time to keep on not unfriendly terms with Germany &
Austria! We have of course told them that this is nonsense, that you can't
make war on limited liability terms, & that therefore they must come in
with us 'all in all or not at all'. . . .

---

[1] On 2 Mar. Carden, the Admiral commanding at the Dardanelles, estimated that, given
good weather, his fleet would break through to the Sea of Marmara in 14 days. The Admiralty
issued an optimistic communiqué; and the grain price fell sharply in Chicago in the expectation that, with the Allied fleet in Constantinople, Russia would resume the export of wheat.

'Armaments . . . I think we shall have to "take over" the principal firms' (Letter 335)

THE administrative problem of securing increased armaments production
bristled with contentious political issues. It was necessary, not only to
obtain increased output from the established armament makers, but to draw
into munitions work hundreds of firms which would be quite unfamiliar
with it. The labour shortages which had resulted from the raising of the
Kitchener armies had to be made good by 'dilution', that is, by the employment of semi-skilled workers and women. The principal political obstacles
in the way of these objectives were Kitchener and the trade unions.

Kitchener, who resented French's demands for limitless ammunition,[1]
was concerned to keep the whole War Office domain under his own hand.

Admiral of the Fleet Lord Fisher of Kilverstone: an etching by Francis Dodd. On L. G. Brock's copy Fisher added his signature and the words:

'"His eye was not dim nor his natural force abated" (see Deuteronomy Chap. 34, verse 7) but he didn't go over Jordan!'

Asquith with Sir John French, when visiting the B.E.F., June 1915

Edwin and Venetia Montagu canvassing

He objected to revealing future munitions requirements to politicians and civilian officials; in his view such secrets, which revealed the size and shape of the armies being created, should be confined to his Master General of the Ordnance and himself. The trade unions objected to giving up traditional practices and restrictions when the most obvious result of doing so would be to increase the owners' profits.

Lloyd George quickly freed the Master General from the Treasury's normal expenditure controls; and in October 1914 he secured the appointment of a 'Shells Committee' of the cabinet under Kitchener's chairmanship. The committee met six times and arranged for the Government to underwrite the cost of expanding some of the armaments works; but Kitchener resented its operations and succeeded in putting an end to them. Lloyd George returned to the charge in February 1915; and on 5 March Asquith presided over a meeting which recommended the establishment of a new munitions committee with executive powers. Montagu's scheme of an Army Contracts Directorate with a minister in charge (Letter 335) was intended to provide administrative machinery for this committee. By 18 March (Letter 355) Lloyd George had emerged as the only possible Director; but he would take the post only if he were given complete control over contracts and Kitchener would not yield on this.

Lloyd George had meanwhile achieved an important success with the trade unions. The union leaders met him at the Treasury on 17, 18, and 19 March and agreed to accept and operate 'dilution'. In return they were promised that traditional practices would be restored at the end of the war, that wartime profits would be restricted, and that they were to share in the direction of wartime industry. On 22 March Asquith, Lloyd George, Churchill, Montagu, and Balfour met and hammered out a formula for the powers of the intended munitions committee (Letters 361 and 362). Kitchener would not accept the meeting's conclusions and Lloyd George threatened to wash his hands of the whole business (Letter 372). Kitchener now made a last-minute defensive move: on 7 April there was a press announcement that he had set up his own War Office Armaments Output Committee. On the previous day, however, Asquith had held a final meeting and on 8 April he told Kitchener that he had appointed a Munitions Committee, with Lloyd George as chairman, 'to ensure the promptest and most efficient application of all the available resources of the country to the manufacture and supply of munitions of war for the army and navy'; the Committee had 'full authority to take all steps necessary for that purpose' (Letter 390). The creation of this Committee was announced in the press on 14 April and in the Commons on the following day.

These proceedings hardly gave an impression of unity and dispatch at cabinet level. The new Munitions Committee, Balfour told Bonar Law

(3 April), 'ought to have been appointed seven months ago'.[2] If the public had known of all that underlay the press communiqués they would have been even less reassured. The Committee had no sooner started work than Kitchener upbraided Lloyd George in cabinet for revealing secret information to it (Letters 394 and 395). Armament production was not put on a satisfactory basis until the reconstruction of the Government in May allowed Lloyd George to leave the Treasury for the newly created Ministry of Munitions. By then Asquith had ceased writing regularly to Venetia.

[1] For Kitchener's complaints after the Neuve Chapelle Battle see Letter 355, n. 2.
[2] S. H. Zebel, *Balfour* (1973), p. 203. See also W. A. S. Hewins's speech, 21 Apr.: *Parl. Deb.*, lxxi. 277–92.

335

Walmer Castle,
Kent.

Sat. 6 March 1915 [ii]

My darling – I sent off a letter as we drove through Deal this morning at the Post Office there in hopes that it may reach you to-morrow (Sunday) morning. After lunch Violet & I had a drive through Ramsgate & Broadstairs, and when we got back we found that Goonie & Clemmie had arrived. Winston does not come till to-morrow. It was a relief to get your telegram & I hope that 'Ever so well' applies not only to your dear hands but to the anaemia or whatever it is that is wrong with your circulation. I am of course most anxious to know your plans – whether you stay on or return, & if the latter on which day. I long more than ever to see you again.

Bongie has brought down a heap of stuff – some of it of a highly difficult & contentious kind. So far as things at home are concerned, the thorniest question is how to get more labour & plant for making armaments & other things needed for the war. I think we shall have to 'take over' the principal firms, leaving the management in its present hands, but keeping the whole business, especially the division of profits during the war, the distribution of work & of labour, and the wages to be paid to the workmen, under Government supervision. We shall want a special Minister to look after it, if this is done, & I incline to the Assyrian. (I am not sure that I won't go into the country & make one or two speeches on the subject: what do you say?) He sent me an excellent mem[m] on the subject this morning, in a letter of gigantic proportions wh. dealt with his own personal aspirations, the relative claims of colleagues, & other delicate matters of the same order. I will tell you more about this when I see you next.

In regard to things abroad, there have emerged two most infernal problems: I say 'emerged', because they have always been there latent & in the background. What I tell you about them is *most secret*. The first is that there are significant indications that, before very long, Italy may come in on the side of the allies. That seems natural enough, but what is strange is that Russia strongly objects.

She thinks that Italy has kept out during the stress of the war, that she will demand an exorbitant territorial price, and that the Three Allies shd. continue to keep the thing entirely in their own hands. Both the French & ourselves I need hardly say take quite a different view.

The other question (and this is if possible *more* secret) is the future of Constantinople, & the Straits. It has become quite clear that Russia means to incorporate them in her own Empire. That is the secret of her intense & obstinate hostility to the idea of allowing the Greeks to take any share in the present operations & their consequences. When this becomes known (if it does) it is not unlikely that Greece, Bulgaria, & Roumania will all protest most vehemently. It is rather a matter of sentiment with Greece, but Bulgaria & still more Roumania – as the map shows you – will feel that they run a risk of having their exit from the Black Sea put permanently at the mercy of Russia. I really don't know how it will be viewed in France or in this country: it is of course a complete reversal of our old traditional policy. Personally I have always been & am in favour of Russia's claim, subject to proper conditions as to non-fortification of the Straits, and as to free commercial transit. With command of the Sea we could always block the entrance. It is monstrous that Russia shd have only 2 ports – Archangel & Vladivostock, both of wh. are ice-bound during the winter.

There, darling, that is enough of 'mundane' dust for one letter, isn't it? Think over these things & let me know your thoughts. When I go to bed to-night I will write you something of a different kind. I am *longing* to hear from you. You are the breath of my life, and the last words of my 1st Sonnet are the *literal truth*.

336

Walmer

Sat Midnight 6 March 1915 [iii]

. . . I sat next Clemmie at dinner & she talked a lot about Neil & his engagement: she has rather a feeling for him. The thing that will amuse you is that Ll. George came to lunch at the Admiralty, & was told of Neil's adventure: on which he commented with much pleasure – 'lucky man' – 'charming young lady' – 'I sat next her at the Prime Minister's, at Downing

St, & found her quite delightful' &c &c. They began to smell a rat, and said 'who do you mean?' 'Isn't she called *Venetia* Stanley?' 'Yes, but this one is called Victoria'.[1] 'Good God – poor Neil – I am so sorry'. There is a dew-drop for you!

The Assyrian's letter to me to-day is a most extraordinary & characteristic document. I am not sure that I won't show it to you – tho' I am sure it was meant for no eyes but mine. . . .

[1] The Earl of Derby's only daughter: she was married to Neil Primrose in Apr. 1915.

337

Walmer Castle,
Kent.

Sunday 7 March 1915 [i]

. . . Winston wires that he cannot get away, wh. does not surprise me, as he is absorbed in his Dardanelles & in catching German ships. By the way one of the amusing parts of the Assyrian's diatribe was his violent invective against poor W, especially from the point of view of his possible candidature for the Indian Viceroyalty. I don't know who put this idea into his head. I feel sure that you didn't, tho' you have once or twice urged it upon me. 'Impetuous & wrong-headed energy, little power of adaptability, great obstinacy, lack of principle &c &c' – these are a few of the flowers from a luxuriant posy of abuse. I can see that tho' he acquiesces in the veto put upon his own ambitions in that quarter, he still hankers a little and is disposed to argue the other way. *Faute de mieux*, he favours McKenna! What do you say to that? It is not easy to picture him & Pamela in their howdahs, holding the 'gorgeous East in fee'.[1] But apart from looks and manners – which after all are of secondary importance – he would do the job with his characteristic efficiency, & probably, poor man, not be more unpopular there than he is here. I have a very genuine respect for him. . . .

. . . Winston has again changed his mind & now says he will come to dinner. Clemmie says he is hopelessly undecided in small things. They are pounding away again to-day at the Dardanelles, having incidentally had a battering match with the forts of Smyrna.[2] . . .

Later. I have just come in from a rather arduous match with the Lord Chief Justice, whom I am glad to say I just managed to beat. He is very nice to play with. I asked him who was the best man who now appears before the Courts, and he said that both he & the best of the other Judges put the Impeccable an easy first – before Carson Finlay Duke & all the other swells. I was glad to hear this. He finds your friend Buckmaster[3] a little too unbalanced & peppery, and apt to 'put out his quills'.

Clemmie tells me you were present at a curious scene at Somatoff's or some such place, where Mrs Keppel offered her a dress, wh. she was too proud & 'well brought up' to accept, notwithstanding your advice to the contrary. Clemmie is very 'particular', isn't she?[4]

Goonie says that Jack has been offered a place on his staff by Sir Ian Hamilton, if he goes to the Dardanelles.[5]

This letter is little better than a bundle of snips & chips of gossip. But I gave you, dear sweet, a heavy dose of politics yesterday, and very likely shall do so again to-morrow. I want very much to know what you think of my idea of making one or perhaps two speeches in the country on the recruiting & mobilisation, not of the Army, but of labour. It is no good doing it if it is likely to be a fiasco, but for the time this is much the most serious feature of the whole situation. I should be much guided by your judgment.

I am hoping that I may get a letter from you here in the morning, and another in London. I *never* wanted them so much. Russia, Italy, Constantinople, Greece, Bulgaria, Labour, Welsh Church – are a few of my 'crosses'. But neither alone, nor together, would they weigh more than a feather in the scale, beside the thought that I had lost or forfeited my share in you. . . .

[1] Wordsworth, 'On the Extinction of the Venetian Republic'.

[2] Churchill told the War Council, 3 Mar., that there was by now a risk of enemy submarines reaching the Dardanelles and that Smyrna must be made useless as a base for them.

[3] Sir Stanley Buckmaster, K.C., Solicitor-General and Director of the Press Bureau.

[4] In Aug. 1914 Mrs Churchill at once returned an emerald and diamond ring sent her by a shipowner (and Conservative M.P.). Her husband commended her warmly for this.

[5] Hamilton was not told definitely of his appointment until 12 Mar. He seems, from Violet Asquith's diary, to have owed it chiefly to Asquith; Kitchener had thought of General Sir Leslie Rundle. It was an important command to give to a general who, in Asquith's view (Sept. 1914), had 'too much feather in his brain' (Letter 169).

338

Walmer

Sunday midnight 7 March 1915 [ii]

My darling – I am afraid I sent you rather a snippety letter to-day. I can say honestly, before I go to bed, that there has not been an hour since I got up this morning when you have not been in my thoughts – the more so perhaps because they had to feed on memories & imaginations. It has been of its kind quite a 'nice' Sunday: both Clemmie & Goonie played up – the latter, by the way, is quite convinced that she has had a success with Kitchener, & scorned my suggestion that he was insensitive to female blandishments. The men too did their best, & I am really fond of Rufus. Winston appeared at about tea time, & was in his best form: he left immediately after dinner in one of his special trains. He agrees with me that there are now probably not more than 3 German submarines patrolling & 'blockading' our coasts. One of the funniest results of this last development is that we have a whole flotilla of our own submarines, huddled together in Dover Harbour, & afraid to go out, lest they should be rammed or sunk by British Merchant ships, which now go at once for every periscope that appears above the surface. . . .

. . . I *long* to have a talk with you about all these & many other things. Without you I am only one half of a pair of scissors! Good night – my most beloved.

IV

E.S.M. to B.V.S.

7 March 1915

Dearest,

Goodnight. Bless you a million times.

It was a wonderful weekend and Browning did me a lot of good. And if you are going to become a bust and me a statue to missed opportunity it just confirms my opinion *its got to be* and that right soon.

Bye-the-bye the bust was a bride – whose are you pray?[1]

Yrs tremendously
E.S.M.

[1] Asquith, Venetia, and Edwin all found Browning's poem 'The Statue and the Bust' a useful source of quotation: see Letters 185 and 203. The poem opens with the wedding of the woman who later has the bust made.

339

H of C

Monday 8 March 1915 4 p.m

. . . My love for you has grown day by day & month by month & (now) year by year: till it absorbs and inspires all my life. I could not if I would, and I would not if I could, arrest its flow, or limit its extent, or lower by a single degree its intensity, or make it a less sovereign & dominating factor in my thoughts & purposes & hopes. It has rescued me (little as anyone but you knows it) from sterility, impotence,[1] despair. It enables me in the daily stress of almost intolerable burdens & anxieties to see visions & dream dreams. . . .

[1] For the change in usage of such words see p. 7, n. †.

340

Tu 9 March 1915

My own darling – it was more than delicious to see you & talk to you & be near you – but how disappointingly short! . . .

. . . I went away feeling that I had only just begun to talk with you. There were such masses of things I meant to say – about your Post Office, and about (to mention one of the least) Lady Warwick, and about the whole future of the War, & how we are to stand with this Power or that – small or great. Somehow, by some impish freak of conversation, just when I am on the point of opening 'rather' big things, you with your 'enigmatic' smile (and some other wiles) switch it off! What a fiend you are! But (to parody Milton) I would rather 'do time' with you in Hell, than sing anthems & Hallelujahs . . . in Heaven. . . .

. . . I went to the Lucys'[1] where I found a most boring company, Lord & Lady Inchcape, Lord Justice Bankes, Sir Guy & Lady Granet, & one or two other dim people. But I had a certain compensation. For I found myself between my hostess Lady Lucy – & who do you think? None other than Mrs Kendal – née Miss Madge Robertson. I hardly think I have ever talked to her before. I told her (what you know) of my first theatrical adventure: she was interested & amused, but persisted in calling me 'Sir' (which you never do – do you?). She admitted that *Dreams* was one of the worst of her brother Tom Robertson's plays – but said that he had induced her to act in it, because he thought that (in those days) she looked better than any other actress in a riding habit! (I remember well my thrill when I saw her come on the stage in that riding habit, with a whip, & a good old chimney pot Victorian hat).[2] She belonged, like the Terrys & the Kembles, to a family wh. had been for generations on the stage, & she says she has play-bills of her grandmothers & great grandfathers wh. go back to the reign of Queen Anne. I had really a good talk with her (so unlike the people we ordinarily meet) which redeemed my evening, & on the plea of 'urgent affairs' I escaped from the rest about 10.30. . . .

¹ Sir Henry Lucy had been well known for many years as a parliamentary journalist. He contributed the 'Essence of Parliament' to *Punch* from 1881 to 1916.
² See Letter 315.

'A horrible mess over the Welsh Church' (Letter 341)

WHEN the Act disestablishing the Welsh Church was put into cold storage, along with Home Rule, it was intended that nothing should be done towards bringing it into effect while the war lasted. The fact that the Church of Wales could not provide under war conditions against partial disendowment had been the principal argument for the postponement. It soon appeared, however, that postponement had not deprived the Welsh Church Commissioners of their authority to take preparatory steps towards disendowment, and that they were in fact taking such steps. The Duke of Devonshire accordingly gave notice in the Lords of a bill to make postponement complete. Beauchamp then promised a Government bill, if the Duke would withdraw his proposals, and if the Opposition would promise not to prevent the Act from coming into effect after the war. Lansdowne gave the necessary undertaking and the Government bill was passed by the Lords. On a less controversial issue a wartime bargain of this kind with the Opposition would have been readily approved. Even on a measure such as this, passed laboriously under the Parliament Act, the bargain might have been accepted without demur, if the Welsh Nonconformist M.P.s been properly consulted. McKenna's failure to hold enough consultations with this important block of Liberal Members brought Asquith and Lloyd George into action (Letters 350 and 351).

The Welsh Church Act finally came into effect on 31 March 1920.¹

¹ Discussions on the Postponement Bill proved inconclusive and the Government announced on 26 July 1915 that it would be withdrawn. For the subsequent proceedings see K. O. Morgan, *Wales in British Politics* (3rd edn., 1980), pp. 286–90.

341

Wed 10 March 1915

. . . As you were inclined to reproach me for destroying the report of my appearance before the bar of the Infernal Tribunal, I have reconstructed it [Letter 342], leaving out the final sentence of which I told you. . . .

You may think the portrait a little over-flattened in some features, and not quite in drawing as a whole. It is not meant to be myself, as *I* see it, or (I hope) as *you* see it, but as it might present itself to a fairly intelligent observer. And as always happens with that class of critic, he never gets within 1000 miles of the central truth – what Wordsworth calls the pulse of the machine. . . .

We had our War Council this morning,[1] wh. was attended for the first time by Lansdowne & Bonar Law.[2] They did not contribute very much. The main question was what we are to demand in return for the recognition of Russia's ultimate claim to Constantinople & the Straits. I told them in the end that the discussion had resembled that of a gang of buccaneers. We did not come to any more definite conclusion than to send a reply that our assent to Russia's proposal[3] was subject to the reservation that both we & France should get a substantial share of the carcase of the Turk. I thought (I was very silent myself) that Grey did the best, and perhaps next to him A.J.B. We lunched with Grey & his one-armed brother Charles,[4] a nice creature with the family stammer. We dine to-night with the Bencks.

McKenna has got us into a horrible mess over the Welsh Church Bill, through not keeping the little gang of Welsh members, who are as touchy as they are stupid, well in hand, and nobbling them in advance. The terms of the new Bill are really very favourable to them, if they cd. only understand it.[5] We shall not rise now until Monday or probably Tuesday. . . .

Joan Balfour[6] has suddenly become engaged to a Lascelles, Lord Harewood's son, and as he goes back to the front on Monday they are to be married to-morrow. I can't go to the wedding (praise Heaven! tho' I know you think I am fond of these functions) because we have a Cabinet in the morning to try & settle up all the Labour difficulties.[7]

I wonder whether you really like your return to the life of squalor & routine? Subject to health, I think you are right to go on, and from my own selfish point of view it is always an underlying joy to know that you are not more than 5 (instead of 200) miles away. My most beloved, I hope I haven't been overloading you with the expression of what I feel. One of the things I liked best in your . . . letter was that you said you were sure that what I had told you was true. There is indeed 'none upon Earth', or in the Heavens above, or in the most golden dreams of imagination, that can or even could be what you are to me. *Write.* Your *own.*

[1] At this War Council meeting Kitchener announced that he could now release the 29th Division to the Dardanelles.

[2] To concede Russia's claim to the Straits from the Black Sea to the Mediterranean meant committing future Governments, and was thus a move needing inter-party agreement. On 15 Mar. Bonar Law put an end to any thoughts of prolonging this co-operation by telling Asquith that he and Lansdowne could not attend further meetings without weakening their support with their party and thereby making themselves impotent to help the Government. See also pp. 420–1.

³ The Committee of Imperial Defence had taken the view in 1903, during Balfour's Government, that excluding Russia from Constantinople did not represent a vital British interest.

⁴ He had lost an arm during the fighting in East Africa early in the war: see Letter 155.

⁵ See p. 468. The Welsh Members, Asquith told the House (15 Mar.), 'are among my most faithful and loyal supporters; and [their] confidence and affection I prize almost more than I can express'.

⁶ A niece of A. J. Balfour.

⁷ See pp. 460–1.

342

SCENE – The Infernal Tribunal

On the Bench – Rhadamanthus
At the Bar – Self-released Shade

RHAD: (loquitur): So here you are, my friend – before your time. I am rarely surprised, but your premature appearance gives me a slight and welcome shock of something approaching to astonishment.

You, of all people! *Que Diable!*

Let me (in self-justification) dwell for a moment on the improbabilities of the case – which is nearly unique, even in my infernal experience.

You were, in the world above, almost a classical example of *Luck*. You were endowed at birth with brains above the average. You had, further, some qualities of temperament which are exceptionally useful for mundane success – energy under the guise of lethargy;[1] a faculty for working quickly, which is more effective in the long run than plodding perseverance; patience (which is one of the rarest of human qualities); a temperate but persistent ambition; a clear mind, a certain facility and lucidity of speech; intellectual, but not moral, irritability; a natural tendency to understand and appreciate the opponent's point of view; and, as time went on, and your nature matured, a growing sense of proportion, which had its effect both upon friends and foes, and which, coupled with detachment from any temptation to intrigue, and, in regard to material interests and profits, an unaffected indifference, secured for you the substantial advantage of personality and authority.

The really great men of the world are the geniuses and saints. You belonged to neither category. Your intellectual equipment (well cultivated and trained) still left you far short of the one; your spiritual limitations, and your endowment of the 'old Adam', left you still shorter of the other.

Nevertheless, with all these curtailments and shortcomings, you were what is called in the slang vocabulary of your time a 'good get out'.

The same *Luck* helped you in external things – in unforeseen opportunities, in the disappearance of possible competitors, in the special political conditions of your time: above all (at a most critical and fateful moment in your career) in the sudden outburst of the Great War.[2]

Everything was going well for you; the Fates, often malignant, or at least perverse, seemed to be conspiring to help you. I had almost given up hope, for years to come, of seeing you here, at my bar, and yet by your choice, *here you are.*

THE SHADE (interrupting): There is a modicum of truth, and a good deal of plausibility, in your rather prolix allocution. But, so far, you have not got near the essential and dominating fact.

RHAD. You mean, I suppose, that I have omitted any reference to the softer and more emotional side of your not very complex nature. Very well. I agree that, in this respect, you rather took in your contemporaries. The world in which you lived regarded you as hard, calculating, insensitive. In almost all the popular 'appreciations' which as a conspicuous personage you provoked, you were depicted as shy, reserved, unforthcoming, cold-blooded. Even those who saw more clearly did not credit you with more than a certain capacity for the enjoyment of comfort and luxury, with a moderate fondness for social pleasures, and (perhaps) a slight weakness for the companionship of clever and attractive women. As I am the embodiment and Minister of strict justice, I will go a step further. You hated and eschewed domestic dissension, and your sons and daughters were genuinely fond of you. So, in a sense, were your colleagues and political followers. At first they looked rather askance at your leadership, with wistful retrospective glances at the much-lamented shade of the defunct C.B.[3] It is odd, but true, that in course of time – apart from old friends like Haldane, E. Grey and Crewe – you gained the loyal attachment of men so diverse as Lloyd George & Winston Churchill, as Illingworth, McKenna & Montagu. Some people, sadly wanting in perspective, went so far as to call you 'chivalrous'; it would be nearer the truth to say that you had, or acquired, a rather specialised faculty of insight and manipulation in dealing with diversities of character and temperament. But the conclusion, by whatever road it is reached, is the same: that you ought not to have left them in the lurch.

THE SHADE: 'Tired with all these, for restful Death I cried.'[4]

RHAD: Pooh! You know very well that that was not the reason for your precipitate appearance here. You had excellent health, a good digestion, an adequate capacity for sleep, unabated authority in your Cabinet, big events to confront and provide for. No man can have had less temptation to violate the 'canon fixed by the Everlasting against self-slaughter'.[5]

THE SHADE: Not bad! I could have made the same speech, without preparation, in the House of Commons. Its only defect is that it ignores the central reality of my life.

RHAD: What was that?

THE SHADE: It is something beyond the ken of your damned tribunal. Give me my sentence, and call up the next Ghost.

*   *   *

(Curtain)[6]

[1] For the dangers of this 'guise' in war see pp. 116–18.
[2] For the implied admission that the war had saved him from political disaster over Home Rule see p. 111.
[3] Sir Henry Campbell-Bannerman, Liberal Prime Minister, Dec. 1905 – Apr. 1908.
[4] Shakespeare, *Sonnet 66*.
[5] Or that the Everlasting had not fixt
His canon 'gainst self-slaughter.
Hamlet, 1.ii
[6] See Letter 348 for the sentence of the court.

343

Thurs 11 March 1915 [i]

My darling – would you, do you think, care rather more for me if I cared rather less for you? (It is what is called an academic question, as I am not a free agent in the matter.) I wonder. One is tempted to think that the sense of complete and unshakeable security might tend to act as a sedative. I was thinking of this last night – not because I was discontented or 'unhappy'. You give me *so* much; and it was delicious to get your dear little letter this morning written after the prison gates had once more closed behind you. . . .

344

Thurs. 11 March 15 [ii]

O, my darling, what a tragi-comedy it was to-day! First of all, I had made sure, not receiving any telegram, that you weren't coming till to-morrow. Then when I came to that dreary collection of odds & ends at the luncheon table I was thunderstruck to see you there. And even so, bad as the conditions were, it was an additional grievance to have to make conversation with that accomplished bore – Mme de L. And, finally, it was the climax to have missed the chance afterwards of at any rate an hour with you, because I had 3 or 4 of the most trumpery questions in the world, and am now (3.40) practically free.

Everything was out of gear – except the joy of seeing you, which (as you know) I put first among human delights. And to-morrow blank, & Sat, & Sunday, & perhaps Monday. It is too sad! But you must be sweet & generous, and write to me *every day*. . . .

I wrote this morning a few lines to dear old Birrell, on the line that we ought not to sorrow overmuch that the ship, after so much tossing on the waves, and such weary waiting, was at last in port.[1] *Do* write him something: I am sure it would touch and console him. I have known them both intimately since about '86 or '87, and there has rarely been a more interesting & delightful couple. She had a most excellent sense of humour, & great cultivation: she knew more about Balzac than anyone in England, & in old days I used to urge her to write a book about him. Perhaps unwisely: most of our friends' books are sadly disappointing. She suffered the most tragic experience of any woman I have known: twice married,[2] & in each case she had an idiot son. But he will be very solitary, and we must try & be companions to him. I feel sure he will soon begin to press his claim to be released from Ireland.

I was looking at your hands at lunch, & was delighted to see how 'nice' they are becoming. I only hope they won't have a relapse, in tending the victims of spotted fever & dementia.

It is only at odd moments that one realises the inversion of everything normal & even conceivable brought about by the war. Of which there is no better illustration than your occupations & mine, a year ago & now. But it has brought us – you & me – closer & nearer together, and made me realise, what before I more or less dimly perceived, that to me you are *everything*. . . .

If you can, beloved, write me one line to D^g St to-night, and to-morrow & Sat. to Walmer. Tell me everything about your life & thoughts and (if you can) something of what I should most love to know. Love of my life – your own.

[1] Mrs Birrell had died that morning. For her last illness see Letter 290.
[2] Her first husband had been Lionel, Lord Tennyson's younger son. She had three sons by her first marriage and two by her second.

345

Friday morning 12 March 1915 [i]

. . . Maud Cunard was quite *incroyable* in my 2 minutes' interview with her after lunch yesterday. She rattled off 3 propositions which she says she is quite determined to carry through: (1) that A.J.B. should be given the Garter (2) that Runciman shd. go to Ireland in place of Birrell (3) that a fund should be raised to secure me an income of £20,000 a year after the War. They are all about equally feasible, but naturally the third is the one that appeals most to my fancy. She appears later in the afternoon to have made a peremptory demand on Beauchamp to give me Walmer.[1] She certainly adds to the gaiety of life & is one of the persons we should miss.

The unhappy McKenna made another attempt to pacify his Welsh flock yesterday afternoon at the House, but the *moutons enragés*. . . . nearly tore him to pieces. . . . As you know, I have never loved them, but there is no doubt that they have a real grievance in the way they have been mishandled. They believe (not altogether without reason) that they have been both flouted & hoodwinked by McK. . . .

. . . Ian Hamilton leaves probably to-day to take the military command at the Dardanelles. I have just been reading the Admiralty secret report of the operations so far;[2] they are making progress, but it is slow, and there are a large number of howitzers & concealed guns (not in the forts) on both shores wh. give them a good deal of trouble, and have made a lot of holes in the ships, tho' so far the damage done is not serious. I think the Admiral is quite right to proceed very cautiously. Winston is rather for spurring him on.[3] It is characteristic of W. that he has worked out since midnight & now sent me a time table, acc. to wh. Ian Hamilton by leaving Charing Cross at 5 *this* afternoon can reach the Dardanelles by *Monday* (taking a 30 knot cruiser at Marseilles). It sounds almost incredible, doesn't it?[4]. . .

Later. I was interrupted by a visit from Rosebery, of all people. We sat in my room upstairs where (as we recalled) Mr Gladstone in his old age used to have the Cabinets. He being very deaf we sat in two circles around a round table. Rosebery's own Cabinets were the most disagreeable gatherings in wh. it has ever been my lot to take part. He came to suggest names of possible successors to old Warre, the Provost of Eton, who is by way of being moribund, & mentioned Durnford & Dr James of King's.[5] I told him I thought we had better return to the old traditions when the post was held by diplomatists & statesmen *en disponibilité* – Sir Henry Wotton[6] &c; and that he should take it himself. He was evidently much attracted by the idea, and promised to consider it. I think it capital, don't you? that he should spend a more or less green old age as Provost of Eton! A.J.B. is another possible candidate: our only 2 ex-Prime Ministers.

Since then we have had a rather interesting Committee consisting of Grey, myself, Winston, Impeccable, & Assyrian, to draw up a reply to the Pecksniffian American note.[7] These things are much better done so than in a huge unwieldy Cabinet, and it is a kind of work in wh. Simon especially shines. I consider that his curve is moving steadily upward, now that he is convalescent from the malaise of last autumn.

Winston remarked to me (& it is true) how well our ladies who were at dinner last night have withstood the ravages of middle age, with the exception perhaps of Ian Hamilton's wife, whom I remember when she still possessed the characteristic allurements of an Anglo-Indian Garrison Queen.[8]

Later still. We have just got through one of our rather menagerie luncheons: Abp. of Canterbury, Phil Burne Jones, Frances Horner, Katharine, Assyrian, Barbara Wilson, Geoffrey &c &c. When at 10 min. to 3 the Servant came & said to me 'The motor is waiting', I had an acute pang, wh. I hope I disguised. For this (3.30) is our regular Friday hour, and without it I feel the week is mutilated. . . .

I wonder what you will be doing to-morrow, when I suppose you have an afternoon 'out'. I feel horribly jealous of whoever it is – male or female – in whose company you spend those precious free hours. I trust & hope & believe that, at moments at any rate, you will think of me. . . .

There is rather a 'nice' thing about me in *Punch*'s Essence of Parliament this week.[9]. . .

[1] Balfour was awarded the O.M. in 1916; but he did not become a K.G. until 1922. For the suggestion that Asquith should continue to occupy Walmer Castle see Letter 230.

[2] Presumably Carden's telegram to Admiralty, 10 Mar.: *Churchill Companion Docs., 1914–1916*, pp. 661–2. On Mar. 12 Violet Asquith wrote to Rupert Brooke:

The authorities still seem to think it quite possible that if all goes well at sea Turkish resistance might collapse, and that there may be no serious fighting, only a formal entry into Constantinople.

[3] Although Asquith had begun to learn the essential nature of the naval problem at the Dardanelles, he seems still not to have realized that this was not how much the warships might be damaged, but whether the minesweepers could operate against a strong current when under fire. In the naval attack on 18 Mar. the *Gaulois* of the French squadron was the only battleship to be seriously damaged by shellfire alone. The *Albion, Majestic,* and *Ocean* each suffered only a single fatal casualty from shellfire.

[4] Hamilton and his party left Charing Cross at 5 p.m. on Saturday 13 Mar. They had with them Kitchener's instructions, an inaccurate map, a three-years-old handbook on the Turkish army, and a pre-war report on the Dardanelles defences. They arrived on 17 Mar., just in time to watch the naval attack the next day: see p. 439.

[5] Edmond Warre remained Provost, however, until 1918, when he was succeeded by M. R.

James, who was himself succeeded as Provost of King's, Cambridge, by Walter Durnford. James was the first ever to preside in turn over both the foundations of King Henry VI. The succession to Warre remained a subject of conversation for the rest of Asquith's premiership: see C. à Court Repington, *First World War* (1920), i. 286.

⁶ Diplomat and poet: Provost of Eton, 1624–39.

⁷ On 1 Mar. Asquith announced (Letters 326, n. 3 and 328, n. 2) that, as the British were being subjected to a ruthless and illegal submarine campaign, they were obliged to respond by preventing 'commodities of any kind from reaching or leaving Germany'. This elicited the 'Pecksniffian American note' (5 Mar.), enquiring how this reprisal was to be put into effect. The British Order in Council, 11 Mar. gave the answer. Grey delivered this to Page (15 Mar.) with a note explaining 'that subject to the paramount necessity of restricting German trade His Majesty's Government have made it their first aim to minimize inconvenience to neutral commerce'. They would therefore restrict the confiscation of ships and cargoes to an absolute minimum. Though the Order in Council aroused considerable anger in the copper and cotton States, Pres. Wilson's note in reply to it (30 Mar.) was studiously moderate.

⁸ Hamilton married in 1887 while serving in India, and remained there until 1898.

⁹ The Prime Minister's 'personality is worth to the Empire an army in the field, a squadron of *Queen Elizabeths* at sea' (*Punch*, 10 Mar.: see Letter 340, n. 1).

346

In train

Friday 12 March 1915 [ii]

My darling – I got your dear little letter just before I was starting for the train. I am sorry that there has been any trouble about your letters coming by messenger. I have only sent them that way when I thought you might be disappointed at not receiving them the same evening. But I forgot that you were living more or less under Convent rules, and I won't in future shock the Hospital etiquette, except on Sunday morning, when it is the only way of communicating with you. I should like to know whether the letter wh. I gave this afternoon to be posted between 4 & 5 reached you this evening by supper time.

I am glad that you still don't think that I write too often. It is the greatest pleasure I have in life – except 2 others, which are greater still – namely seeing you, & hearing from you. I sometimes think it is selfish to write you such a lot about things both big & small. But I couldn't bear not to share them with you, and you have told me again & again, & I believe you, that you are interested in them all. It makes my life incomparably more vivid, and gives me the feeling that it is better worth living. So I shan't stop – until you tell me, or I have to submit to the decree of the 'blind Fury with the abhorred shears'.¹

My travelling companions are Margot who is fast asleep in one corner of the carriage, & Geoffrey who is smoking a pipe – his newly acquired vice – in the other. Jack Pease Violet & Bluey are also coming down to-night, and to-morrow Viola & I forget who else. . . .

. . . I had a visit from that ruffian Bob Cecil, who is trying to manufacture after his fashion a case of 'breach of faith' against us for not pushing thro' the Welsh Bill against the whole of the Welsh Members, before we rise.[2] Happily I wrote to him last Tuesday – the day the Bill was brought in in the Lords – that I could give no assurance that the Welsh wd. not require further time for its fuller consideration. If he makes one of his foul attacks it will have the incidental effect of angering the Welsh & perhaps making them more tractable. . . .

E. Grey was in one of his most gloomy moods to-day – convinced that the Russians were going to have another heavy knock & be driven out of Warsaw,[3] and more than doubtful of the Dardanelles adventure. He is curiously up & down – mostly down. . . .

[1] Milton, *Lycidas*, l. 75.
[2] Lord Robert Cecil held so strong a view about Welsh Disestablishment that he resigned from the Lloyd George Government in 1919 when the final steps were to be taken to bring the measure into effect.
[3] Warsaw did not fall until 4 Aug. 1915.

347

Walmer Castle,
Kent.

Sat. 13 March 1915 [ii]

. . . I send you the Sentence pronounced by the Judge, when the Shade had come to the end of his rather tactless & disrespectful protests. . . .

To come down for a moment to something very mundane, I think I told you that H Samuel had written an almost dithyrambic memorandum urging that in the carving up of the Turks' Asiatic dominions, we should take Palestine, into which the scattered Jews cd. in time swarm back from all quarters of the globe, and in due course obtain Home Rule. (What an attractive community!) Curiously enough, the only other partisan of this proposal is Lloyd George, who, I need not say, does not care a damn for the Jews or their past or their future, but who thinks it would be an outrage to let the Christian Holy Places – Bethlehem, Mount of Olives, Jerusalem &c – pass into the possession or under the protectorate of 'Agnostic Atheistic France'! Isn't it singular that the same conclusion shd. be capable of being come to by such different roads? Kitchener, who 'surveyed' Palestine when he was a young Engineer, has a very poor opinion of the place, wh. even Samuel admits to be 'not larger than Wales, much of it barren mountain, &

part of it waterless' &, what is more to the point, without a single decent harbour. So he (K) is all for Alexandretta, and leaving the Jews & the Holy Places to look after themselves. . . .

348

Walmer Castle,
Kent.

The Judge Pronounces Sentence:

Shade at the Bar,

The sentence of the Court upon you is that you go back to the World whence you came: not for you the 'Sleep Eternal in an Eternal Night': to the same drab dull world from which you sought, before your time, to escape.

There you are to be born again in a new body, with the bare average of faculties & brains, and are to live up to the allotted span a toilsome monotonous existence – an unconsidered item in the dim millions of mankind. You will not even be a madman or a criminal. You will have no big moments, no exceptional chances, no 'roses & raptures'.[1] You & your environment will be equally home-spun and humdrum.

Poetry, art, politics, the living interests and ideals of your country & your age, will be to you a sealed book. You will not even have the curiosity to try & break the seal. From birth till death you will be surrounded by, imprisoned in, contented with, the Commonplace.

Thus does Infernal Justice redress the balance of the Upper World, and secure an equal lot for the Sons of Men.

[1] A. C. Swinburne, *Dolores*. Asquith reverses the two words.

349

Walmer Castle,
Kent.

Sunday 14 March 1915

My darling – you sent me a most heavenly letter this morning, one of your very best, and there can be no higher praise. Only one thing in it I minded – your saying that you had had an attack of cerebrospinal-meningitis, which I have always understood to be one of the most insidious & fatal of diseases. Is it true? or were you trying to frighten me by giving an ultra-scientific name to a very bad headache? And are you quite right again? At times I tremble for your health in that foul environment, with its 'stuffy atmosphere of disease'.

As regards to-morrow the question whether I shall be free at 4.45 depends entirely on whether we can dispose of or cut down the Welsh Church squabble. Could you by chance come to the House about that time or a little before, & find momentary refuge in Mrs Lowther's Gallery, or in my room or Bongie's? It would be too tantalising not to see you when you were so near. I fared *very badly* this last week. Thank God after Monday there is no House for a month to come – so perhaps if to-morrow turns out a disappointment I might pick you up when you are 'out' on Wed. aft & drive you back to prison? Would that be at all possible darling?

Dearest I quite understood about sending the letters by messenger, and you were sweetness itself in the way you put it. There was a time – just after you went to the Hospital – when I was really afraid I might be over-burdening you with my multitudinous & incessant missives. But I am satisfied now that, however many & long, they give you real pleasure, and perhaps sometimes even more. Thank you my most beloved for what you say about them to-day. I am afraid it is more than half selfishness on my part that makes me write so much to you. I don't feel that I have lived a *real* day, unless from hour to hour I tell you my thoughts & experiences. That has never happened to me before, and I assure you it gives a new vividness to life.

To-day is a good illustration; it is very fine & they have all gone off to Church or to golf, and during the morning I have been the solitary inmate of the house. My pouch had a full crop of tiresome & boring things, which I have now disposed of: not one of them of sufficient interest to be worth quoting to you. I should have some excuse therefore for feeling a little dull; but I don't the least, simply because I can sit back & talk to you by pencil, almost as easily as if your dear face were close to mine. And I know that if my letter is the merest 'chronicle of small beer', you will find in it (even if you have to look between the lines, poor sweet!) things that will interest you.

I am glad that you were pleased with what you read in *Punch*[1] . . . I would rather you valued & cared for my speeches and thought them up to my best than have the praise and applause of the whole world. . . .

Nothing more has been done in the matter of the labour speeches, and it may be better to wait a little to see how the new Bill[2] affects both employers & workmen. . . .

[1] See Letter 345, n. 9.
[2] The Defence of the Realm (Amendment No. 2) Bill, which Lloyd George had introduced in the Commons on 9 Mar. The Government already had authority to take over, or control the

output of, any factory producing war material. By this new Bill, which received the Royal Assent on 16 Mar., these powers were extended to cover any works which might be used for war production. For the suggestion about 'labour speeches' see Letter 335.

V

E.S.M. to B.V.S.

14 March 1915

You've no idea how mad I've felt since last Saturday – incipiently mad. I hope you will – I'm sure madness doesn't bother *you*.
Oh my very dear one

How very clearly you do depict a situation to the stupid.

I see you Wednesday.

By no possibility can I see you the rest of the week, I send you a reminder Wednesday night – no reply, (of course poor thing you cant write letters, I'm not grumbling). Yet you can go out all Thursday with Violet, you are about something Friday, I fail Saturday, but you can see Bongie today. Yet do I give in. *Never.* I love you more than love. Come to lunch tomorrow!

Yrs. tremendously, and however foolishly, devoted

E.S.M.

350

Monday 15 March 15 [i]

. . . We have just got through our Welsh Church impasse, so far as the House is concerned, with considerable success. Bob Cecil was (wisely) moderate, & that little whipper snapper Ormsby Gore, who married the Cecil girl, inconceivably caddish & ill-bred in a gratuitous attack upon Mond whom they can't forgive for being a German & a Jew.[1] I made a quiet temporising lubricating sort of speech (the 'facility' which your darling partiality thinks an understatement came to my aid): with the result that B. Law was like heather honey, & gave me his benediction! So do seemingly intractable situations melt into solutions: and I was particularly glad that it was not necessary to repudiate, or rebuke, or even refer to McKenna.[2] I rather wish you had been there, tho' the House was half-empty & there was only subdued excitement, but from an artistic point of view it was not uninteresting. . . .

Your Mother suggested Penrhos for Whitsuntide – so I didn't like to suggest an earlier date. You must come to Walmer for Sunday *April 11th*: I think the Bencks are coming & we will have some other choice spirits: we cd. go down there on the Friday. Do my darling make this a fixed day in your Calendar. I want you so much to see it & pronounce your judgement. All our female guests yesterday cried out with one voice 'Perish India'![3]. . .

[1] Ormsby Gore asked: 'What does the Honourable Member for Swansea Town do for the Welsh Army?' Sir Alfred Mond referred to the time and money which he had spent in helping to raise the Welsh units, and pointed out that he had been one of the first members of the executive committee for the London Welsh Bn., and one of the first guarantors of the funds of the Welsh Army Council. Ormsby Gore retracted and Asquith, who followed him, referred to his 'handsome and manly apology'.

[2] See Letter 345.

[3] See Letter 243, n. 3.

351

Monday 15 March 15 [ii] 10.30 p.m.

. . . I wish you had been there: not because it was a great or dramatic occasion, but one that required a lot of handling. I went out after I spoke (or as soon as I decently could) to write to you: and then I am glad to say that I got back to the House to hear Ll. George make one of his best speeches. I don't suppose there were more than 100 men in the House; but (as poor old John Burns said to me once, when he had spent a Sunday at Sandringham with King Edward) he 'pulled out all his stops'. He went straight for his old Welsh comrades, & in particular for Ellis Griffith (who made a poisonous & malignant speech), in his very best style.[1] I have rarely heard a more courageous speech – quite impromptu – with all those attractive, histrionic, modulations of tone & gesture which only the Celtic & Slavonic races have at command. It would have given you real artistic pleasure to listen to it. Afterwards, at my invitation, the whole Welsh party came to my room, where I was fortified by the presence of Ll G. & McKenna: their feathers had been a good deal ruffled by L.G's pronouncement; and I addressed them like a Father. (This wd really have amused you almost more than the other, had you been behind a curtain, playing the part of Huck.)[2] I hope & believe they have gone back to their mountains & vales with the fear of God in their consciences: and a certain apprehension of fiery vengeance, if they don't 'toe the line' (what a phrase!) of reason & common sense.

In a small way, quite a dramatic issue from what might have been a tragic situation.

Since then I have dined at Grillions, where I had quite a good talk with the Impeccable, the Abp. of Canterbury, & G. Curzon (of Kedleston). It is one of the reasons (wh. I know don't quite commend themselves to you) why I try always to go there on Monday evenings during the Session. Nowhere else do you find yourself in such an incongruous environment . . .

. . . After the others had gone at Grillion's to-night, I opened to the Impeccable the imminent departure of poor Birrell from Ireland. It was very curious & interesting, as a revelation of character. Knowing my man, I began by saying that Ireland was for the time being a backwater: a first-rate Civil Servant there, in the person of Nathan;[3] therefore, for the moment, a fit place in wh. to put a solid 2nd rate man like Jack Pease. I couldn't possibly ask him J.S. to leave his responsible duties for such a small affair &c &c (You can imagine how I embroidered the argument). There was a rather faint & watery response: he acknowledged (for the first time) that I had done him a good turn last August in preventing him from committing political suicide.[4] But he *hated* the Law – judgeships, Lord Chancellorships &c – and was wedded to politics. He evidently chafes & frets in his present cage. I said that his proper post in due time was that of Home Secretary, but M^{c}K (in spite of his recent indiscretion) could not & ought not to be displaced. So he (the Sinless John) must still possess his soul in patience. I wish you had been there to hear our conversation. He was polite, acquiescent, even grateful in a way. But I am sure he went home with a raw place in his soul.

Isn't it 'rather' tragic to have to plant these barbs in the bosom of those whom one regards & even cares for? Do you sympathise? or do you think one ought to be quite callous & insensitive?

The one thing I long for is (you know I am a dreamer of dreams) to have *you* always close at hand to counsel & restrain.

If J.P. goes to Ireland (wh. I don't like, but prefer to the only possible alternative, Herb. Samuel) what *am* I to do? It looks as if the finger of Fate pointed in the direction of sending the Assyrian to the Education Office! There is nothing he wd like less, I imagine: but when one has got into the Cabinet, fairly early in life, one must take the 'rubs of the green' . . .

[1] Griffith insinuated that the Government were more inclined to conciliate the Tories than the Welsh Nonconformists among their own supporters. Lloyd George appealed to the Liberals of Wales to grant 'an extension of six months to the Church when some of its leading men are engaged in the war'.

[2] Venetia's dog had been present though unnoticed 'on a famous occasion': see Letter 258.

[3] Sir Matthew Nathan had been transferred in 1914 from the chairmanship of the Board of Inland Revenue to be Under-Secretary in Dublin, succeeding Sir James Dougherty (Letter 107, n. 6).

[4] Simon had wanted to resign in protest against Britain's intervention in the war. Asquith had succeeded in dissuading him: see Letters 112, 114, and 115.

352

My own most darling – I have just finished my solitary drive thro' the mean streets, and the crowded City, and along the Embankment; till I found myself here, almost before I realised that I had made my journey – back from the Heaven of your nearness to the old familiar groove of work & worry. It was delicious to find you in such high spirits & such wonderful looks. And although I gibed at you (with a pretence of sincerity) for your 'cruelty', and at one moment & another was genuinely baffled by your thought-provoking smile, the abiding memory of our heavenly hour together is of your incomparable sweetness, and of the power, in which you surpass all other women, to understand and anticipate and respond. It is a marvellous gift, and I praise the Gods that you bestow it so largely upon me. It is quite true that there is an ingredient of selfishness in my love, but you give me always – as I said the other day – 'gold' for my 'brass'. An hour with you is worth to me a whole week of the company of the wisest and best and most attractive and forthcoming of all our race. This is not a 'compliment', but sober, solid, sane, & sincere *truth*. I send you this now – fresh from my heart, as I am fresh from the healing life-giving touch of your beloved hands. . . .

353

My darling – I hoped to have sent you a few lines before midnight – so that you might have got them at or after breakfast time to-morrow. But we were kept so late playing very indifferent Bridge at the Farquhars that I did not get back in time; and after what has happened I hardly dare send this in the morning by messenger! It was a regular banquet of many courses, of which I only partook of about 2 – wh. I now hear perturbed my hostess & my neighbour Lady Ripon, the former because she thought I didn't relish her highly elaborated cuisine, & the latter because she thought that such a failure in gluttony portended illness. Of course as you saw to-day I am quite well, but I am rather taking a leaf out of your book in the way of eating. There was the usual social lot who move in that milieu – Keppels, Becketts, Mrs Sassoon &c,[1] and amongst those one is not accustomed so often to meet, the young D[ss] of Sutherland – pretty of a rather flimsy type, Ld Durham (whom I always like to talk to) dear old Harry Chaplin,[2] & A.J.B. Horace Farquhar – a survival of the mid-Victorian beaux –[3] told me how in his young days in the City he used to sell pearls to old Baron Lionel Rothschild –[4]

the father of Natty, Leo &c.[5] The old Jew always used to have on his table in his office in New Court a little chest in wh. he hoarded his pearls, and in the intervals of business handled & fondled them. A good investment too – H.F. told me that a necklace of pearls wh. he gave his wife 20 or 30 years ago, having paid about £7000 for it, is now worth from £40,000 to £45,000. Isn't this a rather disgusting form of unearned increment? – for it only goes to the very rich. I was pleased – in such an environment – to get out of Bridge with a loss of only 15/-.

After I got back from my lonely drive & had disposed of such arrears as there were here, I took refuge at the Athenaeum & tried to read a new book by Maurice Hewlett – *The Lovers' Tale*[6] – all about Ireland in the days of the Vikings. I didn't make much progress with it, for my thoughts were, not 1000, but I suppose about 5 miles away in a dreary corner of the East End. I begin to think that I am losing the power of concentration, upon wh. I was apt to pride myself. I don't know what will happen if I do. Can you suggest a remedy? Counter-concentration is only too easy!

Masterton Smith has sent me a little volume by John Bailey[7] – an excellent critic – on Milton, & before I go to bed, where I ought by now to be, I am going to try & read it. It is good discipline at any rate, but I fear I shall break down. You know very well who is responsible for all this, and I can see you smile & give that slight toss of your head wh. I know & love so well.

Good night my best beloved – I will send this by the first post in the morning, & more will follow as the day goes on.

My last thought to-night is of you, as will be my first thought in the morning, & my *best* thoughts all through the day.

Write me a sweet little letter.

Your lover.

[1] Friends of Edward VII. For Mrs Keppel see Letter 303, n. 2. Rupert Beckett was a Leeds banker. His wife had just stayed at Walmer; Asquith reported that she had 'kept her looks and her youth wonderfully'. The Arthur Sassoons had entertained Edward VII at Tulchan Lodge and at Hove. In youth Mrs Sassoon had been a 'Soul' as well as a member of 'the Prince's set'.

[2] Henry Chaplin had also been a friend of Edward VII. The Duchess of Sutherland and the Earl of Durham were close to George V's court. The Duke of Sutherland's father had died in 1913; for his mother, who was still prominent in society, see Letter 164.

[3] Farquhar was a banker and courtier: Master of the Household from 1901 to 1907, when his activities with Siberian Proprietary Mines Ltd. had aroused unfavourable press comment. Since then he had been an Extra Lord-in-Waiting. Treasurer of the Conservative party from 1911 until dismissed by Bonar Law in 1923.

[4] He was a baron of the Austrian Empire and in 1838 obtained Queen Victoria's leave for his brothers and himself to use this style. He died in 1879 when Farquhar was 35.

[5] The three sons were Nathaniel Mayer, a Liberal M.P. 1865–85, when he was raised to the peerage; Alfred Charles; and Leopold. Asquith was 'Natty's' guest at Tring when first in society. For Leopold see Letter 214, text and n. 1.

[6] Hewlett had been well known as a historical novelist since the publication of *The Forest Lovers* in 1898.

[7] Published in 1915: Home University Library.

354

. . . I am looking forward more than I can say to either to-morrow or Friday. I have discovered a later train on Friday, leaving about 6.20, wh. goes to Faversham, whence it is quite an easy motor drive to Walmer. So one needn't be so damnably hurried!

Do you remember that this week is the first anniversary of that dismal Curragh business which had such unforeseen consequences? I remember as if it were yesterday that I was playing Bridge after dinner on the Friday[1] at Mansfield St, when I was summoned here to a midnight conclave with Seely French & Co.[2] For 3 weeks at least no one thought or talked of anything else, and now it is all as dead & securely buried as Queen Anne. In fact when one looks back at the recurring almost weekly 'crises' of last spring & summer, and contrasts them with the atmosphere in wh. we now live, it wd. also seem as if we had passed into another world. But I shall never forget how in all that petty succession of worries, wh. were real enough at the time, you were my truest & most trusted counsellor, and my never failing stay. When I say now what seem sometimes to you to be extravagant things about you, don't forget (as I don't) that I have proved your quality.

It is St Patricks Day, and I had an early call from John Redmond who brought me some bunches of shamrock, & with them a string of grievances about the Irish Volunteers.[3] I must have another go at K. on that subject, unwelcome as it is. I spoke to him of Birrell's possible retirement (Sir M. Nathan, I think I told you, is inclined to believe that after all he will stay). Redmond is aghast at the thought, and says that B. ought to be kept on at any cost – even if he never goes near the Office, wh. is being admirably run by Nathan. He didn't even like to discuss other names, but I told him he had better do so, if only to indicate which in his opinion was the worst. I ruled out the Impeccable (I think to his relief) and when it came to a choice between Samuel & Pease, he declared himself – this will please you – strongly anti-Pease. He has a considerable respect, tho' not much liking, for Samuel, but shudders at the gibes which Healy[4] & others would pour forth at the spectacle of Dublin Castle ruled by a brace of Jews. (By the way, the Assyrian has just produced a very racy memorandum on the subject of the restoration of the Chosen Race to the Promised Land. It contains some rather vicious digs at Cousin Herbert, of whom he 'doubts whether he cd. translate one paragraph or phrase of his Memorandum into Hebrew'. He denounces the whole proposal as 'a rather presumptuous and almost blasphemous (!) attempt to forestall Divine Agency in the collection of the Jews' – language wh. I confess rather amazes me.)[5]

Redmond has received a present of a record Irish Wolfhound, no less than 9½ hands high, for the new Irish corps. It seems to be almost too big to give to a battalion or regiment, but one never heard of a whole Division having a Mascot. I advised him to hand the beast over to the General, & leave him to parcel it out at his discretion. I expect it is the kind of animal wh., if you had your way, one would find in complete occupation of all the available seats in your little sitting room at Alderley. . . .

Later I am writing in the Cabinet room in the interludes of a very strenuous controversy – three cornered – between the Impeccable, McKenna, & Hobhouse as to the terms of a new Marconi contract.[6] I am called in as a sort of arbitrator, and I need not tell you that I loathe both the thing & its still unsavoury name. . . .

[1] 20 Mar. 1914.
[2] See Letter 49.
[3] See pp. 236–7.
[4] Though an Irish nationalist (and later first Governor-General of the Irish Free State), T. M. Healy was highly critical of Redmond.
[5] For Samuel's memorandum see pp. 402–3 and Letter 281. For Montagu's rejoinder see Asquith MSS vol. 27, f. 38 and I. Friedman, *The Question of Palestine, 1914–1918* (1973), pp. 22–4. It was not circulated to the cabinet (Violet Asquith's diary, Mar. 1915). He and Herbert Samuel were first cousins.
[6] See Letter 268.

VI

B.V.S. to E.S.M.

Wednesday evening [17–18 March 1915]

Dearest I was very glad to see you again this afternoon, but (& I dont want to draw a pathetic picture of my lot, because it doesnt in the least take you in, tho' I also think if you really knew what its like you'd think one had every cause to be wretched, but I'm not) I don't think you can realise what a very little way 3 hours 3 times a week goes, particularly when nearly an hour of that time must be spent in driving & in getting to & from this place. So much as I should like to see you every day it cant be done. But of course I think its divine of you to want it.

I got back just in time, did two hours 'work' & then went to a foolish lecture & now after some talk with other 'nurses' over a box of biscuits, must put out the light & pretend at any rate that I'm part asleep. I'll finish in the morning.

6.40 Thursday (does that wring your heart at all). I've looked at this piece of paper & the above line for about 5 minutes, but as might be expected my head is an entire void. Today doesnt present a very attractive appearance to me, not even the hope of seeing Reggie[1] & only the very faint one of seeing him tomorrow. I'll send you a telegram Saturday if I can lunch, but if you dont hear you'll know that I cant get away. I'm more than doubtful so dont not go to Walmer or anywhere else on the chance. . . .

[Postscript] Why dont you ever write to me, damn you? Even if only to curse me it gives me something to collect when I go for my letters. . . .

[1] Reginald McKenna.

355

Thurs 18 March 1915 [i] Noon

. . . Bluey gave a rather characteristic little dinner last night: Countess Benck (no Count) E. Grey McKennae & E. Drummond. It was 'rather nice', and Pamela & I won a modest sum at Bridge. E. Grey is in better form than he was – less inclined to fits of the jumps – and is looking forward to 10 days on some remote Scotch salmon rises at the beginning of April. M^cK, I regret to say, is for the moment rather under a cloud, as no one can quite understand what he did or didn't say to the Welsh about their Bill.

I spent the best part of an hour with the King who was very amiable, and indulged his humour (such as it is) at the expense of Winston's 'joy-rides' – he went yesterday on one of his 24 hours' excursions to the front – and similar topics. He also developed at considerable length his personal views on racing and the war: how he runs his horses still (to keep up the industry) but never sets foot on a racecourse; and how Ascot – if it comes off at all – is to be confined to racing in the morning – no grand stand, enclosure, luncheons – &c &c. I don't know a better reflection than his talk of what one imagines to be for the moment the average opinion of the man in the tube. . . .

Just as I was beginning to write this, there was a sudden incursion into the Cabinet room (like an Atlantic tornado) of Maud Cunard & Diana Manners – the latter looking particularly well. Maud had her usual lot of small & big axes to grind: A.J.B. for the Garter, a certain Ld Oranmore of Ireland for anything that is going, Thomas Beecham for God knows what, and the raising of a fund to give me £15,000 or £20,000 a year when the War is over![1] . . .

Before lunch K came to see me & we had an interesting talk. He is really distressed & pre-occupied by the reckless way in wh. our men expended their ammunition – particularly shells – last week. It works out (*entre nous*) at 2 shells per square yard gained![2] He has just sent me a private letter from Rawlinson, wh. confirms what we suspected – that the whole operation, successful tho' expensive as it was, just failed of being the most brilliant success in the whole war thro' the mishandling at a critical moment of *one* Division. The General (quite a good man, Davies) has been sent home.[3] These things are very tragic. K. also showed me a very interesting telegram from Ian Hamilton who got to the Dardanelles on Tues. night. The Admiralty have been very over-sanguine as to what they cd. do by ships alone. Every night the Turks under German direction repair their fortifications: both coasts bristle with howitzers & field guns (outside the forts) in concealed emplacements; and the channel is sown with complicated & constantly renewed mine-fields. The French General D'Amade (a good man who won fame in Morocco) arrived at the same time as I.H: and together they are going to make a really thorough & I hope scientific survey of the whole situation.[4] Carden (our Admiral) has fallen sick & gone back to Malta: perhaps a good thing, as de Robeck his successor is supposed to be a much better man.

K. spoke to me *very confidentially* about French. He says he is not a really scientific soldier: a good & capable leader in the field; but without adequate equipment of expert knowledge for the huge task of commanding 450,000 men.

K. is going out there at the end of the week to confer with Joffre, and to put things on a solid basis.

Meanwhile here at home all sorts of things are going on, and it is quite on the cards (this is *most secret*) that I may create a new office for Ll. George ('Director of War Contracts' or something of the kind) & relieve him of his present duties. I shan't do anything without consulting you, wh. makes it all the more necessary that we shd. spend to-morrow aft. together. Darling I have at least a million more things to say, but I am bombarded with telegrams & interviews; and (since I mustn't use a messenger) I must send this at once that it may get to you thro' the post by supper time.

For your amusement, I enclose with it another fragment of the 'Portrait'. Tell me what you think of it to-morrow.

I never loved nor *needed* you more.

Your own

[1] For two of these proposals see Letter 345. Lord Oranmore, a Conservative, had been an Irish Representative Peer since 1902.

[2] Frances Stevenson recorded Kitchener as commenting on Neuve Chapelle to Lloyd George and Balfour: 'I told French that he had wasted the ammunition. . . . he is far too extravagant. . . . it isn't the men I mind. I can replace the men at once; but I can't replace the

shells so easily.' For the exchange on this between French and Kitchener see D. Lloyd George, *War Memoirs*, pp. 113–15, and Hankey, *Supreme Command*, i. 312.

[3] The fact that there was no breakthrough at Neuve Chapelle was not due solely to mishandling by the 8th Division's commander (who had his own complaints about Rawlinson: Robert Blake (ed.), *Private Papers of Douglas Haig* (1952), pp. 87–8 and 91). The attack was originally planned as part of a combined operation with Foch's army: see Letter 255, n. 2. When Foch became so heavily committed elsewhere that he could not take his part Sir John French made the questionable decision to go ahead on his own. Haig's tactical planning and preparation were good; but the battle spelled out the lesson that an advance on a narrow front with limited artillery support and inadequate infantry reserves had no chance against a brave and competent defence. The lesson was not learned. In that the attackers inflicted almost as many casualties as they suffered, the Neuve Chapelle offensive was less disastrous than those which followed. For the sense of insecurity which made French reluctant to admit his mistakes see Richard Holmes, *The Little Field-Marshal* (1981), p. 275.

[4] Ian Hamilton's 'thorough survey' revealed that the Bulair Isthmus was too heavily defended to allow a landing there. This ruled out the possibility of dealing with the Turkish garrison in the Peninsula by isolating them from their base. See pp. 439–40.

356

A Portrait: [Part 3[1]]

It was characteristic of her tendency to minimise moral dimensions, where she herself was concerned, that even when she took up unpalatable tasks (like hospital nursing), she quite sincerely disclaimed the imputation of 'high-mindedness'. She attributed her action not to unselfishness, or a sense of duty, or a desire to relieve suffering, but to the joint operation of two purely self-regarding motives: the one positive and the other negative. The positive motive (so she declared) was her calculation that she would emerge, after three months of drudgery, with a whetted appetite and zest for the pleasures of the world. The negative motive was that, during the three months, she would at any rate escape the more tiresome routine of daily life under war conditions in a country house.

When asked whether the interests of other people did not come in at all, she would reply that she had calculated that, on the whole, she would give as much pleasure to those she was fond of, and perhaps receive as much from them, in the one form of seclusion as in the other.

There is a want of proportion, and therefore of accuracy, in minimising, just as there is in exaggerating: as she would perhaps have admitted. Self-deception takes a thousand different forms: with most people it tends to make them idealise their own motives and conduct; with her it moved in the exactly opposite direction.

Nor was this attitude of hers towards herself due in any way to a cynical temper. She had a rich capacity for admiration, was intensely ambitious for her friends, and was beyond measure rejoiced at any recognition by the world of the qualities and faculties in them which had attracted herself.

[1] For previous Parts see Letters 287 and 309.

VII

E.S.M. to B.V.S.

18 March 1915

My very dearest,

If you like a letter every day you shall have one, even if its only a line. . . .

I am awfully done and have just, 8.5, left a smelly Treasury crowded with people. Things go fairly well and I think I am being useful.

I am being pressed to go to Walmer tomorrow but nothing will induce me to go if theres a slight off distant chance of seeing you for 5 minutes.

Wire me when and I'll meet you at hospital on Saturday. I cant lunch Reggie[1] tomorrow but could you tea?

Yrs ever and more than ever,
E.S.Montagu

3 hours are not much I agree. But if you felt as I do and you dont and never will, I'd have my way.

[1] Reginald McKenna.

357

In motor

Friday 19 March 15 [i]

My darling you have just left me & I feel very desolate. You were (as you always are) your *real* self to-day: sweet, resolute, undeceiving. I know no woman, & have never known one, who could be in any comparable degree all three things at once. I don't say there is no pain in it, but it is at such moments, in the fresh bitterness of parting, and with the clouded uncertainties of an impenetrable future,[1] that I realise how wise and heaven-blessed I was to have found & appropriated & encased in my heart of hearts, what the Scripture calls the pearl of great price.

If by some *coup foudroyant* in this solitary drive I were to come to an end, I should die happy in the thought & love of you, who have enriched & redeemed my life. Moses was ready to be blotted out of the book of life for the sake of the Chosen People. Danton said 'que mon nom soit flétri, que la

France soit libre'. Sadly futile aspirations both of them – judged by results; in the one case a scattered & unattractive tribe: in the other, the most disappointing experiment in the annals of freedom. But I should be more than content if I could think that I left behind me, in your heart, the memory of devoted worship & undivided and unconquerable love. That at any rate you will always have.

It was divine being with you & near you, watching you, hearing you; and looking back upon our heavenly hour I am sorry that I dwelt so much on gloomy forecasts of a selfish kind. My darling you know that I should never quarrel with what on full reflection you thought right & best for yourself – unless, indeed, it meant cutting me out of your life. That I could not endure. But you won't ever do that – will you?

I can't say more.

Write me a sweet little letter. I am going to post this at the next office I find.

Most precious, you are all the light of all my days – the love & glory of my life. Your own.

<hr>

[1] Asquith probably refers here to Venetia's intention to go abroad to nurse.

358

Friday 19 March 1915 [ii] night

. . . This last 2 years I have lived *literally* every day in your company, sharing with you things great & small, big political issues, little social gossip, stories & jokes & odd bits of poetry or biography – everything that came into one's mind that I thought wd. interest or amuse or distract you even for half a moment. The most ideal comradeship that a man, 'immersed' as they say in affairs, ever had with a woman since the foundation of things. And from being first a luxury, then a recurring pleasure, it has become to me not far off from being a necessity. I cannot imagine a day passing in wh. I would not tell you my doings & my thoughts & hopes & fears; with the certainty of sympathy & understanding & response, the wisest counsel, the most tender & unselfish help.

So you can realise the unspeakable blankness – the tragic pall of black unrelieved midnight darkness – wh. wd overspread me if I had to go on living & working & worrying, I won't say without you (for you won't doom me to that, I know) but with all the avenues closed or only open in dim distant far off vistas. I thought I had braced myself to confront it in prospect – before the war, in June & July – when you had planned that damnable journey to Australia *via* India.[1] But now it is a million times more difficult,

& when I think of it (wh. I never do when I can help) I feel like Hezekiah in the Old Testament who 'turned his face to the wall'.[2]

Darling – I don't want to seem exacting or greedy or overbearing. You must frame your life according to what you like, & to what gives you the fullest outlet & the largest possibilities of interest & pleasure-yielding experience. And as you know I am not such a selfish hound as ever to bark or growl. But my overpowering & absorbing love gives me an excuse for trying to make you realise what it means to me. . . .

You used an unintentionally cruel phrase this afternoon – about 'cutting one's loss'. Good God! – but you didn't really mean it. . . .

The one thing I shd. curse myself for, would be that I had caused you even a momentary twinge of unhappiness. I love to think of you always serene and self-sovereign – but once & again moved out of your serenity by the thought that always & everywhere *I* am your own.

[1] See Letter 93.
[2] 2 Kings 20:2.

VIII

B.V.S. to E.S.M.

36 Smith Square,
Westminster.
                                      Friday 19 March 1915[1]

I'm terribly afraid tomorrow is bound to be a failure but if you liked, & weren't busy wd you pick me up at Mansfield St anytime after a quarter to 11, & not later than 11.15 and we'd drive back together. This is rather a foul suggestion as it entails a long dreary solitary drive for you & I shall more than understand if you say you cant. Perhaps you'd like to let me know as if you werent coming I dont think I should go to Mansfield St at all. You'd have found Aggie, Barbara, Pamela & me if you'd lunched & of course dear Reggie.[2] He was very sweet. If you want to go to Walmer early you will wont you.

I shall see you Wednesday anyway 4.30.

                                                    Yrs
                                                    Venetia

[1] Venetia wrote on Friday afternoon, before her drive with H.H.A. (see Letter 357). The conversation during that drive seems to have been about Venetia's intention to go abroad to nurse. See Letters 359 and 360.
[2] Lady Jekyll; her daughters, Barbara McLaren and Pamela McKenna; and the latter's husband, Reginald McKenna.

IX

E.S.M. to B.V.S.

19 March 1915

Dearest,

Oh will you never understand?

I'd come a thousand times to dine with you, and a thousand times back alone and so if you cant lunch I'll be at Mansfield Street tomorrow morning at 10.45. Theres nothing 'foul' about it.

But I fear you never will understand, and your placid suggestion, ('foul' if you like) that I can possess my soul in patience till Wednesday ought to make anyone but a d——d fool forget it all.

Yrs very madly
E.S.M.

359

Walmer Castle,
Kent.

Sat. 20 March 1915

. . . I am afraid lest you may find in both [the letters of 19 March] too much insistence on my own feelings & point of view, as tho' I were trying for *my own sake* to put something like pressure on you. But believe me it is not so. I should not be truthful – as I always am with you – if I did not let you see the inside of my mind & heart, as I believe & know you always, without any reserve, let me see yours. That is the very essence & foundation of our *divine* relationship. But I have never tried – have I? – to bias your judgment in the disposition & ordering of your life, and so long as I am secure in my most prized of all possessions – the love & confidence which you give me – I have perfect faith & trust in your wisdom, and in your unsurpassed capacity to guide yourself.

So forgive me, sweetest, if in the tumult of my own thoughts I said more than I ought. After all, you ought to find it easy to pardon even the importunate expression of intense & overmastering love. . . .

360

Walmer Castle,
Kent.

Sunday 21 March 1915

My beloved – I got your darling letter just before dinner last night &
delighted in it. I am glad you were able to read the epileptic meanderings
that I produced in the motor . . .

It was only as lately as 5 on Friday that we parted, & I feel as if we had
been separated for an age. What would a real *long* separation mean? I agree
with you that we had better for the moment at any rate drop an 'unpleasant
subject'. It may after all never become actual & it is always a foolish thing to
live in advance through woes wh. may never come. Only darling remember
that I didn't & don't call you *selfish* for taking such chances as come of
enlarging & colouring your life. I could always trust you anywhere to make
the best & most of what was around you, & I have never a moment's fear of
your sinking below your best self. And your 'best self' is in my eyes &
judgement the most complete & most alluring that woman can provide.
Only always *think* of me & love me as much as you can.

About *Sanine* I don't quite know what to say.[1] Of course it is every now &
again fiendishly clever, and Sanine himself is a brilliant sketch of the futile
introspective nebulous sensual 'Intellectual' wh. modern Russia produces.
None of the women have for me a particle of attraction, and the love affair
between the sister & the stagey cavalry officer is quite repellently crude.
What I mind (not being as you know very prudish) in the younger Russians
(Gorky, Tchekoff, & this man) is the love of foulness & squalor for their
own sakes; they are dragged in without any relevance or dramatic interest.
This was not so with the great writers such as Tolstoi & Dostoieffsky; their
excursions into the nasty & the loathsome always have a purpose.

Our party here is quite fairly successful, thanks largely to a most beautiful day wh. has taken & kept them out of doors. Guendolen Osborne has a
great deal of attraction, some insight, & a good sense of humour. I talked to
her at dinner about Raymond: she admits that his character rather baffles
her, but thinks that a good deal of his apparent insensitiveness is really
self-defensive. She seems to know Cys the best of the boys. By the way, the
question of Raymond joining Willcocks's staff still hangs fire: I think he will
most likely go.[2]

Of Lady Essex & Lady Kitty there is nothing new to be said: and Margot's
middle-aged young man, Lancelot Smith, is quite a chip of the old Hugh
Smith block: precise, cheerful, business-like, and not very much more.[3]

The Assyrian who has gone back to London to have his weekly gambol with Edward Grey, was in fairly good form, tho' I think rather exhausted by a week spent in Ll. George's company. He is a good deal exercised by the hypnotic ascendancy wh. he thinks A.J.B. is gaining over Ll.G. as well as Winston. He regards A.J.B. as secretly but genuinely hostile to me,[4] and as a dangerous confidant, when these impulsive rhetoricians pour all their grievances against K. & the rest of their colleagues into his ears. Winston it appears has even gone so far as to suggest (not to me) that he A.J.B. shd be put in charge of the Foreign Office when Grey goes next week for his fishing holiday! The Assyrian says that talking politics &c with him B. is like talking with a 'clever woman'. I rather agree; there is only one woman in the world with whom I have or ever could talk politics to any profit; and she alas! is in a Hospital. He has a fertile ingenious thoroughly unsound mind, and a judgment wh. in the long run is of no value because he has no real knowledge of human beings. Do you think darling I ought to put myself on my guard against this new danger? Tell me.

I am distressed about your letter going wrong – they have been telephoning about it between Walmer & London half the day – but you wd. know that it was accident & not neglect. I hear you have got it now (6 p.m)

Violet seems rather obscure as to what you & she are going to do to-morrow afternoon. Do you think by any chance you cd. arrange that I should drive you back to your prison by 6? I *so long* to see you, my most dear.

I must send this now in the hope that you will get it first thing. My angel – you are with me night & day: the author & finisher of everything that is worth living in my life. Your own.

[1] English translation (published Oct. 1914) of a novel by M. Artzibashef (Mikhail Artsuibashev). It had been banned when published in Russia in 1907. A hundred thousand copies were sold of the German edition despite similar censorship troubles there.
[2] Lt.-Gen. Sir James Willcocks commanded the Indian Corps on the Western Front. For Raymond's plans see also Letters 372 and 374.
[3] Hugh Smith had been Governor of the Bank of England, 1897–9. His son Lancelot, a stockbroker, was the chief delegate in the British Mission to Sweden, 1915, and Chairman of the Committee for Restriction of Imports.
[4] 'That cool grace, easy mind and intellectual courtesy takes [sic] the eye off like the 3 card trick. He is a bitter party opponent': Margot Asquith to Lloyd George, 24 Mar., asking Ll.G. to warn Churchill against Balfour.

X

B.V.S. to E.S.M.

[21 March 1915]

I wonder if you'd like to let me have the motor tomorrow if you did I would pick you up at a few minutes after 5 if you really felt you could face the Whitechaple [*sic*] road again.

Let me know when you want to be picked up.

Are you having lunch at Walmer, be very nice to Margot so she asks you again on the 11th. The P.M. doesn't dare ask Diana tho' he longs to.[1]

Venetia

[1] Margot disapproved of the 'Coterie' in which Lady Diana Manners was prominent. For their relations see P. Ziegler, *Diana Cooper* (1981), pp. 60–1.

361

Monday 22 March 1915 [i]

My own darling – what a tantalising glimpse. I won't say I had rather not have seen you, because to see you even for a second is a foretaste of heaven; but I do mind it being so short & so unsatisfying. I hope you got my little card, to explain why a dim hope I had of taking you back to the prison this afternoon was necessarily frustrated. It is a vile & ill-arranged world, and the more I live in it the less I like it.

So you took the Communion yesterday? for the *third* time in your life? You don't localise the Church in which you practised this rare ceremonial rite.

What did you think of the Coleridge poem? Your others are quite a first rate selection (except perhaps the Swinburne). In reading Bailey on Milton last night, I came across these lines from *Comus*, which exactly state the truth so far as you & I are concerned:

> If this fail
> The pillared Firmament is rottenness,
> And Earth's base built on stubble.[1]

That at any rate is how I feel. 'Mind'? How much do I mind? I am glad you realise, my most entirely & only beloved, the length & breadth & depth of *that*. Of course, if it were less in any of its dimensions, it wouldn't be worth *my* giving or *your* taking. I like you to think it the most 'wonderful thing'. At any rate it is *all* that I have or ever *shall have*, darling & it is always &

wholly yours & only yours. You ask where do *I* 'come in'? As you say, the answer might vary from day to day, & even from hour to hour. I never feel quite sure; speculating about it is one of the pre-occupations of my life; 'in dreams a King, in waking no such matter':[2] & perhaps mostly 'waking'. But I build up out of the dew of hope & the gossamer of fancy, & other such insubstantial materials an airy structure – perhaps the 'baseless fabric of a vision'[3] – which I try to think of in terms of reality. I wonder if you can imagine what that means – I think you can. Faint shadowy suggestions; then, for a moment or more, clear cut outlines; blurred again by doubts & fears; reconstructed in a fitful phase of faith; blown to pieces in a sudden tempest of despondency & even despair: and then emerging again in an iridescent rainbow which I shall follow & follow until it ceases to shine & lure.

My own darling – I am writing in the stress & tumult of a windy & wordy controversy about munitions &c between Ll. G. Winston & A.J.B – and I daren't abstract myself more.

I will write you a real letter to-night. But this I felt I *must* say – at once & now. It moves me *so* much that you should say what you do.

I love you more than life.

You will get my real letter to-morrow morning.

Your own.

[1] Milton, *Comus*, ll. 597–9.
[2] Shakespeare, *Sonnet 87*.
[3] *The Tempest*, IV. i. In this, as in the preceding quotation, Asquith gives a slightly inaccurate version.

362

Monday 22 March 1915 [ii] 7.15 p.m.

. . . I had a longish interview with Cambon, who is rather nervous about an approaching interview between Kitchener, & Joffre & Millerand. He wanted to hurry it up, as his Government are apparently afraid that K. may plan out the disposition & theatre of operations of his new Armies without due consultation with them. K. has since seen Cambon, & he will probably go to France for the interview at the end of this week. Meanwhile – this, of course, is *secret* – he is going to-morrow (Tues. evening) to Dover to dine with Sir J. French, who is coming over for a few hours, on board a man of war.

We then had our little Committee, wh. consisted of myself, Ll. G. A.J.B. Winston & the Assyrian, to consider the much vexed question of putting the contracts for munitions &c on a proper footing. The discussion was quite a good one, & I think we came to some rational (and unanimous) conclusions. But we may have some difficulty with K, and I am going to suggest to Ll. G (who is to be Chairman of the new Committee) that he shd. take on the Assyrian as his curate. Winston is fairly pleased with the situation in the Dardanelles,[1] and K. (who has just been here for a talk) appears to be not dissatisfied. I must go & dress for dinner.

Later 11. pm I have just come back from a men's dinner at Rosebury's: R., Kenyon (Br. Museum), E. T. Cook, H. Fisher, Edgar, Soveral, Mathews, &c.[2] Not at all interesting – except for the wonderful pictures & portraits wh. R has on his walls.[3] On the whole, my experience of men's dinners without women is a *minus* mark. Certainly to-night, when there was a really good cohort of intelligent & rather distinguished men, points that way. It was simply a competition in the telling of old chestnut stories. . . .

Whatever you do, or contemplate, now or hereafter, means *everything* to me.

As I have told you, I don't want in any way (even if I could) to circumscribe or curtail your free life. You, & *you alone*, are the judge of that. But, if ever you felt a moment's doubt, do remember that to *me* the whole world, with all it involves, depends upon *you*. Don't be angry that I am so insistent, and write me a *sweet* letter.

Your own devoted *lover*.

[1] Churchill can hardly have been as 'pleased' as he made out to the Prime Minister: Esher noted, 20 Mar., 'Winston . . . very excited and "jumpy" about the Dardanelles; he says he will be ruined if the attack fails' (*Churchill: Companion Docs., 1914–1916*, p. 719). De Robeck telegraphed on 21 Mar. that the ships could not deal with the 'howitzer and field gun fire' so that 'a strong military [as opposed to civilian] mine sweeping force' was essential. 'Until preparation for this thoroughly completed', de Robeck added, 'I do not propose engaging the forts by direct attack' (ibid., p. 720). Asquith did not know that on the day on which he wrote this letter de Robeck and Hamilton had been agreeing to postpone further naval attacks until the army was ready to land on the Gallipoli peninsula in mid-Apr.

[2] H. A. L. Fisher, the Vice-Chancellor of Sheffield University, was a member of the Royal Commission on the Indian public services and well known in political circles. The Marquis de Soveral, lately Portuguese Ambassador in London, had been a close friend of Edward VII. Sir Charles Mathews was Director of Public Prosecutions.

[3] Rosebery had been a collector since the 1880s.

XI

E.S.M. to B.V.S.

22 March 1915

Oh my dear I was sorry about today. I wanted to tell you about Walmer and since. But I went to a Cabinet Committee and couldnt get away.[1] I was a failure there. Why does Winston hate me so? Find out for me I want to try and get over it.

But please dont keep me till Thursday. Cant I see you tomorrow – any time – a wire will take me to Mansfield or Hospital – only engagement cabinet at 12.

Let me see you Wednesday too. Lady Sheffield drive you back to hospital! I will.

On Thursday will you dine with Duff?[2] Do. I would give you dinner here if you prefer it – but in that case you must tell me who to ask for my set are all dining with Duff.

Yrs longingly
Ed S.

[1] See Letters 360 and 362.   [2] Alfred Duff Cooper.

'That most voracious, slippery, and perfidious power – Italy'
(Letter 363)

THOUGH Italy was nominally bound to Germany and Austria-Hungary through the Triple Alliance, it had long been recognized that she could not expose her coasts to the British navy; and she declared her neutrality on 3 August 1914. In 1859, 1866, and 1870 the creators of the Italian state had seized the chances afforded by war in Europe to forward their plans; and in 1914 their successors hoped to exploit the belligerents' needs in order to gain the Tyrol, Istria, and the Dalmatian coast.

The Italian Government first approached the Central Powers, their old Triple Alliance 'partners'. Germany would have allowed the claims. But the Austrians stood firm; and on 4 March Italy turned to the Allies – Britain, France, and Russia. The Dalmatian coast was the main difficulty. In August 1914 the Russians would have conceded it. By the following March, however, Sazonov thought that Austria-Hungary could be defeated without Italian help; and he was even more anxious than Asquith (Letter 363) not to block the Serbs' way to the Adriatic. He aimed to make the Bulgarians allies by promising them Serb territory in Macedonia, so that he needed the possibility of compensations on the Adriatic for Serbia. Russian military help for Serbia being an impossibility, the Russian Government recognized a strong obligation to give the Serbs diplomatic aid. Russia had long been the protector of the Slavs of south-east Europe. This concern extended to Dalmatia which contained a million Slavs and only ten thousand Italians.

It was possible to reach a compromise because neither Russia nor Italy was in a position to be wholly intransigent. Sazonov might be confident of victory against Austria: the Grand Duke Nicholas, the Russian Comman-der-in-Chief, was not. On the other hand, the Italians feared that if they held out for too much Austria might be beaten without their help. As usual the Austrians moved too late: they offered concessions to Italy only after the Treaty of London had been signed on 26 April (Letter 408). When the Italian Government made no reply, information about the offer was given to Giolitti, the master manipulator of Italian politics, and the leading advocate of Italian neutrality. He engineered the fall of the Government. But war-fever, fanned by d'Annunzio the poet and leaders of the extreme left such as Mussolini, was too strong for such tactics to succeed;[1] and on 23 May, in what their Prime Minister termed a spirit of 'sacred egoism', the Italians declared war on Austria-Hungary. The declaration fell within the terms of the London Treaty which pledged Italy to join the Allies within a month of signing. It did not come soon enough to save Asquith's Liberal Government (p. 598).

[1] All the Italian claims were against the Austrians, who would have no need to oblige a neutral Italy in victory, and no power to do so in defeat. Even Giolitti could not counter that argument.

363

Tue. 23 March 15 [i]

. . . Coming up in the motor yesterday in rather a bleak mood, I deliber-ately set to work to make things worse with me by drawing a picture of you, not as seen by me or even by yourself, but by the most 'crabbing' & malignant of critics. Your looks, your 'accomplishments', your brain, your heart, even your clothes were passed one after another in the most hostile possible review. Isn't it a foul & perverse kind of game? But what do you suppose was the result? After the Devil's advocate had done his worst, with pitiless & unshrinking malevolence, and with the Devil's own cunning, I was left *more* in love than ever before! How do you account for that? I wish you would tell me.

3 p.m. We had a longish Cabinet this morning. The news from the Dardanelles is not very good: there are more mines & concealed guns than they ever counted upon: and the Admiral seems to be rather in a funk.[1] Ian Hamilton has not yet sent his report, but the soldiers cannot be ready for any big concerted operation before about 14th April. I agree with Winston & K that the Navy ought to make another big push, so soon as the weather clears.[2] If they wait & wait, until the army is fully prepared, they may fall into a spell of bad weather, & (what is worse) find that submarines, Austrian or German, have arrived on the scene.

All this was rather kept back from the Cabinet, who spent their time in discussing how cheaply we can purchase the immediate intervention of that most voracious, slippery, & perfidious Power – Italy. She opens her mouth very wide, particularly on the Dalmatian coast, and we must not allow her to block the Serbs' access to the sea. But short of that, she is worth purchasing: tho' I shall always think that on a great scene she has played the meanest and pettiest of parts.

(My darling – where are you & what are you doing now? I haven't a notion: for aught I know you might be tending your spotted patient, or gleaning the aftermath of one of the Assyrian's luncheon parties. I *hate* to be so much in the dark: *do* tell me in future. There is a growl for you, but I think not wholly undeserved.)

I was going on to tell you about our luncheon, which I suppose was designed for Queen Alexandra's benefit. She shied off, it appears, & instead proposed herself to tea on *Friday*. This I vetoed at once, for reasons wh. you may perhaps conjecture: so now she is put off till next week. The party was one of our choice studies in incongruity: Lord & Lady Farquhar, Paderewski, A. J. B., Ll. George, Anne Islington, Moyra Cavendish, Lady Ripon, Violet, Sir A. Keogh &c &c.[3] In such a milieu, the best thing is not to strike out, but to float hither & thither as the waves & tides carry you. That is what I did.

Violet told me of her time with you yesterday afternoon. It wd. have been I see no good anyway, even if I had been able to drive you back. You must tell me what you are doing to-morrow (Wed). Thursday I come to you at Mansfield St. about 5.45. Where are you dining? We unfortunately are engaged since a long time to Mrs Arthur Sassoon. . . .

There is rather a lull in things this afternoon, & as I look out of the window it seems fine & fairly warm – just one of the days when we – you & I – used to launch out into space, to Hitchin, or Wanborough; and when 'jaded with the rush & glare of the interminable Hours' (where does that come?) I have so often felt the healing & inspiration & guidance which you alone, my most worshipped, of men or women can give. How I shd. love it to-day! But you are so far away. Do you know M. Arnold's lines (I don't believe you ever read very much, except the 'Scholar Gipsy', of those 'handsome volumes' wh. I gave you) about the Resurrection:

> He is not here: far off he lies
> In the lorn Syrian town;
> And on his grave, with $\begin{cases}\text{shining?} \\ \text{sleepless eyes,}\end{cases}$
> The Syrian stars look down.[4]

At least I think that is how it goes. What are the things I most hate? Distance, Absence, Silence. What are the things I most love? They can't be catalogued, because they are all summed up in one – and that one is *You*. Your own.

[1] De Robeck's telegram, after his conference with Hamilton on 22 Mar., does not justify the suggestion that he was 'rather in a funk': *Churchill: Companion Docs., 1914–1916*, pp. 723–4.

[2] For Asquith's more considered view see Letter 366.

[3] For Lord Farquhar see Letter 353, n. 3. Paderewski, the famous pianist, was establishing branches in London and Paris of a 'General Committee for the Victims of the War in Poland' founded in Jan. 1915. For Lady Islington, Lady Moyra Cavendish, and Sir Alfred Keogh see Letters 12, n. 6; 180; and 172, n. 6. The Marchioness of Ripon had been one of the 'Souls' in the 1890s and is portrayed in Margot Asquith's *Autobiography*, i. 193–4.

[4] 'Obermann Once More'. The passage starts:
   Now he is dead. Far hence he lies. . . .
If 'shining' is read Asquith has the other three lines correctly.

364

Tues 23 March 15 [ii]

My darling – after I finished writing to you this afternoon & had disposed of a lot of tiresome small things, the sun was so bright that I got into the motor 'to take the air'. I hadn't an idea where to go: so I drove first to Mansfield St (of all places) and inquired whether you were to be there any time to-morrow. I didn't in the least expect an answer (of course they didn't know) but for the moment it appeased (negatively) my desire to know about your movements. I then went & had my hair cut, wh. you will probably agree was a judicious way of spending $\frac{1}{4}$ of an hour, and after considering & rejecting the idea of going up in solitude to Hampstead to see the sunset, I drifted to the Athenaeum & tried to read a book on Modern English Essayists. It wasn't at all good, except that I agree with the author in putting Hazlitt very high: there are few better critics anywhere.

Isn't this rather a pathetic record of a singularly fruitless quest? At one moment I even thought of driving to your Hospital, but I knew that I shouldn't see you without upsetting all the conventional rules & raising the

Devil's own to-do. I had really better have stayed at home and read the latest memoranda on Alexandretta, or the Export of Coal, or the purchase of the interned German ships, or any of the other juicy by-products of the war, wh. are for the moment to the front. But I felt restless, and at any rate I have polished off the barber for some time to come. . . .

I had a welcome letter to-day from Oc posted at Malta quite a fortnight ago. . . . He finds Patrick[1] good company with an amazing memory. They seem to have had nothing to do on ship board except getting their men vaccinated & inoculated against typhoid. I suppose by now they are stretching their legs at Alexandria.

11 p.m. I have just returned (with the Countess Benck) from dining at the Horners. She & Soveral & Lady Essex & Sir J. Cowans & Edgar – with R & Kath – were the party. Very nice & quite good talk. Raymond is going out on Willcocks's staff as soon as it can be arranged:[2] I suppose next week. . . . Do you realise that it is now just upon Wed morning & that the last 'scrap of paper'[3] I have received from you was written on Sunday? I am not even perfectly sanguine that I shall get a letter when I wake up. So please send me a telegram in the course of the morning to indicate what you are doing, & whether it is possible (& where) to see you.

Cowans told me to-night that we have now 160,000 horses in France (every loss being regularly supplied) & send out from here every day 1000 tons of hay. Anthony[4] & his lot must be longing for a real cavalry advance. . . .

What delicious hours those are to look back upon when we read things together in your little room at Alderley! Those damned dogs too! How I hated them, and yet somehow they fitted into the picture. Darling, I know I have a lot of ragged edges – as Browning says in 'Xmas Eve'

> T'were to be wished the flaws were fewer
> In the earthen vessel that holds the treasure,
>
> . . . . . .
> But the main thing is, does it hold good measure?[5]

Do you think it does?

[1] P. H. Shaw-Stewart. A Fellow of All Souls. 'All Shaws are charlatans', said Raymond Asquith, 'and all Stewarts are pretenders; besides his nose is as sharp as a pen.'
[2] He did not go. See Letters 372 and 374.
[3] For the popularity of this phrase see Letter 298.
[4] Henley, husband of Venetia's sister Sylvia.
[5] Robert Browning, 'Christmas Eve', xxii. An echo of 2 Corinthians 4:7.

XII

E.S.M. to B.V.S.

23 March 1915

. . . It looks as if what you wanted to say was 'Please understand I am not in love with you and on reflection the idea is abominant or something of that kind.'

Such a sentiment would be death. On the other hand you wont pretend will you? I am slow of understanding and very apprehensive. . . .

365

Wed 24 March 1915 [i] 3 p.m.

My own most darling – I confess it was rather a blow not to get anything from you – letter or telegram – this morning. And I began (like a fool, which I am, tho' nobody but you really knows it) to fear once again that I had over tired you with my incessant stream of letters & appeals. Happily my faith in you is of the kind that not only moves mountains, but (what is much more difficult) perseveres when the ground is flat & sky is drab.

And now at last it has been rewarded by receiving your little letter of yesterday. I suppose you couldn't post it till this morning. I only hope you are writing me something to-day. I wrote you two letters yesterday – one in early aft. the other just before midnight – wh. were both (I am afraid) rather in the nature of *cris de coeur*. But you oughtn't very much to mind that: there are times when it comes over me like a swelling & overmastering tide and bears everything else before it.

It is indeed a bleak and disappointing prospect that you unfold for the moment. Especially for to-morrow (Thursday) wh. I have been counting on & living for. What is the precise import of a 'bandaging class'? Does it mean that you won't get out at all – morning or afternoon? I shall be practically free at any hour – except for lunching at the Rutlands! – so if there is a loophole, however tiny, let me know *in the morning*. I could drive you back, if that were possible.

If one has to wait for Friday, do come to lunch here, & we could go out immediately afterwards, & I should be independent of the trains – for (as I discovered last week) I can easily motor on to Walmer; and so far from boring me, the solitary drive has great compensations in the fresh thought of your dear & precious presence, and even in my jerky efforts to put on paper what I think & feel.

Do give me as much time as you can. That is where I 'come in'! and you mustn't think that I am greedy & jealous & exacting. I *am* in fact – all three – but I suffer from it on the whole much more than you do – isn't that true? Thank God, as you say, the time of greater freedom is drawing near.

There is nothing much doing to-day – no Cabinets or Councils or Com-mittees, & only small & rather tiresome things to dispose of. The great thing at the moment is to draw Italy in – selfish, slippery, & perfidious as she has shown herself to be: and one must not be too squeamish about the price to be paid. Hankey is the only person I have seen: he is a good deal exercised about the Dardanelles.[1]

You wrote in such haste that you say nothing about some of the things on wh. I wanted to get your opinion. That is the worst of hardly ever seeing you. For instance you don't allude to what I wrote about A. J. B. McKenna (I need not say) regards him with almost as much suspicion as the Assyrian – as a poisonous snake in the grass. How can I get on without talking to you, when you are too busy to write? Answer – if you can. I know you can't – and *you* know how dependent I have become. You may say it is my fault & not yours: but the fact remains.

I think I shall take a course of Milton. This is not a bad supplement to Hamlet's soliloquies on self-slaughter &c:

> Sad cure, for who would lose,
> Though full of pain, this intellectual being,
> Those thoughts wh. travel thro' Eternity,
> To perish rather, swallowed up & lost
> In the wide womb of uncreated Nature,
> Devoid of sense & motion.[2]

There is no doubt his is the finest English & the most perfect art of all our poets.

We had at lunch to-day the new Belgian Minister & his wife, as well as Massingham, Waxworks, Maud Wyndham, Katharine & some others. (I wish you had proposed yourself yesterday.) The Belge is on the whole the best I have met of his race: he is the leader of the Liberal Opposition there[3] – the Ministry being Conservative & Clerical – and has taken this post under them for patriotic reasons. I much preferred him to Broqueville & the others I have met.

We dine to-night with the Harcourts.

Perhaps I will write to you again later in the day. Shall I? I am afraid of asking you too many questions, but darling how can I help [it]? You have the keys of my life: to whom else could I go?

I hate these 'to-morrows' which creep in their petty pace with hopes deferred, & receding visions, and fresh topics growing stale, Happily one thing never gets colder – and never could.

Write me a few sweet consoling lines – heart of my heart. I *so* wanted you.

Your own.

---

[1] On 20 Mar. Hankey sent the Prime Minister a memo. in which he pointed out: 'The capture of the Dardanelles as a joint naval and military operation has not been thought out in any detail.' He begged Asquith to ensure that the necessary staff work was done by appointing a 'naval and military technical committee'. In the absence of such a committee he feared a 'repetition of the naval fiasco' (a strong term for the naval losses on 18 Mar.).

[2] *Paradise Lost*, ii. 146 ff.; slightly misquoted.

[3] Paul Hymans.

366

Wed 24 March 15 [ii]

. . . K came to see me & gave me an account of his talk with French on the man of war at Dover last night. F. strenuously denied that he had let off too much ammunition from his big guns in the fighting at Neuve Chapelle.[1] On the general position he was as optimistic as ever, but rather complained that Joffre was too apt to treat him 'like a Corporal'. K. is going over himself on Sunday to make things square with Joffre, and can be trusted not only to hold his own but to carry the war into the enemy's country. K. also talked at length about the proposed new War Supplies Committee of Ll. George, Assyrian & Co.[2] He is naturally rather suspicious of its intruding into his own domain & upsetting some of his plans & arrangements. On the whole he spoke very fairly & temperately, & to-morrow morning I hope to get to a *modus vivendi* between him & Ll. G. . . .

. . .*11.30 p.m.* Winston came to talk about the Dardanelles. The weather is infamous there, & the Naval experts seem to be suffering from a fit of nerves. They are now disposed to wait till the troops can assist them in force, which ought to be not later than about April 10th. Winston thinks & I agree with him, that the ships, as soon as the weather clears, & the aeroplanes can detect the condition of the forts & the positions of the concealed guns, ought to make another push: & I hope this will be done.[3]

We dined at the Harcourts: the Maguires, Mrs Keppel, Ld. Reading, Fritz Ponsonby: nothing very interesting, & a little Bridge after dinner. . . .

I wonder if you can realise how, at *every* hour of the day, I am thinking of you, picturing your supposed environments, envying the people (even the spotted patient) who are within range of your eyes & hands, wondering what is passing in your mind & thoughts, fearing & hoping for the future, and *loving* beyond measure. . . .

[1] It was calculated that the British had used as much artillery ammunition during the Neuve Chapelle Battle as in the entire South African War.

[2] For this Committee see pp. 461–2. It went under various titles: by the end of Mar. Asquith was calling it the Munitions Committee (Letter 376). It was also sometimes termed the Treasury Committee, its chairman being the Chancellor of the Exchequer.

[3] Churchill's naval advisers would not let him instruct de Robeck to make another full-scale naval attack as soon as possible. The most the First Lord could do in his personal telegram, 24 Mar. (*Churchill: Companion Docs., 1914–1916*, pp. 728–30), was to ask: 'What has happened . . . to make you alter your intention of renewing the attack as soon as the weather is favourable?' Even this telegram brought a fresh threat of resignation from Fisher.

'Nationalising the drink trade' (Letter 367)

IN 1915 the public house was almost the only place of recreation for most industrial workers; and the high wages and disruption of wartime soon increased drunkenness until it threatened output in the munitions works and shipyards. 'Drink is doing more damage . . . than all the German submarines put together,' Lloyd George declared on 28 February;[1] and he decided to mount a great campaign to repair this. Such a campaign had attractions for a leading radical. The drink trade had given massive support to the Conservatives for a generation; and curbing its operations had long been a feature of Liberal programmes. The difficulties, on the other hand, were immense (Letter 380). Any move towards 'local prohibition' would cause working-class resentment (Letter 375). The other alternative, a state monopoly of drink, would be unacceptable to what Asquith called 'the professional temperance lot', who were influential in the Liberal party: it would also unbalance the Government's financial arrangements. There was some suspicion that the Government were using drink as an excuse for their failures in supplying munitions.

Though the King (Letter 375) and Kitchener took the pledge for the duration, Lloyd George had no quick success. His increases in the taxes on drink were withdrawn (Letter 416, n. 6); but the Amending Bill (No. 3) to the Defence of the Realm Act received the Royal Assent on 19 May. Under this Act any area of importance for the production and transport of war materials might be placed under special control for the sale of alcohol. A Liquor Traffic Central Control Board was set up, with Lord D'Abernon as chairman. This possessed, and used, extensive powers.

[1] Speech at Bangor: see D. Lloyd George, *War Memoirs*, p. 194.

367

Thurs. 25 March 1915 [i]

My darling – it was sweet of you to send your little letter of last night this morning: it makes all the difference to me not to have to wait in suspense for it. It is sad to think that you are not visible even for a moment all day to-day. But I count on to-morrow & shall pick you up at the Admiralty soon after 3.

Massingham told Margot yesterday a 'horrible tale', which he swears can be proved true on the best authority. It is that Winston is 'intriguing hard' to supplant E. Grey at the Foreign Office & to put A.J.B. in his place. I gave you the other day a milder version of the same story, which the suspicious mind of the Assyrian had treasured up. There is no doubt that Winston is at the moment a complete victim to B's superficial charm; he has him at the Admiralty night & day, and I am afraid tells him a lot of things which he ought to keep to himself, or at any rate to his colleagues. Since I began the last sentence, Ll. George has been here for his favourite morning indulgence (it corresponds in him to the dram drinking of the Clyde workmen) – a 10 minutes discursive discussion of things in general. I asked him what he thought of the Massingham story, & rather to my surprise he said he believed it was substantially true. He thinks that Winston has for the time at any rate allowed himself to be 'swallowed whole' by A.J.B, on whom he, L.G., after working with him for a week or two, is now disposed to be very severe. It is a pity isn't it? that Winston hasn't a better sense of proportion, and also a larger endowment of the instinct of loyalty. As you know, like you, I am really fond of him: but I regard his future with many misgivings. Your little Indian plan for him[1] commands I am afraid no favour in any quarter: the mere mention of it makes the Assyrian foam at the mouth, and is received with less demonstrative but equally emphatic disapproval by the 2 or 3 others to whom I have casually hinted at it. He will never get to the top in English politics, with all his wonderful gifts; to speak with the tongues of men & angels, and to spend laborious days & nights in administration, is no good, if a man does not inspire trust.

You & I (as we have often agreed) are not imbued with the missionary spirit, and are disposed to be content to take our friends as we find them. But to change W. *au fond* is a task wh. wd tax the combined powers of St. Bernard & John Wesley.

By the way it is characteristic of LG's versatility of interest & mind, that tho' he was on his way to a deputation of workmen whom he is going to try to cajole to accept his terms, and has to go through a similar proceeding with the employers to-morrow,[2] he is for the moment red-hot with a plan, or rather an idea, for nationalising the drink trade! He has had a lot of brewers with him at & after breakfast, and has already made an appointment with 2 skilled accountants to go into figures at 3 this afternoon. I warned him to go very warily: a State monopoly in drink would I think be a most dangerous thing politically. But I am all for surveying the ground, particularly on the lines of compensation & public control. The professional Temperance lot – Leif Jones & Co – wd. be aghast if they suspected that anything of the kind was on the stocks.[3]. . .

E. Grey is coming directly to talk about things, & I shall put to him the desirability of having Crewe rather than Haldane as his substitute when he goes off fishing.[4]. . .

[1] Presumably the suggestion that Churchill should become Viceroy of India when the war ended. See Letters 290, 295, and 337.

[2] Lloyd George had secured his main objects with the representatives of 35 trade unions and labour organizations on 17, 18, and 19 Mar. In the meetings to which Asquith refers it was hoped to consolidate the position won.

[3] For Leif Jones see Letter 36, n. 1. He was President of the principal temperance organization, the United Kingdom Alliance, 1906–31.

[4] There had been an outcry about Haldane's spells in the Foreign Office (Letter 234, n. 6); and Asquith greatly respected Crewe's judgement, as the latter's place at the head of the 'tripos list' shows (Letter 324). Early in Mar. Lloyd George had wanted Balfour to manage the Foreign Office when Grey was away. In view of the 'horrible tale' mentioned earlier in the letter it was no doubt thought desirable that Grey should nominate an unobjectionable Liberal of first-class standing as his substitute. Eventually Asquith decided to do the work himself: Letter 373.

368

Thurs. 25 March 1915 [ii] after lunch

. . . E. Grey came . . . & . . . we had a really interesting conversation about the whole international situation – Italy, Roumania, Greece, Bulgaria – the slimness of France, the ambitions of Russia &c &c. Winston & the 'natural man' (whom he very well represents) are anxious that if, when the war ends, Russia has got Constantinople, & Italy Dalmatia, & France Syria, we should be able to appropriate some equivalent share of the spoils – Mesopotamia, with or without Alexandretta, a 'sphere' in Persia, some German colonies &c.

I believe that, at the moment, Grey & I are the *only* two men who doubt & distrust any such settlement. We both think that in the real interest of our own future, the best thing would be if, at the end of the War, we could say that (apart from regularising the status of Egypt & Cyprus, & perhaps picking up a few Pacific islands for Australia & New Zealand) we have taken & gained nothing. And that not from a merely moral & sentimental point of view (which, however, with our record of *perfide Albion*, & the universal cormorant, counts for something) but from purely material considerations. Taking on Mesopotamia, for instance – with or without Alexandretta (I suppose you haven't got a map, but I cd. explain this in 2 minutes) means spending millions in irrigation & development with no immediate or early return; keeping up quite a large army white & coloured in an unfamiliar country; tackling every kind of tangled administrative question, worse than we have ever had in India, with a hornet's nest of Arab tribes; and, even if that were all set right, having a perpetual menace on our flank in Kurdistan, just like Afghanistan & the Pathan tribes who overshadow the Punjab. (My own sweet, are you getting bored & bewildered? I don't think you are, but I pour out to you both my first & my last thoughts sooner than to any colleague; and I love & pine for your judgment upon them.)

The great thing for the moment is to bring in Italy, voracious as she is: and to attain this, if possible, Grey is postponing his holiday until Wed in next week. . . .

We went to the lunch in Arlington St,[1] wh. was almost a State affair. I sat (happy I!) between 2 Duchesses – Rutland & Marlborough.[2] The latter by the way was more sensible than I have seen her lately, and we had quite an interesting discussion of the paradox that Englishmen marry American women, but that hardly any Englishwoman can be induced to marry an American man. . . .

I have just heard that McKenna is coming to see me. I loathe the whole scheme of the Universe, at times: here to-day, for instance, I have had in person or in writing E. Grey, Ll George, Kitchener, now McKenna, & inevitably sooner or later Winston. . . .

[1] No. 16, the Duke of Rutland's London house.
[2] Consuelo, daughter of William Vanderbilt.

369

In motor

Fr 26 March 1915 [i]

My own beloved – you have just left me, and since you are not by me I much prefer to take my 3 hours' drive in solitude. The first thing I do when I get to my destination will be to write to Knutsford & clinch Millbank. I can't tell you the joy with wh. the prospect fills me, or how delicious it is to remember that you said it was for my sake. It is the most heavenly present you have ever given me.[1]

Among our many divine Friday drives – how many I wonder? some day I will try to count them – to-day's was one of the best. To begin with, you never looked so sweet & beautiful. And then you were angelic with my bad temper, of wh. I am rather ashamed. And we never had a more intimate & delicious talk about the things that really matter. A perfect understanding. You may often be tempted to think that my love is selfish. And so in a true sense it is. But I can honestly say that in its selfishness there is no dross of coarseness or unworthiness. I give to you & shall always give to the day of my death – near or far off as we may be – whatever is best in me. The meaner pettier things – of wh. I have more than enough – are refined & expelled by contact with you, ever closer knowledge of you, ever growing devotion to the ideal I have always dreamt of, & thank God have at last realised. You have done that for me. And it is worth a million times over the bitterness of absence, the pains of uncertainty & suspense, the intermittent consciousness on my side of disparities too obvious to be named, the lowering clouds of future possibilities.

I don't really believe that you could have 'choked it off'. But it is no good speculating about that. There it is – for better or for worse – the core of my life – something (I won't say more) that can never be effaced from yours.

You might send me a flower from Covent Garden to-morrow in remembrance of to-day. I will put it with the one I keep from your last foray.

I shall come for you on Monday at M.St 5.10.

I am speeding along through Kent – the gloaming is just setting in – & I shall post this at Maidstone. We have just been stopped in a village by 4 men in uniform with note books. One of them opened the door & when I asked what was the matter requested that I 'would kindly give him my name' – wh. I did. He looked poor man rather crestfallen & remarked apologetically that it was 'for the Defence of London'! . . .

---

[1] 'Millbank' was the Queen Alexandra Military Hospital, next to the Tate Gallery (which absorbed the hospital buildings in 1977). It is not clear why the plan for Venetia to nurse there came to nothing. *Testament of Youth* (1933), ch. 9, includes a picture of 'Millbank' during 1918; the author, Vera Brittain, was nursing there when the war ended.

370

Walmer

Friday 26 March 1915 [ii] Midnight

My own most darling – I didn't get here (after posting my epileptic letter to you at Maidstone) until $\frac{1}{4}$ to 9. I found Hugh here, & we had a most pleasant little dinner *à deux*, and since then for nearly $1\frac{1}{2}$ hours have played a colossal game of Chess. You will, I hope, be glad, and I am afraid be surprised to hear that I was victorious.

I couldn't help thinking in the intervals of conversation & play of what we said, in perhaps not a very serious interlude of our drive to-day, about the men that you of your generation might think of marrying (I assume without anything like strong & passionate inclination). Of those I know, and I know them almost all, I should (perhaps from paternal partiality) put Raymond easily first. I think he has more charm, as well as more intellect, than any of his generation. But after him (now that our dear Archie is gone)[2] I shd. certainly put Hugh second. I am, of course, quite alive to what he lacks – initiative, adventure, settled convictions & purposes, perhaps what you in the Hospital wd. call a deficiency of red corpuscles – but he is good to look at (wh. counts for something) has great natural grace & charm of manner, is really cultivated (how could one live at close quarters with a man or woman to whom poetry & literature were a sealed book?) writes & talks well, and is, apart from a few rather angular inherited prejudices, the best of company. But enough of Hugh.[3]

One thing is quite certain (whoever may be the man or woman) one can't take on marriage as a kind of side-show; and that is equally true whether it turns out a success, or a *succès d'estime*, or a failure, or a tragedy. Nothing afterwards is ever quite the same, and given anything like normal conditions there is no intimacy or confidence with another which is not or *may not* be *à trois*.

With your divine intuition you know what I mean when I say it is not & cannot be so with *me*. I won't write more about this. There are some things that can only be said. . . .

[1] When Asquith wrote in a moving car his writing, though naturally less neat than usual, remained astonishingly legible.

[2] For Archie Gordon's death see p. 1.

[3] Hugh Godley was a Parliamentary draftsman, and became Assistant Parliamentary Counsel in 1917.

371

Walmer Castle,
Kent.

Sat 27 March 1915 [ii] (later)

. . . No news in the F.O. telegrams this morning, except that Russia still vetoes the Italian demand for the Dalmatian coast. She will allow her the bit from Zara to Sebenico[1] (alas! you have no map) but insists on the rest going to Serbia or being neutralised. On the merits, Russia is quite right, but it is so important to bring in Italy at once, greedy & slippery as she is, that we ought not to be too precise in haggling over this or that. As I told you yesterday, Roumania is now a certainty – at any rate after the 1st May.[2] If in addition we cd. rope in both Italy & Bulgaria (Austria being now almost *in extremis*) we ought to be within sight of the end of the war. This I am afraid is the only *mundane* thing I have to contribute – and you told me yesterday that you liked that & the *other* to be mixed like a salad. . . .

It is here a day of glorious sun, with a rather biting North East wind: against wh. Hugh & I struggled, & conscientiously played our 12 holes this morning. We are not disposed to face it again. . . .

None of our guests have yet (3.30) arrived, and I am in the mood to wish that they wd all miss their trains, & not turn up for another 24 hours . . .

What are you doing I wonder now? & to-morrow? Encouraged by last Sunday's experience, are you going again to Communion? I fancy *not*. The one most hateful thing is *unreality*. There is nothing that more strengthens & intensifies my love (on the *rational* side) than your unshakeable & untemptable *Honesty*. I always know that you tell me *less* rather than *more* of what you feel & think. I am honest too – with you. I can truly say that I have never uttered a word or epithet of exaggeration – still less of make-believe – in all my now countless attempts to make you realise what you are to me. I won't say – for it wd not be true – that I have deliberately understated; but the reality passes beyond the resources of language (at least of mine!). . . .

. . . I feel a new spring of hope, now that your Millbank affair has a prospect of being fixed. I wrote a tactful (!) letter to Lord Kn.[3] What fun we shall have visiting the Hospital together. . . .

[1] Zara (Zadar) to Sebenico (Sibenik): a stretch of the Dalmatian coast north-west of Spalato (Split).
[2] Romania did not declare war on the side of the Allies until Aug. 1916.
[3] Lord Knutsford.

372

Walmer Castle,
Kent.

Sunday 28 March '15

My own darling – your delicious tube letter arrived this morning & has brightened my day. I am sure that your letter to Lord K. cost you a wrench.[1] I shall never forget your sweetness in letting the thought of me 'come in', & help to turn the scale.

I was greatly interested by your account of your talk with Edgar &

Raymond. I suspect there is a good deal of truth in what the latter said. The pleasure-hunt wh. raged so furiously shews signs of slackening down. . . .

I have a tiresome pouch or set of pouches this morning from Bongie. There is a truly royal row on the stocks between Kitchener & Ll. George in regard to the proposed Committee on munitions. Neither is disposed to give way: K. threatens to give up his office, and Ll. G to wash his hands of the whole business, leaving on record all sorts of solemn protests & warnings. The Assyrian, who revels in gloomy situations, sends me an only partially legible dirge of considerable length, ending (as these things generally do) with the much underscored statement: 'it is imperative that *you* should step in'! So 'step in' I fear I must; and bad as it looks, I don't know that it is more hopeless than some of the jobs I have had to do, & have always told you darling about, during the last 2 years or so.

There is also a troublesome business between the Press Bureau & the London papers, who complain that if the people are 'being unduly soothed & elated' the responsibility lies with the Gov^t & not with the Press. It is the old story – of news & particularly bad news being kept back or mutilated, with the result that the public are too optimistic & lethargic. I am not fond of the Press, as you know, but there is some truth in this particular complaint, & I am afraid I shall have to see them.[2]

You had a very nice lot of people at the dinner on Friday, & I am delighted that you were so well placed. Our party here is going off quite well. The weather is bright tho windy & cold, and the oldest inhabitant – in this instance Hugh – admits that he has never seen the coast of France half so clearly. It looks just like the cliffs you see on the other side of a moderately broad lake. I went in the motor this afternoon with Ettie & Mrs Sassoon & the Impeccable our usual drive thro' Dover & Folkestone to Lympne, and thence we extended it to Belcaire, wh. was happily untenanted, so we went in. Neither Ettie nor Sir J.S. cd. find words to describe their horror & disgust. It is unchanged since you & I were there, except that in one room (in wh. we used to sit) the undefiled white wall is now covered with a glittering surface of highly burnished mustard-gold, on which are frescoes of a darker shade, representing elephants in different attitudes.[3] I am more lenient because I recall our Sunday there, and the drive down, & Canterbury Cathedral, & a delicious talk we had before dinner. . . .

Ettie is in very good form: she incidentally disclosed her age to-day, she is 47 or 48: her vitality and vividness of interest both in persons & things are in refreshing contrast to that of many much younger people whom we know. I haven't had so much talk with her for years: in old days I was constantly at Taplow.[4] I shall never forget making my first acquaintance with her, while Helen was still alive, one Sunday at Jowett's at Balliol. She was then quite young – I suppose not more than 23; we had a long walk together & became friends, wh. we have remained ever since. She might have been one of the most considerable women of her time, but she made rather a stupid marriage,[5] and, tho' she loves to please people, she is rather lacking in the best kinds of ambition. Still she is a remarkable person, and has made a great deal of her life.

Raymond has given up the Willcocks idea, as he now hears that there is quite a good chance of his being drafted into the 1st battalion & so going to the front.[6] I am afraid Katharine won't like this; nor naturally do I. But he must take his chance like the rest. . . .

[1] Applying to Lord Knutsford to nurse at Millbank entailed giving up plans to do war nursing overseas.

[2] See Letter 381.

[3] This mural by José Maria Sert, the Spanish artist and designer (for whom see Letter 84, n. 1), was obliterated when Port Lympne was occupied by the armed services during the 1939–45 war. The Czech airmen billeted in the house seem to have shared Asquith's views about the elephants.

[4] Ettie, Lady Desborough, had been one of the 'Souls' in the 1880s and 1890s. She had been the mistress of Taplow Court, the Grenfells' house on the Thames near Maidenhead, since her marriage in 1887.

[5] At the age of 19. When W. H. Grenfell was courting her, one of her cousins, Mabell Gore, wrote:

If you do not absolutely hate him I should marry him, I think; . . . everyone says he is an absolute angel; and he may be a little dull, but after all what a comfort it is to be cleverer than one's husband.   N. Mosley, *Julian Grenfell* (1976), p. 8.

[6] To make sure of going overseas he joined the 3rd Bn. of the Grenadier Guards in July. He reached the Front in France in Oct. 1915.

'A Tragic History of Intrigue' (Letter 373)

BY the last week of March it was clear that the Neuve Chapelle attack had been costly and indecisive (Letter 355) and that the navy had been checked at the Dardanelles (Letters 363 and 366): the naval losses in the Straits on 18 March were soon to be magnified by *The Times* into 'a very considerable disaster'. These reverses came on the British just as they had begun to realize that they were in for a long war. Criticism of the man in charge of the war effort was the inevitable result. Some Liberals took the criticism to mean that Tory plots were being hatched to weaken or discredit the Prime Minister, and so to bring down the Government and promote a coalition. It was imputed that the plotters were being helped from inside the cabinet. Massingham of the *Nation* warned Margot Asquith that Churchill was scheming to substitute a Tory for one of the premier's closest associates by making Balfour Foreign Secretary (Letter 367). On 29 March Donald of the *Daily Chronicle* published a counterblast to the press criticisms.[1] He denounced the 'innuendos and suggestions' that the premier was 'not fit for his task'. McKenna at once saw Asquith and suggested the source of the suggestions. Lloyd George had been applauded for some weeks in the Northcliffe press; this showed him, in McKenna's eyes, to be thrusting for the premiership.

The suspicions of Massingham and McKenna are not hard to explain. Churchill's regard for Balfour and his hankering after conscription and coalition were notorious (Letter 134; pp. 420–1; Letter 295); and the state of Grey's eyesight made a change at the Foreign Office quite probable. It was widely known that Lloyd George had suggested a coalition in 1910 during the constitutional crisis. He had referred in conversation during the last few weeks to the premier's shortcomings. Early in March he had told Sir George Riddell, who managed the *News of the World*, that Asquith lacked initiative and took no steps to control and co-ordinate the Government's activities.[2] But all this did not constitute a plot. Anything less conspiratorial than Churchill's views on wartime government would be hard to imagine. Lloyd George was not yet strong enough to bid for the premiership and he had no interest in promoting a coalition. He welcomed new Conservative admirers; but his main concern was to show his old supporters that, however warlike he had become, he was still a radical. He had deserved a good press for the Treasury Agreements with management and labour (p. 461); but, as he knew better than most, a run of luck seldom lasts in politics. Drink (p. 507) was soon to land him in trouble.

The episode of this non-plot was more significant than Asquith made it out to be in this letter. The honeymoon period of the party truce had ended. Though no one was plotting against the Prime Minister, many criticized him: see pp. 353–4. During April Liberal papers began to join the critical chorus; and on 20 April, as will be recounted, Asquith made a damaging mistake.

---

[1] On the same day *The Times* announced: 'The country has courage; the government apparently has not'; and the *Morning Post*, reviewing recent failures concluded: 'Only under the rule of a *roi fainéant* could the offences have come.'

[2] G. A. Riddell, *War Diary* (1933), p. 65.

373

My own most beloved & most dear, when I got back here I found your darling letter: I cannot tell you in any words what a blow it is to me not to see you this afternoon. I have built so many hopes & desires upon it. And, tho' I quite recognise your arguments as to the expediency of listening to Lord Kn., and am *quite* sure that you were absolutely right, as you always are in matters of judgment (and many others), I feel like some one who has had his day turned suddenly from possible sunshine into assured & unrelieved darkness.

How I mind it! I loved the last sentences in your dear letter in wh. I thought & knew that you felt the same.

It is especially sad to me to-day, because I longed above everything to talk to you frankly & fully about the strange & new situation wh. is now being evolved.

There is, as you see in the Tory press, a dead set being made against me personally. Witness the articles in *The Times* & the *Morning Post*.

As you know, I am fairly indifferent to press criticism. I honestly don't care one damn about that. McKenna came to see me just before lunch, with a tragic history of intrigue. The idea is that Northcliffe (for some unknown reason) has been engineering a campaign to supplant me by Ll. G! M^cK is of course quite certain that Ll. G, & perhaps Winston are 'in it'. Which I don't believe. However, he (M^cK) has a certain amount of evidence as to Ll. G to go upon. I can't write it down, wh. makes me the more irritated that we couldn't have had our drive & talk this afternoon. For, as you know well, yours is my best & most trusted opinion.

I lunched with the Assyrian, *tête à tête*, and his loyalty is a certain & invaluable asset. Of course he is rather anti-M^cK, whom he suspects as a mischief maker.

I asked him what wd happen if the so-called 'intrigue' were to come off, & I was supposed to go. He replied without a moment's hesitation that the *whole* Cabinet, including Ll. G. & Winston, would go with me, & make any alternative impossible.

This gave me pleasure, as I am sure it will you, my most darling & precious. Aren't you rather glad that I who have given my whole soul & life to you, should be assured that all these men, mostly clever & able, all thoroughly competent, should after an experience in some cases of 10, in almost all of 7 years, be prepared to sacrifice everything personal or political for your true & devoted lover? . . .

I have determined to take over the F.O.[1] after Grey leaves on this Wed:

with fitful visits to the Wharf. So we might do something: it means that I shall be in or near London. . . .

¹ The negotiations with Italy were still at a delicate stage.

374

Monday 29 March 15 [ii] *7 p.m.*

. . . Since I wrote I have had two really very interesting interviews: indeed three. The first was with, of all persons in the world, Katharine, who is very much perturbed about Raymond & his immediate future. I summoned E. Grey, Bongie, & Hankey into Council with her: and we came to the sage, tho' not very exciting, conclusion that for the moment he shd. go on here with his battalion & take his musketry course; in the hope (wh. Hankey thinks quite possible) that the transfer of one or more of Willcocks's existing staff to the Dardanelles will make a natural vacancy for him.¹

SIR EDWARD GREY
(Punch)

After that, I had a talk of some length with E. Grey (who by the way – so the Assyrian informs me – has played Bridge in those silken & well warmed tents for the last 3 successive nights till 1. a.m, but who is, nevertheless, so jaded with the pressure of work, that he is going off on Wed. night, for a fortnight's salmon fishing. I don't say this the least ill-naturedly: for he both deserves & absolutely needs the change).

The Italians are (he tells me) slightly contracting the orifice of their wide & greedy mouth, & wd. now be content to neutralise the Dalmatian coast from Spalato southwards (wh. means that it wd. effectively belong to Serbia) provided they can keep & fortify the outlying islands. The Russians are still on the haggle, & it is not likely that any final agreement will be reached before Wednesday. In the circumstances I told him (for it is rather a critical situation) that I wd. take on the Foreign Office work, instead of either Haldane or Crewe, for at any rate a week or 8 days i.e. until we go to Walmer on Friday in next week. This was a great relief to him, & he was as nearly warm as it is natural to him to be in his acknowledgements.

Finally, I had an extraordinary & really very interesting talk with Ll. George. (I told you in my earlier letter of McKenna's visit, & his & Montagu's views about the supposed 'intrigue'.) We first tried to get at a working arrangement with Kitchener about the munitions committee &c, and I think we hit upon something that ought to do. Then, before he left, I said I thought it right to tell him that, only to-day, I had heard the sinister and, as I believed, absurd interpretations wh. were being given to the articles in *The Times, Observer, Morning Post* &c. I have never seen him more moved. He made a most bitter onslaught on McKenna whom he believes, thro' his animosity against Winston,[2] to be the villain of the piece & the principal mischief-maker. He vehemently disclaimed having anything to do with the affair: Kitchener, he said, is the real culprit because, in spite of every warning, he has neglected up to the 11th hour a proper provision of munitions: & K. being a Tory, or supposed to be one, the Tory press, afraid to attack him, are making me the target of their criticism. As for himself (Ll. G) he declared that he owed everything to me; that I had stuck to him & protected him & defended him when every man's hand was against him; and that he wd rather (1) break stones (2) dig potatoes (3) be hanged & quartered (these were metaphors used at different stages of his broken but impassioned harangue) than do an act, or say a word, or harbour a thought, that was disloyal to me. And he said that every one of our colleagues felt the same. His eyes were wet with tears, and I am sure that, with all his Celtic capacity for impulsive & momentary fervour, he was quite sincere.

I wish you had been (as *Huck* once was) secreted *perdue* behind a screen. It would have interested, & I think touched, you a good deal. Of course, I assured him that I had never for a moment doubted him – wh. is quite true: & he warmly wrung my hand & abruptly left the room. Darling, does that interest you?

(The suspicious Assyrian thinks that A.J.B. has had a hand in this silly & malicious business.). . .

---

[1] When on his way to the Front in Oct. 1915 Raymond told Katharine of the 'loathing and contempt' of the regimental officers for those on the staff. If she could hear the former talk, he added, she would not regret that he had not applied for the staff, 'though, of course, one may

find in the end that there are more uncomfortable things than general abuse': John Jolliffe, *Raymond Asquith* (1980), p. 205.

[2] I.e. McKenna's animosity. For McKenna's resentment over his supersession at the Admiralty see Letter 284, text and nn. 5–6.

375

Tues 30 March 15 [i]

. . . We have just finished our Cabinet: the Italian thing still hangs fire owing to the difficulties raised by Russia, but it looks rather more promising than it did some days ago. Kitchener returned last night from his visit to Joffre, wh. went off pleasantly enough. It is impossible to get the French Generals & Staff to look at anything but their own trenches & what lies in front of them. As soon as their ammunition is in full supply they are going in concert with French to make a great push, and seem to be quite confident that they can drive the Germans back to the Meuse.[1] There was a great discussion as to the desirability of prohibiting the sale of alcohol, or at any rate of spirits & wine, during the war. There is no doubt that opinion is moving that way, tho' the cost in loss of revenue & in necessary compensations to the trade would be enormous. One of the quaintest results of the anti-drink campaign, & the King's 'close-cellar' policy, is that Margot (of all people) is violently hostile, and full of compassion for the drinkless workers, and of indignation against those who 'would rob a poor man of his beer'.[2] The unhappy Assyrian is reported by Bongie & Eliz[th], who saw him this morning, to be in real distress of mind about his banquet on Thursday, where Ll.G. is to be one of the guests. To drink or not to drink? . . .

I had a small conclave here this morning – K, Winston, myself, & Hankey – to go over carefully & quickly the situation, actual & prospective, at the Dardanelles. There are risks, & it will in any event be an expensive operation, but I am sure we are right to go through with it.[3]

This is the really critical month of the war; an actual equilibrium, with perhaps a slight turn in favour of the allies: the possible belligerents (Italy, Greece, Bulgaria, Roumania) all hanging in the balance; everyone anxious about their own & their opponents' supplies of ammunition: and so much depending upon whether the coin turns up Heads or Tails at the Dardanelles.

If all (or most) of these doubtful hazards go well for us, the war ought to be over in 3 months. But we have had little, & ought not to count on more, of the favours of fortune: so all one can do is to possess one's soul in patience. . . .

The most serious thing I have done to-day is to try to compose the Kitch[r] – Ll. G. dispute about the new Committee. I think I shall probably succeed – particularly as L.G. is now 'off' thinking of nothing but drink, & K. is preoccupied with shells! . . .

. . . I sent you a telegram this morning that Lord K.[4] had sent in your name. I now enclose his letter. I am sure you will bristle with pride & self-complacency at the words wh. I have underlined. Who is the 'Matron in Chief of the Army Nursing' to whom he alludes? If there is still any difficulty (wh. I doubt) one might exercise a little influence upon her.

We have just finished lunch, where were E. Grey, the Assyrian, the Bud, Barbara M[c]L, & poor unfortunate Sir Berkeley Milne.[5] With the last I talked a lot about the Dardanelles, wh. of course he knows very well. It is one of the most tragic things in life to see a man who, having come very nearly to the top of his profession, at the critical moment, perhaps more from ill-luck than incompetence, broke down. The Assyrian gave me a fairly picturesque account of how he spent 3 hours of last evening in the domestic tent, celebrating with his family, under the priestly headship of Ld Swaythling,[6] the Passover. It seems quite out of drawing; but Dizzy was not far wrong when he proclaimed the enduring ascendancy of Race.[7] . . .

[1] For the French attack, 9 May, in Artois see Letter 255, n. 2. In this sector the Allies had not reached the Meuse by 11 Nov. 1918.

[2] The King's offer 'to set an example by giving up all alcoholic liquor himself and issuing orders against its consumption in the Royal Household' had been conveyed to the cabinet that day in a letter to Lloyd George. It was gratefully accepted, Lloyd George replying that, if this pledge were made public 'all classes', he was certain, 'would hasten to follow the lead thus given by the Sovereign'. The newspapers announced 'the King's pledge' on 1 Apr. Margot Asquith was personally abstemious, and periodically anxious about the intemperance, as she saw it, of various relatives and friends. Her opposition on class grounds to the prohibition scheme is a good example of her acute, though highly erratic, political sense.

[3] De Robeck's message to Churchill, 28 Mar., represented the virtual abandonment of a largely naval attempt on the Dardanelles:

I now think it possible there may be minefields above the Narrows of which we know very little . . . Of course there will still be the howitzers which are so difficult to locate from the sea. In my opinion Gallipoli Peninsula will have to be taken and held by land force before Dardanelles can be passed with certainty by capital ships fitted to deal with *Goeben* and by the colliers and other vessels without which the utility of capital ships is very limited.

[4] Knutsford.

[5] Sir Berkeley Milne's conduct as C.-in-C. Mediterranean was the subject of an Admiralty inquiry when the *Goeben* and *Breslau* escaped to Constantinople (Letter 122). His 'dispositions and measures' were approved, the blame being placed on his subordinate; and this finding was published. He was relieved of his command, however, and, in spite of Margot Asquith's pleas to Churchill, not re-employed.

[6] Montagu's elder brother, the head of the family, and of the merchant bank, Samuel Montagu and Co., since their father's death in 1911.

[7] For 'all is race' see Letter 281, n. 6.

376

Tues. 30 March 1915 [ii] 6 p.m.

My darling – the Queen's visit[1] is just over, having lasted the best part of an hour. She was pleased & interested in what we had to show of the house wh. she hadn't seen since Mr Gladstone's days, and she has an excellent sense of humour. She examined all the blotting books of the different Ministers in the Cabinet room, which are full for the most part of rather crude drawings (especially Ll. George's), and when she came to one that was absolutely blank she remarked 'Here is a man who pays attention.' Whose do you think it was? McKinnon Wood's! A pretty good shot, as he hardly ever utters. Unfortunately she is now deafer than any two posts.

I told you I was going to have an interview *à trois* with Ll. G. & M^{c}K. So they came here at 3.30 and we had an hour together. It was as you may imagine at moments 'rather' exciting. L.G. began on a very stormy note, accusing M^{c}K of having inspired Donald[2] to write the article in the *Chronicle* wh. was headed 'Intrigue agst the P.M', and in one sentence of which (only one) his name was mentioned. M^{c}K as hotly denied that he had ever said or suggested to Donald that Ll. G. was in the 'plot', while admitting that he had had a talk with him on the subject of the attacks in the Tory press. Ll. G. proceeded to accuse M^{c}K of always seeing imaginary plots: e.g. in this very matter, Winston's supposed campaign against Grey. To wh. M^{c}K rejoined that the person he really suspected was A.J.B, with whom we all agreed Winston was much too intimate. There was a lot of hitting & counter-hitting between them, but I am glad to say that in the end I not only lowered the temperature, but got them into first an accommodating & in the end an almost friendly mood. I told them that I was absolutely certain none of my colleagues was otherwise than perfectly loyal: that the use of the word 'Intrigue' instead of 'Attack' was calculated to suggest a movement against me from *within* rather than from without; and that while M^{c}K. never meant that *that* shd. be conveyed to the world, it was not unnatural that Ll. G. shd have thought otherwise, and even imagined that he was pointed to as the supposed traitor. And so on – you can well imagine the kind of thing. It was at first & for some time a thoroughly disagreeable interview, wh. I do not wish to go through again, but the sky gradually cleared, and the result shows that it is (as I think) always wise to have these things 'out' at once & not allow the personal virus to curdle, or get inflamed, by suppression, or half-hearted approaches at compromise.

I have now got to perform a similar, but I hope easier, operation as between K. & Ll. G. in the matter of the Munitions Committee.

So I don't for the moment sleep quite on a bed of roses.

I cannot tell you, my best beloved, how wise I thought all that you said in your letter to-day on these subjects: especially in reference to the personal qualities of Winston & M^{c}K. Your intuition never fails you, and there is *no* colleague whose judgment I trust so much. . . .

. . . Do you hear that Geoffrey Howard has an 'affair' with Miss Kitty Methuen, ex-charmer of S. Africa,[3] wh. some people think means business. I once spent a Sat to Mond. with her: she is pretty, experienced, and has a good deal of a kind of attraction, tho' not for me. I am going to close this now & post it myself – so as to get a breath of air: I have not been for a moment out of the house to-day and feel rather heavy about the head. . . .

[1] Queen Alexandra: see Letter 363. 'She was', Asquith wrote on her death, 'the one royalty I really loved.'

[2] Robert Donald, Editor, *Daily Chronicle*, 1902–18.

[3] Her father, Field Marshal Lord Methuen, had held the military command in South Africa, 1908–12. For the occasion on which Asquith met her see Letter 4.

377

Tu. 30 March 1915 [iii] 11.30 p.m.

. . . I had a most characteristic letter from Winston, just before dinner. He said he had refused Ll. G's invitation to come to our interview this afternoon: because (as he said) 'I feel that my case is safe in your hands'. That bears out what you said in your most darling letter – that (whatever happens) W. is really loyal to me. I am sure, & have never doubted, that he is. So that silly 'plot' is done with. . . .

. . . Your letter to-day has made a new man of me. I shall always remember it, because it came just at a moment when I was beginning to be a little doubtful about myself.

Not for the first, or the tenth time, you have re-adjusted my point of view, re-created my fading resolves, and given me new confidence & life.

I bless & adore you: and all my life is yours. Dearest & best, good night. *Your own.*

378

Tu 30 March 1915 [iv] nearly 1 a.m.

My darling – I didn't tell you in any of my numerous letters to-day about one really dramatic moment in my interview with Ll. G. & M^{c}K. They were getting very *acharnés*[1] – bandying charges, & apparently quite irreconcilable. I was, I confess, rather disgusted, and inclined to chuck the whole thing (for the moment). So I said, sitting in the chair wh. I always occupy at the Cabinet: 'Very well: in another week I shall have sat in this chair for 7 years. If I have the slightest reason to think that there is anyone among you who has even the faintest doubt or suspicion about me, I will gladly (for what have I to gain or lose?) abandon this chair, & never sit in it again.' I wish you cd. have seen them! Their mutual anger dissolved like a frost under a sudden thaw: and they both with a united voice exclaimed: 'The day you leave that chair, the rest of us disappear, never to return!' And I am sure they meant it. Wasn't it rather a fine moment for me? And I said to myself (this ought to make you realise what you are) Would God, that my darling was here! She might then take a measure of what she means & is & will always be to me.

I only tell you this (not as you know out of vanity) because I like you to know that in every crisis of my life the thought & love of you dominates everything else.[2] . . .

[1] Heated, embattled.
[2] Beaverbrook described this incident in *Politicians and the War* (1928), i. 149, as if it occurred at least two months later, after the formation of the coalition.

379

Wed 31 March 1915 [i]

My darling – I sent you this morning a little pencil letter wh. I wrote late last night. I hope you will get it before evening, for it will tell you that I was thinking of you. One incidental drawback – among many – of the way in which you spent Monday afternoon is that I never got my *flower*. Did you remember that yesterday was the anniversary of my taking over the War Office? I shall never forget the heavenly letter I got from you (you were at Alderley) that morning. It is sweet of you darling to wish that I shd. take them all in turn, tho' I don't myself much fancy a few weeks spent at the Post Office or the Local Government Board. I had a foretaste of what is to come this morning, when I spent the best part of an hour with Grey & Imperiali at the F.O. The Italians have abated or at any rate softened down some of their demands about the Dalmatian coast, but the Russians are still obdurate & precious time is being lost. I think I said to you yesterday that we may be driven to playing our last diplomatic card – a personal message from the King to the Czar.

Did I tell you that the King is going to announce that during the war he will banish alcohol from his table? It will be curious to see how far his example will be followed.[1] The Doctors will have quite a busy time in giving certificates of exemption 'on grounds of health'. Ll. George informs me that Winston & the Assyrian have already declared that they shall apply for them. . . .

Later. 3 p.m. No letter yet! but I still hope it will come. We have had a curious luncheon party. . . . Dear old Morley was in quite good form: not the least bitter or superior, and we made a compact that if, in the coming revival of Puritan austerity, we are all ostensibly driven to soda-water and ginger beer, he will see that his villa at Wimbledon is kept as a house of ease & reasonable indulgence. He only stipulated that it should not be open to *all* his & my late colleagues. I fancy he wd. exclude the whole lot, with perhaps about 4 exceptions. I suspect that he is busily engaged in writing his memoirs,[2] wh. ought to be very good reading, tho' some people I have known & know will appear in very lurid colours.

I can't quite make out your plan of life my darling to-day – whether you were free morning or afternoon. . . . But I still have hopes of to-morrow. We are dining with Maud Cunard to-night: to which I don't much look forward. Puffin will arrive in a few minutes, to begin his Easter holidays.

[1] Asquith was shortly to receive a telegram from his son Arthur (Oc), sent on behalf of the Naval Division: 'Reported spread of temperance alarms and amazes us. Stand fast.' Haldane followed the King's lead, apparently to the detriment of his health.

[2] Morley's *Recollections* were published in 2 vols. in 1917, and his *Memorandum on Resignation* after his death.

380

Wed 31 March 15 [ii] after midnight

My darling – I am in a rather depressed mood to-night, mainly I think (& know) because I have not heard from you to-day. I expect you were in great difficulties about writing: otherwise I know I shd have had a letter. I have also just begun to struggle with the F.O boxes – no light matter. And no sooner had I settled the row between Ll. G & M^cK over the 'plot', & all but settled the earlier row between LG & K, than this versatile & volatile personage goes off at score on the question of drink, about wh. he has completely lost his head. His mind apparently oscillates from hour to hour between the two poles of absurdity: cutting off all drink from the working man, wh. wd. lead to something like a universal strike; and buying out (at this moment of all others) the whole liquor trade of the country, and replacing it by a huge State monopoly, wh. wd ruin our finances & create a vast engine of possible corruption. He is a wonderful person in some ways, but is totally devoid of either perspective or judgment: and on the whole during these 7 years he has given me more worry than any other colleague.

So you see, darling, I am in especial need at the moment of your 'steadying hand' & 'healing breath' – if I may quote from a 'poet', whose works are only known to you & me.[1]

We dined at a restaurant with Maud Cunard, under conditions which both you & I dislike. There were lots of good elements – A.J.B., Cust, Frances Horner, Hugh &c &c. but the result . . . was chaotic & unsatisfying. I sat next Diana Manners, with whom I had a good talk. . . .

[1] See Letter 291.

381

Thurs. 1 Ap 15 [i] 3 p.m.

. . . To-morrow I shall come for you at the Admiralty at 3. I am not at all sure that I shan't have to come here both Sat & Sunday for some part of the day at any rate. So *do* think if we couldn't get together somehow, either of those days. This is one of the possible compensations for taking over the F.O. You looked very well, & I observed that the dactyls[1] were in almost suspiciously good condition. Of course, I would have gone back with you to M. St. & to the prison, but for my beastly pre-occupations.

I rather wish you could have again played the part of Huck, & been in this room during the deputations. There were (in what you called the prayer-meeting) no less than 25 editors of 'leading' London papers: such a cohort of possible mischief-makers has rarely been assembled under the same roof.[2] On the other hand, I had in my *zareeba* a formidable phalanx: Kitchener, Winston, McKenna, Buckmaster & some others. They (the deputation) developed & dwelt upon all the grievances of the Press since the war broke out: optimism, concealment, & the rest. Their spokesmen were Harry Lawson,[3] Spender, & Donald of the *Chronicle*. I had to improvise a reply, & tho' it was not good I think it perhaps served its purpose: I say this because not only K., but Winston himself, refused to add anything. I won't bore you with details, but in effect I told them there were two kinds of 'optimism': (1) *true*, wh. meant confidence in our cause & its ultimate success, however the tide of fortune ebbed or flowed from day to day: to wh. I pleaded guilty (2) *false*, wh. means blinding your own eyes & other people's to the actual realities & prospects of the situation, and, in that temper, doctoring or manipulating the facts: wh. I repudiated. We had, I think, & both K & Winston agreed, a real clearance of the air; and in the end we buried all hatchets, & started a new era of 'confidence & co-partnership', on the basis that the newspapers should concentrate & appoint one Super-Press-Man, who can always come on their behalf to see me, or K, or Winston. Altogether a well-spent hour. Then I had interviews with Bluey & the Impeccable, who both came to lunch. What would or wouldn't I give to be able to see you in the intervals of the day, & talk over things as they arise! Fate is a fiend! Simon Lovat (recovered)[4] & Laura & Edgar also came to lunch.

My F.O. things thicken around me, & as soon as I have finished this I have to have interviews with Imperiali (whom Winston calls the Ice-Cream man)[5] & Cambon. I can see that the right thing for the moment is to put all the pressure one can on the Italians rather than on the Russians, whose position is *au fond* reasonable. I don't really mind this addition to my labours: there is a lot of interest of a kind about it; and, unless I can be with you, I may just as well, or better, be in the workshop. (I wish Bongie wdn't come in every 2 minutes, instead of accumulating his stuff.)

Darling, I will if I can write to you later so that you will get something to-morrow morning. *Don't* for God's sake disappoint me in the aft. Do you realise how little I have seen of you for a whole week – of you who are the light & centre & supreme blessing of all I do & of all I am. *Boundless* love.

[1] The Greek word for fingers.
[2] For the genesis of this meeting see Letter 372.
[3] His father had founded the *Daily Telegraph*; and he had been its managing proprietor since 1903.
[4] He was then commanding the Highland Mounted Brigade. Invalided home with dysentery soon after the Brigade reached the Dardanelles, he became Director of Forestry in the B.E.F., Feb. 1917.
[5] The manufacture and sale of ice-cream were then largely in Italian hands.

382

Thurs. 1 April 1915 [ii] 7.15 p.m.

My darling – haven't I often said to you that one never gets to the end of human nature? In this very room, in which only two days ago Ll. G. & M^cK were fighting like fish-wives, in the interview wh. I described to you, the same pair have just been and spent over ½ an hour with me, cooing like sucking doves in a concerted chorus of argument and appeal, to bring me round to take a favourable view of Ll. G's latest scheme for buying out the drink trade at a cost of some 250 millions! You never saw two people on such friendly & even intimate terms, or in such complete & happy accord. Isn't it a good reason for not taking *short* views either of people or things?

I am bound to say that they left me entirely unconvinced, and indeed neither of them has had time to think out even the elements of the problem.

Upon one point we were all agreed – that it is not the least use even bringing such a proposition before the Cabinet in these days, unless you are first reasonably sure that you will get the support of the Tories,[1] the bulk of the Temperance people, & the Labour party. Ll. G., whose sanguine temper is never easily daunted, is accordingly going to utilise his Easter holidays in a daring attempt to 'nobble' & reconcile all these warring interests.

I spent most of the afternoon at the F.O. & saw in turn the Italian French & Russian Ambassadors. I had a stiff argument with the Italian, who was afraid to concede anything, to persuade him (in gentle terms) that his greedy country was being offered by the Allies far more than she had any right to expect, and ought to be well content without asking for more. I am disposed to think that they will give way, tho' I pressed Benck. to make it easier for them, at the last moment, by dropping a not very important Russian requirement. . . .

11 p.m. I have just come back from Clemmie's birthday party. You didn't lose very much by not being there, tho' it was quite 'nice'. The Bud, Anne Islington, Alex Thynne (a thundering bore),[2] Masterton Smith, Basil Blackwood,[3] &c. The Bud is divided between her engagement to your Hospital, and a desire to sit in a factory & make fuses for shells, in which she has been encouraged by Lord Moulton,[4] whom she met last night at dinner. I told her that, in my opinion, the fabrication of fuses in a crowded room of women & girls would be more monotonous in the long run, & not more useful, than even your 'Charrington' & 'Milward'.[5] She is rather difficult to measure – not that there is *very* much, according to any standard . . . as the American said of Evan,[6] she 'has no message for me'. . . .

[1] Bonar Law wanted to free the Conservative party 'from the incubus of being tied to the [drink] trade, which has done us far more harm than good', and he thought that Lloyd George's scheme would be 'a great reform'. He told Lloyd George, 7 Apr.:

If the information in possession of the government causes them to decide that it is necessary for the successful prosecution of the war that the state should take over the production and distribution of alcohol with adequate compensation to the existing interests we shall not as a party oppose the proposal.

Robert Blake, *The Unknown Prime Minister* (1955), p. 239.

[2] Brother of the 5th Marquess of Bath; Conservative M.P. for Bath since Jan. 1910; killed in action, 1918.

[3] Brother of the 2nd Marquess of Dufferin and Ava; had been wounded, Oct. 1914; killed in action, 1917.

[4] Great patent lawyer; Lord of Appeal in Ordinary, 1912; presided over committee organizing manufacture of high explosives and propellants and created Explosives Supply Department.

[5] The two wards in the London Hospital in which Venetia served. For Charrington see Letter 250, n. 1. Milward had been opened in 1831 and named after a benefactor.

[6] Probably Evan Charteris of the Parliamentary Bar; an uncle of Lady Cynthia, 'Beb' Asquith's wife.

383

Fr. 2 Ap 1915

My own beloved – something (wh. rarely happens) went a little wrong this afternoon: I am sure it was my fault & not yours. I am *so* sorry, & forgive me, if I was to blame. You were very sweet at the end of our drive; and I hope to-morrow will be possible.

You will, at any rate, wire to me here to-morrow Sat. morning: and if you can, come to lunch.

If that is impossible, try to suggest something for Sunday.

I am just starting with Violet for the Wharf in a (to me for the moment) congenial atmosphere of wind & rain.

Do reassure me, life of my life. Otherwise –

All my heart's love. Yr.

XIII

E.S.M. to B.V.S

2 April 1915

What has happened?

I felt as you must have been aware that our last meeting left me very forelorn [*sic*] about the great adventure I dream of – still. . . .

Can you lunch tomorrow?

XIV

E.S.M. to B.V.S.

Treasury Chambers,
Whitehall, S.W.

[3 April 1915][1]

Venetia, very dearest of women,

           I don't see how I can get up from Wharf tomorrow. P.M. etc. will want to know reason and I can't very well in the circumstances you permit, tell them. *Unless you send* for me! But *please* be at my house as near 6.30 as possible and *wire to tell me to come* – that's what I want! I want you to ask me to come and I'll find a way.

Indeed my Venetia we must have a tremendous talk again and that at once, for I find my life quite frightful and I want to urge an effort.

Remember I have your promise that I shall not be 'Hugh-ed'.[2] I rely on that and can wait for ever. But I really can't without some talk put up with what Hugh never had to put up with, the presence of the P.M.

Can you possibly expect me to go on being allowed to see you only when he is not free and refused either interview or speech or message except when he is busy or away.

I dreamed of a gradual ending of this but I am told you are getting more an element than ever in his life – the thing is taking up more of his time than ever – and all the time I've got to wait!

You drove yesterday, you lunch today, you could not even let me know when I might see you till you saw what he wanted and I am allowed 6.30 tomorrow because he won't be in London.

I want him to have fun – no fun can be like being with you – but can a lover *who means business* put up with it. I hope you won't forget I dreamed the dream afresh because you said *you* had altered your view, and *you* fanned the hopes anew where they had been stifled.

Don't think I blame you or reproach you. I had rather suffer twenty thousand times as much as never hope at all. But I want now that you should put an end to the restraints on your liberty.

You may say 'I can't do this for you' 'You don't attract me sufficiently'. So be it then do it for yourself. Take the only steps which will enable you to look out on the various projects in life which present themselves as a free agent and stop a state of affairs where you can do nothing without first seeing what effect it has on a relationship you are too slack to end.

I wouldn't mind if I didn't see in that relationship, unsatisfaction for you and trouble for him, absorption [?] and possibly loss of grip eventually.

I love him; I have every reason to: but I believe I write in his interests.

As for you, Venetia this letter ought to show I am just mad sleepless, frantic for you and want to see daylight.

So let's have a talk. Wire me Wharf, when!

Yours through all devotedly
Ed. S. Montagu

---

[1] The original is lost and the copy made for Mrs Gendel has no date. The internal evidence strongly suggests 3 Apr.

[2] To be 'Hugh-ed' was to be kept dangling indefinitely and then rejected, this being the fate which Hugh Godley was held to have suffered at Violet's hands. See Letters 74, n. 2; XXVIII, (p. 565).

384

The Wharf.

Easter Sunday 4 Ap 15

My own darling, My solitary drive back to Downing St was in the company of heavenly memories: you were never more sweet or sincere; and the little cloudlet of the day before was quite dispersed. I shall count yesterday's as one of our *Friday* drives: so as to keep the record quite perfect. I did a little F.O. business and then bowled down here at double quick time in Dunn's Rolls Royce. The Assyrian had already arrived and Evan Charteris came before dinner. He has been most of the time with the flying men at the front, and has interesting things to report. With R & Kath & V & Eliz^th we made quite a 'nice' little party. If only you were here!

When I got to my bedroom at night I started the 'Chapter of Autobiography', wh. I promised you & in wh. you seemed to be interested. I send you, just as a sample, the first section, which brings one up to the critical moment . . .

We have had a glut of presents this morning, as the garden was strewn with Easter eggs of various colours & sizes, in wh. Puffin had concealed all manner of small luxuries, including a dagger for Katharine, and a beautiful tie for me. We had quite an arduous hunt & some of the eggs are supposed to be still undiscovered. . . .

. . . I am cudgelling my brains to discover some bridge over the gap between Italian greed & Russian suspicion. . . .

It is just noon, and for seclusion in this tiny house, I am writing in my bedroom where I have just been visited by Katharine. I told her that Hankey who is spending this Sunday at the front, was keeping his eyes open to discover, if possible, a suitable staff place for Raymond.[1] Then we looked over my little stock of books together and had a very pleasant desultory talk. Amongst other things, I asked her what she thought about the Resurrection associated with this festival in the Calendar: she said her ideas on the subject were rather fluid, and with a view to crystallising them she has taken off Butler's *Fair Haven*[2] & is now reading it in the garden. She is a most attractive creature when really known, and I am very fond of her, and (I think) she of me. . . .

My darling – if I ever seem to you either touchy or exigent, you mustn't misunderstand it. I love you with my whole soul – and *always* shall.

[1] When Raymond was finally manoeuvred by his father and others into a G.H.Q. post in

Jan. 1916 he was much chagrined. After a few months he returned to regimental duty with the Grenadier Guards and was killed in the Somme Battle on 15 Sept. 1916. See John Jolliffe, *Raymond Asquith: Life and Letters* (1980), p. 235–96.

[2] By Samuel Butler (1835–1902), an ironical examination of the miraculous elements in Christian doctrine. The 1st edn. (1873) was anonymous. Butler had studied for the Anglican priesthood, and had become sceptical about these elements in the doctrine while doing so. Katharine Asquith later became a Roman Catholic.

385

Chapter of Autobiography

I knew what an angel of comfort and help she had shown herself to Violet. In the second general election of that year (Nov and Dec 1910) she and Violet and I had great 'fun' together travelling about to meetings, the occasion I best remember being our visit to Bluey's constituency of Accrington,[1] and our evening afterwards in the grim and frost-bitten atmosphere of Shuttleworth at Gawthorpe.[2]

So things went on, with long intervals of absence and separation; but always, when we came together again, we resumed, without effort, as though it had never been broken off, the old delightful attitude of true companionship. The only new things I noticed in particular were her interest in and knowledge of poetry, and her really remarkable memory, not only for words, but for things and places.

This first stage of our intimacy (in which there was not a touch of romance, and hardly of sentiment) came to its climax when I went to Sicily with Montagu as a companion, I think at the end of 1911 or beginning of 1912. Violet and Venetia joined us there, and we had together one of the most interesting and delightful fortnights in all our lives.

It was when we had got back to England, and I was spending most of my Sundays in the late winter and early spring at a house lent to me on the outskirts of the New Forest[3] (I remember it was on the eve of the Coal Strike, which gave me one of the most trying experiences – up to then – of my public life)[4] that she came down with us for the usual 'week-end'.

I was sitting with her in the dining room on Sunday morning – the others being out in the garden or walking – and we were talking and laughing just on our old accustomed terms. Suddenly, in a single instant, without premonition on my part or any challenge on hers, the scales dropped from my eyes; the familiar features & smile & gestures & words assumed an absolutely new perspective; what had been completely hidden from me was in a flash half-revealed, and I dimly felt, hardly knowing, not at all understanding it, that I had come to a turning point in my life.[5]

[1] For this visit to Accrington and Burnley see Letter 201, n. 3.

2 Lord Shuttleworth's house near Burnley.
3 Hurstly, Boldre, near Lymington. See Appendix 3.
4 Sunday, 25 Feb. 1912. The coal strike began at midnight, 29 Feb.
5 For another reference to this 'revelation' see Letter 305.

386

Monday 5 Ap 1915

. . . I wrote some more [Autobiography] late last night which brings the 'Confessions' (you see I am treading in the footsteps of St Augustine & Rousseau) down to a certain date in the spring of 1912 when you came for a night to Ewelme:¹ which perhaps you have forgotten but I never forget. So you notice that I didn't make much progress in the matter of time. I find that as I go on, it is all so woven in with the texture of my whole life, that there is constant danger of prolixity & digression, and of losing for a moment or more the main thread. Do you understand this? When I left off, I was fast approaching the visit to Penrhos² on our way to the *first* Dublin meeting (July '12). . . .

I rejoiced to find your darling letter waiting for me here: tho' I hope it won't be the *last* from the Hospital: surely between now & Wed. there is ·time for *one* more.

I note that you get your release on Wed. morn. I know you can't dine here, but couldn't I see you before dinner at M'field St, or the Admiralty? You know how I *long* to . . .

. . . On the whole I don't believe you cd. have spent these 3 particular months under more tolerable & satisfying conditions, and you easily might under less. From a purely selfish point of view I find that I regret them less than I expected. True, I have not seen nearly enough of you, but a good deal more than I should have done if you had been at Alderley. We have had divine drives every week, and letters more frequent & intimate – and, so far as yours are concerned, more delicious in every way – than ever before. . . .

Don't forget that you drive down with me to Walmer on Friday. I particularly want to show you the country between Maidstone & Canterbury, wh. I don't think you know. . . .

. . . The Italians are still holding out for their 1½ lb. of flesh, but I do not mean to give them up, particularly now that it is clear that Roumania will be inclined to hang back until they definitely come in. The delay in the Dardanelles is very unfortunate: visible progress, and still more a theatrical coup, in that quarter would have goaded all the laggard States including Greece & Bulgaria into the arena. Meanwhile the Bulgarians, by way of a little fun, have been raiding the Greek & Serbian frontiers. It doesn't seem, however, to be a very serious affair. I begin to think that – if one could be completely detached from domestic politics – the F.O. would be an interesting & congenial job; there is such a lot of variety about it, even in the piping times of peace. I prefer it vastly to my last experimental *démarche* – the W.O. Happily I have Eric Drummond at hand. I forget which are the others in which you fancied I might find occasional diversion: I think it was the Colonies and India? . . .

. . . I am just come (in the Autobiog.) to the stage in our drives when we began to talk not only of persons & books but of things, & of my interests, politics &c; and I began to acquire the habit, first of taking you into confidence, & then of consulting & relying on your judgment.[3] It seems odd that that should have had a *beginning*: so natural and inevitable does it now appear to be. But no one would have guessed it. Darling try to write me a *line* (it need not be more) to-morrow – a last line from behind your iron bars. *My love*, I live for you. . . .

[1] See p. 2.
[2] He stayed one night at Penrhos before speaking in Dublin on 19 July.
[3] This part of the 'Autobiography' has not survived.

387

Tu. 6 Ap 15 [ii] 11.15 p.m.

. . . I want to send you one last line – Jan 6 to Ap 6 – after these three months, to reach you, if possible, before you shake the dust off your feet to-morrow morning.[1]

I have poured an incessant stream of letters in upon you. And you have been more than angelic in writing to me. I feel as if a phase of our two-fold life was going to be closed down. And, as always happens when one chapter comes to an end, one speculates, with both hope and fear, where we shall be at the end of the next.

You know well where I shall be.

I had a hopeful talk with Imperiali at the F.O. this afternoon, and I am much more sanguine than I was 24 hours ago about Italy. It would be a great reward for a week or 10 days at the F.O. if that could be brought off – wouldn't it, most beloved? . . .

[1] Venetia was leaving the London Hospital at the end of her training.

388

Foreign Office

Wed 7 Ap. 1915

. . . I have had some talk here with Nicolson, who is delighted with the turn which the Italian negotiations are taking. Sazonoff[1] in his last message says in effect that he will leave the question of 'neutralisation' to me.[2]. . .

Hankey has just been in: very anxious about the Dardanelles,[3] which he says Robertson (Chief of French's staff) describes as the stiffest operation anyone cd. undertake. Now that things look better with Italy & Roumania, Hankey strongly urges postponement – lest a check there shd. set back the whole situation. There is a great deal of force in this: what do you think? I am disposed to say that, before any landing is attempted, we shd. get from Sir I. Hamilton on the spot a considered review of the prospects. It is one of the cases in which military & diplomatic considerations are completely intertwined. . . .

[1] Russian Minister for Foreign Affairs, 1910–16.
[2] The Italians were willing to see southern Dalmatia allocated to Serbia provided it was 'neutralized'.
[3] At an informal meeting of the War Council on 6 Apr., attended by Asquith, Churchill, and Kitchener, Hankey maintained that a landing at Gallipoli would be extremely hazardous, against Churchill who 'anticipated no difficulty' in effecting one. On 8 Apr., urged by Balfour, Churchill agreed that it would be best to conclude the agreement with Italy before mounting the Gallipoli assault, and that it would be permissible to postpone the landings for a week to allow this.

389

8 Ap. 1915. [i]

. . . I remember, as if it were yesterday, this day 7 years ago.[1]
I spent it at Biarritz with the good King Edward,[2] whose hand I kissed after breakfast, and began the chapter of my life, which still continues – when to end, who knows? But I want you to know, darling, that all the later part of it has been transformed, put on a different level, lit up, even in its darkest & dreariest hours, by *you* – the thought of you, the memory of you, the hope of you. . . .

[1] On which he had become Prime Minister.
[2] Edward VII had been at Biarritz for some weeks when Campbell-Bannerman resigned. He suffered from serious bronchial attacks and needed a warmer climate than England in early April. Asquith had been sounded before the resignation about going to Biarritz to kiss hands and had answered 'that he would be glad to come out as it would be an advantage to be abroad

during the difficult time of forming a cabinet'. The arrangement was criticized in *The Times*, however, as a slight on the constitution; and the King resented the fact that Asquith did nothing to repel this criticism.

390

Thur. 8 Ap. 1915 [ii]

. . . Ll. George has been here expounding his great scheme (or idea, for it has hardly put on the bones & flesh of a scheme) for buying out & nationalising the liquor trade. He is engaged in his usual process of 'roping in' everybody – Opposition leaders, Labour men, Temperance men &c – and is persuaded that he will succeed in getting them all.

Meanwhile I have appointed a 'Munitions' Committee with the fullest possible powers.

All love.

XV

E.S.M. to B.V.S.

Walmer Castle

[Late evening Saturday 10 April 1915][1]

Dearest,

I have got to take to the Margot habit in despair and send you a little note.[2]

Glowing with happiness at staying with you it has resulted in my being like a caged beast raging up and down at a delectable being separated by the bars of a cage.

Time – the biggest part of my stay here – has gone by with hardly a word to satisfy my appetite and I've been all the time consumed with hunger and jealousy.

I could not let him go to town alone – could I, even though I should have loved to get that golden opportunity.

If only you felt as sorry about it as I do – (always the same 'if'!) Shall I ever have any rights.

I shall be ready tomorrow for the walk that must not be tampered with and I want to arrange something for Monday.

Yrs separated, yearning, anxious
E S Montagu

[1] Both Edwin and Venetia were at Walmer on 10 Apr. The weekend was not a success. Venetia fell ill (Letter 391) and Edwin felt frustrated.

² This suggests that the note was written while Edwin and Venetia were still both at Walmer. Margot wrote notes to her guests 'at all hours of the day and night' (*Autobiography of Margot Asquith*, one-volume edn., 1962: Introduction by Mark Bonham Carter, p. xxxiii).

XVI

B.V.S. to E.S.M.

Admiralty, Whitehall

Monday [12 April 1915]

How can you be so bloody, & why? Is it merely horror at the old generation when compared with the young.

Even Raymond wondered what was the matter.

This I suppose is worthy of Margot.

Anyhow we mustnt quarrel, but you were bloody to me.

Venetia

[Postscript] This was the vituperative Margot line I wrote you last night!¹ I still repeat you were bloody, but *do* dine at Winstons & anyhow come & see me before dinner, anytime after 6.

. ¹ See last letter, XV, n. 2.

XVII

E.S.M. to B.V.S.

12 April 1915

I tried to telephone to you just after you left but was told you had gone to bed with lightning celerity!

My dear one, if as seems certain I have offended you please forgive me. I have no sort of knowledge of what I have done. All I know is that you hardly spoke in the later part of the evening, carefully arranged that I could not possibly drive you home (as I had hoped to do), made it quite impossible that I should dine at Winston's tomorrow night, and went off with hardly a goodnight.

I want awfully to know if I'm to be allowed to see you before you go away. Please remember that I'm feeling wretchedly ill and that I go to bed feeling more miserable than I have done for weeks. Send me across a line of consolation if you can.

Yrs.

E.S.M.

391

Tu 13 Ap '15

Most beloved – I am *so* distressed that your head continues to trouble you, tho' you look so like your real self.

I enjoyed our expedition to the Hospital this afternoon, & it was a great pleasure to realise the scenes in wh. so much of your recent life has been spent. The whole thing, apart from that, was very interesting.

I will write you a real letter to-morrow, & perhaps send you the little Treasury of Sonnets: so that, if you have any spare hours at Alderley these next days, you may fill up one or another of the blank sheets – with whatever seems to you worthy of what is already there, and that is all of the best.

I wasn't able to tell you to-day of other things. They are anxious that I shd. go to Newcastle & speak to masters & men in the course of the next few days. I know you wd. think I ought.

It is sad that you are going away: *do* get perfectly well. . . .

XVIII

B.V.S. to E.S.M.

Admiralty, Whitehall

[13 April 1915]

My darling (I begin like this not because I find you expect it but because I want to). . . .

Dont fail me on Friday. I want you very much, and write me one line to say you still love me. Can you,

Love,
Venetia

[Postscript] In the cold light of morning I'm full of shame at my foul vulgarity.

XIX

E.S.M. to B.V.S.

Treasury Chambers

[13 April 1915]

My dear Venetia

After a wakeful night, and taking into account every circumstance, what happened before dinner and later, I came to the conclusion, though I never loved you more than I do at the moment, that I fear the contemplated venture is bound to fail and we had better agree to abandon it.

Dearest one, I want what you cant give, I want what I cant earn, I take selfishly what I fear makes little difference to you and heaps to the man I owe all my life to.

I am supremely miserable. You ask for an assurance of my love. You have it amply. Your sweet and more-than-tear begetting letter has made it burstingly and lastingly vigorous. My beloved it is true. You have often said something was lacking in you. I only know that it is lacking so far as I am concerned.

I will certainly come on Friday.[1] I cant keep away. I long to see you again. Let's talk about it once more. But I thought I ought to make you know whats today in my mind. Somehow I think we shall still try it. And yet I fear –

Write *me* darling one line of goodbye till Friday.

Yrs

Ed S Montagu

[1] Edwin was invited to Alderley for Friday, 16 Apr. See Letter 392, para 1.

392

Wed 14 Ap 1915

My most dear – I had a faint hope that before you left to-day you might have sent me a line, especially as I know you will not get home until after post time. But I have no doubt you were too busy – one way or another. I only wish that I could spend a really quiet Saturday & Sunday with you at Alderley, free from the manifold distractions of our customary week-ends at Walmer & elsewhere. Unhappily that is reserved for more fortunate people.

This is not a complaint, still less a grievance, but *it is* a profound regret.

What do you think of Sir A. Sinclair? Was there any kind of rapprochement between him & the Bud?[1]

I drove back – some time after we parted – to Windsor, where I arrived just before dinner time.[2] It was not an exhilarating evening, the only addition to our party being Col. Ames & his wife. I suppose you have seen him at one time or another: the tallest man in the British army, an actual 6 ft. 8 in. in his stockings (I remember him as a Life Guardsman at the first Jubilee), who has to have everything specially made for him, clothes, boots, even his bed: a terrible handicap – all thro' life. He is a harmless rather vain kind of man,[3] & told us that he has a nephew who is 6 ft. 9 in. who has been busy recruiting, and when asked why he was not at the front had to reply 'I shd. like to be, but I am only 17'! Soveral was the sheet anchor of the party, with perhaps Lady Minto.[4] The Prince of Wales has developed wonderfully, & Margot had a really good talk with him. But the only really clever person there was my old friend Lady K. Coke (aged about 80), of whom I once told you. She enlarged her reminiscences by telling me that she stayed as a child for 2 summers running with the Duke of Wellington at Walmer,[5] & was present at the wedding of the Empress Frederick (mother of the Kaiser) sometime about the year 1858.[6] She has far more wits than any of the younger women about the Court, of whom the only one to catch the eye even for a moment was Portia Cadogan – Lady Meux's daughter.[7] I gladly shook the dust off my tyres at 10 this morning, & got back to a more natural atmosphere.

(Darling – it is 4 p.m, & what wd. I not give to be in the train with you now, with the prospect of 2 perfect days in the company of Huck, walking to the little wooden house, or in your room with the garish & wonderful casket reading Browning & the Sonnets. I am sending you in another cover my little Treasury: will you be sweet, & write on the blank sheets, during these 2 or 3 days, what occurs to you as fit to accompany & supplement what is already there?)

Rodd telegraphs last night that the delay in Italy is due only to the necessity of consulting the King, & that he is sanguine that it will be all right. If so, it will be the best thing that has happened since the War began, and I know that you will be even more glad than I that I had that week at the F.O.

I send you – *to keep secret or destroy*, as you think best – a letter I got about noon from K, recording the result of his private interview this morning with Sir J. French. It shows how wicked was the lie invented by *The Times* yesterday that our lack of ammunition at the front was holding back not only our own Army but the French.[8] Of course, you won't breathe a word of it.

It is now arranged that I shall go to Newcastle next week – Tues, Wed, or Thurs – and address a big town's meeting on the whole subject. I think it might be a good occasion, if only I can make the most of it. I am sure, sweetest & most wise, that you agree. If *only* you could be there! Could you? I should speak just 1000 times better!

I had a good talk with Crewe before lunch. We are both against prolonging Hardinge's term, (wh. the King wishes), and, as his successor K. will be unavailable next Nov, & even then, & still more later, would be too old for the climate &c. I think K. will be content with a Dukedom, K.G., & if he wants it, some more money. We had again, with many sighs of sympathy & regret, to pass over Mr Wu; Islington is quite impossible; Carmichael begins to show signs of dotage: and the choice seems to be reduced to Beauchamp & Bron. Crewe is rather strongly (for him) in favour of Bron, for whom there is much to be said, if Nan is still unwedded & will go with him as Vice-reine. But he is rather farouche, & hates the ceremonial side of things, wh. counts for a lot of India, and wh. the Beauchamps (as we know from various indications at Walmer) wd. take *au grand sérieux*. Tell me what is your judgment about this.

Darling – this looks as if it were going to be an interminable letter, and you can lay it aside now if you like, & take breath before I start again. In the course of my conversation with Crewe, I got on to the liquor question, and repeated my unalterable objections to Ll. G's scheme of nationalising the trade. As I expected, Crewe (who seems to have been very silent on the Committee) completely agreed with me, and the elusive McKenna has just been here (I am writing from H. of C.) to recant his temporary lapse & assure me that he also is quite convinced that the thing is for practical purposes a chimera. I had already told Bongie to summon the Cabinet Committee for to-morrow morning, in order that I might put my foot on it, when suddenly to my great surprise (I ought by now to have exhausted the faculty of being surprised) Ll. G. himself appears in this room, with an 'alternative' scheme – concocted I imagine in the course of the morning – of the most modest dimensions. He told me that he saw that I was unconvinced & probably unconvinceable in regard to his big plan (wh. he still says is favoured by every other authority, including the leading Editors): but that he wd. never go on with anything that I disapproved, and so had devised a substitute. I haven't yet had time to study it, but I see that it is confined to the Munition & Camp areas, in which there is much to be said for assuming State control. I expect we shall be able to arrive on these lines at quite a workable solution.

Isn't it wonderful how things that seem intractable have a way of smoothing themselves out?

My angel – I am sure your patience is more than exhausted, tho' I cd. easily write you 3 sheets more. But I won't. Aren't you 'rather' grateful? I cherish what you said in our last drive to the Hospital (a divine drive) on Sat week – that between you & me things are 'absolutely unchanged'. I could not bear to think what wd. be my case if it were otherwise. Write me a sweet full letter to-morrow (Thurs) so that I may get it on Friday morning. I shall go on telling you *everything* – inside & outside: until you tell me to stop. And if ever that shd. come, I shd say with Hamlet 'The rest is silence'. And the curtain would fall. But that is not going to be – is it? My own love & hope.

Your own.

[1] See Letters 411 and 412.

[2] He and Margot stayed two nights at the Castle, 12 and 13 Apr.

[3] He had retired in 1906 and, having rejoined on the outbreak of war, commanded the 2nd Life Guards Reserve Regt. He did not serve abroad.

[4] Both were experienced in court life, the first having been Portuguese Ambassador and having known Edward VII well, and the second being the wife of an ex-Viceroy of India. The 'King's Pledge' (Letter 375, n. 2) did not make a visit more agreeable for some of his guests. 'I hear a sad account of Windsor Castle "on the water waggon",' wrote Lady Desborough.

[5] Lady Katharine's mother, the Countess of Wilton, had been the Duke of Wellington's closest woman friend from 1838 to 1848. On one occasion when her children were at Walmer, and he was called to London, he wrote to her, 'They were sorry to part from me as I was to part from them': 7th Duke of Wellington (ed.), *Wellington and His Friends* (1965), pp. 125–6.

[6] The Princess Royal was married to Prince Frederick William of Prussia, as he then was, on 25 Jan. 1858, two months after her 17th birthday.

[7] She was always known by this name, though christened Sybil. Her father, Viscount Chelsea, died in 1908: Admiral Sir Hedworth Meux was her mother's second husband.

[8] See p. 558. Venetia returned this letter in July 1915. After the war Asquith used it to refute the charges in French's book, *1914*. He gave the text in a speech (3 June 1919), and allowed a facsimile reproduction in his article in *Pearson's Magazine*, Dec. 1921.

XX

E.S.M. to B.V.S.

14 April 1915

Please don't take too seriously my solemn words this morning. My letter was half finished when I got your letter. To say that I am not puzzled by the situation would be untrue. . . . But I was not angry, I only want to understand your motive.

But its enough that I love you and let's leave discussion till _Friday_ for which day I am _longing._

393

Thurs. 15 Ap. 1915

My darling – I am sitting in the Cabinet room at a really interesting Committee – Ll. G., Crewe, M^cK, M^cK Wood, Samuel, Assyrian, Lord

Reading, C. Roberts (who is very good) & one or two others – on the great Drink Problem. I have never before attended a meeting of this particular Committee, & only came to-day in order, if possible, to administer the *coup de grâce* to the Nationalisation proposals. Ll. G. did not press it against my judgment, & has produced an ingenious substitute of much more modest dimensions, which we are now discussing.

Later. I had to stop at this point & take part in the conversation. The whole thing bristles with the most contentious points, but it is a gain to have got it down from the Alpine (or Cambrian) altitudes to the sober level of business & common-sense. The two men who seemed to me to shew most acuteness & knowledge in the discussion were McKenna & Chas. Roberts, tho' both Reading & Simon were good. The result is that Ll. G. is going to open a new series of *pour parlers* with brewers, teetotallers & the whole motley crowd of interests. There is a flavour of comedy about the whole thing. . . .

I am glad to say that to-day we have a telegram which makes Italian co-operation a practical certainty. It has to be kept absolutely *secret*, because she wants a whole month from the signature of the agreement, in order to mobilise & to formulate diplomatically her pretext for war! (the latter by no means an easy task, even for the countrymen of Machiavelli & Cavour). . . .

394

Friday 16 Ap 1915 [i]

My darling – it was delightful to get your letter this morning. How I wish I were going to spend Sunday with you in your tranquil solitudes! But I have no luck that way. So you think I was 'unsympathetic' with your afflictions last Sunday? Do you? And that all I cared about was being deprived of the selfish pleasure of companionship? I know you don't mean it. I was really *very* anxious about you; it seemed such an unnatural kind of temporary paralysis. I believe it must have been the reaction after your 3 months of steady wearing routine. I see from what you say that you have not quite shaken it off yet. Darling you know well how I feel about these things.

So far as I can follow it, I think your Goethe quotation as applied to Ll. G. very pertinent; but I am not sure that I have quite made it all out. I suppose this is hardly the time to begin furbishing up again one's rusty *German*.

This Cabinet is singularly wanting in scholars; in fact besides myself (if I am one) there are only 2 others, Crewe & the Impeccable, now that Morley has gone. The Impecc. & I have been solacing ourselves for the particularly dreary discussions of the Cabinet by hunting out a line in Hesiod[1] wh. was once quoted by Dr Johnson. Perhaps you think that a rather indifferent kind of sport.

We had something very like an orgie in celebration of Violet's birthday last night – a big dinner followed by a performance by a male Japanese dancer with naked feet & a Russian accompanist – both imported for the occasion by Maud Cunard. Wu will no doubt give you a graphic account of it. As Katharine said to me (about 1 a.m) we can no longer throw stones at the giddy set which dances nightly in the small hours. Not that I personally have ever been much of a stone-thrower. I had rather a good talk with Diana who sat by me at dinner, & was not I thought in her best looks. There was a good deal of spirit about the whole thing & I think the people enjoyed themselves. *Later.* Since I began this, I have been through a rather stormy experience, wh. I know you will keep *entirely to yourself* with your tried and practised discretion, in the company of your Ministerial week-end guests. As soon as the Cabinet met, K who was evidently a good deal perturbed, went off at score, abusing Ll. G. for having disclosed at the Munitions Committee the figures wh. he (K) had confidentially communicated to the Cabinet of the Armies now in the field & actually or prospectively at home.[2] He declared that he could be no longer responsible for the War Office under such conditions, tendered his resignation, rose from his chair, & was about to leave the room. Ll. G. & Winston were both (the former having quite a presentable case) aggressive and tactless, and the situation was for the moment of the worst – particularly as Grey – a good deal to Ll. G's chagrin – strongly championed Kitchener, and McKenna was almost openly gloating over the imminent shipwreck of the Committee, wh. as you know he has always hated & sought to frustrate. And all this came literally like a bolt out of the blue, for I had not the faintest premonition of it.

So I thought of *you*, & pulled myself together, and by dint of appeals & warnings & gives & takes & all sorts of devices & expedients, succeeded in getting us back into more or less smooth water & clear air: so that we finished by an animated discussion of Hobhouse's scheme for increasing the pay of Postal Servants! Still it leaves a disagreeable taste in one's mouth – particularly as Ll G (who of course is not quite *au fond* a gentleman) let slip in the course of the altercation some most injurious & wounding innuendoes wh. K will be more than human to forget.

I daren't tell any one else, and it is an unspeakable relief to be able always in these trying moments to unbosom myself to you, my most wise & dear.

Do write a line if you can by *early* post to-morrow Sat. to *Walmer* so that I may get it Sunday morning. Literally *one* line wd. suffice to make me happy. . . .

Maud Cunard has just appeared with 2 new books for me: a Terence & a

Sallust both printed by Baskerville[3] & in good condition. She is a wonderful woman, & one never knows what is the latest hare that she is pursuing. . . .

What will you write in the little Treasury? 'Fear no more' & 'Tired with all these',[4] I shd love: also one more Ronsard. I so agree with what you say of Milton's Sonnets as compared with Shakespeare's. Perhaps you might go a little further afield, and give me one or two things out of your own book, wh. we ought to have gone over together last Sunday.

I have just had a moving parting with my servant George whom you remember so well in Sicily & elsewhere. He has got a Commission in the Middlesex Reg[t] & joins them at Cork on Monday.[5] He has been with me everywhere for 6 years & is far the best servant I have ever had. I don't know what I shall do without him. Divine one, I must post this now before I start for Walmer. You are dearer to me than the whole world, and I never loved you as I do to-day.

[1] The Greek didactic poet of the 8th century B.C.

[2] Balfour, who served on the Munitions Committee wrote:

The War Office have a natural objection to stating the number of men they propose to put in the field on any particular date; and probably the Committee would be reluctant to press them upon such points of policy. This reticence, however, makes it extremely difficult to draw up trustworthy statistical estimates of the amount of munitions of war that will be required at different dates.   D. Lloyd George, *War Memoirs*, p. 111.

For a recent statement of the problem, written from Kitchener's standpoint, see G. H. Cassar, *Kitchener* (1977), ch. 16; for the opposite view see R. J. Q. Adams, *Arms and the Wizard* (1978), ch. 2.

[3] Part of the famous quarto series printed in 1772–3.

[4] The song from *Cymbeline*, IV.ii, and Shakespeare, *Sonnet 66*.

[5] George Wicks's commission was signed by Kitchener. He was promoted to Lt. in July 1917, and demobilized in Dec. 1919, his final year of service being spent in Baluchistan with the 1st Bn. of the Duke of Wellington's Regt. He married and eventually settled in Devon, his wife's home county. He died at South Tawton, near Okehampton, in Apr. 1977, aged 92.

395

Walmer Castle,
Kent.

Friday midnight 16 Ap 15 [ii]

. . . I wrote to you earlier my first impressions & my fresh recollection of what took place at the Cabinet this morning. I know that to you it is all secret – a thing we share with no one else. I have naturally been thinking about it since, and when the others had gone to bed I have been talking it over with Crewe, whose judgment you know I rate highest among my colleagues. Not for years – & he agrees with me – have I on reflection been more disillusioned & from the personal point of view depressed. The man who comes out of it best is Kitchener – clumsy & tactless in expression as he often is: as Crewe says, one who has been all his life accustomed either to take or to give orders, and who therefore finds it difficult to accommodate himself to the give & take of Cabinet discussion & comradeship. He was really moved to-day, though I am sure he wd. not have persisted in resignation, and showed in the end a largeness of mind & temper wh. I greatly admire. On the other hand, the people who ought to have known better showed themselves at their worst. Winston was pretty bad, but he is impulsive & borne along on the flood of his too copious tongue,[1] and in the end was frankly regretful & made amends. The two who came out really worst were Ll. G, who almost got down to the level of a petty police court advocate, & McKenna, who played the part of a wrecker, pure & simple. It will take me a long time to forget & forgive their attitude and you know well that I am not prone to be censorious or resentful. It is a great satisfaction to me to find that Crewe completely agrees. I *hate* this side of politics, when it compels one to revise for the worse one's estimate of men whom one likes, and who to me personally have been & are (I believe) quite sincerely loyal. A very depressing day. Darling – I hope you don't mind my pouring into your ears all these confidences, and that you don't think I have lost my sense of perspective & proportion. If only you were always near me! how much stronger & wiser I should be! . . .

[1] See Letters 289, 321.

XXI

Margot Asquith to E.S.M.

10 Downing Street

16 April 1915

Dearest Mr. Montagu

I value this letter[1] very deeply so return it *at once*. I wrote a letter to Henry at 5 A.M. Monday or Tues[2] 13th & gave it to George[3] to put in his motor (going up to London for cabinet). He sat down directly he arrived here in cabinet room & wrote enclosed & sent it down by special messenger.[4] I got it at 1.30 – wasnt it sweet of him.

I had thought him just a little rough in answer when I asked him if he was tired or cold Monday evening – this was all – but I was terribly out of spirits & tho to him I may be cocky, snobby, anything you like – I am *fundamentally* humble & without any form of vanity (I know as well as Blanche that tho' I'm well made & have got an alert expression I'm plain, severe, crisp & candid). I have as you know often wondered if Venetia hadn't ousted me faintly – not very much – but enough to wound bewilder & humiliate me – (I have been chaffed about her more than once). Venetia as I said to Henry has many fine points: she is unselfish & kind but she leads (not in Hospital) the kind of life I hate (after being out 10 years!⁵) & she is not *candid* with me. She has not much atmosphere of moral or intellectual sensibility & in old days she always made mischief between Violet and me just when Violet was *most* devoted to me but in spite of all this I really have no sort of personal dislike & *always* suggest Venetia for everything – Meetings (Newcastle),⁶ Walmer, Wharf, Debates, dinners etc. etc. My jealousy is *not* small as from *wounded vanity* it is <u>Love</u> for Henry (and the *knowledge* alas! that I am no longer young & I daresay – in fact I always observe – as men get older they like different kinds of women) & the passionate longing that nothing & no one should even hang a chiffon or tissue paper veil between him & me even once a month – our relationship is absolutely unique. Every night however late I go & sit on his knee in my nightgown & we tell each other everything – he shows me *all* his letters & all Venetia's & tells me every secret,⁷ things he tells no one in the world but then he doesnt know poor little Violet's curious nature & thinks what he says before her to Cys or Eric⁸ or Bongy she will of course discuss with me (like Oc's wire on Drink⁹ & other trifling *family* things) he cannot imagine that it is an extra pleasure to Violet to know something I dont: I think she wd. exclude me if she could from everything – not from dislike but from vanity. The desire to be of more importance – this is so deep down in her rather thin nature that she is unconscious of it. The idea of sharing her joys and pleasures takes away from them.

Even little Davies¹⁰ said to me 'Wont you join Cys and me sometimes he loves you very much' I couldnt answer him for tears – I see Puff and Elizabeth unconsciously closing up when they think I'm being neglected in tiny *family* (purely family) ways – they dont like it.

When H. arrived Tues night at the Castle & came into my room where I was lying in the dark he took me in his arms & tears were on his cheek, he said my letter had touched him so terribly he had thought of nothing else (he told me Venetia had lunched & he spoke of her with great sweetness). Tear all this up & dont think me wanting in Reverence or diffidence in writing it to you. *Your* part to play is to persuade both Violet & Venetia that if they dont marry they will be miserable formidable egoists and amateurs

Your loving
Margot

¹ The enclosure, which follows as Letter XXII, p. 548.
² Tuesday is correct: Margot was sketchy on dates.
³ George Wicks: see Letter 394, n. 5.
⁴ Asquith went to London for the day (13 Apr.) while staying at Windsor Castle. Margot remained at Windsor.

[5] Like her friends, Venetia had been a débutante at 18.

[6] See Letter 391.

[7] This can hardly have been true. In view of Margot's weakness for imaginative exaggeration it is impossible to judge how much she was shown.

[8] Eric Drummond: one of Asquith's Secretaries, seconded from the Foreign Office (see Letter 317).

[9] For this wire see Letter 379, n. 1.

[10] Another of Asquith's Secretaries: see Letter 264, n. 2.

XXII

H.H.A. to Margot Asquith

13 April 1915 [enclosure of Margot's, 16 April]

My own darling – Your letter made me sad, and I hasten to tell you that you have *no* cause for the doubts & fears wh. it expresses, or suggests.

You have & always will have (as no one knows so well as I) far too large a nature – the largest I have known – to harbour anything in the nature of petty jealousies. But you would have just reason for complaint, & more, if it were true that I was transferring my confidence from you to anyone else. My fondness for Venetia has never interfered & never could with our relationship.

She has *au fond* a fine character as well as great intelligence, and often does less than justice to herself (as over the Hospital business) by her minimising way of talking. She is even now trying to arrange for a fresh spell of what is to her not at all congenial work.

I wish, with you, that Violet had rather more of the same sense of the futility of much of the life they have been leading.

But to come back to the main point, I *never consciously* keep things from you & tell them to others. These last 3 years I have lived under a perpetual strain, the like of which has I suppose been experienced by very few men living or dead. It is no exaggeration to say that I have on hand more often half-a-dozen problems than a single one – personal, political, parliamentary &c – most days of the week. I am reputed to be of serene 'imperturbable' temperament, and I do my best in the way of self-control. But I admit that I am often irritated & impatient, and that then I become curt & perhaps taciturn. I fear you have suffered from this more than anyone,[1] and I am deeply sorry, but believe me darling it has not been due to want of confidence & love. Those remain, and will always, unchanged.

Ever your own husband

A delightful letter from Puff.

[1] The passage from 'These last three years' to 'more than anyone' was reproduced in Spender and Asquith, ii. 230, in a discussion of the press attacks against Asquith during 1916. Asquith's first biographers gave neither the date of the letter nor any account of how it came to be written.

396

Walmer Castle,
Kent.

Sat. morning 17th Ap 15 [i]

. . . Reading over what I wrote last night I am afraid it sounds rather querulous, but I won't alter it, because I always tell you what I am feeling at the moment. I think it is on the whole a good thing that people can't *re-edit* their lives. The second edition would no doubt contain a lot both of erasures and of insertion; but it would be very far from reproducing the real person. That is the supreme value of letters, especially daily letters like ours. I don't think if I tried that I could hide anything (except the most trivial) from you now. . . .

[Indian Viceroyalty: letter from Willingdon, forwarded to H.H.A.] . . . He says Hardinge is too tired, & Carmichael too worn out. He thinks Islington wd. 'do all right, probably very well indeed', but suggests Albert Grey – a thoroughly bad choice: a feather-headed loose-tongued gas-bag – altho' in some ways the best of fellows – is the last kind of head-piece that is wanted in India. Don't you agree?[1]

I must begin (you know my dilatory ways) to think of something to say at Newcastle on Tuesday. . . .

. . . I have got nothing the least new or distracting to read. . . .

[1] Earl Grey had been Governor-General of Canada, 1904–11.

397

Walmer Castle,
Kent.

Sat. aft. 17 Ap 15 [ii]

. . . It has been a wonderful day in the way of sun & sky: quite perfect on the links wh. were swarming with larks. Crewe tho' a very agreeable is a rather trying play-fellow, owing to the extraordinary deliberation of his methods. I calculated at last that I could have repeated to myself the Lords

Prayer and the Apostles' Creed between the time when he begins to address the ball on the tee and the final impact of the club upon it.

Kitchener arrived quite unexpectedly at tea time having motored over from his place at Broome. He spoke quite nicely & quietly about the incidents of the last Cabinet. He had a few not very important bits of business to discuss, but reported a most untoward affair – the torpedoing by a Turkish Destroyer somewhere near Smyrna of one of our transports, wh. was carrying 1000 troops from Egypt to the Dardanelles: whether they were lost or saved we didn't yet know. It is almost inconceivable that the Naval people shd be so intolerably careless as either not to know that the Turks had such a vessel there, (they have been bombarding Smyrna off & on for weeks) or, if they did know, not to provide proper protective escort for the transports. No transport has yet been sunk in the whole war. Doesn't it shake one's confidence in them, coming on the top of so many mishaps & miscalculations & incomplete successes?[1]

K referred to his talk with Sir J. French (I suppose you got the letter). He (K) says he is supplying not only our troops but the French with ammunition: at any rate with the explosive (toluol) without which their shells won't go off.[2]

While he was still here (he is now gone) your Mother arrived in the company of Ld. Morley. She is looking extremely well, and I have just been showing her round the place in the failing light. She is delighted with it, & like everyone else reproaches me with my folly & want of foresight in not taking it. Soveral & Lady Meux have also come: so we are now full up to the lid for our last Sunday.[3] . . .

7.15 p.m Your most beloved little letter has just arrived and lifted a load from me. It was *most* sweet of you my darling to write it when you were feeling so slack & done up, and so like you. I am distressed to think of you feeling drowsy & inactive, but I am not altogether surprised. I am sure it is the reaction, wh. must come in some form or other, after your long & exhausting routine. . . .

. . . For God's sake be strong & well, and your own self: it matters *so* much. . . .

---

[1] The facts were less bad than the report made out. The torpedoes went under the transport's keel and the crew and troops, having abandoned ship, were soon scrambling back on board. British destroyers chased the attacking ship which ran for shore and was beached off Chios. There were some casualties from the transport by drowning.

[2] The British army had replaced lyddite with trinitrotoluene for its high explosive shell fillings shortly before the war.

[3] The period during which the Asquiths had been lent Walmer was ending.

XXIII

B.V.S. to E.S.M.

Alderley Park,
Chelford,
Cheshire.

Sunday [18 April 1915]

My darling (you'll think this I suppose merely a sign that I'm an accommodating woman & ready to comply in small things if I think it makes you happier). What can I say to you after this short time that you've been gone. That I want you back fearfully. Yes I do. And I have'nt in my time written this to Bongie, the P.M., Raymond and half a dozen others. [T]his Sunday has made it very difficult to go on writing to the P.M. as tho' nothing had happened. Darling what am I to do? Obviously what I ought to do would be to try to carry on as I've been doing, you've both been fairly happy under that regime, and as there can be no hard and fast rule of right and wrong and as I feel none of that that people call duty towards themselves, that would be the simplest plan. But are you both happy and can I make you so if I'm not and should I be now? Then again when to tell him. Just before Newcastle,[1] oh no not then, then just after something else will turn up & *if* I'm ready to tell him then you (who are far the fonder of him of us two) will have scruples, & so we shall go on till in a short time you'll loathe me. Why cant I marry you and yet go on making him happy, but you'd neither of you think that fun & I suppose my suggesting it or thinking it possible shows to you how peculiar I am emotionally. . . .

. . . If I go to Servia its only shifting the whole responsibility & giving up.

. . . I am so perplexed and wretched, I want so much to be happy and yet not to make anyone else unhappy. You made everything seem so simple, but now you are gone its as mangled as ever. . . .

Darling I *think* I love you
Venetia

[1] Asquith's projected speech to munition workers: see Letter 391.

398

Monday 19 Ap. 1915 [i]

My darling – It was a great delight to get your little Sat. letter this morning. I hoped I might perhaps have found another written Sunday when I got back here at lunch time. I am afraid you were still feeling slack & not in the mood for writing. I don't wonder – tho' for myself it is always the other way. I mean that the more weary & depressed I may feel, the greater relief it is to unburden myself to you. I talked to your Mother about Newcastle, and you know well that I wd. rather have you in the audience than anyone of the 3 or 4 or 5000 who may be there. But it is not like an ordinary meeting: it will be almost if not quite entirely men from the yards: and it wd be difficult locally to suggest any outside element. I don't regret it quite as much as I should, if I thought you were quite well & fit. I should mind more than anything that you shd. run any risk of extra fatigue as you now are.

I am writing this in the Cabinet, where we are at present discussing in rather a desultory way Italy, Greece, Bulgaria &c &c.

Geoffrey – who is with you to-night – came to announce his engagement to Kitty Methuen. I think I told you I spent a Sunday in her company a year & a half ago: quite pretty & attractive, and with a good deal of experience in the breaking and mending of hearts. I am told she is very much in love with G, and I hope it is all for the best. . . .

You don't say anything in your Sat letter of our Cabinet troubles. I wondered what impression you got from my narrative, and from what I said about particular persons & their attitude. I am very keen to know your opinion about these matters. The volcano is merely slumbering & may break out into eruption at any moment – for there is nothing better than a patched up truce of the thinnest and most precarious kind between K & Ll. G. Our Assyrian friend, who passes backwards & forwards between the wielders of the two temporarily sheathed swords, is in a mood of prolonged depression. He wrote me a most melancholy letter from Alderley, accusing himself of having misled me, whom he induced to prefer his judgment to McKenna's!

We are now in the thick of an animated tho' not as yet intemperate discussion of the great problem of drink. Everybody agrees as to the importance of providing canteens, inside or just outside the works, where good food & decent drink can be supplied to the men, at a reasonable price, under Government control. The controversy is mainly about *prohibition*, which has for the moment few friends except the Lord Chancellor & McKenna & rather half-heartedly the Ch^r of the Ex^r & the Impeccable. Winston has talked some excellent sense about the whole question: also Harcourt, & especially Birrell (I have never written to you under quite such peculiar conditions: for every 2 or 3 minutes I am constrained to burst or break in to the debate: so I think I will bring this to a close now, & send you a postscript at night). . . .

Later ($\frac{1}{4}$ to 6) The Cabinet is now over & I will add a line before post-time.

We did some really good work of the *destructive* kind. The Great Purchase Folly is as dead as Queen Anne: tho' M‘Kenna & Runciman are still disposed to drop a perfunctory tear over its grave: not, however, for love of it, but to discredit its successor & substitute. To-day I am glad to say we also cleared out of the way *total prohibition* whether of spirits, or of heavy beers. Nothing can be more absurd than to prevent the yokels of Bucks or Kerry from enjoying their modest & accustomed drink because some men engaged in ship-building on the Tyne or Clyde are drinking too much. Altogether the thing is beginning to assume more rational dimensions, and before long they will have nearly reached my own 'reactionary' view, that the main thing to be done is to limit hours of opening, provide really good food & drink in accessible places, & perhaps clap a substantial addition on the taxes on spirits & wine.

I have accumulated a little rather scanty material for my speech to-morrow, and hope that the long train journey may (as it often has before) come to my rescue and get my thoughts going. . . .

Grey is very depressed about his eyes which he thinks are doomed. I am not sure that it would not be better for him to go away for a good time now. . . .

399

Monday midnight 19 Ap 1915 [ii]

My own darling – when I got home just now I received & read your letter of Sunday. It is in many ways the most wonderful & insight-full (if there is such a word) that you have ever written me. I understand every word of it, and (what is more important) I can read between the lines.

It is quite true that you have (as no one else ever had or could have) the 'potentiality of making me wretched'. I have long known this. But, on the other hand, you have given me, & continue to give me, the supreme happiness of my life; which has been a different & far richer & nobler thing since I have shared it with you. So that if to-morrow you were to be taken from me – I don't mean by death, but by some veil or barrier, wh. necessarily made our confidence less free & entire & complete – I should still bless you as the chief joy & the real Saviour of my life. Without you, I should have gone under, & 'not Heaven itself upon the past has power'.[1] Love – such as mine for you – makes one terribly & inordinately selfish; and I am so conscious of that, that, if you were to tell me to-morrow that you were going to be married, I hope I should have strength not to utter a word of protest or dissuasion.

I should honestly try to the best of my judgment to forecast your chances of happiness; and, from that point of view, I should mind *quite enormously, who & what* was the man. But whoever it was – through no fault of yours my beloved & best, but entirely thro' mine, for you have never deceived or deluded me for a single moment – life wd have lost for me its fountain, its inspiration, its outlook. You say it wd. make no difference in your 'feelings for me' and I am sure you speak the truth. But read over some of our Sonnets, and you will realise, dimly perhaps, but imaginatively, the difference it must make – not in *love*; that wd always remain to my last living breath – : but in expression, in intercourse, in confidence, in the thousand things big & little, grave & gay, light or serious, which have been woven into the web of our unique & divine intimacy.

Darlingest, forgive me if I have written brutally & exactingly.

My one overpowering desire is that you should be *happy* in the fullest sense – with all the powers and possibilities of the most glorious nature that I have ever known and that I should never stand in the way of this. You have given me everything that is best in my life; sustained, inspired, blessed it; and it, and all that I am or can be, are *yours* now and for ever.

Your own

I must try & think of something to say at Newcastle! Good night, most dear.

---

¹ Dryden, *Translations from Horace, Ode 29 of Book iii*; a favourite quotation. Asquith was to quote this again in his 'farewell' letter to Venetia: see p. 606.

XXIV

E.S.M. to B.V.S.

10 Downing Street

19 April 1915

My very dear one,

I have never received I need not tell you, a letter so thrilling and delicious as yours this morning. God bless you for it! The result is that I am not the only member of the Cabinet writing to you during its deliberations.¹

You tell me that I make things seem simple while I am with you. Good Lord! is this sarcasm. I tell you I do not know what to do. I simply can't face, and that's an end of it, hurting the P.M. I blame myself night and day for landing him in this munitions evil. In a way that's his fault for ever trusting my judgment or giving me any position of responsibility. How can I [aim] a blow in the dark of this magnitude. I saw dear old Geoffrey radiant going to see him and incur his blessing.² And my heart bled to contrast his position with my own. Of course the conventional view is that he has no right to claim your loyalty but neither you or I are conventional or could convince ourselves that this is right. Can you suggest any wise friend I could consult or is this impossible. I owe all to the P.M. I love him. I can't be guilty for my own happiness of hurting him.

. . . And yet when we get together . . . we forget the future in the wonderful present, forget that . . . I am absolutely unfitted by being a coward and a Jew to go on in politics, . . . that we owe everything to the P.M.

. . . As for the rest is not perhaps the best way without going to Serbia gently by being a little withdrawing to regain your freedom and then lets start afresh. . . . So you really *think* you love me in the true sense of the word! I know that I do. This will remain even if marriage becomes impossible.

. . . I do not see how we can invent a new triangle. I cannot share you, nor can he. May I one day find courage to ask you to define your plans still more.

. . . Yours very disjointedly and disturbedly (Winston is gassing all the time). . . .

Ed

[1] See Letter 398.
[2] For Howard's engagement to Kitty Methuen see Letter 398.

400

In train – between York & Newcastle

Tues 20 Ap '15 [i]

My darling – don't drop the possessive prefix, I love it – I got your sweet little letter this morning & have just been reading it again. 'Sorting' my letters must be by now a heavy task: I wonder how many they amount to? Soon they will begin to tax the holding capacity even of the Alderley casket. Yours I am glad to say are accumulating into a goodly & growing pile. I am sure it is already a record in correspondence since man & woman first took to writing to one another.

Don't trouble about your additions to the Treasury until you find yourself in the mood: tho' I long more than I can say to see & read what you will put there. It is my most precious possession, and never passes even for a moment into other hands.

We left Kings X at 10 and had a little send-off: not to be compared to that memorable one a year ago, when my last sight as we swept out of the Station was your dear face, with an expression on it that I shall never forget.[1] I have been trying to put together my speech, wh. I fear will be rather banal: it has been at any rate, for reasons you will readily guess, a real effort in the concentration of thought. . . .

. . . I will try to make my love for you more *unselfish*, and more worthy of you, my darling.

I must stop now & get back to my speech. I will write to-morrow to Alderley, where I assume you are likely to remain. I know you are thinking of me & wishing me good luck. . . .

Central Station Hotel,
Newcastle-on-Tyne.

Later. We got here about 3.30 — a crowd at the Station, Lord Mayor, Military & Naval Officers &c. Happily this hotel is part of the Station. I found they had prepared a longish river expedition in a launch wh. wd have left me hardly any time before the meeting (7.30) especially as they insist on my meeting a damned Committee at 6.45. So I cried off on the pretext that I was busy, & Margot & the 2 girls have gone instead. I am afraid the crowd was rather baffled & disappointed, but I really must look at the notes for my speech wh. were made in the train, with all sorts of other thoughts now & again, as Wordsworth says, 'slipping in between'.

So I have a blessed 1½ hours of peace & solitude, wh. I shall employ partly in my conventional task, & partly (I expect) in reading over again some letters I carry in my pocket: which is not at all conventional.

Do you think I should have been a happier man if (in some ways) I had been more conventional?. . .

---

[1] In Apr. 1914 Asquith had travelled to his East Fife constituency to be re-elected on becoming Secretary of State for War. He was seen off at King's Cross by some 200 Liberal M.P.s, and by Venetia.

401

[20 Ap 15 ii][1]

My darling — whatever you do, don't (in Coventry Patmore's phrase) 'cheapen Paradise'.[2] If you did, I shd. make my account with Purgatorio, or for preference with the worst & most punishing circle of the Inferno itself. After all, it doesn't matter very much what will ultimately (perhaps soon) happen to me; but for *you* I want the <u>*very best*</u> that any woman — in this or any time — can have: for remember *Mimnermus in Church:*

> Your chilly stars I can forgo,
> This warm, kind world is all I know.[3]

And I should love to think, when I am allowed to peep through the bars of the beyond, that I shd. see you where I want to see you, & where you deserve to be. Much better for me than meeting a disembodied & anaemic Beatrice, with angels & archangels & the whole company of Heaven, genuflecting, & chanting Hosannas, and practising a vapid immortality. So whatever you may be tempted to do, my own darlingest, don't 'spoil the bread & spill the wine'. *Don't.* . . .

. . . I know that fate . . . has *just* cut me off from the chance of the best tho' it has given me, & please God will still give me, the richest plenitude of love & happiness that has fallen to the lot of any man of my time. But if – like that old aboriginal Jew, named Moses – I may not enter the promised land, but only catch a transient glimpse of it from the distant peak of Pisgah, I should still love to think of it always, with its milk & honey & grapes & the rest, wh. I am not allowed to taste, as possessed and enjoyed by someone, more love-inspiring & heart-filling, & therefore worthier than I could ever hope to be. Think of this. Let me, at any rate, live and die with that dream unspoiled, that vision unblurred, that supreme & sustaining hope still capable of being fulfilled. I *know* you won't disappoint me there.

Sweetest & noblest – forgive all this. You know & understand me: and *you* I *worship and love.*

[1] An undated pencil note, probably written late at night after returning from the Newcastle meeting.
[2] *The Angel in the House* bk. I, c. iii, Prelude 3 'Unthrift': see Letter 75, n. 2.
[3] By William Johnson Cory, in *Ionica:* 'Mimnermus in Church'.

XXV

B.V.S. to E.S.M.

Alderley Park
                                                                    20 April 1915

My darling . . . Isnt it cruel that 3 years ago that summer at Penrhos I didnt like you enough[1] (tho' you tell me also that you didnt really love me much either) because then, tho' the P.M. had already begun to think he was fond of me, it wouldn't really have mattered to him, & now? Will it? What a fool I've been haven't I. You, being prejudiced in my favour, may say that I've made him very happy for 3 years, but I know quite well that if it hadnt been me it would have been someone else or a series of others who would have made him just as happy. I feel so ungrateful to him & yet at times I resent very bitterly that he should stand in the way. And yet I know you are right & that it wd be almost impossible for me to go to him & say 'In spite of the fact that you've again and again told me that if I were to marry life would have nothing left to offer you, I am going to marry Edwin.' How could he have been so cruel as to say that to me. But I must see you, he has no claim on me has he?

You suggest that I should gradually detach & free myself. But do you know what that would mean to someone like me? I should perhaps for a week see nothing of him, make excuses for not doing so, then there'd be a scene & in order to mollify & propitiate and make him happy again I should say anything he wanted. And in all this can you understand how completely unmoved I am?

My darling dont be angry with me and think me worse than I am, there must be some way out. . . .

. . . Isn't it a depressing thought that among all our friends and relations (except perhaps my mother) there isn't one who wd be otherwise than annoyed if we were to marry? Particularly our families[2]. . . .

[1] See p. 5.
[2] Too gloomy a forecast, especially about Edwin's family: see pp. 602–4.

The Newcastle Speech: 'The people on the spot think that my visit has done good' (Letter 402)

ASQUITH travelled to Newcastle armed with the following assurance from Kitchener:

14 April. I have had a talk with French. He told me I could let you know that with the present supply of ammunition he will have as much as his troops will be able to use on the next forward movement.

On the basis of this note he told the munition workers:

I do not believe that any army . . . has ever either entered upon a campaign or been maintained during a campaign with better or more adequate equipment. I saw a statement the other day that the operations . . . of our army . . . were being crippled, or at any rate hampered, by our failure to provide the necessary ammunition. There is not a word of truth in that statement.

Thus Asquith transformed an assurance about ammunition supply in a forthcoming operation into one which referred not only to that but to recent operations such as the Neuve Chapelle attack. It was perhaps the most extraordinary, and the most damaging, blunder of his wartime premiership.

A few weeks later, in the discussions preceding the formation of the coalition, Asquith blamed Kitchener for accepting French's assurance and passing it on.[1] French certainly gave it. His claim after the war that he had not done so, and had been misunderstood by Kitchener, must be dismissed. He wrote to Kitchener on 2 May: 'The ammunition will be all right.'[2] What he said should have been suspected, if only because it ran counter to so many of his other statements. He had told Kitchener that the Neuve Chapelle offensive had been mounted with the absolute minimum of artillery support (Letter 366). For weeks he had been stressing the need for 'munitions . . . always more munitions' in every interview which he gave. Kitchener and Asquith ought to have remembered how strongly Joffre was pressing the British to attack.

French had pinned great hopes on the offensive planned at Aubers Ridge; he would be tempted to slur over the difficulties of mounting it.[3] Apart from this, it is surprising that Asquith had not heard about the B.E.F.'s shortage of shells from officers on leave who had firsthand experience of it. He had made a statement which no one who knew the Western Front could believe. Twenty-five years later Harold Macmillan was talking to Dalton about the fall of Chamberlain's Government. 'It is like 1915,' Macmillan said,

when old Asquith told Parliament that there were plenty of shells; and soldier M.P.s came back from the front and said 'That's a bloody lie: we only had three shells a day at Festubert.'[4]

Most of the London press was soon in full cry. Here was the Prime Minister making a statement about the supply of shells which was at variance with everything his colleagues were saying. Asquith could now be depicted, not only as failing to co-ordinate the country's war effort, but as ignorant of the most crucial facts about war production.[5]

[1] See Charles Petrie, *Austen Chamberlain* (1939–40), ii. 22–3. On this occasion, as in his speech, Asquith gave an exaggerated account of the assurance given him.

[2] G. Arthur, *Kitchener* (1920), iii. 236.

[3] See French to Mrs Winifred Bennett, 8 May: 'I am just on the eve of commencing what I believe will grow into one of the greatest battles in the history of the World' (French MSS, Imperial War Museum). 'Aubers Ridge' is the name given to the 9 May battle in the *Military Operations* volumes of the Official History. It is sometimes called the battle of Festubert.

[4] J. P. Mackintosh (ed.), *British Prime Ministers of the 20th Century*, i (1977), 263: from Dalton's diary, 16 May 1940.

[5] Despite much speculation Asquith refused to divulge who had reassured him about ammunition supply. He persuaded Lord Hugh Cecil to withdraw a parliamentary question (*The Times*, 24 June) and dealt summarily with the two questions asked (*Parl. Deb.* lxxii. 608, 1452). For the rumours see Cynthia Asquith, *Diaries, 1915–1918* (1968), pp. 44 and 47–8.

402

In train

Wed 21 Ap 1915 [i]

My darling – I wish you could have been at the meeting last night, tho' I quite recognise that it was impossible. You wd. have enjoyed the spectacle: an audience of about 5000, all men, very patient & attentive, and now & then enthusiastic in the right kind of way. I avoided as far as possible the scolding lecturing note, and the people on the spot think that my visit has done good.

Almost as interesting was the visit paid this morning to Armstrong's works. I wished all the time that you were there. They are making shells as fast as they can turn them out in a lot of huge sheds, almost all of which have been built where there were green fields at the beginning of the war, and where they now employ *13,000* instead of *1,300* men & women.[1] We saw the whole process of making shells, fuses &c, and I felt rather disposed to go back on the advice I gave to the Bud not to go in for this kind of occupation. There were masses of girls who looked quite healthy & alert, working the neatest & prettiest little machines, wh. they learn if they are at all clever to handle in 3 days, & if stupid in not more than a fortnight. The 15 inch gun like those in the *Queen Elizabeth* is a terrific fellow to look at, when you see him just after birth, as it were in his cradle. But I wont bore you with further description. Perhaps the most noteworthy man there was Meade Faulkner, who is one of the principal directors of Armstrong's & better known to us as the author of those excellent novels *Nebuly Coat, Moonfleet* &c. You know them? He is about 6 ft. 6 ins in height, with a rather melancholy face & voice, and the general air of a transplanted hidalgo.[2]

I am not good as you know at mechanical things, but I shd. have liked to see more. We had to hurry off to catch the train. . . .

[1] Armstrong's Ammunition Department was at Scotswood, though it formed part of the Elswick Works.

[2] Falkner, whose name Asquith misspells, entered Armstrong's by a tutorial route. He tutored the sons of Andrew Noble who succeeded Armstrong in 1890 as chairman of the firm. Three of his novels were published between 1898 and 1903, the manuscript of a fourth being lost in a train. Apart from his activities as a business man and novelist, he was a book collector and palaeographer and a benefactor of libraries; and the beauties of Burford in the Cotswolds owe much to his generosity. He received many decorations from foreign governments for his armament activities, and one from the Pope for palaeography. His best adventure story, *Moonfleet*, has been filmed.

403

Wed 21 Ap 1915 [ii] Midnight

. . . It is true as you say that Geoffrey is very exalté. Pauline Cotton who is first cousin to his 'Kitty'[1] writes that she pities him. This is probably cousinly candour: she thinks Geoffrey's lady an accomplished 'flirt', and not very real; but adds (by the way of compensation) that she is a convinced & resolute Liberal!

Wu has just been here: his Mother, who has been seriously ill, is apparently better: and he dilated on Geoffrey (who seems to be entirely dependent, materially, on the incalculable caprices of his Mother)[2] & on Ll. G's latest liquor phases. . . .

Meanwhile (between ourselves) Fisher, who came here before dinner, believes that a big thing is at last imminent between our Navy & the Germans in the North Sea. The cry of Wolf has been so often heard in this sphere, that I am still rather sceptical. But it may come off at last. . . .

[1] Pauline Stapleton-Cotton's mother was Lord Methuen's sister.

[2] Rosalind, widow of the 12th Earl of Carlisle, was a crusader for teetotalism and women's suffrage. Asquith did not favour the expenditure of money and time on those two causes.

XXVI

B.V.S. to E.S.M.

Alderley Park
21 April 1915

My darling I've been in a terrible frame of mind all today and have written you an odious letter which I shant send as if you got it you'd probably refuse to come here & I want you very much. . . .

Were you rather disgusted by my letter yesterday, I was rather ashamed of it, & more so when this morning I got a wonderful letter from the P.M. which shows me how wrong I was to think he only thought of his own happiness & never of mine.[1] I think I'll show it you if you like.

We wont think of those things for a little but just be very happy . . .

[1] Probably Letter 399.

XXVII

E.S.M. to B.V.S.

21 April 1915

Dearest and most darling Venetia

. . . As regards the Prime. I can't see the way out – but best beloved, we must find one . . . for we ought not to waste time.

Don't think my relations will object. I think they will be rather pleased – if you are brave enough to come into the fold, right in.[1] Are you? And do you love me enough to face this. I have more to say on this when we meet . . .

Yrs absolutely lost without you
Edw S.

[Postscript] . . . I am drunk with anxiety to see you. Venetia! Do you love me? _Answer_ that. Think of the year we've wasted already.

[1] That is, to be converted to the Jewish faith.

404

Thurs. 22 Ap 1915 [i]

Beloved, it was a joy to get your most sweet letter this morning. I am so glad that you liked my speech: if you think it good, I don't care a twopenny damn what anyone else thinks about it – let alone Northcliffe & his obscene crew.[1] I don't think we shall hear much more now on this particular line of attack, as after a very curious rapprochement between K & Ll.G, you wd. see that the latter was allowed – for the first time – to give a number of most convincing figures to the House yesterday. . . .

. . . It is a heavenly thought that you will be back here on Monday, and I devoutly hope that we may travel back together to Alderley on Friday, and that I may have a peaceful Sat & Sunday in your dear company. That is the best 'rest-cure', and strength-restorer, and doubt-killer, and soul-inspirer, and (above all) *life-giver*, that I could possibly have.

No, I am afraid there is a great deal of the dross of selfishness in what I shd. like to think the pure gold of my love. But I love you to say & I am sure you say it sincerely, that it has been the 'one thing in the world that has only brought you happiness'. One cannot believe that such a thing is doomed (as Shakespeare says in *Measure for Measure*) 'to lie in cold obstruction & to rot'.

I wonder if you have made any progress with my 'Treasury'? I am writing this at the House between my questions & having to go in to pay a tribute to the Serjeant at Arms (!) & to listen to Jack Tennant & Walter Long.[2] I will try & add something on the bench.

Later – on Treasury Bench – we have all paid our little *éloges* to the expiring Serjeant at Arms (wh. B. Law pronounces *Surjeant*). . . .

We had a prolonged but peaceful Cabinet this morning. French seems to have done a really good thing in taking what is called 'Hill 60',[3] as it is the only high ground from which the Germans cd. make observations for shelling Ypres & the neighbourhood. The casualties are heavy but not excessive.

Sazonoff, who is a pettifogger of the Old Bailey type, has I am glad to say caved in; and there is now every prospect that the agreement with Italy may be signed by the end of this week. That will be – if it does come off – the best piece of work we have got through for months. I know that you will rejoice at it – for my sake, among other reasons.

We then 'took to Drink' – wh. is now narrowed down, & shrinks every day. What we have got to is, that there will be no prohibition either of spirits or of wine or of beer; that in the selected 'Munition' areas, wh. are also being whittled down, the Gov[t] will have *power* to take over the public houses &, where the houses are 'tied', the breweries wh. own & locally supply them; and that, in these districts, we shall set up in the public houses, or outside or inside the works, canteens wh. will provide good food & wholesome drink, alcoholic & other, at reasonable prices & in not immoderate quantity. The most controversial outstanding point is whether we should buy out the owners, or only give them compensation. Ll George is strongly for the former, as in the long run the cheapest plan; and at the end of the war the State could, if it pleased, resell the houses either to their late owners, or to the municipalities, or to some Trust Company. Others – such as Harcourt, McK Wood, the Assyrian &, at least in the way of inclination, I myself – would prefer not to saddle ourselves even provisionally with the ownership, but to give fairly liberal compensation. I think the 'purchase' party will win for the moment, but I much doubt their plan surviving H. of Commons discussion. We shall have another Cabinet on the subject on Monday. I shan't be surprised if it turns out that no Parliamentary agreement is possible, and that we shall have to abandon legislation, & fall back on the powers given by the Defence of the Realm Act to the Executive. . . .

. . . (Jack is just perorating in a rather purple patch – & is being succeeded by Walter Long. There are, I suppose, at the outside about 60 or 70 men in the House; and the atmosphere is far from electric. Bluey is sitting next me, and we talk at intervals about Hesiod and Sidonius Apollinaris:[4] it is a *real* pleasure to me – who as you know have a pedantic side – to have a scholar like him for a colleague; with no sealed books or dumb notes. What a long digression!)

After W. Long had gone on for the best part of an hour in his discursive over-emphatic fashion, I got up and made a few 'sympathetic remarks' about disabled soldiers & officers who are not promoted as quickly & as often as they think they deserve. And that ends my connection with the debate.

Violet went to Ireland last night & the others are going this evening to a kind of charitable operatic performance somewhere in the Waterloo Road, where Elizabeth is to 'oblige' by a short speech on Shakespeare! So we have improvised a little dinner at the Assyrian's with Birrell & E Drummond & one or two kindred spirits: wh. will be restful at any rate.

I am going to take Puffin to a play to-morrow (Fr) night: so I shall not go to the Wharf till Saturday. Please darling write *here* to-morrow. . . .

[1] The Times expressed 'deep disappointment' over Asquith's 'somewhat petty attempts' at Newcastle 'to prove that he and his colleagues have made no miscalculations and no mistakes'. The Daily Mail asked how the Prime Minister's statements could be reconciled with those of Kitchener and Lloyd George proclaiming an acute shortage of munitions. Criticism of the speech was by no means confined to these Northcliffe papers. To the Pall Mall Gazette it was 'too guarded . . . and uninspiring'. The Daily Express thought it 'mischievous to a degree'.

[2] On the Army Estimates.

[3] 'Hill 60' was a mound formed by the earth excavated from a railway cutting. Having mined it by a tunnelling operation, the British captured it on the evening of 17 Apr. with only 7 casualties, and held it despite three days of counter-attacks. It was retaken by the Germans, however, on 5 May, having cost the British 5th Div. over 100 officers and 3,000 men.

[4] For Hesiod see Letter 394, n. 1. Sidonius Apollinaris was a 5th-century A.D. Latin poet and Bishop of Clermont, chiefly known through the surviving texts of many of his letters.

405

Thursday 22 Ap 1915 [ii]

My own darling – you will tell me, won't you? the real truth at once. However hard it may be to me.

I would rather know the worst – without disguise or delay. You once said a thing that wounded me – only once – about 'cutting the loss'.

Do tell me – yes or no! Then I can settle my account.

The only thing I mind is suspense & uncertainty. Deliver me from that.

Your own lover.

XXVIII

E.S.M. to B.V.S.

22 April 1915

My darling

Will you let me say that I am very apprehensive about your last letter and feel it best to say so. We shan't make progress by concealment and therefore I almost wish you had sent me the odious letter you describe yourself as having written and suppressed. . . .

. . . Yes you had better let me see the P.M.'s letter to you for I feel I don't understand exactly how things are between you. I should have thought after last weekend particularly that if you could be as you were with the P.M. you were never much in love with him or were not now in love with me. For if the P.M. means nothing to you then you could go on giving him false coin but if I meant anything to you, you could not go on loving him.

When he writes you letters such as you describe, it would seem that I disappear and I presume you write him letters in reply which make it all the more difficult for you to alter things. Am I right? and yet these very letters might be your opportunity of regaining freedom!

Venetia, my beloved, one thing is quite certain. Your plan of being happy as we are won't do. If we are going to marry let us decide to do so and then attack our difficulties. But don't let's sit on our haunches for another three years, sliding along without the necessary vim to face the situation. I am not a Hugh[1] and although I would wait for you any length of time I think your proposal is not half worthy of you. I fear I must assume after your last letter that you love the P.M. If that is so the sole question is whether you propose to let that love fill your life as long as it will last? If so don't let me go on in a concealed and semirequited love of you but tell me so – and I will try and find courage to bear it and you should not be influenced by the fact that I feel life has no further value worth worrying about and that I shall probably clear right out of everything and go my own way with never an effort. . . .

Don't ask me to think of you – I do so all day and every day. And although I talk heroics I fear you know that I will willingly understand and take anything I can get – After all there are other obstacles to our plans besides the P.M. !². . .

---

[1] See Letters 74, n. 2, and XIV, n. 2 (p. 530).

[2] Edwin refers to his father's will, whereby he would lose his share of the inheritance if he married someone who was not of the Jewish faith.

'The miners are threatening to come out'
(Letters 406 and 416)

THE Board of Trade figures showed that working-class costs had increased by 20 per cent between July 1914 and 1 March 1915, the increase for food being 24 per cent. Miners' wages had been settled previously district by district; but the Miners' Federation of Great Britain now mounted a campaign for a nation-wide wage increase of 20 per cent. The rates of productivity and profit varied widely between one region and another; and the owners and managers resisted the demand for a single national settlement. A meeting at the Board of Trade on 21 April left the miners highly dissatisfied: Runciman acted, they thought, more as 'a capitalist partisan' than as 'an outside, intelligent, government official'. They saw the Prime Minister on 23 April and he arranged a meeting between the two sides for 29 April (Letter 406).

At this meeting Asquith offered, in the words of the miners' report, 'to settle the method of settling this matter' if both sides were willing to be bound by his decision. Each side tried without success to extract from the premier exactly what this formula meant. Owners and miners met on 30 April but failed to agree. The owners offered to recommend district awards of 10 per cent; the miners offered to settle for a national 12½ per cent, but only if this was agreed and effected immediately. On 1 May, after a bitter debate, the Miners' conference accepted the leaders' advice and voted by 438 to 279 to put the matter in Asquith's hands.

On 5 May Asquith decided against a national award. He wired the miners' executive to say that war conditions justified an immediate increase. This was to be negotiated through the local bodies within a week. If any coalfield failed to produce an agreement within the week the Government would appoint an umpire. The result was an average increase of about 10 per cent. The local variation was quite wide, prosperous mining areas such as the Midlands and Yorkshire gaining some 17½ per cent.

The miners' leaders did not blame Asquith. For all their tough talk to him in the April meetings they knew the difficulties of a wartime strike. They had also to recognize that coal prices were lagging behind the general price rise. In terms of the prices and profits in their own industry the settlements were not ungenerous. There was a notorious miners' strike in South Wales in July 1915; but this was not directly connected with Asquith's award in May. National wage bargaining for the mines was conceded later in the war, when the industry was moving into government control 'for the duration'. It survived in shadowy form until 1926 and was decisively re-established in the second war.

406

Friday 23 Ap. '15 [i]

My darling – thank you so much for your dear little note this morning. I am sorry you find the conditions of life at Alderley so unstimulating. At any rate you will have some infusion from outside at the end of this week, and next week you will be among your old haunts again. I feel pretty sure now (indeed, I have so arranged, unless the Heavens fall) of being able to return with you on Friday. Let us treat that as a fixed point.

I have just come back from the Memorial service for young Gladstone[1] at St Margaret's. There were some rather weird prayers of a Byzantine flavour, including a 'Contakion' (whatever that is) of the 'Faithful Departed', which must have been imported direct from the liturgies of the Greek Church. Our anti-Roman High Churchmen (like the Gladstones) have a great weakness in that direction. Another innovation, which I approve, was the omission of the Dead March at the end of the service. There were quite a lot of people there.

Since my return I have been interviewed by the Assyrian, who is a good deal exercised over Ll. George's drink schemes even in their latest whittled down form, and by Geoffrey Howard, who tells me that the Temperance people are going to meet on Monday and to announce their irreconcilable hostility to any form of 'purchase' – of however limited a kind. I am only surprised that they have not given tongue before. He is going to bring his 'Kitty' to lunch to-day. I will tell you afterwards what my second impressions are.

There is a nasty telegram from Petrograd this morning, reporting (only at second hand) that the Germans have succeeded in getting 2 submarines to Constantinople, & hope to get in 6 more. This would or might play the devil with the situation & I hope it is not true. If the weather is favourable there ought to be something doing to-morrow.

I am going with Puffin, who is nearing the end of his holidays, to see a play called *Quinneys*[2] wh. is well spoken of to-night. I go to the Wharf to-morrow. Unless (wh. is not likely) you cd. send a line there on Sat. morning by the early post, please darling address to Downing St.

I am now going to greet Geoffrey and the young person.

Later. I sat next 'Kitty' at lunch. She is not in any sense a beauty, but has rather attractive blue grey eyes, an irregular nose, & prettyish fair hair. She is quite intelligent to talk to, with a good sense of humour: she reminded me that when we last met & went to Church I had applied to her the Psalmist's epithet 'froward'. On the whole, *attrayant* but not the least *foudroyant*. I cannot conceive what was the invisible bond wh. drew her & Geoffrey together – who can, in these cases? – but when one thinks of the Hennessys &c, I am sure he is quite to be congratulated.

By the way did you ever come across at the Hospital an anaesthetic called 'Nikalgin'? Spender, who was also at lunch, says it is a wonderful American invention, only producing local insensitiveness, with no unconsciousness or sickness or other reactions. Mrs S. runs a hospital at Faversham where it is much used.[3]

This afternoon I have had rather an unpleasant revival of the memories of 1912, when as you remember I spent the best part of 6 weeks over the Coal Strike. The miners are threatening to come out for a *national* advance of wages of 20 per cent to meet the extra cost of living, and the owners (among whom I believe 'Uncle Hugh' has not yet appeared) insist that whatever is given shd. be given locally in view of the circumstances of each particular area. There was an impasse at the Board of Trade, so Runciman brought me in, & I have just been listening to a deputation of about 20 representative miners, who tried to put forward their case. I have so far succeeded that the owners will now agree to meet the men here next week – wh. is something: for if they quarrel, as is likely & indeed certain, one may be able to put the screw on both. But it is an unwelcome addition to the cares of life.

What were you doing in Manchester?

Darling let me know what time you are coming up on Monday, & whether I can see you that evening or Tuesday before dinner, at or soon after 6.

A wave of distress and uncertainty came over me last night, as you would see from the little letter I wrote you. I hope it didn't worry you, & I am sure you would understand. You are so true & courageous that I know you would always tell me everything. Some one once wrote a book that had considerable notoriety in early Victorian times called *The Eclipse of Faith*.[4] My Faith is – as Wordsworth says – 'subject neither to eclipse or wane'.[5] But sometimes it longs – perhaps irrationally – for re-assurance.

Beloved – most beloved – you are my *life*.

[1] William, grandson of W. E. Gladstone; M.P. for Kilmarnock Burghs from 1911. Commissioned Royal Welch Fusiliers, Sept. 1914. Reached the Front 21 Mar., killed 14 Apr. Bryce had suggested to Asquith, 19 Mar., that this promising man should be found a place on the staff.

[2] By H. A. Vachell. Henry Ainley played Joseph Quinney.

[3] Spinal analgesia was then a comparatively new technique.

[4] By Henry Rogers, a Congregationalist, who was a professor at Spring Hill College, Birmingham. This defence of Christian doctrine was published anonymously in 1852 and ran through 6 edns. in 3 years.

[5] *Excursion*, iv. 72.

407

Friday midnight 23 Ap 15 [ii]

My darling – I can't tell you what I feel about Rupert Brooke's death.[1] It has given me more pain than any loss in the war. We have seen a great deal of him all this autumn & winter,[2] he & Oc being fellow officers, & the closest companions & friends. And Violet & he had a real friendship – perhaps the germ at any rate (as I once said to you) of something more.[3] He was clean-cut & beautiful to look at, and had a streak of something more than talent: his last Sonnets struck a fine note.[4] Altogether, *by far* the most attractive & winning of the younger men whom I have got to know since the war began. . . .

Why should people like myself be allowed to linger on the stage, when so much vividness & promise is cut prematurely off?

And in the stress of such an event – so unforeseeable, so apparently irrational & wasteful – one gets a dazed, dim, premonitory feeling, that the next blow may come even nearer home. My much loved Oc – or Beb, who went off to-night to the front in France. Who cd. have thought it possible or even conceivable a year ago?

[1] Brooke died on the afternoon of 23 Apr. and was buried that evening on Skyros. By the following evening the ships carrying the assault troops for the Gallipoli landings were moving to their battle stations.

[2] He had stayed twice at Walmer and had recovered from influenza at 10 Downing St.

[3] On the voyage to the Mediterranean Brooke had written to Violet: 'I had rather be with you than with anyone in the world.' According to Virginia Woolf, Violet said in 1916 that she had loved Brooke 'as she had never loved any man'.

[4] The War Sonnets had appeared in *New Numbers* in Mar. *1914 and Other Poems* was not published until June 1915.

408

Sat. morning 24 Ap 1915

We have 2 cars in hospital, and have damaged by bad driving a third, wh. had been lent to us by the munificent Dunn: so Bluey is going to drive . . . me & Eliz^th . . . [to the Wharf] in his. . . .

I hope that the Italian thing will be signed to-day or to-morrow.[1] The Miners trouble is rather threatening, but I think it will yield to tactful handling. . . .

[1] See Letter 410, n. 1.

409

The Wharf,
Sutton Courtney,
Berks.

Sunday 25 Ap 1915

. . . We have a very odd party here (scratched together after all kinds of desperate & futile experiments by Miss Way).[1]. . .

I had a good letter from Violet from Dublin yesterday describing her new milieu: a house adorned with many photographs of the Nathan family, 'which, rather unexpectedly, point to Matthew as the beau of the breed'. She had not as yet seen the Wimbornes. She says rather an apt thing by the way of Lady Scott 'she has just the wrong amount of intelligence – I mean too much for its quality'. I know people like that, don't you? especially women. Happily yours is mixed in just the right proportion: which is one (tho' not more than *one*) of the reasons why I love you so much, & find such joy in our intercourse. Of course, Violet hadn't heard when she wrote of poor Rupert's death.[2] Eddie Marsh (who adored him) is quite broken hearted.

I wonder what you are doing? Last night, by way of a sedative, I took to reading again Dill's excellent book on Roman Society from Nero to M. Aurelius.[3] Many good judges think that that 100 years was the happiest in the history of the world. But towards the end of it at any rate (as Renan says) 'le monde s'attristait'. Nothing is new under the sun. I see that Pliny complains of the want of deference & reverence (!) of young people for their elders: 'ipsi sibi exempla sunt' – 'they are their own models' – like Diana Manners, & some others we know. There was something delightfully hospitable & catholic in the later Paganism, just before Christianity began to break all the crockery. The Emperor Alexander Severus used to have daily Matins in a chapel which was decorated with images of Abraham, Orpheus, & Christ.

Darling I don't often ramble off like this into the byways of the past, and I dare say you think I have fallen into one of my 'pedantic' moods. Whatever they may be, I fear I always make you their victim.

I have just (to change topics) been reading a rather able mem^m by Hankey, in wh. he gives a number of reasons for thinking that the German High Fleet will come out 'in earnest' in a few days' time. One of them is the hope of keeping K's first Army – wh. is now ready – at home. Another, to strike a blow at our prestige before the Italian & Roumanian business (of wh. they no doubt know a lot) is finally clinched. I see from a note that Fisher entirely agrees with him. It wd. be a gambler's throw, but rather an attractive one.[4]. . .

[1] Asquith told Violet that Miss Way had invited 34 ladies in vain.

[2] Lady Scott, who was a fellow guest in Dublin, wrote in her diary: 'That night Violet heard Rupert Brooke was dead. She minded awfully and sobbed for hours. I stayed with her till two; but I am the worst hand at comforting I ever knew. . . . Poor Violet, I liked her much better when she was a poor, weak, mizzy, little impotent thing than I do in all her brilliance.'

[3] Published 1904. Samuel Dill had been Professor of Greek at Queen's College, Belfast, since 1890; but he was best known for his books on Roman society.

[4] Hankey wrote on 22 Apr., Fisher similarly to Churchill the next day. Churchill had issued a warning on 24 Mar.:

A long series of indications in the intercepts points to a general offensive movement by the German High Seas Fleet at no distant date. . . . Every precaution should therefore be taken during April.

The Germans were reported to have put to sea on 17 Apr. but to have thought better of it. Their High Seas Fleet ventured out on the night of 17–18 May, but only to cover minelaying operations in the Dogger Bank.

410

Monday Midnight 26 Ap 1915

My own darlingest – to see you again, & be with you, & hear your voice, and above all to feel that everything is unchanged, has made a new creature of me. You are the best and richest of life-givers. . . .

. . . My own most dear & sweet – you were never more what I think & dream of you than to-day. Nor shall I ever forget your appreciation of what I have done, or tried to do, to bring in Italy.[1] In all the momentous things of life, you are the star of my faith, and the anchor of my hope, and the crown of any success I have. And that must be your compensation for the worries & anxieties wh. I fear I sometimes cause you. Believe me, they do not spring from caprice or silly weakness. They are the price which love pays for the best thing that life can bring. . . .

I hope & believe that this is going to be a good week for us – a little shadowed tho' it may be by your perhaps too unconditional compliance to Sir H. Norman.[2] Inoculation is at any rate a useful arresting asset. . . .

To-morrow . . . (unless the Heavens fall) I shall come to you in the motor at Mansfield St between 5.45 & 6, and we will have one of our divine drives. I wish that brute Bluey had asked me to dine! And we will make plans for the following days. . . .

[1] The secret treaty pledging Italy to fight beside the Allies within a month had been signed that day.

[2] A well-known Liberal M.P. who, with his wife, ran the war hospital at Wimereux, near Boulogne, where Venetia was going to nurse.

XXIX

E.S.M. to B.V.S.

10 Downing Street

26 April 1915

My very darling

. . . You will dine alone with me tomorrow? I shall have heaps to tell you as I shall see my brother tomorrow.[1] Dearest I have been most depressed since I met Barbara at lunch and heard you were going to France. I can't bear to think I shan't see you for long times but I must ask you in any case if you do go to postpone your departure till everything is settled. . . .

[1] Lord Swaythling, Edwin's eldest brother, was a trustee under their father's will.

411

Tues. 27 Ap 1915 Midnight

My darlingest – We had a heavenly drive this afternoon – hadn't we? You were divine, as you always are: and in some ways so extraordinary & unique, that I feel at odd moments puzzled & bewildered. I wonder sometimes whether any one else than me has, or could have, more power of provoking or compelling a response? Not that I am in the least unsatisfied or ungrateful – as you know well. . . .

I went straight back to the House, & (happily) strayed in & took my seat on the bench, to find Austen Chamberlain on his legs complaining that neither the P.M. nor the For. Sec[y] had thought it worth while to be present at the debate on our prisoners in Germany! So I got up, as soon as he sat down, & made a short speech wh. was full of sympathy, & seemed to satisfy the situation. Luck![1]

I dined at the Admiralty: W & Clemmie & Goonie, Sir A. Sinclair (quite an attractive young soldier) & the ex-Colonel – now Brigadier Seely. The Bud came in afterwards while we were playing Bridge, & reported that she had found you & Bluey playing also with M[c]Kenna. What an ill-arranged evening! You & I & Bluey & Frances wd have made an excellent quartette – don't you think? . . .

. . . The Bud retired to a distant sofa with Sir A.S.: I wish that cd. be brought off – they are made for one another. . . .

. . . It was strange – what you said to-day – of your detachment from yourself & your own future. It fills me with surprise & forebodings. What I mean is – that I can never bring myself to understand your under-estimate of yourself – wh., to me, is an almost unimaginable array of glorious possibilities (if only you were ambitious!) . . .

I am far from happy about other things – foreign & domestic. I have to make a fresh draft every day upon my already over-drawn account of optimism, but *you* redeem it. Send me a little line to say whether you are bound to Violet – *or free after 6*. That wd. be heavenly. Everything else, and everyone else is *flat*, stale, unprofitable. Your lover always.

Are you sure that you don't want to be 'unlettered'?

[1] Despite George V's protests, the 39 officers and men taken from U-boats since the start of unrestricted submarine warfare had been 'separately interned' from 'honourable prisoners of war' and subjected to 'special conditions': *Parl. Deb.* lxxi. 573. This had led to reprisals against 39 British prisoners of war in Germany, all of them officers chosen for their prominence (*The Times*, 26 Apr., 6b). Asquith began his speech by explaining that his 'absence during the earlier part of the debate was not due to any want of sense of the importance of the subject-matter under discussion'.

412

Wed. 28 Ap 1915 [i]

My darling – as I have often told you this is an ill-managed world, and to-day is an illustration. The House is almost empty, discussing the Post Office vote: the sun is at its best: I could get away with ease, & we might have had a delicious drive between 5.30 & 7.30 to Richmond or into space!

And now I have your little message, which bars the door to anything. Sweet darling, I know it is not your fault. . . .

I am rather anxious about your taking the inoculation so soon. May it not possibly disable you on Sat or Sunday? – which would be the grimmest of tragedies. I *do* look forward to our time together at Alderley.

Frances Horner came to lunch & told me of your proceedings last night. She says she got so tired that in the end she couldn't move, & nearly spent the night at Bluey's. She, lucky woman, is dining again in your company to-night. I wish Barbara[1] had asked me; like Bluey, she is a very poor friend at a pinch. . . .

Nellie Hozier was at lunch to-day and I ventured on a little mild chaff about her prolonged session with the young Scottish laird last night: but I fear he has the cannyness of his race. And yet she wd. be an excellent investment – wouldn't she?[2]

To-day's news of the Dardanelles is quite good, & illustrates the truth that in this extraordinary war all the oldest, as well as the most modern, devices come in. The Trojan Horse, for instance. 2000 soldiers who were unable to land were shut up in a collier, the decks covered with coal, & the sides made openable & flappable. And then when night came on, she was run ashore, and they emerged from their cupboard, & were all safely landed.[3] I dare say they told you this at lunch. It is quite one of the romantic by-episodes of the War. I am afraid there have been very heavy losses, but so far we hear nothing of the Naval Division. . . .

My most beloved, I have come to the conclusion that, when you were created, as much was *left out of you* as would make the whole of an ordinary average woman! *Some* of the things we were speaking of yesterday: I hoped to continue our talk to-day: we will on Sat & Sunday. But the things that were kept, and wh. I have learnt to know so well & to adore so deeply, were worth a billion times as much. Such is my sober judgment. It is hateful that you shd be so near & yet so far. Write me one little line of consolation & help – most entirely dear: the love of my life.

[1] Barbara McLaren, Pamela McKenna's sister: see next letter.
[2] She married Lt.-Col. Bertram Romilly in Dec. 1915.
[3] Not a correct version of what happened to the *River Clyde* on 25 Apr. She was run aground at Sedd-el-Bahr, near the tip of the Gallipoli peninsula, at 6.22 a.m. after an hour's bombardment of the shore positions. The Turks, who had crept back into their trenches when the bombardment ended, poured a murderous fire into the assaulting troops; and the lighters could not be fixed between ship and shore. A second attempt at 4 p.m. to bring the remaining troops off the *River Clyde* was little more successful; but during the night they were landed without a single casualty. Though the parallel with the Trojan Horse occurred to those at Gallipoli as well as to Asquith, it was far from close, since the Turks could not have mistaken the nature of the ship's mission at Sedd-el-Bahr. The *River Clyde* (renamed as *Maruja y Aurora*) plied as a collier on the Spanish coast until 1966.

413

Wed April 28, 1915 [ii] Midnight

My darling – After a long rather dreary afternoon at the House (in the course of which I wrote to you) I thought I would try to get some of the sunlight – wh. I had hoped to spend in your company. So about 7 I sallied forth & wandered in solitude thro' the slums of Westminster, ultimately dropping my little letter (like a postman, tho' without a ring or knock) into the slit in the door of 8 L. Coll. St.[1] Oddly enough at almost the next street corner I met Aggie,[2] who had been visiting the sick-bed of Pamela. I 'passed the time of day' with her, and rambled on.

¹ The McLarens' house in Little College Street.
² Lady Jekyll: she had been visiting her daughter, Pamela McKenna, whose house in Smith Square was close to Little College Street.

XXX

E.S.M. to B.V.S.

[28 April 1915]

. . . I have just had another talk with my brother. He has devised a glorious (comparatively) new plan far quicker and less ridiculous. So I quiver with new hope but will explain all to you today.

To tell you the honest truth, nothing worries me now but *you*. I cant expect to be loved much or nearly as much as I love *you* – it ought to satisfy me to be loved at all, but dearest you are a perplexing person.

You decide to spend your life with me if it can be done, then without a word to me fix up 3 months at least in France. You come to London and use most of your time there being inoculated! . . .

You no longer dislike being alone with me (Thank God for that) yet you seem not to mind much if convention, or social duty prevents!

Forgive dearest all these growls. My new plan is so simple that nothing else matters . . .

414

Thurs. 29 Ap. 15.

Thank you so much most dear for your little letter wh. I got this morning. Of course you are right to stay in bed to-day. I only hope the temperature will come & go, so that you will be fit to travel without risk to-morrow.[1] I trust you won't have more than the usual amount of malaise. . . .

Violet . . . came to see me late & we had rather an intimate talk – some of it about *you*, whom she loves with a good deal of understanding. . . .

. . . I think always of you, and long for you to be happy: if possible, in a way that won't make me *very* unhappy! All love.

¹ Asquith was to spend the weekend at Alderley, travelling there by train with Venetia on 30 Apr.: see Letter XXXIV, p. 579.

XXXI

E.S.M. to B.V.S.

30 April 1915 [misdated 29] [i]

Most desperately beloved of all women,

Yesterday was the greatest day of my life. Its net result was that the most wonderful woman in the world delivered herself into my safe keeping, into my hands for better or worse, in the hope that with me she could lead a happier life than was possible without me, or with any other man.

. . . Despite all my gloomy warnings and safeguardings, I will do my best – I will try to alter lifelong and crusted habits and adopt all your suggestions to fashion myself into the husband of your desire. . . .

As to the rest, I want you to become a Jewess just as a woman who marries a Frenchman becomes a Frenchwoman, but in this case you become naturalised before. As to the religion it seems always to me the easiest of religions and makes no demands of me save a very rare visit to synagogue and Passover at my mother's (do you remember saying how amused you would be at that!!) You have no use for formulated religion, nor have I, still less for ceremonial masquerading as religion.

As regards our children. I have always believed that no religious teaching was the right thing and I mean to stick to that. If they want to know they shall be told that their father was born a Jew and remained throughout life a Jew – that their mother was a Jew by adoption and that they were therefore born Jews. If they want a religion to practise although you and I practised none, they can choose their own.

You are right in saying that they are likely to have more non-Jewish than Jewish friends and therefore they are likely to care nothing about their label. If they want to marry Xians or Hindus they will have no criticism from me, nor shall I think any worse of them for wanting to. But if they choose to stick to the flag (which I do not think likely because I would regard it as unloving to try and influence them in any way) I shall be pleased. . . .

I never think of myself as one. It's a thought which does not intrude. You won't find it will. But all I ask is that when we are attacked or scorned, you regard yourself as one of us by adoption, that you have thrown your lot with us, and that honestly is the only time I ever find one thinks of it at all. . . .

That is really all. If you can do this I shall be more than satisfied.

Will you take my advice? It is this. Think of the fun we shall have together, think of our lives from happiness to happiness, think of all the things we can do together, think of the great happiness of the children we have so often discussed, think of having a wonderful life, go baldheaded for the disagreeablenesses, go through with them bravely and lets get on with our fun. All else matters very little. Don't make an obstacle of words, say things which make life easier even if it costs an effort, and do hurry up my beloved. . . .

. . . Come to me soon. I agree about money. Let them say what they like.[1] We wont increase our difficulties by poverty. Just dismiss the matter by saying to me 'I will go through with it and do it'. . . .

Yours most lovingly,

E.

[1] Venetia had presumably referred to the likelihood that her conversion would be seen, not as a natural move by a woman who was marrying into a Jewish family, but as a precaution against forfeiting a fortune.

XXXII

E.S.M. TO B.V.S.

[30 April 1915][1] [ii]

Venetia dearest, you have a right to satisfy yourself of my love. Can you return it? Can you be honest with yourself in returning it?

Can you make a true foundation. It might well be that you can say at best that you think life will be more or less good with me. It has not been very happy lately. It has lacked direction and responsibility. It has contained elements which perhaps you want to get rid of even at the cost of some void. It has no future of aim, purpose or fulness. You will therefore exchange it for something loveless perhaps but the best available. If that is your true view for all that you hold dear say so. It will then be for me to say if I will give it to you & pour my love unrequited to the only woman and say that I am indeed happy to do so, that from my Venetia I have no right to expect more, that I am lucky to get so much.

As a matter of fact I dont think I should say so. I think I should in permanent unhappiness go away to my lonely furrow, with all hope gone and a colourless future of painful egoism. For when I thought I had little emotion, love, passion, exclusive and deep feeling to give, I felt that for such as I had to give, I could not expect much in return. But now that I know you are of the very element of my being, that you are of my life, that I could find for you something approximating to sacrifice and courage, that you alone are of my waking and sleeping, that I want nothing else but you, to know that my love was not returned would kill. Once, wonderful one, you wrote that you thought you loved me! Can you say you really do. . . .

Please dont be angry with me. You can hurt me now as no one else in the world can or could and as I thought no one ever would be able to. You wont will you. I am not digging up by the roots. I am asking for a firm foundation, an assurance which I shall believe and accept for always and then – oh for such fun. Come back to me at once.

Yrs devotedly – your husband in the near future
Edwin S.

[Postscript] Are you tired of all this. Please forgive me for boring you. Could you relieve me and send me to Picket happy by telegraphing tomorrow morning to this address

> (1) Alls well.
> or (2) Curse you.
> or (3) Am doubtful . . .

. . . I had to tell Bongie last night!

[1] The letters which Edwin wrote to Venetia on 30 Apr. give a vivid illustration of his quick changes of mood. He did not date Letter XXXII; but it contains (in an unpublished passage) a reference to Lloyd George's luncheon for the French Minister of Finance, Alexandre Ribot; and this establishes that it was written on 30 Apr.

XXXIII

E.S.M. to B.V.S.

30 April 1915 [iii]

Darling, darling

Since writing to you I am more than ever certain that a lot I wrote was overdone and that I've got your love. Thank God! How slowly time passes. . . .

Are you engaged Thursday? I've got an invitation to dine with P.M. Shall I meet you? . . .

XXXIV

B.V.S. to E.S.M.

In train

30 April 1915

Darling, I wish I felt the faintest inspiration, but this infernal train shakes so that I find it impossible to concentrate either my mind or my pen. Opposite me sits the P.M. in a more cheerful frame of mind I think, but I've a feeling in my bones that this party isnt going to be a success, I feel I shall quarrel with Bongie, be odious to the P.M., & have to avoid Violet's questions if she bothers to ask any. . . .

. . . I'm no fun to be in love with. . . . my supply of emotion is a thin and meagre one, but such as it is, bad in quantity and quality, its yours.

And you mustnt be always examining it under a microscope or subjecting it to severe tests because it wont stand it!

We can have such fun together & I'm sure could be so really happy & if that cant be made a good basis for marriage I dont know that I shall ever find a better. We've both I'm bound to say always put ourselves before the other in the most unprepossessing terms. You take every opportunity of telling me that nothing that I want will ever make you alter your mode of life, and I am always impressing on you the fact that I'm completely & coldbloodedly detached from all interest in my life. It doesnt sound good on paper. And yet I'm simply longing for you to be here, & miss you horribly. Its again such a lovely day & we should have been so happy. . . .

God, how bored I feel, how glorious one's life ought to be & how bloody it is. But I was happy yesterday, thank you so much. . . .

I hope this isnt a horrible letter, I'm never sure. . . .

XXXV

E.S.M. to B.V.S.

1 May 1915 [i]

A diary of a miserable day.

Awake 6.0 . . . 2 hrs, before post – what a fool I was to write as I did[1] – I've lost my V. and I'm so certain if I'd shown a little more confidence she was mine. . . .

2.45 p.m. . . . Can find no body to talk to, Katharine away, Bongie away, am done and near suicide. . . .

Get letter. Thank God things are better. How I wish I'd never written so exacting a letter. . . .

I'll never be a fool again.

¹ See Letter XXXII (pp. 577–8).

XXXVI

E.S.M. to B.V.S.

1 May 1915 [ii]

My darling

A thousand thanks for your letter. God what a day I've spent. . . .

I am quite happy now although the day has been a black one.

I will learn from it to trust. . . .

Forgive me for my doubts and be my own Venetia, the woman of women. . . .

415

Alderley Park,
Chelford,
Cheshire.

Sunday morning 6.30 2 May 15

My darling – I thought once or twice yesterday, for the first time in our intercourse, that I rather bored you, and that you would have been more relieved than sorry if some one had joined us & shared our talk. This has puzzled me & made me rather unhappy during the night —

Forgive me: but I *must* tell you.

I love you more than ever.

XXXVII

B.V.S. to E.S.M.

Alderley Park

2 May 1915

. . . Boulogne, darling, is clinched I go on Monday week.[1] Dont be angry with me for settling this, I know it must seem to you to show lamentable lukewarmness, but it isnt that I want to postpone things but I do want to have a slight first hand experience of what the conditions are like not 60 miles away from a vast war. . . .

My dearest you have been an angel to me all this time, your patience & generosity to me have been wonderful.

I think we'll come up from Winston's Sunday after dinner[2] & have a last long glorious talk.

I've not said anything to mother yet, I find it impossible to talk of my affairs.

I've *loathed* this Sunday in spite of Birrell,[3] & felt quite miserable. . . .

[1] To nurse in Lady Norman's war hospital at Wimereux.
[2] From Churchill's weekend retreat, Hoe Farm, Hascombe, Surrey. See Appendix 3.
[3] Violet enjoyed the weekend, writing in her diary: 'I travelled down with Birrell and Bongie – we had a very good talk. . . . I have never known Alderley so nice. . . . I went for peaceful potters about the garden with Birrell in the mornings and divine motor drives in the afternoon.'

416

Monday 3 May 1915

. . . I had a heavenly time at Alderley to look back upon during these coming weeks of separation & absence. True there were some depressing moments, for which I hold myself accountable. I only hope I did not infect you with any of my bad spirits. Our walk & talk in the garden this morning was perfect, and will be to me a golden memory. I know you will always tell me everything. As for me I could not love you *more*, but I try hard to make my love more unselfish and more worthy of you.

I have been busy ever since I got here – first, with Runciman & his Board of Trade men over the Coal business. I don't mean to burn my fingers in that very combustible milieu: so I have told them to get express assurances at once from both sides, before I do anything, that they will abide by & carry out my decision – whatever it may be. It certainly can't please both, and will probably not please either.[1]

Then I had a rather interesting talk with K. He is strong for our retorting against the Germans with asphyxiating shells.[2] The news from the Dardanelles is satisfactory, & K. has no doubt that we shall break through.[3] The interesting place for the moment is the Flanders side of France. Relations are very strained between Joffre & French, who thinks that the French have behaved disgracefully for the last 10 days. The result of their running away, & taking no effective step to recover the ground, is that he has had to draw back his line over a mile. (This is *Secret*.)[4] K, however, for the first time takes a very optimistic view of this part of the field. He thinks that he has evidence that the Germans have resolved to fall back (on a considerable scale): in fact to shorten their line, and substantially reduce their number in the west.[5] If this is true (of course, it is also *very* private), it looks as if they knew by this time that Italy is coming in, and were preparing to meet the new dangers in the East & South. K. is happier than I have seen him for a long time.

Next, there appeared Ll. George, attended by the Assyrian & Jack Pease. He came ostensibly to talk about to-morrow's Budget, which will be a humdrum affair. But as usual, he launched out into irrelevant topics: amongst others, an interview he had had to-day with Bonar Law on the subject of the Drink taxes. B.L. seems to have told him frankly that the Tory party was so much in the hands of the Trade that they must oppose them root & branch. Ll. G. replied that, if so, he could not persist with them, but would throw the whole responsibility for doing nothing in that direction on the Tories. B.L. said that this might be awkward; but I don't suppose he really minds the least.[6] Finally I had E. Grey, who talked at length about his eyes. In the end we arranged that he shd. go away for a month in about a fortnight from now: when the Italian business will have become public property.[7] . . .

. . . Most dear & precious, think of me, and believe in my deep & deathless love.

---

[1] See p. 566.

[2] On 22 Apr. at the start of their attack on Ypres the Germans had used chlorine gas, emitted from cylinders, against two French divisions. The British and French had both disregarded the signs they had received of this impending gas attack. The French broke; and the Canadians immediately to the south had to extend their front dangerously. This second battle of Ypres continued until 24 May.

[3] Kitchener presumably argued that the part of the operation already accomplished, namely the landing itself, must be the most difficult. On 28 Apr. he had ordered a Territorial Div. and an Indian Brigade from Egypt as reinforcements for Hamilton. The general Turkish counter-attack, started on 1 May, had made no progress. Kitchener's confidence was misplaced. When Hamilton attacked on 6 May he made no more progress than the Turks had done. By 8 May he had no reserves left and not many shells; and he held only two small bridgeheads, about 13 miles from each other and covering scarcely 5 square miles between them. See p. 598.

⁴ The fact that French had lost this ground was of little importance; but, like many of his fellow commanders, he believed, though without any corroborative evidence, that tactical retreats impaired the morale of his troops. When Smith-Dorrien refused to try to regain the ground by counter-attacks he was sent home and replaced as 2nd Army Commander by Plumer. With great skill the latter advanced just far enough E. of Ypres to satisfy his C.-in-C.

⁵ Since mid-April the Germans had passed an army of 8 divs. from West to East. This had just won a great victory at Gorlice and would soon clear the Russians out of Galicia. This massive effort to save Austria did not entail a shortening of the German lines in the West.

⁶ Lloyd George was compelled to abandon almost all of the increases in beer, wine, and spirit duties which he had put before the Commons on 29 Apr. Opposition to his proposals was by no means confined to the Conservatives: increasing the spirit duties, for instance, was extremely unpopular with the Irish Nationalists. Asquith was right to assume that the protests were too widespread for the Tories to be saddled with the responsibility for Lloyd George's retreat. Later in the war Lloyd George secured large increases in the taxes on drink.

⁷ On 4 May the Italian Government denounced the Triple Alliance, which had bound it nominally to Germany and Austria, and so made public its warlike intentions.

XXXVIII

E.S.M. to B.V.S.

3 May 1915

. . . I am miserable about Boulogne. Well so be it, only swear to me you will be back by a certain date, and lets try and fix all things before you go. Will you? Give me the whole of this week regardless of anybody.¹. . .

Let's be married next month !². . .

¹ Despite this plea Venetia went for drives with Asquith on the Wednesday and the Friday: Letters 418 and 420.
² They were married on 26 July 1915: see p. 606 below.

417

Tu. 4 May 15 Midnight

My darling – I don't think you were really *very* glad to see me this evening, though you were as good, & quick at seeing things, and as kind, as you have ever been. I feel I have the uncanny instinct of a clinical thermometer in measuring your moods & tenses – normal, sub-normal, & sometimes, but how rarely, super-normal.

I walked almost the whole way back to Downing St (nearly run over) ruminating over these things. I sometimes think that Northcliffe & his obscene crew may perhaps be right – that, whatever the rest of the world may say, I am, if not an imposter, at any rate a failure, & *au fond*, a fool. What is the real test?

I suppose most people would say that I had got at least a fair share of what men desire, & struggle for, & aim at. But then comes in the Gospel question: What shall it profit a man to gain the whole world, & lose his own soul?

There, I fear, I am in peril of breaking down. For 'my own soul' is not wholly, or whole-heartedly, engaged (even now) in the things that seem, & probably are, of supreme importance.

And to *you?* 'the little more & the little less': such a *slight* difference! I sometimes *long* for your detachment: 'to thee the reed is as the oak'.[1]

Most sweet – I don't know in what mood this may catch you. Perhaps you will toss your head (a gesture not described in the passport) and purse your lip, & pucker for an instant, the 'pencill'd brow', and ejaculate 'poor dear' – 'I *adore* Mikky'! (or Huck). When you do that, I feel that I should like to be 'imprisoned in the viewless winds'[2] & 'consign' to the dust-heap. And – . . . .

. . . To me, at this moment, (I am just going to bed & I hope to sleep) the world is (as Hamlet says) 'a foul & pestilent congregation of vapours'.

Good night – divine one.

---

[1] *Cymbeline*, IV. ii: 'Fear no more the heat o' the sun'. 'Consign' in the 6th para. of the letter is from the same poem.
[2] *Measure for Measure*, III. i.

418

Wed 5 May 1915 Midnight

My own beloved – how glad & grateful I am that you wrote your letter this morning, before we had our drive. It made such a difference, and enabled us to clear out of our wonderful sky (the *most* wonderful sky ever known) the only lowering shadow of a possible dread. I have had some very good times – as well as some very bad ones – in my life: but for a single hour of perfect delight & happiness I should find from 5.30 to 6.30 to-day difficult to beat. I never saw you look more lovely, and there was in your divine eyes every now & again a soft & beatific radiance that I shall remember to my dying day. And apart from what is outside (tho' I can never separate what is without & within) I have never known you more wise in insight, more large in imagination, more sensitive in response, more noble in all the things that make a woman worthy of a man's devotion & worship.

After you left, I said to myself, with more assurance & certainty than ever, that in knowing you & loving you I had won the supreme prize of my life. And so, darlingest, I shall *always* think: you are the greatest gift of the Gods.

Don't let us ever go back *one inch* from where we were when we parted to-day. Will you try? To me it needs no trying. Promise me this.

And if, in moments when I am tempted to think of the might-have-been (do you remember some lines I sent you on your birthday in 1913?)[1] I seem jealous or exacting or exorbitant, you will remember always – won't you? – that these are the penalties, justly exacted by fate, for the supreme absorbing happiness of the great love of a life.

You say, in your minimising way, that it makes *you* happy to know that you help & sustain & inspire me. Darling – I owe you *everything*. Without you, where should I have been? or be now?

It is not, after all, such an unequal partnership. I give you all the love that any man can ever give: you give me the life blood of all that I do, or can ever hope to do.

We will leave the future, till it comes; and when it comes I will try to face it with courage & to be worthy of you. Meanwhile, we will let nothing spoil our unique & divine intimacy. You can hardly imagine how much happier & more buoyant I feel than I did this time last night.

I am so glad that our lightning shopping resulted in *The Bag*. I have hopes that it will make you every day mix your smallest doings with thoughts of me.

I went to the House & made a little speech on prisoners,[2] and since then have played mild Bridge with Jack Pease & Mikky (who received your message that you couldn't lunch with him); but all the time I was breathing 'an ampler aether, a diviner air' – like St Paul when he was lifted into the Third Heaven – 'whether in the body, or out of the body, I cannot tell'. Most dear, will you send me one little line in the course of the day to-morrow (Thurs) to tell me (what I know) that you *understand?*

For life, till death, you are the love of my heart, the joy & glory of my life. Your own.

Don't forget Friday!

[1] Letter 18.
[2] Asquith promised that records would be kept of maltreatment of British prisoners of war in German camps 'in order that when the proper hour comes . . . the means of convicting and punishing the offenders . . . may be put in force'. The American Ambassador to Germany was active in trying to help the 39 British officers who had been placed in solitary confinement in reprisal against the Admiralty's treatment of the U-boat prisoners: see Letter 411, text and n. 1. Asquith read to the House a note which Grey had just sent to the Ambassador. For the latter's account of his efforts see J. W. Gerard, *My Four Years in Germany* (1917), ch. 10.

419

7 May 1915 [i]

My darling – I have seen Norman. He is going by the same train as you on Monday (2.30 Victoria) & will look after you & Violet if she goes.[1]

He says the only important thing is to get your passport *visé'*d by the *French* authorities here as of *Monday's* date; and that if I sent yours & Violet's to the French Embassy they would do this at once & save endless waiting on Sat or Monday at the Consulate.

He doesn't seem to attach importance to the police permit, but it is as well to have it. There is an infinitude of red tape.

You will have heard about Oc's wound: happily it does not seem to be really serious.[2]

I shall be with you at M. St. just before 3.30. *All love.*

[1] Violet Asquith planned to go to Wimereux on an experimental basis.
[2] He soon recovered from this knee wound.

420

Friday May 7. 1915 [ii] Midnight

My most darling – what do I think of Simon? the dullest, dustiest, most limited, and hide-bound creature (having sparks of great intelligence, and an almost immeasurable capacity for getting on in life) that ever had, & failed to recognise, the supreme chance of sitting next the best companion in the whole world. This, however, is by the way.

We had one of the most heavenly of our drives – hadn't we? When shall we have such another? I despair when I think of the Fridays that lie before me. I wonder if you feel the same. I will undertake to say that, in the hundred or more of our drives, there has been a greater interchange of 'Fun', in the best & widest sense, than has ever happened in our time, or perhaps my time, between any man and any woman. (This will rather amuse you: George Moore, French's friend, said to Margot (apropos of the *Times* attacks):[1] 'Northcliffe thinks he can get rid of the P.M: there is only one person who can do that'. M: 'Who'? Moore: 'God'.) Very simple isn't it, darling? Whoever possesses that power, can exercise it effectively & without a moment's delay, when any veil is dropped between me & you – soul of my life. . . .

. . . Whatever the future has in store for you in the way of companionship and intimacy (with some undisclosed person, whom in advance I loathe more than words can say) I shall be ready at the day of judgment to mention that I had the best of it! 'Poor darling' (I almost hear you say) 'he has for once, at any rate, rather a swollen head.'

Perhaps: but my conviction is unshaken & unshakeable. 'For the time being' – you said to-day. God knows how long or how short a time that means. Long or short, it measures out the supreme & crowning happiness of my life. The rest will be silence. . . .

We dined with the Keppels (while you were at your music hall) – the only unusual person there being Sir S. Jameson, the hero of that antiquated & futile adventure that used to be called the 'Raid'. *Au fond*, a nice, simple, not very effectual creature.[2]

I mind *very much* that I should not be with you this last Sunday,[3] – more than any words can say. Such (in D[r] Chalmers's historic phrase) is my 'unbridled appetency'.[4]

Most sweet, you will write me a little farewell letter to D[g] St on Sunday – won't you? . . .

I think this week has taught us to know one another better than ever before – if that were possible. . . .

[1] On 4 May *The Times* made play with the discrepancies between Asquith's Newcastle speech (pp. 558–9) and other Government statements. Its first leader two days later on the organization of manpower ended with the comment: 'We have still far to travel before we can claim, as a nation, that we are really "at war".' On 7 May the methods of recruiting for government posts were criticized, with the conclusion: 'The government cannot effectively appeal either for recruits or for economy unless they give a better lead themselves.'

[2] On 29 Dec. 1895 Leander Starr Jameson, Cecil Rhodes's chief lieutenant, led a force of about 700 into the Transvaal in the hope of inducing the *uitlanders* in Johannesburg to rise against the Boer régime which denied them full citizens' rights. The 'Jameson Raid', which was mounted against the advice both of Rhodes's subordinates in Cape Town and of the Johannesburg 'reformers', ended in a humiliating fiasco. The raiders were surrounded by Boer commandos 14 miles from Johannesburg and forced to surrender. Jameson and others were convicted under the Foreign Enlistment Act and imprisoned. Jameson recovered from this catastrophe and became Prime Minister of Cape Colony (1904–08). Kipling's 'If' is said to have been inspired by his career. By 1915 his health was frail; he died in November 1917.

[3] Venetia was to spend Sunday at Hoe Farm, Hascombe, Surrey, with the Churchills.

[4] When Chalmers visited Carlingford Castle in 1842 he was told that the nearby villagers spoke Gaelic; and an old woman was given sixpence to demonstrate this. On being asked to translate her remarks into English she incurred Chalmers's reproof for her 'unbridled appetency' by demanding another sixpence: W. Hanna, *Chalmers* (Edinburgh, 1850–52), iv. 444.

421

The Wharf,
Sutton Courtney,
Berks.

Sunday 9 May 1915

My darling – I am not going to write you a farewell letter, for after all you will not be more than 100 miles from London all the time, although separated from me by the salt estranging sea, and by this ridiculous barrier of passports & permits. At least, I try to look at the situation in its comparatively mild geographical aspect. But of course it is all, more or less, a voluntary & calculated self-deception. I have *never* felt parting with anyone so much.

We have quite a nice party here – Ll. George, the Chief Justice, Bongie, your Sylvia (of whom I am fond) & Violet. And it is a lovely day. I am going presently to drive into Oxford to have a glimpse of Puffin,[1] & this afternoon I will take Sylvia round the country in a motor. But my thoughts all the time are far away, always in your company; re-living the past, clinging to the present, at moments diving dubiously into the future: altho' this last is a propensity wh. I try to hold in check.

I was looking last night thro' the *Two Gentlemen of Verona*, wh. I had not read for ages, & wh. is not a very rich quarry for our purpose.[2] These 2 lines sum up a lot of the misadventures in people's lives. 'She dreams on him that has forgot her love: You dote on her that cares not for your love'. Not that I think them appropriate to our case, which is of the rarest kind.

Beloved, I want you to know that you take with you, and, all the time you are away, you will be surrounded by, the deepest love and devotion of all my life. And I shall live on the thought of what you have been & are to me, and of what you are *in yourself* – the one incarnation of all that I worship.

Your *lover – for all time.*

[1] Anthony Asquith was at Summer Fields Preparatory School in north Oxford.
[2] The project was to collect favourite passages from Shakespeare's plays. Venetia completed it and gave the volume containing the transcriptions to Asquith for Christmas, 1915.

422

Monday 10 May 1915 Midnight

My own most loved – I suppose it is true (as the Scripture says) that all things work together for good for those who deserve them. Two days ago, at any rate, I shd. have expected you to be interned at Wimereux by now, &

could not have hoped for a sight of you for a month or 6 weeks. But Providence has happily ordered otherwise.[1]

Naturally, I don't like to think of you as laid low & suffering. But when I saw you in that too brief 10 minutes this evening, I went away with the impression that I had never seen you more lovely & loveable to look at, or, to all appearance, in better health & stronger vigour. But praise be to Allah, the doctors think otherwise, for it means at any rate *one* more (perhaps even more than one) opportunity of being with you.

I wonder what it is? My diagnosis (for what it is worth) points to the aftermath of inoculation, & rejects the facile hypothesis of 'German' measles, or, as Cynthia calls it, the 'Hun-pox'. Anyhow I shall come & see you (unless I am forbidden) at 6 on Tuesday.

I have just come back from a small man's party at Glenconner's: E. Grey and I & Jack Tennant & Drummond played a little Bridge (you will be glad to hear that at $\frac{1}{2}^{d}$s I made 57/-)

I walked back with the Assyrian from Mansfield St, and we had (as always) good conversation. I don't honestly believe that, at this moment, there are 2 persons in the world (of opposite sexes) from whom I cd. more confidently count, whatever troubles or trials I had to encounter, for whole-hearted love & devotion than you & he: of course, in quite different ways & senses. But – you remember well (for I have quoted it to you before) Beaumont's line:

'They have most power to hurt us whom we love' – perhaps it wd be better said: 'who us love'.[2]

Darling – shall I try to tell you what you have been & are to me? First, outwardly & physically, unapproachable & unique. Then, in temperament & character, often baffling & elusive, but always more interesting & attracting & compelling than any woman I have ever seen or known. In solid intellect, and real insight into all situations, great or small, incomparably first. And above all, & beyond all, in the intimacy of perfect confidence & understanding, for 2 years past, the pole-star & lode-star of my life.

This is plain unadorned truth. . . .

You are everything to me. God make you happy, & help me (you assisting & inspiring) to make the most of what is left in my life. Your own.

---

[1] Venetia had been taken ill during the weekend before her intended departure for Wimereux.

[2] Beaumont and Fletcher, *The Maid's Tragedy*, v. iv, a favourite quotation: see Letter 73.

423

Tues 11 May 1915 [i]

My darling – I got your sweet little pencil letter just as I was coming down to the House. I begin to be afraid that my diagnosis was wrong, & that the country leech was right. It is *too* disappointing. I fear you have a lot of *malaise* & discomfort, without the compensations (such as they are) of feeling that you are in for a 'heroic' complaint. I am coming between 6 & 7 (when I shall leave this) to see Sylvia & hear Parkie's latest report. Meanwhile alas! you are as secluded as if you were in the most jealously guarded Harem in Stamboul.

I don't know whether in the circumstances I ought to write you a *real* letter (which may increase your head-ache) or only 'a few lines' which you can toss easily aside: as some one said of a cup of mild Cocoa, 'made without trouble, drunk without regret'. But I have never yet written you a *Cocoa* letter – have I? so I won't begin now. You can, at any rate, put it aside if it bores you by its length, until to-morrow: I hope in a coffer of safety.

We had a Cabinet this morning of a rather straggling kind. There is no very good news from any quarter, but K. is still fairly hopeful about the Russians, who generally manage, after a hard knock, to swing back again.[1] There was a lot of talk about the *Lusitania*[2] & the United States. The one thing to fear & avoid is that they shd. be provoked, in order to save their travelling millionaires from the risk of being torpedoed, to prohibit the export of munitions of war to us: wh. wd. be almost *fatal*. I don't think that, in their present mood, they are the least likely to do anything of the kind: but in view of possibilities K. has conceived the grandiose idea of transplanting to Canada the 3 or 4 big works wh. are now making guns & shells for us in the States. Meanwhile that truly wonderful product which is called 'American opinion' is pursuing its usual mysterious & incalculable course. Bryan advises his fellow-countrymen not to 'rock the boat' (rather a good phrase); and, by way of setting an example of 'calmness', we learn that President Wilson had a round of golf in the morning, & a motor-drive in the afternoon: supplemented (as now appears) by a speech in the evening to 'Americans of alien birth', stuffed with even more than the usual allowance of swollen & sterile platitudes.[3]

We had (by way of change) Mr Selfridge to lunch to-day: a capital fellow to whom I took quite a liking. He has just returned from Berlin, where he found everybody confident & cheerful & persuaded that they have still 2 million fighting men in reserve. Do you remember selling at his shop, & buying me that charming blue muffler that I always wear in the motor?[4]

I wonder if you have been able to read a line of any of my books: a poor lot, which I wd. have made very different if I had dreamt that you were going to be stricken like this. On the whole, I shd. advise you – in any nice interval when you can read in comfort – to try *Resurrection* in preference to *My Novel*.[5]

The House is dull as a duck pond this afternoon, & it is cursed ill-luck that we couldn't have had a drive in this beautiful sun, or an hour of divine talk alone together after 6.

Oc seems to have had what the General calls a 'miraculous escape' from a broken knee, wh. wd. have lamed him for life. He is now on the high seas *en route* for Alexandria, whence the General thinks they will send him home. Violet is still in doubt whether or not to go out there to him. Lane says that Edward Horner's is a bad wound: he can neither be operated on or moved; but there is quite a good chance of recovery.[6] The latest casualties from the Dardanelles are Wilding (the lawn-tennis player, attached to the ridiculous armoured cars) killed, and Josiah Wedgwood MP (of the same) wounded.[7] So far, of our friends, Patrick & Francis MacLaren[8] have escaped. It is a bloody business & a slow one, but K. is sending out 2 more Divisions, and I think we shall certainly push through.[9]

Most loved, I am so glad that you liked the letter I sent you this morning. It came from the deepest depths of my heart, & was a real confession of faith. You know me so well that I am sure you didn't think that there was in it a single note of exaggeration. Does it give you any solace in your tiresome seclusion to realise how much you have done, & how much you mean, and what a supreme life-giving power you are? What don't I owe you?

I count – or wish I could – the hours till I see you again. If you are well enough, you will send me in my solitude & anxiety a few pencil lines, as often as you can, won't you darling?

I went thro' *Measure for Measure* by way of distraction: a truly marvellous treasure-house. I mustn't weary your dear eyes any more. You know well that the *love of you is my life*.

[1] Towards the end of May the Russians organized a front behind the San and Dniester rivers. By then, however, they had lost, to Mackensen's army alone, 153,000 prisoners and 128 guns.

[2] On 7 May the *Lusitania* was torpedoed by a U-boat off the Old Head of Kinsale, 1,198 people, including 124 Americans, being drowned. This British liner was in normal passenger service, though its cargo included 173 tons of ammunition. The sinking formed part of the German policy of intimidation which was aimed at paralysing American trade with the Allies.

[3] The golf and the motor drive on 8 May were part of the President's Saturday routine. On the evening of 10 May he spoke in the Philadelphia Convention Hall, and told some 4,000 newly naturalized Americans: 'There is such a thing as a man being too proud to fight.' The remark was much criticized. When questioned about it by a friend Wilson said: 'That was just one of the foolish things a man does. I have a bad habit of thinking out loud.' When he met Wilson soon after the Armistice Asquith was 'very favourably impressed' by the President's 'erudition and gift of concise talking': Lady Scott, *Self-Portrait of an Artist* (1949), p. 172.

[4] Selfridge was an American citizen (who did not take British naturalization until 1937).

His store in Oxford St. had opened in 1909. He acted as a purchasing agent for the French Government during the war. For the charity venture to which Asquith refers see Letter 48.

⁵ That is, Tolstoy in preference to Bulwer-Lytton.

⁶ Sir Arbuthnot Lane, the surgeon, was one of the party which had been allowed (with Asquith's help and through the influence of George Moore at G.H.Q.) to cross the Channel and visit the wounded Edward Horner. Edward lost a kidney, but recovered. Sent to Egypt in 1916, he pulled strings to return to the Western Front and was killed during the Battle of Cambrai, Nov. 1917.

⁷ For the armoured cars and their machine-guns see Letter 298, n. 2. A. F. Wilding was the Wimbledon singles champion in 1913, and one of the winning pair in the men's doubles in 1914.

⁸ Patrick Shaw-Stewart and Francis McLaren survived the Dardanelles; but both were killed in 1917.

⁹ Neither Asquith nor the generals realized that the Front was by now almost as stable on the Gallipoli Peninsula as in France: in each attempt to advance the attackers found the odds to be with the defence. See p. 440.

424

Tuesday 11 May 1915 [ii] Midnight

My darling – I went from the House to Mansfield St. about 6.30 to see Sylvia & get the latest report from Parkie, wh. was ambiguous, and left one in doubt as to the real source & nature of your illness. I am afraid you had a miserable night, & for the most part a bad day, but you seemed this evening to be freer from pain & temperature. Of course I was not allowed to see you. I do trust for better & more reassuring news in the morning. I can't bear to think of you with head-ache & depression, and 'all the wheels of being slow'.[1] It is, however, great luck that *it* – whatever it is – declared itself on Sunday, and that you did not go out to the Normen,[2] to find your darling self laid low & stricken there.

I have just come back from dining with Revelstoke at Carlton House Terrace – the Bencks, E. Grey, Lady Desborough & Mrs Leo Rothschild. Quite 'nice' & peaceable, & a little mild Bridge. I am not sure that you know him – John Baring? He has been now, to my knowledge, for over 20 years more or less in love with Ettie: as has been (for about the same space of time) Evan Charteris. The years have rattled by, & every kind of water has passed under the bridge: but *plus ça change, plus c'est la même chose* – an almost unique instance of *double* constancy.[3]

Nathalie comes back on Thursday, & they hope that Jasper,[4] who is no longer in the fighting line, will get leave at the same time.[5] . . .

¹ Tennyson, *In Memoriam*, 50.

² As in the Mastermen and the McKennae.

³ See N. Mosley, *Julian Grenfell* (1976), pp. 41–6. There was a break in Revelstoke's 'constancy': he courted Mrs Nancy Shaw from 1904 until her marriage to Waldorf Astor two years later. When Asquith wrote, Evan Charteris appears to have been attached to the

Countess of Essex, as well as to Lady Desborough: Cynthia Asquith, *Diaries, 1915–1918* (1968), pp. 33–4.

  [4] Jasper Ridley had married Nathalie Benckendorff in 1911.

  [5] The letter is incomplete, stopping at the end of the first double sheet. Probably Asquith had intended to finish it the following morning, but was too overwhelmed to do so when he received Venetia's letter announcing her engagement.

425

Wed 12 May 1915

Most Loved –

As you know well, *this* breaks my heart.

I couldn't bear to come and see you.

I can only pray God to bless you – and help me.

Yours.

PART IV

Epilogue

VENETIA could not have married without making Asquith unhappy. He
needed to share his 'thoughts and experiences' with her 'from hour to hour'.
To be able to do this he had to feel that no one else shared her heart and so
possessed the right to be made free of the confidences which he poured out to
her. He therefore took for granted that her engagement to be married would
necessarily sever his lifeline of communication to her: from that moment
the flow of 'the divine daily confidence' would cease. When she warned him
on 18 April of what might lie ahead (see p. 551), she had written that
marriage would not alter her 'feelings for him'. He had replied:

I am sure you speak the truth. But . . . you will realise . . . the difference it must
make – not in *love*; that would always remain to my last living breath – but in
expression, in intercourse, in confidence, in the thousand things big and little, grave
and gay, light or serious, which have been woven into the web of our unique and
divine intimacy (Letter 399).

He expected that she would tell him who was courting her and had her
favour, so that he would have a little time in which to brace himself for the
deprivation to come. He hoped anxiously that if he had to be supplanted in
her heart it would be by a man 'more love-inspiring and heart-filling and
therefore worthier' than himself (Letter 401).

Venetia's letter of 11 May shattered all Asquith's illusions. The girl he
had idolized was prepared to marry someone he thought utterly unworthy
of her; and this entailed renouncing Christianity for what all the world
would regard as mercenary reasons. He may have thought that she was
doing this to escape the burden of his friendship. The 'divine daily confidence' was not merely severed, but brutally dishonoured. In its last few
weeks, at the very least, he now saw it as a humiliating sham.

Venetia seems to have indicated in the letter that she was unwilling to
enter into explanations or discussions. Asquith at once made a confidante of
Sylvia Henley, the sister nearest to Venetia in age, and the only person with
whom he could discuss Venetia's doings with freedom. He wrote three
times to Sylvia on 12 May. This inaugurated a flow of letters which lasted

for some years, and in which those to Venetia were often echoed.[1] Sylvia had a husband at the war and young children. She could not take Venetia's place; but her letters helped Asquith at a critical time.

In his second letter to Sylvia, Asquith wrote:

I never had any illusions, as I often told Venetia, and she also was always most frank about it – as to her some day getting married. It was obvious and inevitable, and I have always braced myself (or tried to) to face that contingency.

But *this*! We have always treated it as a kind of freakish, but quite unimaginable, adventure.

I don't believe there are two living people who, each in their separate ways, are more devoted to me than she and Montagu: and it is the irony of fortune that they two shd. combine to deal a death-blow to me. You know how I rate Venetia: I put her quite first. And for 2, nearly 3, years she & I have shared every confidence. That, of course, must have come to an end, whenever she resolved to marry.

But (I say again!) *this*! I am really fond of him, recognise his intellectual merits, find him excellent company, & have always been able to reckon on his loyalty & devotion. Anything but this!

It is not merely the prohibitive physical side (bad as that is) – I won't say anything about race & religion, tho' they are not quite negligible factors. But he is not a *man*: a bundle of moods & nerves & symptoms, intensely self-absorbed, and – but I won't go on with the dismal catalogue. . . .

Even so, I could have borne it more easily, if she had been *frank* with me: especially that last Sunday at Alderley, when I feel sure it had been practically settled.

She says, at the end of a sadly meagre letter today: 'I can't help feeling, after all the joy you've given me, that mine is a very *treacherous* return.'

Poor darling! I wouldn't have put it like that. But in essence it is true: and it leaves me sore and humiliated.

Sylvia's help could not reconcile Asquith to Venetia's silence. At midnight on 14 May he wrote to the friend he had lost:

This is too terrible. No Hell can be so bad. Cannot you send me one word? It is *so* unnatural. Only one word?

Venetia responded with enough encouragement for letters to be resumed for a little, though with none of the old freedom. Asquith wrote on 17 May:

Darling your most revealing and heart-rending letter has just come. What am I to say? What can I say? I was able to keep silence for the two most miserable days of my life, and then it became unbearable; and like you I felt that it was cruel and unnatural, and that anything was better. So I scrawled my 2 or 3 agonised sentences, and thank God you once more speak to me and I to you.

When I think that, only a week ago, I should never have thought twice about what I was saying & writing to you, but put down every word & thought that came into my head, while now I dread lest, without knowing it, I may give you acute pain by anything I write – I am able to measure the distance wh. it has taken so short a time to travel.

Inevitably Venetia resented the advice which followed to 'take time' before making her final decision. Inevitably she read into Asquith's letters a tone of reproach. A flurry of explanations followed: five letters seem to have passed between them on 21 May. After much indecision he asked for a farewell half-hour and they met on 23 May, the day before she left for Wimereux.

It would be absurd, she told Edwin on 24 May, to pretend that the Prime Minister's unhappiness did not affect her very deeply:

How could it not? For three years he has been to me the most wonderful friend & companion, and to see him just now made wretched by me is, and should be if I pretend to any heart at all, a real sorrow.

Three weeks later, from the other world across the Channel, she gave Edwin this retrospect of her last weeks in England:

When I think of that . . . fortnight, . . . how ghastly it was, how ill and miserable I felt, those three days spent at Alderley and the last Saturday and Sunday were the only ones which I didn't end in floods of tears. How awful you must have thought me but how good and patient and understanding you were to me . . . I really now bless that 'fever' at Hoe. If it hadn't been for that I should have gone away on the Monday with nothing settled, meaning to write to the P.M. from here and as likely as not, for you know my havering nature too well, still be in the same position as before and have it all to go through. It's over at any rate.

*   *   *

Venetia's foredoomed search for a quiet week in which to tell Asquith ended ironically: she dropped her bombshell in one of the worst weeks of his whole premiership. The letter which gave him such anguish reached him early on 12 May. That morning's papers carried extracts from the Bryce Report on German atrocities. The hatred engendered by the Zeppelin raids, the gas attacks, and the sinking of the *Lusitania*, now rose to the pitch of fury: anti-German rioting and looting reached serious proportions that day. Far more menacing for the Government, however, was the new conviction that 'Prussianism' must be stamped out and the war fought to a finish whatever the cost, for very few Conservatives believed Asquith and his Liberal colleagues to be capable of ruthless, 'all out' war-making.[2] Conscription was the touchstone. In the changed mood the impression grew that the cabinet were refusing to prepare for it, not because it would be impracticable, but because their whole past made them revolt against this kind of compulsion. When Haldane told the Lords on 13 May that he could 'conceive a state of things in which the Government might resort to conscription', press reactions showed a wide gulf between the parties on an issue which could not be postponed much longer.

To sustain the impression that they knew how to make war the cabinet needed a success. There was one in prospect, in that the Treaty of London signed on 26 April pledged Italy to 'enter the field' with the Allies within a month (p. 500). On 13 May, however, the Italian Government tendered their resignations; Italy's march to war was not going as planned. Some even more severe jolts awaited the War Council when they assembled on 14 May. A dispatch and a leader in that morning's *Times* attributed the failure of the Aubers Ridge offensive of 9 May to shell shortages created by the Government's failure to organize munitions output. The Council were told that there was no chance of an early breakthrough either at the Dardanelles or in the West. Hamilton's force was still pinned into its two small Gallipoli bridgeheads. As for de Robeck, one of his battleships, the *Goliath*, had been sunk; his super-Dreadnought, the *Queen Elizabeth*, had been given back to the Grand Fleet; and enemy submarines had made their appearance in the Eastern Mediterranean. Kitchener argued that the Germans' recent successes against Russia would enable them to switch troops back to the Western Front; 'he felt some doubt as to whether the French could hold' against the resulting attacks.

After the Council Churchill and Fisher spent about half an hour together and decided on the naval reinforcements for the Dardanelles. At about 5 a.m. the next morning, 15 May, Fisher received four memoranda from Churchill embodying the arrangements agreed, but adding to them. For Fisher the additions were the last straw. He sent Churchill and Asquith his resignation. It was his ninth; this time he meant it. He went into hiding and dispatched a note to Bonar Law hinting at what he had done. The latter called on Lloyd George early on Monday, 17 May, and learned that the First Sea Lord had indeed resigned. A little later Asquith, Lloyd George, and Bonar Law met in No. 10; and it was agreed after a very brief discussion that the Government ought to be reconstructed as a coalition.

The effect of Asquith's private grief on his actions in forming the coalition has been much discussed. Mr Roy Jenkins attributes some of the premier's conduct during the crisis to his personal troubles. By this view 'it was most unlike Asquith' not to play for a short delay in order to gain the prestige of Italy's entry into the war; and it was equally unlike him, when 'at his best', to be coerced into dismissing Haldane after one of the most discreditable smear campaigns in British history.[3]

This view may well be right; but the evidence cited by Mr Jenkins is not conclusive. In the event Italy declared war on 23 May; but that could not have been predicted with any great confidence six days earlier. By 17 May it was clear that Salandra enjoyed massive popular support for entering the war, and that his chances of staying in office were good; but the Chamber did not pass the War Powers Bill until 20 May. Asquith did not have the prime requirement for staving off the attack in the Commons until good news came from Italy: he lacked a Liberal of the standing to replace Churchill who could restore stability at the Admiralty. Nor is it certain that his decision to replace Haldane originated in coercion exercised by the Conservative leaders. According to Austen Chamberlain, Asquith sketched the possible distribution of offices at his first meeting with Bonar Law. In this sketch Haldane was to 'retire from the Lord Chancellorship'.[4] Asquith was sad at this ousting of his old friend; and later in the negotiations he naturally made much of the Liberal objections to it. He greatly resented the scurrilous Tory campaign against Haldane; but it is not certain that his decision about the Lord Chancellorship resulted solely from Opposition pressure.[5]

The question so often asked, whether Asquith's distress at the news of Venetia's engagement made him inefficient at a critical moment, is far too narrow. He was acutely worried about his friendship with Venetia for weeks before her letter of 11 May at last told him the truth. During the May crisis itself he acted with undeniable skill and vigour. No doubt personal distress made him uncharacteristically emotional once or twice. This does not seem to have impaired his performance. It was indeed the emotional nature of his appeal to the Liberal back-benchers on 19 May which made it so effective. Depressing the position of Bonar Law in the new Government may have been mistaken; but, if so, it was a thoroughly Asquithian mistake, and not the careless error of a premier who was distraught.

It is possible that the search for a quiet week in which to break the news was wholly mistaken. In a crisis Asquith missed Venetia's support and counsel terribly. But as he told her on 15 May, the worse the crisis, the less time he had to brood on his woes. He suffered cruelly when Venetia broke the news and ended the dream; but to dream for longer might not have done him good. The friendship was no longer helping him quite as it had done during the first weeks of the war: his state had turned from dependence into obsession. Edwin was not an impartial judge; but he may have been right when he told Venetia in April 1915 (Letter XIV, p. 530) that the Prime Minister's relationship with her spelled 'trouble for him . . . and possibly loss of grip eventually'.

*   *   *

When she left for Wimereux Venetia asked Edwin 'to help . . . and protect' Asquith. Edwin was very ready to do so and wrote to her:

Margot said to me yesterday that she thought I loved him as much as I did you. That of course is not true but I love him more than any other man and I need no stimulus to do all I can for him.

Edwin went to The Wharf on 29 May determined to discuss the engagement with Asquith, however great the latter's reluctance to do so.* 'I had a talk, the first, with the P.M. about you,' he reported to Venetia on 31 May:

He was just too noble and splendid for words. He warned me before I began that he might wound me though he would try not to. I said I wanted to make my case and that I would rather hear his criticisms from himself and not from anyone else. He did not disapprove, he had only doubts if change of religion was too much like a transaction, and he feared we would not be happy. He told Katharine afterwards the religious point was only subsidiary and all he minded were his doubts as to our love. He told me that he hoped and prayed his doubts were not well founded and ended by blessing me and wishing us both well.

To Sylvia Henley Asquith poured out the thoughts on the Jewish side of the question which he had withheld from Edwin:

I thought . . . of what the abjuration of Christianity plus the substitution of 'Judaism' really would mean even to a person who had no dogmatic beliefs. The more I thought of it (in I hope a detached & impersonal way) the more repugnant & even repulsive it seemed. In the first instance, (as M. admitted to me to-day) you have to declare – expressly or by implication – that Xtianity is a gross imposture . . . – in other words to turn your back . . . on the main force wh. has created the West . . . has remoulded & transformed the world, & made us what we are. And after that 'gran rifiuto',† you have to declare positively (& not negatively) that you adopt in its place the narrow, sterile, tribal creed, wh. has . . . kept alive & separate the Israelite sept. . . . And that *this* should be the fate of our darling noble Venetia! It makes me sick to think of it. . . .

When he wrote this Asquith was at the start of his first visit to the Western Front. He returned via Boulogne and met Venetia there at her initiative. She convinced him at last that her determination to go through with the religious change and the marriage would not weaken; and that evening she wrote urging him not to allow her marriage to disrupt their friendship. On 11 June he replied:

Most loved – Your letter written on the night of the Thursday [3 June] when I last saw you wandered about, & did not reach me till Tuesday in this week. My impulse, as you will readily believe, was to reply at once; but I thought it better for both of us that I should think about it, & the whole agonising problems [*sic*] wh. it raises,

---

* On 12 May Asquith had written to Edwin:
  'My Dear Montagu,
     You are more than fortunate, and I pray that Heaven will bring you both all happiness.
                                                                   Yrs always, H. H. A.'
† Great renunciation.

before writing an answer. That fact in itself is almost too tragic for words. For the best part of 3 years, it has been so natural & easy & inevitable for me to write to you – every day, twice a day: if opportunity had offered at almost every hour of the day or night. And to have to pause, & take thought, & consider what I should say, is such a new, and I should only a month ago have said such an *unthinkable* experience, that, even now, I can hardly realise its possibility.

You talk of your 'gross selfishness'. My darling I am (as I have always been) more selfish for you than I cd. ever be for myself. You were the centre & mainspring of my life: everything in it hung upon you: there was not an act or a thought (as you know well) wh. I did not share with you.

No one – not even you, who know me so well – can ever imagine what your letter on the 12th May (exactly a month ago!) meant to me. Believe me, I have never in word or even in thought reproached you. I know why you were silent: you were undecided, you were considerate. You dreaded to prepare the way for the breaking of my heart. Do you remember that day when we went & bought your little bag? & had a short delicious drive? And I felt so happy & assured (like a damned fool).* And you never breathed a hint. I think it might have been easier if you had taken your courage in both hands, and –. But I love and honour you so much that even now I don't dare to say that you were not right. You have given me so much more than I can give or could give to you (tho' there was nothing I had, or was capable of, that I wd. not have given) that in all the terrible & heart-rending hours that made my life a veritable hell, I have never (*most sweet* – I assure you this is true) felt that I had any title to complain.

Say *beloved* that you believe me!

But your letter (quite a divine one, worthy in every way of my loved & worshipped Venetia) is addressed not to the unforgettable past, but to the undisclosed & impenetrable future.

Most dear, what can I say? You say that your old love for me is not impaired or altered by what has now come to you, and that in spite of what you contemplate, with all that it involves, that love will persist, constant & unchanged. You don't need to be told that mine will never cease or wane, until I die.

Don't, don't, I implore you darling think for a second that I am cruel or callous. Have I ever been? When have I been unkind or insensitive? Look back on the whole time we have spent together, in the most perfect & heavenly intimacy that could exist between man & woman. Was it ever clouded for a moment by suspicion, or jealousy, or doubt, or even a shadow of reserve? You know well, *it never was*.

But how can you think it possible – you don't, I know – that things can ever again be as they were? I had the *best* that a man had or could have. Don't, for God's sake, think me selfish or exorbitant, if I shrink from the second best. I told Montagu the other day in the only talk I have ever had or wish to have with him on the subject that I don't care what happens to me or to him – that I wouldn't lift a finger to save either him or myself from instant death if I could be sure that in that way you wd. be happy.

---

* Letter 418, dated 5 May.

That is all I care for.

You say, & I devoutly hope & pray that you are right, that you believe you love him enough to make sure of your happiness with him.

My best, you must give me time.

Don't force me to sadder & adamantine resolutions. Don't think me hard if I seem for the time to stand aloof. Don't press me now to say anything – except that I love you – always, everywhere.

> Your heart-broken and *ever devoted*

My very dearest – I hope this won't give you as much pain to read as it has given me to write it. I love you.

Venetia read this with relief and wrote to Edwin (14 June):

I had a divine letter from the P.M. this morning. He is an angel. But you needn't be in the least afraid that he or I will ever renew our old relationship. Nothing would induce him to. I know because his letter was an answer to one from me . . . in which I urged him not to let my marriage make the slightest difference to his feelings, it hadn't altered mine so why shouldn't we both go on getting happiness in that way. Darling why do I tell you this. No I'm right to tell it you, but it was cruel to write that to him because it must have shown him more clearly than anything else I've ever written how little I really cared for him. Bongie was right I suppose I oughtn't to have gone in to see him. I shall urge my daughters to marry young, if they can . . . before they've had time to make friends who they'll regret. They can do that afterwards.

Asquith's family were divided over the marriage. Violet, deeply shocked by the engagement, and naturally inclined to take her father's part, lectured both Edwin and Venetia at length. Edwin was hurt by her outspoken criticism; Venetia treated it more calmly, and wrote to Violet:

I think I have quite made up my mind to be married to E. in such a way as not to separate him from ever from his family. . . . It won't change me, I shan't live religiously or spiritually a different life than if I'd married any complete free thinker, the only thing is that by this very formal compliance I make two people (of whom [Edwin] is very fond, his mother and brother) reconciled & happy and myself live in greater comfort. Of course there would be absolutley no difficulty about doing it if this bloody money weren't involved, but I do admit I mind the fact that nearly everyone will think it has been done for that alone. It doesn't sound convincing when one says the other thing. They won't quite believe it & you who love me must (if you believe it too, try & reconcile yourselves to the idea.

Margot wrote roundly to Violet on 7 June: 'They are both old enough to know their minds & no one must tease them now. There's a good deal of bosh in the religious campaign *au fond* tho' superficially it takes one in.' Arthur Asquith, writing from Gallipoli, told Violet in August: 'I hate the whole business; but my social self-indulgence is such that the crimes of my friends rarely make me wish to forgo their society.'

Raymond Asquith and his wife Katharine supported the marriage from the start. 'K. is fearfully splendid,' Edwin wrote on 31 May. 'She has no doubts at all as to the whole thing, and thinks Violet is making a ridiculous fuss and that the P.M. is wrong.' Katharine continued to argue the cause with Violet. She was the only member of the Asquith family to attend the wedding.

Raymond told Conrad Russell that he was 'entirely in favour of the Stanley–Montagu match'. He went on:

Of course I see your point when you say you wouldn't like to go to bed with Edwin. I don't mind admitting that I shouldn't myself. But you must remember that women are not refined, sensitive, delicate-minded creatures like you and me: none of them have much physical squeamishness and Venetia far less than most. You say she must have weighed the consequences and so she did, quite carefully: but what frightened her most was not the prospect of the bed being too full but of the board being too empty. She was afraid that her friends might give her up in disgust; but after sounding a few of them – Katharine e.g. and Diana – she concluded that it would be all right and decided to flout the interested disapproval of Mr. H. H. and the idiotic indignation of Miss V. Asquith.

Your character sketch of Edwin is done in much too dark colours. You are obviously prejudiced against him by the fact (if fact it be) that he steals birds' eggs, a vice utterly immaterial in a bride-groom. I agree that he has not a drop of European blood, but then neither has he a drop of American. I don't agree that he is a wet-blanket in Society. He is moody certainly, but is capable of being extremely amusing and (specially during the last year) has succeeded in attracting some very critical and some very beautiful women. He is broad-minded, free from cant, open to new impressions, tolerant of new people. I do not think he will be either a dull or a tyrannical husband, and I understand that the terms of alliance permit a wide licence to both parties to indulge such extra-conjugal caprices as either may be lucky enough to conceive.[6] . . .

There was a similar division of opinion among the Stanleys. It was not likely that Lord Sheffield, then aged 77, would approve his daughter's intention to change her religion. His daughter-in-law Margaret could remember his 'once mentioning the possibility of such a marriage' to her, and being 'very vehement in his denunciation of it'. She and her husband, Sir Arthur Stanley (the Governor of Victoria), were 'horribly surprised' by the news but were too far away to take part in the family discussions.[7] This gave Venetia's other brother Oliver, who was on her side, a good chance of 'doing battle with Lord Sheffield'; and the latter's agreement was finally obtained, although he continued to regard the matter with 'deep distaste'.

Of Lady Sheffield, whom Edwin found 'sweet beyond words', Margaret Stanley wrote: 'M. in Law's letters are very characteristic, all contradicting each other gloriously – I think really her main feeling is one rather of relief that V is settled off at last, and that she will not be harassed by her vagaries any more.'[8]

Edwin's was the only one of the three families chiefly concerned where approval of the marriage seems to have been unanimous. 'I think they will be rather pleased', he had told Venetia in April, 'if you are brave enough to come into the fold, right in.' On 27 May he wrote to her in Wimereux:

I bring to my people a wonderful recruit, who calls herself one of us, who stands by us . . . Lord Swaythling [Edwin's brother] . . . wants to do all he can and all my family long for it.

On 9 June Edwin reported his sister Lilian to be urging

speed as the best way to cut the cable. . . . I asked her again what is demanded of you afterwards. She agreed wholeheartedly nothing but the avowal *if challenged* that you have adopted citizenship of our citadel.

*   *   *

Edwin's enquiries about the minimum required of the convert were pertinent, for Venetia was as candid to him on this question as she had been to Violet. On 6 June she told him:

Were I to be washed 1000 times in the waters of the Jordan & to go through every rite and ceremony the strictest Jewish creed involved, I should not feel I had changed my race or nationality. I go through the formula required because you want it for your mother's sake, and also (I'm going to be quite honest) because I think one is happier rich than poor. . . . Religion you know I care nothing about and shan't attempt to bring up my children in any. . . . The whole of it amounts to this – I shall nominally call myself one of you, but that is the limit of what will happen & I am sure that your children will not regard themselves as in any way different from their friends. . . . But I want you to tell me if this most superficial acquiescence is enough? Darlingest don't think I am being influenced by what anyone has said. This is only a question between you and me, I don't want to deceive you about my intentions. It is not whether I am right or wrong to change my label, but whether I am changing it enough, I can't do it more. I shall never think of myself as a Jew, any more than I think of you as one.

Edwin had propounded essentially the same view in April (Letter XXXI, p. 576). What worried him was not the absence in Venetia of any sense of conversion, but her flippant attitude to the formalities. On 28 May she had written about the Revd. Morris Joseph, who was to conduct her 'admission preparation':

I can't face old Joseph's book,[9] it's *too* boring, also I'm afraid it would be useless as I should have forgotten it all by the time I got home so I shall mug up all about the Paschal Lamb when I get home. . . .

On 14 June she wrote:

As for old Joseph and all his tribe we'll settle with him in half no time. . . . I wish he could be squared by writing, it would save time, but I suppose he can't.

Edwin sent more books and warned that a 'breaking point' might come – 'when they may say we have done everything we can and it is clear you are not in earnest . . .' Venetia accepted the books, but wrote:

I'm not sure a little judicious cramming of old Joseph's at the last moment won't be more efficacious . . . as I've a fairly good verbal memory I might *hope* to flatter the old boy by some verbatim quotations.

Long before the initial harassments of the engagement ended Edwin acquired yet another worry. Despite the heat, noise, and fleas of the hospital Venetia took so well to war nursing that she did not want to come home. She had planned to spend a month at Wimereux; but on 9 June she wrote, 'I just can't come home, my desire for a new sensation is too strong.' There might, she admitted, be 'an element of shrinking' in her wish to stay, since the hospital, if dull, had been 'very peaceful and impersonal'. When on 14 June she wrote, 'I'm thinking of trying to get moved to a large clearing hospital at Hazebrouck which might be better,' Edwin became so alarmed that he crossed the Channel to beg her to fix a date for her return. Finally, on 5 July, he told her that her application must reach the Jewish authorities within a week, and that two of the ministers who were to admit her were under orders for the front as chaplains. Venetia at last buckled down to 'Joseph's book' ('I think I'm rather good at it, I hope he won't expect a character sketch of Moses or anything of the kind'), returned home on 10 July, and was received into the faith.

On 15 July Asquith went to his wife's room to show her a letter, and there found, as he wrote to Sylvia,

Venetia in conversation with her. We were, I think, both rather taken aback for the moment; and she went off almost at once to see Violet [who had been ill]. After a time I thought it better to break such ice as there is as naturally as may be: so I went myself to the sick room. . . . I stayed for a few minutes talking to them both. . . . Violet did not think Venetia in at all high spirits, and said that she rather avoided her own concerns. . . . They are, however, on the best of terms.

After another short meeting on 21 July, he wrote again to Sylvia:

It is the only consoling thought I have that there is not the shadow of a cloud – except what was inevitable – between us.

His wedding present was two silver boxes, chosen by Sylvia. On 24 July he wrote to Venetia in farewell:

I thought it was better for both of us not to say good-bye to-day. It was not (as you know well) want of feeling, or of a sense of the full meaning of your new departure, now approaching within a measurable number of hours.

'Not Heaven itself upon the Past has power.'[10]

But when (as is inevitable now) I have to survey the past, in the light (if it is light) – perhaps I ought rather to call it twilight – of the impending & unescapable [sic] future, I should wish you always to remember that I am conscious of many things, on my part, which fell short of what I should have wished them to be: that I treasure, as among the best things that any companionship could give, unforgettable and undying memories: and that I pray without ceasing to 'whatever gods there be' that you may have a complete, and (so far as may be) an unclouded life.

Will you always also remember an old & favourite text of mine (on which I never found it necessary to preach to you): 'It is the Spirit that prevaileth.'[11]

Always & everywhere
Your loving

The wedding took place in Lord Swaythling's house on 26 July. Asquith wrote to Sylvia:

I think I told you in my letter that Venetia had sent me – dated her wedding day – a feeling message. I won't enclose it, because I had rather that we read it together, as we will to-morrow.

But (you will understand) I feel at this moment as tho' the world stood still; and that, immediately after, everything was upside down; and that all values had lost their meaning; and that white was black (or at least grey); and that the 'oracles were dumb'.[12] . . .

*   *   *

The sad ending to his romance with Venetia may have told on Asquith's performance as Prime Minister of the coalition from May 1915 to December 1916; but there can be no certainty about this. At most it was no more than a contributory factor in his decline. After the coalition had been formed he wrestled with appalling difficulties and suffered new blows, including the crushing one of Raymond's death in action in September 1916. By December of that year his long premiership had worn him out; he had grown a little careless, even about governmental crises.

An attempt to judge Asquith's leadership of the coalition would lie far outside the scope of this edition.[13] When his letters to Venetia were written he was near his peak; and if some lines of Browning of which he was fond had been applied to him there would have been no doubt about the answer to the question in them:

> It were to be wished the flaws were fewer
> In the earthen vessel holding treasure,

. . . . . .
But the main thing is, does it hold good measure?[14]

*   *   *

Montagu remained close to his chief until the end of Asquith's premiership. When the coalition was formed in May 1915 he lost his cabinet place and returned to the Treasury as Financial Secretary; but he re-entered the cabinet in January 1916. He had been 'indefatigable', Asquith told Sylvia Henley on 2 January, in helping to solve the conscription crisis. 'My dear Montagu,' Asquith wrote at Easter 1916, ' . . . For ten years your friendship and devotion have never failed me; and each successive trouble in these harassing times brings me fresh proof of the value of your affection and counsel.'

Montagu succeeded Lloyd George as Minister of Munitions in June 1916. 'I am enormously impressed with Montagu and his administration of . . . Munitions,' Hankey noted the following November.[15] A month later Asquith was ousted from the premiership. Montagu refused the place offered him in the new Government, though he might well have accepted a better one;[16] but in June 1917 he became Lloyd George's Secretary of State for India. Asquith was outraged at being 'deserted' in this way. 'Such a combination of noble motives,' he wrote scornfully to Lady Scott, on receiving Montagu's explanatory letter.[17]

For the next few years Asquith met the Montagus as little as possible. He disapproved, with reason, of Venetia's post-war milieu; and he referred, in March 1922, to her membership of a 'rotten social gang . . . who lead a futile and devastating life'.[18] In that month Montagu fell foul of Curzon by indiscreet championship of the Indian Government's pro-Turkish views. He was forced to resign; he lost his seat in the election a few months later; and his political career was ended. Surveying the fate of Montagu and other 'renegades' when the polls were declared, Asquith told Mrs Harrisson: 'The thing that gives me the most satisfaction is to gloat over the corpses . . . left on the battlefield'.[19] Both men had suffered at Lloyd George's hands, however; and a *rapprochement* followed. By October 1923 Montagu was once again the Asquiths' guest.

By all accounts the Montagus' marriage was hardly a continuing success. A daughter was born in February 1923 and named Judith Venetia. 'Whenever [Edwin] talked about the future,' Duff Cooper recalled, 'he would interject: "But I, of course, shall be dead by then." '[20] In November 1924, aged 45, Edwin died. He had left instructions, written on the eve of his marriage, that he should not be buried in a graveyard and that there should be no funeral service. Although the second request was disregarded, and full Jewish rites were performed, Edwin was buried in the grounds of Breccles[21] in the Norfolk countryside that he loved. A circle of stones surrounds the grave, and on one is cut the words, 'I say that one shall remember me even afterward.'

In November 1927 Asquith paid his last visit to Venetia. He wrote from The Wharf:

Dearest – it was with a sad heart & heavy feet that I turned my back upon Breccles: I had enjoyed every minute of my little visit & long to come again when the flowers are all out. It was most good of you to take me in, a 'sheer hulk' in need of refitting in your sheltered and delightful haven . . . Bluey (as always) imparted his own distinctive & stimulating flavour. It is a great refreshment to come within reach of a spray from that pungent & aromatic reservoir.

We accomplished the journey here without missing our way and at a good pace. I feel much better for the change. I am staying on here for a few days & hope to have Margot's company on Sunday for a day or two. Parkie has just arrived by motor: in most characteristic form. He didn't waste much time over me and my 'symptoms' . . .

. . . I haven't grappled yet with 'Red Sky in the Morning',[22] but I must soon take it in hand. It looks as if I should be more or less immured here for most of the autumn. Happily I have occupation. Give my love to your Judith, whose acquaintance I should like to improve. Much love

Yrs always

H.

Judith Montagu, then aged four, remembered the tears on Asquith's cheeks as he said: 'This then is the child.' Asquith concealed in his letter that he was seriously unwell. At various times in 1927 he had suffered from a loss of power in one leg. When he reached Sutton Courtney from Breccles this trouble returned and he could not get out of the car without help. He never left The Wharf again and died in February 1928.

When Venetia died in August 1948 the cremation, which was private, was not accompanied by any religious ceremony. The ashes were placed in Edwin's grave. Until Judith Montagu sorted through the papers she had inherited from her mother, she did not know that these included any of Asquith's letters.

Notes to Epilogue

1. Asquith seems to have stopped writing regularly in 1919, though Mrs Henley continued after that to visit The Wharf with her children. Some 390 of his letters to her survive; but the series is almost certainly incomplete, as nothing is extant for Sept. 1915. Asquith also became very friendly before the end of 1915 with Lady Scott. For his suggestion, which came to nothing, that Lady Diana Manners might take Venetia's place see P. Ziegler, *Diana Cooper* (1981), p. 60. Violet was due to leave for Egypt when the break with Venetia came. She found a note from her father on her pillow: 'Don't go from me now – I need you:' *Winston Churchill as I Knew Him*, p. 385.

2. On 2 May the Conservative *Observer* (edited by J. L. Garvin) called for an end to the 'harassing fire of criticism' aimed at ministers. On 9 May the same paper advocated 'a Government of Public Safety' on a coalition basis.

3. See pp. 322–3.

4. Austen Chamberlain MSS, AC2/2/25; Birmingham University. This passage is not reproduced in Petrie, *Austen Chamberlain*, ii. 23. See Stephen Koss, *Lord Haldane* (1969), pp. 210–14. If the account in Austen Chamberlain's memo is accepted, Asquith may merely have anticipated what the Conservative leaders would in any case have demanded. Willingness to jettison Haldane would have been compatible with intense resentment at the scurrilous campaign waged against him. The Conservatives may well have claimed that their leaders had achieved the ejection of Haldane.

5. Asquith's failure to write to Haldane at this point may perhaps be ascribed to his personal preoccupations.

6. John Jolliffe, *Raymond Asquith* (1980), p. 202.

7. Margaret Stanley to Sylvia Henley, 29 June 1915: Bodleian Library, dep. c. 629.

8. Margaret Stanley to her mother, Mrs Evans Gordon, 28 July 1915 (State Library of Victoria): quotation in Adelaide Lubbock, *People in Glass Houses* (1977), p. 82.

9. *Judaism as Creed and Life* (2nd edn., 1910): the significance of the paschal sacrifice in the Passover Festival is explained in book ii, ch. 4.

10. Dryden, *Translations from Horace, Ode 29 of Book iii*, often quoted by Asquith.

11. 'It is the spirit that quickeneth': St John, 6:63.

12. Milton, *Hymn on the Morning of Christ's Nativity*, 1.173.

13. For critical comments on Asquith's performance during his coalition premiership see Petrie, op. cit. ii. 55; Austen Chamberlain, *Down the Years* (1935), pp. 111, 116; Lady Scott, *Self-Portrait of an Artist*, p. 137 (Austen Chamberlain); John Fair, *British Inter-party Conferences* (1980), p. 322 (Selborne); Martin Pugh, *Electoral Reform in War and Peace* (1978), p. 119 (MacCallum Scott); A. C. Benson's diary, 'Sunday' [29 Aug. 1915], Magdalene College, Cambridge (Randall Davidson), cited in David Newsome, *On the Edge of Paradise* (1980), p. 326. For a more balanced comment see B.E.C. Dugdale, *Balfour* (1936), ii. 157.

14. See Letter 364.

15. Diary, 29 Nov.

16. For the terms in which he turned down the Financial Secretaryship to the Treasury see his letter to Lloyd George, 13 Dec. 1916: Lloyd George MSS, House of Lords F/39/3/1.

17. 23 June 1917: Kennet MSS.

18. To Hilda Harrisson, 20 March: not included in *H.H.A.: Letters to a Friend* (2 vols., 1933–4). The extract is taken from a typescript, the originals having apparently been destroyed; see *The Times*, 7 Feb. 1972. See also P. Ziegler, *Diana Cooper* (1981), p. 106; Laura, Duchess of Marlborough, *Laughter from a Cloud* (1980), p. 111.

19. *H. H. A.: Letters to a Friend*, ii. 37.

20. *Old Men Forget* (1953), p. 52.

21. See Appendix 3.

22. By Margaret Kennedy: published a few weeks earlier. She was married to David Davies, who had been one of Asquith's Secretaries. See Letters 264 and 303.

Judy Gendel

BY PATRICK LEIGH FERMOR

JUDY GENDEL was full of contradictions. She wasn't remotely like anyone else. Intelligence and flair and an innate competence at almost everything – except, sometimes, her own interests – were gifts which, even when she was very young, impressed Prime Ministers, presidential candidates and heads of colleges. She grew up in an active, sharply faceted world where ability, intellect and wit were prized; and, a precocious and observant only child, and a lonely one, she absorbed it all and she might have played a vigorous part in the wings of politics, like a heroine in Disraeli or Trollope. The gifts, inherited and acquired, were always there; but, in any conflict between head and heart, the heart won every time, and – to the mistaken disappointment of elders who looked on lives as parabolas – her energies took a turning where ambition played no part. Feelings of early isolation, perhaps, set the companionship of friends higher than anything. She loved them and lived for their company. Some lives must be assessed by the warmth with which friendship is lavished and returned, and in these rare terms, Judy's was an entire success. Her friendships covered a wide and varied range. They sprang up spontaneously from affinity or contrast, from the delights of reciprocal stimulus in conversation, from loving warmth and romantic impulse; and all of them, wrapped in a snowballing mythology of private humour and back-reference, were fostered by a genius for unpremeditated feasting and fun and improvization and a passion for the comic and the odd. In spite of her excellent brain, she was free of all vanity or arrogance: a teasing suggestion that the literary range of her mother's friends, though wide and dazzling, stopped short at Belloc, immured her next day behind a palisade of books. She was generous and unguarded; a confident, ungrudging and uncircumspect spirit marked all she did with a headlong zest that was only briefly reined in, now and then, by spells of depression and languor. She lived at full tilt; quite literally, once in Italy, when, to dodge the swarming Roman reporters on an expedition for the sake of a celebrated visiting friend, she assembled her small troop, on horseback and by stealth, among some remote Etruscan tombs. When, outmanoeuvring her, a score of concealed photographers suddenly rose from a streamside hazel-copse, up went her cry of 'Come on!', and everyone broke into a gallop, across the brook, through the ragged volley of flashbulbs, to thunder away over the Maremma and to safety. . . .

These Poussin landscapes were a permanent background after her happy marriage to the art-historian, Milton Gendel. Romanesque churches, ruins in mountain villages in Upper Latium, in the Sabine Hills and the Campagna became the goals of exciting hunts for little-known frescoes and abstruse stylistic data: quests that gave rise to picnics by remote silvan basilicas or crumbling Orsini castles; all the more joyful later on, thanks to their captivating little daughter Anna. (No solitude or isolation here!) Such days ended with after-dinner talk and laughter under the cross-vaults of their house on the Tiber Island above the Fabrician Bridge, and they often lasted till the Tiber was yellow with the Roman dawn, for she hated things to break up.

We know that candles burning at both ends, unlike more careful tapers, may not last the night. But, after the momentary shadow of dismay and loss, the memory of Judy's warm-hearted, spirited, and generous vitality shines brighter than a Christmas tree.

(1972)

Appendices

Appendix 1: Previous Use of the Letters

DURING the 1920s both Asquith and Beaverbrook published extracts from the Letters into which they introduced various distortions. When Asquith (or the Earl of Oxford and Asquith, as he had by then become) was preparing his *Memories and Reflections* in old age, he asked some of his women friends to lend him letters which might help him with his narrative. Venetia had a typed copy prepared for him.[1] She reproduced what she called 'extracts from Mr A's letters leaving out all sentimentalities'.[2] The first six chapters in the second volume of *Memories and Reflections* consist largely of these extracts which are taken from about 120 of the Letters to her. Parts of letters to Mrs Henley, Lady Scott, and Mrs Harrisson appear in the rest of the volume. The reader is given the names of the three last; but Asquith was unwilling to reveal the extent of his correspondence with Venetia. He therefore began the first chapter by discussing the ethics of publishing diaries, adding:

I have not myself, except for a brief period, kept what is technically called a 'Diary'; but I have been in the habit of jotting down irregularly my impressions of noteworthy persons and incidents while they were still fresh in my memory. . . . For the period I now approach I have drawn freely upon such of these contemporary notes as were accessible, and also upon letters to a few intimate friends, which they have been good enough to place at my disposal.

By changing a few words in Venetia's typed copy Asquith succeeded in concealing that the 'notes' had been made, not to help his own memory, but to interest and concern his correspondent. He died in February 1928 before *Memories and Reflections* appeared, and the two volumes were seen through the press by an experienced journalist, Alexander Mackintosh. The second volume was serialized in thirty-four issues of the *Daily Telegraph* during April, May, and June 1928. Every one of these newspaper articles, and the two leaders commenting on them, were headlined as Asquith's 'diary'. When J. A. Spender and Cyril Asquith produced the authorized *Life* some four years later they revealed in a footnote that the 'contemporary notes' consisted largely of letters to correspondents such as Venetia.[3] This footnote has been much disregarded and the extracts in *Memories and Reflections* are cited in a number of well-known works as being from Asquith's diary. Violet Asquith (by then Lady Asquith of Yarnbury) saw the complete text of the Letters to Venetia in March 1964. However, in *Winston Churchill as I Knew Him*, which appeared in the following year, she cited the extracts either as Asquith's 'contemporary notes', or as 'daily notes', or as his 'diary'.

Asquith also altered Letters when he encountered phrases which seemed liable to bring discredit on the Liberals or himself. He had written on 2 August 1914, 'I suppose a good ¾ of our own party in the . . . Commons are for absolute non-interference at any price.' This estimate became 'a good number'. On 21 August he had told Venetia of a long cabinet 'mostly about rather boring details connected with the war'. 'Rather boring' was deleted. No sign was left in the published version of the alterations and omissions which had been made.

Beaverbrook had gone to work some years earlier. By 1919 Venetia was reported to be his mistress;[4] and at various times she made extracts from the Letters for him. When forwarding those for March and April 1915 she wrote of Asquith:

I have done him a dirty turn once (tho' I am not fatuous enough to imagine it was more than quite momentary) so I'm very anxious that you should know a lot about him. I'm confident that the more you do the more you will appreciate his very great and exceptional qualities. I wish chance had thrown you together, for I'm sure you wd have been friends.

Beaverbrook used these extracts in *Politicians and the War*, vol. 1 (1928).[5] Neither in this nor in other similar cases did he indicate his source. The freedom with which he treated the extracts may be illustrated by his placing the fourth of the Letters which Asquith wrote to Venetia on 30 March 1915 (Letter 378) in an account of the functioning of the coalition cabinet, the passage being thus misplaced by at least two months.[6] Beaverbrook also invested the Letters with somewhat legendary features. Writing to Churchill in October 1925 he implied that the whole series 'from May of 1914 up to early in 1915' had been written 'from the cabinet room'.[7] He instructed Robert Bruce Lockhart to refer in an *Evening Standard* book review (4 April 1929) to the day when Asquith's Letters, written 'during the most critical years of the war', would see the light. 'When they do,' the reviewer wrote, 'England will realize that in the former Liberal Prime Minister she has acquired a letter writer as eloquent as Horace Walpole and as romantic as Dean Swift.'

The effect of these various operations may be illustrated from a passage in Letter 127 (21 August 1914) about the cabinet discussion on Turkey which is reproduced both in *Memories and Reflections* and in *Politicians and the War*. In her typed copy Venetia gave the passage in full, with several mistranscriptions, one of which transferred the Prime Minister's views to Masterman. She included Asquith's final comment: 'There's a picture for you of a united and *most* efficient cabinet!' Asquith crossed out this last sentence and four of the ministers' names. The passage was then made still shorter, probably by Alexander Mackintosh. In the 'Asquith-Mackintosh version', as finally published, the comments on Haldane, Simon, and Hobhouse were omitted, presumably because of their critical tone, part of the one on Runciman being transferred to Haldane.

Beaverbrook did not share the anxiety of Asquith and Mackintosh to protect Liberal reputations. When he used the same letter in *Politicians and the War* he named Haldane and Hobhouse and gave the critical comments on them. 'Precise and uninspiring' against Simon was altered to 'the last word in logic'. The comments are attributed to 'a keen observer'. As Beaverbrook was working from Venetia's copies, he had an overlong passage on Masterman and none on Asquith. He supplied the latter deficiency by giving his version of the Prime Minister's usual preoccupation. 'Asquith', he wrote, 'appeared anxious, with the best of reasons, to avoid a split at any cost.'

Roy Jenkins had access to all the extant letters for his important biography, *Asquith* (1964), as did Randolph Churchill and Martin Gilbert for *Churchill*. The quotations in these two works are far more reliable than the extracts which appeared during the 1920s.[8] Some passages have appeared both in *Memories and Reflections* and in one of the *Churchill* volumes. Where this has happened the earlier version has not always been recognized as no more than the unreliable rendering of an extract which was later published more accurately. Thus the editors of *The Letters and Papers of Chaim Weizmann*,[9] Series A, Volume 7, cite Asquith's 'diary entry' for 13 March 1915 from *Memories and Reflections*, and his letter of the same date to Venetia Stanley from Gilbert's *Churchill*, as two separate sources, not knowing that the first is merely an inaccurate version of the second.

Notes to Appendix 1

1. There is a complete copy in the Beaverbrook MSS, House of Lords, G/9, and an incomplete one, marked by Asquith for his publisher, in the Bonham Carter MSS. The extracts, which extend to 123 typed pages, relate to the period 26 July 1914 to 11 May 1915.
2. To Beaverbrook, 9 Apr. 1928: Beaverbrook MSS.
3. I.217, n. 2. But Spender and Asquith continued to refer to the letters as 'aides-mémoire': for instance, ii.92,228.
4. See P. Ziegler, *Diana Cooper* (1981), p. 106.
5. There are thus two sets of extracts in the Beaverbrook MSS, G/9. The earlier ones are largely in Venetia's hand, though some were re-copied by Lady Jean Campbell. The later set consists of the typescript described in n. 1 above. It was sent to Beaverbrook after Asquith's death: see n. 2. See also A. J. P. Taylor, *Beaverbrook* (1972), p. 103.
6. *Politicians and the War*, i.149. Some of the inaccuracies were introduced by Venetia or by her helpers. Thus Asquith's comment (Letter 114) that the German ultimatum to Belgium showed 'almost Austrian crassness' was omitted from the typescript, the omission being unmarked. Venetia may have removed this phrase deliberately, thinking in retrospect that it looked unstatesmanlike. More probably she simply failed to realize how revealing it was. For Beaverbrook's inaccuracies in *Politicians and the War* see P. Fraser, *Historical Journal*, xxv (1982), 147–66.
7. *Churchill: Companion Docs.*, *1922–1929*, p. 561. Of the 425 Letters in the present edition it can be seen that 15 were written in part when Asquith was on duty – 6 from the Treasury Bench in the House, 4 during cabinet discussions, 3 during committees, one during a C.I.D. meeting, and one while the War Council was in session. Asquith may have written a number of others when he was alone in the cabinet room.
8. The quotations in Jenkins are not entirely reliable, however; and the inaccuracies have not been corrected in the revised edition (1978).
9. Ed. L. Stein (1975).

Appendix 2: Schedule of the Letters

THE series of more than 560 Letters from Asquith to Venetia Stanley seems to be complete except that Venetia probably did not keep the earliest Letters. No letter from Venetia to Asquith has survived (except for one fragment preserved by accident: see Letter 9a) and her replies were almost certainly destroyed by Asquith himself.

In the following Schedule, the letters marked with an asterisk are given, wholly or in part, in this edition.

On 11 May 1915 Venetia wrote to tell Asquith that she was going to marry Edwin Montagu. His reply, dated 12 May, which marked the end of their close relationship, also ends the series selected for this edition. Some of the letters written by Asquith after 12 May are quoted in the Epilogue. These are marked † in the Schedule.

The total number of letters per month is given in brackets.

The methods used for inserting some of the letters which passed between Edwin Montagu and Venetia Stanley are outlined on pp. xvii and xviii.

1910	September	10th*, 13th. (2)
1911	September	15th, 17th. (2)
1912	March	20th, 21st, 26th. (3)
	April	1st*, 2nd, 7th, 14th, 20th. (5)
	May	6th, 14th, undated note. (3)
	June	10th, 18th, 23rd, undated poem. (4)
	July	4th, 12th, 13th*, 24th, 30th. (5)
	August	5th, 14th*. (2)
	September	14th*. (1)
	October	18th. (1)
	December	2nd, 27th, undated poem, 31st. (4)
1913	January	6th*, 7th*, 9th, 11th, 16th*, 20th*, 22nd*, 27th*. (8)
	February	3rd, 10th, 18th*. (3)
	March	16th, 22nd. (2)
	April	'April 1913' poems**, 7th*, 8th, 11th. (5)
	May	11th, 15th, 22nd. (3)
	June	11th, 24th. (2)
	July	9th, undated poem*. (2)
	August	3rd, 19th, 21st*, 22nd*. (4)
	September	3rd*, 16th. (2)
	October	2nd, 13th, 18th. (3)
	November	18th. (1)
	December	8th*, 9th, 10th, 11th, 12th, 13th, 15th*, 16th, 17th*, 18th, 20th, 21st, 23rd, 24th, 26th. (15)

1914 January 3rd*, 5th, 6th*, 7th, 9th*, 10th, 12th, 15th, 21st*, 27th*, 28th*. (11)

February 3rd*, 4th*, 5th*, 6th*, 7th, 9th, 11th(i)*, 11th(ii)*, 12th*, 15th*, 16th*, 17th, 18th, 19th*, 21st, 24th, 26th(i)*, 26th(ii)*, 27th. (19)

March 2nd, 3rd*, 5th, 7th*, 9th*, 10th*, 11th, 14th*, 16th*, 17th*, 19th*, 21st*, 22nd*, 23rd*, 25th*, 26th*, 27th, 30th*, 31st. (19)

April 4th, 7th*, 9th*, 10th*, 11th*, 13th, 14th, 15th, 17th*, 18th*, 21st, 22nd*, 25th. (13)

May 1st*, 3rd*, 4th, 5th*, 7th*, 11th*, 12th*, 13th*, 17th, 19th*, 24th*, 25th*, 'Locutiones'*. (13)

June 6th*, 7th*, Whitsuntide*, 8th*, 9th*, 11th*, 14th*, 15th*, 17th(i)*, 17th(ii)*, 18th*, 22nd, 24th*, 25th*, 29th, 30th*. (16)

July 2nd(i)*, 2nd(ii)*, 3rd*, 4th*, 6th*, 7th, 8th*, 9th*, 10th*, 13th*, 14th*, 15th*, 16th(i), 16th(ii), 17th*, 18th(i), 18th(ii)*, 19th, 20th(i)*, 20th(ii), 20th(iii)*, 22nd*, 23rd, 24th*, 25th*, 26th*, 27th*, 28th(i)*, 28th(ii)*, 29th*, 30th*, 31st*. (32)

August 1st*, 2nd*, 3rd*, 4th*, 5th*, 6th*, 7th, 8th*, 9th*, 10th*, 11th*, 12th*, 17th*, 18th*, 19th*, 20th*, 21st*, 22nd(i)*, 22nd(ii)*, 23rd*, 24th(i)*, 24th(ii)*, 25th*, 26th*, 27th*, 28th(i)*, 28th(ii)*, 29th*, 30th*, 31st*. (30)

September 1st*, 2nd*, 3rd*, 4th*, 5th*, 6th*, 7th, 8th*, 9th*, 10th*, 12th(i)*, 12th(ii)*, 13th(i)*, 13th(ii)*, 14th(i)*, 14th(ii)*, 15th(i)*, 15th(ii)*, 15th(iii)*, 16th(i)*, 16th(ii)*, 17th(i)*, 17th(ii)*, 18th, 19th*, 20th*, 21st*, 22nd*, 23rd, 28th*, 29th*, 30th*. (32)

October 1st*, 2nd*, 3rd*, 4th*, 5th*, 6th*, 7th*, 8th*, 9th*, 10th*, 11th*, 12th*, 13th(i)*, 13th(ii)*, 14th*, 15th, 20th*, 21st*, 22nd*, 23rd*, 24th*, 25th*, 26th, 27th*, 28th*, 29th*, 30th(i)*, 30th(ii)*, 31st(i)*, 31st(ii)*. (30)

November 1st, 2nd(i)*, 2nd(ii)*, 3rd(i)*, 3rd(ii)*, 4th*, 5th(i)*, 5th(ii)*, 6th(i)*, 6th(ii)*, 7th*, 8th*, 9th, 10th*, 12th*, 16th(i), 16th(ii)*, 17th*, 18th*, 21st*, 22nd, 24th*, 27th, 28th(i)*, 28th(ii)*, 29th*, 30th*. (27)

December 2nd, 4th*, 5th(i)*, 5th(ii)*, 6th*, 8th*, 16th, 17th, 18th(i)*, 18th(ii)*, 19th(i)*, 19th(ii)*, 20th(i)*, 20th(ii)*, 21st*, 22nd*, 23rd*, 24th*, 25th*, 26th*, 27th*, 28th*, 29th(i)*, 29th(ii)*, 30th(i)*, 30th(ii)*, 31st*. (27)

1915 January 1st(i)*, 1st(ii)*, 2nd, 3rd*, 5th(i)*, 5th(ii)*, 6th(i)*, 6th(ii)*, 7th*, 8th*, 9th*, 10th*, 11th*, 12th(i)*, 12th(ii)*, 13th(i)*, 13th(ii)*, 14th*, 15th(i)*, 15th(ii)*, 16th*, 17th(i)*, 17th(ii)*, 18th(i)*, 18th(ii), 20th(i)*, 20th(ii)*, 20th(iii)*, 21st(i), 21st(ii)*, 21st(iii), 22nd(i)*, 22nd(ii)*, 23rd*, 24th*, 25th*,

	26th(i)*, 26th(ii)*, 26th(iii)*, 27th(i)*, 27th(ii)*, 28th*, 29th(i)*, 29th(ii)*, 30th*. (45)
February	1st*, 3rd(i)*, 'Portrait' Pt.1*, 3rd(ii)*, 4th*, 5th, 6th*, Sonnet*, 7th*, 8th*, 9th(i)*, 9th(ii)*, 9th(iii)*, 10th(i)*, 10th(ii)*, 11th(i)*, 11th(ii)*, 12th*, 13th(i)*, Sonnet, 13th(ii)*, 14th(i)*, 14th(ii)*, 15th(i)*, 15th(ii), 15th(iii)*, 16th, 17th(i)*, 'Portrait' Pt.2*, 17th(ii)*, Sonnet*, 18th(i)*, 18th(ii)*, 19th*, 20th*, 21st*, 22nd(i)*, 22nd(ii), 23rd*, 24th(i)*, 24th(ii)*, 25th(i), 25th(ii)*, 26th(i)*, 26th(ii)*, 26th(iii)*, 27th*, 28th*. (48)
March	1st(i)*, 1st(ii)*, 4th(i)*, 4th(ii)*, 4th(iii)*, 5th(i)*, 5th(ii)*, 6th(i)*, 6th(ii)*, 6th(iii)*, 7th(i)*, 7th(ii)*, 8th*, 9th*, 10th*, 'Infernal Tribunal'*, 11th(i)*, 11th(ii)*, 12th(i)*, 12th(ii)*, 13th(i), 13th(ii)*, 'The Judge'*, 14th*, 15th(i)*, 15th(ii)*, 16th(i)*, 16th(ii)*, 17th*, 18th(i)*, 'Portrait' Pt.3*, 18th(ii), 19th(i)*, 19th(ii)*, 20th*, 21st*, 22nd(i)*, 22nd(ii)*, 23rd(i)*, 23rd(ii)*, 24th(i)*, 24th(ii)*, 25th(i)*, 25th(ii)*, 25th(iii), 26th(i)*, 26th(ii)*, 27th(i), 27th(ii)*, 28th*, 29th(i)*, 29th(ii)*, 30th(i)*, 30th(ii)*, 30th(iii)*, 30th(iv)*, 31st(i)*, 31st(ii)*. (58)
April	1st(i)*, 1st(ii)*, 2nd*, 4th*, 'Autobiography'*, 5th*, 6th(i), 6th(ii)*, 7th*, 8th(i)*, 8th(ii)*, 13th*, 14th*, 15th*, 16th(i)*, 16th(ii)*, 17th(i)*, 17th(ii)*, 19th(i)*, 19th(ii)*, 20th(i)*, 20th(ii)*, 21st(i)*, 21st(ii)*, 22nd(i)*, 22nd(ii)*, 23rd(i)*, 23rd(ii)*, 24th*, 25th*, 26th*, 27th*, 28th(i)*, 28th(ii)*, 29th*. (35)
May	2nd*, 3rd*, 4th*, 5th*, 7th(i)*, 7th(ii)*, 9th*, 10th*, 11th(i)*, 11th(ii)*, 12th*, 14th†, 15th, 17th†, 20th(i), 20th(ii)†, 21st(i), 21st(ii), 21st(iii), 22nd. (20)
June	3rd, 11th†. (2)
July	14th, 20th, 24th†. (3)
October	19th. (1)
November	2nd. (1)
December	9th, 27th. (2)
1927 November	11th†. (1)

Appendix 3: Houses

ALDERLEY PARK: The Stanley family had been connected with Alderley, Cheshire, since the 15th century. The house mentioned in the Letters was a large mansion built in the early 19th century; most of it was pulled down in 1934.

ARCHERFIELD HOUSE: 3 miles W. of North Berwick and about a mile from the Firth of Forth. Built by William Nisbet *c.* 1700 and enlarged by Robert Adam in 1790. Lent to the Asquiths by Frank Tennant, 1907–12, one of the attractions being a private 9-hole golf course. The interior of the house was gutted in 1962–3.

BELCAIRE: Sir Philip Sassoon's house, near Lympne, Kent. Originally a manor-house, but substantially rebuilt by Herbert Baker before and after the First World War and renamed Port Lympne.

BRECCLES HALL: Norfolk. An Elizabethan brick house, repaired by Detmar Blow soon after 1900, and enlarged, and altered inside, by Lutyens, 1908. Acquired by Edwin and Venetia Montagu early in their marriage.

BROOME PARK: Kent. A 17th-century house acquired by Kitchener in 1911.

BUCKHURST: Sussex. Built by George Stanley Repton in the 1830s. Leased in Asquith's time to the Benson family. Some of the extensions by Lutyens which they commissioned have since been removed.

CLOVELLY COURT: On the N. Devon coast. Owned by Margot Asquith's friends, the Hamlyns. The house was much damaged by fire in the Second World War.

EASTON GREY: An 18th-century manor-house on the Avon about 4 miles W. of Malmesbury, Wiltshire. The home of Asquith's widowed sister-in-law, Lucy Graham-Smith.

ESHER PLACE: Surrey. A large mansion (incorporating part of an earlier house) built for Sir Edgar Vincent, 1895–8, by G. T. Robinson and A. Duchêne, with sunken gardens by Lutyens.

EWELME DOWN: Oxfordshire. Built *c.* 1910 by Walter Cave for Frank Lawson.

GAWTHORPE HALL: Lancashire. Built 1600–5 for the Revd. Lawrence Shuttle-worth; drastically restored by Charles Barry, 1849–51. Still the family seat.

GLEN: S.-W. of Innerleithen, Peeblesshire (Borders). Built in Scottish baronial style for Margot Asquith's father, Sir Charles Tennant, 1854–8, by David Bryce.

GUNNERSBURY PARK: Middlesex. Had been owned by the Rothschild family since 1850. Two adjacent main houses, the earlier (about 1834) by Sydney Smirke.

HACKWOOD PARK: Hampshire. A late 17th-century house, remodelled early in the 19th by Lewis Wyatt. Leased in Asquith's time by Curzon.

HOE FARM: Near Godalming, Surrey. A Tudor farmhouse, converted *c.* 1900 by Lutyens. Winston Churchill was the tenant in 1915. See illustration facing p. 429.

HOPEMAN LODGE: Moray. Thomas Gordon-Duff, Margot Asquith's brother-in-law, lent the house, then new, to Asquith in 1913.

HURSTLY: Hampshire. This substantial house (now divided, after some demolition) was lent by a cousin in 1912 to Asquith, who described it as 'a nice little villa in the New Forest'. See illustration facing p. 141.

INNES HOUSE: Moray. Originally a 17th-century house by William Ayton, enlarged in the mid-18th century, rebuilt and restored for Frank Tennant, 1911–16.

LYMPNE CASTLE: Kent. Acquired in a derelict state for Frank Tennant in 1906 and restored, with large additions, by R. S. Lorimer.

MANSFIELD STREET, NO. 18: Near Portland Place, W.1. Part of a development by Robert and James Adam, 1770–5. Town residence of Lord Sheffield.

MELLS: Manor-house, W. of Frome, Somerset. The home of Sir John and Lady Horner, who had made extensive restorations to the Elizabethan original.

MUNSTEAD HOUSE: Near Godalming, Surrey. Designed by J. J. Stevenson, 1877–8, and partly remodelled by Lutyens, 1900.

NUNEHAM PARK: This manor-house near Oxford, and the church and village adjoining, were built for the 1st Earl Harcourt by Stiff Leadbetter in the 18th century.

PENRHOS: The second of Lord Sheffield's country houses, on the Anglesey coast, near Holyhead, was a Tudor house with 18th- and 19th-century additions by James Defferd. It is now a ruin. See illustration facing p. 333.

QUEEN ANNE'S GATE, NO. 24: Edwin Montagu's house, bought Jan. 1913.

SKIBO CASTLE: Sutherland. Designed for Andrew Carnegie by Ross and Macbeth in 1899. Put up for sale by Carnegie's only daughter, 1982.

STANWAY: Gloucestershire. Built in Elizabethan and Stuart times by the Tracy family, from whom it descended to the Earl of Wemyss. Additions were made, 1859–60, by William Burn, and to the N.E. wing in 1913 by Detmar Blow.

WALMER CASTLE: Kent. Official residence of the Lord Warden of the Cinque Ports. A Tudor castle first enlarged and made residential in the 18th century, and further altered in 1863 by George Devey. See illustration of drawing-room facing p. 333.

THE WHARF: On the Thames at Sutton Courtney, Oxfordshire. The Asquiths acquired it (partly from Lady Tree) in 1912 and had the 18th-century structure converted and enlarged by Walter Cave. See illustration facing p. 141.

WILSFORD MANOR: Wiltshire. Built 1904–6 by Detmar Blow, in local 17th-century style.

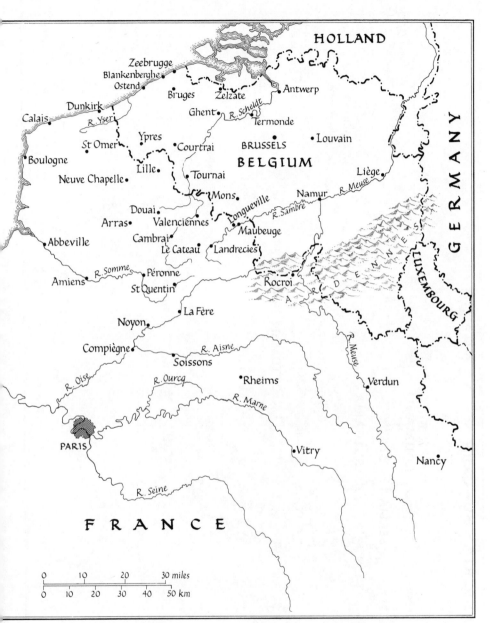

HOLLAND

Zeebrugge
Blankenberghe
Ostend
Bruges
Zelzate
Antwerp
Dunkirk
Calais
R. Yser
Ghent
R. Scheldt
Termonde
Ypres
St Omer
Courtrai
Louvain
Boulogne
Lille
BRUSSELS
BELGIUM
Neuve Chapelle
Tournai
Liège
Mons
R. Meuse
Douai
Longueville
Namur
Arras
Valenciennes
R. Sambre
Maubeuge
Abbeville
Cambrai
Le Cateau
Landrecies
R. Somme
Péronne
Rocroi
Amiens
St Quentin
A R D E N N E S
La Fère
Noyon
R. Meuse
GERMANY
LUXEMBOURG
Compiègne
R. Aisne
R. Oise
Soissons
R. Ourcq
Rheims
Verdun
R. Marne
PARIS
Vitry
Nancy
R. Seine

F R A N C E

0   10   20   30 miles

0   10   20   30   40   50 km

FRANCE AND THE LOW COUNTRIES, 1914

THE DARDANELLES

Sea of Marmara

Bulair

Gallipoli

Chanak
The Narrows

Cape Helles

0 10 20 miles
0 10 20 30 km

AUSTRIA–HUNGARY

RUSSIA

Black Sea

ISTRIA

BOSNIA

Zara
Sebenico
Spalato
DALMATIA

TRANSYLVANIA

ROUMANIA

R. Danube

SERBIA

MONTE-NEGRO

BULGARIA

Adriatic Sea

ALBANIA

MACEDONIA

Salonika

GREECE

Constantinople

Sea of Marmara

Gallipoli

LEMNOS
Mudros Bay

OTTOMAN EMPIRE

Smyrna

Alexandretta

SYRIA

PALESTINE

ITALY

SICILY

CRETE

CYPRUS

Mediterranean Sea

EGYPT

Cairo

0 100 200 300 miles
0 100 200 300 400 500 km

THE EASTERN MEDITERRANEAN, 1915

Family Trees

THE families are shown as they were at May 1915 (the same treatment being given to ranks and titles in the Index). Names of those mentioned in the Letters are given in italics.

Trees of the large Tennant connection can be found in N. Crathorne, *Tennant's Stalk* (1973), pp. 236–43.

THE ASQUITHS, at May 1915

Herbert Henry
(1852–1928)

m. 1st 1877 Helen   m. 2ndly 1894 Margot
(1855–1891),   (1868–1945),
dau. of Dr. F. Melland   dau. of Sir Charles Tennant, Bt.

Raymond   Herbert ('Beb')   Arthur ('Oc')   Violet   Cyril ('Cys')   Elizabeth   Anthony ('Puffin')
(1878–1916)   (1881-1947)   (1883–1939)   (1887–1969)   (1890–1954)   (1897–1945)   (1902–1968)
m. 1907 Katharine m. 1910 Cynthia
(1885–1976)   (1887–1960)
dau. of Sir John Horner dau. of 9th Earl of Wemyss

                 2 sons

Helen   Perdita
(b.1908)   (b.1910)

THE STANLEYS OF ALDERLEY, at May 1915

Edward, 2nd Baron Stanley of Alderley (1802–1869)
m. 1826 Henrietta Maria, dau. of 13th Visc. Dillon

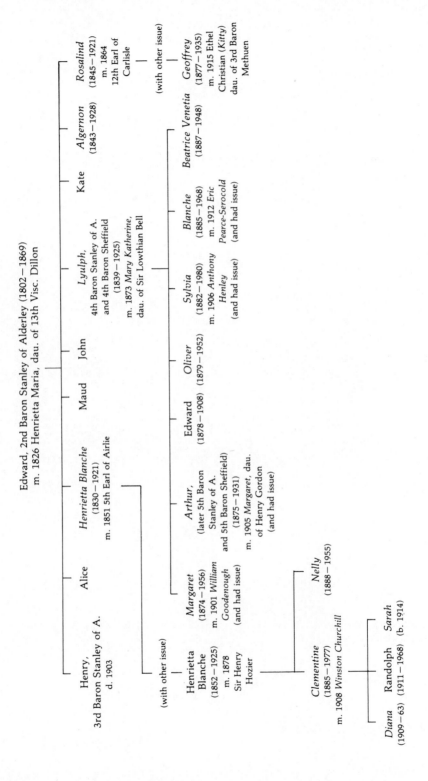

Biographical Notes

ABERDEEN, 7th Earl of: Marquess of, 1916 (1847–1934). Grandson of the Crimean War Prime Minister. Lord-Lieutenant of Ireland briefly in 1886, Governor-General of Canada, 1893–8, and Irish Lord-Lieutenant again, 1906–15. The Irish Nationalists laughed at him but liked him; he had, as one of their papers put it, 'opened everything in Dublin except the Parliament House in College Green and the safe containing the Crown Jewels'. Lady Aberdeen's well-meant interferences eventually landed her in trouble (Letter 197, n. 3).

ASQUITH, Arthur ('Oc') (1883–1939). Asquith's 3rd and favourite son, universally popular; thought by his sister-in-law Cynthia 'a great dear – genial and sane to a fault'. In a remarkable war career rose to be Brig.-Gen.; D.S.O. and two bars. Four times wounded: for first occasion see Letter 419; on fourth lost a leg below the knee.

ASQUITH, Emma Alice Margaret (Margot), later Countess of Oxford and Asquith (1862–1945). 6th daughter of Sir Charles Tennant, a wealthy Scottish industrialist. She and her sister Laura (d. 1886) became youthful society favourites; and she went on to be a central figure in 'The Souls'. Married H. H. Asquith, as his second wife, 1894. Of her 5 children only 2 (Elizabeth and Anthony) survived infancy. Her unbridled and critical tongue made her enemies; and in the years with which the Letters are concerned she was a prey to nervous illness. See illustration facing p. 140.

ASQUITH, Herbert Henry, cr. Earl of Oxford and Asquith, 1925 (1852–1928). Born Morley, Yorkshire. Lost his father, a small employer, at age of 8. Relatives paid (partly on a loan basis) for his education at City of London School. Scholar of Balliol, 1870–4; successful Oxford undergraduate. Called to the Bar, 1876. Married Helen Melland, daughter of a Manchester doctor, 1877 (5 children). M.P. for East Fife, 1886–1918. Q.C., 1890. Wife's death from typhoid, Sept. 1891. Home Secretary, 1892–5. Married Margot Tennant, May 1894 (2 children survived infancy). A leader of the Liberal Imperialist group during the party's Boer War troubles. Chancellor of the Exchequer, Dec. 1905–Apr. 1908, then Prime Minister to Dec. 1916.

ASQUITH, Raymond (1878–1916). Asquith's eldest, and most variously gifted, son. A Winchester and Balliol Scholar; at Oxford, prizeman, Pres. of Union. Called to Bar, 1904. Married Katharine Horner, 1907 (2 daughters, 1 son). Prospective Liberal candidate, Derby, 1913. Enlisted Queen's Westminsters, 1914; transferred, July 1915, to 3rd Bn., Grenadier Guards. Killed in action, 15 Sept. 1916. Until he went to the war, found the world 'a little barren of motives'.

ASQUITH, Violet; cr. Life Peeress, 1964 (Baroness Asquith of Yarnbury) (1887–
1969). Asquith's 4th child, and only daughter, by his first wife. Privately educated, widely read in English literature, and a good linguist. Fiercely devoted to
her father, with whom she had talked of politicians and politics since childhood (in
one of his 'political letters' to her he ends by expressing pleasure that she can now
do up her gaiters). Married Maurice Bonham Carter, July 1915 (two daughters, 2
sons). 'There is a thin crust of nonsense,' Raymond Asquith wrote of her to his
wife in 1910; 'but . . . if you put your foot quickly through it the birds begin to
sing and everything is all right.' See illustraton facing p. 428.

BAKER, Harold Trevor ('Bluey') (1877–1960). Winchester and New College; the
equal in promise of Raymond Asquith, to whom he was one year senior. Had
private means. Liberal M.P., 1910–18. Financial Sec., War Office, 1912–15. He
became slightly deaf, and was perhaps deficient in vital force; in the Liberal
decline this prevented him from scaling the heights.

BALFOUR, A. J., cr. Earl of, 1922 (1848–1930). Entered Parliament, 1874; made his
name as Chief Sec. for Ireland, 1887–91; Prime Minister, 1902–5. Led the
Conservatives in the Commons, 1891–1911; then was forced to resign, replaced
by the more obviously combative Bonar Law. Respected by Asquith, suspected by
Margot. 'That cool grace, easy mind, and intellectual courtesy takes [sic] the eye
off like the three card trick,' she wrote in Mar. 1915; 'he is a bitter party
opponent.'

BATTENBERG, Admiral Prince Louis of; Marquess of Milford Haven, 1917 (1854–
1921). Eldest son of Prince Alexander of Hesse, lived in England from boyhood;
married Princess Victoria of Hesse, granddaughter of Queen Victoria. Naturalized and entered Royal Navy, 1868; 1st Sea Lord, 1912–Oct. 1914.

BERTIE, Sir Francis; cr. Baron, 1915; Visc., 1918 (1844–1919). Ambassador to
Rome, 1903; Ambassador to Paris, 1905–18. 'He had the gift', Grey wrote, 'of
making himself trusted . . . in a rare degree.'

BIRRELL, Augustine (1850–1933). Barrister and author (*Obiter Dicta*, 1884, 1887,
1924). Entered Parliament, 1889; Chief Sec. for Ireland, 1907–16. One of Asquith's oldest friends. Hobhouse thought him (Aug. 1912) 'cynical, amusing, a
bad administrator, but high principled and with plenty of courage'.

BONHAM CARTER, Maurice ('Bongie') (1880–1960). Asquith's Principal Private Sec.
Devoted to his chief, whose elder daughter, Violet, he married (July 1915). A
great success at house parties: 'imitates ducks, cocks, etc.', Raymond Asquith
reported (1906), 'without a moment's intermission'. For Asquith's criticism of
one of his secretarial habits see Letter 184.

BRYCE, James: cr. Visc., 1914 (1838–1922). Regius Professor of Civil Law, Oxford,
1870–93. Entered Parliament, 1880; Pres. Board of Trade, 1894, Chief Sec. for
Ireland, 1905. Ambassador to America, 1907–13. 'Looks like Father Time,'
Asquith reported (Feb. 1914). 'but could still . . . discourse at a moment's notice
and at any required length on any topic, human or divine' (Letter 30).

BUCKMASTER, Sir Stanley; cr. Baron, 1915; Visc., 1933 (1861–1934). Barrister.

Entered Parliament, 1906; Solicitor-General, 1913; Lord Chancellor, May 1915. Asquith thought him *'very* able' (Letter 194).

CANTERBURY, Archbishop of; Randall Davidson (1848–1930). Bp. of Rochester (1891), Winchester (1895). Abp. of Canterbury, 1903–28. He and Asquith were somewhat critical of each other: see p. 12 and Letter 126.

CARSON, Sir Edward; cr. Baron, 1921 (1854–1935). Barrister. Born in Dublin. Entered Parliament (M.P. for Dublin University), 1892. Q.C., 1894 (Oscar Wilde trial, 1895). Solicitor-General, 1896. Leader of Ulster Unionists, 1910; Ulster Volunteer Force and Covenant, 1912. Attorney-General, May 1915. The 'uncrowned king of Ulster'. 'By temperament opposed to every government' (Beaverbrook).

CASSEL, Sir Ernest (1852–1921). Financier and philanthropist. Born in Cologne, naturalized as a British subject, 1878. Knighted, 1899. Privy Councillor, 1902. Edward VII benefited from his financial advice. At the time of the Letters a lonely figure: his wife had died in 1881 and their only child, a daughter, in 1911. See Letter 39.

CHURCHILL, WINSTON LEONARD SPENCER (1874–1965). Elder son of Lord Randolph Churchill (1849–95) and of Jennie (1854–1921), daughter of Leonard Jerome of New York. Commissioned 4th Queen's Own Hussars, Feb. 1895. Smelled powder Cuba, 1895; North West Frontier, 1897; Omdurman, 1898; South Africa, 1899–1900 (taken prisoner, escaped from Pretoria). Described these experiences in four books, published 1898–1900. Conservative M.P., Oldham, Oct. 1900. Opposed tariff reform, and joined Liberals, May 1904. Colonial Under-Secretary, Dec. 1905. Liberal M.P., North West Manchester, Jan. 1906, his two-volume life of his father appearing the day after his election address. P.C., May 1907. President, Board of Trade, Apr. 1908. Defeated N.W. Manchester, elected, Dundee. Described by colleague at this stage as 'full of the poor whom he has just discovered. He thinks he is called by providence to do something for them.' Home Secretary, 1910. First Lord of the Admiralty, Oct. 1911 (exchanging offices with a resentful McKenna: see Letter 284). Instituted Admiralty War Staff, Jan. 1912. Modified his pacific radicalism, plunged into defence problems, and, to the annoyance of Lloyd George, when the Letters take up the story, would 'only talk of boilers'.

Conservative Prime Minister, 1940–5, 1951–5.

Married, Sept. 1908, CLEMENTINE (1885–1977), daughter of Sir Henry and Lady Blanche Hozier, the latter being Venetia's first cousin. 'Clemmie' was not an intellectual and the Asquiths tended to under-value her sterling qualities. 'She is beautiful,' Raymond Asquith wrote in 1905; '. . . she is certainly nothing else.' Her wary relationship with Venetia and Violet Asquith is described in Mary Soames, *Clementine Churchill* (1979), pp. 62–3.

CREWE, 1st Marquess of (1858–1945). Succeeded to a peerage when 27. Viceroy of Ireland, 1892; Lord Pres. of Council, 1905; Sec. for Colonies, 1908; Lord Privy Seal, 1908–11 and 1912–15; Sec. for India, 1910–15. Asquith greatly respected his judgement (Letter 324) but found him a tiresomely slow performer on the golf course.

CUNARD, Maud, later 'Emerald' (1872–1948). Exotic, cultivated American (née Burke), married to Sir Bache Cunard, heir to the shipping fortune. Helped Thomas Beecham, who was her lover, to stage his Covent Garden seasons. Often tried to persuade Asquith to further her purposes by use of his patronage.

D'ABERNON, Baron, cr. 1914; Visc., 1926; Sir Edgar Vincent (1857–1941). After Coldstream Guards, showed administrative talent and became Governor of Imperial Ottoman Bank, 1889. His financial operations succeeded: the Bank's did not. Left Constantinople, 1897, and bought Esher Place (Appendix 3). Conservative M.P., 1899–1906. Opposed tariff reform and stood unsuccessfully as a Liberal, 1910. Tall, handsome, quick-minded, a pungent conversationalist. His wife had been one of London's 'reigning beauties' in the 1890s.

DRUMMOND, Eric (1876–1951). Entered Foreign Office, 1900. One of the Prime Minister's Private Secs., 1912–15. Heir presumptive to Earldom of Perth (and succeeded, 1937): 'the only radical of his family', as a Conservative paper called him. For Asquith's high opinion of him see Letter 317.

FISHER, John Arbuthnot ('Jacky'), 1st Baron, cr. 1908 (1841–1920). Served in Baltic Fleet during Crimean War. Controller of Navy, 1892–7: responsible for programme of shipbuilding following Naval Defence Act, 1889. 2nd Sea Lord, 1902; 1st Sea Lord, 1904–10 and Oct. 1914–May 1915: see p. 294. Responsible for Britain's lead in 'all-big-gun' battleships and battle-cruisers (*Dreadnought* launched, 1906). Flamboyant, the creator of greatly needed changes and of much discord. Somewhat oriental in appearance: see Letter 199 and illustration facing p. 460.

FOCH, General Ferdinand (1851–1929). The great star of the École de Guerre. Aged 62 at outbreak of war. Apostle of the offensive, but learned much about defensive warfare round Nancy in Aug. 1914, and S. of the Marne when the German advance was at its limit. Sent, 4 Oct. 1914, to northern part of Front, as 'deputy' to Joffre, to co-ordinate French, British, and Belgian forces there. Showed great tact with Sir John French (see Letter 193, n. 7).

FRENCH, Sir John; cr. Visc., Jan. 1916; Earl of Ypres, 1922 (1852–1925). See p. 164 and illustration facing p. 461. Entered Navy at 14, but left to join Army, 1870. After success in Boer War, Lt.-Gen. and K.C.M.G., 1902. Inspector-Gen. of Forces, 1907; C.I.G.S., 1912; Field Marshal, 1913. Resigned after Curragh 'Mutiny', 1914. C.-in-C., B.E.F., 1914 till superseded, Dec. 1915. His book, *1914*, about the opening months of the campaign is misleading at several points.

GEORGE V, King (1865–1937). 2nd son of Edward VII. Cr. Duke of York on elder brother's death, 1892. Married Princess Victoria Mary of Teck, 1893. Prince of Wales, 1901. Succeeded to throne, May 1910. For Asquith's patronizing view of him see Letter 27, n. 2.

GREY, Sir Edward, 3rd Bt.; cr. Visc., July 1916 (1862–1933). Sent down from Balliol for idleness, 1884. Entered Parliament, 1885. A mainstay, with Asquith and Haldane, of the Liberal Imperialist group during party splits occasioned by Boer War. Foreign Sec. from 1905 until Asquith's fall, Dec. 1916. Married, as his 2nd wife, Pamela Glenconner, 1922; she died, 1928. F.R.S., 1914. Asquith admired and relied on him, but thought him 'too *nervy*' for the highest political courage (Letter 217). He came second, after Crewe, in the 'class list' of Feb. 1915 (Letter 324). See drawing, p. 518.

HAIG, Sir Douglas; cr. Earl, 1919 (1861–1928). Staff Officer to Sir John French, Boer War, both being cavalrymen. Summoned by Haldane to work on military reorganization, 1906. Commanded 1st Corps, B.E.F., Aug. 1914: 1st Army, Jan. 1915. Came to national prominence after 1st battle of Ypres (Oct.–Nov. 1914). His reputation stood high during the period of the Letters: see Letter 243.

HALDANE, Richard Burdon; cr. Visc., 1911 (1856–1928). Barrister. Entered Parliament, 1885. Sec. of State for War, 1905–12; Lord Chancellor, 1912–15. F.R.S., 1906; F.B.A., 1914; O.M., 1915. One of Asquith's closest friends in the 1880s. Told his mother (Feb. 1920) that Margot had 'done much to make it difficult in the years gone by for Asquith to rise to the occasion'. For his wartime troubles see pp. 322–3.

HAMILTON, Gen. Sir Ian (1853–1947). Began his military career with a long spell of Indian service. Wounded, his left arm being crippled, Majuba Hill, 1881. A.D.C. to C.-in-C., India (Roberts), 1886. Distinguished service in Boer War. Q.M.G., 1903. Accompanied Japanese armies in Russo-Japanese War, 1904–5. Commanded anti-invasion forces, 1914–15; Dardanelles army, March–Oct. 1915. Distinguished and intelligent, he lacked the tough, ruthless realism of the great commander.

HANKEY, Maurice (1877–1963). Commissioned Royal Marine Artillery; transferred, 1902, to Naval Intelligence. Committee of Imperial Defence, Asst. Sec., 1908; Sec., 1912. Acted as Sec. to War Council from its formation, Nov. 1914. 'Without Hankey we should not have won the war' (Balfour).

HENLEY, The Hon. Mrs Sylvia (1882–1980). The 2nd of Lord Sheffield's 4 daughters. Married Anthony Henley, 1906. For some years after the break with Venetia, Asquith's chief correspondent and confidante. In the 1970s, when one of the last survivors from his circle, appeared in an evening gown made for her by Paquin in 1913.

HORNER, Lady (Frances) (1858–1940). Daughter of William Graham, India merchant, Liberal M.P., and friend of the Pre-Raphaelites. Married, 1883, John Horner of Mells, Somerset. Asquith came to know her in 1892 and corresponded with her regularly when first a widower. 'Jack' Horner became K.C.V.O., 1907. Raymond Asquith married their daughter Katharine in the same year.

HOWARD, Geoffrey (1877–1935). Son of 12th Earl of Carlisle and of Lord Sheffield's sister, Rosalind, the temperance crusader. Venetia's cousin. M.P., 1906–10, 1911–18, 1923–4 (a faithful Asquithian). Vice-Chamberlain, H.M.'s Household, 1911–15. Lord of the Treasury, 1915–16. Married 'Kitty' Methuen, 15 May 1915.

ILLINGWORTH, Percy (1869–1915). M.P., Shipley, 1906–15. Chairman, Yorkshire Liberal Federation. Liberal Chief Whip from 1912. Nonconformist; sportsman; formerly Capt., Imperial Yeomanry. His death (Jan. 1915) was a serious blow to Asquith.

JELLICOE, Adm. Sir John; cr. Earl, 1925 (1859–1935). Transferred to Admiralty for building programme, at Fisher's insistence, 1889, and recalled by Fisher again, 1904. Controller of Navy, 1908; 2nd Sea Lord, 1912. C.-in-C., Grand Fleet, Aug. 1914. 1st Sea Lord, Nov. 1916–Dec. 1917. Sincere, considerate, professionally competent. Not good at delegation: apt to wear himself out.

JOFFRE, Gen. Joseph Jacques Césaire (1852–1931). Took part in defence of Paris, 1870. Service in Indo-China and Africa. Of sound republican credentials. Vice-Pres. of Supreme War Council, and thus C.-in-C. in case of war, 1911 (third choice for the post). Massive, paunchy, and silent; strong-willed, and untroubled by self-doubt. C.-in-C., French armies, Western Front, Aug. 1914–Dec. 1916.

KAISER, The: Wilhelm II, German Emperor and King of Prussia (1859–1941). Grandson of Queen Victoria. Succeeded father, 1888. In 1908 publication of some of his remarks in the *Daily Telegraph* weakened his political position in Germany; and the replacement of Bülow as Chancellor by Bethmann-Hollweg did nothing to strengthen it. Thereafter in no position to restrain the General Staff, or those who preferred the apparently warlike Crown Prince to the theatrical, but apprehensive, Emperor.

KEPPEL, The Hon. Mrs Alice (1868–1947). Married, 1891, 3rd son of 7th Earl of Albermarle. Edward VII's intimate friend during the last 12 years of his life. Greatly admired by Foreign Office for her 'wonderful discretion and . . . excellent influence' on the King (Hardinge). 'A plucky woman of fashion; human, adventurous, and gay, who, in spite of doing what she liked all her life, has never made an enemy' (Margot Asquith).

KITCHENER, Horatio Herbert; cr. Earl Kitchener of Khartoum, June 1914 (1850–1916). Served briefly with French Army in latter part of Franco–Prussian War, 1871, after qualifying for a commission in Royal Engineers. Successful campaigns in Egypt and Sudan (battle of Omdurman, 1898). Roberts's Chief of Staff, then C.-in-C., Boer War. C.-in-C. India, 1902–9, where he worsted the Viceroy (Curzon). British Agent and Consul-General, Egypt, 1911–14. Sec. of State for War, Aug. 1914 to death on H.M.S. *Hampshire*, June 1916. See pp. 152–4 and drawing, p. 195.

LAW, Andrew Bonar (1858–1923). Born in Canada, brought up in Glasgow. Joined family firm and later William Jacks & Co., iron merchants. Entered Parliament, 1900. Profiting from the split between Austen Chamberlain's supporters and Long's, became Conservative leader in the Commons, 1911. Much underrated by Asquith. Colonial Sec., May 1915. Chancellor of the Exchequer and Leader of the Commons, Dec. 1916. Prime Minister, 1922–3. See illustration facing p. 332.

LICHNOWSKY, Prince Karl Max (1860–1928). German diplomat: various legations, 1884–9; recalled to Foreign Office by Bülow. German Ambassador in London, 1912. Worked hard for pacific relations between England and Germany, but carried no weight in Berlin.

LLOYD GEORGE, David: cr. Earl, 1945 (1863–1945). Schoolmaster's son, orphaned in infancy, brought up by his uncle, a shoemaker and Baptist preacher in the radical Welsh tradition. Solicitor, 1884. M.P., Carnarvon Boroughs, 1890 (to 1945). Became a national figure, and the radicals' standard-bearer, by championing the Boers against Joe Chamberlain's imperialism and the Nonconformists against Balfour's Education Bill. Pres. Board of Trade, 1905; Chancellor of Exchequer, 1908. Introduced People's Budget, 1909; National Insurance, 1911. Under slight cloud from the end of 1912 to the outbreak of war from Marconi scandal and fiasco of 1914 Budget (Letters 7 and 83). Minister of Munitions, May 1915; War Secretary, July 1916; Prime Minister, Dec. 1916–Oct. 1922.

MACDONALD, Ramsay (1866–1937). Secretary, Labour Representation Committee, 1900. Entered Parliament, 1906. Chairman, Labour Party, 1906–9; Chairman, Parliamentary Labour Group, 1911–14. Went as volunteer to British ambulance unit with Belgian army, Dec. 1914, but was sent back to England.

Prime Minister of Labour Governments, 1924, 1929–31; and of a 'National' Government, 1931–5.

MCKENNA, Reginald (1863–1943). Barrister. Entered Parliament, 1895. Pres. Board of Educn., 1907; 1st Lord of Admiralty, 1908. Married Pamela Jekyll, 1908. Home Sec., 1911–15; Chancellor of Exchequer, 1915. Asquith admired his courage and intellect, but thought him 'singularly rasping and unpersuasive in argument'. His appearance seemed to Margot 'ugly in a pathetic and insignificant way'.

MASTERMAN, Charles (1874–1927). Entered Parliament, 1906. 1st Chairman of National Insurance Commission, 1911. Chancellor of Duchy of Lancaster, 1914. Resigned, 1915. The Letters touch on his electoral misfortunes: a casualty of the old law which required a minister to be re-elected on taking office. Brilliant, but not tough enough for politics.

MILLERAND, Alexandre (1859–1943). French lawyer. Elected to Chamber of Deputies, 1885, and became leader of the Socialist left, who later disowned him as he gravitated towards the centre. Minister of Public Works in Briand's first cabinet, 1909; Minister of War under Poincaré, 1912–13; again Minister of War, 1914. For Asquith's view of him see Letters 143 and 272.

MONTAGU, The Hon. Edwin Samuel (1879–1924). 2nd son of a wealthy merchant banker (cr. Lord Swaythling, 1907). Pres. of Union, Cambridge University, 1902. Liberal M.P., Chesterton Div. of Cambridgeshire, 1906–22. Private Sec. to Asquith when Chancellor of Exchequer and Prime Minister. Parlty. Under-Sec. for India, 1910–14 (toured India, 1912–13); Financial Sec. to Treasury, 1914–15; Chancellor of Duchy of Lancaster, Jan. 1915; Minister of Munitions, 1916; Sec. of State for India, 1917 until resignation, Mar. 1922. See illustrations facing pp. 140, 332, 461.

MORLEY, John, Visc., 1908 (1838–1923). Journalist and barrister. Entered Parliament, 1883. Chief Sec. for Ireland, 1886 and 1892–5; Sec. of State for India, 1905; Lord Privy Seal, 1910 until resignation, 4 Aug. 1914. O.M., 1902. His many successful books included the authorized *Life of Gladstone*, 1903.

MORRELL, Lady Ottoline (1873–1938). Half-sister of the 6th Duke of Portland. Became Asquith's close friend in 1898. Married Philip Morrell, 1902; he won a

Liberal seat in 1906 and another in December 1910. By 1908 she had established her Bloomsbury salon; and in 1913 she bought Garsington Manor, near Oxford. In both places, hostess to a scintillating company of intimates and acquaintances. 'Lady Ottoline', Nijinsky said, 'is so tall, so beautiful, so like a giraffe.'

NORTHCLIFFE, (Alfred Harmsworth) cr. Baron, 1905; Visc., 1917 (1865–1922). Father of modern popular journalism. Proprietor of *Daily Mail*, 1896, *The Times*, 1908, and other papers. Campaigned before 1914 for compulsory military service and gave warnings of Germany's warlike intentions. Greatly distrusted by Asquith and by many other Liberals.

PAGE, Walter Hines (1855–1918). Journalist from 1880 to 1911 when sent to London as Ambassador by Woodrow Wilson. A devoted and resourceful friend to Britain during the war.

PARSONS, Viola (1884–1938). Daughter of Sir Herbert Beerbohm Tree, with whom she acted. Tried unsuccessfully for an operatic career. Married, July 1912, Alan Parsons. 'In all the changes and chances of the last 10 years,' Asquith wrote to her, Jan. 1919, 'I have always been able to rely on your clear insight and staunch loyalty.'

PEASE, Joseph ('Jack'): cr. Baron Gainford, 1917 (1860–1943). Entered Parliament, 1892. Liberal Chief Whip, 1908; Chancellor of Duchy of Lancaster, 1910; Pres. Board of Educn., 1911–15. Asquith thought him 'a solid 2nd rate man' (Letter 351).

REDMOND, John (1856–1918). Barrister. From a family of Catholic gentry in Wexford. Entered Parliament, 1880. Leader of the Parnellite group after the Irish party split, 1891. Chairman of the reunited Irish M.P.s, 1900. Able and patient parliamentarian, but knew little of Ulster, and not much of extremist movements, such as Sinn Fein, in the rest of Ireland.

RUNCIMAN, Walter; cr. Visc., 1937 (1870–1949). Son of a shipowner. Entered Parliament, 1899. Pres. Board of Educn., 1908; Pres. Board of Agriculture and Fisheries, 1911; Pres. Board of Trade, 1914–Dec. 1916. Like other Asquithians lost his seat, 1918.

SCOTT, Lady (1878–1947). Orphaned at an early age, spent childhood in Edinburgh. Became a well-known sculptress. Married, 1908, Captain Scott, Antarctic explorer, who d. returning from S. Pole, 1912. From May 1915 to Dec. 1916 one of the Premier's confidantes. Married, 1922, Hilton Young, who was cr., 1935, Lord Kennet of the Dene.

SEELY, Col. J. E. B.; cr. Lord Mottistone, 1933 (1868–1947). Barrister. Fought in Boer War. Entered Parliament as Conservative, 1900, but crossed the floor; Liberal M.P., 1906. Sec. of State for War, 1912. Resigned after Curragh 'Mutiny', 1914. Handsome, immensely self-confident, but politically, in the eyes of Esher (and some others), 'a goose'. Left London to join French's staff, 11 Aug. 1914. For his distinguished war career see Letter 276, n. 2.

SIMON, Sir John: cr. Visc., 1940 (1873–1954). Fellow of All Souls, 1897. Called to Bar, 1899. A brilliant advocate, he took silk only 9 years later. Entered Parliament, 1906. Solicitor-General, 1910. Attorney-General, in cabinet, 1913; Home Sec., 1915–16. A shy man, made more reserved by his first wife's death (1902). 'The Impeccable', to Asquith.

SPENDER, J. A. (1862–1942). Editor, *Westminster Gazette*, 1896–1922. Asquith's biographer, with Cyril Asquith (1932), and one of the very few journalists whom Asquith respected.

STANLEY, Beatrice Venetia (1887–1948). Youngest child of Edward Lyulph Stanley (who succeeded as Lord Stanley of Alderley, 1903, and as Lord Sheffield, 1909) and of Mary Katharine, daughter of Sir Lowthian Bell, Bt. Married, 26 July 1915, Edwin Samuel Montagu (who d. 1924). Daughter, Judith, b. 1923, the original editor (when Mrs Milton Gendel) of these letters.

WILSON, Lt.-Gen. Sir Henry (1864–1922). Failed to gain admission into Woolwich twice, into Sandhurst three times. Finally obtained commission via Irish Militia. Commandant, Staff College, 1907–10. Spoke French fluently; formed friendship with Foch and became principal advocate of collaboration of B.E.F. with French Army. Director of Military Operations, 1910–14. Advised Opposition leaders throughout final pre-war phase of Home Rule. Sub-Chief of Staff to Sir J. French, Aug. 1914. Chief Liaison Officer with Joffre's HQ and Lt.-Gen., Feb. 1915. By November 1914 Asquith knew enough of Wilson's doings to call him 'that poisonous mischief-maker' (Letter 205).

WIMBORNE, 2nd Baron, succ. 1914; Visc., 1918; Ivor Guest (1873–1939). Conservative M.P., 1900. Crossed floor with his cousin Winston Churchill in protest at tariff reform. Liberal M.P., 1906. Obliged Liberal leaders by accepting a peerage, 1910 (Ld. Ashby St. Ledgers, 1910–14). Paymaster-General, 1910–12. Irish Viceroy, 1915–18. Cynthia Asquith, visiting Viceregal Lodge, Aug. 1915, found him 'just a fairly frank bounder'.

Index

✳

THE index entries give:

(a) Letter numbers for Asquith's writings and for the attached footnotes.

(b) Page numbers only, for all other editorial passages; where there are page numbers they are given at the end of an entry, or subentry, in **bold** type.

(c) The roman number of the Letter, followed by its page number in brackets, for the Letters of Edwin Montagu and Venetia, e.g. XVI **(537)**.

The ranks and titles shown are those held in 1915. Where someone is better known under their later title, or married name, this has sometimes been added in brackets. An asterisk against a name indicates an entry in the Biographical Notes.

Houses, and places in the U.K., have been indexed only if they are important in the Letters. The houses of historical interest are listed in Appendix 3. People have not been indexed where they are mentioned only as sources of information. The title 'The Hon.' is usually omitted.

Where possible the longer entries follow a roughly chronological arrangement.